MARKETING COMMUNICATIONS
A European Perspective

Third Edition

Patrick De Pelsmacker

Maggie Geuens

Joeri Van den Bergh

 Prentice Hall
FINANCIAL TIMES

An imprint of **Pearson Education**

Harlow, England • London • New York • Boston • San Francisco • Toronto • Sydney • Singapore • Hong Kong
Tokyo • Seoul • Taipei • New Delhi • Cape Town • Madrid • Mexico City • Amsterdam • Munich • Paris • Milan

Pearson Education Limited

Edinburgh Gate
Harlow
Essex CM20 2JE
England

and Associated Companies throughout the world

Visit us on the World Wide Web at:
www.pearsoned.co.uk

———————————

First published 2001
Second edition published 2004
Third edition published 2007

© Pearson Education Limited 2001, 2004, 2007

ISBN-13: 978-0-273-70693-9
ISBN-10: 0-273-70693-4

British Library Cataloguing-in-Publication Data
A catalogue record for this book is available from the British Library.

Library of Congress Cataloguing-in-Publication data
A catalog record for this book is available from the Library of Congress

10 9 8 7 6 5 4 3 2 1
11 10 09 08 07

Typeset in 10/12.5pt Sabon by 35
Printed by Ashford Colour Press Ltd, Gosport

The publisher's policy is to use paper manufactured from sustainable forests.

We dedicate this book to Isabel, Vita, Jan, Jolien and Jelle

Contents

Supporting resources

Visit **www.pearsoned.co.uk/depelsmacker** to find valuable online resources

For instructors
- Complete, downloadable Instructor's Manual
- PowerPoint slides for every chapter that can be downloaded and used for presentations

For more information please contact your local Pearson Education sales representative or visit
www.pearsoned.co.uk/depelsmacker

About the authors

Patrick De Pelsmacker (b. 1957) holds a PhD in economics (University of Ghent, Belgium). He is Professor of Marketing at the University of Antwerp, Belgium and part-time Professor of Marketing at the University of Ghent. He has also worked at the University of Brussels (VUB). He is or has been a regular guest lecturer at various institutes, such as the Rotterdam School of Management (The Netherlands), the Swedish Institute of Management (Brussels, Stockholm), the China-Europe Management Centre (Antwerp), the Centre for Management Training (University of Warsaw, Poland), the Institute of Business Studies (Moscow, Russia) and Ca'Foscari University (Venice, Italy). He also has teaching experience in management and marketing programmes in France, Thailand, Indonesia, the Philippines, Vietnam, Italy, the Czech Republic, Hungary and Romania. He has undertaken numerous in-company training and consultancy assignments.

His field of interest is mainly in marketing research techniques, consumer behaviour and marketing communications. He has co-authored textbooks on marketing research techniques, and has written over eighty articles in various journals, including *Applied Economics, International Journal of Research in Marketing, Journal of Advertising, Psychology and Marketing, International Journal of Advertising, Journal of Marketing Communications, Advances in Consumer Research, Journal of Business Ethics, Journal of Consumer Affairs, Journal of International Consumer Marketing, Journal of Euro-Asian Economics, International Marketing Review, Educational and Psychological Measurements*, and *Psychological Reports*. He has contributed to more than twenty books and over sixty research reports and working papers on various marketing-related topics.

Maggie Geuens (b. 1969) holds a PhD in Applied Economics at the University of Antwerp, Belgium, where she also worked as an assistant professor. Currently she is Professor of Marketing at the University of Ghent. She is academic director of the Brand Management Centre at the Vlerick Leuven Gent Management School. She also has teaching experience in The Netherlands, Italy, Kazakhstan, Russia and Vietnam. She is involved in in-company training and consultancy on a regular basis.

Her main field of research interest is in advertising and consumer behaviour. She has co-authored a book, *Marketing Management*, and has contributed to books and to over twenty working papers and research reports in this field, and has published in journals such as *International Journal of Advertising, Journal of Marketing Communications, Psychology and Marketing, International Marketing Review, Journal of Advertising, Journal of Health Communication, Psychologica Belgica, Journal of Business Research, Tourism Management, Advances in Consumer Research, Psychological Review, Educational and Psychological Measurement* and *Journal of Consumer and Market Research*.

Joeri Van den Bergh (b. 1971) holds a masters degree in marketing (University of Ghent and the Vlerick Leuven Gent Management School). He started his career as a researcher at the Marketing Communication Research Centre, and later became senior researcher, involved in the activities of this Centre, as well as the Kids and Teens Marketing Centre, and the Senior Consumer Marketing Centre. He is co-founder and managing partner of InSites Consulting, the European online market research pioneer. He is a regular teacher in various marketing programmes, has been involved in in-company training and consultancy, and is a Counsellor of the Board of Ancienne Belgique (AB), a large concert venue in Belgium.

His main field of interest is marketing communications, and especially internet communications and research techniques. He has contributed to various books and to over thirty research reports in these fields. He has published in journals including *International Journal of Advertising* and the *Journal of International Consumer Marketing*.

Preface

Marketing communications are not only one of the most visible and widely discussed instruments of the marketing mix, with an overwhelming impact on both society and business, they are also one of the most fascinating. Every private consumer and business executive is exposed to advertising. They make use of sales promotions, are approached by sales persons, visit trade fairs and exhibitions, buy famous or not so famous brands, are a target of public relations activity, are exposed to sponsorship efforts, receive direct mail, telemarketing or research calls and visit stores in which no stone is left unturned to influence their buying behaviour.

Furthermore, an increasing number of consumers are regular users of the Internet. Marketing executives constantly face the challenge of integrating their promotional effort into strategic management and marketing plans. They must integrate the various instruments of the marketing communications mix, build successful brands, try to find out how marketing communications can be instrumental in achieving company objectives, and how they can be applied in specific marketing situations.

Following the success of the first two editions, this third edition of *Marketing Communications: A European Perspective* continues to offer a comprehensive overview of the cornerstones, techniques and applications of marketing in a European context.

The market

This book is geared to undergraduate and postgraduate students who have attended introductory courses in marketing, and who want to extend their knowledge to various aspects of marketing communications. The book can also be used by marketing communication professionals who want an overview of the whole field and may find inspiration and new angles to their marketing communications practice in the many examples, cases and research results that are covered in this text.

Organisation

The book is organised as follows. Chapter 1 provides a global overview of marketing and corporate communications and discusses the crucial topic of the integration of marketing communications activity. One of the major objectives of marketing communications is to build and maintain strong brands. Branding is covered in Chapter 2. The following chapter discusses the groundwork of all marketing communications activity. It is devoted to the intriguing question of how communications influence consumers.

In subsequent chapters the different steps in the marketing communications plan and the various instruments and techniques of marketing communications are covered. Separate chapters are devoted to the definition of target groups (4) and objectives (5) and to budgeting issues (6).

Chapters 7–17 cover each of the marketing communications instruments. Chapters 7–9 address advertising-related issues, including media planning and advertising research. Subsequent chapters each cover one tool of the marketing communications mix: public relations (10), sponsorship (11), sales promotion (12), direct marketing (13), point-of-purchase communications (14), exhibitions and trade fairs (15), personal selling (16) and e-communications (17). Marketing is not just about selling consumer products to individual end consumers. A large part of day-to-day marketing communications effort takes place in a business-to-business context. This is discussed in Chapter 18. Business is becoming increasingly global. Communicating in an international context is discussed in Chapter 19.

Pedagogy

To help reinforce key learning points, each chapter includes the following:

- Chapter Outline, which presents the contents of the chapter graphically.
- Chapter Objectives, Summaries and Review Questions assist the reader in understanding the important elements and help test one's knowledge.
- Main text organised in sections and subsections to help students digest and retain the information.
- Tables, figures, outlines and other illustrative material help the reader grasp the essential facts.
- Separate highlights throughout text cover extended examples, mini-cases, interesting research results or more technical issues.
- Suggested further readings offer the opportunity to refer to other, more specialised or specific sources of information on many subjects.
- An extensive European or global case study.

Distinctive characteristics

- This is not just a book about advertising, supplemented by a brief discussion of the other instruments of the marketing mix. Although advertising-related topics are thoroughly discussed, the book is comprehensive in that it covers *all* instruments of the marketing communications mix.
- The book has a consistent European focus. Although research results and examples from other parts of the world are covered, the main focus is the application of marketing communications concepts in a European environment.

- Every chapter contains an extensive European or global case study in a wide variety of industries, markets and countries. Most of these cases contain original and in-depth material, often provided by the marketing executives of the brands and companies discussed. Challenging case questions are designed to encourage the reader to apply the concepts from the chapter to the solution of the case at hand. Furthermore, many of these cases can be used with more than one chapter.
- Two chapters are devoted to the application of marketing communications principles and techniques in specific circumstances, such as business-to-business or international context.
- A number of chapters focus extensively on particularly important and/or relatively new fields of interest related to marketing communications. This is the case for the chapters on branding, how communications work, and e-communications.
- Throughout the text, numerous examples, case studies and research results from various countries, industries and markets are given, to illustrate and make the concepts as practice-oriented as possible.

New to the third edition

While the structure of the third edition of this book and its chapters has largely remained the same as the second edition, case studies, vignettes, examples and references have been updated and new materials have been added in every chapter. Some of the new material draws upon the following companies and organisations: Ford, Delvaux, Galler, Kitkat, Ferrari, Acer, Microsoft, Samsung, McDonald's, Virgin, Handicap International and Unicef.

Furthermore, most end-of-chapter cases have been updated and several new cases and vignettes have been added: Biotherm, Umicore, Electrolux, Mobistar, Barco and Suez. New theories, frameworks and research results were added in many chapters, amongst others ethical issues, integrating communication efforts, creativity in advertising, new consumer groups and new trends. The chapter on e-communications has been thoroughly updated to reflect the most recent evolutions and best-practice applications in this fast-growing area.

Finally, we are proud to offer instructor and student support materials at our website: **http://www.booksites.net/dePelsmacker**. Visit this site to find valuable teaching and learning materials on *Marketing Communications*.

Authors' acknowledgements

While we assume full responsibility for the content of the whole book, important parts of it could not have been written without the help and support of numerous people. We would particularly like to thank the following people, and hope we have not forgotten anyone.

Geert Ailliet
Roger Bennett (London Metropolitan University)
Malaika Brengman (Free University of Brussels)
Frank Caron (Jouret Management)
Kristiaan Cloots (FreeMobility & CIA)
Danny Cools (Sony I.T.E.)
Laurent De Hauwere, Pia Steen Hansen, Vincent Maenhaut, Sandra Deblander (Tele Atlas)
Serge Dekoninck (Saatchi and Saatchi Business Communication)
Dimitri De Lauw, Sofie Huygelen, Wouter Van den Herreweghen, Fons Van Dijck (VVL/BBDO)
Ann Galland (Barco)
Derek Gosselin, Rick Grant, Julie Vitek, Katja Damman (Suez)
Mark Hofmans, Siegfried Högl (GfK)
Martin Kingdon (Retail Marketing In-Store Services)
Wim Lagae (Lessius Hogeschool)
Nigel Lawrence (Dunnhumby)
Thomas Leysen, Eddy Cornelis (Umicore)
Pascal Libyn and Filip Eeckhoudt (RISC)
Klaus Lommatsch (Duval Guillaume)
Yuri Malinin (Mediafirst Russia)
Robin McCammon (General Motors)

Danny Meadows-Klue (IAB Europe)
Patrick Mertens (De Kie)
Marc Michils (Quattro Saatchi and Saatchi)
Geert Neutens (Artex)
Jorgen Nygaard Andreassen (Fedma)
Josefien Overeem (CV News)
Johan Ral, Christine De Pauw (European Communication Strategies)
Veerle Ringoir (Bacardi-Martini)
Dirk Schyvinck (Dexia)
Katharina Thiessen, Benjamin Michahelles (Beiersdorf AG)
Freddy Vander Mijnsbrugge
Georges Van Nevel (DVN)
Chris Van Roey (Mobistar)
Theo van Roy (Hints and Hits)
Joëlle Van Ryckevorsel, Teresa di Campello (L'Oréal)
Jan Verhaege (Etap Yachting)
A number of reviewers: Paul Copley, University of Northumbria; Claude Pecheux, Les Facultés Universitaires Catholiques de Mons; Jane Underhill, University of Northumbria; Tania Van den Bergh, Arteveldehogeschool, Flanders, Belgium

Finally, we would like to thank Pearson Education for supporting and publishing the third edition of this book. In particular we thank the following: David Cox, Senior Acquisitions Editor; Elizabeth Rix, Desk Editor; Adam Renvoize and Colin Reed, Senior Designers for cover and text, respectively; Angela Hawksbee, Senior Project Controller and Andrew Harrison, Editorial Assistant.

Publisher's acknowledgements

We are grateful to the following for permission to reproduce copyright material:

Plate 1   InSites Consulting
Plate 2   Artex NV
Plate 3   Barco
Plate 4   Mobistar
Plate 5   European Communication Strategies
Plate 6   Dexia Bank
Plate 7   Gesamtverband Werbeagenturen GWA & J. Walter Thompson
Plate 8   Leo Burnett
Plate 9   VF Corporation
Plate 10   Leo Burnett
Plate 11   Leo Burnett
Plate 13   Gesamtverband Werbeagenturen GWA & McCann-Erickson Europe
Plate 14   British Tourist Authority
Plate 15   Gesamtverband Werbeagenturen GWA & Euro RSCG Works
Plate 16   The Advertising Archives
Plate 17   Gesamtverband Werbeagenturen GWA & Abbott Mead Vickers BBDO
Plate 19   Federation of European Direct Marketing
Plate 20   Smart Center Antwerpen
Plate 21   Iglo-Ola, a Division of Unilever Belgium
Plate 23   Etap Yachting NV
Plate 24   Unilever, Inc.
Plate 25   Umicore
Plate 26   DHL Worldwide Network
Plate 27   V&S Vin & Spirit AB
Plate 29   Reticel

We are grateful to Guardian Newspapers Limited for permission to reproduce an extract on pages 124–125 from 'From lad mag to dad mag' by Hilly Janes published in *The Guardian*, 9th April 2003 © Hilly Janes 2003.

Table No. 4.6 from *The $100 Billion Allowance: Accessing the Global Teen market*, by E. Moses. © 200 Wiley. Reprinted with permission of John Wiley & Sons, Inc.; Table No. 6.2 Reprinted by permission of *Harvard Business Review*. The relation between share of invoice and market share. From Ad Spending: Maintaining Market Share by Jones, J.P., 68(1)/1990. Copyright © by the Harvard Business School Publishing Corporation; all rights reserved; Table No. 7.1 from IP Peaktime Television Key Facts, 2004 (www.ipb.be), reprinted by permission of IP NETWORK INTERNATIONAL, 45 Boulevard Pierre, FRIEDEN, LUXEMBOURG; Table 16.6 adapted from Dalrymple, D.J. & Cron, W. L. (1992), *Sales Management*. New York: John Wiley & Sons. © 1992 Wiley. Reprinted with permission of John Wiley & Sons, Inc.; Figures 6.4 & 6.5 reprinted by permission of *Harvard Business Review*. Relation between SOM & SOV in market dynamics. From Ad Spending: Growing market share by J.C. Schroer, 68(1)/1990. Copyright © by Harvard Business School Publishing Corporation; all rights reserved; Figure No. 13.4 reprinted by permission of Harvard Business School Press. From *The Loyalty Effect: The Hidden Force Behind Growth, Profits and lasting Value* by F.F. Reichheld, Boston, MA 2001. Copyright © 2001 by Harvard Business School Publishing Corporation; all rights reserved; Figure No. 16.1 from Dalrymple, D.J. & Cron, W.L. (1992), *Sales Management*. New York: John Wiley & Sons. © 1992 Wiley. Reprinted with permission of John Wiley & Sons, Inc.

Every effort has been made by the publisher to obtain permission from the appropriate source to reproduce material which appears in this book. In some instances we have been unable to trace the owners of copyright material, and we would appreciate any information that would enable us to do so.

Chapter 1

Integrated communications

Chapter outline

Chapter objectives

This chapter will help you to:

- Situate marketing communications in the marketing mix
- Get an overview of the instruments of the marketing communications mix
- Understand what integrated marketing and corporate communications mean, and their organisational implications
- Learn to know the factors leading to integrated communications
- Get an overview of the different levels of integration
- Understand why fully integrated communications are not easily implemented
- Get an overview of the essential steps in the marketing communications plan

Introduction

The integration of the various instruments of the marketing mix is one of the major principles of sound marketing strategy. Obviously, this integration principle also applies to
the various instruments of the communications mix. In fact, integrated communications
have been practised by good marketing communicators for decades. Why, then, has the
concept of 'integrated marketing communications' (IMC) in recent years developed into
one of the basic new trends or buzz words in marketing communications? Is IMC really
fundamentally new? Or is it an old idea which has rarely, if ever, been realised? In other
words, is it something everybody agrees on which should have been activated years ago,
but for all kinds of practical reasons was not? Or is it nothing more than traditional
marketing and advertising dressed up in fancy words and a new language?[1] Whatever
the case, the integration of the various instruments of the communications mix is
favourably influenced and necessitated by a number of important trends in marketing
today. At the same time, barriers to change, and to the successful implementation of
IMC, remain strong. The latter may explain why such an obvious concept as IMC, leading to a more homogeneous and therefore more effective communications effort, has
not been put into practice much earlier. As a result, integrated communications have a
number of practical and organisational consequences that influence the way in which
communicators organise their communications function, the way in which they deal
with communications consultants such as PR and advertising agencies, and indeed the
way in which communications consultants organise themselves.

Marketing and the instruments of the marketing mix

Marketing is the process of planning and executing the conception, pricing, promotion
and distribution of ideas, goods and services to create and exchange value, and satisfy
individual and organisational objectives.[2]

Given the marketing objectives and goals, the target segments and the market position that has to be defended, the tools of the marketing plan have to be decided upon.
The marketer has a number of tools to hand: the instruments of the marketing mix.
Traditionally, these instruments are divided into four categories, called the 4 Ps of the
marketing mix. In Table 1.1 some of the tools of the marketing mix are shown.

The **product** tool consists of three layers. The core product is the unique benefit that
is being marketed. In fact it is the position, the unique place in the mind of the consumer, that will be focused upon. Often the brand is a summary, a visualisation of this
core benefit and all the associations it leads to. The core product has to be translated
into a tangible product. Product features, a certain level of quality, the available options,
design and packaging are important instruments by which a core benefit can be made
tangible. Finally, the augmented product gives the tangible product more value and
more customer appeal. The augmented product can be defined as the 'service layer' on
top of the tangible product. It includes elements such as prompt delivery, installation
service, after-sales service and management of complaints.

Price is the only marketing instrument that does not cost anything, but provides the
resources to spend on production and marketing activity. The list price is the 'official'
price of a product. However, discounts and incentives of all kinds can be used to make

Table 1.1 Instruments of the marketing mix

Product	Price	Place	Promotion
Benefits	List price	Channels	Advertising
Features	Discounts	Logistics	Public relations
Options	Credit terms	Inventory	Sponsorship
Quality	Payment periods	Transport	Sales promotions
Design	Incentives	Assortments	Direct marketing
Branding		Locations	Point-of-purchase
Packaging			Exhibitions and trade fairs
Services			Personal selling
Warranties			Internet

the product more attractive. Systems of down payments and payment periods, combined with attractive interest rates, can also be used to make the offering more attractive and ensure that the immediate budget constraint is less of a problem for the consumer. The price instrument is an ambiguous tool. On the one hand, price cuts are an effective way to attract consumers. On the other, price cuts mean losing margin and profit. Furthermore, the customer gets used to discounts and may gradually be educated to buy on price and be a brand-switcher. The regular use of the price instrument is incompatible with building a strong position and a strong brand on the basis of product characteristics or benefits. Therefore good marketing can be defined as avoiding the price tool as much as possible.

By means of **place or distribution** the company manages the process of bringing the product from the production site to the customer. This involves transporting the product, keeping an inventory, selecting wholesalers and retailers, deciding on which types of outlet the product will be distributed in, and the assortment of products to be offered in the various outlets. Distribution strategy also implies maintaining co-operation between the company and the distribution channel, and finding new ways to distribute products, such as infomercials (programme-length advertising and selling) and e-commerce.

Promotion or marketing communications (MC) are the fourth and most visible instruments of the marketing mix. They involve all instruments by means of which the company communicates with its target groups and stakeholders to promote its products or the company as a whole. The instruments of the communications mix are introduced in the next section.

Good marketing is integrated marketing. Two principles are important when designing and implementing a marketing mix, i.e. **consistency** and **synergy**. Marketing instruments have to be combined in such a way that the company's offering is consistently marketed. In other words, all marketing instruments have to work in the same direction, and not conflict with each other. The ice cream brand Häagen-Dazs is positioned as a high-quality treat for sophisticated young adults. This core product or basic positioning is reflected in the whole marketing mix. The product itself is of excellent quality and made from the best ingredients. The brand name sounds – at least to an American public – exotic, maybe Scandinavian. The price is high, emphasising the exclusive character and the top quality of the brand. Distribution is relatively exclusive. The product is available in special shops or in separate freezers in supermarkets. Marketing communications reflect the sophistication and special, erotic atmosphere of the brand positioning. Similarly, a watch, the basic benefit of which is low cost, will be a very simple product with no special features or design. No strong brand name will be developed, and the basic marketing instrument will be price. The watch will have to be widely available, especially in discount stores and hypermarkets. Promotion will be limited to in-store communications or a simple presentation of the product in the retailer's advertising campaign.

Playtex: building a strong lingerie brand

Playtex is one of the leading lingerie brands in Europe. It holds number 2 position in the European market, with 6.2% market share. The major brand strength consists of the image it enjoys of possessing know-how, quality and comfort. Serious weaknesses, on the other hand, are that Playtex, as compared to other benchmark brands, scores worst of all on characteristics such as youth, modernity and seductiveness. According to consumers, Playtex is the most outdated and most old-fashioned brand. In a French qualitative study the following comments were reported: 'Playtex is for women who hide themselves, who don't dare to be sexy or provocative' and 'Playtex is for farmer's wives and pregnant women'. Furthermore, Playtex faces the threat of a customer base that is getting older: 55% of Playtex consumers are over 50. An opportunity seems to be the underwire bras market, both in volume and image. Underwire bras have a market share of 74% in France, 65% in Spain, 40% in Germany and 30% in Italy. In order to avoid having continuously to swim against the tide and greying or dying, together with its target group, Playtex launched a wired/coordinated bra line 'Stylis by Playtex'. This product line is aimed at 25–35 year olds and is positioned on seductiveness. In a segment in which the company has no image credibility, Playtex is faced with the challenge of creating interest in the brand. In contrast with the previous informational, functional-oriented campaigns, the communications campaign for Stylis by Playtex had to rule out any demonstration of comfort since this reduces the perception of seductiveness. However, both elements needed to be stressed: seductiveness and comfort, with the latter being expressed through both physical and psychological well-being. Unlike other brands, Playtex also focuses on the fact that women are more than 'clothes hangers' by using the slogan 'women whose minds are in as great shape as their body'. To differentiate itself further from competitors, Playtex decided to use TV commercials instead of print advertising and billboards. The results were remarkable, leading to a bronze Euro Effie award in 1998. Consumers' perceptions consist of a revolutionised image, a positive change and a brand for all women, but especially young women. Recall of product features ranged from 89% ('seductive bras') to 97% ('bras that feel comfortable'). Actual sales as compared to objectives are on average 21% higher. Increase in sales after four months was 71% in Spain, 85% in Germany and 45% in Italy.[3]

The second important principle is synergy. Marketing mix instruments have to be designed in such a way that the effects of the tools are mutually reinforcing. A brand will become stronger if it is advertised and available in the appropriate distribution outlets. Sales staff will be more successful if their activities are supported by public relations activity, price incentives or advertising campaigns. The effect of sponsorship will be multiplied if combined with sales promotion activity and public relations campaigns generating media exposure of the sponsored event. Intensive distribution will be more effective when combined with in-store communications and advertising, etc. Successful marketing depends on a well-integrated, synergetic and interactive marketing mix.

The same principles apply to marketing and corporate communication. In each of the chapters on communication instruments attention will be devoted to consistency and synergy in integrating communication instruments.

The communications mix

Often advertising is considered a synonym of marketing communications because it is the most visible tool of the communications mix. But, of course, a large variety of communications instruments exists, each with its own typical characteristics, strengths and weaknesses. The tools of the communications mix were presented in the last column of Table 1.1.

Advertising is non-personal mass communication using mass media (such as TV, radio, newspapers, magazines, billboards, etc.), the content of which is determined and paid for by a clearly identified sender (the company).

Sales promotions are sales-stimulating campaigns, such as price cuts, couponing, loyalty programmes, competitions, free samples, etc.

Sponsorship implies that the sponsor provides funds, goods, services and/or know-how. The sponsee will help the sponsor with communications objectives such as building brand awareness or reinforcing brand or corporate image. Sports, arts, media, education, science and social projects and institutions, and television programmes can be sponsored. Events are often linked to sponsorship. A company can sponsor an event or organise its own events, for instance for its sales team, its clients and prospects, its personnel, its distribution network, etc.

Public relations consist of all the communications a company instigates with its audiences or stakeholders. Stakeholders are groups of individuals or organisations with whom the company wants to create goodwill. Press releases and conferences, some of the major public relations tools, should generate publicity. Publicity is impersonal mass communication in mass media, but it is not paid for by a company and the content is written by journalists (which means that negative publicity is also possible).

Point-of-purchase communications are communications at the point of purchase or point of sales (i.e. the shop). It includes several communications tools such as displays, advertising within the shop, merchandising, article presentations, store layout, etc.

Exhibitions and trade fairs are, particularly in business-to-business and industrial markets, of great importance for contacting prospects, users and purchasers.

Direct marketing communications are a personal and direct way to communicate with customers and potential clients or prospects. Personalised brochures and leaflets (with feedback potential), direct mailings, telemarketing actions, direct response advertising, etc. are possible ways of using direct marketing communications.

Personal selling is the oral presentation and/or demonstration of one or more salespersons aimed at selling the products or services of a company. It is a personal contact between a company representative and a prospect or client.

E-communications offer new ways to communicate interactively with different stakeholders. The internet, together with e-commerce, combines communicating with selling. Mobile marketing uses the possibilities of text, video and sound transfer to mobile phones. Interactive digital television has the potential to transform traditional advertising into interactive communication on television.

Marketing communications try to influence or persuade the (potential) consumer by conveying a message. This message transfer may be directed to certain known and individually addressed persons, in which case it is called personal communications. The message transfer may also take place to a number of receivers who cannot be identified, using mass media to reach a broad audience. This is called mass communications. Personal communications are mainly direct and interactive marketing actions and personal selling.

Table 1.2 Personal versus mass marketing communications

	Personal communications	*Mass communications*
Reach of big audience		
■ Speed	Slow (selling), faster (DM)	Fast
■ Costs/reached person	High	Low
Influence on individual		
■ Attention value	High	Low
■ Selective perception	Relatively lower	High
■ Comprehension	High	Moderate–low
Feedback		
■ Direction	Two-way	One-way
■ Speed of feedback	High	Low
■ Measuring effectiveness	Accurate	Difficult

All other promotional tools are mass communications. Table 1.2 compares personal and mass marketing communications using different criteria. This comparison does of course generalise. The practical implications of the selection mix depend on the situation and the creative implementation and execution of the communications instruments. For instance a bad mailshot could also lead to higher selective perception and lower attributed attention.

Apple: combining personal and mass communications

The following illustrates the difference between personal and mass communications by applying both to a marketing communications strategy for the Apple Imac computer.

Personal communications
An Apple salesperson demonstrates the new Apple Imac to a group of clients or prospects. It will take some time before he has visited a large group of prospects (slow speed). To reach one prospect, the company will have to pay the labour costs of half a day (costs per person reached are high). Once the salesperson has made an appointment, the chance of the message being skipped or avoided is low and he or she will have the attention of the audience. He or she will be able to give a clear explanation and will know straightaway if the prospect has questions to ask or has not understood everything. The salesperson will be able to answer questions and listen to the needs of the prospect (two-way communication). The speed of feedback is very high: the prospect will or will not buy. As a consequence, effectiveness is easy to measure: sales/number of sales visits, etc.

Mass communications
Apple uses advertising on TV and in magazines to promote its new Imac computer. With TV advertising in prime time it reaches millions of viewers in a few seconds (high speed). Although advertising is not cheap, the cost per contact will be substantially lower than in the case of the salesperson. The attention TV viewers attribute to advertising is a lot lower: they may be talking with family members, reading, leaving the room for refreshments, etc. Selective exposure is high: zapping TV commercials, skipping ads in magazines, etc. It is difficult to transmit a clear message to everybody in 30 seconds or in one print ad. Ad viewers may have questions but cannot respond (one-way communication). The speed of feedback is low, and effectiveness may be assessed only later by looking at sales figures or brand-awareness scores. Effectiveness is often difficult to measure: market research is needed and is often subject to inherent methodological weaknesses. (See also Chapter 9.)

Another way of categorising marketing communications instruments is to differenti-ate between theme or image communications and action communications.

In **image** or **theme communications** the advertiser tries to tell the target group some-thing about the brand or products and services offered. The goal of image communications could be to improve relations with target groups, increase customer satisfaction or rein-force brand awareness and brand preference. This might eventually lead to a positive influence on the (buying) behaviour of the target group. Theme communications are also known as above-the-line communications, as opposed to below-the-line or action communications. This difference (the line) refers to the fee an advertising agency used to earn. All above-the-line promotional tools used to lead to a 15% commission fee on media space purchased. Consequently, above-the-line communications are synonymous with mass media advertising (TV, radio, magazines, newspapers, cinema, billboards, etc.). Below-the-line or **action communications** tools were communications instruments for which the 15% rule was not applicable. This terminology has since lost its import-ance because most agencies now charge a fixed fee or hourly fee rather than using the commission system.

Action communications seek to influence the buying behaviour of target groups and to persuade the consumer to purchase the product. The primary goal is to stimulate purchases. In practice, theme and action campaigns are not always that easy to discern. Sometimes the primary goal of advertising is to sell, as in advertisements announcing promotions or direct response ads. Visits from sales teams may also have the purpose of creating goodwill rather than selling. Theme promotions such as sampling gadgets to increase brand awareness are also used.

Eurocard/MasterCard: imbuing a well-known brand with richer emotional qualities

Europay International and its local partners market the Eurocard/MasterCard all across Europe. All countries differ in terms of the relative strength of the Eurocard/MasterCard, its target audi-ences and its major marketing objectives. For example, in central Europe, the main objective is to introduce the concept of credit cards; in Germany to motivate and capture first-time card applicants; in France to maintain market share. This has meant that locally generated campaign and media strategies and tactics have been applied throughout the years. In 2000 a global campaign was launched to build brand awareness and to create a stronger emotional bond with the target audiences. This image-building campaign was intended to differentiate an essentially generic brand with well-known functional qualities from its competitors. The European-wide target group for the campaign was defined as people who use their credit cards intelligently and responsibly, essentially to achieve good things in their lives for their families, their friends, their colleagues and themselves. Eurocard/MasterCard users are supposed to be more family-oriented, more in line with values of personal balance and harmony, rather than hedonistic and materialistic. The basic selling idea is 'Eurocard/MasterCard: the best way to pay for everything that matters'. The creative expression is 'There are some things that money can't buy – for everything else there's Eurocard/MasterCard'.

Television advertising has been used to launch, consolidate and leverage the concept of higher-level emotional values throughout Europe. The concept has been leveraged across all media and has also been used in below-the-line campaigns. Eurocard/MasterCard was a sponsor of the UEFA Euro 2000 and the UEFA Champions League soccer competitions. In all

▶

countries, the campaign was extended into various other media. For instance, in France, print and outdoor have become a key part of the media schedule; in the UK, cinema and national press were added; in Italy, radio and press were used. Both in Italy and in Germany, an internet site was set up, linked to the sponsorship of the Champions League. Research indicates that consumers value the campaign as sensitive and intelligent. It is considered to be advertising that clearly understands people as individuals and addresses them in an adult and positive manner. After the advertising campaign unprompted brand awareness in nine European markets had increased by 3% to 37%. Unprompted advertising awareness has moved up from 5% to 11%.[4]

Integration of marketing communications

Integrated marketing communications have been defined in a number of ways, stressing various aspects, benefits and organisational consequences of IMC. Putting it very generally,

> *'it is a new way of looking at the whole, where once we saw only parts such as advertising, public relations, sales promotion, purchasing, employee communication, and so forth, to look at it the way the consumer sees it – as a flow of information from indistinguishable sources'.*[5]

It is the integration of specialised communications functions that previously operated with varying degrees of autonomy. It is seamless, through-the-line communication.[6] The American Association of Advertising Agencies uses the following definition of IMC:

> *'a concept of marketing communication planning that recognises the added value of a comprehensive plan that evaluates the strategic roles of a variety of communication disciplines, e.g. general advertising, direct response, sales promotion and public relations – and combines these disciplines to provide clarity, consistency and maximum communication impact'.*[7]

The various definitions incorporate the same core idea: communications instruments that traditionally have been used independently of each other are combined in such a way that a synergetic effect is reached, and the resulting communications effort becomes 'seamless' or homogeneous. The major benefit of IMC is that a consistent set of messages is conveyed to all target audiences by means of all available forms of contact and message channels. Communications should become more effective and efficient as a result of the consistency and the synergetic effect between tools and messages. In other words, IMC has an added value when compared with traditional marketing communications.[8]

The rationale behind this new way of looking at marketing communications – and certainly the most relevant issue in the whole IMC discussion – is the consumer point of view. The consumer does not recognise the subtle differences between advertising, sponsorship, direct mailing, sales promotions, events or trade fairs. To him or her, these are all very similar and indistinguishable ways a company employs to persuade the consumer to buy its products. Therefore, it is very confusing and less persuasive to be confronted with inconsistent messages. Consumers may be more sensitive to commonalities and discrepancies among messages than to the specific communications vehicles used to transmit them.[9] IMC may therefore also be defined from the customer's point of view. It is in the field of communications where the receiver is offered sources,

Figure 1.1 The marketing mix and integrated marketing communications

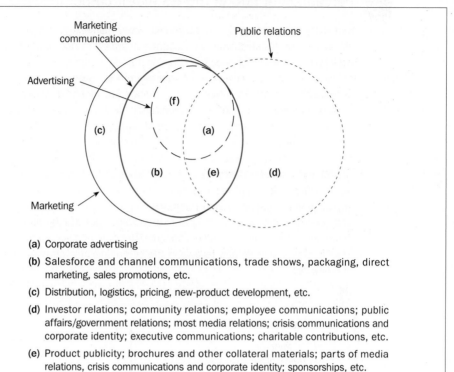

(a) Corporate advertising

(b) Salesforce and channel communications, trade shows, packaging, direct marketing, sales promotions, etc.

(c) Distribution, logistics, pricing, new-product development, etc.

(d) Investor relations; community relations; employee communications; public affairs/government relations; most media relations; crisis communications and corporate identity; executive communications; charitable contributions, etc.

(e) Product publicity; brochures and other collateral materials; parts of media relations, crisis communications and corporate identity; sponsorships, etc.

(f) Traditional mass-media advertising

Source: Hutton, J.H. (1996), 'Integrated Marketing Communication and the Evolution of Marketing Thought', *Journal of Business Research*, 37, 155–62.

messages, instruments and media in such a way that an added value is created in terms of a faster or better comprehension of the communication. Integration occurs at the consumer or perceiver level. It is the task of the communicator to facilitate this integration at the consumer level by presenting the messages in an integrated way.[10] In fact, there is a need to manage each point of contact between the consumer and the product or organisation.[11] In Figure 1.1, an overview is given of various elements of the communications mix, and the potentially integrating role of marketing communications.[12]

Integrated marketing communications do not happen automatically. All the elements of the communications mix have to be carefully planned in such a way that they form a consistent and coherent integrated communications plan. As a consequence, IMC can only be implemented successfully if there is also a strategic integration of the various departments that are responsible for parts of the communications function. Indeed, advertising, public relations, sales promotions and personal selling in most companies are traditionally managed by separate divisions that seldom communicate with each other, let alone take account of each other's priorities or integrate their efforts. Successful IMC rests on the existence of one communications manager who has the authority to supervise and integrate all the specialised communications functions of the organisation. Often this will imply a radical change in the structure of the organisation, and that may be the most important reason why IMC has not been implemented in most companies.

Perception of IMC in the US motor carrier industry

In a study of the perception of US motor carrier marketing managers, 192 respondents were asked to report for which communications functions they used each of the marketing communications tools they employed. The subjects framed five communications functions as the steps of the individual-level new product adoption model. Sixteen marketing communications tools were mentioned. The map below was generated by means of correspondence analysis on the basis of the number of times a communications tool was assigned to a specific communications function. It is a graphical representation of how appropriate the marketing managers perceive the role of each tool in each stage of the new product adoption process. The horizontal axis of the map primarily represents the various stages in the adoption process. All mass communication tools are clustered in the left-hand side of the map, close to the first stages of the adoption process (awareness and interest). Internet and e-mail are positioned close to the interest and evaluation stages. Telemarketing is more closely associated with generating trial, while personal selling is more closely associated with gaining adoption. Although integrated marketing communications advocates consistency in all the communications tools used, each tool still has a specific role to play in the communication strategy accompanying the launch of a new product.[13]

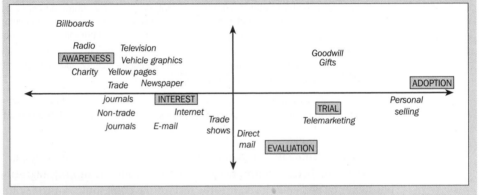

Source: Garber, L.L. and Dotson, M.J. (2002), 'A Method for the Selection of Appropriate Business-to-Business Integrated Marketing Communications Mixes', *Journal of Marketing Communications*, 8(1), 1–18.

In Table 1.3, some major differences between 'classic' communications and integrated communications are summarised.[14] In this overview the focus is on the changing nature of communications and the changing attitude of the consumer. Both necessitate a seamless integration of communications instruments. Traditional communications strategies are based on mass media, delivering generalised transaction-oriented messages. Integrated communications are much more personalised, customer-oriented, relationship-based and interactive. It is not only aimed at changing awareness and attitudes, but also at directly influencing behaviour. Integration is not synonymous with relationship marketing, satisfaction management or interactive communications. These principles may well be put in practice by means of a 'classic' communications strategy. However, by means of integrated communications the key objectives of modern marketing can be reached much more effectively.

Table 1.3 Classic and integrated communications

Classic communications	Integrated communications
Aimed at acquisition	Aimed at retention, relationship management
Mass communications	Selective communications
Monologue	Dialogue
Information is sent	Information is requested
Information provision	Information – self service
Sender takes initiative	Receiver takes initiative
Persuasive 'hold up'	Provide information
Effect through repetition	Effect through relevance
Offensive	Defensive
Hard sell	Soft sell
Salience of brand	Confidence in brand
Transaction-oriented	Relationship-oriented
Attitude change	Satisfaction
Modern: linear, massive	Postmodern: cyclical, fragmented

Based on: van Raaij, W.F. (1998), 'Integratie van Communicatie: vanuit de Zender of vanuit de Ontvanger' (Integration of Communication: Starting from the Sender or the Receiver?), in Damoiseaux, V.M.G., van Ruler, A.A. and Weisink, A., *Effectiviteit in Communicatiemanagement (Effectiveness in Communication Management)*. Deventer: Samson, 169–84.

Combining marketing communications tools to create synergies

Integrating the various tools can lead to synergies in a number of ways. Here are some examples:

- The sales team have an easier job if their product or company is well known as a result of sponsorship or advertising.
- In-store or point-of-purchase communications that are consistent with advertising are much more effective.
- A promotional campaign that is supported by advertising is generally more successful.
- Direct mailing is more effective when prepared by an awareness-increasing advertising campaign and supported by a sales promotion campaign.
- Public relations, corporate advertising and sponsorship can have synergetic effects on company image-building.
- Websites will be more frequently visited when announced in mass media advertising.
- Advertising for a trade show will be more effective if an incentive to visit the stand is offered.

Integration of corporate communications

Corporate communications can be defined as the total integrated approach to the communications activity generated by all functional departments of a company, aimed at establishing and maintaining the link between strategic objectives, the corporate identity and the corporate image in line.[15] Corporate communications have three main objectives:

1 To establish joint strategic starting points of the organisation that will have to be translated into consistent communications, in other words, to define a corporate identity that is in line with corporate strategy.

2 To reduce the gap between the desired identity and the image of the company (corporate image) that exists with its target groups.

3 To organise and control the implementation of all the communications efforts of a company, in line with the two above-mentioned principles.

Corporate strategy, culture, personality and identity

Corporate communications can be defined as the visualisation of corporate identity. To understand what the core concept of corporate identity means, its link with a number of related concepts has to be discussed. This is presented in Figure 1.2.[16]

Just as individuals have personalities, so do organisations. Corporate identity is derived from strategic priorities, corporate culture, corporate structure and industry identity. Corporate culture can be defined as 'the deeper level of basic assumptions and beliefs that are shared by members of an organisation, that operate unconsciously and define in a basic "taken for granted" fashion an organisation's view of itself and its environment'.[17] Put more simply, corporate culture can be defined as 'the way we do things around here'. It is determined by factors such as the corporate philosophy, values, mission, principles, guidelines, history, the founder of the company and the country of origin.[18] Corporate culture consists of a number of levels. The first level includes the physical aspects of the company, such as the atmospherics of the building (look and style) and the way visitors are treated. The second level consists of the values held by employees, such as the importance of honesty in doing business, the service-mindedness of the sales staff and the responsiveness to customer complaints.

Figure 1.2 **Corporate strategy, culture, personality, and corporate identity and its components**

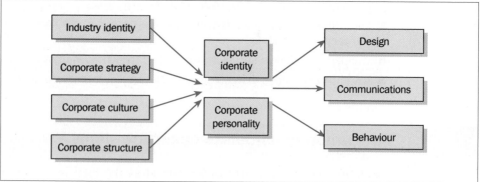

Source: Melewar, T.C. (2003), 'Determinants of the Corporate Identity Construct: A Review of the Literature', *Journal of Marketing Communications*, 9(4), 195–220.

The third level is achieved when everyone in the company develops a firm belief in the corporate culture characteristics, and behaves accordingly without questioning them. This third level is sometimes considered to be synonymous with corporate personality. This concept refers to the values held by personnel within the organisation. It is defined as the collective, commonly shared understanding of the organisation's distinctive values and characteristics. It encompasses corporate philosophy, mission, strategy and principles, and as such is a major component of the corporate identity or even its main determining factor.[19] A well-established corporate personality rests on a number of prerequisites. First of all, employees have to know and understand the company mission: what it wants to achieve, what its place in society should be, what the values and beliefs of the company are and how it wants to attain its goals. Furthermore, the employees should be involved in achieving these goals. They have to believe firmly in the company's basic mission and objectives, and be prepared to behave in a way that is consistent with this set of basic principles and objectives. As a result, the corporate personality is the set of characteristics of a company and a company's behaviour that are considered important, even self-evident, by managers and employees. It is based on the tradition and the characteristics of the company, its employees and its environment.

Corporate identity is also embedded in corporate strategy. Long-term strategic objectives will determine and shape the desired corporate personality: the company's mission will reflect the desired personality and corporate culture; positioning decisions will reflect the priorities that companies hold as to their chosen personality. On the other hand, the corporate personality will also determine the strategic options. Corporate culture and corporate personality are a very persistent part of the internal company environment, and as such cannot be changed overnight. Corporate strategy will always to a certain extent have to be based on the most persistent elements of the corporate personality, or at least take them into account.

Corporate identity is also influenced by industry identity and corporate structure. Industry identity involves underlying economic and technical characteristics of an industry, such as industry size, growth, competitiveness and technology levels. A strong generic or industry-wide identity (e.g. the banking industry) often forces companies to have similar strategies and missions. Corporate structure consists of organisational structure and brand structure. Organisational structure is concerned with the lines of communication and reporting responsibilities within the organisation. It relates to the degree of centralisation and decentralisation, and often has a major influence on brand structure.

Three different types of brand structure can be distinguished:[20]

1 *Monolithic identity*: the whole company presents itself as a unity, both in visual appearance and communications, and in behaviour. Companies such as IBM, McDonald's and BP are good examples of that type of corporate identity.

2 *Endorsed identity*: subsidiaries have their own identity and style, but the parent company is always clearly present in the background. Subsidiaries often have their own tradition and style which is considered to be a valuable marketing tool, but the endorsement of the mother company is strategically perceived as equally important. Examples are General Motors, Danone, and Kraft.

3 *Branded identity*: each division or even product line has its own identity and style, and the various product lines of the company do not seem to have anything to do

with each other. Often, this type of company has developed as a result of mergers and acquisitions of existing companies with a strong identity and/or companies that opt for 'interbrand competition', i.e. the strategic option that each brand or product line has to defend its own position, even if it means that they have to compete with other brands of the same company. Examples are Procter & Gamble and Lever.

Obviously, the choice of a specific type of corporate identity will depend on the strategic priorities defined, and will have a great impact on brand strategy and marketing and corporate communications.

Corporate identity is the set of meanings by which a company allows itself to be known and through which it allows people to describe, remember and relate to it. It is the way the company chooses to present itself to its relevant target audiences by means of symbolism, communications and behaviour. It is the tangible manifestation, the visual statement, of the personality (shared values) or corporate culture of an organisation. Corporate identity is what the company is, what it does and how it does it. It relates to the products and brands a company offers, how they are distributed, how the company communicates with publics or stakeholders, and how the company behaves.[21]

Corporate communications have to be based on, and be consistent with, the important elements of the corporate identity of the company. For instance, companies that are committed challengers in the markets in which they operate will be more aggressive communicators, may be using more direct guerrilla types of marketing and thus communications strategies involving head-on sales promotion and comparative advertising techniques. Also the principles of value marketers, like The Body Shop, will be reflected in all their communications efforts. Sponsorship will be used to link the company's image to environmental causes such as wildlife concerns, and in-store communications techniques will be used to convey the message of avoiding waste by recycling and simple, low-cost packaging.

But building and maintaining a corporate identity is more than just consistently using the traditional tools to communicate its core elements. Everything the company does, and all the material the company uses, should be an integral part of the effort to convey a homogeneous and consistent identity. Corporate symbolism or corporate design, more specifically a consistent house style on business cards, letter heads, vehicles, gifts, clothes, equipment, packaging, etc. is an integral part of the corporate identity, or at least of the way in which it is made visible.

The visualisation of the corporate identity: logos and slogans

The company name, logo and slogan are vital elements of the house style of a company and important elements of corporate design. They are the visualisation of the corporate identity.
   Logos and slogans should have a number of characteristics:

■ A logo should be the long-term visualisation of the company's strategy. One logo and one slogan should be used for the whole company. The slogan should be a perfect summary of the company's identity.

■ Logos and slogans have to be distinctive. They are tools of differentiation between the company and its competitors. As a result, slogans that are relevant but too general should be avoided, as well as logos that are too similar to the ones used by the competition. The same goes for company names, for that matter. Often, images and colours are much more important factors in recognising a logo or a brand and attributing it to the correct product than the verbal elements of a brand (the brand name).

■ Additionally, slogans should be relevant for the consumer, otherwise they will not be able to contribute to the development of a distinctive corporate image.

■ The logo and slogan should be timeless, but modifiable. All too often logos refer to a short-term objective, or to an issue that seemed important at the time it was designed, but loses all its relevance after some time. Since logos and slogans should visualise the long-term image of the company, they should have a timeless capacity that allows them to be used for a long period of time. Having said that, the perception of what is beautiful changes over time. Logos should be modifiable in that the corporate design should be adaptable to changing aesthetic preferences over time, without radically altering the whole house style.

The logo of a local government body is shown. The name of the local community starts with an E, which is recognisable in the three horizontal lines in the logo. The lines are coloured green in the original because the government wants to create an ecological image. The building on the logo is the new community centre, which opened at the time of the design of the logo. Needless to say, this logo is neither universal nor timeless, let alone easy to understand or to integrate in other communication tools.

■ Slogans, but especially logos, should be usable in all circumstances and in all communications instruments and tools. This includes advertisements, mailings and annual reports, but also business cards, letterheads, envelopes, brochures, trucks, walls, films, ties, pens, press releases, etc. They should be equally distinctive on a business card and on a large truck. The company should be able to combine them with other logos, to include them in communications tools with different colours, with all kinds of letter formats and shapes. (See Plate 1.)

Corporate design is not just a matter of logos and slogans. Here are a number of examples in which intelligent design has contributed to the corporate or brand identity:

– the shape of the container (Toilet Duck, Absolut Vodka);
– a distinctive opening device (Grolsch beer);
– the packaging material (Ferrero Rocher; Absolut Vodka);
– the colour of the packaging (Marlboro);
– the use of a personality (KFC and Colonel Sanders, the Marlboro cowboy).

Besides communications and corporate design, corporate behaviour is also an important factor in making the corporate identity visible. The saying 'actions speak louder than words' is very applicable to corporate identity issues. The way in which the employees of a McDonald's restaurant behave is an integral part of the corporate identity of the company. The self-proclaimed customer-friendliness of a bank (e.g. by means of an advertising campaign) may be completely destroyed by behaviour that is inconsistent with this principle. A mineral water, using 'purity' as its main selling proposition, cannot afford actions that may be perceived as a threat to this purity, e.g. manufacturing processes involving potentially toxic chemicals or a lack of hygiene during the bottling process. Internal marketing, and internal communications as a part of it, will be extremely important in convincing and training staff to develop behaviour that is consistent with the desired corporate identity.

Paying attention to the corporate identity is of growing importance for a number of reasons:

- The business environment is undergoing rapid changes, altering the structure and the strategic direction of companies. Mergers, acquisitions, changing competitive environments, etc. change the nature of markets in radical ways. Corporate identity should therefore be constantly monitored and reviewed, along with the rapidly changing strategies.

- It is increasingly difficult for companies to differentiate themselves and their products from each other. Developing a distinctive corporate identity can be of crucial importance in developing a unique market position.

- Companies tend to become more global, and hence the danger of inconsistent communications by the various business units becomes greater. Developing a common corporate identity can be the basis of a more consistent communications strategy.

- Important economies of scale can be achieved by ensuring that all forms of communication by a company are consistent with one another. A good starting point is the development of a common base, i.e. a common corporate identity that is based on well-defined strategic options.

- A well-established corporate identity can lead to increased motivation of the company's own employees. Feeling 'part of a family' may stimulate them to do a better job.

- A corporate identity that is communicated convincingly creates confidence and goodwill with external target groups of stakeholders. Shareholders and investors may have more confidence, relations with the government may be better, higher quality employees may be attracted, and the general public may have a more favourable attitude.

Code of conduct of the Belgian Association of Communication Companies

Advertisers and communication professionals value freedom in marketing communication as a fundamental principle of free-market economy. However, responsibility comes with freedom. The Belgian ACC, a professional organisation of communication agencies, adopted a moral code of conduct that encompasses ten principles of ethical communication, above and beyond the legal requirements that are laid down in advertising regulations.[22] All members of the ACC endorse this code. These principles are:

- Marketing communications must not mislead the consumer;

- Marketing communications may not abuse the good faith of the consumer or, particularly in the case of children and youngsters, their lack of knowledge and experience;

- Marketing communications must be recognisable as such, whatever the medium or the format used. It must also be clear who the sender is;

- All marketing communications based on facts must be verifiable;

- Marketing communications may not discriminate or insult people on the basis of race, nationality, religion, sex, sexual disposition or age;

▶

- Marketing communications must respect people's privacy;
- ACC members always strive for the best possible advice, without fear or prejudice, and always act in the best interest of their customers;
- ACC members always honour their commitments to customers, suppliers and employees;
- ACC members respect other professional codes in the industry, such as the ones of the Jury for Honest Practices in Advertising, the code for sponsoring and advertising on television, and the legal limitations to advertising towards children;
- ACC members respect each other.

Needless to say this code of conduct is an ambitious one, and can easily conflict with old habits (such as certain types of humour in advertising) and emerging practices (such as data mining, and product placement and branded entertainment) in marketing communications.

Source: ACC (2006) code of conduct, ACC: Brussels.

Corporate image and corporate reputation

The corporate image is the stakeholder's perception of the way an organisation presents itself. It is the result of the interaction of all experiences, beliefs, feelings, knowledge and impressions of each stakeholder about an organisation. It is a subjective and multidimensional impression of the organisation. The corporate identity resides in the organisation, but the corporate image resides in the heads of the stakeholders.[23] The corporate image is not always consistent with the desired corporate identity; in other words, an image gap may exist.

Corporate reputation is the evaluation or esteem in which an organisation's image is held. It is based on experience with the company and/or exposure to communications, behaviour and symbolism. While corporate image can be quite transient and short-term in nature, corporate reputation is more firmly embedded in the mind of an individual. Images may change, but the corporate reputation is not easily altered in the short run. It implies credibility, trustworthiness, reliability and responsibility.[24] It refers to how stakeholders view and believe in the core identity and image components of the company.

The corporate image is influenced by a number of factors, the corporate identity and its communication being only two of them. These factors are presented in Figure 1.3.[25]

Corporate identity or corporate culture and corporate strategy are important determining factors or cornerstones of the corporate image, as well as marketing and external corporate communications. But the company's employees also play an important role. Their communications with external target groups and their behaviour in their contacts with these groups will to a large extent determine how the company is perceived. Therefore, internal communications are very important to corporate identity-building and corporate communications. Misfits between the perception of the employees and the desired corporate identity may therefore lead to an undesirable image gap.

Several problems of internal marketing and internal communications can be distinguished. First of all, strategy may not be internally communicated at all. Second, strategies may be communicated but incompatible with the historic corporate identity, organisational behaviour or the communications. Finally, strategy may be communicated, understood and compatible, but employees may lack the tools to translate it into

Figure 1.3 Factors influencing the corporate image

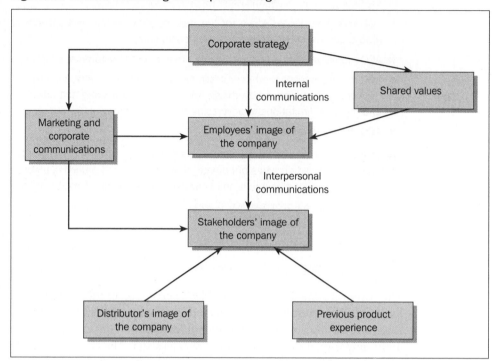

Based on: Dowling, G.R. (1986), 'Managing Your Corporate Images', *Industrial Marketing Management*, 15, 109–15.

reality. Ideally, good strategy is communicated internally, and is compatible and workable. The interdependency of internal and external communications cannot be neglected. Advertising claims that are unrealistic, or external communications that are perceived as silly or inappropriate, will lead to gaps between the external communications of the company and the employees' behaviour and their communications with target groups. Prerequisites for an effective internal communications strategy are an environment that values free expression of ideas, tools such as suggestion boxes, quality circles, meetings and committees, and the willingness of the management to take suggestions and criticism into account.

Besides their own staff, other intermediate audiences, such as the distribution channel or advertising agencies, may have an influence on the corporate image. Finally, reality is an important factor: product experience is, to put it in operant conditioning terms, a powerful reinforcer or punisher in the development of a corporate image. In Figure 1.4 the complex reality of corporate image management is summarised.

Corporate image may also be defined as the attitude of members of the target groups towards the company. Indeed, image and attitude are two sides of the same coin. The concept of 'image' is used to describe the characteristics of an object, such as a company, while the word 'attitude' is used to describe the characteristics of a person. Attitude and image are composed of three dimensions:

1 *Beliefs, the cognitive dimension of the attitude.* People may hold certain beliefs about a company, for instance, that it is a good company to work for, or that it manufactures high-quality products.

Figure 1.4 Important factors in corporate image management

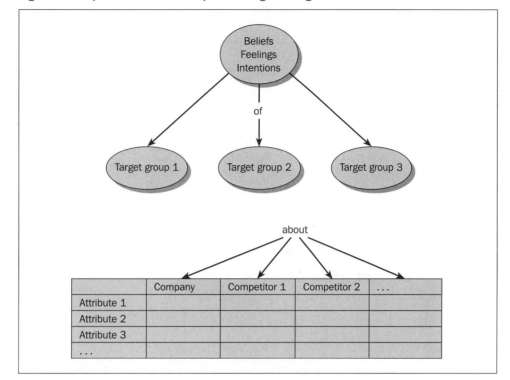

2 *Emotional feelings, the affective component of the attitude.* People may dislike a company for its social or environmental policies, or its handling of a crisis.

3 *Behavioural intentions.* Target group members may be inclined to buy products of a company, or to go and work there.

Corporate communications should focus on all three components of attitude formation.

Images are not good or bad as such. The corporate image is not monolithic, but multidimensional. People's attitudes towards a company are based on a number of image attributes, and the extent to which they are perceived as important. Companies may be judged on the basis of attributes such as the quality of their products, the nature of their external communications, their value system, the friendliness of their personnel, their environmental policy, etc. Evidently, not all attributes are equally important. Target group members make an (implicit) ranking of corporate image attributes. As a result, the corporate image may be conceptualised as the weighted average of perceptions on a number of corporate image dimensions. In Figure 1.5 the multidimensional corporate image of a financial newspaper is shown and compared with two of its competitors.

This figure also illustrates another important aspect of corporate images. Image attributes are not perceived as good or bad, but as better or worse than some benchmark. Indeed, the corporate image of a company should always be compared with a standard or a norm. This can be the competitors' images, or the company's image in the past, or some kind of normative expectation. Especially when measuring and interpreting the results of corporate image research, this will be an important consideration.

Figure 1.5 The multidimensional corporate image of a financial newspaper and two of its competitors

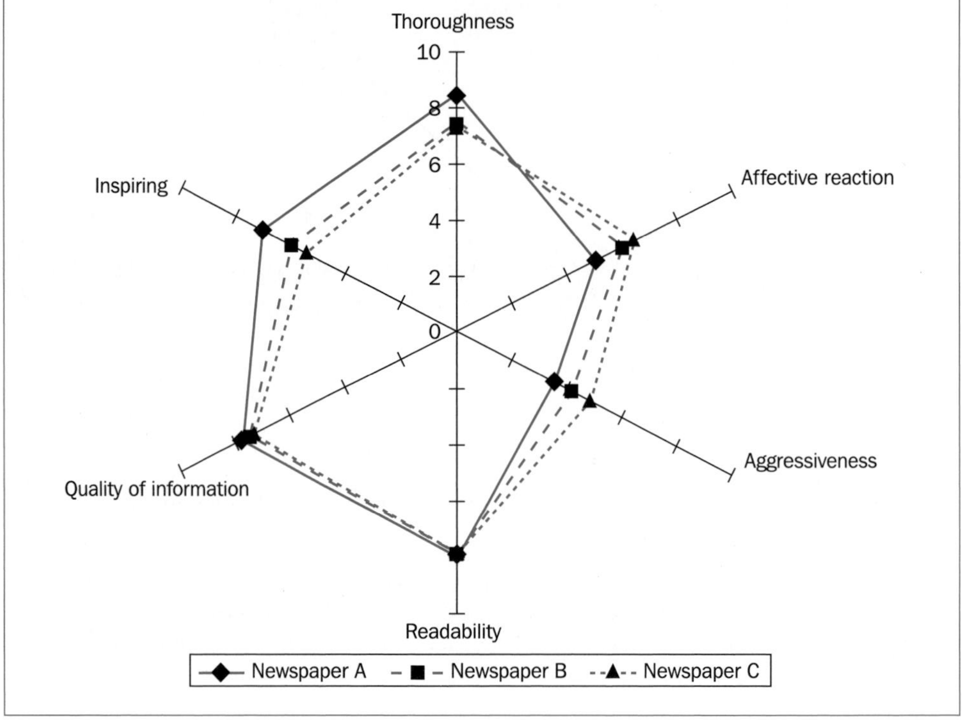

Based on: De Pelsmacker, P. and Mielants, C. (1998), 'Tijdspiegel, een Analyse van de Lezers van de *Financieel-Economische Tijd*' (Time Mirror, an Analysis of the Readership of *De Financieel-Economische Tijd*), Antwerp: University of Antwerp.

Finally, some aspects of the corporate image may differ from one target group to another. Employees may see the company as customer-unfriendly, and selling low-quality products, while the media or the distribution channel may have a totally different perception.

Corporate social responsibility in Cyprus

Corporate social responsibility (CSR) refers to a company's obligation, beyond that required by law or economics, to pursue long-term goals that are good for society. CSR refers to various types of activities and behaviours, such as ethical behaviour, sustainable development, environmentally friendly behaviour and philanthropic activity. CSR is a synonym for 'good citizenship'. Social responsibility can be used to build strong brands and a positive corporate image and reputation. In a pilot study involving 40 managers and directors of Cypriot companies, the corporate social responsibility practices were identified. They are summarised in the following table. The figures refer to the percentage of the respondents that indicated they practice the principle. Although, on the basis of these results, CSR appears to be of major concern to companies in Cyprus, the low response rate of 1% in this study seems to indicate the opposite.[26]

General	%
Engages in fair and honest business	68
Sets high standards of behaviour for all employees	54
Exercises ethical oversight of the executive and board levels	37
Initiates and engages in genuine dialogue with stakeholders	32
Develops and publishes both internally and externally a Code of Conduct	37
Applies confidentiality and anonymity with regard to privileged information	54
Community	
Fosters a reciprocal relationship between the corporation and the community	73
Invests in the communities in which the corporation operates	51
Launches community development activities	27
Encourages employee participation in community projects	42
Consumers	
Respects the rights of consumers	68
Offers quality products and services	83
Provides information that is truthful, honest and useful	76
Avoids false and misleading advertising	68
Discloses all substantial risks associated with product or service usage	34
Avoids engaging in price fixing	37
Employees	
Provides a family-friendly work environment	63
Provides an equitable reward and wage system for employees	61
Engages in open and flexible communication with employees	54
Engages in employment diversity in hiring and promoting women	46
Encourages employees to treat one another with dignity and fairness	59
Investors	
Strives for a competitive return on investments	37
Engages in fair and honest business practices in the relationship with stakeholders	54
Suppliers	
Engages in fair trading transactions with suppliers	76
Environment commitment	
Demonstrates a commitment to sustainable development	54
Demonstrates a commitment to the environment	73

Source: Doukakis, I., Krambia-Kapardis, M. and Katsioloudes, M. (2003), 'Corporate Social Responsibility: A Pilot Study into the Realities of the Business Sector in Cyprus', in Bennett, R. *New Challenges for Corporate and Marketing Communications. Proceedings of the Eighth International Conference on Marketing and Corporate Communications.* London: London Metropolitan University, 64–80.

What is the value of a positive corporate image?

- It gives the company authority and it is the basis for success and continuity.

- Consumers buy products, often not just because of their intrinsic quality, but also because of the reputation and the value they attach to the company marketing the products. A positive corporate image creates an emotional surplus, which can be a more persistent long-term competitive advantage than whatever specific product characteristic.

- A positive corporate image is particularly important for companies the customers of which are not deeply involved in the product category. Such customers will base their buying decisions on limited information, such as the impression they have of the company's value. But even when the customer is highly involved, but does not have the capability of judging the value of the company's offerings (because the available information is too complex, or product quality is difficult to assess, as in the case of services), the corporate image can be the decisive factor in the customer's decision.

- It creates a goodwill surplus which avoids or diminishes problems with government, pressure groups, consumer organisations, etc. in times of crisis.
- It supports the company in attracting more easily the people that are crucial for its success, such as investors, analysts, employees, and partners.

Integrated corporate communications should take all these considerations into account.

Factors leading to integrated marketing and corporate communications

A number of important changes and trends have created the need and urge to integrate marketing and corporate communications and to facilitate them. In Table 1.4 key IMC drivers are listed.

There is a widespread belief that mass media communications are becoming increasingly less effective. Communications clutter, resulting from increasing advertising pressure, leads to increased irritation and advertising avoidance behaviour and to a situation in which advertising in traditional, undifferentiated and impersonalised media is less and less capable of attracting attention, let alone of convincing consumers. As a result of more and more advertisers claiming media time and space, mass media are increasingly expensive. Furthermore, traditional mass media communications are primarily capable of stimulating awareness and attitudes, but much less of stimulating or directly influencing demand. The need for marketing strategies influencing behaviour directly has further eroded the attractiveness of traditional mass media. Using more

Table 1.4 **Key drivers of integrated communications**

- Loss of faith in mass media advertising
- Media cost inflation
- Need for more impact
- Need for more cost-effectiveness and efficiency
- Media fragmentation
- Audience fragmentation
- Increased reliance on highly targeted communication methods
- Low levels of brand differentiation
- Increased need for greater levels of accountability
- Technological evolutions
- Greater levels of audience communications literacy
- Overlapping audiences
- More complex decision-making units
- Need to build more customer loyalty
- Move towards relationship marketing
- Globalisation of marketing strategies

media and more channels and tools to reach the consumer effectively increases the need for integration of these tools.

New forms of communications: advertorials and infomercials

Traditional mass media can be used to create new forms of communication to escape from message clutter. One of these new types is the advertorial (advertisement + editorial). For instance, a television programme can take viewers into department stores to introduce them to the latest fashion and beauty trends. At a certain moment in time, the show directs the customers to certain brands, the marketers of which have sponsored the programme. The viewers only learn about the sponsors at the end of the show. After the show, consumers are offered the opportunity to order a newsletter containing information about the featured products. Similarly, the Walt Disney Studios sponsor an entertaining movie news show. At the end of the show it is revealed that it was paid for by Buena Vista (Disney's film distribution company). Of course, most consumers are not aware of the close link between Disney and Buena Vista.[27] As becomes clear from the examples, these new forms of communication may raise some serious ethical questions.

   Another type of creative communication on television is the infomercial (information + commercial) or programme-length advertising. During an 'informative programme' a product is presented and demonstrated to the consumer, who is urged to order it by telephone. Infomercials are very behaviour-oriented and try to bridge the gap between not knowing the product and ordering it in half an hour's time.[28]

The recession at the beginning of the 1990s increased cost-awareness and the need for more cost-effective and efficient marketing. The time horizon of companies became more short-term-oriented. As a result there is a greater need for directly effective marketing strategies and for instruments the effectiveness of which can be assessed and can be assessed instantaneously. There is, in other words, a growing need for increased levels of accountability. Consequently, mass media are supplemented with, or replaced by, other communications tools with allegedly more impact, that focus much more on influencing the behaviour of individual consumers directly, and the effectiveness of which can be measured precisely, such as direct marketing and interactive marketing communications. Adding more and more diversified tools to the communications mix leads to more media being used and more fragmented media, and increases the need for integration of marketing communications. As a spin-off from this integration of fragmented communications tools, it becomes less and less relevant to measure the effect of one single element in the communications mix, such as advertising. The measurement of communications effectiveness will have to focus on techniques such as monitoring and tracking, which assess the effectiveness of a total campaign at the brand level.

Audiences and markets tend to become more and more fragmented, making mass media less effective and increasing the need for more specialised and fragmented media. Communications tend to become customised for narrower and narrower markets, and customer contact is established by means of multimedia methods. There is an increasing reliance on highly targeted communications methods, such as database techniques and boutique channel (highly targeted television channel) advertising.[29] Integrated marketing communications are about co-ordinating multiple and diverse tools targeted at multiple and diverse audiences.[30]

New creative ways to reach target audiences

Marketers are constantly looking for new, efficient and creative ways to reach their audiences. Here are some examples.

Extremely short ads

Master Lock, the American lock company, produced a 'zap-proof' and 'snack-proof' ad: the one-second commercial. The goal of such extremely short ads is to prevent consumers using the commercial break to zap to another channel. Although one can question whether it is possible to convey any information in just one second, Master Lock is convinced that it is sufficient on the condition that the advertising company is well known and uses a very familiar logo or image. Between June and August 1998, Master Lock aired 400 one-second ads. So far, no other company has announced similar campaigns.[31]

Free products in exchange for commercial messages

The Californian multimedia company Free-PC offered a free computer to 10,000 consumers.[32] In exchange for a Compaq with internet access, the consumers have to accept that almost half of the 4.2 gigabyte hard disk is occupied by advertisements. The banners appear on the side of the screen and are frequently adapted when the user is online. The advertising companies choose which messages the user receives. Well-known companies such as Disney, credit card company MBNA, and internet car dealer Autobyte! seemed to have a lot of faith in this project and enlisted as advertisers. Whether advertisers are really willing to pay for the costs of the PCs remains to be seen. However, this is not so inconceivable since it seems to be part of a trend that can already be witnessed in the mobile phone market. More and more phone providers offer free telephones in exchange for subscribing to their network. The same goes for internet providers. British Telecom and LineOne announced that they were dropping their subscription fees. Furthermore, phone companies are offering free phone calls as long as the consumer is willing to accept that his or her phone call will be interrupted by an advertising message every five minutes. Again, although free phone calls to friends seem to be an attractive offer, the future will show whether the consumer is willing to take the advertising messages that accompany it.

Troopers

Sometimes it is difficult to motivate people to go to a musical or a play because they live too far away, or are not in the habit of going. The Belgian company Music Hall tries to change this by hiring 'Troopers'.[33] Troopers are preferably people who are very sociable and have lots of friends and acquaintances. The goal is that every Trooper tries to motivate his or her friends to go and see, for example, *Les Misérables* together. In exchange, the Trooper receives a price reduction on each ticket, the total of which he or she can keep for him or herself or split with the group. The advantage for Music Hall is obvious: they can reduce their advertising budget and reach people who would not otherwise have bought a ticket.

Advertising for animals

In January 1999 the first commercial for animals was aired on the British channel ITV.[34] Whiskas announced it in the media and asked the British people to observe their cat's responses. According to a first test, 60% of cats paid immediate attention to hearing the mice and bird sounds, and a minority approached the TV to sniff and pat the screen. The goal of the advertising agency, Saatchi and Saatchi, seems to have been obtained: 'Sell to the one that does not consume. Be consumed by the one that does not buy'. Whiskas' research department was overwhelmed with responses and the question from, amongst others, Japanese production houses to extend the campaign.

▶

Stealth tactics

The New York advertising agency Big Fat Inc. organises campaigns that can be labelled as undercover, stealth or guerrilla marketing. Key influencers of the target group promote products or brands by means of so-called real life product placement. For instance, a group of young and attractive role models are paid to hang around in trendy bars, to order a new drink, say vodka-mineral water, and to talk about it in such a way that the other visitors of the bar are positively exposed to the new drink in a real-life situation. Nestlé organises wake-up calls for students. Fifteen minutes after the wake-up call, someone rings the doorbell to offer the student a cup of Nestlé coffee. The technique as such is not new. Years ago, the cognac brand Hennessy hired people to order Hennessy in bars.[35]

High exposure

The Dutch agency MediMountain sells advertising space on ski lifts in the Alps. Millions of tourists are exposed to the commercial messages on 650 ski lifts in 165 ski areas in Switzerland, France, Austria, Italy and Slovenia. Advertising on ski lifts has an enormous advantage for the advertiser: forced and unchallenged exposure is high during a substantial amount of time.[36]

Most markets in well-developed countries are mature. This means that a lot of products and brands are of similar quality. Low levels of brand differentiation increase the need to make the difference by means of communications. Therefore, some argue 'that the basic reason for [the increased attention for] integrated marketing communications is that marketing communications will be the only sustainable competitive advantage of marketing organisations in the 1990s and into the twenty-first century'.[37]

Mainly as a result of technological evolutions and innovations, new marketing and marketing communications tools are becoming available. Scanning and database technology allow more in-depth knowledge of the consumer and especially a more personalised and direct approach of the consumer. Interactive media, such as the internet, have contributed to a situation in which the relationship between the sender and the receiver of messages is less unidirectional. Direct marketing and direct response communications also lead to a situation in which communications become more and more receiver-directed.[38] Together with increased communications literacy on the part of the consumer, this leads to a market situation in which much of the power is at the receiving end, i.e. the receiving consumer decides what he or she will be exposed to and how he or she will react to it. Indeed, the marketing situation has gradually shifted from a situation in which all the power of knowledge and control was in the hands of the manufacturer to a market in which the retailers are the strongest party. Today the balance is shifting towards a market in which the consumer is the most powerful agent.[39] In fact, one could argue that integration is mainly technology-driven. New technologies and applications, such as the internet, make the consumer less accessible, and force companies into a more integrated approach towards a fragmented and increasingly interactive communications situation which will make marketing communications more credible and more convincing.

Organisations are increasingly communicating with multiple audiences and stakeholders. Many of these stakeholders overlap. An employee may be a shareholder, a community leader may be a supplier, members of stakeholder groups are target customers, and all of them are exposed to different media. Furthermore, decision-making units in many of these stakeholder groups are increasingly complex, implying that they have to be reached by means of different communications tools and channels. It is not necessary to give exactly the same message to all these audiences; on the contrary, messages will have to be adapted to the stakeholders' needs. Nevertheless, it is very important not to convey contradictory messages. Consistent communication has to reflect the mission, corporate identity and core propositions of the organisation to all target groups. Integrated communications provide a mechanism for identifying and avoiding message conflicts when communicating with these overlapping and complex target groups.

One of the trends in marketing today is the increasing importance of building customer loyalty instead of attracting and seducing new customers. This trend towards relationship marketing implies a much more 'soft sell' approach. Integrated marketing communications focus upon building a long-term relationship with target groups by means of consistent interactive communications, rather than aggressively persuading the consumer to buy a company's products.

Finally, markets are becoming increasingly global. Phenomena such as the internet, but also the globalisation of mass media and the increasing exposure of consumers and stakeholders to international communication stimuli, increase the need for consistency in everything the company communicates in all countries in which it markets its products.[40]

Marketing communication professionals' views on new trends

In November 2005 two surveys were held in two different groups of marketing communication professionals.[41] The purpose of these studies was to explore the extent to which the concept of Integrated Marketing Communications was understood and applied, and to find out how these professionals perceived the future of marketing communications. The following remarkable results were found in the first study, which was based on 150 responses:

■ Only half of the respondents said they understood the concept of IMC (defining it as 'consistency over time and channels') and only one in three claimed to practise it.

■ Seven out of ten pay attention to multi-channel reinforcement.

■ Strangely enough, four out of five claim to be organised for IMC and advocate IMC to build strong brands (amongst whom, apparently, a number who said they did not know the concept).

■ On average 9–10 marketing communications media and channels are used per campaign.

■ 43% agree that the efficiency of traditional above-the-line instruments is decreasing. On the other hand, a similar percentage thinks that these instruments are the best guarantee for communication effectiveness.

■ 80% believe that in five years' time marketing communications as we know it will still be the same.

■ 53% believe that the Internet is indispensable in a marketing communications campaign, but 40% think it is overrated as a communications channel.

■ 43% believes in the disrupting effects of interactive television.

■ The share of 'old' media is universally projected to decrease, at the benefit of 'new', interactive media.

■ Half of the respondents claim to measure the return on communication investments; 12% state that they do not even measure communication effectiveness.

■ The planning horizon of 80% of the respondents is less than one year.

▶

The second study was conducted in a different sample of 40 marketing communication professionals. The table below gives an indication of the type of marketing communication activities and instruments are more or less important, and are expected to grow more or less. Remarkably, direct and short-term instruments are very important, and are projected to become even more important in the future. Corporate communication efforts are, at least in this small group, not so important, and are going to be even less important in the future.

Table 1.5 Importance and projected growth in communications activities

Very important and fast growth	Very important and moderate growth	Very important and slow growth
■ Sales promotion ■ Direct communication ■ Catalogues	■ Internal communication	■ Trade fairs
Moderately important and fast growth	**Moderately important and moderate growth**	**Moderately important and slow growth**
None	■ Product/brand advertising ■ Product/brand sponsorship ■ Web communication	None
Less important and fast growth	**Less important and moderate growth**	**Less important and slow growth**
None	■ Product/brand public relations	■ Corporate sponsorship ■ Investor relations ■ Corporate public relations ■ Corporate advertising

Levels of integration

Companies cannot be expected to integrate their communications efforts fully overnight. Several stages or levels of integration can be distinguished. In Table 1.6 seven categories or levels of integration are distinguished.

Table 1.6 Levels of integration

- ■ Awareness
- ■ Image integration
- ■ Functional integration
- ■ Co-ordinated integration
- ■ Consumer-based integration
- ■ Stakeholder-based integration
- ■ Relationship management integration

Source: Duncan, T. and Caywood, C. (1996), 'The Concept, Process and Evolution of Integrated Marketing Communication', in Thorson, E. and Moore, J. (eds), *Integrated Communication: Synergy of Pervasive Voices*. Mahwah: Lawrence Erlbaum Associates, 13–34.

The first five levels imply the integration of the communications effort mainly at the consumer or marketing communications level. The first two levels focus on conveying the same image and brand awareness through all the marketing communications tools. The next step is the functional integration of all the tools (advertising, sales promotions, sponsorship) into one marketing communications department. In stage four, the marketing tools and the marketing PR function are co-ordinated. Finally, in stage five marketing communications and marketing PR are functionally integrated into one system through which harmonised and consistent messages are conveyed to all actual and potential consumers. In stages six and seven, corporate communications and marketing communications efforts are integrated into one system. Indeed, companies not only communicate with (potential) customers, but with all stakeholders. In fully integrated communications messages, tools, instruments and media, targeted to all stakeholders, are co-ordinated and eventually integrated into a comprehensive system of consistent relationship marketing.[42]

Another way of looking at integration levels implies four stages.[43] First of all, the company can define an integrated *mission*, i.e. the basic values and objectives of the company, which are based on the corporate identity. From this basic mission a number of *propositions* are derived, i.e. concrete propositions to the target groups. A 'one voice' approach implies the consistent integration of mission and propositions. Propositions can be creatively translated into *concepts* or messages with a certain content and format. A concept can be a theme, a core message, a specific style or a slogan. The fourth level is the integration of *execution*. This implies uniformity in layout, design, typography, logo, colours, visual triggers and other elements of the house style. Successful IMC implies that a 'one voice' approach is developed, which serves as a starting point for integrated concepts and execution.

Evidently, a company's communications are more than communicating with marketing target groups. A variety of other audiences and stakeholders need to be considered too. In the next integration stage all communications to all target groups are harmonised. In a truly integrated communications environment, corporate identity definition, corporate reputation and image-building, stakeholder communications and marketing communications are fully integrated. The integration of marketing communications in an international company is not complete until it is achieved across national and international boundaries.

Barriers to integrated communications

Integrated marketing communications are far from a reality in most companies. A number of strong barriers prevent IMC being implemented quickly and efficiently. They are listed in Figure 1.6.

Over many years companies have grown used to extreme specialisation in marketing communications. The various instruments of the communications mix are managed by separate individuals or departments. Traditionally, the strategic power is the exclusive domain of advertising, PR is largely reactive, and sales promotion and personal selling are mainly tactical. Specialisation is rewarded and highly regarded, and the need for, or benefits of, integration are overlooked.

Figure 1.6 Barriers to integrated communications

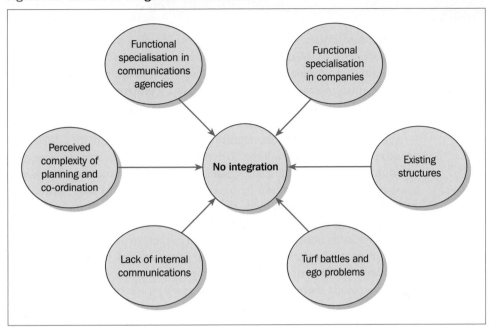

The various instruments of the communications mix have traditionally been managed by different organisational entities as discrete activities. Financial structures and frameworks have been in place for many years.[44] Often the idea of IMC is incompatible with traditional hierarchical and brand management structures. These structures may or may not be changed easily. Ideally, integrated marketing communications can best be effected when all communications activities are physically integrated into one department. But people are generally conservative and reluctant to change. Turf battles and ego problems are important barriers to IMC. The parochialism of managers and their fear of budget cutbacks in their areas of control, and of reductions in authority and power, lead to defending the status quo. PR departments especially are reluctant to integrate because they often consider IMC as the encroachment of ad people on PR professionals and a form of marketing imperialism.[45]

If not all communications activities of a company are integrated into one department, at least the sharing of information, the communications across divisions and the co-ordination of all communications activities have to be organised. Often, the combination of lack of internal communication and the perceived complexity of planning and co-ordination are important barriers to the organisation of IMC.

Finally, the functional specialisation of external communications agencies and their fragmentation in overspecialised disciplines make the full integration of communications even more cumbersome. The role of communications consultants is discussed in the following section.

Client–agency relations and IMC

Communications agencies are traditionally as functionally specialised as the various departments of the companies that hire their expertise. Besides advertising agencies there are direct marketing consultants, PR agencies, sales promotion agencies, media planning companies, internet experts, designers, etc. Companies that want to engage in integrated communications face the difficult task of choosing an agency that can offer all these fields of expertise 'under one roof' or work with a multitude of specialised agents, in which case they face the task of integrating their advice and activities. Ideally, one would expect advertising or PR consultants to evolve to 'full service' agencies that can provide all communications support in an integrated way. Although the need for an integrated approach is increasingly recognised by agencies, and more and more different communications tasks are expected from them, there are a number of structural problems. Research shows that in integrated agencies, often the advertising function is in command. In other words, the agency is not really integrated, but rather an advertising agency that accepts other communications tasks.[46] Advertising agencies and PR agencies in particular seem to perceive conflicts of interest that hamper the integration of communications functions.[47] Furthermore, there seems to be a (perceived) trade-off between the level of integration of an agency and the level of expertise provided. Companies seeking top quality expertise in different fields of marketing communications may be better off using specialised agencies and integrating their advice themselves.[48]

The question as to how the client–agent relationship in the perspective of IMC is managed at present and will be managed in the future is a matter of uncertainty and debate. Several models can be assumed:

- The company plans its integrated communications and subsequently seeks specialised external experts for each communication instrument.
- The company develops a communications plan and contacts an integrated communications agency that carries out the plan.
- The company works with one integrated communications agency. The strategic communications plan is jointly developed and the agency carries out the whole plan.
- The company develops a plan, in co-operation with one (specialised) agency (e.g. an advertising agency), and the agency subcontracts specialised PR, sales promotion, direct marketing, etc. experts.

Research does not provide an answer as to the way in which these client–agency relationships are generally organised now, or how they will evolve in the future. Each of the scenarios mentioned can be found in different companies.[49]

The integrated communications plan

The different communications tools will be used in an integrated marketing communications mix, according to a communications plan that will have to be integrated into the strategic marketing plan. The essential steps in the communications plan are shown in Table 1.7.

Table 1.7 The communications plan

- Situation analysis and marketing objectives: *Why?*
- Target groups: *Who?*
- Communications objectives: *What?*
- Tools, techniques, channels and media: *How and where?*
- Budgets: *How much?*
- Measurement of results: *How effective?*

Since marketing communications have to be embedded in the strategic marketing plan, the first step is to analyse the marketing communications environment and the marketing strategy, and assess where the marketing communications activity should fit in. From this analysis, target groups and objectives and goals of the marketing communications effort can be derived. Next, which instruments, techniques and media to use and to what extent will be agreed. On the basis of this plan a budget can be established, and the communications plan can be implemented. Finally, the effectiveness of the campaign has to be assessed.

In the following chapters branding (Chapter 2) and how communications can influence consumers (Chapter 3) are discussed. Branding is an important core issue, since brands are often the link between marketing strategy and its communication. In subsequent chapters the various stages in the marketing communications plan are discussed, and per instrument a detailed overview of the planning stages is provided. Furthermore, marketing communications can only be effective if they are based on a thorough understanding of how communications can influence behaviour. The components of the marketing communications plan are discussed in more depth in the following chapters: target groups (Chapter 4), objectives (Chapter 5), budgets (Chapter 6) and tools (Chapters 7–17). In the last two chapters special topics in marketing communications are covered. Communications instruments can be used in various market environments. Sometimes this implies that they have to be thoroughly adapted to the specific circumstances in which they are used. In Chapter 18 business-to-business communications are covered. The international context, and its implications for marketing communications, is covered in Chapter 19.

Summary

Integrated communications are the integration of formerly specialised communications functions into one organisational system that conveys a consistent set of messages to all target audiences. Integrated marketing and corporate communications manage each point of contact between the consumer or other target groups and the product or the organisation. Several key drivers of IMC can be identified, such as loss of faith in mass media advertising, the need for enhanced cost-effectiveness, media and target audience fragmentation and overlap, more complex decision-making units, the need to build customer loyalty, relationship marketing and, last but not least, the evolution of technology. Integrating the marketing effort is not an easy process. Companies evolve only gradually to a truly integrated communications system. This slow evolution is caused by a number of important barriers to integration, such as the functional specialisation in companies, existing structures, the lack of internal communications and the perceived complexity of planning and co-ordination. The client–agency relationship and agency structures are profoundly impacted by the evolution towards IMC. In integrated communications many instruments are used. They are embedded in a communications plan that has to be integrated in the strategic marketing plan.

Review questions

1 Give a brief overview of the instruments of the communications mix.

2 What are integrated communications and in what way do they differ from 'classic' communications?

3 How do corporate strategy, culture and personality influence corporate indentity?

4 How does corporate identity influence corporate communication?

5 What factors have to be taken into account in corporate image management, and what is the role of communications?

6 What are the factors that reinforce the need for integrated communications, and how can the latter provide an answer to contemporary marketing communications problems?

7 What are the levels of integration a company can go through?

8 What are the barriers to integrated marketing communications?

9 In what way can the communications activities of companies and external communications consultants be integrated?

Further reading

Argenti, P. and Forman, J. (2002), *The Power of Corporate Communication: Crafting the Voice and Image of your Business*. McGraw-Hill Trade.

Duncan, T. (2002), *IMC. Using Advertising and Promotion to Build Brands*. McGraw-Hill Higher Education.

Gronstedt, A. (2002), *The Customer Century: Lessons from World Class Companies in Integrated Communications*. London: Routledge.

Kitchen, P.J. and De Pelsmacher, P. (2005), *Integrated Marketing Communication: A Primer*. London: Routledge.

Kitchen, P.J. and Schultz, D.E. (2001), *Raising the Corporate Umbrella: Corporate Communications in the 21st Century*. Palgrave Macmillan.

Kitchen, P.J., De Pelsmacher, P. Schultz, D.E. and Eagle, L. (eds) (2006), *A Reader in Marketing Communications*. London: Routledge.

Schultz, D.E. and Kitchen, P.J. (2000), *Communicating Globally: An Integrated Marketing Approach*. Lincolnwood IL: NTC Business Books.

www.reputationinstitute.com (Reputation Institute)

www.henrystewart.com/journals/crr (Corporate Reputation Review)

Case 1

Marie Jo and PrimaDonna: when luxury meets quality

Van de Velde SA, founded in 1919 in Belgium, is a famous supplier of figure-enhancing, high-quality women's lingerie. It has production operations in Hungary and Tunisia, and subcontractors in China, France and Germany. Van de Velde is market leader in the Benelux countries in the luxurious lingerie market, is one of the three main market players in the other EU countries, and is also present in the US and Southeast Asia. Perfection and quality have always been the key characteristics of Van de Velde's products. However, from the late 1970s, Van de Velde started to combine its sense of perfection and quality with elegant creativity. Since 1981 the creative line 'Marie Jo' successfully tapped into the trend of seeking for individual experiences and paying attention to one's personal charisma. The lingerie that women burnt in the 1960s became the symbol of the 'new' independent, assertive female. Three new brands have been added: in 1990 PrimaDonna was taken over, in 1997 Marie Jo L'Aventure was introduced and in 2001 Marie Jo L'Exclusive was introduced, leading Van de Velde into the top segment of the luxury lingerie market (from 2005 onwards, the L'Exclusive brand disappeared). Van de Velde believes that luxury products create their own markets:

> 'It is a characteristic of mankind to distinguish oneself through luxury, beauty and originality. Linked with quality, luxury is a hard to beat competitive advantage. This is also true or even truer when the economy is not doing very well.'

The excellent results of Van de Velde can be considered as proof of the above statement. The company realised a turnover of more than €100 million in 2004, which is an increase of 9.5% compared to 2003. Core markets are the Benelux (38% of turnover), Germany (25%) and France (15%). The Marie Jo brands account for 58% and the Prima Donna brand for 42%. Van de Velde's mission is to offer lingerie with high-quality design, perfect wearing comfort and luxury, beauty and originality. It wants to help customers to be successful by offering a wide assortment, and by providing extensive and relevant services. The objectives of the company are to be top in every European market of luxury lingerie

and to be the market reference point for creativity and product and service quality. The most important competitors of Van de Velde in the luxury market are La Perla, Lise Charmel, Aubade, Barbara, Simone Pérèle, Chantelle and Lejaby.

Brand positioning

The luxury lingerie market in Belgium, The Netherlands, France, Germany, Switzerland, Austria and the Scandinavian countries is estimated to consist of about 40 million women, representing a market potential of about €1.5 billion. The Van de Velde share is approximately 20%. In this segment, consumers pay an average price of between €50 and €90 per item. However, even in the segment of the luxury lingerie market, subsegments can be discerned. Therefore, Van de Velde designs, produces and commercialises different brands, of which each has its own unique style and each is clearly positioned in different subsegments of the market (see Case Table 1.1).

Every year 300 new products are introduced under these three brand names. All of the products are consistently communicated with the value

Case Table 1.1

Van de Velde's brand portfolio

Marie Jo	Refined, luxurious and fashionable. Women mainly buy it to please themselves, but partly also to please their partner. It is a brand for self-conscious, ambitious and assertive women. It is the *accessible luxury* product line.
Marie Jo L'Aventure	*Pure and minimalist*, without frills, represents a young and dynamic lifestyle. It is a brand for extrovert, energetic, spontaneous and pure young women looking for *sober lingerie*.
PrimaDonna	*Fashion* and luxury *for larger cups* (up to H cups). Besides luxury and fashion, fit and comfort are the main benefits.

propositions shown in Case Table 1.1, season after season, year after year.

Integrated marketing communications

Van de Velde uses through-the-line communications to try to reach both specialty lingerie retailers and the end consumer. About 8% of the turnover is spent on marketing communications. The communication objectives can be defined as creating awareness for its products by means of informing the consumer about new collections as well as building a strong brand by creating a unique brand image. Throughout Europe a consistent marketing communications approach is used: both the same message and the same MC tools are employed. Obviously different tools are used depending on the two broad target groups: retailers and consumers.

Retailer communications. Thirty-eight sales representatives have direct contact with 4,000 specialty lingerie retailers. To keep the retailers motivated, their concerns are always taken into account. For example, instead of using the website to sell lingerie, Van de Velde lists the retailers' addresses where Van de Velde products are for sale. Moreover, Van de Velde prints brochures on which the retailer can put his or her address before it is distributed to the consumers. Retailers receive 1,500 free brochures to distribute amongst their (potential) customers. If they want more than 1,500 they have to pay for them. For every brand and every season a different brochure is produced. Besides brochures, Van de Velde's communications mix directed to retailers consists of mailings, point-of-sales material (such as posters, pancartes, books), support in local advertising, retailer contests and retailer visits by the sales representatives. For example, twice a year a multi-brand mailing containing a Newsmagazine per brand is sent to all 4,000 retailers. This way retailers are informed in advance of when, where and what will appear in the media, in the brochures and POS communication. In between the winter and summer seasons, another mailing is sent. This means that at least four times a year, every retailer receives some information on the Van de Velde brands. Van de Velde tries to establish close relationships with its retailers and tries to be as prominent in the stores as possible. In the luxury lingerie market women first decide on which store to visit, and afterwards they decide on the brand. Therefore, in-store communications and being present with as many brands as possible is very important. Even so, it is not profitable to

try to build a good relationship with every store. In view of the size of the retailer group and the costs involved in establishing good relationships, Van de Velde segments its retailers according to their value to the company. First of all, an individual retailer value is calculated based on the retailer's turnover, age of customers, number of employees, size of window, location, etc. Next, a product value is computed: how much of the individual Van de Velde brands are sold by the retailer, how much of the collection is sold, etc. Thirdly, a communication value is computed on the basis of the retailer's response to diverse marketing communications actions undertaken by Van de Velde, such as previous direct mail actions, Van de Velde's newsletter, whether point-of-sales material was actually used or not, etc. This segmentation is taken into account for fine-tuning the MC support: the higher the value of the retailers to Van de Velde, the higher the marketing communications investments.

Consumer communications. Van de Velde's main communications tool is its brochure. This is used both as a tool for action (purchase response on seeing the new collection) and image (brand building) communication. Besides distributing brochures by means of the retailers, Van de Velde uses its brochures to advertise in womens and lifestyle magazines. In this case, a brochure is inserted in a magazine or a gatefold-encart (showing retailer pictures and addresses) is used. In France and Finland this brochure contains all four brands instead of just one brand. For this type of magazine advertising, Van de Velde opts for reach instead of frequency, meaning it reaches many women of the target group once instead of reaching a limited part of the target group frequently. Moreover, the choice of magazines is also very important. Van de Velde opts for magazines that are selective on the target group, meaning that they avoid mass magazines but go for magazines of which the readers resemble Van de Velde's target group of the upper-upper-class (see Case Table 1.2).

Another communications tool targeted at the end consumer is the website. The website is mainly used as an information channel to support the brand and the collection. Therefore, every season the site is updated. However, the website is also an interactive communications tool in the sense that visitors can send e-cards (with nice pictures of models wearing one of Van de Velde's brands) or can order gift cheques. For the gift cheques visitors can click through to local dealers. Moreover, men who would like to give their partner a nice lingerie gift, but do not know

Case Table 1.2
Magazine use in selected countries

Country	Magazines used in 2002
Austria	Cosmopolitan, Marie Claire, Elle, Gala, Brigitte, Amica
Belgium	Gael, Feeling, Weekend Knack, Nouveau, Elle, Cosmopolitan, Marie Claire, Loving You
Denmark	Cosmopolitan Inland, Marie Claire Inland, Elle Inland, Gala, Femina, Eurowoman
France	Gala, Madame Figaro, Point de Vue
Germany	Brigitte Inland, Cosmopolitan Inland, Marie Claire Inland, Elle Inland, Gala
Luxemburg	Femmes Magazine, Info Magazine
The Netherlands	Nouveau, Elle, Cosmopolitan, Marie Claire, Feeling, Loving You, Body Perfection
Switzerland	Femina
UK	Elle, Cosmopolitan

her size, can find some tips on the site for calculating the right size.

Of Van de Velde's total communications budget, about 60% is spent on the brochures and consumer advertising (see Plate 2), 20% goes to retailer communication (direct mailings) and another 20% is spent on point-of-sales communications and local media to support retailers.

Communications effectiveness

Van de Velde realises that the way to achieve effective communications is using the same claims, the same tone of voice, the same positioning and the same values for the same brand, season after season, year after year. Moreover, every communications tool, be it a poster, a brochure, a website or a magazine ad, has to be consistent with the brand's value proposition. Although every year 300 new products are launched under the Marie Jo, Marie Jo L'Aventure and PrimaDonna brand names, the style is very recognisable to consumers. Every Marie Jo picture, for example, is shot in the studio, and the model will always look into the camera, while every PrimaDonna ad is shot on an external location, stressing more the fashion and creative appeal. This integrated marketing communications approach clearly pays off. In 1998 the impact of a Marie Jo booklet in *Feeling* was compared to an average Belgian print ad. The Marie Jo insert was well recognised, people's knowledge of which brand the booklet was for was above average (attribution), the booklet was liked, and was considered original and informative (see Case Figure 1.1).

In other countries the communications also seem to be effective. A 2002 communications analysis carried out by the German magazine *Brigitte* reveals that over the years Marie Jo has increased in awareness, liking and actual purchase (see Case Figure 1.2).

The fact that Van de Velde uses the right advertising appeal for its target groups is also evident from the 2003 impact scores of two ads that appeared in *Gala*. Nine out of ten French consumers had seen

Case Figure 1.1 Impact scores of a 1998 Marie Jo booklet in *Feeling*

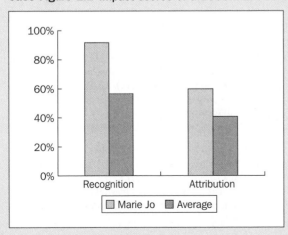
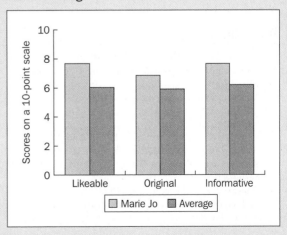

Case Figure 1.2
Brand potential of Marie Jo in Germany

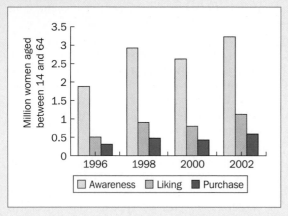

at least one of the two ads. Moreover, the ad really made the consumers want to buy Marie Jo (see Case Table 1.3).

This case study shows the power of integrating marketing communications tools targeted at retailers and consumers and doing this in a consistent way over the years.

Questions

1 Evaluate the communications mix Van de Velde uses to reach its consumers. What do you think of the type and number of different communications tools that are used?

2 Considering the three brands in Van de Velde's portfolio, would you advise the company to use a different communications mix for some of the brands? Would some or all of the brands benefit from another approach?

3 Should Van de Velde try harder to establish a relationship with the end consumers? If so, how could it do that?

4 Does Van de Velde use an appropriate marketing communications mix to communicate with its retailers? What are the strong and weak points of its approach?

5 Do you think it was a good idea to extend the Marie Jo brand (Marie Jo L'Aventure) or would it have been better to launch the latter product under a completely different brand name?

6 Which level of marketing communications integration does Van de Velde seem to be using?

Sources: http://profiles.wisi.com/profiles/scripts/corpinfo.asp?cusip=C056C8040; Annual Report 2004; www.mariejo.com; Information provided by Geert Neutens, Artex Marketing & Communication.

Case Table 1.3 Impact scores of *Gala* ads

Ad	Seen	Read	Like	Ad fits magazine	Makes me want to buy
Marie Jo 1	88	48	81	84	73
Marie Jo 2	85	50	92	88	85
Average apparel	84	46	66	80	50
Average all sectors	80	43	62	78	48

* Cells are percentages.

References

1 Schultz, D.E. (1996), 'The Inevitability of Integrated Communication', *Journal of Business Research*, 37, 139–46.
2 American Marketing Association (1985).
3 Euro Effie (1998).
4 Euro Effie (2001).
5 Schultz, D.E., Tannenbaum, S.I. and Lauterborn, R.F. (1992), *Integrated Marketing Communication: Putting it Together and Making it Work*. Lincolnwood, IL: NTC Business Books.
6 Duncan, T.R. and Everett, S.E. (1993), 'Client Perceptions of Integrated Marketing Communication', *Journal of Advertising Research* (May/June), 30–9.
7 Duncan, T.R. and Everett, S.E. (1993), 'Client Perceptions of Integrated Marketing Communication', *Journal of Advertising Research* (May/June), 30–9.
8 Payne, A. and Holt, S. (2001), 'Diagnosing Customer Value: Integrating the Value Process and Relationship Marketing', *British Journal of Management*, 12, 159–82.
9 Englis, B.G. and Solomon, M.R. (1996), 'Using Consumption Constellations to Develop Integrated Communication Strategies', *Journal of Business Research*, 37, 183–91.
10 Schultz, D.E. (1996), 'The Inevitability of Integrated Communication', *Journal of Business Research*, 37, 139–46.

11 Englis, B.G. and Solomon, M.R. (1996), 'Using Consumption Constellations to Develop Integrated Communication Strategies', *Journal of Business Research*, 37, 183–91.

12 Hutton, J.H. (1996), 'Integrated Marketing Communication and Evolution of Marketing Thought', *Journal of Business Research*, 37, 155–62.

13 Garber, L.G. and Dotson, M.J. (2002), 'A Method for the Selection of Appropriate Business-to-Business Integrated Marketing Communications Mixes', *Journal of Marketing Communications*, 8(1), 1–18.

14 Based on: van Raaij, W.F. (1998), 'Integratie van Communicatie: vanuit de zender of vanuit de Ontvanger?' ('Integration of Communication: Starting from the sender or the receiver?'), in Damoiseaux, V.M.G., van Ruler, A.A. and Weisink, A., *Effectiviteit in Communicatiemanagement (Effectiveness in Communication Management)*. Deventer: Samson, 169–84.

15 Jackson, P. (1987), *Corporate Communications for Managers*. London: Pitman.

16 Melewar, T.C. (2003), 'Determinants of the Corporate Identity Construct: A Review of the Literature', *Journal of Marketing Communications*, 9(4), 195–220.

17 Schein, E.H. (1984), 'Coming to a New Awareness of Corporate Culture', *Sloan Management Review*, 25 (winter), 3–16.

18 Melewar, T.C. (2003), 'Determinants of the Corporate Identity Construct: A Review of the Literature', *Journal of Marketing Communications*, 9(4), 195–220.

19 Cornelissen, J. and Harris, P. (1999), *Two Perspectives on Corporate Identity: As the Expression of the Corporate Personality and as the Essential Self*. ICCIS Working Paper Series, Strathclyde: University of Strathclyde.

20 Olins, W. (1990), *Corporate Identity: Making Business Strategy Visible through Design*. London: Thames & Hudson.

21 Olins, W. (1990), *Corporate Identity: Making Business Strategy Visible through Design*. London: Thames & Hudson.

22 ACC (2006), Code of Conduct.

23 Cornelissen, J. and Harris, P. (1999), *Two Perspectives on Corporate Identity: As the Expression of the Corporate Personality and as the Essential Self*. ICCIS Working Paper Series, Strathclyde: University of Strathclyde.

24 Fombrun, C. (1996), *Reputation: Realising Value from the Corporate Image*, Harvard: Harvard Business School Press.

25 Dowling, G.R. (1986), 'Managing Your Corporate Images', *Industrial Marketing Management*, 15, 109–15.

26 Doukakis, I., Krambia-Kapardis, M. and Katsioloudes, M. (2003), 'Corporate Responsibility: A Pilot Study into the Realities of the Business Sector in Cyprus', in Bennett, R. *New Challenges for Corporate and Marketing Communications. Proceedings of the Eighth International Conference on Marketing and Corporate Communications*. London: London Metropolitan University, 64–80.

27 Zinkhan, G.M. and Watson, R.T. (1996), 'Advertising Trends: Innovation and the Process of Creative Destruction', *Journal of Business Research*, 37, 163–71.

28 Evans, C.R. (1994), *Marketing Channels. Infomercials and the Future of Televised Marketing*, Englewood Cliffs, NJ: Prentice Hall.

29 De Pelsmacker, P. and Roozen, I. (1993), 'Trends in Marketingtechnieken van Vandaag' ('Trends in Marketing Techniques Today'), *No Ideas No Marketing, congresverslagen 12e congres van Stiching Marketing*, 75–88.

30 Stewart, D.W. (1996), 'Market-Back Approach to the Design of Integrated Communications Programs: A Change in Paradigm and a Focus on Determinants of Success', *Journal of Business Research*, 37, 147–53.

31 'Televisiepubliciteit in één knipoog' ('TV Advertising in one Eye Glance'), *De Morgen*, 20 August 1998.

32 'Gratis computers in ruil voor reclame' ('Free Computers in Exchange for Advertising'), *De Morgen*, 15 February 1999.

33 'Gezocht: publiek dat zichzelf vermenigvuldigt' ('Wanted: Audience that Multiplies Itself'), *Het Nieuwsblad*, 3 October 1998.

34 'Als het aan de kat lag, keek ze televisie' ('If it Depends on the Cat, then she Watches Television'), *De Morgen*, 28 January 1999.

35 *De Morgen*, 4 August 2001.

36 *De Morgen*, 22 February 2003.

37 Schultz, D.E., Tannenbaum, S.I. and Lauterborn, R.F. (1992), *Integrated Marketing Communications: Putting it Together and Making it Work*. Lincolnwood IL: NTC Business Books.

38 Low, G.S. (2000), 'Correlates of Integrated Marketing Communications', *Journal of Advertising*, 40, 27–39; Liechty, J., Ramaswamy, V. and Cohen, S.H. (2001), 'Choice Menus for Mass Customisation: An Experimental Approach for Analysing Customer Demand with an Application to a Web-based Information Service', *Journal of Marketing Research*, 38, 183–96.

39 Schultz, D.E. (1996), 'The Inevitability of Integrated Communication', *Journal of Business Research*, 37, 139–46.

40 Schultz, D.E. and Kitchen, P.J. (2000), *Communicating Globally: An Integrated Marketing Approach*. Lincolnwood IL: NTC Business Books.

41 Avisio/Tagora (2006), *Trends in Marketing Communications*, Avisio, Antwerp. Dens, N., De Pelsmacker, P., Janssens, W. (2006) *Marketing and Communication in Belgian Companies: Past, Present, Future. Proceedings of the 5th International Congress on Marketing Trends*. Venice, Italy.

42 Duncan, T. and Caywood, C. (1996), 'The Concept, Process and Evolution of Integrated Marketing Communication', in Thorson, E. and Moore, J. (eds), *Integrated Communication; Synergy of Pervasive Voices*. Mahwah: Lawrence Erlbaum Associates, 13–34.

43 van Raaij, W.F. (1997), 'Globalisation of Marketing Communication?', *Journal of Economic Psychology*, 18, 259–70.

44 For a discussion of the structural relationship between PR and advertising departments in organisations, see Grunig, J.A. and Grunig, L.A. (1998), 'The Relationship Between

Public Relations and Marketing in Excellent Organisations: Evidence from the IABC Study', *Journal of Marketing Communications*, 4(3), 141–62.

45 Hutton, J.H. (1996), 'Integrated Marketing Communication and the Evolution of Marketing Thought', *Journal of Business Research*, 37, 155–62.

46 Mitchell, H. (1997), 'Client Perception of Integrated Marketing Communication', in De Pelsmacker, P. and Geuens, M. (eds), *The Changing World of Corporate and Marketing Communication. Proceedings of the 2nd International Conference on Marketing and Corporate Communication*. Antwerp: RUCA, 197–204.

47 Ewing, M.T., De Bussy, N.M. and Caruana, A. (2000), 'Perceived Agency Politics and Conflicts of Interest as Potential Barriers to IMC Orientation', *Journal of Marketing Communications*, 6(2), 107–19.

48 Gronstedt, A. and Thorsen, E. (1996), 'Five Approaches to Organise an Integrated Marketing Communication Agency', *Journal of Advertising Research*, (March/April), 48–58.

49 Borremans, T. (1998), 'Integrated (Marketing) Communication in Practice. Survey among Communication, Public Relations and Advertising Agencies in Belgium', in Kitchen, P.J., *The Changing World of Corporate and Marketing Communication: Towards the Next Millennium. Proceedings of the Third International Conference on Marketing and Corporate Communication*. Glasgow: Strathclyde Graduate Business School, 66–75.

Chapter 2
Branding

Chapter outline

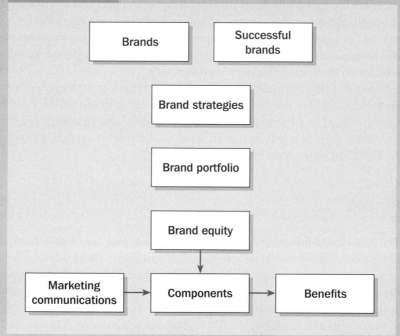

Chapter objectives

This chapter will help you to:

- Understand the various aspects of branding
- Learn about the characteristics of successful brands
- Make the distinction between major types of brand strategies and their advantages and disadvantages
- Form an idea of the composition of a brand portfolio
- Understand the concept of brand value or brand equity and its major components
- Assess the benefits of branding for the consumer and the manufacturer
- Get an overview of how marketing communications contribute to brand strength

Introduction

Since the early days of marketing, brands have always been important. Consistent and long-term investment in brand awareness and brand image resulted in famous brands that survived the storms of changing marketing environments and were powerful instruments of marketing strategy. Later, the pressure for short-term results and the changing power balance between manufacturers and retailers has led to a situation in which patient and long-term investment in brand value no longer seems to be a priority. Short-term profit goals seem to be at least as important as long-term investments in goodwill. However, the value of brands in modern marketing strategy, and the important role of marketing communications in building and maintaining brand value, are still recognised. Brands are powerful instruments of strategic marketing and important vehicles on the road to long-term profitability.

What is a good brand? What are suitable branding strategies? Why are brands so important, and for whom? What is the value of a brand (often referred to as brand equity)? What is a brand portfolio and what different functions can brands fulfil in a portfolio? And, last but not least, what is the role of marketing communications in building and supporting brands?

Brands

The American Marketing Association defines a brand as 'a name, term, sign, symbol or design, or a combination of these, intended to identify the goods or services of one seller or group of sellers, and to differentiate them from those of a competitor'. Defined like this, a brand is a set of verbal and/or visual cues, and as such it is a part of a product's tangible features. A brand name is that part of a brand that can be spoken, including letters, words and numbers, like BMW, Danone or Citibank. A brand mark is the element of a brand that cannot be spoken, often a symbol, design or specific packaging, like the Mercedes logo or the Absolut Vodka bottle. A trademark is the legal designation indicating that the owner has exclusive use of the brand.

However, Keller goes beyond the pure constituting brand elements and defines a brand as a product that adds either rational and tangible dimensions (related to product performance) or symbolic, emotional and intangible dimensions (related to what the brand represents) that differentiate it from other products designed to fulfil the same need.[1]

Brand names, as well as other brand elements such as logos, URLs, symbols, characters, spokespeople, jingles, packages and signages, should be memorable, meaningful, likable, adaptable, transferable and protectable.[2] A good brand name is easy for customers to say, spell and recall. Excellent examples are Dell, Bic, Nokia and Ford. To enhance brand recognition and avoid brand confusion, a brand name should also be distinctive and be able to differentiate the product from the competition. Besides being memorable, it is an advantage that brand elements are meaningful; for example, Mr Clean cleaning product, Vanish stain remover, Head & Shoulders shampoo and *Newsweek* magazine reinforce an attribute or benefit association related to the brand positioning. Brand elements should also be tested on their visual and/or verbal likability, or in other words, on their aesthetic appeal. Over time brand elements may loose their appeal, calling for an update. As a consequence, logos, symbols, characters and even brand names often have to be adapted. Nike and Michelin are just a few examples of brands that updated their logo/character over time. Preferably a brand is transferable both across product categories and geographic boundaries. The more specific the brand name, the more difficult it may be to extend the brand to other product categories. Nivea could easily extend its brand to the shampoo, skin care and other markets, but it will be difficult for Head & Shoulders to extend its shampoo brand into skin care. To build a successful global brand, the brand name should be easy to pronounce in different languages. This is the case for neither the soft drink brand Mountain Dew in many non-English-speaking countries nor the Polish vodka brand Wyborowa in non-Polish-speaking countries. Global brand names also have to be culture- or language-neutral in the sense that they do not evoke strange or undesirable connotations in foreign languages. Kodak, Mars and IBM are good examples of this linguistic neutrality. On the other hand, the Rolls-Royce Silver Mist model name sounds strange in Germany (where mist means manure), as does the Finnish defroster Super-Piss in certain European countries, and the toilet paper brand Kräpp in English-speaking parts of the world. Other examples are the Spanish bread brand Bimbo that is associated with an attractive, unintelligent lady in English; the Dutch bread brand Bums reminds English-speaking people of a person's backside and German-speaking people of sex; the Egyptian airline company Misair is not appealing to French-speaking consumers because 'misère' means misery to them.[3] Finally, a brand should be available and easy to protect through registration. Therefore, no generic words should be used. Really successful brand names often become household names, i.e. the brand name is used to indicate the product category in which it was a pioneer. Examples are Xerox, Aspirin and Hoover.

Only with KitKat can you have a break

Protectability is an important prerequisite in building a strong global brand. But slogans as well as brands can be protected. Since 1957 the snack brand KitKat uses the slogan 'have a break, have a KitKat', and Nestlé, the parent company, felt that they had been using this slogan so long that they had the right to patent it. In 1996 the company filed a patent request in the UK, much to the outrage of competitor Mars, who defended the thesis that this slogan was not a brand, but just a sentence that applied to any snack. The British patent bureau agreed, and a long legal fight started. After losing trial after trial, eventually Nestlé went to the European Court of Justice, who finally decided that any phrase that distinguishes a brand from its competitors could be regarded as part of the brand, and could therefore be patented, provided that the slogan has been used long enough, the brand has a substantial market share and is widely available, the majority of consumers link the slogan to the brand, and the marketing company has invested in it substantially. The case has been sent to a British court now, which will have to assess to what extent this particular slogan and brand live up to the criteria. This ruling may have a substantial impact on jurisdiction regarding the protectability of brands and brand components. Marketing actions such as the one by Tetris, who used the slogan 'have a break. Play Tetris' may no longer be allowed.

Source: De Morgen 9 July 2005.

Three categories of brands can be distinguished:

1 **Manufacturer brands** are developed by producers. They are supported by integrated marketing, including pricing, distribution and communications. Levi's, Danone and BMW are examples of manufacturer brands.

2 **Own-label brands** (also called private labels, store or dealer brands) are developed and owned by wholesalers or retailers. There is no link between the manufacturer and the brand. Retailers develop own-label brands to gain more power. It enables them to enhance their store image, generate higher margins and be more independent of the manufacturers of premium brands. Mostly, they compete on the basis of a price benefit compared with manufacturer brands. St Michael (Marks & Spencer), Albert Heijn (The Netherlands) and Derby (Delhaize, Belgium) are examples of store brands. In many product categories, own-label brands pose a serious threat to well-established manufacturer brands. Some own-label brands are as well known as traditional brands, have a good image and are less expensive. Some retailers are using their own-label brands as the key element in their marketing strategy, and support their own brand with a limited number of well-established manufacturer brands to optimise their store image and consumer traffic. Own-brand labels hold a market share (in volume) of 45.4% in the UK, 33.2% in Germany, 22.1% in France, 20.5% in Spain, 20.6% in The Netherlands, 17.1% in Italy and 34.7% in Belgium.[4] As a consequence, brand manufacturers have to take the competition of private labels into account in their own strategy. Six strategic options can be chosen: (1) increase distance from private labels through innovation, (2) increase distance from private labels by investing in brand equity (offer 'more value for money' by stressing brand image, changing packaging, etc.), (3) reduce the price gap, (4) introduce a value-flanker as a me-too strategy, (5) wait and do nothing, and (6) produce (premium) private labels. A recent study in The Netherlands shows that the best strategy for national brands might be to react by investing in innovations and brand image. This is preferred to 'wait and do nothing', although the latter may sometimes be effective (for example, wait until the company is ready to come up with the next innovation). Producing private labels may also be a viable option, especially in product categories with high private-labels market shares or many possibilities for technological differentiation. Producing private labels for retailers has the advantage that it strengthens the ties with the retailer. Furthermore, it can also be very profitable for the company if it has excess capacity. Finally, companies seem to react to the competition with private labels in a more subtle way than to other brands. Decreasing the distance from private labels by price reductions and value flankers is less used. Obviously the latter would sour the relationship with the retailer. Furthermore, it often also seems to have a detrimental impact on the company's and market profitability.[5]

3 **Generic brands** indicate the product category. In fact, the concept is a contradiction in terms. Generics are in fact brandless products. They are usually sold at the lowest prices. In pharmaceutical products, generics are quite successful. The end of the legal protection of a patent allows the introduction of generics at lower prices. Depending upon the country, generics account for a substantial share of pharmaceutical products sales.

Successful brands

Giving a product a brand name does not always guarantee success. Successful brands have to meet a number of conditions[6] (Figure 2.1).

- Successful brands are differentiated. Consumers clearly perceive them as having unique benefits and being different from the competition.

- Top brands are positioned on quality and added value. Superior product quality is a prerequisite for successful branding. Often it is not only the product that is superior but also the additional service which is less easily copied by competitors.

- Leading brands continually innovate to answer changing consumer tastes and to keep ahead of the competition.

- A leading position can only be sustained by having full support and complete commitment of both management and employees.[7] Especially in service branding, internal marketing (i.e. training and communicating with internal staff to convince them of the basic strategic priorities) is vital. The success of a bank, an airline or a restaurant largely depends upon the motivation and quality of the service provider (bank clerk, steward or waiter).

- Brands cannot become success stories without long-term, consistent communications support, making customers aware of their uniqueness and keeping the brand's value trustworthy. Both long-term support and the significant contribution of communications are important. Successful brands are not built overnight. Long-term communications, and more particularly advertising support, is a key factor in the development of successful brands. As already mentioned, brand managers are often tempted to cut investments in brands to increase short-term profitability, thereby affecting the long-term profit potential.

Figure 2.1 Determinants of successful brands

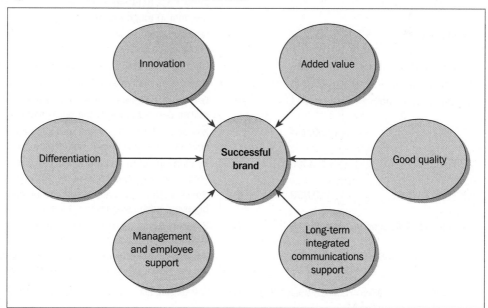

Table 2.1 Top 25 brands worldwide

Brand	2005 Brand Value (millions €)	Per cent change	Description
1 Coca-Cola (US)	53,912	0	Difficulties in adding new diet and energy drinks. Still looking for a zippier global advertising message
2 Microsoft (US)	47,857	−2	Proceeds in hot markets such as TV set-top box software, video games and mobile phones
3 IBM (US)	42,615	−1	Transforming from a computer company to a services and manufacturing company
4 GE (US)	37,522	7	Cutting edge innovations and environmentally friendly products moves GE's image up
5 Intel (US)	28,413	6	The Pentium chips and the Centrino wireless notebooks made Intel famous worldwide
6 Nokia (Finland)	21,119	10	Attack on Apple's iPod by converging cell phones and MP3 players into one device
7 Disney (US)	21,110	−2	Kids are waiting for new, edgier offerings
8 McDonald's (US)	20,770	4	Salads and a hipper image made McDonald's reconnect with consumers
9 Toyota (Japan)	19,830	10	Toyota's hybrids moves its image up
10 Marlboro (US)	16,917	−4	Big in US, struggling in Europe
11 Mercedes (Germany)	15,973	−6	Quality problems and strategic errors hurt the brand
12 Citi (US)	15,942	0	A history in global markets helped Citi to counter recent scandals
13 Hewlett-Packard (US)	15,063	−10	Increased competition in the printer market, performance improvements necessary to win the battle from Dell and IBM
14 American Express (US)	14,818	5	On the rise since banks can issue its cards
15 Gilette (US)	13,999	5	The battery-powered M3Power razor leads Gillette to a sales record (now merged with P&G).
16 BMW (Germany)	13,673	8	Perfect mix between engineering and marketing even opens the door in tough markets
17 Cisco (US)	13,247	4	New focus on small business, effective partnership with Microsoft to tackle Internet security
18 Louis Vuitton (France)	12,836	N/A	Uma Thurman leads the world's richest luxury brand to the sky
19 Honda (Japan)	12,605	6	Consumers become more and more fond of Honda
20 Samsung (Korea)	11,941	19	One big global brand and an explosion of popular cell phones makes Samsung one of the big winner's in brand value
21 Dell (US)	10,564	15	Market leader in PC market and aggressively moving in printers, TVs and laptops to counter the decreasing PC demand
22 Ford (US)	10,506	−9	Mustang is doing well, but not so for SUVs and pickups. Ford's truck profits are also under attack by fierce competition
23 Pepsi (US)	9,899	3	Stressing Diet Pepsi and Hispanic marketing, combined with big-event advertising on the Super Bowl and Oscars pays off
24 Nescafé (Switzerland)	9,773	3	By ready to drink products such as Ice Java coffee coolers Nescafé can stand up to Starbucks
25 Merrill Lynch (US)	9,595	5	Revamping its retail brokerage business was a success and makes Merrill Lynch the best performer in the industry

Based on: 'The 100 Top Brands', *Business Week*, 1 August 2005, 90–4. (Original data was in US$, recalculated taking the exchange rate of April 27 2006: 1 USD = .7984 €.)

In Table 2.1 an overview is given of Interbrand's 2005 ranking of 25 of the world's most valuable brands. Interbrand calculates brand values on the basis of cash flows. Absolute winners in the top 100 ranking are Ebay (55), HSBC (29) and Samsung (20) who respectively gained 21%, 20% and 19% in brand value as compared to 2004. The biggest losers in 2005 were Sony (28), Morgan Stanley (33) and Volkswagen (48) who saw their brand value decline with respectively 16%, 15% and 12%.[8]

Brandchannel

Every year Brandchannel organises a brand poll in which readers are asked to vote for the brands that had most impact on them that year. In 2005, 2,500 people from 99 countries participated. The most impactful brands differ from the list presented above. Also, as pointed out in the figure below, the top five shows many differences between regions. Asia-Pacific consumers seem to be fond of electronics while Central and Latin American consumers love drinks.

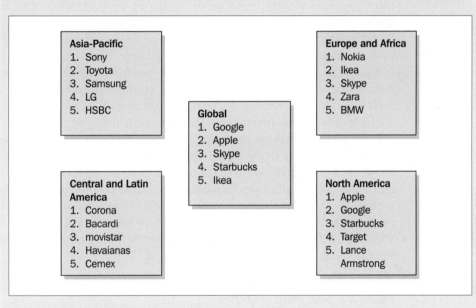

Asia-Pacific
1. Sony
2. Toyota
3. Samsung
4. LG
5. HSBC

Global
1. Google
2. Apple
3. Skype
4. Starbucks
5. Ikea

Europe and Africa
1. Nokia
2. Ikea
3. Skype
4. Zara
5. BMW

Central and Latin America
1. Corona
2. Bacardi
3. movistar
4. Havaianas
5. Cemex

North America
1. Apple
2. Google
3. Starbucks
4. Target
5. Lance Armstrong

Source: Rusch, R.D. (2006), 'The search is over: Google wins in 2005', 23 January, www.brandchannel.com

Brand strategies

A brand strategy starts with the decision whether or not to put a brand name on a product. It can be argued that, for some product categories, branding is not essential and may even be useless. This is especially true for undifferentiated and homogeneous products. Since branding is an essential element in pull marketing strategies, the products for which a push strategy is indicated have less need of formal branding. The latter may be the case for industrial products such as steel and raw materials, or complex machinery like transmission equipment or capacitors. However, except for generics, hardly any brandless consumer product can be imagined, although in some consumer product categories such as fresh fruit, vegetables, meat and bread, branded goods are the exception rather than the rule. Marketers cannot live with undifferentiated products and will always look for extra marketable value. A brand is an excellent vehicle by means of which a product can be differentiated from the competition.

Once the decision to go for branded products has been taken, a company must decide on its overall brand strategy. This strategy will also guide the branding of new product introductions. In Figure 2.2, the basic brand strategies are shown. First of all, a product can be given one brand name, or several (mostly two) brands can be used to position it. In the case of one brand name, four different strategies can be followed. Sticking to existing product categories and using the same brand name for all new product introductions in a product category is called line extension. This strategy is used very frequently. Examples are Stimorol's flavours black'n'blue and roseberry, or the 'made in Kellogg's country' assortment of breakfast cereals. Marketers may want to expand the variety of their offerings, try to accommodate the needs of new consumer segments, react to successful competitive products, crowd the product space and deter competitive entry, enhance the image of the parent brand or try to command more shelf space from retailers. Overall, it improves the competitive position of the brand by offering consumers more variety, as a result of which they are not inclined to look to competitive brands to satisfy their needs. Moreover, there seem to be strong spillover effects from advertising the line extension on choice of the parent brand. Advertising of Yoplait non-fat yoghurt, for example, increased sales of Yoplait yoghurt even more than advertising of Yoplait yoghurt itself.[9] Line extension strategies have a number of obvious advantages. The favourable image of the brand is carried over to the new products that are marketed with the same brand name, and the past communications investments in the brand are more efficiently used to market more products. However, a line extension also has a number of disadvantages, the most important being that the original brand loses its meaning and clear positioning.[10] Another disadvantage is the risk of cannibalisation. A new product may cannibalise the company's other products instead of taking market share away from the competition, the net result of which could be that the line extension is not very profitable. Finally, an unsuccessful extension can harm sales of the parent brand.[11]

Figure 2.2 Basic brand strategies

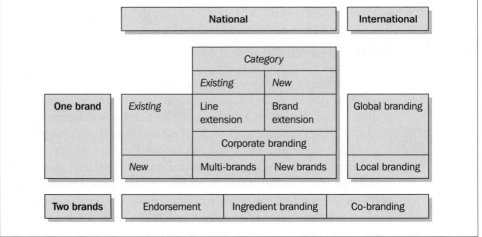

Brand extension, or **brand stretching**, occurs when an existing brand is used to market products in a different product category. Examples are Adidas glasses, Microsoft XBox videogame system, Apple iPod digital music player and Nesquick cereals. The basic rationale behind brand extensions is the same as the one behind line extensions, i.e. limiting the risk of failure of new product introductions by capitalising upon the image and reputation of a successful existing brand, and at the same time trying to save the huge advertising expenses of launching a totally new brand. Research indicates that brand extensions tend to be more effective than new brand introductions. In one study 30% of new brands survived four years after their introduction, as opposed to 50% of the brand extension launches.[12] Furthermore, brand extensions capture more market share and require less advertising.[13] However, the risks of brand extensions are great. First of all, if the brand image does not fit the new product category or the new market segments well, the new introduction may not be successful.[14] Bic tried to launch a low-price perfume and failed. Recent research, however, shows that an incongruent brand extension can overcome initial negative responses if the exstension is backed by sufficient advertising support. Respondents who were exposed to an ad five times responded significantly more positively (or less negatively) than respondents who saw the ad only once.[15] Secondly, there is the risk of brand dilution. This occurs when the brand name is used for so many different product categories that the brand personality becomes fuzzy and the brand's value deteriorates.[16] If Virgin had not continuously articulated the abstract characteristics of its origin (i.e. fun, hip and subversive) in all its products, it could have been detrimental to use the brand name Virgin for products so fundamentally different as airlines, compact discs and soft drinks. By stressing its abstract characteristics, Virgin seems to become virtually product-independent, embodying a mere brand concept or image.[17]

Brand extension losers and winners

A 2005 survey on brand extensions in which branding and marketing professionals could vote for the best and worst brand extensions showed that key factors for successful extensions are a strong brand and a loyal consumer. Moreover, the most successful extensions came from 'companies that really know their customers, and know the limitations of their brands even more so'. Winners were, amongst others, Starbucks coffee liqueur, Tide to Go stain removal pen and Iams pet insurance. Harley-Davidson's cake decorating kits and Evian's water-filled bra won the votes of worst brand extensions.

Source: TippingSprung, 'Top Brand Extensions', December 2005, www.brandchannel.com

A special case of extension strategies is **corporate branding**. In this case the name of the company is used for all the company's products. This strategy is often used by service companies like banks and insurance companies for which the reputation and the endorsement of a reliable company is very important. For the same reason it is also very valuable for high-technology products. Potential customers have more faith in a long-established and experienced company with a good reputation, which will be able to offer consistent high-quality support in the future. Corporate branding is very similar to the other extension strategies and therefore has the same advantages and disadvantages. One additional disadvantage is that a corporate branding strategy is relatively inflexible. Specific niches that are not associated with the corporate reputation cannot efficiently be targeted on the basis of a corporate branding strategy.[18]

Samsung, the new electronics giant

About ten years ago, Samsung Electronics Co. still was a lower-end consumer electronics producer bringing its product on the market under a handful of brand names including Wiseview,
Tantus and Yepp. To move up the value chain, the company had to build a stronger identity.
Therefore, the company got rid of its other brands and invested in building a strong corporate
brand. Next, it focused on better quality, a nicer design and innovation. To be in users' presence 24 hours a day, seven days a week, the company chose to first focus on a new line of
mobile phones and digital TVs. These are also products with which consumers are more likely
to form a strong bond. Building a strong image in these categories opens doors to other categories. Samsung's strategy is clearly paying off. Over the past five years, Samsung realised
the biggest gain in value of any of the Global 100 brand, namely 186%. By now, it has even
surpassed Sony in overall brand value. Successful strategies get copied: LG Electronics Inc. is
currently following Samsung's example by elevating its products under the single brand LG. The
company entered the Global 100 brands list in 2005 at number 97.

Source: Berner, R., Kiley, D. (2005), 'Global Brands: Interbrand rank the companies that best built their images-and
made them stick', *Business Week*, 1 August, 86–9.

A brand strategy in which different names are used for products or product ranges
in the same product category is called multi-branding. This is frequently used by companies like Procter & Gamble and Mars. Procter & Gamble, for instance, has a number
of different detergent brands. However, the traditional multi-branding companies also
use brand stretching. For instance, Fairy and Dreft are brands used in both dishwashing
liquids and laundry detergents. The advocates of multi-branding argue that this strategy
permits finer segmentation and positioning. Each brand is fully capable of building
its own personality and perceived benefit and of appealing to the specific segment it is
targeted on. The obvious disadvantage of this strategy is that individual brands cannot
benefit from the leveraging effect of existing brands.

Companies using the multi-branding strategy will also be inclined to use new brands
when they introduce a product in a new product category. But introducing new brands
may also be called for when none of the company's brands is suited to be used in the
new product category. For instance, Toyota established a new name for its luxurious
car range, the Lexus.

Western brand thinking has mainly been shaped by Procter & Gamble, Unilever,
Henkel and Mars. The key feature here was differentiation: every possible segment
should be serviced with a new brand. Japanese brand thinking, on the other hand,
used to focus on harmony and loyalty: trust, authenticity, credibility and expertise is
based on the company and the values it stands for. Therefore, all products refer to
the company and are not stand-alone items.[19] In the 1990s, some claimed that the
corporate brand would be the only successful option for brand building in the future.[20]
A recent study shows that this does not appear to be true, at least not as far as fast-
moving consumer goods are concerned. Comparing brand strategies of the twenty top
suppliers of UK grocery retailers (involving about 400 products) between 1994 and 2004,
showed a significant drop in the use of corporate brands to the advantage of mixed
brands. More than 60% of the products used some form of mixed branding in 2004.
The researchers assume that the reason for the recent shift away from corporate brands

can be sought in risk avoidance (inspired by recent scandals that broke brands like Enron), the need for precise targeting and the benefits of mixed branding.[21]

When a company introduces a product abroad, it can also choose between an extension or a 'new brand' strategy. If the existing brand has the required global characteristics, is already known in the new country, or if the company is committed to building global brands, a global strategy will be used. Globalisation increases the value of the brand (see below) and enables the company to benefit from transnational efficiencies in advertising, since television channels targeted at consumer segments in different countries, such as Eurosport and MTV, increase the 'footprint' of ads broadcast through these channels. Examples of global brands are Coca-Cola, Nike and McDonald's. On the other hand, local brands often have a long tradition in specific countries, as a result of which the company marketing these brands stays with a localised strategy to benefit optimally from the power of each separate brand. General Motors uses the name Vauxhall in Britain and Opel in the rest of Europe. Procter & Gamble uses the brand name Fairy in some countries and Dreft in others.

Moreover, local brands often are market leaders. Thumbs Up is the leading soft drink in India leaving Coca-Cola behind; Valentine is a more powerful paint brand in France than Dulux; Dreft is a powerful detergent brand in Belgium and the Netherlands; Larios was leader in the Spanish gin market when it was bought by Pernod-Ricard. DBS has a 30% market share in the Norwegian bicycle sector while Crescent accounts for 20% of the Swedish bicycle sector and Kildamoës has 15% of the Danish market. Local brands benefit, amongst other things, from the deep-rooted and powerful bond that has been established with local consumers (i.e. consumers often buy the brand their parents bought) and they are adapted to the economic standards of the home country. These local brands are very attractive for global companies and more and more global companies extend their brand portfolio with local brands.[22]

Companies can also opt for dual branding strategies. Three categories of dual strategies can be distinguished. In an endorsement strategy two brand names of the same company are used, one of them serving as a quality label or endorsement.[23] In fact, this strategy can be situated somewhere between an extension and a multi-brand strategy, and combines the advantages of both, although the disadvantages of the two combined strategies should be taken into account. An example is Kellogg's (Cornflakes, Rice Krispies, Coco Pops, etc.).

With ingredient branding, a basic ingredient of the product is mentioned next to the actual product's name. Examples are Intel, Nutrasweet, Woolmark, Goretex, and Tetrapak. The advantages are that both brands can benefit from the synergy effects of combining the two strong brands. Furthermore, communications costs can be shared.[24] A prerequisite for ingredient branding is that the ingredient has to be essential, differentiating and of consistently high quality.[25]

Finally, in co-branding, companies combine their efforts to introduce a product with two brand names in an attempt to carry over the image of the two original brands to the new product. Examples are Braun and Oral B launching an electric toothbrush, and Kimberley Clark introducing a toilet paper carrying the Scottex and Kleenex brand names. The advantages are the same as with ingredient branding. Additionally, the research and development (R&D) costs can be shared. Obviously, the combination should result in a perfect perceptual fit, both from a product and target market point of view.[26]

Cobranding cars and laptops

For owners of a Ferrari or a Hummer, or for people who are frustrated because they cannot afford one of these expensive luxury vehicles, laptop manufacturers have started to market computers with the look and feel of these famous car makes. Acer has launched a Ferrari laptop line, with the well-known Rosso Corso paint of the Ferrari cars. And also the brand of the car is mentioned on the laptop and the mouse. The US PC-brand Itronix launched a Hummer look-alike laptop, with the style of the famous American SUV-car. The strategy behind these co-branding initiatives is in both cases the penetration of Western markets. The Korean brand Acer wants to increase its sales in Europe, and Itronix is a largely unknown brand. By putting their own brand in the background and stress famous brands on their products, they hope to raise awareness and sales.

Source: De Morgen, 12 January 2006.

Brand portfolio

Building a strong brand is one thing, sustaining brand equity in the long run is something else. Besides a well-balanced marketing programme and continuous and consistent integrated marketing communications support, it may be necessary to adapt the brand portfolio over time. A brand portfolio can be defined as the set of all brands and brand lines that a company possesses. The rationale behind every brand portfolio should be threefold. First of all, a company should try to maximise market coverage in a sense that different market segments can be serviced. Secondly, brand overlap has to be minimised in a way that brands are not competing among themselves. Notwithstanding, some overlap may be necessary, or as the CEO of Liz Claiborne put it: 'Cannibalization is inevitable, but it's much better to steal market share from yourself than to sit back and let somebody else do it'.[27] Thirdly, every brand in the brand portfolio should have an added value for the company. For example, in 2000 Unilever decided to trim its brand portfolio from about 1,600 to 400 leading brands. Two criteria were used to select the leading brands: (1) *brand appeal* meaning the appeal of the brand to the consumer and how well the brand meets the expected consumer needs over five to ten years, and (2) *prospects for sustained growth* indicating the brand potential to justify significant investments in technology, innovation and brand communication. Focussing on the 400 brands with a positive growth rate (such as Dove, Lipton, Magnum, Calvin Klein) allowed Unilever to reduce overheads and to focus resources where they were most effective.[28]

Brands in a portfolio usually serve different functions and can be classified as bastion, flanker, fighter and prestige brands (see Figure 2.3). Bastions provide most profit for the company, often follow a premium price strategy, are characterised by a high level of psycho-social meaning and are generally considered as high-performance brands. In order to protect bastion brands, flanker, fighter or prestige brands can be introduced. A flanker brand follows a similar price–profit ratio as the bastion brand, is also characterised by a high psycho-social meaning and perceived performance level, but usually appeals to a different, smaller market segment (niche). Fighter brands are sold at a lower price, situated between the price of the bastion and discount brands. Its

Figure 2.3 A brand portfolio model

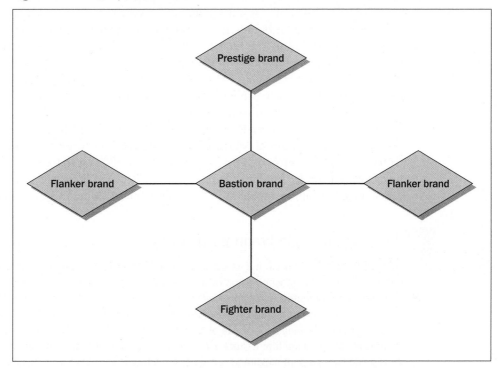

Based on: Riezebos, R. (2003), *Brand Management*. Harlow: Prentice Hall/Financial Times.

quality perception is usually lower than that of the bastion and flanker brands. **Prestige brands** are high-quality, luxurious brands targeted at a smaller segment, looking for status and high psycho-social meaning.[29]

Coca-Cola bought Orangina as a flanker brand for its bastion brand Fanta. Procter & Gamble's shampoo bastion brand is Pantène while Head & Shoulders can be considered as a flanker brand. Philip Morris introduced Basic as a fighter brand to protect Marlboro, just as Procter & Gamble launched Bonux to protect Dash and the Volkswagen Group acquired Seat and Skoda to safeguard Volkswagen. Finally, Toyota, Nissan and Ford have Lexus, Infinity and Jaguar as prestige brands.[30]

Brand equity

In the previous sections it has been argued that brands are valuable assets for marketing. Brand equity is a concept that is used to indicate the value of a brand. It is the value added to a product by virtue of its brand name.[31] In fact, a distinction should be made between consumer brand equity and financial brand equity.[32] The latter refers to the financial value of the brand for the company, the former to the underlying customer- and marketing-related components of brand equity. In practice, the concept of brand equity is used to describe both. Economically speaking, the value of a brand is the sum of all discounted future income streams attributable to the brand.

When looking at the balance sheet of companies marketing branded products, one generally only finds buildings, machines and inventories there. Seldom is the goodwill built up in well-known brands shown. However, whenever a company is involved in mergers or acquisitions, the financial value of the brand portfolio becomes of great importance. Some say that the brand portfolio is the most valuable asset of a company. John Stuart, former president of Quaker Oats, illustrated this by stating: 'If we were to split up the company, you can have all the buildings, I will take the brands. I am sure I will be more successful than you.' As a result, huge amounts of money are paid for brand portfolios. Nestlé took over Rowntree (KitKat, After Eight, Rolo) for US$4.5 billion. The British concern Grand Metropolitan took over the American company Pillsbury for $5.5 billion, thereby paying a premium of over 50% on share value.[33] Gillette took over Duracell for $7 billion dollars.[34] Hewlett-Packard is valued at $18,866 billion, Dell at $13,231 billion, Apple at $7,985 billion and IBM at $53,376 billion.[35]

Building strategic brand portfolio's

Beiersdorf AG, the German manufacturer of body-care products, wound-healing products and adhesive bandages, reached a turnover of €4.742 billion in 2002.[36] Two-thirds of this turnover could be attributed to the 'cosmed' division, with Nivea as leading brand. In 2002 Nivea held position 91 in Interbrand's 'world's most valuable brands' list. Its brand value equalled $2.397 billion, showing an increase of 16% compared to 2001.[37] Nivea was growing twice as fast as its direct competitor L'Oréal and four times as fast as Procter & Gamble and Unilever. This made Nivea a potential brand for takeover. Rumours were that several companies, including Procter & Gamble, were lining up to bid. It goes without saying that Nivea would be of strategic importance to Procter & Gamble. A takeover of Nivea would help Procter & Gamble (producer of Oil of Olay) close the gap on L'Oréal in the global skin-care market. Moreover, it would help Procter & Gample to get a stronger foothold in Western Europe.[38] In such situations, the takeover price can be much higher than the estimated brand value. Several examples prove this. Coca-Cola, for example, paid a billion dollars for Orangina, almost three times the brand's turnover. Unlike Pepsi, which is not interested in orange soft drinks, Orangina was a strategic product to add to Coca-Cola's brand portfolio. Indeed, by taking over Orangina, Coca-Cola holds both the number one brand – Fanta – and the number two brand – Orangina – in the sector. Moreover, both brands hold a very distinctive positioning so that different segments are serviced.[39]

How can the financial brand value be calculated? Different calculation methods exist. Interbrand, one of the leading brand valuation companies, uses four criteria:[40]

- A *financial analysis* to identify business earnings.
- A *market analysis* to determine what proportion of those earnings are attributable to the brand ('branding index').
- A *brand analysis*, to find out how strong the brand is in the perception of consumers ('brand strength score').
- A *legal analysis*, to establish how well a brand is legally protected.

Using these four categories, experts determine financial brand equity. In Table 2.2 an example is given of the importance of the brand (branding index), relative to other

Table 2.2 The relative importance of brands (%)

Industry	Tangibles	Brand	Other intangibles
Utilities	70	0	30
Industrial	70	5	25
Pharmaceutical	40	10	50
Retail	70	15	15
Info tech	30	20	50
Automotive	50	30	20
Financial services	20	30	50
Food and drink	40	55	5
Luxury goods	25	70	5

Source: Perrier, R. (1997), *Brand Valuation*. London: Premier Books and Interbrand Group. Reproduced with permission of R. Perrier, Interbrand Group Ltd.

assets, in a number of industries.[41] Especially in consumer product companies, the brand accounts for a large part of the business earnings. In information technology and pharmaceutical companies, other intangibles, such as patents and the quality of personnel, are relatively more important. In industrial sectors, tangible assets play a major role. Obviously these percentages are only averages, and the situation may be significantly different from one company to the next. The higher the branding index or the importance of a brand for a company, the more branding strategy and brand support in terms of marketing communications will be important for the company's economic success.

Another important aspect of the brand valuation system is the brand strength score. This is based on seven criteria with different weights. They are summarised in Table 2.3. The most important criteria are leadership and internationality (each accounting for 25% of the score). Obviously, a leading brand is generally a more stable and valuable property. Additionally, brands that have proved to be successful in different countries are assumed to be a more stable and robust asset. Customer loyalty accounts for 15%. Strong brands are brands with a loyal customer base. Brands that have been supported consistently by marketing investments, that show an increasing long-term trend and that are in markets in which branding is relatively important are also assumed to be more valuable. Finally, the value of well-protected brands is, of course, more secure.

Table 2.3 The brand strength index

Factor	Relative importance (%)
Leadership	25
Internationality	25
Stability	15
Market	10
Trend	10
Support	10
Protection	5

Source: Perrier, R. (1997), *Brand Valuation*. London: Premier Books and Interbrand Group. Reproduced with permission of R. Perrier, Interbrand Group Ltd.

For a marketer, consumer brand equity is more important than financial brand value. The former type of brand equity, representing the 'marketing value' of a brand, can be measured in different ways, all of them trying to capture the extent to which the brand gives the product extra marketing strength. In Figure 2.4, the components of consumer brand equity are presented.[42] Each of the brand equity factors are determined and influenced by marketing communications strategy, and lead to a number of benefits. These are discussed in the following sections. In this section the components of brand equity are looked at more closely.

A well-known brand is more valuable than an unknown brand. Consumers have more faith in a well-known brand. **Brand awareness** is also necessary to penetrate the consideration set of consumers. The more a brand is in the consideration set of consumers, the greater the chance that it will be purchased and that consumers will become loyal to it.[43] Furthermore, brand awareness leads to more interest and processing of advertising for the brand, thereby enhancing the effectiveness of marketing communications.[44] Brand awareness is more than just being aware of the fact that the brand exists. It also includes knowing what the product stands for, and its attributes and characteristics, such as the brand logo, the manufacturing company, functional, situational and symbolic characteristics, price, quality, performance and advertising characteristics.

Perceived quality is the consumer's judgement about a product's overall excellence or superiority, relative to alternatives.[45] It is influenced by intrinsic and extrinsic cues. Intrinsic cues refer to concrete, physical properties of a product, such as features, colour, taste, miles per gallon. These cues lead to more abstract beliefs in the quality of the product and the benefits it can provide.[46] Extrinsic cues are product-related, but

Figure 2.4 Components of consumer brand equity

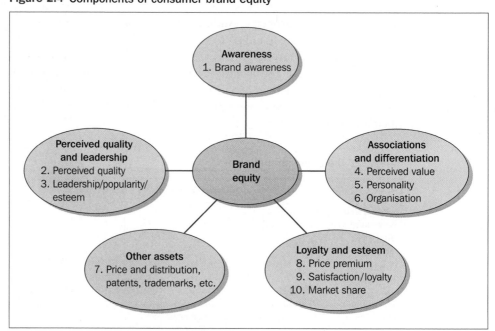

Based on: Aaker, D.A. (1996), *Building Strong Brands*. New York: Free Press.

not part of the physical product. Extrinsic cues are used by consumers to judge the intrinsic quality of a brand. Examples are price, level of advertising, warranty and, last but not least, the brand name. The brand name is an important extrinsic signal for a chunk of intrinsic cues.[47] In an experiment, the difference in perception between Pepsi and Coke Light was tested in the UK. A blind test showed a preference for Pepsi by 51% of the consumers and for Coke by 44%. However, a tasting test with the brand exposed showed a preference for Coke by 65% of the consumers and for Pepsi by 23%.[48] This illustrates the power of the brand as an extrinsic cue of perceived quality on brand preference. The **leadership** dimension reflects to what degree a brand can be considered as a leading and popular brand in the product category. More broadly, it also pertains to the extent that consumers hold the brand in high esteem.

Brand association structures can be conceptualised in different ways. The evoked associations of a brand can be hard, i.e. tangible/functional attributes such as speed, user friendliness or number of flights per day. Associations can also be soft, such as trustworthiness, fun or excitement. Associations can also be made with the corporate image of the provider of the product (IBM or Macintosh), with the product itself or with the users of a product (cellular telephones).[49] Moreover, associations can pertain to the perceived value of the brand as compared to other brands and the extent to which the brand is different from competitive brands.

Arch Deluxe: an expensive McFlop

McDonald's has focused on kids and families for years. In response to the greying of the population and an expanding older market, McDonald's tried to capture the more adult audience. To this end the company launched the Deluxe line, 'hamburgers for adults', with a sophisticated, grown-up taste. The line included the Fish Filet Deluxe, Grilled Chicken Deluxe, Crispy Chicken Deluxe and as flagship the Arch Deluxe. The new line was launched by a $100 million ad campaign. Both the products and the campaign were very different from what people expected and were used to from McDonald's. The ads showed kids looking puzzled at the complex hamburger and making 'yucky faces'. Ronald was even shown in 'adult' activities like golf and pool. McDonald's key values and key consumer associations are friendliness, cleanliness, consistency, simplicity and convenience. That is what people expect to get from McDonald's and that is the reason why they go to McDonald's. Not to get a sophisticated burger at a high price. McDonald's gradually discontinued the line and currently only a few sandwiches (such as Chicken McGrill) are still available. It is estimated that McDonald's lost about $300 million in research, production and marketing for the Deluxe line. The Deluxe line is considered as one of the biggest marketing flops in history, on the same level as New Coke.

Sources: Haig, M. (2005), *Brand Failures: The truth about the 100 biggest branding mistakes of all time*, Kogan Page. Horowitz, A., Athitakis, M. and Lasswell, M. (2004), *The Dumbest Moments in Business History*, New York: Portfolio. http://en.wikipedia.org/wiki/Arch_Deluxe

Brands can have a symbolic meaning or personality, a certain charisma. Examples are Marlboro, Goodyear and Absolut Vodka.[50] Brand personality can be defined as a set of associations that differentiate the brand from competing products and represents the core value of the product.[51] A brand's personality is stronger if its elements are deliberately co-ordinated, if the personality sought is distinctive and kept consistent over time.[52] More recently, Jennifer Aaker developed the Brand Personality Scale (BPS) to measure a brand's personality.[53] The BPS distinguishes five personality dimensions: (1) sincerity (down-to-earth, honest, wholesome and cheerful), (2) excitement (daring, spirited, imaginative and up to date), (3) competence (reliable, intelligent and successful), (4) sophistication (upper class and charming), and (5) ruggedness (outdoorsy and tough). In her US study, MTV scored highly on excitement, CNN on competence, Levi's on ruggedness, Revlon on sophistication and Campbell on sincerity, while other brands scored highly on more than one factor. However, in a later crosscultural study in Japan and Spain, only three of the five factors emerged. Both in Japan and Spain, the 'ruggedness' dimension was replaced by 'peacefulness', while in Spain 'competence' disappeared in favour of a 'passion' dimension.[54] In the current competitive environment, engineering brand symbolism and a brand personality is becoming more important.[55] The success of Lego, for example, is not only linked to its physical attributes, being the simple and distinctive Lego bricks, but also to the psychological meaning of a company committed to fostering creative imagination.[56]

The structure of the 'ladder' of meanings that a brand can deliver is often presented as a 'means–end chain', with six levels (associations) (Table 2.4).[57] First of all, a brand suggests a number of both concrete and abstract attributes. Concrete attributes can be the Absolut Vodka bottle or the lubricating strip on a Gillette razor. Abstract attributes can be the level of technology in a Saab car or the good taste of Danone yoghurt. These attributes lead to functional and psycho-social benefits. A functional benefit of Elsève hairspray is that you avoid sticky hair. The psycho-social benefit of Nespresso coffee may be that guests feel happy and have more fun drinking it. Finally, brands are also associated with instrumental and end values. Using Dolce and Gabbana perfume may enable you to impress others (instrumental values), leading to a higher level of self-esteem (end-value). The concept of means–end chains is derived from the fact that the attributes (means) lead to benefits, which eventually lead to values (ends). For instance, Dorito crisps are made of corn and have a special flavour, as a result they are tasty and guests have more fun and enjoy visiting you, which makes you a good host, leading to the desired end-value of higher self-esteem. The final goal of consumption and brand choice is to satisfy end-value needs.

Table 2.4 Means–end chains and brand association structures

	Concrete attributes	Abstract attributes	Functional benefits	Psycho-social benefits	Instrumental values	End-values
Bacardi Breezer	Less alcohol	Filling	I drink less alcohol	I avoid the negatives of alcohol	I am more able to socialise and can really enjoy my company	I get the feeling I belong to the group
50cl cola can	Too much to drink	Cola gets warm	I cannot drink it all	I throw it away	I am wasting money	I feel irresponsible
Spicy Doritos	Flavour	Strong taste	I eat less	I don't get fat	I maintain a good figure	I feel good about myself

Based on: Reynolds, T.J. and Gutman, J. (2001), 'Laddering Theory, Method, Analysis, and Interpretation', in: Reynolds, T.J. and Olson, J.C. (2001), *Understanding Consumer Decision Making. The Means-End Approach to Marketing and Advertising Strategy*, Mahwah, NJ: Lawrence Erlbaum Associates, 25–62.

Finally, in assessing brand association structures, not only the evoked associations should be measured, but also their desirability, strength and uniqueness,[58] i.e. the extent to which customers value the associations they make, and the extent to which the brand is perceived to be the only one that evokes that particular set of associations.

Other assets also determine brand equity, such as patents and trademarks, quality of staff, labels, support by the distribution, shelf space, the number of stores carrying the brand, the percentage of people that have easy access to the brand, etc.

The first four factors of brand equity do not imply any real behaviour on the part of the consumer. Evidently, real brand strength will be translated into consumers buying the brand and being loyal to it. Behind every powerful brand stands a group of loyal consumers. In fact, the real company asset is brand loyalty, not the brand itself.[59] Different levels of loyalty can be distinguished (Figure 2.5). Evidently, a strong brand implies that as many customers as possible are satisfied, committed buyers. Not only will committed buyers repurchase the brand, they will also actively promote your brand to others and function as real ambassadors. Striving for customer loyalty is also a cost-saving strategy. Research indicates that the cost of attracting new customers can be as much as six times greater than the cost of retaining existing customers.[60] One way to retain loyal customers and committed buyers is to address marketing programmes in a way that consumers are offered an experience instead of a product. For example, marketers and consumers can jointly build brand communities where brand experiences can be build and/or shared. A brand community is 'a specialised, non-geographically bound community, based on a structured set of social relationships among users of a brand'.[61] Jeep, for example, organises brand fests such as Jeep Jamborees (regional rallies focussing on off-road trail driving), Camp Jeep (national rally offering lifestyle and product-related activities) and Jeep 101 (off-road driving course), all attracting a

Figure 2.5 The loyalty pyramid

wide range of Jeep owners and their friends. Even Jeep owners who come to the event with a feeling of being different from the others seem to leave the event believing they belong to a broader community. Brand communities also exist for Harley-Davidson (Harley Owner Groups, HOGs) and Apple. Certainly, customers who feel they belong to a brand community will remain brand loyal. Moreover, the experiences gathered by means of the brand community increase word-of-mouth leading to many friends also buying the brand.[62]

Benefits of branding

Strong brands have a number of benefits for the company, the retailer and the consumer.[63] Strong brands help the **consumer** to locate and identify products and evaluate their quality. It makes it easier for the consumer to develop attitudes and expectations. A brand name serves as a shorthand label for a large bundle of associations and the whole brand personality. Branding makes shopping more efficient in that it reduces the amount of decision-making time required and the perceived risk of purchase, as a result of the fact that a brand promises a constant level of quality. It gives consumers the ability to assess quickly the value and quality of new products by association with a well-known brand name. Furthermore, the consumer derives a psychological reward, since some brands, like Rolex or Lexus, are regarded as status symbols. Finally, branding increases the innovation potential of manufacturers, thus leading to more variety and consumer choice.

Retailers also benefit from strong brands because they improve the image of the store, and as a result attract customers. Strong brands often result in lower selling costs and a higher inventory turn. Furthermore, retailers benefit from the marketing support the brand gets, by means of advertising, sales promotion and in-store communications.

Last but not least, **manufacturers** benefit greatly from high-equity brands.[64] In Table 2.5, the benefits for the manufacturer are summarised per brand-equity component. High brand awareness puts the brand in the evoked set of many consumers, and may even give it a prominent place in this evoked set. The more a brand is in the evoked set of consumers, the more probable it becomes that the consumer is going to buy it. Promotional support is facilitated.

Well-known brands are also capable of developing favourable attitudes and perceptions more easily, again leading to more sales. Additionally, well-known brands can lead to more interest and trust by retailers, resulting in easier access to the distribution channel. Well-known brands also increase the power of the manufacturer over the retailer. As already mentioned, a brand name serves as a shorthand signal for favourable brand associations. Brand awareness also gives the company and the brand a sense of trustworthiness and the image of commitment.

Higher perceived quality gives the consumer a good reason to buy the product. Higher perceived quality as well as a positive brand personality and higher customer loyalty give the company the opportunity of charging a premium price. Furthermore, it protects the company against future price competition. Brand associations and high quality perception enable the manufacturer to create a differential advantage, to build up a defence against the competition and to target and position products in a more sophisticated way. The same brand equity components also give the manufacturer an

Table 2.5 Brand equity components and branding benefits

Brand equity components	Benefits
Brand awareness	■ Brand in evoked set ■ Influence on attitude and perceptions ■ Anchor for associations ■ Signal of substance/commitment
Perceived quality	■ Price premium ■ Differentiation/positioning ■ Reason to buy ■ Channel member interest ■ Brand extension potential
Strong brand associations	■ Differentiation/positioning ■ High price premium ■ Memory retrieval potential ■ Reason to buy ■ Brand extension potential
High brand loyalty	■ Reduced marketing costs ■ Trade leverage ■ Attracting new customers ■ Time to respond to competitive threats

efficient base for line or brand extensions. The image and personality of the brand is easily carried over to the new product, giving it a head start. An extensive set of brand associations helps the consumer retrieve information from memory, thus facilitating the purchasing process and biasing it towards the brand.

A strong brand is capable of fostering brand loyalty. It is a vehicle in forging stable relationships between the consumer and the manufacturer. It reduces the marketing cost, because it is cheaper to retain an existing loyal customer than to win over a new one. Brand loyalty leads to more support from the distribution channel and makes the company less vulnerable to competitive action. Overall, the most important consequence of possessing strong brands is that it can generate higher and more stable sales and profits.

Marketing communications and brand equity

In general, the role of marketing communications is to communicate the essence of brand personality and provide the continuity for a partnership between the brand and the consumer.

A number of communications tools can be used to reinforce brand equity. Others, on the other hand, should be avoided. Taking a long-term perspective of brand management, managerial efforts can be classified in two types of activities: brand-building and brand-harming activities.[65] High advertising spending is an example of a brand-building activity. Frequent use of price promotions, on the other hand, dilutes the brand in the long run and can therefore be classified as a brand-harming activity. Indeed, price cuts and other types of immediate material incentives may reduce the quality perception of brands and the potential of the brand to command a premium price. On the other hand, loyalty promotions may serve both as a reward for loyal customers and as a means of enhancing the loyalty-creating effect of brand strength with new customers.

The 'junk mail' image of direct mailing could also harm the brand. A beautiful and convincing image campaign may be completely overturned and destroyed by frequent, straightforward, hard-sell direct mailing campaigns. On the other hand, public relations, if well handled, and corporate image-building can be valuable brand-building activities for corporate brands. McDonald's did not open a restaurant in Moscow because of its immediate profit potential. The worldwide coverage of the event in the media gave it massive free publicity and positioned the company as very international and forward-looking. On the other hand, Perrier reacted so clumsily to the problem of benzene in its mineral water that the image of the brand was seriously damaged. Consistent corporate identity and corporate image-building through packaging and design add to building and maintaining the long-term network of associations, one of the factors of brand equity.[66]

Colours and symbols as brand-building tools

Corporate identity-building can lead to powerful associations between colours or symbols and brand names. Consider the following examples:

- Golden arches symbolise McDonald's.
- The circle with the triangular star is Mercedes.
- Three stripes on a shoe is Adidas.
- A stylised lion is the ING Bank.
- IBM owns dark blue in business machines.
- Yellow belongs to Kodak in photography.
- In batteries, bronze and black is Duracell.

No doubt, advertising is the key tool of marketing communications when it comes to building and sustaining strong brands. Advertising can build brand equity in several ways. It can influence brand attitude and build brand awareness and associations. It also influences the consumer's memory structure for a brand and enables him or her to retrieve brand information more easily.[67] This can be effected by means of formal or content-related advertising techniques, using emotional cues as well as informational appeals. In Figure 2.6, the relationships between brand equity components and a number of advertising models are shown.[68] A single ad, and certainly a whole campaign, may combine several appeals simultaneously to build and maintain brand equity.

The main objective of awareness-salience advertising is to create advertising recall, advertising awareness and impact, leading to brand awareness and brand salience. Often, this type of advertising will be used in the introduction stage of the brand life cycle. Multiple awareness-building media such as billboards and television can be used, and campaign pressure will be substantial.

Figure 2.6 Brand equity components and advertising models

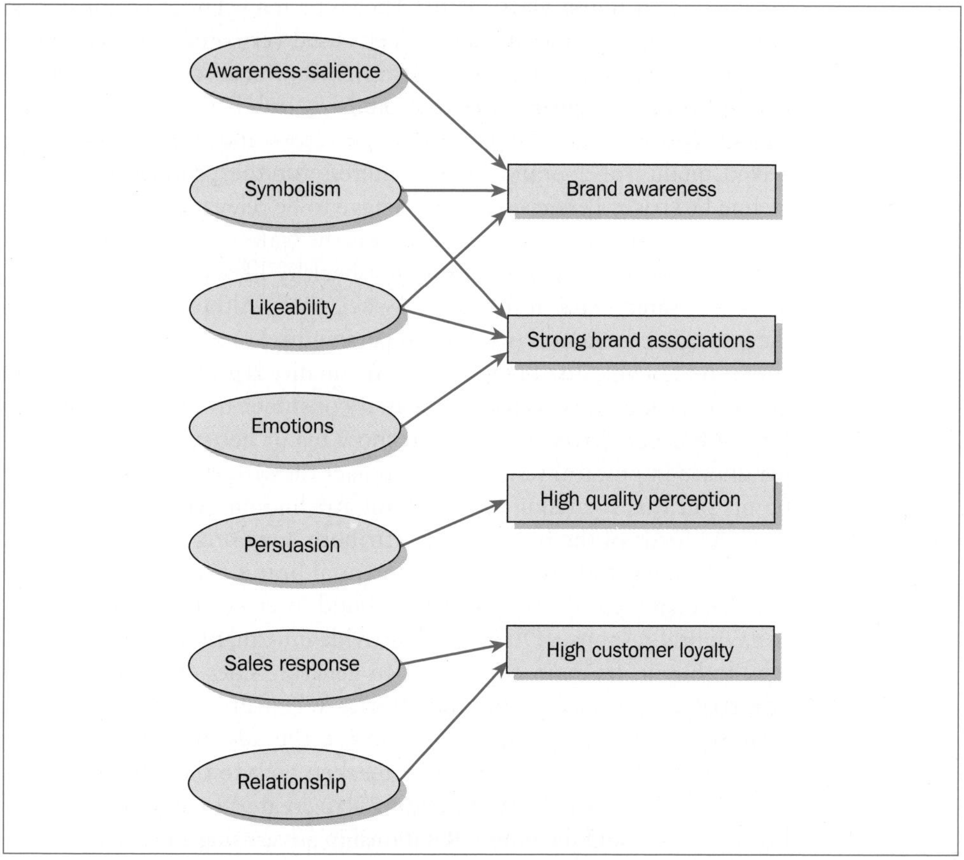

Based on: Franzen, G. (1998), *Merken en Reclame (Brands and Advertising)*. Kluwer Bedrijfsinformatie.

Symbolism advertising tries to communicate symbolic brand meanings and brand personality traits. Besides building brand awareness, it serves the purpose of creating associations between the brand name and brand symbols, such as a logo, a design and packaging, but also between the brand and its user types. In doing so, it tries to develop advertising involvement and meaningful brand attitudes. The Benetton campaigns and the Absolut Vodka campaigns are good examples, as well as the Coca-Cola Light 11.30 break ads which show a delivery boy drinking Coke Light. In most perfume ads models (or celebrities) are shown, which suggest what type of consumer the product is made for.

Likeable ads create advertising involvement and try to make the likeability carry over to the brand, the result being brand likeability and reinforcement of brand attitudes. Ad creativity, humour and celebrity endorsement are techniques that can be used to create likeable ads. The 'Whassup' Budweiser campaign is an example of this advertising technique.

To build a relationship with a brand, the consumer does not need only information and symbolic cues. Emotions can be a very strong relationship-building factor. Advertising may use a likeable, friendly atmosphere, stimulate emotions such as excitement, fun, carefreeness and nostalgia to build emotional brand associations, create empathy and rein-force brand attitudes. The Gillette ('The best a man can get') campaign is a good example of this strategy. Emotional advertising is used very often.[69] It can be very powerful, and is indeed often more effective than straightforward 'selling is telling' advertising.[70]

Persuasion advertising tries to establish a link between a brand and an attribute or benefit. It tries to get the main message across and as such helps to enhance the per-ceived quality of a brand, builds interest for the product and makes the consumer inclined to try it. Persuasion appeals have to be relevant and credible in order to lead to purchase intention. Volvo used to stress the 'safety' factor in most of its ads. Bio from Danone tries to associate itself with a healthy lifestyle, and Intel always tries to rein-force the 'safety' and 'technology' associations. Although brand managers often stress the intangible attributes (values and personality) of a brand, consumers often base their choice on tangible attributes. Therefore, quality is a very important brand characteristic and persuasion advertising may help a consumer to justify his or her product choice. Even a Porsche driver who likes to show his or her success wants to rationalise his or her choice in physical terms (speed, power, design, etc.).[71] On the other hand, research points out that focussing too much on attribute information to promote a brand may shift the focus of the brand to the attribute, lowering brand equity to a certain extent and reducing the attractiveness of potential brand extensions.[72]

Sales response advertising tries to build interest in the brand and provoke a direct behavioural response. Often it will provide information on where to find the brand and why to buy it. Its main objective is to generate sales. This strategy is closest to action advertising and sales promotion efforts. When Procter & Gamble launched Febreze, a spray to eliminate odours from fabrics, the ads informed the consumer where the product could be found in the supermarket: next to the fabric softeners.

The ultimate goal of brand-building is to create a long-term and firm link between the loyal customer and the brand. **Relationship advertising** stresses the value of the brand for the consumer, reinforces emotional involvement, brand associations and personality, and favourable attitudes. Most image campaigns can be considerded relationship advertising. Virtually all perfume brands use this form of advertising.

In Chapter 3 (How marketing communications work) and Chapter 7 (Advertising) these issues will be explored in more depth, and other marketing communications models will be discussed.

Summary

A brand is a name, term, sign, symbol or design, intended to differentiate the products of one company from those of the competitors. Brand names should be memorable, meaningful, likeable, adaptable, transferable and protectable. There are different categories of brands. To compete with manufacturer brands, distributors introduce own-label brands and generic products. Successful brands have a number of common characteristics. The products are original, of good quality and differentiated from the competition, and the brand is supported by the management, employees and characterised by additional service and integrated communications support in a long-term perspective. Companies can choose different strategies for their brands. Besides co-branding with other brands, an extension or multi-brand strategy can be adopted. Also corporate branding, i.e. using the same company name for all company products, is a possibility. Not only does brand equity have to be built, it also has to be sustained over time. In this respect, the brand portfolio may have to be adapted once in a while. It is important that the portfolio maximises market coverage, minimises brand overlap and is efficiently composed. To protect the main brand (bastion brand), flanker, fighter and prestige brands may be useful. Brand strength is measured on the basis of a number of factors, such as leadership, internationality and stability. The marketing value of a brand, or brand equity, is composed of five factors: brand awareness, perceived quality, strong brand associations, high brand loyalty and other assets such as legal protection and a good distribution network. Strong brands lead to a number of benefits for the company, the consumer and the retailer. Brand equity is developed and supported by means of consistent, long-term, integrated marketing communications. Different communications models can be considered to do this, such as the awareness-salience, symbolism, likeability, emotion, persuasion, relationship and sales response strategy.

Review questions

1 What is a brand? What are the characteristics of a good brand? What types of brand can be distinguished?

2 What are the characteristics of successful brands?

3 What are the benefits and disadvantages of line and brand stretching versus multi-branding? What are the implications of the two types of strategy for marketing communications?

4 What is a brand portfolio and what different functions can the composing brands serve?

5 What is brand equity and what are its main components?

6 How can marketing communications influence brand equity?

7 What are the benefits of strong brands for the consumer and for the manufacturer?

Further reading

Aaker, D. and Joachimsthaler, E. (2002), *Brand Leadership*. New York, NY: Free Press.

de Chernatony, L. (2006), *From Brand Vision to Brand Evaluation*. Oxford: Butterworth-Heinemann.

Haig, M. (2005), *Brand Failures: The Truth About the 100 Biggest Mistakes of all Time*. London: Kogan Page.

Journal of Brand Management.

Journal of Product and Brand Management.

Kapferer, J.N. (2004), *The New Strategic Brand Management*. London: Kogan Page.

Keller, K.L. (2003), *Strategic Brand Management. Building, Measuring, and Managing Brand Equity. 2nd Edition*. Upper Saddle River, NJ: Prentice Hall.

Riezebos, R. (2003), *Brand Management*. Harlow: Financial Times/Pearson Education.

Case 2

Barco, Visibly yours

Barco was founded in Belgium in 1934 by Lucien De Puydt who specialised in the assembly of radios with American components. He called the company 'The Belgian-American Radio Corporation', or Barco. In the 1940s, Barco picked up with an innovation in communication technology, namely television. From the 1960s onwards, Barco started to diversify in different sectors. Today, Barco is a world leader concerning display and visualisation solutions for professional markets. The company is still active in a huge variety of markets, served by five different divisions. Markets include Medical Imaging, Media & Entertainment, Infrastructure & Utilities, Traffic & Transportation, Defence & Security, Education & Training, Manufacturing industries and Corporate AV. Worldwide, Barco has 4,222 employees and its sales mounted to about €712 million in 2005, an increase of 6% as compared to 2004. Barco is present in about 90 countries and is visible almost everywhere (screens at pop concerts and sports events, screens in planes, screens in hospitals, screens for company presentations, etc., but since they are active in business-to-business markets, hardly any consumer knows the company. In this way, Barco is one of the world's best kept secrets. To become more visible and to build a stronger brand, Barco recently adopted a corporate branding strategy which was effected in its 'one company, one image' programme. In the next paragraphs, we describe Barco's strategic and branding orientation in 2002 and how the company has evolved since then.

The Barco Brand, 2002

Barco's strategic orientation is characterised by a vertical market expansion. Moreover, Barco not only wants to expand, the objective of the company is to be number one or two in all the markets it serves. If it cannot obtain this (anymore) in a certain market, it moves out of it and looks for other opportunities in display and visualisation solutions. Such a strategic objective and orientation requires a strong corporate brand. Indeed, since professional customers also have less and less time to evaluate different alternatives, branding can make an important difference for the ultimate decision. The company firmly believes that high-quality products, services and technologies can make Barco successful, but unfortunately they cannot make Barco unique since they can be easily copied. Therefore, a strong corporate brand was pursued to guarantee long-term success, since this could be even more important in a high tech B-to-B environment than in B-to-C markets.

Concerning brand identity, Barco saw the following elements as core building blocks: quality, reliability, technological advantage, performance and being the category reference. Many of Barco's employees are engineers that are convinced of the quality of its products. Moreover, since Barco's products easily 'sold themselves' in the past, they were convinced that the customers' perception matched their own beliefs. An image study in 2002 revealed, though, that Barco was perceived as company-centred, technical, technology-driven, purely factual without an emotional link, not containing a 'feel good' factor or possessing much likeability. In short, a rather distant and boring brand. Some of the customers even said they just bought Barco because there was not yet a competitor around for some of the products, adding 'as soon as an alternative comes into the market, we will buy from them'. No need to tell that this was an unpleasant message for Barco. Apparently, price, quality and technology are not the only things that matter for B-to-B markets.

To counter some of the negative image associations, Barco started a branding programme to give the company 'a human face'. They wanted to move from 'distant and boring' to 'personal and emotional' by a translation of the following elements:

Traditional branding	Emotional branding
- Customers	- People
- Products	- Experience
- Honesty	- Trust
- Quality	- Preference
- Notoriety	- Aspiration
- Identity	- Personality
- Function	- Feel
- Ubiquity	- Presence
- Communication	- Dialogue
- Service	- Relationship

ations were made in completely different templates, etc. The divisions not only looked different, they also felt as if they belonged to a different company. For example, when a customer asked information about projectors at a show where LCD screens were on display, an employee could just simply answer 'oh, that's not us, you need to talk to the Barco projector guys' without trying to help the customer.

To achieve a consistent and uniform reflection of the Barco brand in product design and to obtain one image for the five divisions (instead of a different image for each of the five divisions), a Brand Charter was created. The company chose to invest in a strong corporate brand instead of in a multitude of individual brands. This way the Barco image can be leveraged to all other existing and future image solutions.

Realising that building brand equity takes time, the following stepped procedure was worked out:

On top of the image problems mentioned before, each division appeared to have its own 'look and feel' and communicated in different ways to the customers. Different colours were used, the corporate slogan was used by some but not all divisions, company present-

Case Figure 2.1 Brand positioning

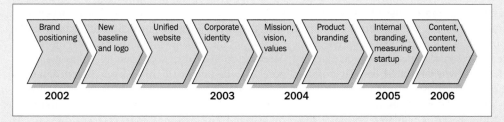

Brand positioning (see chart)

New baseline and logo (the Barco signature)
As mentioned before, the different divisions used different housestyles and logos. One had red letters on a white background, another black letters on a white background, another one white letters on a red background, etc. The logos were also put in different sizes, at different places on any type of marketing tools or collateral, and worse, even by means of different techniques on the products. To underline the new company positioning, the Barco logo was rejuvenated and an updated logo was introduced, in which each division could recognise some of its previous elements. For all collateral, the square logo contains both the Barco name and the company baseline 'Visibly yours' (see Plate 3). On the products,

the baseline is omitted and the preferred method of rendering is in grey metal. In the Brand Charter, which came into being in the course of 2004, strict guidelines are included on where and how to put the logo on the products.

Concerning the slogan, Barco asked its employees to come up with alternatives for the existing slogan 'innovators in image processing'. They were told the slogan should refer to the fact that Barco is active in visualisation solutions, that its products are applicable everywhere, and that the company is customer-centred and user-friendly (i.e. emotional rather than technical). Moreover, the slogan had to be simple and believable. Some 350 responses were received, consisting of, amongst others, 'enhancing your vision', 'vision beyond experience', 'bringing vision to life', 'vision and beyond', 'just look' and 'visibly yours'.

The latter one was deemed perfect since Barco can be very visible, noticeable in every individual's life without them knowing so. Furthermore, throughout the day, Barco is with you, whatever you do, wherever you go, wherever you look. The new logo and slogan was introduced by a one-minute company flash that were shown to all employees during an internal event. By having everyone involved from the beginning, Barco was able to accomplish the objective of making people belong to one and the same company. The company flash also became the standard screensaver on every employee's PC companywide.

Unified website

Until 2002, Barco used to have some forty different websites. Barco gradually closed them all and currently has only one integrated website. *Ad hoc* protests against closing a site since 'this site is important for our customers' could be countered by measuring the traffic on the sites and confronting regions, countries or business units with on the one hand the cost of keeping the site and on the other hand the number of actual visitors. A unified 'one company, one image, one look' site was the first step that was taken. The site was restructured so that each market Barco serves had its own dedicated market portal. Some remnants of divisional structure, however, could still be seen in the products overview page. Currently, in 2006, Barco is planning to make the site more customer-friendly by strategically reorganising the site with an even more accessible market and product entry right from the homepage itself.

Corporate identity

A corporate identity book and an identity website were created. Both tools were designed to be a useful working tool containing the necessary rules of the game, while at the same time allowing everyone to be innovative and creative. The objective was to enable all divisions and all business units to fit into the 'one company, one image, one look' strategy. The result is that all marketing communication tools currently have the same look and feel worldwide. From whichever division or business unit a brochure is, everyone recognises it to be about Barco products and solutions.

Mission, vision, values

Since the five divisions also differed in this respect, a new set of mission, vision and values were developed. Again care was taken to co-develop everything with all divisions so that a sense of 'we developed this' was reached. At the moment all are convinced of the following. As imaging is revolutionising the world, accurate processing and display of visual information has become critical in the business world. Because of the increasing complexity, user-friendly solutions are a necessity. In line with this vision, Barco describes its mission as 'to excel in creating stakeholder value, by offering user-friendly imaging solutions to selected professional markets worldwide'. As a guiding principle for Barco's daily operations and business relations, the following five corporate values were defined:

Case Table 2.1 Barco corporate values

Customer focus	Barco wants to be a close business partner that speaks the customer's language, that is alert and responsive, that understands and anticipates his needs.
Integrity	Relationships with customers, suppliers and society in general are marked by integrity. Barco wants to be a long-term partner earning respect, credibility and trust through quality, service, openness and responsiveness.
Creativity	Barco is continuously looking for fresh horizons, new technologies and creative ideas. Originality is an invitation for people to participate in an ambitious project, to express Barco's authenticity through their own personalities.
Passion for achievement	Employees share the same work spirit and passion to meet goals and deadlines. They are driven by the kicks of exploring new technologies, the pleasure of designing award-winning solutions and the satisfaction of creating added value.
Team spirit	Barco staff are driven by a healthy team spirit. They share the same vision and join hands to achieve their goals.

Product branding

Barco decided to stop using product names. Everyone was in favour of using Barco as a master brand. Therefore, Barco switched from individual product names to alphanumerical codes. The advantages of this strategy are multiple. First of all, it enhances brand recognition without additional costs. Secondly, it facilitates the strategic move from products to solutions, stressing much more the added value of the solution than of the separate components. For example, instead of building brand awareness for 'Osyris', 'arrival management software' could be stressed. Thirdly, it saves costs since trade marking product brands is no longer required. Fourthly, it describes and organises solutions by a generic terminology. Finally, the use of generic names improves results on search engines.

Internal branding

Rucci, Kirn and Quinn (1998) demonstrated that engagement and commitment of employees towards the brand and the company has a significant impact on how they treat customers and consequently, on customers' perceptions and business performance. They showed that companies that were rated by their employees as a great place to work, witnessed a 25% growth in share and dividend returns compared to 6.3% for the other companies. Keeping this in mind,

Barco continuously delivered important efforts to involve employees in each of the brand process steps. In 2005 a study was carried out (Vlesich Brand Management Centre, 2005) to investigate to what extent Barco's employees can be considered as brand ambassadors. To this end, employees filled out a brand ambassador scale consisting of a cognitive (e.g. 'I know the core values of Barco by heart'), an affective (e.g. 'I am a true Barco fan') and a behavioural component (e.g. 'I spontaneously say good things about Barco to people in my environment'). All items were rated on a six-point scale (1 = totally disagree, 6 = totally agree). A mean across all items of lower or equal to three means that the employee is rather a brand resister than a brand ambassador, a mean between three and four is considered to be indicative for brand neutrals, a mean between four and five indicates moderate brand advocates, and means between five and six refer to true ambassadors. Barco scored very well: more than two thirds of the employees scored on average higher than four on six! A small 4% can be considered as brand resisters. (Case Figure 2.2)

Moreover, both the employees' and customers' perception of Barco was measured to investigate whether there was a gap between the company's vision, employee and customer brand experience. (Case Figure 2.3)

Case Figure 2.2 Brand ambassadorship Barco

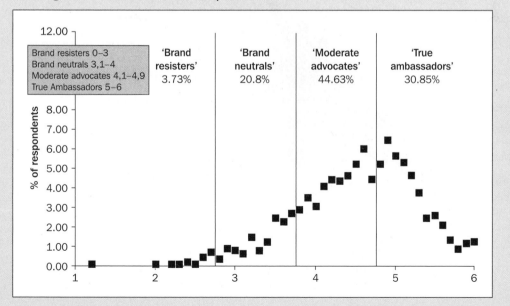

Case Figure 2.3 Gap?

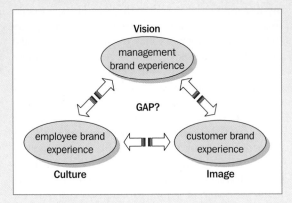

Comparing management's goals with employee and customer perception, it is obvious that in 2005 Barco still scored high on innovativeness, intelligence, technical orientation and reliability, but rather poorly on sensitiveness, emotionality, friendliness and

excitement (see Case Figure 2.4). As far as the core elements of the brand personality are concerned, no considerable differences were discovered neither between divisions nor across countries.

Content, content, content

By creating a higher level of intelligent content and by adhering to the principle of talking the language of the customer (both online and offline), Barco believes this will eventually lead to increased sales and ROI in key markets. Just a few examples:

Corporate marketing has set up a sound product portfolio strategy and brand architecture by defining both the brand charter and product branding principles. In addition, the department is steering regional marketing to make sure that the overall company strategy is executed in a consistent way all over the globe.

The website is continuously being further developed as a fully-fledged marketing tool so that it can

Case Figure 2.4 Elements of the brand personality

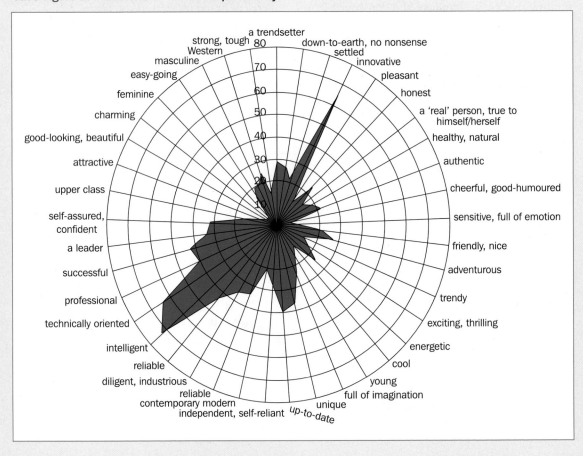

support the full sales cycle, from new customer acquisition over sales support to after sales and service. The content is gradually being personalised to the specific needs of the various target audiences of the company (e.g. announcement of relevant training programmes coming up, service features for the products the web visitor already owns, announcing updates of products, etc.). Improved collection methods of personal data will also lead to enhanced databases and more opportunities for future marketing research and marketing actions.

'You'll See' campaign

To support the above-mentioned branding process, to help retain its innovative image and make the brand more 'emotional', Barco launched a communication campaign in 2005 that will run for at least two years. As part of its long-term strategy, the management defined a 'Barco claim' consisting of the following three elements:

■ A rational promise stressing Barco's user-friendly imaging solutions to make you see better and more with your own eyes.

■ An emotional promise referring to the fact that smart professionals worldwide choose first-class Barco solutions.

■ A communication style based on passion to make the world see better.

The Barco claim was translated into the 'You'll see' campaign which led the foundation for all marketing and communications tools. 'You'll see' is about the desire to see more, to learn more, to feel more and ultimately to know more. A desire that Barco answers in all the markets it is active in. It is based on the customer insight that whether you're a scientist, a pilot, a teacher, an advertiser, an operator, a radiologist or an entertainer, all professionals share a passion for insight. Several pictures of children of various races were shot: a child looking at the sea, a child looking over a wall, a child looking at a tree, a child standing on a bike in order to peep through a small window, etc. All pictures were accompanied with a head or baseline like 'there's more to see', 'there's more to enjoy', 'there's more to observe', 'there's more to manage', 'there's more to explore' or 'there's more to master' (for an example, see Plate 3). These pictures are used for a company

calendar (distributed to all employees and external relations worldwide), for posters and roll-up displays (for use in offices, at tradeshows and on events), in corporate advertisements, for the company brochure, the annual report etc. Besides these pictures, a company commercial was also made to be used in offices, at tradeshows, in presentations, at company events, in demo centres, at press conferences, etc. Moreover, Barco's divisions and international offices can mix and match the pictures in their different marketing communications tools, be it product brochures, product ads, human resources ads, posters for tradeshows, roadshows, customer and dealer events, for use in the offices, etc.

In the space of four years, Barco managed to lay the foundations for a strong corporate brand. Moreover, this was realised with a very limited budget. To guide the brand in even more stricter lines in the future, Barco needs a more analytical approach from now onwards. To this end, the corporate marketing division is gradually moving from a communication-driven, hands-on approach to a more analytical, consultative approach based on metrics. Indeed, measuring all aspects related to brand equity is essential for a good brand policy. It gives early warnings and gives the company directions on how to keep the brand 'on track'.

Based on: Information provided by Ann Galland, Corporate Director Marketing, Annual Report 2005, www.barco.com, Rucci, A.J., Kirn, S.P. and Quinn, R.T. (1998), The employee–customer profit chain at Sears, *Harvard Business Review,* 76 (1): 82, and the 'Internal Branding' research report of the Vlesich Brand Management Centre, Vlerick Leuven Gent Management School, 2005.

Questions

1 What branding strategy did Barco use in the past? Which one is it currently using?

2 What are the advantages and disadvantages of the current branding strategy?

3 Currently Barco is active in several markets. Would you advise Barco to do more brand extensions in the future? Would you advise them to focus on less markets?

4 What are the major strengths of the Barco brand?

5 Do you think Barco has a high Brand Strength Index? What about its customer brand equity?

6 Which of the advertising models shown in Figure 2.6 does Barco use in its 'You'll see' campaign? Do you think this was a good choice? Why (not)?

References

1 Keller, K.L. (2003), *Building, Measuring, and Managing Brand Equity. 2nd Edition*. Upper Saddle River, NJ: Prentice Hall.

2 Keller, K.L. (2003), *Building, Measuring, and Managing Brand Equity. 2nd Edition*. Upper Saddle River, NJ: Prentice Hall.

3 Riezebos, R. (2003), *Brand Management*. Harlow: Financial Times/Pearson Education.

4 Bengès-Sennou, F., Bontems, P., Réquillart, V. (2004). 'Economics of private labels: a survey of literature', *Journal of Agricultural and Food Industrial Organisation*, 2004, 2(1), Article 3. Available at: http://www.bepress.com/jofio/vol/iss1/art3.

5 Verhoef, P.C., Nijssen, E.J. and Sloot, L.M. (2002), 'Strategic Reactions of National Brand Manufacturers towards Private Labels: An Empirical Study in the Netherlands', *European Journal of Marketing*, 2002, 36, 11, 1309–26; Hoch, S.J. (1996), 'How Should National Brands Think About Private Labels?', *Sloan Management Review*, 34(4), 57–67.

6 Doyle, P. (2000), *Value-based Marketing*. Chichester: John Wiley & Sons; Green, D.H., Barclay, D.W. and Ryans, A.B. (1995), 'Entry Strategy and Long-term Performance: Conceptualization and Empirical Examination'. *Journal of Marketing*, 59(4), 1–16; Tellis, G.J. and Golder, P.N. (1996), 'First to Market, First to Fail? Real Causes of Enduring Market Leadership'. *MIT Sloan Management Review*, 1 January.

7 de Chernatony, L. (2006), *From Brand Vision to Brand Evaluation*. Oxford: Butterworth-Heinemann; Tellis, G.J. and Golder, P.N. (1996), 'First to Market, First to Fail? Real Causes of Enduring Market Leadership'. *MIT Sloan Management Review*, 1 January.

8 Anonymous (2005), 'The 100 Top Brands', *Business Week*, 1 August, 90–4; www.interbrand.com.

9 Balachander, S. and Ghose, S. (2003), 'Reciprocal Spillover Effects: A Strategic Benefit of Brand Extensions', *Journal of Marketing*, 67, 1, 4–13.

10 Ries, A. and Trout, J. (2002), *The 22 Immutable Laws of Marketing*. New York: HarperCollins.

11 Swaminathan, V., Fox, R.J. and Reddy, S.K. (2001), 'The Impact of Brand Extension Introduction on Choice', *Journal of Marketing*, 65, 4, 1–15.

12 Kapferer, J.N. (1997), *Strategic Brand Management*. New York: The Free Press.

13 Keller, K.L. (2003), *Building, Measuring, and Managing Brand Equity. 2nd Edition*. Upper Saddle River, NJ: Prentice Hall; Smith, D.C. and Park, C.W. (1992), 'The Effects of Brand Extensions on Market Share and Advertising Efficiency', *Journal of Marketing Research* (August), 296–313.

14 Grime, I., Diamantopoulos, A. and Smith, G. (2002), 'Consumer Evaluations of Extensions and their Effects on the Core Brand: Key Issues and Research Propositions', *European Journal of Marketing*, 36, 11, 1415–38.

15 Lane, V.R. (2000), 'The Impact of Ad Repetition and Ad Content on Consumer Perceptions of Incongruent Extensions', *Journal of Marketing*, 64 (April), 80–91.

16 Trout, J. (1996), *The New Positioning*. New York: McGraw-Hill.

17 Berthon, P., Holbrook, M.B. and Hulbert, J.M. (2003), 'Understanding and Managing the Brand Space', *MIT Sloan Management Review*, 44, 2, 49–54.

18 Murphy, J. (1990), *Brand Strategy*. Englewood Cliffs, NJ: Prentice Hall.

19 Tanaka, H. (1993), 'Branding in Japan', in Aaker, D.A. and Biel, A.L. (eds), *Brand Equity and Advertising. Advertising's Role in Building Strong Brands*. Hillsdale, NJ: Lawrence Erlbaum Associates, 51–66; Kapferer, J.N. (2000), *(Re)Inventing the Brand. Can Top Brands Survive the New Market Realities?* London: Kogan Page.

20 King, S. (1991), 'Brand-building in the 1990s', *Journal of Marketing Management*, 7(3), 3–13.

21 Laforet, S., Saunders, J. (2005), 'Managing brand portfolios: how strategies have changed', *Journal of Advertising Research*, September, 314–27.

22 Kapferer, J.N. (2001), *(Re)Inventing the Brand. Can Top Brands Survive the New Market Realities?* London: Kogan Page.

23 Riezebos, R. (2003), *Brand Management. A Theoretical and Practical Approach*. Harlow: Financial Times/Prentice Hall.

24 Kemper, C.K. (1997), 'Ingredient Branding', *Die Betriebswirtschaft*, 57(2), 271–4.

25 Freter, H. and Baumgarth, C. (1996), 'Komplexer als Konsumgüter-Marketing' ('More Complex than Consumer Product Marketing'), *Markenartikel*, 58(10), 482–9; Bugdahl, V. (1996), 'Ingredient Branding – Eine Marketing Strategie für Mehrere Nutzniesser' ('Ingredient Branding – A Brand Strategy for More than One Beneficiary'), *Markenartikel*, 58(3), 110–13.

26 Simonin, B.L. and Ruth, J.A. (1998), 'Is a Company Known by the Company It Keeps? Assessing the Spillover Effects of Brand Alliances on Consumer Brand Attitudes', *Journal of Marketing Research*, 35, 2, 30–42; Samu, S., Shanker Krishnan H. and Smith, R.E. (1999), 'Using Advertising Alliances for New Product Introduction: Interactions between Product Complementarity and Promotional Strategies', *Journal of Marketing*, 63, 1, 57–74.

27 Keller, K.L. (2003), *Building, Measuring, and Managing Brand Equity. 2nd Edition*. Upper Saddle River, NJ: Prentice Hall.

28 www.unilever.com/pressreleases/2000/EnglishNews_988.asp

29 Riezebos, R. (2003), *Brand Management. A Theoretical and Practical Approach*. Harlow: Financial Times/Prentice Hall.

30 Riezebos, R. (2003), *Brand Management. A Theoretical and Practical Approach*. Harlow: Financial Times/Prentice Hall.

31 Yoo, B., Donthu, N. and Lee, S. (2000), 'An Examination of Selected Marketing Mix Elements and Brand Equity',

Journal of the Academy of Marketing Science, 28, 195–212.

32 Keller, K.L. (2003), *Building, Measuring, and Managing Brand Equity. 2nd Edition.* Upper Saddle River, NJ: Prentice Hall.

33 Franzen, G. (1998), *Merken en Reclame (Brands and Advertising).* Kluwer Bedrijfsinformatie.

34 Perrier, R. (1997), *Brand Valuation.* London: Premier Books and Interbrand Group.

35 Anonymous (2005), 'The 100 top brands', *Business Week*, 1 August, 90–4.

36 www.beiersdorf.com

37 www.interbrand.com

38 www.uktop100.reuters.com

39 Kapferer, J.N. (2001), *(Re)Inventing the Brand. Can Top Brands Survive the New Market Realities?* London: Kogan Page.

40 Perrier, R. (1997), *Brand Valuation.* London: Premier Books and Interbrand Group.

41 Perrier, R. (1997), *Brand Valuation.* London: Premier Books and Interbrand Group.

42 Aaker, D.A. (1996), *Building Strong Brands.* New York: Free Press.

43 Keller, L.K. (1993), 'Conceptualizing, Measuring and Managing Customer Based Brand Equity', *Journal of Marketing*, 57(1), 1–22.

44 De Pelsmacker, P. and Geuens, M. (1999), 'The Advertising Effectiveness of Different Levels of Intensity of Humour and Warmth and the Moderating Role of Top of Mind Awareness and Degree of Product Use', *Journal of Marketing Communication*, 5, 113–29.

45 Aaker, D.A. (1996), *Building Strong Brands.* New York: The Free Press.

46 Kirmani, A. and Zeithaml, V.A. (1993), 'Advertising, Perceived Quality and Brand Image', in Aaker, D.A. and Biel, A.L. (eds), *Brand Equity and Advertising. Advertising's Role in Building Strong Brands.* Hillsdale, NJ: Lawrence Erlbaum Associates, 143–62.

47 Zeithaml, V.A. (1988), 'Consumer Perception of Price, Quality and Value: A Means–End Model and Synthesis of Evidence', *Journal of Marketing*, 52(3), 2–22.

48 De Chernatony, L. and McDonald, M.H.B. (1992), *Creating Powerful Brands: The Strategic Route to Success in Consumer, Industrial and Service Markets.* Oxford: Butterworth-Heinemann.

49 Biel, A.L. (1993), 'Converting Image into Equity', in Aaker, D.A. and Biel, A.L. (eds), *Brand Equity and Advertising. Advertising's Role in Building Strong Brands.* Hillsdale, NJ: Lawrence Erlbaum Associates, 67–82.

50 Smothers, N. (1993), 'Can Products and Brands Have Charisma?', in Aaker, D.A. and Biel, A.L. (eds), *Brand Equity and Advertising. Advertising's Role in Building Strong Brands.* Hillsdale, NJ: Lawrence Erlbaum Associates, 97–112.

51 Broniarczyk, S. and Alba, J. (1994), 'The Importance of the Brand in Brand Extension', *Journal of Marketing Research*, 21(2), 214–28.

52 Batra, R., Lehmann, D.R. and Singh, D. (1993), 'The Brand Personality Component of Brand Goodwill: Some Antecedents and Consequences', in Aaker, D.A. and Biel, A.L. (eds), *Brand Equity and Advertising. Advertising's Role in Building Strong Brands.* Hillsdale, NJ: Lawrence Erlbaum Associates, 83–96.

53 Aaker, J.L. (1997), 'Dimensions of Brand Personality', *Journal of Marketing Research* (August), 347–56.

54 Aaker, J.L., Benet-Martinez, V. and Garolera, J. (2001), 'Consumption Symbols as Carriers of Culture: A Study of Japanese and Spanish Brand Personality Constructs', *Journal of Personality and Social Psychology*, 81(3), 492–508.

55 Tan Tsu Wee, T. and Chua Han Ming, M. (2003), 'Leveraging on Symbolic Values and Meanings in Branding', *Journal of Brand Management*, 10, 3, 208–18.

56 Anonymous (2002), 'Branding @ Lego, McDonald's and JCB', *Strategic Direction*, 18, 10, 7–9.

57 Reynolds, T.J., Olson, J.C. (2001), *Understanding Consumer Decision Making. The Means–End Approach to Marketing and Advertising Strategy*, Mahwah, NJ: Lawrence Erlbaum Associates.

58 Keller, K.L. (2003), *Building, Measuring, and Managing Brand Equity. 2nd Edition.* Upper Saddle River, NJ: Prentice Hall.

59 Perrier, R. (1997), *Brand Valuation.* London: Premier Books and Interbrand Group.

60 Dekimpe, M.G., Steenkamp, J.B.E.M., Mellens, M. and Vanden Abeele, P. (1997), 'Decline and Variability in Brand Loyalty', *International Journal of Research in Marketing*, 11(3), 261–74.

61 Muniz, A. and O'Guinn, T. (2001), 'Brand Community', *Journal of Consumer Research*, 27 (March), 412–32.

62 McAlexander, J.H., Schouten, J.W. and Koenig, H.F. (2002), 'Building Brand Community', *Journal of Marketing*, 66, 1, 38–54.

63 Webster, F.E. (2000), 'Understanding the Relationships Among Brands, Consumers and Resellers', *Journal of the Academy of Marketing Science*, 28, 1, 17–23.

64 Brassington, F. and Pettitt, S. (2003), *Principles of Marketing.* London: Pitman Publishing.

65 Yoo, B., Donthu, N. and Lee, S. (2000), 'An Examination of Selected Marketing Mix Elements and Brand Equity', *Journal of the Academy of Marketing Science*, 28, 195–212.

66 Biel, A.L. (1993), 'Converting Image into Equity', in Aaker, D.A. and Biel, A.L. (eds), *Brand Equity and Advertising. Advertising's Role in Building Strong Brands.* Hillsdale, NJ: Lawrence Erlbaum Associates, 67–82.

67 Edell, J.A. and Chapman Moore, M. (1993), 'The Impact and Memorability of Ad-Induced Feelings: Implications for Brand Equity', in Aaker, D.A. and Biel, A.L. (eds), *Brand Equity and Advertising. Advertising's Role in Building Strong Brands.* Hillsdale, NJ: Lawrence Erlbaum Associates, 195–212.

68 Franzen, G. (1998), *Merken en Reclame (Brands and Advertising).* Kluwer Bedrijfsinformatie.

69 De Pelsmacker, P. and Geuens, M. (1997), 'Emotional Appeals and Information Cues in Belgian Magazine

Advertisements', *International Journal of Advertising*, 16(2), 123–47.

70 Geuens, M. and De Pelsmacker, P. (1998), 'Feelings Evoked by Warmth, Eroticism and Humour in Alcohol Advertisements', *Journal of Marketing and Consumer Research*, 1, online, 17p.+links. http/www.jcmr.org

71 Kapferer, J.N. (2001), *(Re)Inventing the Brand. Can Top Brands Survive the New Market Realities?* London: Kogan Page.

72 Van Osselaer, S.M.J. and Alba, J.W. (2003), 'Locus of Equity and Brand Extension', *Journal of Consumer Research*, 29, March, 539–50.

Chapter 3

How marketing communications work

Chapter outline

| Hierarchy of effects |
| Attitude formation and change |

High elaboration likelihood Cognitive attitude formation	Low elaboration likelihood Cognitive attitude formation
High elaboration likelihood Affective attitude formation	Low elaboration likelihood Affective attitude formation
High elaboration likelihood Behavioural attitude formation	Low elaboration likelihood Behavioural attitude formation

| Irritation |
| Brand confusion |

Chapter objectives

This chapter will help you to:

- Get an idea of how hierarchy-of-effects models describe how communications works
- Understand the importance of attitude formation in the consumer persuasion process
- Distinguish the basic types of attitude formation and change processes and marketing communications models
- Learn about the importance of elaboration likelihood and cognitive, affective and behavioural processes for marketing communications
- Understand the causes and consequences of ad-evoked irritation
- Learn what causes brand confusion in advertising

Introduction

Often it is hard to predict how a consumer will respond to advertising or how someone will process a communications message. Several factors have an impact on this: consumer goals, characteristics of the product type, the situation the consumer is in (hurried or distracted by others, for example), involvement in the product category, and social, psychological or cultural factors. In this chapter an overview of the different ways in which a consumer might process marketing communications is given. One type of explanatory framework that has dominated the marketing communications literature for decades is the hierarchy-of-effects models. Later, modifications of these models were presented, and the focus has shifted towards attitude formation models of response to marketing communications. Consumer involvement and cognitive, affective and behavioural aspects of message processing have been studied intensively. One thing we have learnt so far is that no single theory can explain it all. Some models are applicable in some situations for some kinds of people and for some categories of products. Because of this complexity, it is not surprising that marketing communications do not always work as they should. At the end of the chapter, two phenomena an advertiser would like to avoid – irritation and brand confusion – are discussed.

Hierarchy-of-effects models

Hierarchy-of-effects models[1] are some of the oldest marketing communications models. The first was published in 1898, and their influence on marketing thought remained important until the 1980s. In general, a hierarchy-of-effects model assumes that things have to happen in a certain order, implying that the earlier effects form necessary conditions in order for the later effects to occur.[2] According to these models, consumers go through three different stages in responding to marketing communications, namely a cognitive, an affective and a conative stage, or a think–feel–do sequence. During the **cognitive stage** consumers engage in mental (thinking) processes which lead to awareness and knowledge of the brand communicated. In the **affective stage** emotional or feeling responses occur which are associated with the advertised brand and attitudes towards the brand are formed. A difference with the previous stage is that consumers may become aware and gather information continuously and effortlessly, while affective reactions may only be formed when the need for an evaluation arises. The **conative or behavioural stage** refers to undertaking actions with respect to the advertised brand, such as buying it.

Consumers are assumed to go through the three stages in a well-defined sequence. The majority of the hierarchy models claim a cognitive–affective–conative sequence. In other words, consumers should first learn or become aware of a brand such as Fitness breakfast cereal, for instance. Afterwards they develop affective responses or form an attitude towards Fitness, which might be that Fitness is tasty and healthy. Finally, this feeling or attitude makes the consumers want to buy Fitness. The task of marketing communications is then to lead the consumers through these successive stages. Table 3.1 gives some examples of hierarchy models that follow this traditional sequence. The Lavidge and Steiner model is the one most frequently referred to in the literature.

Table 3.1 Hierarchy-of-effects models

Year	Model	Cognitive	Affective	Conative
1900	AIDA, St Elmo Lewis	Attention	Interest, desire	Action
1911	AIDAS, Sheldon	Attention	Interest, desire	Action, satisfaction
1921	AIDCA, Kitson	Attention	Interest, desire, conviction	Action
1961	ACCA (or DAGMAR), Colley	Awareness, comprehension	Conviction	Action
1961	**Lavidge and Steiner**	**Awareness, knowledge**	**Liking, preference, conviction**	**Purchase**
1962	AIETA, Rogers	Awareness	Interest, evaluation	Trial, adaption
1971	ACALTA, Robertson	Awareness, comprehension	Attitude, legitimation	Trial, adoption

Based on: Barry, T.E. and Howard, D.J. (1990), 'A Review and Critique of the Hierarchy of Effects in Advertising', *International Journal of Advertising*, 9, 121–35.

However, a lot of disagreement exists regarding the sequence of the different stages, and several researchers have developed alternative models. An example is the 'low involvement' hierarchy according to which consumers, after frequent exposure to marketing messages, might buy the product, and decide afterwards how they feel about it (cognitive–conative–affective hierarchy). Another possibility is that consumers' affective responses towards a product lead them to buy it and, if necessary, they reflect on it later. This would suggest an affective–conative–cognitive sequence.

Vaughn[3] proposed an integration of the different sequence models and presented a model, known as the Foot–Cone–Belding (FCB) grid. Four different situations are distinguished, based on two dimensions, i.e. the high–low involvement and the think–feel dimension. **Involvement** can be defined as the importance people attach to a product or a buying decision, the extent to which one has to think it over and the level of perceived risk associated with an inadequate brand choice. The **think–feel** dimension represents a continuum reflecting the extent to which a decision is made on a cognitive or an affective basis. Here Vaughn takes into account that for certain products such as sugar, mineral water, paper towels, soap and banks, cognitive elements are important, while for products such as cakes, ice cream and perfume, affective elements seem to have more impact on the buying decision process. For example, consumers may wonder whether they are running out of water, or whether they will need paper towels during the next week. This is in contrast to considerations such as what to buy the children for a treat: Kinder Delight or chocolate mousse? In Figure 3.1 the different sequences in each of the four situations are shown.

Purchase decisions in quadrant one are characterised by high involvement and rational decision criteria. Here, the consumer first wants to learn about the product. This could be the case for deciding on an insurance policy or a loan or for buying a new computer or major household appliances. In this quadrant the classical hierarchy of effects would hold. The second quadrant concerns product decisions of high involvement, but for which less information is needed. In this case, the consumer first wants to be emotionally attracted by the brand image, then he or she collects information,

Figure 3.1 **The FCB grid**

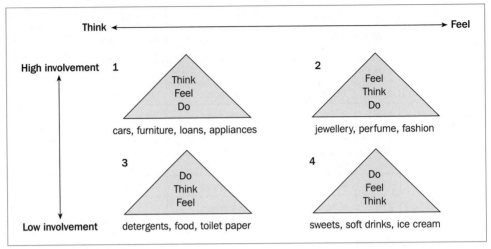

Based on: Vaughn, R. (1980), 'How Advertising Works: A Planning Model', *Journal of Advertising Research*, 20(5), 27–33. Reproduced with permission of ARF, New York.

and finally undertakes some action. Jewellery, perfume, fashion and holidays may be examples that fit in this category. In the third quadrant product decisions are located that require a minimum of cognitive effort and tend to become routinised because of habit formation. The assumed sequence is first buying the product, then learning what its major advantages and disadvantages are, and finally developing an attitude after product or brand usage. Toilet paper, sugar, paper tissues and detergents are expected to be bought without much reflection and only after product experience will an attitude be formed. The fourth quadrant reflects decision-making regarding products which can be termed 'life's little pleasures'. The assumed sequence here is: buy the product, experience an affective response and gather product knowledge afterwards. Examples that fit this category might be soft drinks, ice cream and chocolate bars. For example, consumers buy cake or pizza, eat it and realise that they are really fond of it, but learn afterwards that it makes them fat.

The Rossiter–Percy Grid is an alternative to, or a modification of, the FCB grid which again classifies products and buying decisions in four categories, based on the dimensions high–low involvement and fulfilling a transformational or informational buying motive.[4] Transformational buying motives consist of positive motivations, such as sensory gratification, social approval or intellectual stimulation, while informational buying motives refer to reducing or reversing negative motivations such as solving or avoiding a problem, or normal depletion. Examples of products for which transformational motives prevail are products that give consumers pleasure such as ice cream, cosmetics and perfume. Examples of informational products are detergents, babies' nappies and insurance products.

The advantage of hierarchy-of-effects models and related frameworks is that they incorporate what is their most important contribution, i.e. the recognition of the importance of brand awareness. Hierarchy-of-effects models consider brand awareness as a prerequisite for brand attitude formation. They correctly assume that affective responses cannot be formed or that a purchase cannot take place without having an awareness of the brand. In this respect, it should be mentioned that most companies strive to reach Top-of-Mind Awareness (TOMA) in consumers. TOMA indicates which brand is most salient within a product category. It reflects the first brand that comes to mind when thinking of a particular product category. It is generally acknowledged that brands that are top of mind are more likely to be purchased.

The reintroduction of God in Singapore

You could assume that God does not need to be introduced and that awareness of God is high. This is not what the Love Singapore Movement (a group of 150 churches) thought. They decided to reintroduce God to Singaporian teenagers and young professionals by advertising. The objective of the campaign was to first increase top of mind awareness of God, and secondly to change God's image of 'schoolteacher' into 'someone you wouldn't mind putting on the guest list of your dinner party'. Budgeting for 17 TV commercials and 24 ads in newspapers, Ogilvy & Mather came up with a witty, playful, approachable God spreading messages like: 'I hate rules. That's why I only made 10 of them', 'Bring your umbrella, I might water the plants today', and 'Of course I have a sense of humour. I gave you baboons with bright red asses, didn't I?' Before the ads were on air for a week, the Singapore authorities pulled them out. Therefore, Ogilvy & Mather started using non-traditional media. Buses were painted with the message 'Please don't drink and drive. You're not quite ready to meet me yet', subway waiting places were plastered with the message 'I'm here. God', and SMS was used spreading messages like 'Thank me. It's Friday. God', 'Even I rested on the 7th day. Enjoy. God' and 'Are you coming over to my place later?' (on Sundays). The campaign received incredible attention both in the traditional media and the internet. The campaign was awarded two gold lions and achieved a cult status in no time.[5]

Notwithstanding the important contribution of the classical hierarchy models, several shortcomings have been formulated. A major critique is that empirical support for the fact that consumers go through each stage is still lacking. Significant relations have been observed between ad characteristics and recall, and between ad characteristics and attitudes and purchase intentions, but not between recall and attitudes. This leads to the conclusion that, empirically, no hierarchy of cognitive, affective and conative effects can be observed.[6] Furthermore, hierarchy models do not allow interactions between the different stages, which is very unlikely. Purchase will lead to experience, which will have an important impact on beliefs and attitudes, for example. Therefore, to base marketing communications on hierarchy-of-effects models may not be the most effective or relevant strategy.

Attitude formation and change

Since the 1980s, attitudes have received more and more attention. Attitudes can be defined as a person's overall evaluation of an object, a product, a person, an organisation, an ad, etc. In this view, an attitude towards a particular brand (Ab) can be considered as a measure of how much a person likes or dislikes the brand, or of the extent to which he or she holds a favourable or unfavourable view of it. The reason for this interest in, for example, brand attitudes is the belief that the more favourable brand attitudes are, the more likely a purchase of the brand becomes. Although brand attitudes are relatively stable, they can be changed over time. So, the ultimate challenge for marketing communications is to change attitudes in favour of the company's brand.

Attitudes play an important role in hierarchy-of-effects models too, but in these models they are primarily defined as affective reactions in a hierarchical setting. In fact, an attitude can be assumed to consist of three components (Figure 3.2).[7] The **cognitive component** reflects knowledge, beliefs and evaluations of the object; the **affective component** represents the feelings associated with the object; and the **behavioural component** refers to action readiness (behavioural intentions) with respect to the object.

An example may clarify the distinct components. You may love Timberland shoes (affective component) because you know they are durable and convenient to wear (cognitive component) and that's why you intend to buy Timberland the next time you go shopping (behavioural component). To change attitudes, marketeers might concentrate on changing one of the three components. Gap might stress the fact their clothes are neat, cool and stylish, thereby trying to influence the feelings associated with it by image-building. Communications campaigns trying to influence the consumer on an affective basis often use emotional ads containing no or very few product arguments. Miele might address the quality and durability of its appliances to change consumers' beliefs and evaluations. Marketing communications will probably use many and strong arguments to illustrate the numerous benefits of Miele. Coca-Cola might run a promotion campaign in which consumers can receive a fabulous Coke mobile phone or a Coke sofa in return for a certain amount of cola caps, to induce consumers to buy (a lot of) the brand.

As mentioned before, consumers follow different processes. Not surprisingly, a lot of communications models have been developed, most of them giving an adequate explanation for particular situations only. These different communications models regarding attitude formation and attitude change can be classified along two dimensions.[8] The first refers to the way attitudes are formed – primarily cognitive, affective or behavioural; the second is about the level of elaboration of a message, or central-route versus peripheral-route processing.

Broadly stated, these dimensions are comparable to the ones used in the FCB grid, but no hierarchical conclusions are derived from them. The think–feel dimension of the FCB grid is transformed into a distinction between cognitive, affective and behavioural attitude formation. The involvement dimension of the FCB grid is extended to motivation, ability and opportunity (MAO). By motivation a willingness to engage in behaviour,

Figure 3.2 Attitude components

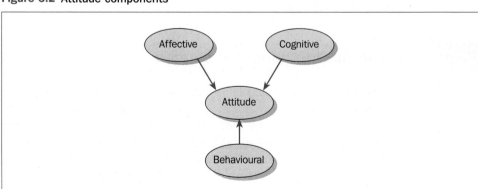

make decisions, pay attention, process information, etc. is meant. Motivation is to a large extent influenced by consumer needs and goals. Consumer needs can be categorised as functional, symbolic or hedonic.[9] Functional needs can be compared to the informational motivation dimension of the Rossiter–Percy Grid and pertain to solving consumer problems. Consumers buy detergents to clean dirty clothes and hire a baby-sitter because they cannot leave their baby unattended. Symbolic needs relate to how we see ourselves and how we would like to be perceived by others. Youngsters may wear Calvin Klein jeans to show they are trendy. Hedonic needs reflect consumers' desires for sensory pleasure. Many tourists buy Belgian chocolates when visiting Belgium because of the delicious taste. Needs/goals can also be classified in approach or promotion goals, and avoidance or prevention goals.[10] The former pertain to positive outcomes while the latter relate to avoiding negative outcomes. For example, consumers can decide to shop at Carrefour because it offers them a nice shopping experience (= approach, promotion) or because they do not have to drive far (= avoidance, prevention). A consumer who plans to buy a new car is probably motivated to process marketing communications on cars. However, the needs or higher order goals that this particular consumer is pursuing have an important impact on information processing and the benefits he or she is receptive to.[11] If the consumer is mainly driven by functional needs, he or she may want clear information on price, safety, fuel consumption, etc., while a status appeal or an ad showing driving sensations may be more effective when symbolic or hedonic needs prevail. The same goes for approach/promotion goals and avoidance/prevention goals: when the former are prevalent then marketing communications should bring a message focussed on positive outcomes (you feel the excitement when driving this car), while for the latter goals a message should emphasise negative outcomes (the excellent air bags will protect you during a crash).[12] So, in order to be persuasive, marketing communications should tap into consumers' motivational concepts and marketers need to understand what goals consumers are trying to accomplish by buying the product.[13]

Being a teenage mum is not that much fun[14]

Teenagers getting pregnant is not a problem of undeveloped countries alone, in many developed countries it also happens more than the society would like. Many young girls see babies as cute and lovely (approach motivation), but do not realise the responsibilities and problems having a baby at such a young age can bring. To convert the approach in a prevention motivation, encourage contraceptive use and raise awareness about teenage pregnancy, Duval Guillaume created for the Belgian public health department a TV spot that promotes a fictitious game. The game is inspired on the Simms, a game that is very popular in teenage girls. The ad starts out like a normal video game commercial: 'Get ready for teenage mum, your ultimate gaming experience . . .'. The player is invited to change diapers around the clock, try to study while your baby cries all night, and manage your relationship with friends while looking after your kid. You see the girl in the game having to choose between picking up the phone or letting her baby have a little accident. Choosing for the baby results in 'friend lost'. The next challenge is to feed the baby who spits the food in his mum's face. At the end, the mum is on her knees, totally exhausted. The voiceover ends with 'your ultimate challenge: not having a nervous breakdown'. Next the text 'Being a teenage mum is not that much fun. Use contraceptives. http://www.laura.be' appears. The ad clearly shows the difficulties of balancing teenagers' needs and wants with the responsibility of a baby. The campaign provoked a lot of discussion, was mentioned on many weblogs and received an award for its creativity and effectiveness.

Although someone is motivated to do something, he or she may be unable to do it. Ability refers to the resources needed to achieve a particular goal. One may be motivated to process a computer ad, but when it is full of technical details one may not be able to process and understand it because of a lack of technical knowledge. A person may be motivated to buy a particular house, but after learning what it is going to cost after renovation, stamp duty, land registration fees, etc. might be unable to buy it because of insufficient money.

Finally, opportunity deals with the extent to which the situation enables a person to obtain the goal set. A consumer may be motivated to buy Danette of Danone, but if the supermarket runs out of Danette, the consumer does not have the opportunity to buy it. A consumer may be motivated to process the information of a particular ad, but if the phone rings, he or she does not have the opportunity to pay attention to it. Also, when the ad contains little or no information, it does not provide the opportunity to elaborate on it.

The effects of the MAO factors on attitude formation and marketing communications processing are presented in the Elaboration Likelihood model (ELM) (Figure 3.3).[15]

Figure 3.3 The Elaboration Likelihood model

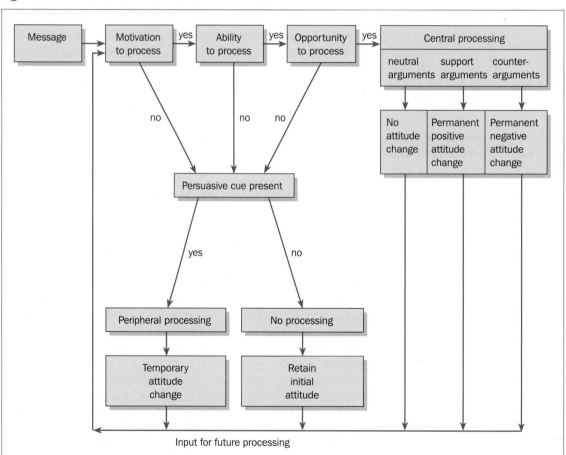

Based on: Petty, R.E. and Cacioppo, J.T. (1986), 'The Elaboration Likelihood Model of Persuasion', *Advances in Experimental Social Psychology*, 19, 123–205. Reproduced with permission of Elsevier.

If motivation, ability and opportunity are all high, the elaboration likelihood is said to be high and consumers are expected to engage in central-route processing. This means that they are willing to elaborate on the information, to evaluate the arguments and find out what the information really has to offer. Depending on the quality and credibility of the arguments, consumers will react by producing counter-, support or neutral arguments, which induce a negative, positive or no attitude change, respectively. For example, when thinking of McDonald's consumers might think of how good McDonald's burgers and fries taste: a support argument. On the other hand, consumers might also think of how unhealthy fast food is: a counter-argument. Furthermore, consumers might just think of the red and yellow colours of a McDonald's restaurant: in effect, a neutral argument. Attitudes formed via the central route prove to be good predictors of later behaviour and are fairly resistant to other persuasive messages.

On the other hand, if one or more of the MAO factors is/are low, consumers are more likely to process the information peripherally. The result of the latter is no real information processing, but an evaluation based on simple, peripheral cues, such as background music, humour, an attractive source or endorser, the number of arguments used, etc.[16] In other words, a favourable brand attitude might be formed because the consumer liked the music in a Levi's commercial or the erotic setting in a Häagen Dazs ad or because the consumer is fond of the polar bears in the Coca-Cola commercial, or because he or she assumed that the high price of the Miele washing machine is a sign of superior quality, or that French wine is invariably good. However, such attitudes do not necessarily last long. If Pepsi launches a campaign with a cute animal, a celebrity or a nice song, consumers may forget about Coca-Cola's nice polar bears and switch their attitude in favour of Pepsi. The reason why consumers start paying more attention to peripheral cues is that in many ads peripheral cues form the only processable information under circumstances of low motivation, limited ability or limited opportunity. Ads without attractive peripheral cues, but with an easy-to-process, product-related message might also work under low MAO, simply because the cognitive resources to form counter-arguments are lacking.

How persuasive is negative information?

For long it has been assumed, both by managers and academics, that negative as compared with equally extreme positive information receives a higher weight in the formation of judgements because negative information would be perceived as more useful or diagnostic for classifying brands into evaluative categories. However, the negativity effect may be overstated. A recent study[17] shows that the negativity effect may only be prevalent when consumers process a message with the goal of forming an accurate impression. In this situation, consumers can be expected to engage in open-minded processing. However, in practice consumers tend to process marketing communications more often with other goals, such as defending prior beliefs and managing their impression with others. A goal of defence motivation can be described as a commitment to a particular brand or object as opposed to being involved in an unbiased, open-minded way.[18] Consumers who are loyal to a certain brand usually do not process information concerning this or competitive brands in an unbiased way, but rather counterargue information that contradicts their original beliefs and support information that confirms the original judgements. Even a weak positive attitude is likely to evoke a consistency motivation (i.e. being averse to processing information [that is contrary] to one's original

▶

attitude), let alone a strong one. In this case, not a negativity effect but a reversed negativity effect was observed. A goal of impression-relevant processing corresponds to processing in a way that satisfies social goals, such as when consumers may need to justify their decisions to family members or friends. In this case, negative and positive information was weighed equally. To conclude, even if consumers are motivated to process marketing communications, the same information may lead to a completely different processing and communication result depending on the type of consumer motivation or processing goal.

At first sight, the above might suggest that the central route pertains to cognitive attitude formation (people carefully think about the substance of the message), while peripheral route processing is more likely to give rise to affective attitude formation (people rely on how the ad makes them feel instead of what the ad really tells). However, reality reveals a more complicated picture. The ELM, as well as other models such as Chaiken's Heuristic-Systematic model (HSM), and Forgas' Affect Infusion model (AIM), assumes that under different MAO conditions, both arguments and affect may give rise to peripheral and central (and even biased) processing.[19] It is not so much the MAO factors, but consumers' goals that might determine whether consumers rely on the substance of the message (i.e. the strength of the claims, the compellingness of the product attributes, etc.) to form a judgement or on their affective responses (i.e. ad-evoked feelings, aesthetic of the product design, charisma of the endorser, etc.). Recent research shows that when individuals focus on ideals (promotion goals, relating to one's hopes, wishes and aspirations such as dreaming of a nice house, an exotic holiday, etc.), they consider affective information as more relevant than the substance of the message and as a consequence are more likely to base their evaluation on affect. On the other hand, when consumers' 'oughts' (prevention goals, relating to one's duties, obligations and responsibilities such as providing for a child's education, looking professional at work) are their driving goal, the opposite result is found.[20] However, how exactly the message substance or affective responses are processed is likely to depend on consumers' elaboration likelihood. Therefore, we distinguish six types of marketing communications models based on two dimensions (see Table 3.2). The first dimension

Table 3.2 Six types of attitude formation and change

		Elaboration likelihood (EL) based on motivation/involvement, ability and opportunity	
		High Elaboration *central-route processing*	*Low Elaboration* *peripheral-route processing*
Attitudes based on:	*Cognitions*	■ Multi-attribute models ■ Self-generated persuasion	■ Heuristic evaluation
	Affect	■ Feelings-as-information model	■ Ad transfer ■ Feelings transfer ■ Classical conditioning ■ Mere exposure effect
	Behaviour	■ Post-experience model ■ Perception–Experience–Memory Model	■ Reinforcement model ■ Routinised response behaviour

pertains to elaboration likelihood which can be either high or low. The second dimension is related to the attitude component on which attitude formation is mainly built, i.e. cognition, affect or behaviour.

High elaboration likelihood, cognitive attitude formation

The models that will be discussed here are relevant if the consumer's motivation, ability and opportunity are high and especially when cognitive elements are important for attitude formation. An example is someone who is going to buy a home video installation and tries to compare objectively the different brands available on several attributes (price, sound quality, etc.) before making a decision.

Multiple attribute models

The most famous multiple attribute model is no doubt the Expectancy-Value model, or Fishbein model.[21] In this model brand attitudes are made up of three elements: relevant product attributes, the extent to which one believes the brand possesses these attributes, and the evaluation of these attributes or how good/bad one thinks it is for a brand to possess these attributes. More specifically, brand attitude is represented by the sum of the products of brand beliefs and attribute evaluations:

$$A_o = \sum_{i=1}^{n} b_{oi} e_i$$

where: A_o = attitude towards object o
b_{oi} = belief of object o possessing attribute i
e_i = evaluation of attribute i
n = number of relevant attributes

In other words, since not all product attributes are equally important for a consumer, product beliefs are weighted by the importance that the consumer attaches to the different product attributes. Table 3.3 shows an example of an attitude towards going to university and going to a polytechnic. In this case, beliefs and evaluations are measured by means of a 7-point Likert scale. A Likert scale is an ordinal scale, but if the scale contains enough categories, it is usually considered an interval scale, as a result of which calculating mean scores across respondents is allowed.[22] An example of a 7-point (going from 1 to 7 or from −3 to +3) Likert scale, is:

To what extent do you think it is difficult to succeed at university?

−3	−2	−1	0	+1	+2	+3

Not at all difficult   Very difficult

In this example the quality of the teachers is most valued (e = 7) and the perception that it is difficult to get a degree seems to be the least important attribute (e = 2). Multiplying these evaluations by the beliefs regarding universities and polytechnics as possessing these characteristics gives the results in the fourth and sixth columns. Summing these products results in a more positive attitude towards going to a university.

Table 3.3 An illustration of the Fishbein model

		Attitude towards going to a university/polytechnic			
		University		*Polytechnic*	
Attribute	e_i	b_i	$e_i \times b_i$	b_i	$e_i \times b_i$
Difficulty	2	+2	+4	+1	+2
Prestige	6	+2	+12	0	0
High cost	3	+1	+3	0	0
Quality of teachers	7	+1	+7	−1	−7
Number of friends	5	−1	−5	+2	+10
High study time	3	+2	+6	0	0
Business-oriented	5	−1	−5	+1	+5
Attitude			**22**		**10**

e_i is measured on a 7-point bipolar scale (1 = bad, 7 = good)
b_i is measured on a 7-point unipolar scale (−3 = unlikely, +3 = likely)

So, if all relevant attributes are measured and correctly evaluated, a university would eventually be chosen.

The Theory of Reasoned Action (TORA) is an extension of the Expectancy-Value model.[23] The model was developed to provide a link between attitude and behavioural intention. The latter is not only determined by attitudes, but also by subjective norm. A subjective norm is comprised of the belief one holds regarding what different reference groups consider as socially desirable behaviour, weighted by the consumer's need or willingness to behave according to the norms of the particular reference group. The latter is referred to as social sensitivity. Certain personalities are more sensitive to social pressure and, as a consequence, are more willing to comply with the rules, norms and beliefs of reference groups than others. An example of socially influenced behaviour is that, even though a child might not be particularly fond of piano lessons, it might take these lessons to please its parents. And although a teenager might not hold a favourable attitude towards smoking, he or she might do so because his or her friends regard it as 'cool' to smoke. Again, some teenagers will be more likely to let themselves be led by the opinions of others. Table 3.4 gives an illustration of how a subjective norm can influence the choice between going to university and going to a polytechnic.

The reference group valued most highly is the friends at school (ss = 6), while the sensitivity or motivation to comply with the opinion of current teachers is the lowest (ss = 3). Multiplying social sensitivity by the opinions of significant others for the different reference groups, and summing all these products, results in a subjective norm of +35 for going to university and +1, for going to a polytechnic. In view of these results as well as the results of Table 3.3, the attitude towards a university is more favourable than the attitude towards a polytechnic.

The Theory of Reasoned Action has been further extended into the Theory of Planned Behaviour (TPB).[24] Fishbein and Ajzen felt this extension was necessary to be able to deal with behaviours over which people have incomplete volitional control. Indeed, behavioural intention can result in actual behaviour only if the consumers themselves can decide to perform or not perform the behaviour. For many consumer behaviours this prerequisite does not pose a problem (for example, choosing between Coke Vanilla or Coke Lemon), but often behaviour also depends on non-motivational

Table 3.4 An illustration of subjective norm effects

Reference group		University			Polytechnic	
		Subjective norm = social sensitivity (ss) × others' opinions (oo)				
		University			*Polytechnic*	
	ss_i	oo_i	$ss_i \times oo_i$		oo_i	$ss_i \times oo_i$
Friends at school	6	+2	+12		−1	−6
Friends in youth club	5	0	0		+1	+5
Friends in sports club	5	−1	−5		+1	+5
Parents	4	+2	+8		−2	−8
Family	4	+1	+4		0	0
Current teachers	3	+2	+6		0	0
Business	5	+2	+10		+1	+5
Subjective norm			**+35**			**+1**

ss_i is measured on a 7-point bipolar scale (1 = low, 7 = high)
oo_i is measured on a 7-point bipolar scale (−3 = negative, +3 = positive)

factors, such as resources (time, money, skills, infrastructure, etc.). For example, a consumer may be willing to go to work by means of public transport, but when he or she lives in a remote village in which hardly any public transport facilities are available, this may be difficult to do. Or, a consumer and his or her significant others may hold very favourable attitudes towards buying a Lamborghini, but when this consumer lacks the money, a cheaper car will be bought in the end (so, in fact, the extension resembles the 'ability' and 'opportunity' factors of MAO). That behavioural control as perceived by the consumer is more predictive of behaviour than actual behavioural control is very important. Perceived behavioural control can be defined as 'the perceived ease or difficulty of performing the behaviour and it is assumed to reflect past experience as well as anticipated impediments and obstacles'.[25] Two individuals enrolling for a foreign language course may have equally strong intentions to learn the foreign language, but if one feels more confident than the other that he or she can master it, he or she is more likely to persevere than the one who feels less confident. Therefore, not actual control but perceived behavioural control is added to TORA to build the Theory of Planned Behaviour. Perceived behavioural control is computed by multiplying control beliefs by perceived power of the particular control belief to pose the behaviour, and the resulting products are summed across the salient control beliefs. For example, for jogging, salient control beliefs appeared to be 'being in poor physical shape' and 'living in an area with good jogging weather'. Figure 3.4 presents the TPB model graphically.

Handicap International

Handicap International was founded in 1982 in France. Afterwards, a network was created with sections in Belgium, Germany, Luxemburg, Switzerland, the UK and the US. Currently, Handicap International is active in about 60 countries with aid programmes for people with disabilities. To collect money for clearing up cluster bombs, a mine awareness programme and a physical rehabilitation centre in Afghanistan, Handicap International uses direct mail as a communication tool. They sent citizens a paper bomb, not bloody pictures or crying people. A strong accompanying letter and a reference to the expertise Handicap International has,

▶

Figure 3.4 The Theory of Reasoned Action (TORA)

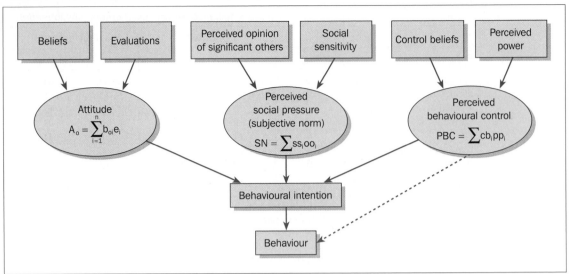

were also included. Since Handicap International is well aware that many people believe their individual efforts do not matter, they clearly indicate what can be done with small sums of money and give people the option to choose one of them. For example, €30 means crutches for one of the victims, with €40 about 10 square metres can be demined, and for €55 you actually give a prosthesis to a cluster bomb victim. This increases donors' perceived behavioural control. The DM action clearly paid off: the response rate amounted to more than 10% and they collected 37% more money than expected. They received a Cuckoo Award for the effectiveness of the campaign.

Source: http://www.handicapinternational.be (28 April 2006), Cuckoo Awards 2005.

The Theory of Planned Behaviour has received considerable attention in the literature. Ajzen constructed a website with more than 400 articles in which TPB was used.[26] These studies deal with a variety of activities, from predicting choice of travel mode, eating and leisure behaviour, healthy lifestyle, condom use, loosing weight, etc.[27] From a database of 185 of these independent studies, it has been shown that the TPB accounted for 27% and 39% of the variance in behaviour and intention, respectively. Moreover, the perceived behavioural control (PBC) construct and attitudes in particular seem to have predictive value, while subjective norm in general accounts for only a small part of the variance in behaviour and intention.[28]

Based on the TPB model, marketing communicators can try to change consumers' attitudes and influence their behaviour in several different ways (Figure 3.5). First, they can try to change brand beliefs. For example, suppose a university has a reputation for granting degrees too easily and not taking the education task seriously enough. If an independent quality control committee finds that this university is offering students a good quality education, the university might use this conclusion in an advertising campaign in order to influence existing beliefs. A second possibility is changing attribute evaluations. For example, when people have the impression that a large university has

Figure 3.5 Marketing communications and the TORA model

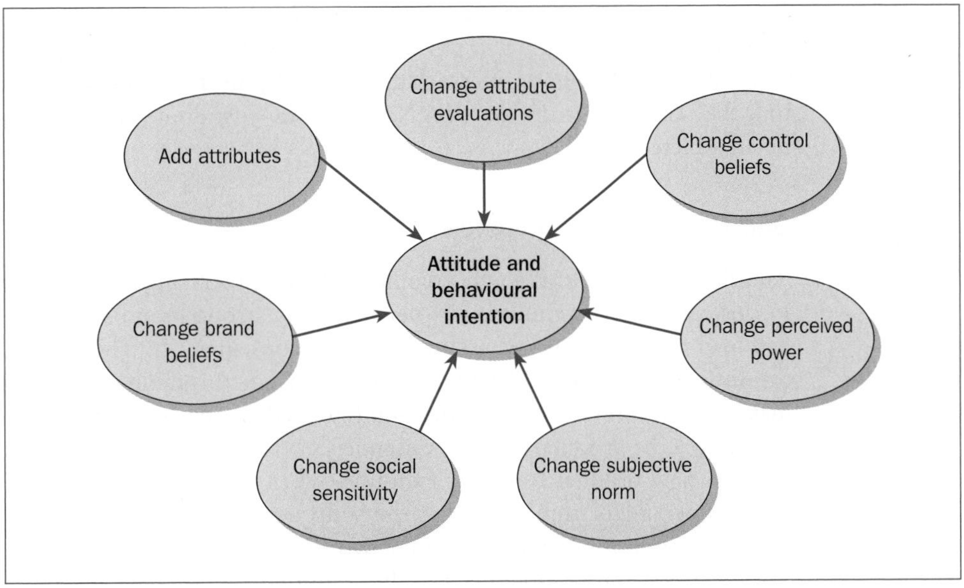

to be good since it is able to attract so many students, a small university can try to change this evaluation by emphasising the benefits of small classes (more personal contact, more time per student, greater supervision, etc.). Finally, attitudes can be changed by **adding attributes**. For example, suppose a university has an exchange contract with foreign universities so that foreign students can take part of the courses while own students can follow courses abroad, the university can emphasise the multicultural environment. By doing so, it might create an additional attribute students take into account when choosing between universities. When Levi's, for example, saw its market share decline, it emphasised Levi's pioneering role in the jeans market and tried to add the fact that Levi's was the first jeans brand as a product attribute that consumers might consider when buying jeans. An example in the beer market is Labatt Ice which underscores the freshness of the beer rather like Cola Light claims 'you have never been refreshed like this before'.

Besides trying to change attitudes, marketers can focus on **changing the opinion of others**. To counter the increase in smoking of young girls, for example, the UK government tried to change the opinions of youngsters by means of a communications campaign of which the main message was that smoking makes you less attractive for the opposite sex. One ad pictured two pairs of kissing lips with the message 'Ever kissed a non-smoker? Taste the difference.' Changing the opinion of others is also prevalent in several children's advertisements. Marketers try to influence children's attitudes so that they start nagging for the product. For example, Kraft tries to show children that Lunchables is a cool school lunch and having it will make all other children jealous. **Raising or lowering social sensitivity** for specific significant others is another possibility. For example, while buying a new car used to be a decision made by the parents, Opel stresses how comfortable, exciting and cool Opel Safira is perceived by children, hoping that parents will take the opinion of their children into account when choosing a particular type and brand of car. Finally, perceived behavioural control can be influenced. Marketers could change control beliefs by showing how easy or convenient to use certain products are. For example, MasterCard uses the slogan 'North. South. East. West. No card is more accepted' to indicate you can pay everywhere with MasterCard (see Plate 13). Another possibility is to focus on increasing perceived power or the confidence of consumers that they can master the activity. Nike stresses 'Just do it', meaning that everyone can be an athlete.

Self-generated persuasion[29]

Another form of central-route, cognitively based processing is self-generated persuasion. In this case, the consumer is not persuaded by strong brand arguments, but by his or her own thoughts, arguments or imagined consequences. These thoughts go beyond the information offered in the ad. The consumer combines the information in the message with previous experience and knowledge, and tries to imagine him- or herself consuming the product and the consequences thereof. Sometimes consumers even come up with new product uses. For example, when seeing an ad for canned lobster soup, a consumer might think of using the soup not as a soup, but as an ingredient for a sauce to use in a fish pasta. In other words, the persuasive process is imagery-based. These self-generated thoughts and the cognitive and affective responses evoked by the imagined brand experience give rise to fairly strong brand beliefs. These beliefs are believed to have a considerable impact on brand attitude.

Low elaboration likelihood, cognitive attitude formation

In this case, one of the MAO factors is low, leading or forcing the consumer to concentrate on peripheral cues. The consumer will try to make inferences on the basis of the cue in order to form a cognitively based attitude. For example, when consumers do not have the time to compare all available brands on relevant attributes, they may infer from a high price that it is a high-quality brand and therefore form a positive attitude towards the brand. This process is called heuristic evaluation.[30] When MAO is low, central information processing is very unlikely to occur and consumers will probably process the communication peripherally. This means that they do not elaborate on the message, but try to make inferences on the basis of ad characteristics. In other words, peripheral cues in the ad are used as a heuristic cue to evaluate the quality of the message and to form a general evaluation of the brand advertised. These inferential beliefs have a significant influence on the attitude people form towards the brand. Heuristic evaluation has also been referred to as the satisficing choice process.[31] Since consumers' MAO factors are not optimal, they lack the motivation, ability or opportunity to gather and process information to find the best choice. They are not looking for direct evidence of performance superiority in this case, but settle for a satisfactory or acceptable brand choice. Therefore, they seek for reassurance or credibility in heuristic cues such as brand name reputation, experts endorsing the brand, price level, etc. Table 3.5 summarises a few ad characteristics that can be used as a heuristic cue.

Another example is the use of celebrities. The heuristic in this case might be 'if Kim Clüsters uses Sanex skin care it has to be a good brand' or 'if Anna Kournikova wears a Shock sportsbra because "only the ball should bounce", it has to be a comfortable and

Table 3.5 Potential heuristic cues

Characteristics	Peripheral cue	Heuristic
Source	Attractiveness Expertise Status Number of sources	The more attractive, the better The more expertise, the better The higher status, the better The more, the better
Message	Number of arguments Repetition Layout	The more, the better The more, the better The more attractive, the better
Product	Price Design Country of origin	The higher, the better The more attractive, the better German is good (cars) The Netherlands is good (cheese) Italian is good (fashion, leather)

Based on: Pieters, R. and van Raaij, F. (1992), *Reclamewerking (How Advertising Works)*. Leiden/Antwerp: Stenfert Kroese Uitgevers.

good bra'. However, using this approach can give rise to problems. A famous Dutch actress, Monique van de Ven, claimed in a TV commercial that she had a mortgage with FBTO, one of the largest Dutch insurance companies. Some insurance agents did not believe her, and after an investigation they found out that she had her mortgage at Aegon, FBTO's competitor. Needless to say, this created a big to-do in The Netherlands which not only harmed the image of FBTO and the actress, but may also lead to negative knock-on effects for the corporation as a whole when it seeks to advertise again. Furthermore, the practice of using false statements in advertising is actionable in court. Therefore, care should be taken that if, for example, Ronaldo announces that he always plays football wearing Nike boots, he in fact always wears Nike, for training as well as for matches. The foregoing illustrates that credibility is crucial to evoke positive cognitive responses, and as a consequence change attitudes in a favourable way.

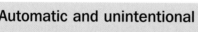

Automatic and unintentional country-of-origin effects

It is generally accepted that consumers think products are better when they are made in countries holding a positive image. These effects have been found in a huge variety of countries. One explanation for these effects is that consumers use country stereotypes as a heuristic to simplify the decision process. An additional and more recent explanation is that a reference to the country in which the product is made spontaneously activates country stereotypes, and that these stereotypes influence the evaluation of the product even when consumers do not intend to use this information in their judgement. In a recent experimental study, consumers had to classify eight fictitious brands of notebooks as either good or bad. In a first stage, consumers were exposed to brand characteristics (processor speed, hard drive capacity and RAM size). On the basis of these characteristics they were taught how they could easily make a distinction between a good and a bad brand. After an unrelated task, consumers were in a second stage re-exposed to the eight brands, but now information was added concerning to where the brand was manufactured (either a positive or a negative image country). Next, consumers had to classify the brands again. Half of the respondents were distracted during this task, while the other half could pay full attention to the classification task. The results showed

▶

that the negative or positive affect associated with the country of origin involuntarily influenced brand judgements. This effect was larger in the distracted group who could not pay full attention to the brand categorisation. This suggests that in case respondents' MAO factors are high (high motivation or involvement, high ability and opportunity) and consumers follow central route processing, automatically activated country stereotypes are more likely to be inhibited, while its impact is largest when one of the MAO-factors is low.[32]

High elaboration likelihood, affective attitude formation

In this category, central processing of affective elements is predominant.

Affect-as-information

Affect has long been considered as a peripheral cue, having an impact only when people have low involvement. However, it is increasingly recognised that affect may play a fundamental role in decision-making. People may judge objects by monitoring their subjective feelings to the target. The Affect-as-Information model posits that consumers may use feelings as a source of information to form an overall evaluation of a product or brand, not by means of a simple association, but through a controlled inferential process or, in other words, in an informed, deliberate manner.[33] A feeling-based inference often referred to is the 'how-do-I-feel-about-it' model. According to this model, consumers evaluate brands/objects by imagining the brand in their minds and asking themselves 'How do I feel about this brand/object?' Next they infer like/dislike or satisfaction/dissatisfaction from the valence of their feelings.[34] Consumers may even infer the strength of their preference from the strength of the feelings the brand or object evokes.[35] Note that we are talking about real feelings (i.e. 'subjective experiences of affective states and responses with a somato-visceral component'), not about affective or hedonic beliefs (such as 'It would be great to spend a weekend in Stockholm').[36] These feelings can be evoked either integrally by looking at the product or imagining the product, or by a pre-existing or contextually-induced mood.[37] However, a prerequisite of the Affect-as-Information model is that when people inspect their feelings to judge a brand or object, they do not inspect their mood states at that moment, but their feelings in response to the brand or object. So, if consumers decide not to go to the movies, it is because the thought of going to the movies makes them feel unpleasant, not because they happen to be in a bad mood. As a consequence, for feelings to influence the product evaluation, they must be perceived as representative of the product, i.e. consumers must be convinced that these feelings are genuine affective responses to this product. Moreover, feelings need not only be representative, they also have to be relevant for the evaluation at hand and match consumers' goals.[38] For example, when a consumer has made an appointment to go to the dentist, the fact that he or she does not feel happy about going may not be considered to be relevant by this person, and he or she might still go. In fact, when consumers' purchase motivations are hedonic rather than functional, the likelihood that they will perceive their feelings as relevant and follow the 'how-do-I-feel-about-it' model is much more likely.[39]

It should be obvious that feelings should not be assigned a heuristic or peripheral role here. Under high elaboration likelihood, people use their feelings because they believe they contain valuable information. When consumers closely scrutinise the arguments in a message, mood and ad-evoked emotions can be considered as an argument or a central cue.[40] One way to elicit strong ad-evoked feelings is to make consumers think of pleasant things in the past, such as the birth of a baby, a wedding, a first romance, etc. Another way is to use nostalgic ads. Nostalgic ads make use of music, movie stars, fashion products, symbols or styles that were popular during a consumer's youth. Research has indicated that early experience performs a determining role in shaping subsequent preferences and that they actually can influence consumers' lifelong preferences.[41] For example, it has been shown that consumers retain a lifelong attachment to the styles of popular music they experienced in their late teens and early twenties.

UNICEF: Don't let war affect the lives of children

UNICEF in Belgium has created a unique, but shocking TV commercial about the impact of war on children. The ad features the blue, Smurf cartoon characters in a war setting. The ad starts out with the traditional Smurf song 'hey, come to Smurf country, welcome to all. Yes, come to Smurf country, the country of pomp and circumstance' on a nice sunny day. Immediately after, the Smurf village is annihilated by warplanes. Smurfs are lying dead all over the street, a baby is crying without its mum or dad being around, . . . The tag-line of the spot read 'Don't let war affect the lives of children'. The ad was meant for the adult population and was aired only after 9 pm in the evening. The objective of the campaign was to raise awareness about the many ways conflict destroys children's lives in general, and to raise money for the rehabilitation of former child soldiers in Burundi in particular. Currently, about 300,000 children are being used as child soldiers worldwide. Moreover, almost one in two of the 3.6 million humans killed in conflicts since 1990 are children. The campaign showed what many children are experiencing in real life. The ad featured Smurfs because Smurfs have been part of Belgian culture since 1958. Adult viewers immediately recognise the blue cartoon figures which make them think back to their youth. The emotional bond they have with the Smurfs made the ad more shocking. Smurfs were deliberately used here to enhance the impact and awareness of the campaign. The campaign has been in the news worldwide, receiving both positive and negative comments. Some think the ad featured unnecessary violence, others praised the creative approach to draw attention to the problem. One way or another, the campaign worked and received an award for its effectiveness.[42]

Low elaboration likelihood, affective attitude formation

While central-route processing and cognitively based attitude formation predominated in the 1960s and 1970s, models characterised by peripheral processing of mainly affective elements have received a lot of attention in the 1990s. The attitude towards the ad (Aad) and feelings transfer, classical conditioning and the mere exposure effect are some models that have been frequently referred to in the literature.

Aad transfer

From the 1980s onwards, research on low involvement, affective processing has boomed. One of the first to indicate that how one evaluates an ad may be transferred to how one evaluates the brand were Mitchell and Olson.[43] They used an ad picturing a kitten and a purely informative ad. Their conclusion was that both brand attitude (Ab) and purchase intention were influenced not only by brand beliefs, but also to a great extent by the attitude towards the ad. Another study found that the difference in brand preference before and after exposure to advertising was twice as positive for consumers who liked the ad a lot as compared to consumers who had a neutral Aad.[44] When consumers feel indifferent towards the available brands as a consequence of low brand differentiation or insignificant consequences of a non-optimal choice, their choice goal is likely to be to buy the first brand that they like.[45]

Ad likeability might be an important factor because of its ability to attract attention and facilitate information processing. Peripheral cues such as humour, music, animals and children may attract attention, induce curiosity which lead consumers to watch the whole ad, and induce a favourable Aad which can lead to a favourable Ab.

The Aad transfer model receiving most empirical support is the dual mediation model (Figure 3.6).[46] According to this model the evaluation of the ad not only has an immediate impact on the evaluation of the brand, but also an indirect effect on brand attitude via brand cognitions.

The reasoning behind this model is that consumers who hold a positive attitude towards the communication are more likely to be receptive to arguments in favour of the brand advertised. For example, if you like the Frisk commercial in which a cook accidentally drops a Frisk in an aquarium, a fish eats it and gets so much energy out of it that he jumps into the next aquarium, then the next and at the end out of the window, you might be less inclined to think of counter-arguments, or you might find yourself thinking of more support arguments (e.g. Frisk gives energy, Frisk is refreshing) because you think the commercial is clever, original and humorous.

Figure 3.6 Dual mediation hypothesis

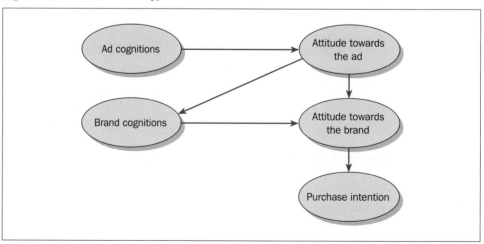

Based on: MacKenzie S.B., Lutz, R.J. and Belch, G.E. (1986), 'The Role of Attitude Toward the Ad as a Mediator of Advertising Effectiveness: A Test of Competing Explanations', *Journal of Marketing Research*, 23, 131. Reproduced with permission of American Marketing Association.

The power of ad likeability

The conclusions of a study in which consumer responses were measured to all ads that were on air in Belgium in two consecutive years are:[47]

■ Emotions are more effective than information.

■ If consumers see emotions, they will feel your ad.

■ If they feel something while they see your commercial, they will like it.

■ If they like your ad, they will like you.

■ If they like you, they will buy you.

Feelings transfer

In line with the foregoing, some researchers suggest that the feelings an ad evokes may be transferred to the attitude towards the ad, the brand attitude and the purchase intention without much deliberation.[48]

Why consider ad-evoked feelings? Several studies show that people in a positive mood make decisions more quickly, use less information, avoid systematic processing, evaluate everything more positively, accept a persuasive message more easily and pay less attention to details.[49] According to some researchers, ad-evoked feelings might even have a greater impact on communications effectiveness than mood.[50] Mood affects brand evaluation only if this evaluation takes place when watching the ad. Since ad-evoked feelings and the brand are associated in a consumer's memory, emotional advertising might influence brand evaluation no matter when the brand evaluation takes place. In this way, thinking of the brand in another situation might activate the feelings associated with it.

Empirical studies investigating the influence of ad-evoked feelings usually find that feelings exert a significant influence on the different stages in the communications process. A recent study investigating 23,000 responses to 240 advertisements shows that ad-evoked feelings (pleasure, arousal, dominance) explain 3% to 30% of the variance in brand interest and purchase intention while brand knowledge and beliefs explained 2% to 13%.[51] The magnitude of the influence of ad-evoked feelings depends on the product category advertised, the specific feelings that are evoked and the type of ad that is tested. Although several researchers are convinced of the importance of ad-evoked feelings for the communications process, no generally agreed instrument exists to measure feelings. Most researchers use a verbal scale consisting of several feeling states for which respondents indicate to what extent they experience them. However, different feeling scales lead to different feeling dimensions which can be deducted from the scales. This makes the research results difficult to compare. Table 3.6 summarises some of the feeling dimensions observed in empirical studies. Nevertheless, we can conclude that affective responses might be predictive of brand choice and as a consequence are a valuable tool for message testing and brand tracking.[52]

Emotional conditioning

Emotional conditioning can be considered an extreme case of feelings transfer, and is based on Pavlov's classic conditioning theory.[53] When dogs see food they begin to

Table 3.6 Feeling dimensions

Holbrook and Batra, 1987, Morris et al., 2002	Homer and Yoon, 1992	Edell and Burke, 1987, Burke and Edell, 1989	Cho and Stout, 1993	Pieters and de Klerk-Warmerdam, 1996	Geuens and De Pelsmacker, 1998
Pleasure	Attention	Upbeat	Upbeat	Unpleasant	Insulted
Arousal	Pleasure	Negative	Irritation	Pleasant of low intensity	Irritated
Dominance	Scepticism	Warm	Warm	Pleasant of high intensity	Interested
	Downbeat				Cheerful
					Carefree

salivate. This is called an unconditioned response since it happens automatically. By frequently pairing a conditioned stimulus (a bell) with an unconditioned stimulus (meat powder), Pavlov was able to get dogs salivating just by hearing the bell (conditioned response). In a marketing context, communications practitioners sometimes try to pair a brand with an emotional response. Figure 3.7 explains the strategy DaimlerChrysler is currently following. Being aware of the fact that Celine Dion is a very popular singer, DaimlerChrysler paid Celine Dion between US$10 million and US$20 million to use songs such as 'I Drove All Night' in a three-year 'Drive and Love' campaign. Chrysler hopes that by frequently pairing Celine Dion's songs with the brand, the love feeling that the songs of Celine Dion evoke will be transferred to Chrysler and will make the brand classy again.[54] Research shows that on the premise of a high exposure frequency and strong emotional content, attitudes towards saturated brands are said to be predominantly formed on the basis of emotional conditioning.[55] Examples of brands that try to benefit from emotional conditioning are Martini, Bacardi Breezer and Häagen-Dazs, which try to associate sexual arousal with their brands.

Figure 3.7 Emotional conditioning at work

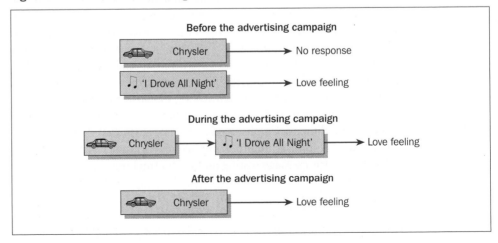

Emotional conditioning worked out well for Häagen-Dazs

Häagen Dazs has used erotic advertising for several years. One of its campaigns features a couple indulging in sexual foreplay. The ice cream is their main attribute, which is put on each other's body and licked off by the other. By frequently combining the ice cream with foreplay, the ice cream itself has sexual connotations for some people. This is illustrated by the statements of some university students who completely identify Häagen Dazs with sex. In an interview one of those students said:[56]

'. . . it was very nice ice cream, we really enjoyed the ice cream and the advertising had a lot of sexual connotations in it and I think we basically liked the connotations of the ads and we liked the idea of that and we believed the idea that Häagen Dazs was sexy because the ads told us it was sexy, so when we had the ice cream in front of us we felt that the pot was very sexy, a sexy pot.'

Furthermore, when the students had a date, they always made sure to buy Häagen Dazs in advance. Today, Haägen-Dazs is still positioned on pleasurable experiences, but the source of the pleasure (the sex) has been replaced by New Age spirituality.[57]

Mere exposure

Hundreds of studies have demonstrated that prior exposure to stimuli (nonsense syllables, words, slogans, pictures, faces, sounds, smells, etc.) increases positive affect towards these stimuli.[58] In the same vein, ad and brand exposures can increase liking of the ad and the brand, and can make it more likely that the advertised brand enters consumers' consideration set.[59] In other words, the mere exposure of consumers to a particular ad, without the consumer actively elaborating on the ad, can influence consumer preferences and behaviour. Indeed, studies show that respondents who were exposed to an ad more than once, as compared to respondents who saw the ad for the first time, appeared to evaluate the ad as more favourable and less dull.[60] For a while, it has been assumed that prior exposures to stimuli acquaint consumers with the stimuli and that this familiarity causes the more positive attitude towards the stimuli. However, several studies indicate that the mere exposure effect on brand attitude does not occur through a subjective feeling of familiarity. When a respondent has been exposed to a particular stimulus before, this exposure can result in a more positive stimulus evaluation even if the respondent cannot remember having seen the stimulus before.[61] A more recent explanation of the mere exposure effect is that prior exposure increases processing fluency at the time consumers have to make a judgement.[62] The fact that consumers have been frequently exposed to a certain ad or brand results in a representation of this stimulus in consumers' memory. When consumers later on want to evaluate the stimulus, for example during a shopping trip, the representation of the stimulus in their memory will facilitate the encoding and processing of the stimulus. As a consequence, processing of the stimulus will be easier and more fluent. Since consumers often do not realise that prior exposures increase processing fluency, they misattribute the source of the processing fluency (i.e. the previous exposures) to liking, truth or acceptability of the ad or brand. Of course, the mere exposure effect is limited and should be seen as a function of learning and satiation.[63] The more novel a stimulus, the more consumers can learn and the more positive the affective response will be.[64] When consumers are confronted too often with a particular message or ad, there is no learning opportunity anymore and they get bored. This can have a boomerang effect on ad and brand attitude. The latter effect is called wear-out and indicates that there is a certain threshold of exposures after which additional exposures result in negative instead of positive communications effects (see Chapter 8).

High elaboration likelihood, behavioural attitude formation

The theories discussed above have often been tested for hypothetical products and/or hypothetical brands, which make them more relevant for new than for established brands. Although using hypothetical stimuli is ideal for eliminating research biasing effects such as brand knowledge, the extent to which the brand has been advertised in the past and the influence of previous campaigns, it disregards a source of information that might have important consequences for the way a consumer processes and evaluates a new marketing message, more specifically personal brand experience through previous brand usage. Post-experience models assume central-route processing of prior brand experiences. So, in this case the consumers are motivated, willing and able to think of previous brand experience and will take this into account in forming an attitude towards the brand, as well as in deciding what brand to buy in the future.

Although incorporating the influence of brand experience is a much more realistic approach to consumer information processing, brand experience has been neglected by most researchers. As a consequence, only a few communications models exist that try to explain its effect on the communications process. However, it is straightforward that brand satisfaction or dissatisfaction will have an impact on the next purchase. For example, if you have been driving a Nissan for six years and you are really satisfied with its design, petrol consumption and after-sales dealer service, the probability that you will buy a Nissan next time is much higher than if you find out that your Nissan consumes much more petrol than your friend's Mazda, spare parts are more expensive than a Ford's, and your Nissan broke down five times in six months. Another example is that when you buy Lay's crisps you expect them to be fresh, otherwise you are very likely to switch brands. An example of a model that incorporates brand experience is the post-experience model.[65] The model assumes relations between the current purchase on the one hand, and previous purchase, previous advertising, previous promotion, current advertising and current promotion on the other. The post-experience model was tested using scanner panel data for an 84-week period on ketchup and detergent brands. The data included household purchase records, store environment information on price and promotion, and advertising exposure records. The results revealed that the current purchase is significantly influenced by previous purchase behaviour, current advertising and current promotion, but not by previous advertising, and negatively by previous promotion. The fact that a brand was previously bought in promotion diminished the probability that the consumer would purchase the brand again in the next period. The latter can be explained by the fact that people who take advantage of promotions are more likely to be brand-switchers who are less inclined to buy the same brand in subsequent purchases. Current advertising also enhanced brand-switching. The results of this study seem to suggest that previous purchase behaviour is indeed the most important explanatory factor of current behaviour and that advertising mainly serves to remind people who have not recently purchased the brand of the fact that it exists.

However, what is the role marketing communications can play for first buys on the one hand, and for other than first-time purchases on the other? The Perception–Experience–Memory model (see Figure 3.8) tries to formulate an answer to this.[66] When consumers do not have brand experience yet, the main function of advertising consists of framing perception. Framing can affect consumers' expectation, anticipation and interpretation. Expectation is concerned with notifying consumers that a particular brand in a certain product category is available and putting the brand in a frame of reference so that the consumers expect to see it. Next, marketing communications should try to create anticipation or hypothesis generation. Research indicates that exposing consumers to an attribute-based ad before brand trial makes consumers more curious about the brand ('Would Red Bull really energise my body and mind, and give me wiiiiings?'), it helps consumers to formulate hypotheses about the brand ('Red Bull will give me a kick'), and it induces the consumers to test their hypotheses during a subsequent trial experience.[67] Besides expectation and anticipation, pre-experience communications may offer an interpretation or a rationale for the anticipation the brand generates. For example, an unfamiliar computer brand could use the Intel Inside logo to assure consumers that it is a trustworthy and high-quality brand.

A next critical function of both pre-experience and post-experience communications is enhancing sensory and social experience. Products may taste better, function better or look nicer and the service may be perceived as friendlier or more knowledgeable just because consumers expect to experience this and anticipate the experience.[68] Moreover, consumers may focus their brand trial evaluation on attributes that they would not have used without the pre- or post-experience advertisement (instead of evaluating Red Bull on taste, carbonation, sugar level, etc. it may be evaluated on the uplifting experience it gives because of the advertising campaign), or marketing communication may change

Figure 3.8 The Perception–Experience–Memory model

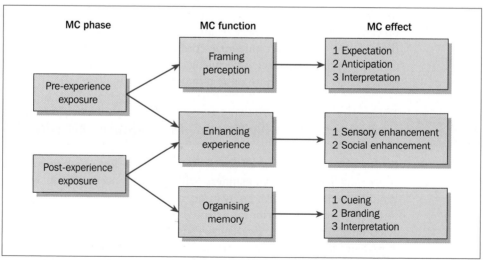

Based on: Hall, B.F. (2002), 'A New Model for Measuring Advertising Effectiveness', *Journal of Advertising Research*, 42 (March/April), 23–31.

the weight that the advertised attributes receive at evaluation (valuing the uplifting experience as more important than taste, refreshment, etc.). On the basis of experiments in which respondents were exposed to an ad alone, to an ad and a product trial, or to a product trial alone, it appeared that a pre-experience ad combined with brand trial resulted in significantly more favourable brand responses than either a brand trial alone or an advertisement alone. More specifically, when an ad and brand trial were combined, the pre-trial ad led consumers to process the brand trial information in a more focused and meaningful way, resulting in more confidently held brand beliefs, a higher expectancy value from the brand (as measured by the Fishbein model) and higher purchase intentions. Moreover, ads appeared to be better in fostering confidently held beliefs about non-experiential attributes (such as the number of calories), while trial was more powerful in creating confidently held experiential attribute beliefs (such as taste).[69] Also, post-experience ads have been shown to enhance the experience of a previous brand trial. This happens when a consumer evaluates his or her brand experience as more favourable when he or she has been exposed to advertising after brand usage as compared to the situation when no advertising followed the brand experience. For example, if you have had Fitness for breakfast and afterwards you see an ad for Fitness which shows all the ingredients and stresses the fact that no sugar is added, it might improve your evaluation of Fitness as a healthy breakfast choice.

A second role of post-experience communications is to organise memory. It offers verbal and visual cues such as jingles, slogans, user imagery, etc., enriching the brand schema and making it more likely that afterwards the brand will be recalled. Increasing brand recall and top-of-mind awareness can increase the possibility that consumers stop buying the competitor's brand and change to the company's brand; in other words, it can stimulate brand-switching. Pepsi, for example, tried to change taste beliefs by stressing 'nothing else is a Pepsi'. On the other hand, post-experience communications may also prevent consumers switching to the competitor's brand.[70] Finally, post-experience communications also helps consumers to interpret their experiences. 'The advertisement not only influences the consumer to feel that the sensory or social experience was a good one, but it also provides reasons to believe that it was'.[71] It is important to remember that marketing communications really is able to improve and reshape objective sensory experience. In an era in which consumers have the feeling that in the majority of product categories brands are converging instead of becoming more distinct,[72] post-experience advertising may offer the extra element for a brand to be perceived as better or more unique than the rest.

Low elaboration likelihood, behavioural attitude formation

In this case, at least one of the MAO factors is low, making well thought through processing less likely. Consumers will rather concentrate on elements of previous brand experience to form an attitude and purchase intention. A typical model for this low-involvement–behavioural-oriented processing is Ehrenberg's **reinforcement model**. According to this model, awareness leads to trial and trial leads to reinforcement. Product experience is the dominant variable in the model, and advertising is supposed to reinforce habits, frame experience (see previous section) and defend consumers' attitudes.[73] A similar model is called **routinised response behaviour** and assumes that a large number of product experiences can lead to routinised response behaviour, especially for low involvement, frequently purchased products such as toilet paper, toothpaste, paper tissues, mineral water or chewing gum.[74] In this case, consumers do not spend much time on deciding which brand to buy, but buy a particular brand out of habit. In other words, previous behaviour guides future behaviour. Although the initial brand choice may have been thoroughly elaborated, routinised response behaviour is characterised by no or very low cognitive effort in which very few possibilities are considered. The fact that routinised response behaviour is a frequently used purchase strategy is illustrated by a study observing consumers who were buying detergents in a supermarket:[75] 83% of the 120 consumers observed took only one brand while no more than 4% picked up more than one brand to investigate them a bit closer. It took the consumers on average 13 seconds to walk down the aisle and choose a detergent. Obviously, no extended problem-solving was used here. Building brand awareness and trying to become top of mind is very important here in order to be included in the limited set of brands that a consumer is willing to consider, to retain brand loyalty and to enhance brand-switching to the own brand.

As becomes obvious from previous sections, a lot of communications models have been presented and all of them found empirical support in some circumstances. However, the key seems to be to define which variables influence the way a consumer deals with marketing communications. Motivation, ability and opportunity certainly are very important variables, although an even more important factor – previous brand experience – has been neglected most of the time. Future research will no doubt try to integrate this variable further and will propose new models. One thing is certain, communications processing is a complex subject and predicting how someone is going to respond to a certain stimulus will always be a cumbersome task. As is the case with consumer behaviour, theories and models can only help us to understand consumers and their responses a bit better. Attention will be devoted now to two phenomena that are major concerns to advertisers, namely irritation and brand confusion.

Causes and consequences of irritation evoked by advertising

When ad-evoked feelings were discussed above, in general only positive feelings were considered. In this section, frequently experienced negative feelings are addressed. Irritation can be defined as 'provoking, annoying, causing displeasure, and momentary impatience'.[76] As mentioned before, a lot of researchers use different feeling scales and as a consequence come up with different feeling dimensions. However, a striking result is that in many studies investigating consumers' responses to advertising, an irritation dimension appears.[77] In other words, irritation seems to be a basic reaction to marketing communications. Two questions arises: What causes irritation? And what are the consequences of ad-evoked irritation for advertising effectiveness?

Causes of irritation

A number of factors can cause irritation. They are shown in Figure 3.9. As for **media**, consumers mention television as one of the most irritating communications media, the

Figure 3.9 Causes of ad-evoked irritation

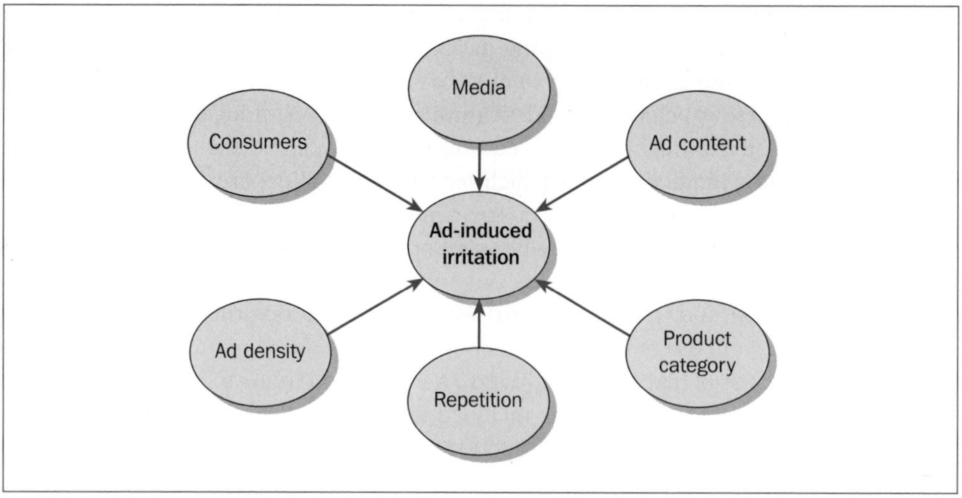

reason being that commercials interrupt programmes.[78] For the same reason, interruption of an ongoing task, as well as for the intrusive character, pop-up ads are also considered to be rather irritating.[79] Concerning irritating ad content, several elements can be identified.[80] First, unbelievable, exaggerated, overdramatised situations such as expert endorsements, testimonials and slice-of-life commercials increase irritation. A good example is a housewife confirming how white Daz makes her laundry. Second, unsympathetic characters in the ad, or picturing an uncomfortable situation such as a quarrel, enhance irritation, as well as hectic, nervous spots. Third, brand comparisons in which the advertised brand always claims to be the best, or showing the brand name too often leads to more irritation. Fourth, information-oriented appeals seem to irritate more than transformational or image-dominant appeals. Furthermore, if information cues are used, it is advisable to follow a 'soft sell' (e.g. availability, quality, taste, etc.) rather than a 'hard sell' (performance, price, etc.) approach and stick to no more than five arguments (four arguments seem to be ideal). Fifth, satire, provocation and eroticism increase irritation, while music, sentimental humour and warmth created by the use of animals or children seem to have an irritation-reducing effect.

With respect to the product category, research results are not really surprising. Products that seem to elicit on average more irritation are female hygiene products, female underwear, laxatives, toothpaste, mouthwash, personal care products, detergents and cleansers.[81] Concerning repetition, consumers seem to react negatively to an ad at low exposure frequency because of the newness of the stimulus. After repeated exposures the ad responses become more and more positive, a phenomenon called 'wear-in'. However, after a certain number of exposures, 'wear-out effects' occur in the sense that negative responses show up again[82] (see also Chapter 8). However, wear-out effects (leading to a higher level of irritation) seem to be more prominent for some types of commercials than others. Complex messages, minor changes in ad execution, short or slow commercials, very warm spots and non-food ads do not seem to experience negative effects of higher exposure levels,[83] while humorous, long, fast-paced, image-dominant and transformational commercials suffer more from high repetition levels.[84]

Ad density or the fact that consumers are exposed to many ads in a short period can also evoke irritation. An experiment in which respondents were exposed to a 30-minute documentary on capital punishment with either three or thirty embedded ads indicated significant differences in evoked irritation.[85]

Consumers react differently to advertising. For instance, a study trying to define consumer segments on the basis of the general attitude towards advertising found a segment of advertising haters as well as a segment of advertising lovers.[86] On the basis of the foregoing, it is obvious that some consumers are more likely to be irritated by advertising than others. Some research results suggest that men and consumers in the 34–41 age group are more irritated by commercials, while irritation seems to increase with increasing levels of education and income.

Consequences of ads evoking irritation

Contradictory hypotheses can be found in the literature regarding the effects of irritating communications. In line with feelings transfer models, one can expect negative evoked feelings, such as irritation, to have a negative influence on ad- and brand-related responses. This has also been referred to as 'the superiority of the pleasant' hypothesis. On the other hand, 'the law of extremes' theory assumes that the relationship between the attitude towards the ad and the attitude towards the brand follows a J-shaped curve (Figure 3.10).[87] The latter means that not only a very positive, but also a very negative Aad can eventually lead to a positive Ab, while communications evoking a moderate instead of an extreme Aad, result in a less positive Ab.

Both models found empirical support. Some studies show negative feelings lead to exclusively negative effects on Ab, brand recall and brand confusion.[88] Moreover, irritation caused by either an unlikeable ad or many ads in a short time period has also been shown to negatively impact unrelated subsequent ads.[89] These results can be explained by the 'law of extremes' theory or the feelings transfer that is likely under low elaboration likelihood, affective attitude formation. Another study[90] found that the

Figure 3.10 The J-shaped relationship between Aad and Ab

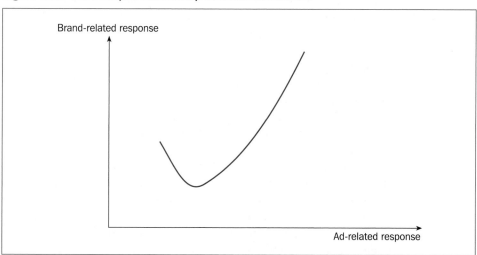

effect of irritating communications depends on the type of buying motive the ad appeals to. As mentioned before, transformational buying motives consist of positive motivations such as sensory gratification, social approval or intellectual stimulation, while informational buying motives refer to reducing or turning of negative motivations such as solving or avoiding a problem, or normal depletion.[91] It turns out that ad-related responses are negatively affected by irritation in any case, but correct brand recall, the attitude towards the brand and purchase intention are only affected negatively by irritating commercials when transformational buying motives are appealed to. In other words, for informational motives, the law of extremes theory seems to be confirmed. People did not like the ad, but the negative feelings were not transferred to the brand. This corresponds with the affect-as-information model that can be expected to apply under high elaboration likelihood affective attitude formation. Consumers experienced negative feelings but depending on their motive they considered these feelings relevant or irrelevant. Only when the feelings were deemed relevant were they taken into account, resulting in a negative impact for transformational purchase motivations. For informational purchase motivations, feelings apparently were not perceived to be relevant and therefore they did not serve as information input. Again, the important role of consumer motivations is shown.

Advertising and brand confusion

The goal of advertising is stimulating the demand for the brand advertised. However, similar products and similar advertising appeals may generate brand confusion, which in turn can lead to an increase in sales of a competitor's instead of the advertiser's brand. Therefore, attention should be devoted to how brand confusion can be avoided by finding out which factors are most likely to cause it.

Brand confusion refers to the fact that a communication for brand X is regarded by the consumer as being a communication for a different brand, Y.[92] In other words, the consumer attributes a wrong brand name to a particular communications stimulus. Besides brand confusion, product confusion can also occur. Product confusion is the phenomenon of attributing a stimulus to a wrong product category. A consumer might, for instance, think that a particular ad is for a bank, while it is in fact for an insurance company. Furthermore, a distinction has to be made between positive and negative brand confusion.[93] Negative brand confusion refers to the extent to which a consumer wrongly thinks that your advertising message is an ad for a competitor's brand, while positive confusion is about wrongly assuming that a competitor's communications campaign is actually a campaign for your brand. It has to be added, though, that positive confusion is not necessarily positive, since the confusion with another brand can harm the current or desired positioning or image of your brand.

A recent study[94] regarding facial care products and perfumes shows that brand confusion is a serious problem. Up to 35% of the people who thought they knew which brand was advertised in an ad in which the brand name was covered, actually confused brands. Another study[95] investigated correct attribution for print ads. For several of the print ads tested, correct brand attribution came to less than 10%. Especially for insurance companies, banks and facial care products, correct brand attribution is low, while for clothing and beer some of the brands are able to get a correct recognition score of 50%. It has to be added, though, that the low numbers in the latter study do not completely relate to brand confusion, since the people who did not have the faintest idea are also included in the analyses. However, the latter group was excluded in the former study.

A number of factors can cause brand confusion (Figure 3.11). Examples are brand and product category-related, consumer-related, message and campaign-related factors. As for brand and product category-related factors, brand name similarity, reduced inter-brand differences with respect to functionality and product presentation,[96] wilful brand imitation by imitating package shape and size, label print style and layout, and package colour,[97] and a high degree of competition in the product category[98] (which is often accompanied by a high advertising clutter) seem to increase the risk of brand confusion. Furthermore, brand confusion often occurs to the disadvantage of low market share brands to the advantage of market leaders or other large market share brands. Message-related factors refer to differences between ads in emotional and informational content, but also in format. With respect to emotional content, for example, it is generally agreed that emotional appeals attract more attention, but when the emotional content distracts the consumers, less brand recall and more brand confusion may result, leading to the phenomenon that everybody knows the ad, but nobody knows the brand advertised. As mentioned before, too much information causes irritation, which in turn can lead to more brand confusion.[99] Format factors that have been shown to lower the level of brand confusion are a clear headline, the use of pictures and showing the product in use. Furthermore, 'the degree of overall similarity of strategy' (DOSS) in information content seems to have increased over time, although ads seem to differ more and more in emotional content.[100] Therefore, the more unique an ad is in terms of ad content and execution, the less likely brand confusion is to occur.[101]

As for campaign-related factors, the campaign budget is negatively related to brand confusion, and the same can be expected for total gross rating points (GRP) or share of voice (see also Chapters 6 and 8).[102] Furthermore, using multiple communications media, and a consistent communications strategy, over time as well as over the different media,

Figure 3.11 Factors affecting brand confusion

may be important factors in reducing or avoiding brand confusion. Concerning consumer characteristics, individuals with a negative attitude towards advertising in general are more likely to confuse brands, since they are more likely to avoid or block out most of the advertising targeted at them. Not only the attitude towards advertising in general, but also the attitude towards a particular ad is of major importance, since a more positive Aad seems to lead to less brand confusion.[103] Furthermore, people who feel more involved or who are more familiar with the product category are less likely to confuse brands since they have more brand and product knowledge.[104] Brand-loyal consumers, on the other hand, are more focused on their favourite brand and, as a consequence, confuse brands more easily.[105] Rather surprisingly, the fact that a consumer had been exposed to an ad a few or several times did not impact the level of brand confusion.

Summary

How marketing communications persuade consumers is largely a black box process that can be explained in many ways. In hierarchy-of-effects models, the consumer is assumed to go through a hierarchical process of cognitive, affective and behavioural responses to communications stimuli. Depending on the type of product and buying situation, this hierarchy may differ. A crucial role in this persuasion process is the formation and change of attitudes. The extent to which attitudes are formed in a stable or less stable way depends on the elaboration likelihood of information processing, which in turn depends on the motivation, the ability and the opportunity to process information. If one of these factors is not present, consumers may be convinced by peripheral stimuli, such as the colours in the ad or the celebrity endorsing the product, rather than by rational product information. The way in which attitudes are formed and changed depends on the high or low likelihood of elaboration on the one hand, and whether attitudes are primarily based on cognitive, affective or conative factors on the other. As a result, six types of attitude formation and communications models can be distinguished. Among the most important of these models are the cognitively based high elaboration likelihood model of Fishbein–Ajzen and the theory of planned behaviour, the affectively oriented feelings-as-information and feeling transfer models. The post-experience, the perception–experience–memory and the routinised response behaviour models focus on the behavioural aspects of attitude formation. Communications do not always have positive effects. A number of media, product and advertisement characteristics can cause irritation and brand confusion, which affect advertising effectiveness.

Review questions

1 What are the contributions and shortcomings of hierarchy-of-effects models, such as the Lavidge and Steiner model and the FCB grid?

2 How are attitudes formed and changed? How can the ELM model explain how communications work?

3 How can the elements in the theory of planned behaviour be used in marketing communications?

4 What is heuristic evaluation and how can it be used in marketing communications?

5 How can the feelings-as-information theory be used in marketing communications?

6 What is the importance of ad-evoked feelings and emotional conditioning in marketing communications?

7 What is the mere exposure effect?

8 How can pre- and post-experience advertising influence brand choice?

9 What causes irritation and what are its consequences for advertising effectiveness?

10 What is brand confusion and what are the factors affecting it?

Further reading

Ajzen, I., 'Theory of Planned Behavior: A Bibliography', online (http://www.unix.oit.umass.edu/~aizen/tpbrefs.html)

Bryant, J. and Zillmann, D. (2002), *Media Effects: Advances in Theory and Research. 2nd Edition*. Hillsdale, NJ: Erlbaum.

Chaiken, S. and Trope, Y. (1999), *Dual-Process Theories in Social Psychology*. New York: Guilford Press.

Davidson, R.J., Scherer, K.R. and Goldsmith, H.H. (2003), *Handbook of Affective Sciences*. Oxford: Oxford University Press.

Forgas, J.P. (2001), *Handbook of Affect and Social Cognition*, Hillsdale, NJ: Lawrence Erlbaum Associates.

Haddock, G. and Maio, G. (2003), *Theoretical Perspectives on Attitudes for the 21st Century*. Philadelphia, PA: Psychology Press.

Higgins, E.T. and Kruglanski, A.W. (2003), *Social Psychology: A General Reader*. Ann Arbor MI: Taylor and Francis.

Ratneshwar, S., Mick, D.G. and Huffman, C. (2000), *The Why of Consumption: Contemporary Perspectives on Consumer Motives, Goals and Desires*. New York: Routledge.

Case 3

Mobistar: always together, never alone

The market of mobile telephone service providers in Belgium

In 1994, Proximus, the mobile brand of the Belgian national public telecom operator Belgacom, was launched, and was thus the historical pioneer in mobile telephone services in Belgium. It benefited from this monopoly position until August 1996, when Mobistar started out as the second company to receive a mobile licence in Belgium. At that time, mobile telecoms were perceived as complicated, expensive, snobbish and reserved to an élite. Mobile phone penetration was about 3%, and early adopters were mainly businessmen, due to the high cost of mobile communications. With its 300,000 customers, Proximus was the historical market leader. Endorsed by the national public company Belgacom, it was the standard and trusted reference of the market. Its customers consisted of early adopters of the new telecom technology; they were trend setters and high spenders. Mobistar challenged this situation by making mobile phones accessible to everyone, and innovated by launching the prepaid card Tempo, the first in Europe.

At the end of 1997, market penetration had grown to 9.4%. The market was more mature and the race was on to get new users. The competitive environment became heavier and more and more aggressive. Proximus launched its own pre-paid card Pay & Go in 1998. It dominated the business market due to its head-start in this segment (changing your phone number was a major obstacle to changing operators) and benefited from Belgacom's network of *télé-boutiques*. A third player entered the arena in 1999: Orange, born from the joint venture between Orange (UK) and KPN (Holland). Orange arrived on the market with an appealing image, revolutionary tariffs (invoicing by the second) and major promotional activities.

Market penetration reached 56.4% at the end of 2000, representing 5,640,000 users. Mobile telephony became a commodity. Products and services offered by operators on the market were very similar and each innovation brought to consumers by one brand was immediately copied by the competition. Brand image became more and more important in the choice for and the loyalty to an operator. Number portability (being able to change operators without changing your number, MNP) became a reality in October 2002, with hard discounts appearing in September 2003. In 2000, Mobistar's main shareholder France Télécom bought the Orange brand on an international level. To avoid monopoly issues in Belgium, France Télécom sold the Orange customers to KPN, which then had to sell its services under another name. This rebranding took place in April 2002. Base was born. After searching for a strategic

positioning for a while, Base opted for a hard discount positioning in October 2003. The media investments used were enormous, the sales offers were of unprecedented aggressiveness. Mobistar had to face up to this unmatched offensive. In 2003 Proximus allied itself with Vodaphone.

As can be seen from Case Table 3.1, the telecom industry is characterised by a very aggressive mass media advertising scene.

A long-term advertising strategy in three phases
Since its launch in 1996, Mobistar has supported its brand by means of extensive integrated marketing communication campaigns. Three phases can be distinguished:

- *Phase 1 (1996–97): build brand awareness.* When first launched, Mobistar's communication strategy was to build brand awareness and show that mobile phones can be neither complex, expensive, nor élitist and that they are for everyone. While building brand awareness, Mobistar positioned itself as the mobile operator that offers accessible, simple, state-of the-art and value for money solutions. The launch of the prepaid card Tempo was the tangible evidence of this positioning from the very start of Mobistar.

- *Phase 2 (1998–2000): build rational brand preference.* After making mobile communications accessible to everyone in the consumer segment,

Case Table 3.1 Mass media advertising investments and share-of-voice (SOV) of telecom operators in Belgium

	Proximus		Mobistar		Orange/Base	
	investment	SOV %	investment	SOV %	investment	SOV %
1996	9.9	64	5.6	36		
1997	14.7	52	13.3	48		
1998	16.4	47	16.9	49	1.5	4
1999	34.7	45	23.3	31	18.3	24
2000	39.0	45	26.3	30	21.3	25
2001	32.3	40	31.9	40	15.7	20
2002	38.9	47	26.7	32	17.9	21
2003	32.0	32	23.3	23	44.2	44
2004	31.5	40	27.0	35	19.3	25

Investment figures are in million Euros.

Source: Mediamark and Peaktime

Mobistar refined its communication strategy while reinforcing its credibility and legitimate place on the market. Mobistar developed its rational brand preference. Communication supported technological developments, product and tariff innovations, improvements to the services, significant personal and professional references.

■ *Phase 3 (2001–04): build emotional brand preference.* After building its rational brand preference, it was time for Mobistar to add an emotional coating to the brand. This also led to a new positioning: 'Mobistar, the bloom-booster': 'Mobistar will help everybody to make their personal life better by helping them develop themselves, to listen and to be listened to. Mobistar helps me to live more intensely and to share this with others whether they be part of my family, friends or professional life.' A strong emotional brand territory is developed to transmit the seven new defined brand values: straightforward, honest, refreshing, optimistic, reliable, friendly and dynamic.

While evolving through these three phases, Mobistar deliberately strove to develop a strong, attractive, consistent and coherent image and create a unique and differentiating communication territory.

Communication and commercial objectives

Consistent with its strategy in the three phases of campaign development, Mobistar formulated three sets of communication objectives:

■ *Phase 1 (1996 to 1997): build awareness*
  – to achieve a total awareness of over 60% by the end of 1997
  – to achieve a top-of-mind of over 20% by the end of 1997.
■ *Phase 2 (1998 to 2000): build credibility*
  – to consolidate the top-of-mind at 25%.
  – to build credibility, especially in the business market.
  – to significantly increase (+30%) the brand image parameters:
    ■ relevance: a brand that matches my needs
    ■ esteem: a brand I can trust
    ■ familiarity: a brand with which I am familiar.
■ *Phase 3 (2001 to 2004): build emotional branding*
  – to achieve the same top-of-mind level as the level of the market share: 33%.
  – to consolidate brand image (+10%) in term of relevance, esteem and familiarity.

– to develop a strong distinctive and coherent brand territory by increasing the attribution of the seven defined brand values from an average score of 34.4% to 45%.
  – to increase the attribution score of the campaigns over and above the market average.
  – to increase emotional proximity by leveraging the likeability of the campaigns to top level.

Similarly, also three sets of commercial objectives were advanced:

■ *Phase 1 (1996–97): 'Launch'*
  – to reach 200,000 customers by the end of 1997.
  – to achieve a market share of 20% by the end of 1997.
■ *Phase 2 (1998–2000): 'Get'*
  – to reach 1,500,000 customers by the end of 2000.
  – to consolidate the market share despite the new competitor on the market.
■ *Phase 3 (2001–04): 'Get/Keep/Increase'*
  – to reach 2,400,000 customers by the end of 2004.
  – to increase the average revenue per user (ARPU) by 10%, by increasing consumption of telecoms.

Target groups

In each of the three phases, target groups of the communication campaign were formulated. The level of segmentation and the nature of the target groups consistently evolves with the communication strategy and objectives:

■ *Phase 1 (1996–97): no segmentation*
  All the active population, potential users of a mobile phone, was targeted to install the new brand.
■ *Phase 2 (1998–2000): socio-demographic segmentation*
  Consumer target:
  – broad public: total 18–54 years
  – post-paid: 25–54 years, social classes 1 to 4
  – pre-paid: 'youngsters' 15–24 years and 'elderly people' 55 years +
  Business target:
  – SMA (Small and Medium Accounts): 63,000 companies, from 5 to 200 employees, telecom is not a priority, decision-makers are often not specialists.

– CMA (Corporate Major Accounts): 1,250 companies, more than 200 employees, telecom is often top priority, contacts are specialist telecom managers.

■ *Phase 3 (2001–04): people segmentation*
The people segmentation, based on the consumer's aspiration and needs, allows us to select the following groups and to get closer to them.

– caring and dependable: family is a very important part of their lives, they like to make others feel good about themselves. Feeling physically safe and financially secure are very important to them, very moral, their self-respect is a core value.

– leisure roamers: they enjoy an active social life but being successful and professional are also important to them – they try to make their life exciting and like to be stylish and give themselves the best.

– playful: feel life is all about having fun and enjoying themselves – social life is at the core of their existence – success in life is mainly a matter of luck – tendency to 'follow' rather than 'lead'.

– rational fun seeker: more focused on having fun than being successful but sensible and serious about finances and home – focuses on own projects and pleasures, looks for a personal sense of accomplishment, likes to feel an individual.

– mobile utilitarian: more focused on being successful than on having fun – internal locus of control and self-motivated, they make things happen – lives dominated by work.

– upmarket aces: driven and ambitious, know what they want – success is not just a matter of luck – believe you have to work hard and play hard, burn the candle at both ends.

Creative strategy

The communication strategy, objectives and target groups were translated into an appropriate creative strategy for each of the three phases:

■ *Phase 1 (1996–97): 'Mobistar, this time it's for you'.* The creative strategy consisted of a struggle to make mobile communications accessible to everyone, and so illustrate Mobistar's conviction that 'One day, we will all have a mobile phone, starting today'. Mobistar undertook to explain this new mode of communication. The brand values –

accessibility, simplicity, state-of-the-art, value for money – are adapted into language that is clear but not ordinary. This is why a modern tone is given to the campaigns to build a strong, distinctive brand. Its character traits are: serenity, joyfulness, friendliness and optimism. The images' colour treatment and the friendly tone of voice were developed to transmit this brand personality.

■ *Phase 2 (1998–2000): 'Mobistar, I know why'.* To affirm its credibility, Mobistar revisited the technique of the testimonial. On the one hand, it undertook a very broad campaign aimed at using the reputations of famous brands and companies by showing that they chose Mobistar and trust it. On the other hand, it also showed that many celebrities recognised for the high level of competence and exigence also chose and prefer Mobistar. (See Plate 4.)

To increase the legitimacy, Mobistar communicated its vision of mobile communications and its added value using empathy, so that everyone can feel concerned. Mobistar continued to consistently use the existing communication code to allow a clear identification and personality.

■ *Phase 3 (2001–04): 'Mobistar. Get more out of life' – 'Mobistar. Brighter together'.* Mobistar radically adopted a more emotional approach to communicate the new 'blooming' brand position through all its communication activities in a consistent way. The approach is definitively 'consumer centric'. A strong creative code was developed in order to express the 'blooming' concept through the symbolism of jumping people, because when people jump they cannot control their facial expressions. The mask falls and a large range of emotions such as enjoyment, pleasure, contentment, a feeling of fullness and surprise at one's own abilities are expressed. Or through facial close-ups able to express those emotions. The creative guidelines (visual and audio) followed, translating the seven values of the brand and its emergence in terms of attribution and impact.

Since its launch and throughout its communications, Mobistar has continuously and deliberately capitalised on its brand territory: joyfulness, friendliness and optimism. It has also developed its own communication codes: the colour treatment, layouts and the friendly tone-of-voice.

Media strategy

Finally, a media strategy was developed, adapted to the specific objectives and targets of the campaign in each phase:

■ *Phase 1 (1996–97): build brand awareness*. The main objective was to create brand awareness for Mobistar as the newcomer on the Belgian mobile telephone market. Media objectives were: create impact and visibility, generate high reach level over a short period of time and maintain high repetition level to further build brand name awareness.

The main media for the launch phase was billboards (42% Share of Investment (SOI) in 1996): a 'natural' media to communicate to people on the move, to people who need mobile phone technology. Furthermore, billboards were also the perfect medium to create impact, build coverage and maintain high repetition level. With the launch of the Tempo card, Mobistar needed more dynamic explanation power, the reason that TV was added to the media mix for product communication. As the objective was also to educate the market (still immature at the time), informative and descriptive media such as magazines and newspapers were used (35% SOI in 1997).

■ *Phase 2 (1998–2000): defend share-of-voice*. The objective also to defend Mobistar's SOV led to increased media investments and thus enlarged the media mix including the six main media. The Mobistar brand name still needed to be sustained towards a broad target, but product segmentation (Prepaid, Postpaid, Business . . .) allowed the brand to start using media selectively. Billboards were still used in awareness building campaigns for specific targets (testimonial campaign for upscale and business targets). Magazines were used for their ability to talk to 'niches' with potential, such as students, elderly people or professionals. At the same time, broad covering media with informative and descriptive power (such as newspapers and radio) were used to sustain promotional offers (mainly of the Middle of the year/End of the year). Finally, as the market became more and more mature, TV was used to enlarge the media coverage and communicate to a broader audience.

■ *Phase 3 (2001–04): optimise media investment*. The media strategy is based on two main principles. The first principle consists of building a media hierarchy to sustain each communication objective:

– emotional: audio-visual media
– rational: billboards, print and ad-hoc media
– tactical: multimedia approach adapted to the importance of the promotion.

The second principle is to maximise the importance of the media presence through:

– limited media mix per action in order to get an optimal share of voice per selected media
– concentrated activity period per action with proportional overweight at the start
– multiplication of the contacts with targeted groups.

Contrary to its competitors Proximus and Base that use heavy sponsorship, Mobistar relies upon its advertising strengths to reach its objectives.

Communication results

Mobistar in every period succeeded in reaching or exceeding its communication objectives:

■ *Phase 1 (1996–97): achieving top awareness in one year*
– Mobistar achieved a total awareness of 90% by the end of 1997 (+50% *vs* objective). This score is very close to Proximus' total awareness of 92%.
– Mobistar obtained a top-of-mind of 22% (+10% *vs* objective).

■ *Phase 2 (1998–2000): achieving top credibility*
– Mobistar consolidated its top-of-mind equal to or above 25%.
– As of mid 2000, Mobistar's credibility objective among the business segment was achieved with resounding success: 100% of credibility (Case Figure 3.1).
– Brand image saw very strong growth in terms of relevance, esteem and familiarity (Case Figure 3.2). The objective to increase the scores by 30% for the period 1997–2000 was overtaken. Mobistar achieved a minimum progression of 40% on brand image for this period. This evolution continues in phase 3.

■ *Phase 3 (2001–04): becoming an emotional brand*
– With 34% of top-of-mind Mobistar reached the fixed objective.
– Brand image was consolidated during the period 2001–04 (see graph in Case Figure 3.2). A minimal growth of 16% is worth highlighting.
– Mobistar achieved an average score of 54.6% for the seven values attribution while the

Case Figure 3.1 Scores on brand image attributes in the business market

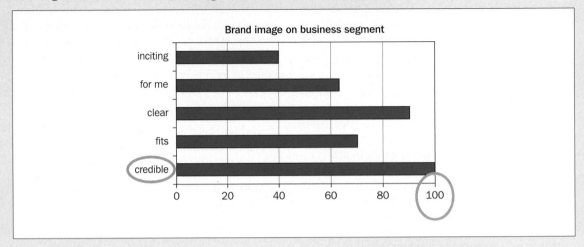

Source: Significant May/June 2000.

Case Figure 3.2 Relevance, esteem and familiarity of the Mobistar brand

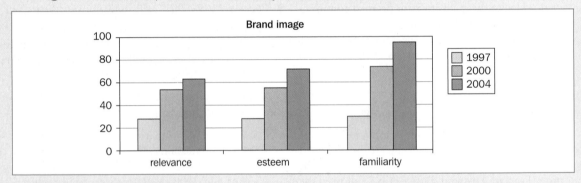

Source: Brand Asset Valuator – Y&R.

average score objective was fixed at 45% (Case Figure 3.3).

- The advertising attribution score strongly increased to reach 24% above the market average (Case Figure 3.4).
- The major TV campaigns exceeded the score of 80% in likeability (barometer Adscores Inra).

Case Figure 3.5 gives a summary of the evolution of the top-of-mind brand awareness scores of each telecom operator over the three campaign phases.

Commercial results
- *Phase 1 (1996–97): successful launch*
  - Mobistar reached 283,000 clients at the end of 1997 (+41.5% *vs* objective).

- Mobistar achieved a market share of 30% (+50% *vs* objective).

- *Phase 2 (1998–2000): exponential growth of the customer base*
  - Mobistar had 1,800,000 customers at the end of 2000. This represents an acquisition of 1,517,000 customers in three years (+20% *vs* objective).
  - Mobistar consolidated and increased its market share to 32.5% which is in line with the commercial objective. Mobistar did not suffer from the launch of the third operator, while Proximus lost 13.5% during this period.

- *Phase 3 (2001–04): strong revenue growth*
  - Mobistar reached 2,846,000 customers by the end of 2004 (+18% *vs* objective).

Case Figure 3.3 Scores on Mobistar value attributes

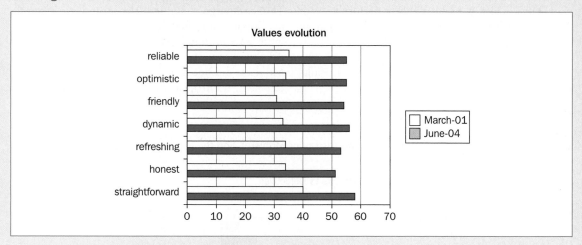

Source: Adscores Inra.

Case Figure 3.4 Advertising attribution score evolution of Mobistar relative to total market

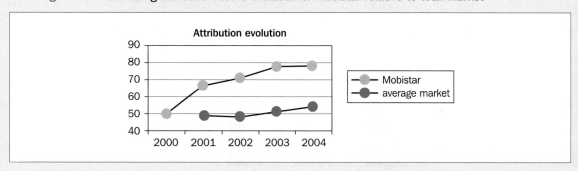

Source: Adscores Inra.

Case Figure 3.5 Top-of-mind brand awareness of the three telecom companies

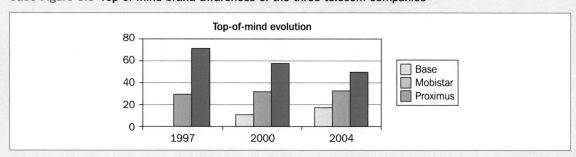

Source: Adscores Inra.

– The average revenue per user has increased by 18%, which is by far the best performance of the market. The competitors' results are flat on this item.

Case Figure 3.6 summarises the commercial results over the three phases.

Wrapping up

The campaigns enabled the brand to strongly develop its emotional proximity to consumers, making it an emotional brand leader (Case Figure 3.7). As the second operator on the Belgium market, Mobistar did not suffer from the launch of the third operator. A European benchmark shows us that this

Case Figure 3.6 Commercial objectives and results of Mobistar and its competitors

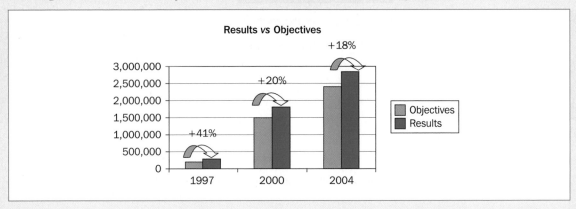

Source: Mobistar.

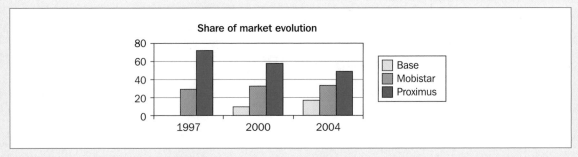

Source: Operators annoucement.

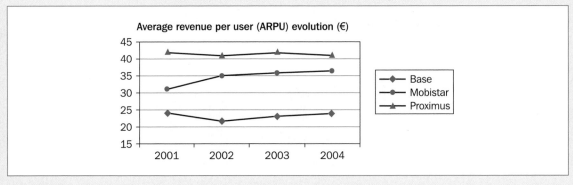

Source: Operators annoucement.

is an exceptional situation. The international brand image survey in Case Figure 3.8 confirms the top power of the brand Mobistar compared to second operators of others markets: France, Switzerland, The Netherlands and the UK.

In a market in which technological advances are easily copied and where the products and services are increasingly similar, Mobistar claims that only the brand image can act as a genuine differentiator. The company considers the scores achieved in the various parameters tied to the advertising campaigns a demonstration of their efficiency.

Questions

1 In its long-term campaign, did Mobistar follow a hierarchy-of-effects approach? Was that the right thing to do? Explain why or why not.

2 In which cell of the FCB-grid would you classify mobile phone services? In which cell can Mobistar be situated or does it aims to be situated? Is that realistic? Has it been successful?

3 Using the classification of attitude formation models in this chapter, which models seem most relevant to explain the processing and impact of the Mobistar campaign?

4 In terms of the Theory of Reasoned Action, how is Mobistar trying to form the intentions towards its brand? What is the role of attitudes, subjective norms and perceived behavioural control?

5 Would you say Mobistar has been effective in reaching its targets, and is this effectiveness attributable to their advertising campaign?

Source: Mobistar Effie Case 2005, Chris Van Roey, Mobistar.

Case Figure 3.7 Emotional proximity of customers to the Proximus, Mobistar and Base brand

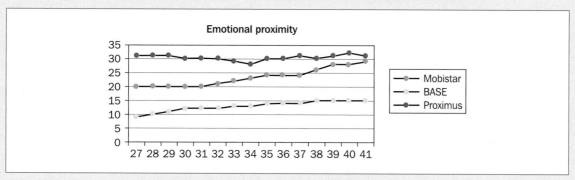

Source: Research International – weeks 2005.

Case Figure 3.8 Brand image parameters of 'second' telecom companies in selected European countries

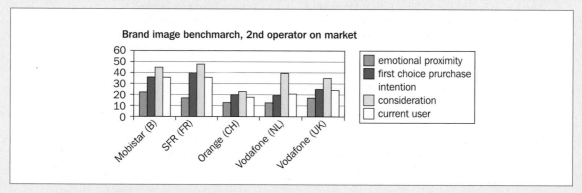

Source: Research International 2004.

References

1 Barry, T.E. and Howard, D.J. (1990), 'A Review and Critique of the Hierarchy of Effects in Advertising', *International Journal of Advertising*, 9, 121–35; Barry, T.E. (2002), 'In Defense of the Hierarchy of Effects: A Rejoinder to Weilbacher', *Journal of Advertising Research*, 42(3), 44–47.

2 Vakratsas, D. and Ambler, T. (1999), 'How Advertising Works: What Do We Really Know?', *Journal of Marketing*, 63, 1 (January), 25–43.

3 Vaughn, R. (1986), 'How Advertising Works: A Planning Model Revisited', *Journal of Advertising Research*, 26(1), 57–66.

4 Rossiter, J.R. and Percy, L. (1997), *Advertising and Promotion Management*. New York: McGraw-Hill.

5 Yoon, S.K. (2001), 'Prophet warning: is nothing sacred?', *Far Eastern Economic Review*, 10 May, http://www.singapore-window.org/sw01/010510re.htm.

6 Barry, T.E. and Howard, D.J. (1990), 'A Review and Critique of the Hierarchy of Effects in Advertising', *International Journal of Advertising*, 9, 121–35; Barry, T.E. (2002), 'In Defense of the Hierarchy of Effects: A Rejoinder to Weilbacher', *Journal of Advertising Research*, 42(3), 44–47.

7 Peter, J.P., Olson, J.C. and Grunert, K.G. (1999), *Consumer Behaviour and Marketing Strategy, European Edition*. London: McGraw-Hill.

8 Hoyer, W.C. and MacInnis, D.J. (2001), *Consumer Behavior*. Boston: Houghton Mifflin.

9 Hoyer, W.D. and MacInnis, D.J. (2001), *Consumer Behavior*, Boston NY: Houghton Mifflin; Park, C.W., Jaworski, B.J. and MacInnis, D.J. (1986), 'Strategic Brand Concept–Image Management', *Journal of Marketing*, 50 (October), 135–145.

10 Aaker, J.L. and Lee, A.Y. (2001), ' "I" Seek Pleasures and "We" Avoid Pains: The Role of Self-Regulatory Goals in Information Processing and Persuasion', *Journal of Consumer Research*, 28 (June), 33–49; Higgins, E.T. (1997), 'Beyond Pleasure and Pain', *American Psychologist*, 52 (December), 1280–1300.

11 Huffman, C., Ratneshwar, S. and Mick, D.G. (2000), 'Consumer Goal Structures and Goal Determination Processes', in Ratneshwar, S., Mick, D.G. and Huffman, C. (eds), *The Why of Consumption: Contemporary Perspectives on Consumer Motives, Goals and Desires*, New York: Routledge, 1–35.

12 Pham, M.T. and Higgins, E.T. (2005), 'Promotion and prevention in consumer decision making: State of the art and theoretical propositions', in S. Ratneshwar and D.G. Mick (eds), *Inside Consumption: Perspectives on Consumer Motives, Goals and Desires*, 8–43, London: Routledge.

13 Baumgartner, H. (2002), 'Toward a Personology of the Consumer', *Journal of Consumer Research*, 29 (September), 286–292.

14 Cuckoo Awards (2005).

15 Petty, R.E. and Cacioppo, J.T. (1986), 'The Elaboration Likelihood Model of Persuasion', *Advances in Experimental Social Psychology*, 19, 123–205.

16 Petty, R.E. and Cacioppo, J.T. (1986), 'The Elaboration Likelihood Model of Persuasion', *Advances in Experimental Social Psychology*, 19, 123–205.

17 Ahluwalia, R. (2002), 'How Prevalent is the Negativity Effect in Consumer Environments?' *Journal of Consumer Research*, 29 (September), 270–9.

18 Chaiken, S., Giner-Sorolla, R. and Chen, S. (1996), 'Beyond Accuracy: Defense and Impression Motives in Heuristic and Systematic Processing', in Gollwitzer, P.M. and Bargh, J.A. (eds), *The Psychology of Action: Linking Cognition and Motivation to Behavior*, New York: Guilford, 553–78.

19 Bosmans, A. (2002), 'Affective Persuasive Communication: Multiple Roles of Affect in Persuading the Consumer', Unpublished Doctoral Dissertation, Belgium: Ghent University; Forgas, J.P. (1995), 'Mood and Judgment: The Affect Infusion Model (AIM)', *Psychological Bulletin*, 117(1), 39–66; Chaiken, S. (1980), 'Heuristic versus Systematic Information Processing in the Use of Source versus Message Cues in Persuasion', *Journal of Personality and Social Psychology*, 39, 752–66; Petty, R.E. and Cacioppo, J.T. (1986), 'The Elaboration Likelihood Model of Persuasion', *Advances in Experimental Psychology*, 19, 123–205.

20 Pham, M.T. and Avnet, T. (2004), 'Ideals and Oughts and the Reliance on Affect versus Substance in Persuasion', *Journal of Consumer Research*, 30 (March), 503–518.

21 Fishbein, M. and Ajzen, I. (1975), *Belief, Attitude, Intention, and Behavior: An Introduction to Theory and Research*. Reading, MA: Addison-Wesley; Ajzen, I. (2002), 'Attitudes', in Fernandez Ballesteros, R. (ed.), *Encyclopedia of Psychological Assessment*, 1, 110–15. London: Sage Publications; Ajzen, I. (1991), 'The Theory of Planned Behavior', *Organizational Behavior and Human Decision Processes*, 50, 179–211.

22 De Pelsmacker, P. and Van Kenhove, P. (2006), *Marktonderzoek. Technieken en Toepassingen (Marketing Research. Techniques and Applications)*. Amsterdam: Pearson Education Benelux.

23 Ajzen, I. (2002), 'Attitudes', in Fernandez Ballesteros, R. (ed.), *Encyclopedia of psychological assessment*, 1, 110–15. London: Sage Publications; Ajzen, I. (1991), 'The Theory of Planned Behavior', *Organizational Behavior and Human Decision Processes*, 50, 179–211.

24 Ajzen, I. (1991), 'The Theory of Planned Behavior', *Organizational Behavior and Human Decision Processes*, 50, 179–211.

25 Ajzen, I. (2002), 'Perceived Behavioral Control, Self-Efficacy, Locus of Control, and the Theory of Planned Behavior', *Journal of Applied Social Psychology*, 32, 665–83.

26 http://www.unix.oit.umass.edu/~aizen/tpbrefs.html

27 Bamberg, S., Ajzen, I. and Schmidt, P. (2003), 'Choice of Travel Mode in the Theory of Planned Behavior: The Roles of Past Behavior, Habit, and Reasoned Action', *Basic and Applied Social Psychology*; Baker, C.W., Little, T.D. and Brownell, K.D. (2003), 'Predicting Adolescent Eating and Activity Behaviors: The Role of Social Norms and Personal Agency', *Health Psychology*, 22, 189–198; Bamberg, S. and Schmidt, P. (2003), 'Incentive, Morality or Habit? Predicting Students' Car Use for University Routes with the Models of Ajzen, Schwartz, and Triandis', *Environment and Behavior*, 35, 1–22; etc. (see http://www.unix.oit.umass.edu/~aizen/tpbrefs.html).

28 Ajzen, I. (1991), 'The Theory of Planned Behavior', *Organizational Behavior and Haman Decision Processes*, 50, 179–211.

29 MacInnis, D.J. and Jaworski, B.J. (1989), 'Information Processing from Advertisements: Toward an Integrative Framework', *Journal of Marketing*, 53, 1–23.

30 MacInnis, D.J. and Jaworski, B.J. (1989), 'Information Processing from Advertisements: Toward an Integrative Framework', *Journal of Marketing*, 53, 1–23.

31 Baker, W.E. and Lutz, R.J. (2000), 'An Empirical Test of an Updated Relevance-Accessibility Model of Advertising Effectiveness', *Journal of Advertising*, 29(1), 1–14.

32 Liu, S.C. and Johnson, K.F. (2005), 'The automatic country-of-origin effects on brand judgements', *Journal of Advertising*, 34(1), 87–97.

33 Schwarz, N. and Clore, G.L. (1996), 'Feelings and Phenomenal Experiences', in Higgins, E.T. and Kruglanski, A.W. (eds), *Social Psychology: Handbook of Basic Principles*, New York: Guilford, 433–65.

34 Pham, M.T. (1998), 'Representativeness, Relevance, and the Use of Feelings in Decision Making', *Journal of Consumer Research*, 25(2), 144–60.

35 Gorn, G.J., Pham, M.T. and Sin, L.Y. (2001), 'When Arousal Influences Ad Evaluation and Valence Does Not (and Vice Versa)', *Journal of Consumer Psychology*, 2(3), 237–56.

36 Pham, M.T., Cohen, J.B., Prajecus, J.W. and Hughes, D.G. (2001), 'Affect Monitoring and the Primacy of Feelings in Judgment', *Journal of Consumer Research*, 28(2), 167–88.

37 Pham, M.T., Cohen, J.B., Prajecus, J.W. and Hughes, D.G. (2001), 'Affect Monitoring and the Primacy of Feelings in Judgment', *Journal of Consumer Research*, 28(2), 167–88.

38 Pham, M.T. (1998), 'Representativeness, Relevance, and the Use of Feelings in Decision Making', *Journal of Consumer Research*, 25(2), 144–60. Bosmans, A. and Baumgartner, H. (2005), Goal-relevant emotional information: When extraneous affect leads to persuasion and when it does not', *Journal of Consumer Research*, 32 (Dec.), 424–34.

39 Pham, M.T. (1998), 'Representativeness, Relevance, and the Use of Feelings in Decision Making', *Journal of Consumer Research*, 25(2), 144–60.

40 Bagozzi, R.P., Gopinath, M. and Nyer, P.U. (1999), 'The Role of Emotions in Marketing', *Journal of the Academy of Marketing Science*, 27(2), 184–206; Forgas, J.P. (1995), 'Mood and Judgment: The Affect Infusion Model (AIM)', *Psychological Bulletin*, 117(1), 39–66.

41 Schindler, M.R. and Holbrook, M.B. (2003), 'Nostalgia for Early Experience as a Determinant of Consumer Preferences', *Psychology and Marketing*, 20(4), 275–302.

42 www.unicef.org, Cuckoo Awards, 2006.

43 Mitchell, A.A. and Olson, J.C. (1981), 'Are Product Attribute Beliefs the Only Mediator of Advertising Effects on Brand Attitude?', *Journal of Marketing, Research*, 18, 318–32.

44 Biel, A.L. (1990), 'Love the Ad. Buy the Product?', *Admap*, 21–5.

45 Baker, W.E. and Lutz, R.J. (2000), 'An Empirical Test of an Updated Relevance-Accessibility Model of Advertising Effectiveness', *Journal of Advertising*, 29(1), 1–14.

46 Brown, S.P. and Stayman, D.M. (1992), 'Antecedents and Consequences of Attitude towards the Ad: A Meta-Analysis', *Journal of Consumer Research*, 19, 34–51.

47 Gouden Gluon Onderzoek (1998), *De Kracht van Emoties*, (Golden Gluon Research, *The Power of Emotions*), PUB, 14, appendix.

48 Bagozzi, R.P., Gopinath, M. and Nyer, P.U. (1999), 'The Role of Emotions in Marketing', *Journal of the Academy of Marketing Science*, 27(2), 184–206.

49 Frijda, N.H. (1987), *The Emotions*. Cambridge: Cambridge University Press; Bower, G.H. (1991), 'Mood Congruity of Social Judgment', in Forgas, J. (ed.), *Emotion and Social Judgment*. Oxford: Pergamon, 31–53.

50 Mitchell, A.A. (1988), 'Current Perspectives and Issues Concerning the Explanation of "Feelings" Advertising Effects', in Hecker, S. and Stewart, D.S. (eds), *Nonverbal Communication in Advertising*. Lexington, MA: Lexington Books, 122–44.

51 Morris, J.D., Woo, C., Geason, J.A. and Kim, J. (2002), 'The Power of Affect: Predicting Intention', *Journal of Advertising Research*, 42(3), 7–17.

52 Morris, J.D., Woo, C., Geason, J.A. and Kim, J. (2002), 'The Power of Affect: Predicting Intention', *Journal of Advertising Research*, 42(3), 7–17.

53 Pavlov, I. (1927), *Conditioned Reflexes*, London: Oxford University Press.

54 Freeman, S. (2003), 'Celine Dion Sings "I Drove All Night" for Chrysler', *Wall Street Journal*, January 16.

55 Kroeber-Riel, W. (1984), 'Effects of Pictorial Elements in Ads Analyzed by Means of Eye Movement Monitoring', *Advances in Consumer Research*, 11, 591–6.

56 Elliott, R. and Ritson, M. (1995), 'Practicing Existential Consumption: The Lived Meaning of Sexuality in Advertising', *Advances in Consumer Research*, 22, 740–5.

57 Anonymous, (2001), 'Is Häagen-Dazs Shrewd to Drop its Sexy Image?', *Marketing*, 6 September.

58 Janiszewski, C. and Meyvis, T. (2001), 'Effects of Brand Logo Complexity, Repetition, and Spacing on

Processing Fluency and Judgment', *Journal of Consumer Research*, 28 (June), 18–32.

59 Shapiro, S. (1999), 'When an Ad's Influence is Beyond Our Conscious Control: Perceptual and Conceptual Fluency Effects Caused by Incidental Ad Exposure', *Journal of Consumer Research*, 26 (June), 16–36.

60 Mano, H. (1996), 'Assessing Emotional Reactions to TV Ads: A Replication and Extension with a Brief Adjective Checklist', *Advances in Consumer Research*, 23, 63–9.

61 Zajonc, R.B. and Markus, H. (1988), 'Affect and Cognition: The Hard Interface', in Izard, C.E., Kagan, J. and Zajonc, R.B. (eds), *Emotions, Cognition and Behaviour*. Cambridge: Cambridge University Press, 73–102.

62 Janiszewski, C. and Meyvis, T. (2001), 'Effects of Brand Logo Complexity, Repetition, and Spacing on Processing Fluency and Judgment', *Journal of Consumer Research*, 28 (June), 18–32.

63 Hoyer, W.C. and MacInnis, D.J. (2001), *Consumer Behaviour*. Boston: Houghton Mifflin.

64 Berlyne, D.E. (1970), 'Novelty, Complexity, and Hedonic Value', *Perception and Psychophysics*, 8 (November), 279–86.

65 Deighton, J., Henderson, C.M. and Neslin, S.A. (1994), 'The Effects of Advertising on Brand Switching and Repeat Purchasing', *Journal of Marketing Research*, 31, 28–43.

66 Hall, B.F. (2002), 'A New Model for Measuring Advertising Effectiveness', *Journal of Advertising Research*, 42 (March/April), 23–31.

67 Kempf, D.S. and Laczniak, R.N. (2001), 'Advertising's Influence on Subsequent Product Trial Processing', *Journal of Advertising*, 30(3), 27–38.

68 Hall, B.F. (2002), 'A New Model for Measuring Advertising Effectiveness', *Journal of Advertising Research*, 42 (March/April), 23–31.

69 Kempf, D.S. and Laczniak, R.N. (2001), 'Advertising's Influence on Subsequent Product Trial Processing', *Journal of Advertising*, 30(3), 27–38.

70 Deighton, J., Henderson, J.M. and Neslin, S.A. (1994), 'The Effects of Advertising on Brand Switching and Repeat Purchasing', *Journal of Marketing Research*, 31(2), 28–43.

71 Kempf, D.S. and Laczniak, R.N. (2001), 'Advertising's Influence on Subsequent Product Trial Processing', *Journal of Advertising*, 30(3), 27–38.

72 Clancy, K.J. and Trout, J. (2002), 'Brand Confusion', *Harvard Business Review*, 80(3).

73 Ehrenberg, A.S.C. (1974), 'Repetititve Advertising and the Consumer', *Journal of Advertising Research*, 14 (April), 25–34; Vakratsas, D. and Ambler, T. (1999), 'What Do We Really Know?', *Journal of Marketing*, 63 (January), 26–43.

74 Peter, J.P. and Olson, J.C. (1993), *Consumer Behaviour and Marketing Strategy*. Burr Ridge, IL: Irwin.

75 Hoyer, W.D. (1984), 'An Examination of Consumer Decision Making for a Common Repeat Purchase Product', *Journal of Consumer Research*, 11, 822–9.

76 Aaker, D.A. and Bruzzone, D.E. (1985), 'Causes of Irritation in Advertising', *Journal of Marketing*, 49 (Spring), 47–57.

77 De Pelsmacker, P. and Van den Bergh, J. (1998), 'Ad Content, Product Category, Campaign Weight and Irritation. A Study of 226 TV Commercials', *Journal of International Consumer Marketing*, 10(4), 5–27.

78 Pasadeos, Y. (1990), 'Perceived Informativeness of and Irritation with Local Advertising', *Journalism Quarterly*, 67, 35–9.

79 Edwards, S.M., Li, H. and Lee, J.H. (2002), 'Forced Exposure and Psychological Reactance: Antecedents and Consequences of the Perceived Intrusiveness of Pop-Up Ads', *Journal of Advertising*, 31(3), 83–95.

80 Aaker, D.A. and Bruzzone, D.E. (1985), 'Causes of Irritation in Advertising', *Journal of Marketing*, 49 (Spring), 47–57; De Pelsmacker, P. and Van den Bergh, J. (1998), 'Ad Content, Product Category, Campaign Weight and Irritation. A Study of 226 TV Commercials', *Journal of International Consumer Marketing*, 10(4), 5–27.

81 De Pelsmacker, P. and Van den Bergh, J. (1998), 'Ad Content, Product Category, Campaign Weight and Irritation. A Study of 226 TV Commercials', *Journal of International Consumer Marketing*, 10(4), 5–27.

82 Pechmann, C. and Stewart, D.W. (1990), *Advertising Repetition: A Critical Review of Wear-In and Wear-Out*. Working paper, Cambridge: Marketing Science Institute.

83 Cox, D.S. and Cox, A.D. (1988), 'What Does Familiarity Breed? Complexity as a Moderator of Repetition Effects in Advertisement Evaluation', *Journal of Consumer Research*, 15, 111–16; Anand, P. and Sternthal, B. (1990), 'Ease of Message Processing as a Moderator of Repetition Effects in Advertising', *Journal of Marketing Research*, 27, 345–53; Schumann, D.W., Petty, R.E. and Clemons, D.S. (1990), 'Predicting the Effectiveness of Different Strategies of Advertising Variation: A Test of the Repetition-Variation Hypothesis', *Journal of Consumer Research*, 17, 192–202.

84 De Pelsmacker, P. and Van den Bergh, J. (1998), 'Ad Content, Product Category, Campaign Weight and Irritation. A Study of 226 TV Commercials', *Journal of International Consumer Marketing*, 10(4), 5–27.

85 Fennis, B.M. and Bakker, A.B. (2001), 'Stay Tuned – We Will Be Back After These Messages: Need to Evaluate Moderates the Transfer of Irritation in Advertising', *Journal of Advertising*, 15(3), 15–25.

86 De Pelsmacker, P. and Geuens, M. (1997), 'Affect Intensity and the General Attitude Towards Advertising', in De Pelsmacker, P. and Geuens, M. (eds), *The Changing World of Marketing and Corporate Communication, Proceedings of the Second International Conference on Marketing and Corporate Communication*. Antwerp: RUCA, 60–2.

87 Moore, D.L. and Hutchinson, J.W. (1983), 'The Effect of Ad Affection Advertising Effectiveness', *Advances in Consumer Research*, 10, 526–31.

88 Burke, M.C. and Edell, J.A. (1989), 'The Impact of Feelings on Ad-Based Affect and Cognition', *Journal of Marketing Research*, 26, 69–83; Stayman, D.M. and Aaker, D.A. (1988), 'Are All the Effects of Ad-Induced Feelings Mediated by Aad?', *Journal of Consumer Research*, 15, 368–73; Aaker, D.A. and Bruzzone, D.E. (1985), 'Causes of Irritation in Advertising', *Journal of Marketing*, 49 (Spring), 47–57; De Pelsmacker, P. and Van den Bergh, J. (1997), *Advertising Content and Brand Confusion*, Research report, Marketing Communication Research Centre, Ghent: De Vlerick School voor Management.

89 Fennis, B.M. and Bakker, A.B. (2001), 'Stay Tuned-We Will Be Back After These Messages: Need to Evaluate Moderates the Transfer of Irritation in Advertising', *Journal of Advertising*, 15(3), 15–25.

90 De Pelsmacker, P., Van den Bergh, J. and Anckaert, P. (1998), *Irritation, Product Type, Consumer Characteristics and Advertising Effectiveness*. Working paper, Marketing Communication Research Centre, Ghent: De Vlerick School voor Management.

91 Rossiter, J.R. and Percy, L. (2000), *Advertising and Promotion Management*, New York: McGraw-Hill.

92 Poiesz, T.B.C. and Verhallen, T.M.M. (1989), 'Brand Confusion in Advertising', *International Journal of Advertising*, 8, 231–44.

93 Poiesz, T.B.C. and Verhallen, T.M.M. (1989), 'Brand Confusion in Advertising', *International Journal of Advertising*, 8, 231–44.

94 Brengman, M., Geuens, M. and De Pelsmacker, P. (2001), 'The Impact of Consumer Characteristics and Campaign Related Factors on Brand Confusion in Print Advertising', *Journal of Marketing Communications*, 7, 231–43.

95 De Pelsmacker, P. and Van den Bergh, J. (1997), *Advertising Content and Brand Confusion*, Research report, Marketing Communication Research Centre, Ghent: De Vlerick School voor Management.

96 Poiesz, T.B.C. and Verhallen, T.M.M. (1989), 'Brand Confusion in Advertising', *International Journal of Advertising*, 8, 231–44.

97 Diamond, S.A. (1981), *Trademark Problems and How to Avoid Them*. Chicago, IL: Crain Communication, Inc.

98 De Pelsmacker, P. and Van den Bergh, J. (1997), *Advertising Content and Brand Confusion*. Research report, Marketing Comunication Research Centre, Ghent: De Vlerick School voor Management.

99 De Pelsmacker, P., Van den Bergh, J. and Anckaert, P. (1998), *Irritation, Product Type, Consumer Characteristics and Advertising Effectiveness*. Working paper, Marketing Communication Research Centre, Ghent: De Vlerick School voor Management.

100 De Pelsmacker, P. and Geuens, M. (1997), 'Emotional Appeals and Information Cues in Belgian Magazine Advertisements', *International Journal of Advertising*, 16(2), 123–47.

101 Poiesz, T.B.C. and Verhallen, T.M.M. (1989), 'Brand Confusion in Advertising', *International Journal of Advertising*, 8, 231–44.

102 Poiesz, T.B.C. and Verhallen, T.M.M. (1989), 'Brand Confusion in Advertising', *International Journal of Advertising*, 8, 231–44.

103 Brengman, M., Geuens, M. and De Pelsmacker, P. (2001), 'The Impact of Consumer Characteristics and Campaign Related Factors on Brand Confusion in Print Advertising', *Journal of Marketing Communications*, 7, 231–43.

104 Foxman, E.R. and Muehling, D.D. (1990), 'An Investigation of Factors Contributing to Consumer Brand Confusion', *Journal of Consumer Affairs*, 24(1), 170–89.

105 Brengman, M., Geuens, M. and De Pelsmacker, P. (2001), 'The Impact of Consumer Characteristics and Campaign Related Factors on Brand Confusion in Print Advertising', *Journal of Marketing Communications*, 7, 231–43.

Chapter 4

Target groups

Chapter outline

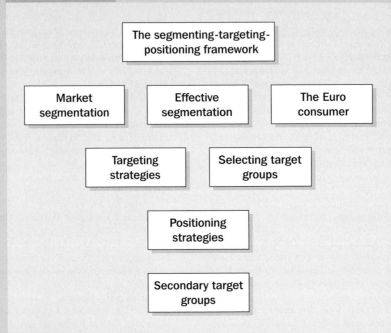

The segmenting-targeting-positioning framework

Market segmentation

Effective segmentation

The Euro consumer

Targeting strategies

Selecting target groups

Positioning strategies

Secondary target groups

Chapter objectives

This chapter will help you to:

- Understand the process of segmenting, targeting and positioning
- Get an overview of the criteria for segmenting markets
- Understand the requirements for good segmentation
- Distinguish the strategies for targeting market segments
- Choose positioning strategies
- Understand the difference between primary target groups and secondary target groups or stakeholders

Introduction

The first step in the strategic marketing planning process is the study of market needs, a situation analysis of current and future market conditions. This can be done by using SWOT analysis, which consists of an internal analysis – strengths and weaknesses of the company or brand – and an external analysis – opportunities and threats in the marketplace. This analysis leads to opportunities for existing product lines in new or existing markets, or new product ideas for new or current markets. In most circumstances a market has different groups of customers or prospects with different needs and subject to different trends. Identifying these different groups and deciding at which group(s) to target the marketing and communications efforts is a major task of communications planning.

Companies can define target markets in a number of ways, based on multiple criteria. Segmenting a market, deciding on target groups or segments to focus on, and establishing a position to defend vis-à-vis these target groups, are at the same time vital components of the strategic marketing plan and basic cornerstones of a communications strategy. Understanding buying motives and behaviour of target groups is an essential element of this groundwork and requires thorough preliminary analysis. The choice of well-defined target groups and positioning decisions should, later in the communications planning, be reflected in the selection of communications objectives, communications instruments, campaign execution and media planning.

The segmenting-targeting-positioning framework

In Table 4.1 the various steps in the segmenting-targeting-positioning (STP) process are shown. The STP exercise starts with a definition of potentially relevant factors on the basis of which a market can be segmented. Market segmentation should ideally lead to more homogeneous subgroups in that the members of one group should react in the same way to marketing stimuli and differ in their reactions to these stimuli from the members of other segments. In other words, it is not sufficient for men and women to be physiologically different. If there is no systematic difference between the two groups in the way they react to marketing stimuli, there is no sound reason to distinguish between them. For example, the furniture market includes different segments such as home and business markets. These segments can be further divided: home markets include student home furniture, design furniture, classic furniture etc.; business markets include, for instance, office furniture (for small/large companies), hotel furniture, etc.

In stage two of the STP process, segmentation variables can be combined to form segmentation profiles. In fact, by combining segmentation variables, multivariate

Table 4.1 Segmenting, targeting and positioning

1 Definition of segmentation criteria
2 Definition of segment profiles
3 Assessment of the attractiveness of segments
4 Selection of target groups
5 Definition of the desired unique position in the mind of targeted consumers

segmentation takes place. Various analytical techniques, such as cluster analysis, conjoint analysis, multidimensional scaling and automatic interaction detection are being used to identify segments on the basis of multiple variables.[1] Once segment profiles have been identified, their attractiveness can be assessed. Segment attractiveness will depend on the size and predicted evolution of sales, buying power and the amount of competition targeted at the same segment.

On the basis of this analysis of attractiveness the marketer will select a number of target groups to focus on, based on their attractiveness and for which the company has relevant strengths. This is called targeting. All further communications objectives, strategies and tactics will be aimed at these specific groups. Hence, the promotional mix may differ depending on the different target markets a company is focussing on in its communications programme. For example, Ikea, the Swedish international 'takeaway' furniture distributor, could target the segment of young home users with a limited budget interested in designer furniture by offering a special designer furniture line. Or it could capitalise on the trend that tele-working and self-employment are increasing and develop a home office furniture line for this targeted segment.

Finally, the company has to define a unique and relevant position for its products in the mind of the target group. Positioning can be defined as the way a product is perceived by the target group on important attributes, the 'place in the mind' a product occupies relative to its competitors. Positioning is a core element of marketing strategy and hence of marketing communications. Indeed, marketing management can be defined as finding and sustaining a unique and defendable image or position for a product. Unlike imitating successful competitors, positioning attempts to claim exclusive 'ownership' of a benefit in the mind of the customer which differentiates it from the competition.[2] This position is the brand or product personality which should always be claimed and supported in the communications strategy.[3] Several examples of successful positioning can be given. Mercedes stands for luxury, Volvo for safety, Miele (dishwashers, washing machines, etc.) for quality, Levi's for the original American jeans, and Duracell batteries for power.

A company's communications can be aimed not only at the targeted group of customers or prospects, but also at other stakeholders. Stakeholders, publics or audiences are secondary target groups. The company does not sell directly to them, but their opinions, attitudes and behaviour are vital to the company's wellbeing in the long run. Examples include shareholders, the media, governments and banks. NCC, one of Scandinavia's leading construction and real estate companies with headquarters in Denmark and offices in Sweden, Norway and Finland has a turnover of about SEK46 billion with 28,000 employees. As it conducts business in many different areas such as telecom infrastructure and road constructions and is quoted on the stock exchange, its corporate communications plan is targeted to employees, government, shareholders and the media.

Market segmentation

Market segmentation is the process of dividing consumers into homogeneous groups, i.e. groups that share needs or react in a comparable way to marketing and communications efforts. Different variables or criteria can be used to segment a market. In Table 4.2, a framework and some examples of variables used to segment consumer markets are

Table 4.2 Consumer market segmentation variables

	Objective	*Inferred (psychographic)*
General	Geographic Demographic (income, gender, age, education, profession, life cycle)	Social class Personality Lifestyle
Specific (behavioural)	Occasion Loyalty status User status Usage rate	Benefit Buyer readiness

presented.[4] Objective segmentation variables are variables that can be measured objectively and straightforwardly. Inferred constructs have to be defined before people can be classified into groups. For instance, the construct 'lifestyle' has to be operationalised before any one consumer can be attributed to a lifestyle group.

General factors are segmentation variables that hold in all behavioural circumstances. A person is always male or female, no matter what buying situation he or she is in. On the basis of specific or behaviour-related variables, consumers can belong to different segments depending on the product class or buying situation concerned. For instance, a person can be a loyal buyer or a heavy user of chocolate or a chocolate brand, but an infrequent and brand-switching consumer of margarine.

Markets can be divided into different geographic segments such as continents, climate, nations, regions or neighbourhoods. Consumer behaviour and buying patterns often denote cultural differences and therefore the place consumers live may require other marketing mix approaches. For instance InBev, one of the biggest international breweries, is selling its Stella lager as an ordinary lager in some European countries such as Belgium and as a premium and more expensive lager in countries such as the UK. This will also imply a different choice of communication tools: sponsoring pop music events to reach the population of students in Belgium while choosing stylish cinema events in Cannes and advertising in glossy trendy magazines such as *The Face* to support the different positioning in the UK. This segmentation method is often combined with other criteria. A marketing area is first defined geographically and subsequently other segments within this broad geographic area are identified.

Demographic segmentation divides the market on the basis of sex, age (see Plate 6), family size, religion, birthplace, race, education, income or social class. These segmentation variables are frequently used, not only because they correlate with other variables such as consumer needs, but also because they are less difficult to measure than others.

For instance, Axe deodorant targets men, promising increased sex appeal in its communications campaign. Diamond targets women in the UK by offering a cheaper car insurance because women are better drivers and female accidents imply less severe damage. Colgate produces strawberry-flavoured toothpaste for children. BMW launched the Compact series for 'smaller' budgets.

Besides differences between younger and older consumers, one can also distinguish between generations or age groups born in a particular period. This makes their buying responses, needs and interests different from those of people of the same age, living in a different time period. Table 4.3 shows characteristics of two generations, i.e. Baby Boomers and Generation X.

Table 4.3 Baby boomers and generation X

Present age	Generation name	Characteristics
40–60	Baby boomers	Luxury, high-quality products, not bargain hunters, less critical of marketing techniques and advertising
30–40	Generation X	High spending, materialistic, ambitious, need for individualism, critical of marketing techniques and advertising

Based on: Herbig, P., Koehler, W. and Day, K. (1993), 'Marketing to the Baby Bust Generation', *Journal of Consumer Marketing*, 10(1), 4–9.

Parental views about advertising to children

Advertising to children has long had a bad reputation and parents are concerned about advertising to children.[5] Burr and Burr[6] have already reported that parents had strong doubts about the honesty of advertising to children and that they displayed a strong degree of cynicism about TV advertising to children and its apparently misleading aspects. Television advertising has been described as manipulative, promoting materialism, stifling creativity and disrupting parent–child relationships.[7] Burr and Burr[8] state that some abuses of advertising are perceived to be unique to child-centred advertising: it manipulates the child, imposes stress and strain on low-income mothers, and arouses desires which would not otherwise be salient. A particularly negative potential effect of children's advertising is the 'pester power' or 'nag factor'.[9] This means that 'advertising encourages children to nag their parents into something that is not good for them, they don't need or the parent cannot afford'.[10] Although in one study 86% of parents say they do not concede to children's demands,[11] it may be a major factor in advertising caused conflicts between parents and children.

Many food ads in children's programmes are perceived to promote unhealthy products (containing too much sugar, fat or salt). The amount of advertising to which children are exposed has the potential to influence children's health attitudes and behaviours.[12] Therefore, besides children's advertising in general, many parents also have negative attitudes towards food advertising in particular. Positive nutritional tendencies lead to objections to TV food advertising aimed at children, and for instance Chan and McNeal[13] concluded that Chinese parents held negative attitudes toward television advertising in general and children's advertising, and food advertising to children in particular, because, according to them, it encourages bad eating habits.

A particular reason for parental concern is that children are being regarded as vulnerable and as not having the cognitive abilities to understand advertising, as well as not being mature enough to make choices that affect them or their health.[14] Although it is widely accepted that children of 5 can understand the difference between a programme and an advertisement, and that, from 8 years onwards, they also understand the commercial intent of advertising,[15] this does not mean they are not influenced by advertising, just like anyone else, and it certainly does not mean that parents feel the same way.

These perceived negative characteristics of children's (food) advertising may only worry parents in so far as they perceive that this advertising has an influence on children. In one study obese children recognised more of the food ads, and there was also a correlation with the amount of food eaten after exposure to ads. The author concluded that exposure to food advertisements promoted consumption.[16] Others claim that advertising is aimed at brand sales, not category sales, and category sales are mostly established long before exposure to ads.[17] Furthermore, 90% of the food is bought by parents, so they control the diet.[18] This leads Young to conclude that 'the route from advertising to obesity is a long and tortuous one'.[19] Although the link between food advertising, eating habits and obesity is unclear, a lot of it promotes (unhealthy) food products, it is claimed to blur the line between diet and nutrition,[20] it is perceived to have the potential to influence children's health attitudes and behaviours.[21] To what extent does this worry parents? Grossbart and Crosby[22] found conflicting evidence on parents' perception of the influence of television advertising on their children. And 20 years later, a UK study involving 1,530 parents also concluded that parents believed children were influenced by advertising, but that they thought that they (the parents) had more influence than ads and that there was a high level of acceptance (as part of modern life).[23] Nevertheless, many parents appear to be actively mediating their children's television viewing behaviour. Many researchers, e.g. Grossbart and Crosby (1984), Nathanson (2001) and Nathanson et al. (2002) have already concluded that parents with negative attitudes towards TV advertising more strictly control their child's viewing behaviour, indicating that they perceive these negative characteristics as influencing children.[24] For instance, Chan and McNeal found that 89% of parents exercise some control over the contents and time of television viewing.[25]

Baby boomers were born in the years immediately after the Second World War. America and Europe in particular saw a huge boom in the number of births in these years. Today the baby boomers are aged between 45 and 65 years and form a large and wealthy group of consumers. As a group they prefer quality products and tend not to look for bargains (unlike their parents), on average they have few children and more women go out to work.[26] This makes the baby boomers an ideal market for luxury and high-quality products, as well as for products for working households: a smaller car meant as the second family car, easy to prepare meals, child minders, etc.

From 1965 to 1980 birth rates in the US and in Europe declined, due *inter alia* to effective contraception and an increased number of divorces, and the people born during this period are referred to as baby busters, generation X or X'ers.[27] Although this segment is smaller than the baby boomers, it is an interesting target market since almost 85% of busters over the age of 15 have a job, but do not seem to be particularly inclined to save much. Furthermore, they often get allowances from their parents, resulting in quite high per capita spending. Baby busters seem to have different characteristics from baby boomers at the same age. First, they hold different values. Baby busters are more materialistic, ambitious and show a greater need for individualism, for keeping their own identity within the society. Second, baby busters have more marketing knowledge, they acknowledge the meaning of marketing and advertising. Third, baby busters as compared to baby boomers are said to be more cynical and more critical of advertising. They reject any attempt to lump them together into a target segment.

Senior consumers are an increasingly important target group with specific characteristics. Here are a number of prejudices and misconceptions regarding seniors as a target group.

Seniors are one large group of non-active people
When marketers think of the mature consumer, they immediately think of hearing aids or false teeth. Of course, there is a part of the senior population, the more dependent part of 75+, who needs these products, but they form only 20% of the total senior population, leaving 80% of the 50+ market very interested in different products and services.

▶

Seniors stop consuming

This is not true. In fact there are a lot of products with a higher penetration rate in the group of seniors than in other demographic groups. Examples are cosmetics (e.g. Nivea launched the Vital line to the 50+ers), but also financial and insurance services. Seniors also have more leisure time which they can use to take cruises or long vacations in 5-star hotels, or they rediscover an old hobby which prompts them to buy certain things. Every consumer market may have opportunities to the target market of mature consumers.

Seniors may harm the brand image

Marketers often fear harming the brand image by addressing it to senior consumers. This can be easily avoided. First, there are some very selective media to use, media that will not be noticed by other demographic groups, for instance *Viover60*, a magazine for seniors in Norway. Second, senior consumers abhor products 'typically directed to a group of seniors'. They explicitly do not want products for older people, because they do not feel old.

Seniors are very brand-loyal

Another prejudice is that a brand should attract its consumers before they are 50, and that older people will not change their preferred brand. This means that marketing efforts to the over 50s will not have any influence and all efforts will be wasted. In a Belgian study among 935 senior consumers, it appeared that 35% of them were very brand loyal, but exactly the same number of them were brand-switchers: 43% indicated that they liked to try out new things. This confirms the findings of Uncles and Ehrenberg, who claim that older consumers are as open to trial or switching as their younger counterparts.[28]

Consumer markets can also be segmented on the basis of household life-cycle criteria. This concept has its origin in sociology in the decade of the 1930s and has been applied in market research since the 1950s. It is founded on the fact that family changes (for instance, marriage, birth and emancipation of children, break-up of the marriage, etc.) affect both income and expenditure of households.[29] Consequently each stage will imply different needs and therefore consumers can be segmented in this manner. Life-cycle segmentation and marketing is extremely popular in the financial sector where CRM software tools (customer relationship marketing: see Chapter 13, Direct marketing) allow marketers to track changes in life cycles of clients as input for a targeted marketing campaign.[30] Studies revealed that the importance attributed to financial choice criteria and financial services varies as consumers pass through the life-cycle stages.[31]

The conceptual framework of household life-cycle stages has been modernised a few times and the most recent consensus is found around the model of Gilly and Ernis (1982) since it excluded only 0.5% of households.[32] Figure 4.1 illustrates this model.

Ninety per cent of men now attend not only their baby's birth, but also the first scan: evidence that men are more involved as parents than ever before. Research published by the equal opportunities commission shows that men undertake one-third of parental childcare in the UK, thanks mainly to the so-called 'swing door' phenomenon. In many families, when dad is home from work, mum is not. She will be out earning her share, leaving her partner in sole charge of the family. A survey in *Management Today* magazine found that three-quarters of men under 55 were likely to attach more importance to their work–life balance than their fathers did. But they are struggling to make that a reality. Almost half of them did not benefit from family-

▶

Figure 4.1 A model of household life cycles

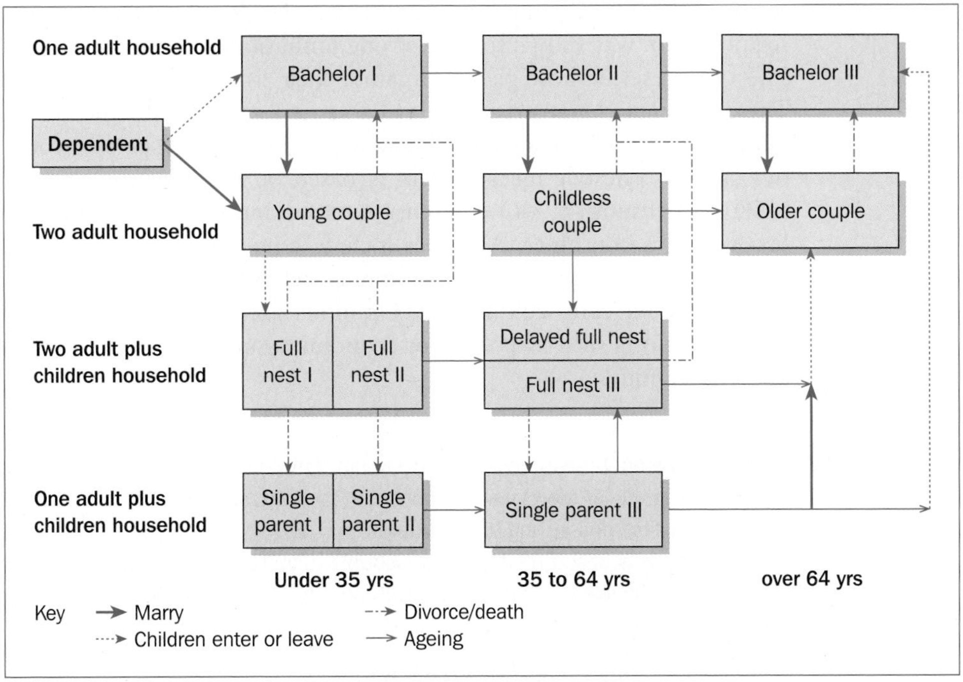

Based on: Gilly, M. and Enis, B. (1982), 'Recycling the Family Life Cycle: A Proposal for Redefinition', in Mitchell, A. (ed.), *Advances in Consumer Research*, 9, Association for Consumer Research, Ann Arbor, MI, 271–6.

friendly policies at work; a third said that work seriously interfered with their private life; a quarter felt as if they had neglected their children recently.

Yet 50% said they would not trade career progression for more time with their family, reflecting, perhaps, feelings of insecurity in the job market. For similar reasons, 20% of fathers work more than 48 hours a week. A survey from the Department of Trade and Industry reveals that employers and working mothers are more willing to embrace flexitime than fathers. But this report coincides with the introduction of paid paternity leave, entitlement to unpaid time off for either parent with children under six, and the right for both sexes to ask employers for flexible work options, which policymakers hope will redress men's perception that work always comes first.

While men can find more objective guides to becoming a parent helpful, those written by female gurus, such as Penelope Leach or Gina Ford, tend to target the mother. Parenting magazines don't hit the spot either. The title of *Mother & Baby*, the bestseller at 80,000 copies a month, says it all. Even the more gender-neutral and culturally hip *Junior* is read largely by women. As for men's lifestyle magazines, there's little attention to self-improvement. Into the vacuum of this knowledge deficit comes *Dad*, created by Show Media, and edited by a founder of Fathers Direct, the national information centre on fatherhood. It is first a men's magazine, but for dads it is entertaining but informative. The first issue (April 2003) is a pilot, available on newsstands throughout the UK but also to be given away to fathers-to-be attending 12-week scans in selected hospitals. From September the distribution will go nationwide twice a year, reaching a potential 670,000 fathers annually, of which 40% are first-timers. Dad's first advertisers are upmarket – among them are Land Rover, Armani and Sony.[33]

Segmenting markets using lifestyle or personality criteria is called psychographic segmentation. Psychographic research was developed when traditional demographic segmentation was shown to have strong limitations in predicting consumer behaviour. Lifestyles describe how people organise their lives and spend their time and money. These external characteristics (playing sports, going to the theatre or restaurant) are linked to a person's personality (for example, a risk-averse person won't take up dangerous sports). Lifestyle measurement is based on the activities, interests and opinions (AIO) of consumers. AIO combines internal and external characteristics to map the life-style of a consumer. Activities include how people spend their money and time, e.g. work, leisure, product use, shopping behaviour, etc. Interests can be in fashion, housing, food, cars, culture, etc. Opinions are attitudes, preferences and ideas on general subjects such as politics or economics, on more specific subjects or on oneself and one's family.

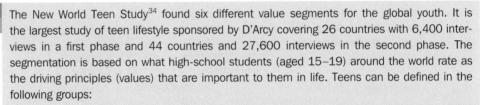

The New World Teen Study[34] found six different value segments for the global youth. It is the largest study of teen lifestyle sponsored by D'Arcy covering 26 countries with 6,400 interviews in a first phase and 44 countries and 27,600 interviews in the second phase. The segmentation is based on what high-school students (aged 15–19) around the world rate as the driving principles (values) that are important to them in life. Teens can be defined in the following groups:

Segment 1: 'Thrills and Chills' (18% worldwide)
This segment is somewhat the stereotype of the trying-to-become-independent hedonist. They have affluent and middle-class parents and have allowance money with which they love to buy 'stuff', not caring about the price for expensive items. They love to go out, meet in pubs and go dating or dancing. They constantly seek out the new, and experimenting is second nature. They are the popular kids in school, the trendsetters that other kids try to copy.

Segment 2: 'Resigned' (14% worldwide)
The resigned have very low expectations and exhibit an inescapable fatalism. They perceive that their lot in the world has already been determined and they are very pessimistic about their chances for economic success. Their looks resemble the ones from the Thrills and Chills segment (lots of body ornaments and colourful hair) but they tend to see the dark side. They come from blue-collar homes, with parents who are factory workers or clerks. The resigned do not participate in many activities outside school; for the resigned the world is grey, and boredom is a major factor.

Segment 3: 'World Savers' (12% worldwide)
This segment consists of the 'good kids', teens that really care about global and local causes, and altruism is the most significant attribute of this value segment. They are doing well in school and are club leaders that join many organisations. They attend the same parties as the Thrills and Chills kids but are not motivated by the new and exciting, rather they are more into romance, relationships and friendships. Grades and higher education are important not only to succeed in finding a better paying job but, more important, to provide careers like doctors, nurses, social workers, environmentalists.

Segment 4: 'Quiet Achievers' (15% worldwide)
Quiet Achievers value anonymity and prefer to stay in the shadows. These teens are the least rebellious of all groups; they study long hours, have strong family ties and realise that ▶

success reflects back upon the family. They avoid going to parties or drinking and have a singular purpose – to study hard and do well in school. Most of the Quiet Achievers live in Asia, especially Thailand and China. The parents of Quiet Achievers have some wealth and they will be keen on investing in computers and other technology that will help with homework.

Segment 5: 'Bootstrappers' (14% worldwide)

Bootstrappers are the starry-eyed optimists who cannot wait for adulthood so they can take the world for all it has to offer. Bootstrappers are highly family-oriented and enjoy spending time with relatives. Their key goal is achievement, but not exclusively scholastic. These teens have hopes and dreams that the world will improve in their lifetime and that they will contribute to this improvement. Geographically, many of the Bootstrapper teens come from emerging nations such as Nigeria, Mexico and India but also comprise 40% of Afro-American teens.

Segment 6: 'Upholders' (16% worldwide)

The Upholders are the most dreamy and childlike teens of the six segments. They are slow to make the leap to adulthood and live sheltered and ordered lives. They are different from the Quiet Achievers in that they do not have overwhelming ambitions to succeed. They are content to rest comfortably in the mainstream of life, remaining unnoticed. The girls want to get married and have families and the boys feel they are fated to have jobs similar to their fathers. Many of these teens will make up the middle-class of their countries. Upholders predominate in Asian countries such as Indonesia and Vietnam that value traditions and extended family relationships.

	Global	France	UK	Spain	Germany	The Netherlands	Turkey	Russia
Thrills and Chills	**18%**	**24%**	**34%**	18%	**37%**	**32%**	**27%**	16%
Resigned	14%	**18%**	**21%**	**21%**	27%	26%	**21%**	12%
World Savers	12%	17%	14%	**24%**	11%	10%	12%	**20%**
Quiet Achievers	15%	9%	8%	7%	4%	7%	5%	**18%**
Bootstrappers	14%	4%	9%	9%	9%	10%	10%	10%
Upholders	**16%**	7%	7%	12%	5%	6%	8%	14%

Note that worldwide, 11% of teenagers could not be classified.

Source: Moses, E. (2000), *The $100 Billion Allowance. Accessing the Global Teen Market*. New York: John Wiley & Sons. © 2000 Wiley. This material is used by permission of John Wiley & Sons, Inc.

When a company divides its market into segments referring to product or brand preferences, or involvement with categories, it adapts a behavioural segmentation. Consumers can be segmented on the basis of the occasion in which they use a product or a brand. For instance, a brand of orange juice can be targeted at a segment of consumers drinking juice at breakfast, but there will also be a segment using orange juice in cocktails in the evening, etc.

Motivational segmentation of young smokers

According to research among 15- and 16-year-old smokers in Sweden, Austria, Poland, Belgium and Scotland, girls smoke to support relationships while boys are more individual smokers. Although many countries prohibit tobacco advertising and different anti-smoking campaigns were launched, the number of youngsters that can't resist a cigarette is still increasing. Remarkable in this evolution is that the growth specifically comes from the girls. People tend

▶

to smoke cigarettes to cope with negative emotions. For boys the predominant emotions they describe are often anger and stress, whereas girls mention a broader range of emotions: not only anger but also frustration, depression and feeling bad. Girls are also definitely more social smokers. They begin their smoking habit influenced by their female peers, share cigarettes to enhance group feelings and support relationships, and tend to smoke only in specific social situations that are linked to a relaxed and cozy atmosphere. The latter is explained by the stigma girls experience when smoking in public. Boys are more individual smokers. They start smoking on their own and don't consider it as a means to stimulate friendship. When asked for negative aspects about smoking, boys stress the effects on their physical fitness while girls feel ashamed that they are considered as 'smokers' and are concerned about the bad smell of cigarettes. The findings of this survey might influence the anti-smoking advertis-ing campaigns. The majority of them focussed on how tobacco affects sporting performance but this study proves that this argument is not well targeted to the growing group of young women.[35]

Markets can also be divided into segments on the basis of customer loyalty. Customers can be loyal to one brand, loyal to a set of brands, or brand-switchers. Obviously, marketing communications efforts can be different when targeting these different groups. Brand-switchers are mainly influenced by material incentives. Sales promotions will therefore be an important tool to get them to buy a product. Brand loyals, on the other hand, do not have to be convinced. Advertising to keep the brand top-of-mind, and loyalty promotions will be the main communications instruments to be used with this group. Consumers that are loyal to a set of brands will have to be approached with a combination of communications tools. Advertising will keep the company's brand in their choice set, while in-store communications and sales promotions will make them choose the company's brand rather than competing brands.

Markets can also be segmented on the basis of the user status of customers. An individual can be a non-user, a potential user, a first-time user, a regular user or an ex-user. Non-users are consumers who will never buy a product. They should therefore be avoided in a marketing communications plan. Men, for example, will never buy sanitary towels for themselves. As a result, a communications plan should avoid talking to them as much as possible. Ex-users are more a target group for customer satisfaction research than for a marketing communications campaign. It will be very hard to regain a customer who has deliberately decided not to use the product anymore. Potential users need to be persuaded to try the product for the first time. Advertising, building awareness and attitude, trial promotions and in-store communications may convince them to have a go. First-time users should be converted into regular users. Advertising, building a favourable attitude and a preference for the brand, together with loyalty promotions, might do the job. Regular users should be confirmed in their favourable attitude and buying behaviour. They may be approached by means of advertising and loyalty promotions.

Markets can also be segmented on the basis of usage rate. Heavy users are of particular interest to the company because they make up the largest part of sales. Light users may be persuaded to buy and consume more of the product by means of special offers or 'basket-filling' promotions, increasing the number of items they buy.

Segmenting on the basis of benefits looked for by consumers can be done by researching all benefits applicable to a certain product category, e.g. a salty snack should be crunchy, taste good and not be expensive. For each of these benefits consumers preferring that benefit are identified and for each benefit products or brands offering that benefit are defined. This segmentation links psychographic, demographic and behavioural variables. A specific benefit for which a brand has a unique strength can be defined, and the communications effort can be targeted at the customer group preferring that particular benefit. As such, benefit segmentation is conceptually very close to positioning.

Finally, consumers can be divided into more homogeneous subgroups on the basis of their buyer readiness. When a potential customer is unaware of a brand, awareness-building advertising and sponsorship will have to be used. For a group of customers already aware of the product, attitude building campaigns are called for. People who are interested in and like the product should be persuaded to try it by means of sales promotions and in-store communications.

Similarly, variables that can be a basis for segmenting industrial or business-to-business marketing can be defined. They are summarised in Table 4.4.[36]

Table 4.4 Business-to-business market segmentation variables

Demographics	Operating variables	Purchasing approaches
■ Industry	■ Technology	■ Purchasing function organisations
■ Company size	■ User/non-user status	■ Power structure
■ Location	■ Customer capabilities	■ Nature of existing relationships
Situational factors	**Personal characteristics**	■ General purchase policies
■ Urgency	■ Buyer/seller similarity	■ Purchasing criteria
■ Specific application	■ Attitudes towards risk	
■ Size of order	■ Loyalty	

Source: Bonoma, V. and Shapiro, B.P. (1983), *Segmenting the Industrial Marketing*. Lexington, MA: Lexington Books. Reproduced with permission.

Requirements for effective segmentation

In stage two of the STP process, segmentation variables can be combined to form segmentation profiles. Segment profiles have to meet a number of requirements to be effective (Figure 4.2). Segments have to be measurable. It should be possible to gather information about segmentation criteria and about the size, composition and purchasing power of each segment. Segments have to be substantial enough to warrant separate and profitable marketing campaigns to be developed particularly for that segment. Segment profiles have to be attainable, i.e. accessible and actionable. The marketing manager must be able to identify the segment members and target the marketing action programme at them separately. Unless most members of the segment visit similar places, shop in similar supermarkets or read similar media, it will be difficult to reach them separately and develop specific stimuli for them. In other words, the chosen segments must be in reach of communications media and distribution channels. Finally, market segmentation should ideally lead to more homogeneous subgroups in that the members of one group should react similarly to marketing stimuli and differ in their reactions to these stimuli from the members of other segments.

Figure 4.2 Requirements for effective segmentation

```
         Attainable              Measurable


                    Effective
                  segmentation


                                    Large
         Different                  enough
```

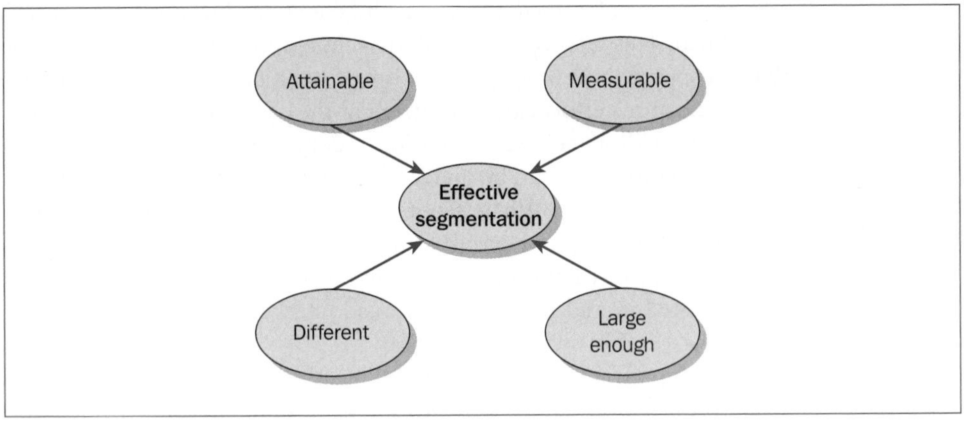

Nike Goddess targeting active women

In its 30-year history, Nike has become one of the undisputed leaders in sport marketing. But although the company is named after a woman – the Greek goddess of victory – until recently 80% of Nike's sales figures came from male customers, even though the market of women's sports apparel had been skyrocketing. According to the NPD Group, women's sports apparel generated sales of more than $15 billion in 2001, $3 billion more than men's apparel. According to data from MRI, today's physically active women are more affluent and more educated than the average woman. Given that the girls who engage in sports or fitness activities at least twice a month are relatively well educated (most have at least a college degree and many have post-graduate degrees as well), it's not surprising that they tend to occupy professional, executive or managerial positions at work and have household incomes of more than €60,000. Not all active women are 18 years old, in fact the most active group of women is 25 to 34 years old.

Considering these evolutions and the increasing popularity of top female athletes, Nike decided to wake up to the women's business and start doing things differently. Until 2002 advertisement campaigns and sponsorship of female athletes weren't enough to target the segment of active women. Since 1986 Nike developed basket-ball shoes for female feet but with moderate success. Now Nike aims to augment sales to women to at least one-third of its yearly return. Nike Goddess initially began as a concept for a women's-only store because Niketown, the retail setting for which the company is best known, is also known to be a turnoff to female customers. The women's section is on the fourth floor. At each floor, women looking for workout shoes or a yoga mat have to wade through displays for basketball, golf and hockey to catch the next escalator up. The feel of the store is dark, loud and harsh. Women weren't comfortable in Nike's flagship stores. As women seem to be more comfortable in an environment that resembles their own homes, Nike Goddess stores have more of a residential feel, with furnishings. At the first Nike Goddess store, located in Newport Beach, California, the mood fits; it has light-blue and white colours, with dark wood floors. Milky-white mannequins with muscles fill the floor-to-ceiling windows. Shoes are displayed on tables or wooden shelves alongside pieces of pottery and white orchids. Overnight, the store can be overhauled to focus on a specific sport or trend – whatever is fashionable for the times.

▶

Designing a new approach to retail was only one element in Nike's effort to connect with women. Another was redesigning the shoes and clothes. Nike's footwear designers worked on 18-month production cycles – making it hard to stay in step with the new styles and colours for women. The apparel group, which worked around 12-month cycles, was better at keeping up with fashion trends but that meant that the clothes weren't co-ordinated with the shoes – a big turnoff for women. The company appointed fashion designers to enlarge the collections and make them more female. On the product development side of the movement towards a more female positioning, Nike introduced the Air Kyoto, the first shoe for yoga (normally practiced in bare feet). Martin Lotti, the Swiss designer who created Air Max Craze and Spector was also the creative brain behind the Kyoto yoga shoe. The upper side of the shoe looks like both sides of a kimono and the sole is black with orange lines that reflect the sand in the Kyoto Zen garden. According to Lotti there are some differences in shoe design for women: the shape of women's feet is different (smaller heel) and as women weigh on average 20% less than men, the shoe soles must be softer and thinner. Darcy Winslow, Nike's global footwear director for women, says the Air Kyoto is the first step in a new journey for women's products at Nike – away from testosterone and a focus on competition and results.

One key insight Nike understood is that for most women, high performance isn't about sports; it's about fitness and about a woman's active nomadic lifestyle. Women go from doing yoga in the morning, to work, to picking up the kids, to going for a run. Nike Goddess has to fit into that kind of life. That's why Nike designers and researchers have spent time scouring trendy workout spots like London's Third Space to pick up on new fitness trends that it calls the '21st-century gym'. And some of the company's designs don't involve workout gear at all, but everyday's clothing.

The last step in the female repositioning was communicating the new values and style. For much of its history, Nike either treated women like men in advertising or didn't think much about them at all. Sometimes, though, Nike got the voice right. Back in 1995, the company ran a campaign titled 'If You Let Me Play' that struck a nerve with most women, who had grown up believing 'I could do anything boys could do'. The campaign featured female athletes talking about how sports could change women's lives, from reducing teen pregnancy to increasing their chances of getting a college education. Nike Goddess had to strike a similar chord with women and be more personal than Nike's traditional ads. Nike launched a dedicated website (www.nikegoddess.com, where apart from a forum, a 30-minutes workout mp3 mix is available for free downloading) and 'magalogs' (catalogues in a magazine format) with titles such as 'The Book of Lies', 'The Art of Contradiction' and 'The Encyclopedia of Addictions'. These 'magalogs' presented short picture stories with models wearing the Nike Goddess collection and became extremely popular among women because of their humoristic and recognisable storylines in Bridget Jones style. For instance, one shows pictures of a girl looking at herself in the mirror of a dressing room and thinking: 'I've been sporting 35 minutes. I've spent 2 hours hesitating whether I would or would not sport tonight. So I've been busy with sporting for 2 hours and 35 minutes. A great improvement!'[37]

Targeting

After segmenting the market, opportunities for each segment should be singled out. The next stage in the process is targeting segments.[38] There are two decisions here: how many segments will the company target, and which segments are most attractive to that company?

Targeting strategies

Market concentration is used when the company chooses one segment and tries to be a market leader within that segment. Market differentiation involves directing the marketing effort to different segments with different marketing and communications strategies. Undifferentiated marketing is using the same strategies to all segments. There are five basic types of targeting strategies.

- **Concentration on one segment**: a company chooses one segment (one product for one market) and develops a marketing mix for that segment. This strategy has some positive aspects. The company will be able to build up expertise and enjoy learning effects. On the other hand, it will be dependent on a single segment (which could suddenly stop growing) and vulnerable to competitors. For instance, Jaguar was a company concentrating on one segment until it was acquired by Ford.

- **Selective specialisation**: a company chooses a number of segments that look attractive. There is no synergy between the segments but every segment looks profitable. Activities in one segment can compensate for other, slower-growing segments. For instance, Richard Branson started with a music label (Virgin) which he sold while launching new services in different segments: travel (holidays, trains, flights and travel guides), entertainment (a new music label V2, virgin megastores, books, radio and internet service providing), telecom (mobile and fixed lines), lifestyle (soft drinks, wines, cosmetics and fitness clubs), energy (water, gas and electricity), finance (credit cards, loans, insurances . . .) and motoring (retailing of cars ands bikes).

- **Product specialisation**: a company concentrates on one product and sells it to different market segments. For instance, a company can sell microscopes to companies, hospitals, universities, schools, labs, etc.

- **Market specialisation**: a company concentrates on one market segment and sells different products to that group of customers, e.g. a company selling microscopes, oscilloscopes, etc.

- **Full market coverage**: a company tries to target all customer groups with all the products they need. For instance, General Motors makes cars (in different classes), four-wheel drive cars, vans, agricultural machines, etc.

The Prosumer: the proactive consumer who is not in a hurry

The term Prosumer was first used by Alvin Toffler in his book *The Third Wave*, 25 years ago. Today this new consumer seems to have officially surfaced. Prosumers want to know, test and compare everything, and judge for themselves. Nobody tells them how to live, eat, wear or listen to. 'Go slow' is their credo. The bombardment of products, chances, obligations, trends, fads and opinions are irrelevant to them. They don't care about the label, and hate pushy marketing communication. The proactive consumer actively develops his own world with the help of companies he/she trusts and new players he/she likes, and with which they build a firm relationship. They read product labels, actively seek new products, discuss about them with other consumers, are responsible for buzz and have an active radar for launching new trends. The advertising agency Euro RSCG estimates that already 25% of the European consumers are Prosumers, and that they have been instrumental in many of the new trends of recent years,

▶

such as exercising more and eating more healthily, do-it-yourself, and more assertive patient–doctor relationships. Consequently, building a relationship with these consumers has become increasingly important: shops have longer opening hours, products are tailor-made, price competition has increased, and the internet plays an increasingly important role. Similar to their ancestors, Prosumers want to belong to 'tribes', hence the success of book clubs, new religious groups, but also product-related communities such as the 'iPod clan'. Prosumers identify themselves with peers on the basis of the shared meaning they attach to products and product attributes (such as the white iPod headsets).

Source: De Morgen, 8 January 2005.

Selecting the right target groups

The second decision is to select the most attractive target groups. To evaluate segments companies have to look at four elements: size and growth of segments, structural attractiveness of a segment, objectives and budgets of a company, and stability of market segments. Current turnover, potential growth and profitability of segments are the first important conditions a marketer should evaluate for each segment. For small companies it could be wiser to target smaller or less attractive niche segments when competition is strong in the larger segments. Structural attractiveness can be analysed by using Porter's model. Current competitors, potential entrants, substitution products, and the power of customers and suppliers influence the attractiveness of segments. Some attractive segments may not fit with the strategic objectives or long-term goals of a company.

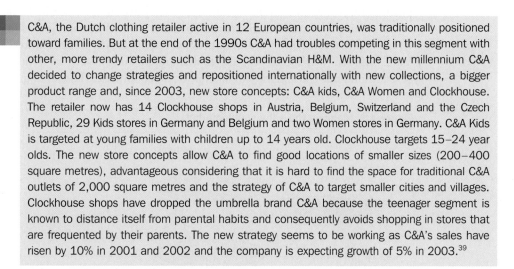

C&A, the Dutch clothing retailer active in 12 European countries, was traditionally positioned toward families. But at the end of the 1990s C&A had troubles competing in this segment with other, more trendy retailers such as the Scandinavian H&M. With the new millennium C&A decided to change strategies and repositioned internationally with new collections, a bigger product range and, since 2003, new store concepts: C&A kids, C&A Women and Clockhouse. The retailer now has 14 Clockhouse shops in Austria, Belgium, Switzerland and the Czech Republic, 29 Kids stores in Germany and Belgium and two Women stores in Germany. C&A Kids is targeted at young families with children up to 14 years old. Clockhouse targets 15–24 year olds. The new store concepts allow C&A to find good locations of smaller sizes (200–400 square metres), advantageous considering that it is hard to find the space for traditional C&A outlets of 2,000 square metres and the strategy of C&A to target smaller cities and villages. Clockhouse shops have dropped the umbrella brand C&A because the teenager segment is known to distance itself from parental habits and consequently avoids shopping in stores that are frequented by their parents. The new strategy seems to be working as C&A's sales have risen by 10% in 2001 and 2002 and the company is expecting growth of 5% in 2003.[39]

Positioning

Positioning a brand or product is differentiating it from competitors in the mind of consumers, e.g. Volvo is a safe car, Duracell batteries last longer, etc. Positioning means taking into account a complicated set of perceptions, feelings and impressions a consumer has about a brand or product. Consumers will position brands in certain associative schemes even if a company is not actively promoting the competitive advantage of its products.

Positioning strategies

Six basic questions should be asked when creating a market position:[40]

1 What position, if any, do we already have in our customer's or prospect's mind?
2 What position do we want?
3 What companies must be outgunned if we are to establish that position?
4 Do we have enough marketing budget to occupy and hold that position?
5 Do we have the guts to stick with one consistent positioning strategy?
6 Does our creative approach match our positioning strategy?

A frequently used visual tool that helps companies position products and brands is 'mapping', based on axes representing the dimensions important to consumers. Every product or brand is given a score on both dimensions and the map shows which products or brands have the same characteristics. Figure 4.3 is a map of the salty snacks market. In the eyes of a consumer, there seems to be a big difference between peanuts and cocktail snack nuts. The latter are competing with fantasy snacks (snacks in different shapes). There's no product considered as natural and different. This is a hole in the market, but to be attractive it should be a profitable hole. There are a number of positioning strategies a company can use.[41] They are summarised in Table 4.5.

Positioning by product **attributes and benefits** is based on a unique selling proposition which makes a company's brand or product special for the target market. For example, Vidal Sassoon Wash&Go was the first shampoo (introduced by Procter & Gamble) offering a unique combination of shampoo and conditioner. Positioning by price/quality

Figure 4.3 Mapping the salty snack market

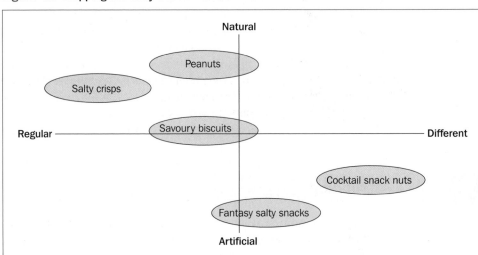

Table 4.5 Positioning strategies

■ Product attributes or benefits	■ Product user
■ Price/quality	■ Competitor
■ Use or application	■ Cultural symbols
■ Product class	

means offering the same or better quality at a lower price than competitors. For instance, Virgin Coke offers a 'good' coke with a brand image comparable to Coca-Cola and Pepsi but at a lower price. Positioning by use or application implies emphasising a specific use or application of the product. For instance, Kellogg's introduced cereals as a snack at hours other than breakfast by offering little variety packages that kids can take to school. Positioning by product class is an alternative to positioning against another brand, e.g. Eurostar offers a fast train connection as an alternative to airline connections. Positioning by product user is associating a product with a specific group of users, e.g. Aquarius, a thirst-quenching isotone drink for sporting men and women, is positioning a brand by a group of product users. In positioning by competitor, comparative advertising is often used. A well-known example is Avis, who use the slogan 'we try harder', to position itself against the market leader in car and truck rental, Hertz. 7-up was positioned as 'the un-cola' and became number three in the soft drinks market. Cultural symbols refer to brand personalities or branding devices such as Tony the Tiger (Kellogg's Frosties), Mr Clean, Captain Iglo, Bibendum (Michelin). These symbols are a visual way of successfully differentiating from competitors. The brand personality or cultural symbol often visualises the key benefit of a product. For instance, Mr Clean is a powerful, clean symbol. Tony the Tiger gives power and strength.

A company may possibly detect different competitive edges, in which case it will have to choose one or more competitive advantages for its positioning strategy. A company can focus on one single advantage for a target group. This exclusive Unique Selling Proposition (USP) will be easier to remember by the target group, especially in low-involvement buying situations. Other companies will stress more than one competitive advantage. This is necessary when two or more competitors claim to be the best in the same attributes. Volvo, for example, claims to be both safe and durable.

Not all differences with competitors are meaningful for an effective differentiation. Every difference could mean an increase in costs to a company, therefore the way a company differentiates its products and brands should be well considered. The chosen USP(s) should be important to the target group, clearly different from what a competitor is offering, superior, easy to communicate, difficult to imitate or copy, affordable for the target group of consumers and profitable for the company.

The more claims a company makes about its brands, the greater the risk of disbelief. Moreover, the different product benefits should be compatible in a consumer's mind: a super-strong detergent that also claims to be mild for the hands won't have any credibility.

There are indeed three possible positioning mistakes a company or brand can make:

■ Underpositioning: a company fails to make a clear differentiation with competitors, e.g. Korean car brands such as Kia or Hyundai: how do they position themselves against Japanese or European cars?

- Overpositioning: extreme positioning on one benefit will reduce the number of interested consumers, e.g. if Ikea only claimed low prices and not quality (Möbelfakta guarantee, for example), Ikea would deter people looking for a durable dining room suite.
- Confusing positioning: inconsistent communications or an inconsistent choice of distribution channels would give a customer a confused image of a company or brand. For example, bath towels claiming exclusive quality but also sold in hypermarkets will have difficulty keeping their positioning.

Developing a positioning strategy

There are seven consecutive steps in the development of a positioning strategy (Table 4.6). First, the company has to identify its major competitors. This competition analysis should go further than the brands in exactly the same product category, but should also include generic competition, i.e. products in different product categories that nevertheless satisfy the same need. For instance, a gift box of chocolates (e.g. Ferrero) is competing not only with other chocolate gift boxes but also with wine, champagne and flowers, which people take when visiting friends or relations. All possible competitors and their effects and evolutions on consumer target group behaviour should be taken into account. Second, the consumers' perception of the products and brands of competitors should be assessed. Questions such as which attributes or benefits are important in this market segment and how is a competitor's product or brand evaluated on these criteria are important.

Determining the positions of competitors' brands and products with respect to each of the relevant attributes is the third step in a positioning development. Consumer research through in-depth interviews, focus groups or full quantitative assessment should be used in this stage. Often, this analysis leads to a 'map' of consumers' perceptions about the relative position of each brand, as illustrated in Figure 4.3. It is not just the relative position of each brand that is important. Each of the targeted segments may have different buying motives or needs and will find other attributes important. Therefore, relative preferences of target groups towards the competing brands have to be studied.

After the first four stages of what is essentially market and consumer research, the company has to decide which position it is going to defend. Ideally, the company will select a position on the basis of one or more attributes that are important in the mind of a consumer and for which the brand is at least as strong as its major competitors. As a positioning decision should be a brand's direction for a number of years, a marketer should consider whether the positioning is appropriate and attainable. Positioning should be based on important attributes, not on fads, and on attributes for which the

Table 4.6 Stages in the development of a positioning strategy

- Identification of competitors
- Assessment of the consumers' perception of competitors
- Determination of positions of competitors
- Analysis of consumers' preferences
- The positioning decision
- Implementation of the positioning
- Monitoring the position

company can hope to defend and maintain its relative strength and reputation. Once a position is chosen, a company has to implement it by supportive marketing and communications activities. All communications instruments, in synergy with all other marketing tools, will have to reflect the selected positioning strategy. The last step in the positioning process is the monitoring stage. The image of the brand and its competitors on important attributes will have to be tracked on a continuous basis to reveal changes in consumer perceptions and in the competitors' positions.

As a result of this tracking analysis, a company may have to alter the position of its brands to keep up with the changing consumer or competitive landscape. There are a number of ways to change a positioning strategy or to reposition a brand:[42]

- *A company can introduce a new brand.* For instance, after major price cuts in the PC branch IBM introduced a new brand 'Ambra' to be competitive in a new context of consumers expecting cheap computers for daily use. Procter & Gamble reintroduced their old Bonux brand as a cheaper laundry powder to fight the competition of own-label brands.

- *A company can change an existing brand.* Compaq used a different strategy to cope with the changing computer trend. Compaq lowered the prices of its existing brand and made basic versions of its computers.

- *Changing the beliefs with regard to the own brand benefits.* Japanese car brands such as Honda and Toyota changed their image of cheap, small and poor-quality cars to an excellent price/quality appreciation.

- *Companies may also attempt to change the beliefs with regard to the benefits of competing brands.* The Body Shop created a less environmentally friendly and animal-friendly image about the cosmetic products of competitors.

- *The importance of attributes may be changed.* Volvo succeeded in increasing the importance of safety as a car attribute.

- Finally, a company can try to *add new attributes to the 'perceptual map' of consumers.* Procter & Gamble introduced the Vizirette to measure out the amount of detergents used in washing machines by explaining to the public that it would improve washing results.

The latter four repositioning strategies are based on the components of the Fishbein model, discussed in Chapter 3. Defending a brand position or image will often be one of the major objectives of a communications campaign. Marketing communications objectives are further explored in the next chapter.

In 1950 Monte Goldman founded Eastpak, originally as Eastern Canvas Products, Inc. The company produced big durable bags that had to survive wars. When Mark Goldman joined his father's company, he convinced him to start making practical bags targeted to students. Not just school bags but comfortable bags for life, with padded backs and organiser pockets for all the things students carry with them through the day. The Eastpak brand name was introduced in 1979 with the mission statement 'to offer authentic, functional backpacks guaranteed for life with progressive designs for the mobile youth' and sold 1,000 pieces in the first year. In 2000 Eastpak sold almost four million backpacks in Europe accounting for €80 million sales. The Eastpak main target group is between 15 and 18 years old. Eastpak is the favourite

▶

backpack for the cool, progressive and trendsetting segment of skaters. About 60% of the skaters segment wants to own an Eastpak. Eastpak's brand values can be summarised as authentic, resistant, unique and naturally cool. In advertising campaigns (see Plate 9) the focus is always on the product and on the durability aspect. The target group itself is never incorporated in the ads because the group of teens does not have role models or popular celebrities. Advertising campaigns have always been on the edge: a cemetery full of back-packs, a skeleton wearing an Eastpak in the desert, dogs standing in a row to make love with the backpack, etc. Above-the-line communications only account for 45% of the brand's communications budget. All other marketing communications are strictly linked to the interest of the target group, for instance skating and BMX events.[43]

Primary and secondary target groups

Communications are seldom limited to primary marketing target groups. An organisation wants to communicate with its customers, but also with other stakeholders, publics or audiences. These groups are called secondary target groups. Stakeholders are 'any group or individual who can affect or is affected by the achievement of an organisation's purpose'.[44] Stakeholders may be internal to an organisation, such as employees, unions or managers, or external, such as authorities, governement, competitors, suppliers, shareholders and customers. An organisation should assess the importance of the different publics influen-cing its operations. Stakeholder analysis determines who has a stake in the organisation and what their motivations and aims are. There are three different possible sources for a stake in a company. The first is based on an equity in the organisation; the second is a market exchange-based relationship; and the third is a stake based on other than marketplace-related influences. These represent the vertical dimension in Table 4.7. The horizontal dimension of this table reflects the type of power stakeholders have in an organisation: this can be formal power to control actions, economic power to influence markets important to the organisation or political power through legislations and regulations.

Stakeholders are important target groups when developing a public relations or a corporate communications campaign. They will be discussed in more depth in Chapter 10 (Public relations).

Table 4.7 Stakeholders

	Equity-based	Exchange-based	Other
Equity	Shareholders Directors Minority interests	Employee/owners	Dissident shareholders
Economic	Preferred debt holders	Suppliers Debt holders Customers Employees Competitors	European Union Local government Foreign governments Consumer lobbies Unions
Influencers	Outside directors Licensing bodies	Regulatory agencies	Trade associations Environmental groups

Besides stakeholders, the company also has to pay attention to groups of people that are important influencers of the target group's buying decisions. For example, a manufacturer of Havana cigars will not only target cigar smokers (primary target group) but also peers, friends and housemates of cigar smokers (in this example also secondary target groups). These persons will have to accept the smoking of the targeted smoker and they will have to recognise the exclusivity of the brand. A cigar smoker will only be satisfied if his acquaintances appreciate his cigars.

Summary

The segmenting-targeting-positioning process is one of the core elements of the strategic marketing plan. Market segmentation is the process of dividing consumers into homogeneous segment profiles. This can be done on the basis of one characteristic of potential consumers, or multiple characteristics can be combined. Segmentation criteria can be behavioural-related, such as buying occasion, loyalty status, usage rate, buyer readiness or benefit sought, or general, such as demographics and psychographics (lifestyle, personality, etc.). Market segments have to be measurable, substantial, attainable, different and large enough. The next stage in the process is to target one or more of these customer groups. Marketing communications can concentrate on one segment, specialise selectively, specialise in specific markets or products, or fully cover the market. Marketers have to define a unique position for their products in the mind of the consumer, based on product attributes or benefits, price/quality, use or application, product class, product users, competitors or cultural symbols. Developing, monitoring and adapting an appropriate position for a brand, a product or a company is a crucial prerequisite for effective marketing communications. Finally, the communications effort can be directed to corporate target groups, such as shareholders, governments, pressure groups, employees and the media.

Review questions

1 What are the stages in the segmenting-targeting-positioning process, and what is the relevance of this process for marketing communications?

2 On the basis of what criteria can markets be segmented? How can market segmentation influence the communications mix?

3 What are segment profiles, and what are the requirements for effective segmentation?

4 Discuss the most important targeting strategies and the selection of target groups.

5 What positioning strategies can a company develop, and what are the consequences for communications strategies?

6 What are the stages in the development of a positioning strategy?

7 How can a product be repositioned?

8 What are secondary target groups and in what respect can they be important for marketing communications?

Further reading

Dibb, S. and Simkin, L. (1996), *The Market Segmentation Workbook. Target Marketing for Marketing Managers.* London: Routledge.

Hooley, G., Saunders, J. and Piercy, N. (2003), *Marketing Strategy and Competitive Positioning.* London: Financial Times Prentice Hall.

Morgan, C. and Levy, D. (2002), *Marketing to the Mindset of Boomers and Their Elders: Using Psychographics and More to Identify and Reach Your Best Targets.* Ithaca, NY: Paramount Market Pub.

Ries, A. and Trout, J. (2001), *Positioning: The Battle for Your Mind.* New York: McGraw-Hill.

Trout, J. (2001), *Differentiate or Die: Survival in Our Era of Killer Competition.* New York: John Wiley & Sons.

Wedel, M. and Kamakura, W. (1999), *Market Segmentation: Conceptual and Methodological Foundations.* Norwell, MA: Kluwer Academic Press.

Case 4

Electrolux: taking care of new born babies and their parents

Electrolux

Electrolux was established in 1919, and has since then evolved into a world leading producer of powered appliances for kitchen and cleaning products, such as refrigerators, washing machines, cookers and vacuum cleaners for both consumer and professional use. Total group sales in 2005 were SEK129.5 billion (approximately 13.9 billion euros), an increase of about 4% compared to the previous year. About 40% of sales are effectuated in Western Europe, and another 40% in North America. In 2005 Electrolux counts 70,000 employees, 30,000 of whom work in Western Europe, and another 21,000 in North America. The company is a market leader in many of the individual product categories in which it competes. In 2005 the Electrolux market share accounted for some 20% in Europe. In the US, the company is the third largest producer with a market share of approximately 23%. Electrolux markets a number of well-known brands, amongst which Electrolux, Electrolux-AEG, and Zanussi in Europe, and Electrolux, Eureka and Frigidaire in the US.

One of the key drivers of the strategy of Electrolux is consumer insight. As CEO and President of Electrolux has stated: 'we focus on really understanding consumer needs and problems related to household work. By increasing our consumer insight, we are able to develop even more new products that solve these needs and problems.' The Electrolux Baby Brochure project fits into this core strategic focus.

The Baby Brochure project

An average consumer has several key triggers in his or her lifetime that drive them to buy a particular or collection of appliances (Case Figure 4.1). 'Being there' when these occur by exposing the brand in a supportive and positive manner will help drive consumers towards the Electrolux brand. In 2004, Electrolux decided to focus on one of these triggers and to launch a practical guide for young families with new babies. Having a new baby can be both rewarding and demanding, and many new parents often remain uncertain of how their appliances can help them meet these new challenges. With the birth of a child, most young parents experience a shift in the way they see the world, as their day-to-day schedules become more complex and the need for support in the household increases. The intention was to produce an extensive booklet that would provide in-depth and practical information related to effective, efficient and safe use of household appliances on

Case Figure 4.1 Overview of key triggers to buy appliances

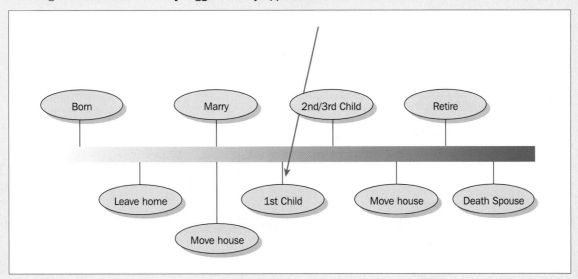

everything from cooking to washing for babies and effective dust and mite reduction to the best way of destroying harmful bacteria around the house. The brochure had to cover a wide range of topics aimed at helping new parents improve their knowledge of household appliances and care for their child: what temperatures baby's clothes should be washed, how to best store breast milk in a deep freezer and how to warm up baby's milk or food. (See Plate 5.) In brief, the intention of the company was to provide added value to new parents through much needed and desired information via an easy to use and keep booklet. The project was also a differentiation opportunity for the company, since no other appliance manufacturer has taken this initiative for this target group of consumers. Moreover, the brochure fits perfectly with the Electrolux 'thinking of you' brand essence, reflecting the brand's commitment to its consumers as it provides new families with effective and useful information at a time of need.

Content and approach

The title of the brochure is 'Enjoy New Life. An appliance guide for baby care'. The information provided is based on household appliance functions (e.g. cooling, heating, freezing, washing . . .) rather than the actual product itself. Information includes hints and tips on saving time, child's health (how long to boil, freeze, cool . . .), interesting facts and figures, advice on what (not) to do, sample recipes,

and reminders to Mum on how to take care of herself too . . . The idea is to provide credible and useful information in a format that allows for both reading (during the time spent in hospital, for instance) and reference in the future (easy to consult). To link in with the 'new baby' feeling, the booklet is produced in the format of a children's book, i.e. hardboard glossy pages which can be kept for references on shelves, etc. Moreover it is 'droolproof'. In order to boost Electrolux's credibility towards this specific target audience, the company looked for high-profile endorsers. The brochure was distributed worldwide through Electrolux's global PR network who had the opportunity to translate and adapt the content for local use (for instance, to meet local regulations and laws), and then printed centrally to lower costs. Each country could choose whether or not to pursue its use, in what numbers, etc. based on local insight. The timeline of the project is given in Case Figure 4.2.

Target groups and communication and distribution strategy

The target groups of the new brochure are all mothers and fathers of new-born babies worldwide. The communication strategy was not primarily to send the brochures to parents directly, but to distribute them via a variety of channels and endorsers that would also leverage the impact of the initiative. Moreover, the PR departments were

Case Figure 4.2 Timeline of the Baby Brochure project

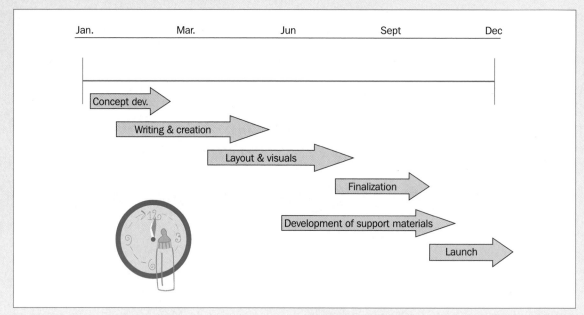

provided with a standard press release about the brochure that could be easily adapted to the local situation. The target groups of the campaign were therefore intermediaries and media. As far as the intermediaries were concerned, the following outlets were targeted:

■ Networks which own and distributes new mother info and sample packs in hospitals

■ Paediatric offices by providing large volumes to paediatric associations, gynaecologists and day-care centres

■ Family organisations, planning centres . . .

■ Retail chains for household appliances and chains of baby shops and supermarkets

■ Provide with appliances

■ Promo-team events

■ Ad as a free bonus to magazines

■ Electronic format downloads on baby websites, chat sites, info sites . . .

■ Internal distribution to staff expecting a new child.

The brochure was also distributed to the press in CD-Rom format, allowing journalists to use text and images freely. Target media were: family magazines, women's magazines, men's magazines, baby and birth magazines, health magazines, relevant sections in daily newspapers (e.g. weekend edition), and online (baby/birth sites, etc.). Additionally, the brochure was also sent directly to consumers upon request, for instance after press coverage. Barter trades were organised with relevant media providing free brochures to readers through, for instance, competitions. The target group and communication/distribution is summarised in Case Figure 4.3.

Supporting activities

The launch of the brochure was supported by an integrated marketing communications campaign. Some of these materials were provided in standardised formats, others were suggested as possible actions to accompany the roll-out, allowing countries to buy into the existing setup to suit their own local needs, yet keeping design and layout centralised. Local markets would pay for production, but layout and design was covered centrally.

All local PR divisions received press packs and printed and electronic versions of the brochure and its components (pictures, drawings . . .).

Furthermore, local branches were allowed to add reduction coupons, or provide consumer contact

Case Figure 4.3 Communication and distribution channels for the Baby Care brochure

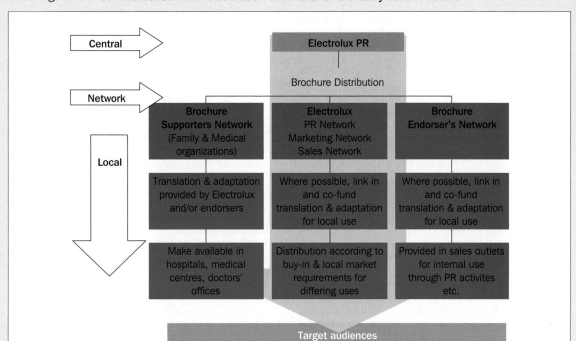

and information data (telephone, e-mail . . .). The brochure could be posted on local relevant websites, activities could be organised with recognised and leading family or medical ambassadors (e.g., paediatrician). For instance, a top-level paediatrician from the University of Brussels approved all the information in the brochure. Activities could be organised with the medical sector (for instance, temporary advice numbers to medical specialists).

The Results

■ The total circulation of the Electrolux Baby Brochure to date (April 2006) amounts to 800,000 copies. By the end of 2006, circulation is expected to reach 1.1 million print copies

■ The Electrolux Baby Brochure has been used in 17 markets so far: Belgium, Croatia, Egypt, Estonia, Germany, Greece, Hungary, Latvia, Lebanon, Lithuania, Poland, Romania, Slovenia, Spain and Turkey

■ Finland, Russia, Kazakhstan and Australia are expected to launch the Baby Brochure in 2006

■ China, The Netherlands and Portugal plan to launch it in 2007

■ In addition, a new upgraded baby website was up and running in May 2006 in 19 languages.

Questions

1 Which segmentation logic did Electrolux use to select the final target group of the Baby care project?

2 Is the approach and concept of the Baby care project supportive for the Electrolux brand *vis-à-vis* its final target groups?

3 Assess the choice of the intermediate target groups (channels) that Electrolux has used. Which are more appropriate than others? Can you think of other channels or instruments to effectively bring the brochure to the parents?

4 Assess the instruments that Electrolux used to promote the brochure. Are they appropriate? Can you think of other instruments?

Sources: www.electrolux.com
Information provided by Ulrich Gartner, Vice President Communications Europe, The Electrolux Group and Frederique Depraetere, Publicity Development Manager, The Electrolux Group.

References

1 Malhotra, N. (1996), *Marketing Research. An Applied Orientation*. Upper Saddle River, NJ: Prentice Hall.

2 Ries, A. and Trout, J. (1986), *Positioning: The Battle for Your Mind*. New York: McGraw-Hill.

3 Bovée, C.L., Thill, J.V., Dovel, G.P. and Wood, M.B. (1995), *Advertising Excellence*. Englewood Cliffs, NJ: McGraw-Hill.

4 See also Dibb, S. and Simkin, L. (1996), *The Market Segmentation Workbook. Target Marketing for Marketing Managers*. London: Routledge; Cathelat, B. (1993), *Socio-Styles. The New Lifestyles Classification System for Identifying and Targeting Consumers and Markets*. London: Kogan Page.

5 Grossbart, S.L. and Crosby, L.A. (1984), 'Understanding the bases of parental concern and reaction to children's food advertising', *Journal of Marketing*, 48(3), 79–92; Chan, K. and McNeal, J.U. (2003), 'Parental concern about television viewing and children's advertising in China', *International Journal for Public Opinion Research*, 15(2), 151–66; Spungin, P. (2004), 'Parent power, not pester power', *International Journal of Advertising and Marketing to Children*, 5(3), 37–40.

6 Burr, P.L. and Burr, R.M. (1976), 'Television advertising to children: What parents are saying about government control', *Journal of Advertising*, 5(4), 37–41.

7 Spungin, P. (2004), 'Parent power, not pester power', *International Journal of Advertising and Marketing to Children*, 5(3), 37–40; Buijzen, M. and Valkenburg, P.M. (2003), 'The unintended effects of television advertising', *Communication Research*, 30(5), 483–503.

8 Burr, P.L. and Burr, R.M. (1977), 'Parental responses to child marketing', *Journal of Advertising Research*, 17(6), 17–20.

9 Young, B. (2003), 'Does food advertising make children obese?', *International Journal of Advertising and Marketing to Children*, 4 (April/June), 19–26; Clarke, B. (2005), 'Responsible marketing,' *Young Consumers*, 6(4), 3–4; Spungin, P. (2004), 'Parent power, not pester power', *International Journal of Advertising and Marketing to Children*, 5(3), 37–40.

10 Spungin, P. (2004), 'Parent power, not pester power', *International Journal of Advertising and Marketing to Children*, 5(3), 37–40.

11 Clarke, B. (2005), 'Responsible marketing,' *Young Consumers*, 6(4), 3–4.

12 Zappa, J.A., Morton, H. and Mehta, K. (2003), 'Television food advertising: counterproductive to children's health? A content analysis using the Australian guide to healthy eating', *Nutrition and Dietics*, 60(2), 78–84; Kunkel, D., Wilcox, B.L., Cantor, J., Palmer, E., Linn, S. and Dowrick, P. (2004), Report of the APA Task Force on advertising to children. Retrieved 7 October 2005 from http://www.apa.org/releases/childrenads.pdf.

13 Chan, K. and McNeal, J.U. (2003), 'Parental concern about television viewing and children's advertising in China', *International Journal for Public Opinion Research*, 15(2), 151–66.

14 Bijmolt, T.H.A., Claassen, W. and Brus, B. (1998), 'Children's understanding of TV advertising: Effects of age, gender and parental influence', *Journal of Consumer Policy*, 21(2), 171–94; Clarke, B. (2005), 'Responsible marketing,' *Young Consumers*, 6(4), 3–4.

15 Bulmer, S.L. (2001), Children's perceptions of advertising. Auckland, Massey University: Working paper 01.05; Preston, C. (2005), 'Advertising to children and social responsibility', *Young Consumers*, 6(4), 61–7; Wright, P., Friestad, M. and Boush, D.M. (2005), 'The development of marketplace persuasion knowledge in children, adolescents, and young adults', *Journal of Public Policy and Marketing*, 24(2), 222–33; Kunkel, D., Wilcox, B.L., Cantor, J., Palmer, E., Linn, S. and Dowrick, P. (2004), Report of the APA Task Force on advertising to children. Retrieved 7 October 2005 from http://www.apa.org/releases/childrenads.pdf.

16 Halford, J.C.G., Gillespie, J., Brown, V., Pontin, E. and Dovey, T.M. (2004), 'Effect of television advertisements for foods on food consumption in children,' *Appetite*, 42, 221–5.

17 Lvovich, S. (2003), 'Advertising and obesity: the research evidence', *International Journal of Advertising and Marketing to Children*, 4 (January/March), 35–40.

18 Clarke, B. (2005), 'Responsible marketing,' *Young Consumers*, 6(4), 3–4.

19 Young, B. (2003), 'Does food advertising make children obese?', *International Journal of Advertising and Marketing to Children*, 4 (April/June), 19–26.

20 Lyna, A. (2005), TV confuses children about which foods are healthy, new study finds. University of Illinois at Urbana–Champaign News release (6 June 2005). Retrieved 28 July 2005, from http://www.news.uiuc.edu/news/05/0606kidfood.htm.

21 Zappa, J.A., Morton, H. and Mehta, K. (2003), 'Television food advertising: counterproductive to children's health? A content analysis using the Australian guide to healthy eating', *Nutrition and Dietics*, 60(2), 78–84.

22 Grossbart, S.L. and Crosby, L.A. (1984), 'Understanding the bases of parental concern and reaction to children's food advertising', *Journal of Marketing*, 48(3), 79–92.

23 Spungin, P. (2004), 'Parent power, not pester power', *International Journal of Advertising and Marketing to Children*, 5(3), 37–40.

24 Nathanson, A.I. (2001), 'Parent and child perspectives on the presence and meaning of parental television mediation', *Journal of Broadcasting and Electronic Media*, 45(2), 210–20; Nathanson, A.I., Eveland Jr., W.P., Park, H.S. and Paul, B. (2002), 'Perceived media influence and efficacy as predictors of caregivers' protective behaviours', *Journal of Broadcasting and Electronic Media*, 46(3), 385–410; Grossbart, S.L. and Crosby, L.A. (1984), 'Understanding the bases of parental concern and reaction to children's food advertising', *Journal of Marketing*, 48(3), 79–92.

25 Chan, K. and McNeal, J.U. (2003), 'Parental concern about television viewing and children's advertising in China',

International Journal for Public Opinion Research, 15(2), 151–66.

26 Peter, J.P. and Olson, J.C. (1993), *Consumer Behavior and Marketing Strategy*, Burr Ridge, IL: Irwin.

27 Herbig, P., Koehler, W. and Day, K. (1993), 'Marketing to the Baby Bust Generation', *Journal of Consumer Marketing*, 10(1), 4–9.

28 Uncles, M. and Ehrenberg, A. (1990), 'Brand Choice among Older Consumers', *Journal of Advertising Research*, 30(4), 19–22.

29 Redondo-Bellon, I., Royo-vela, M. and Aldas-Manzano, J. (2001), 'A Family Life Cycle Model Adapted to the Spanish Environment', *European Journal of Marketing*, 35, 5/6, 612–38.

30 Dumont, E. (2001), 'Is Life Cycle Marketing Outdated?', *Bank Marketing*, (April), 12–13.

31 Javalgi, R.J. and Dion, P. (1999), 'A Life Cycle Segmentation Approach to Marketing Financial Products and Services', *The Services Industries Journal*, 19 (July), 74–96.

32 Gilly, M. and Enis, B. (1982), 'Recycling the Family Life Cycle: A Proposal for Redefinition', in Mitchell, A. (ed.), *Advances in Consumer Research*, 9, Association for Consumer Research, Ann Arbor, MI, 271–6.

33 *The Guardian*, 9 April 2003.

34 Moses, E. (2000), *The $100 Billion Allowance. Accessing the Global Teen Market*. New York: John Wiley & Sons.

35 *De Morgen*, 3 May 2003.

36 Kotler, P. and Keller, K.L. (2006), Marketing Management. Englewood Cliffs, NJ: Prentice Hall.

37 *De Morgen*, 26 October 2002; *Fast Company*, Issue 61, August 2002; *Active Marketer*, December 2002.

38 Kotler, P. and Keller, K.L. (2006), Marketing Management. Englewood Cliffs, NJ: Prentice Hall.

39 *De Morgen*, 2 May 2003.

40 Ries, A. and Trout, J. (1986), *Positioning: The Battle for Your Mind*. New York: McGraw-Hill.

41 Aaker, D.A., Batra, R. and Myers, J.G. (1992), *Advertising Management*. Englewood Cliffs, NJ: Prentice Hall.

42 Leeflang, P.S.H. (1990), *Probleemgebied marketing (Problem Field Marketing)*. Houten: Stenfert Kroese.

43 Geuens, M., Goessaert, G., Mast, G. and Weijters, B. *Case study: Eastpak & JanSport*. Vlerick Leuvan Gent Management School, 2002.

44 Fill, C. (2005), Marketing Communications: Contexts, Strategies and Applications. Harlow: Pearson Education.

Chapter 5

Objectives

Chapter outline

A hierarchy of marketing communications objectives

Stages in the product life cycle and marketing communications objectives

Consumer choice situation and communications objectives

Corporate communications objectives

Chapter objectives

This chapter will help you to:

- Get an overview of the various goals and objectives of marketing communications and corporate communications campaigns
- Understand the relation between stages in the product life cycle (PLC) and communications objectives
- Understand how the consumer choice situation affects communications objectives

According to the DAGMAR model, during the communications process nine effects can be established. When a marketer is defining his or her communications strategies he or she will have to select the most appropriate communications effect or goals from the list above. Every promotional campaign should be organised with one of these communications objectives in mind. The choice of the right goals depends on the problems that have arisen in the preliminary situation analysis of the market, brand positions, competition, opportunities and threats. In that sense, communications objectives are only an intermediary way to reach marketing goals of a higher order, such as sales volumes, market share, distribution penetration, etc.

A good set of communications goals should have a number of characteristics. It should:[3]

- fit in with the overall company and marketing goals;
- be relevant to the identified problems and specific to cope with threats or to build on opportunities in the market;
- be targeted to different target audiences; this implies that different target groups (such as countries, socio-demographic groups, heavy and light users) could need different communications objectives;
- be quantified in order to be measurable which allows you to make a precise evaluation of the campaign results;
- be comprehensive and motivating to all involved persons but at the same time be realistic and achievable;
- be timed to enable specific scheduling of the campaign as well as planning of results evaluation;
- be translated into sub-goals when necessary.

The communications objectives are guidelines for everyone who is involved in campaign development and realisation: marketers, advertising agencies, PR officials and sales promotion agencies, media planners and buyers, and researchers. They are also fundamental to campaign strategy: all phases of the marketing communications plan, such as creative, media and budgeting decisions, should be built on the goals.

As communications objectives are also the criteria against which a campaign's success (or failure) is evaluated, it is important that they are well defined and quantified. Only when goals are measurable are they a management tool enabling you to gauge returns against investments.

Developing category wants

The first basic condition to be fulfilled by a brand is that it should fit within category needs and wants. If buyers cannot perceive the communicated product or brand as an appropriate answer to their needs and demands, they will not be motivated to buy it. Category wants or needs can be defined as the existence of one or more of these buying motives and the perception of the product category as a good means of meeting these motives. Of course, although category need is always necessary before other brand-related objectives work, it is clear that in most cases, i.e. when promotional actions and communications are targeted to category users, it can be considered as already present and thus can be ignored. Indeed, it can be assumed that category wants are already well developed in product categories such as food, detergents, insurances and cars. However, in product categories that are infrequently purchased or infrequently used, such as pain killers, communicating category needs to remind buyers of their present but forgotten need may be useful.

Using category need as a primary communications objective is a must for innovations (see Plate 7). Consumers should first understand which need is satisfied by an innovation and the difference between the 'new category' and known categories should be stressed. When Sony invented the CD player, the first thing to communicate, before building awareness for the Sony brand, was the difference in sound quality compared with the record player. Creating category awareness is also an appropriate goal when non-category users are addressed. For instance, when telecom operators of cellular phone networks communicate to a group of non-owners of a cellular phone they will stress the need for mobile telephones. When they address owners they will stress other benefits such as special rates and special services. Sometimes a manufacturer repositions a product or service to meet other usage occasions or methods of use. Kellogg's introduced Variety cereals in small packages to broaden its cereal market from the breakfast moment to other snack and school moments and consequently takes part in the between-meals market. Category wants can be omitted, refreshed or actively used in market communications in the different situations described above. The following communications goals are not on a category level but focus on the brand.[4]

Brand awareness: recognition and recall

Brand awareness is the association of some physical characteristics such as a brand name, logo, package, style, etc. with a category need. There are two ways brand awareness can be defined. For example, if people think of a soft drink, they may spontaneously think of either Coca-Cola, Fanta or Lipton Ice Tea. This is their top-of-mind brand awareness. In an unaided context people may recall several brands spontaneously. This is brand recall or unaided spontaneous awareness. But it is also possible that people recognise a brand by its package, colour, logo, etc. This is brand recognition or aided awareness. Aided brand awareness is of course less difficult to achieve. Less repetition and thus smaller investments are needed to establish it than brand name recall. Research has shown that the correlation between recall and recognition is on average 50%. Buyers will be better able to recognise brands than to recall brand names spontaneously.[5] On the other hand, brand recall is not a guarantee that the buyer will recognise the brand in a shop.

The question of which awareness goal should be aspired to by a marketer depends on the situational circumstances in which the product or brand is bought. If the purchase decision is made at another time and location than the point of sales (at the office, at home), or when a buyer has to ask explicitly for a certain product or service (e.g. at a drugstore or a pharmacist) brand name recall is needed. This is also true when a shopping list with preferred brand names for every category is made prior to going to a shop, or when somebody is making purchases by phone (airline tickets, courier services, etc.). When the purchase decision is made in the store (and according to a POPAI study this is the case for 60%–80% of all fast moving consumer goods bought in the supermarket – see also Chapter 14), and the buyer can use visual cues such as packages, displays, colours, and logos, brand recognition is more important than brand recall.

All European countries are different in terms of market positions of the Eurocard/MasterCard compared to its major competition (Visa card, American Express, Diner's Club), resulting in a variety of marketing objectives and target audiences from one country to another. For instance, in central Europe Eurocard/MasterCard is still introducing the concept of credit cards (which will require stressing the category needs in advertising), while in Italy the notion of revolving credit is still unknown and in Germany first-time card applicants (youngsters entering the labour market) should be captured. This inevitably has meant that local media and tactics have been applied but all with the basic European advertising strategy that was first launched in Europe in 1998 in mind. Apart from the main advertising objective in this strategy, to build significant brand awareness, Eurocard/MasterCard discovered that its users are more family-oriented and less hedonistic than Visa users. They make the same purchases and spend similar amounts of money but are more in line with values such as personal balance and harmony than with materialistic values. Therefore Eurocard/MasterdCard's aim is to build a stronger emotional bond with the target audience in all countries to differentiate the card and its services from its main competitors. The core selling idea for the card is that Eurocard/MasterCard is the best way to pay for everything that matters. It is expressed by the 'Priceless' campaign stressing the fact that there are some things money can't buy – and for everything else there's Eurocard/MasterCard. As a result of this campaign unprompted brand awareness for Eurocard/MasterCard in its top nine European markets improved by 3% to 37% in April 2001, whereas Visa declined by 3% to 61%. Specifically, the major increases in awareness include Italy (+8%), Spain (+4%) and the UK (+3%).[6]

To stimulate brand recognition, showing the product package or logo in advertising and other communications in exactly the same colours and formats is crucial. The latter implies that media such as radio advertising are less appropriate for brand recognition goals. To build brand recall, repetition of the association between the category and the brand is necessary. Sign-off slogans should therefore always integrate category and brand name. In some cases a marketer should try to attain both brand recall and recognition. A consumer then recalls a brand at home and will search for it at the supermarket or store. For this search process to be successful, brand recognition is needed. Sometimes this dual brand awareness objective is required, since for many product categories consumers limit their search activity based on loyalty to a limited set of brands.

Every communications activity should take brand awareness into account. Even if brand attitude or other objectives are more dominant, it will still be important to support brand awareness. A brand can never have too much brand awareness. Brand awareness should also be established prior to brand attitude and the other communications objectives. If a brand is not known, it would be impossible to build an image, preference or attitude towards that brand. The effect of brand awareness on brand choice and brand purchases is substantial. If two brands are equally valued, the brand with the highest awareness will be purchased more often.[7]

Brand knowledge

Brand knowledge and comprehension mean that target consumers are aware of the most essential brand characteristics, features and benefits. They know the strengths of the brands as compared to competitive brands, they know why they should buy brand X instead of brand Y or Z. Essentially, consumers should be able to recall the brand's positioning. This knowledge may be based on very objective information, but also on brand image and lifestyle positioning. It is clear that what people know about a brand is very subjective and based on past experiences or on beliefs and perceptions.

When Alldays, the Procter & Gamble brand of panty liner, introduced Alldays Tanga (a string panty liner) in May 2000 in markets where competitor Mölnlycke had already launched Libresse String, it was clear that the tried and tested formula of proclaiming a superior product feature which had led to a trusted but rather scientific brand image for the Alldays brand had to be put aside. String underwear became the most fashionable underwear at the beginning of the new millennium, particularly among young women. As research had shown Procter & Gamble that these young women were tired of advertising in the femcare category that took itself too seriously and Alldays Tanga needed to project a younger, more contemporary image, the company decided to shift perceptions of Alldays to a more cosmetic brand by using honest and straight-talking advertising without product demonstrations and scientific language. Alldays Tanga broke the advertising rules of the category by using humour. The TV spot showed a young woman in a club in Ibiza doing strange dance steps (imitated by the rest of the club to the tunes of Bob Sinclair's major club hit 'Can you feel it') because her string panty liner would not stay in place. Market research had showed Procter & Gamble that the only real issue involved with panty liners was the ultimate embarrassment for young women of having to deal with a dislodged panty liner while wearing the most fitted and glamorous clothes. This campaign proved to reflect a well-liked brand imagery, with young women feeling that finally someone in the femcare category was speaking their language. It was also very successful in launching the Tanga product: in Germany, where it was the first major brand string launch, Alldays Tanga's share of the panty liner market was 65% at the end of December 2000, while the main competitor had only 14% share. In Greece where Alldays Tanga was second to market, the brand nearly matched the key competitor's value share six months after launch.[8] This knowledge and comprehension stage is strongly related to the next step in the DAGMAR hierarchy, in which a certain degree of like (or dislike) and preference is added to the information stored in a consumer's memory.

Brand attitude

If consumers are equally aware of a number of brands in a certain product category they will base their brand choice on an evaluation of the different brands. The result of this evaluation is called 'brand attitude'. Brand attitude is the perceived value of a brand to a consumer. Because a brand is stronger (and thus has more loyal customers) when the differentiation with another brand is bigger, brand attitude is an important communication objective (see also Chapter 2).

A marketer should study the current brand attitudes and perceptions and then decide what to do. If there is no brand attitude, and people are unaware of brand benefits, a brand attitude should be created. If there is a moderately favourable brand attitude, the attitude should be reinforced through adapted communications. Improving attitudes among these benefit-aware target groups will lead to more frequent buying and hopefully make customers loyal. A very favourable brand attitude should be maintained to keep all loyal customers satisfied. In marketing practice there's no such thing as a permanently very favourable brand attitude because attitudes are liable to changes as a consequence of dynamic markets and competition power. When a certain brand attitude cannot be improved, it could be a strategic decision to switch to another attitude by repositioning the brand and perhaps finding a better brand proposition for the targeted market.

Existing brand attitudes can also be adapted to appeal to other and new target groups. For instance, Wolverine World Wide, the American company behind Wolverine shoes for workers and Hush Puppies, an American brand of casual footwear, began building the Caterpillar footwear brand in 1994 under licence from Caterpillar Inc., the heavy equipment and engine manufacturer. Caterpillar boots and shoes are now sold in 100 countries on six continents, reflecting the original brand attitude of Caterpillar in a totally different product category. In 1998 the company also acquired the licence from Harley-Davidson to transfer the legendary motorcycles brand image to shoes and boots; in 2000 Wolverine started to manufacture Stanley footwear, positioned as footwear helping workers to 'make something great', bringing the slogan of the well-known manufacturer of construction tools to life in a new category.

If there is a negative prior brand attitude, changing the attitude is necessary. This is a very difficult objective to realise. It might be better – especially when the negative attitude is based on negative experiences – to modify the brand attitude and reposition the brand by appealing to different buying motivations.[9] In January 2003 Christian Dior had to change major elements of its advertising campaign for Dior Addict perfume and cosmetics. The TV spot for the fragrance originally showed a bikini model dipping her finger into a substance on a mirror and holding it up to her nose, then grabbing a bottle of Addict perfume while a voice whispers 'addict' and 'Will you admit it?' The ad initiated the 'Addiction is Not Fashionable' protest campaign and boycott co-ordinated by Faces and Voices of Recovery and MOMStell, a group of parents concerned with addiction and recovery issues. In response to this protest Dior stopped using the tagline 'admit it' in its marketing communications and altered the ads to emphasise the full name of the product 'Dior Addict' instead of 'addict' as a single word.[10]

Purchase facilitation in lingerie shops

A lot of men consider lingerie a sexy present for their loved ones. However, buying bras usually turns out to be a painful and embarrassing experience. Contrary to popular belief (amongst women) most men do not have the faintest idea about the size of the 'natural wealth' of their girlfriends or wives. When asked about size, they give vague indications such as 'more or less like that woman over there' or 'about a handful'. The consequence is that 90% of the women who receive a lingerie set as a present (mostly in December or on Valentine's day) take it back to the shop because it does not fit. A female student of the 'Piet Zwart Institute for Retail and Interior Design' in Rotterdam developed an original new retail concept that aims at facilitating the buying process for men. In the middle of the shop a 'breast wall' is installed. On this wall breast of different sizes and shapes are modelled in gel, and men can 'experience' which size is closest to the one they need. Furthermore, most men do not feel comfortable in lingerie shops and they find it difficult to find their way around. Therefore, the shop is more or less conceived as a do-it-yourself store. There are separate aisles per cup size, and the size is clearly illustrated by means of pictures in each aisle. 'Men know everything about PK's of cars, but have a selective memory about the anatomy of their wives and girlfriends', the designer says. 'We should assist them as much as we can.' In the meantime, the new concept has raised the interest of lingerie retailers and manufacturers all over the world.

Source: De Morgen, 13 January 2006.

Purchase intention

The intention of the buyer to purchase the brand or the product or take other buying-related actions (going to the store, asking for more information) can also be enhanced. For low-involvement buying situations (see Chapter 3), purchase intention should not be stressed in communications. In this case, when a brand is known and a favourable brand attitude exists, this will in many cases lead to buying behaviour whenever the need for a certain category is aroused. In high-involvement situations, however, when perceived buying risks are high, the intention to buy is typically a necessary mediating step between a favourable attitude and the actual purchase. In this case generating purchase intention and trial is necessary.[11] Advertising and sales promotion can stimulate the consumer in that direction.

Purchase facilitation

Purchase facilitation is all about assuring buyers that there are no barriers hindering product or brand purchase. These barriers could be other elements of the marketing mix, such as price, product and place (distribution).

Sometimes availability or price is a problem preventing consumers from buying a product. Communications in this case should minimise the perceived problems. For example, if a certain brand is not widely available in all stores, a list of approved dealers might help the consumers.[12] Point-of-purchase communications may also help to facilitate purchases.

Purchase

Sales are, of course, the main marketing objective. However, in most circumstances it is difficult to use sales goals as a primary communications objective. Nevertheless, there are situations in which, due to the action-oriented context of communications tools, sales could be a good objective. For instance, the main objective of most sales promotions like couponing, price cuts and premiums is the short-term effect on sales. Some direct marketing tools such as direct-response advertising may be evaluated by generated sales. Indeed, in these situations direct sales is the main goal.

TELE2 is an alternative pan-European fixed-line operator specialising in lowest cost residential telephony. By mid-2000 TELE2 had established strong market positions in seven markets in its Southern and Central European region with 3.1 million customers. But with decreasing prices and lower margins occurring, TELE2 had to quickly increase market share to ensure its future in the highly competitive markets of residential telephony. The main communications objective was to bring in new subscribers for TELE2, quite a challenge considering that unlike its competitors, TELE2 has no salesforce, no stores, and no in-store presence. The target group for TELE2 is relatively broad and consists of adults between 20 and 50 years old with a phone bill above the national average. The advertising objectives were to generate new subscriber phone calls to the TELE2 call centres and to build the TELE2 brand attitude of 'best price offer' and 'most simple and clear offer'. In the creative strategy, JW Thompson developed a campaign that in a humorous way illustrated the carefree attitude TELE2 customers have towards using their phone as it is so cheap with TELE2. The headline of the ad campaign was 'It's easier to choose your phone operator'. In this way the agency wanted to express that TELE2 customers can use their phones in ways that are outrageous for normal customers, in ways that would normally send their phone bills through the roof. Direct response television commercials with a toll-free number were used to generate leads and boost awareness, in combination with print advertising for providing the reassuring tariffs information and 'no strings attached' message and also for generating calls via the toll-free number. The campaign generated 7.75 million calls to TELE2's call centres between May 2000 and May 2001 and TELE2 more than doubled its subscribers to 7 million in May 2001. The company also obtained strong brand awareness increases with a top-of-mind awareness that increased by 100% in France, Germany and Italy, 80% in Austria and 30% in Switzerland. Spontaneous awareness rose by 22% in France and 75% in Germany and aided awareness rose by 13% in Austria and 43% in Holland. TELE2 became number one leader in image for providing the 'most favorable prices' in five out of six monitored markets and of 'simple offer' in three out of six markets.[13]

Satisfaction

When a consumer buys a product or service he or she has certain expectations about the purchase. When the product or service lives up to the required and desired benefits or surpasses the expectations, the consumer will be satisfied and thus inclined to choose the same brand whenever he or she buys the product again. Dissatisfied consumers will probably buy a different brand on the next occasion and will complain to relatives and friends. Most marketers are satisfied when consumers finally buy and stop communicating at that point. But it is clear that communications should also be directed to existing customers. The most important reason is that clients are advocates of the brand and products they buy. Word-of-mouth communications can be stimulated and approved by communicating with current customers. Moreover, it is important to reassure consumers about their choice. Cognitive dissonance, i.e. the fact that – due to a choice situation – buyers start to have doubts about that choice, should be avoided to enhance brand loyalty.

Brand loyalty

Brand loyalty is defined as the mental commitment or relation between a consumer and a brand. But there are different types of brand loyalty. Repeat purchase is not the same as brand loyalty. The former is often the result of habit or routine buying rather than of brand preference or brand loyalty. Instead of evaluating alternatives and choosing a new brand for every new purchase, in low-involvement, fast-moving packaged goods consumers tend to buy the same brands again without having a commitment to the brand. This is how brand habits develop. By always using and buying the same brands a positive attitude towards those brands is initiated. Longitudinal tracking in the US, the UK and Germany has shown that brand loyalty is not a characteristic of a brand but of a product category. Brands with a higher market share in that category have a higher 'loyalty' because of their higher penetration rate and not necessarily because the emotional bond with the customer is better. Brand 'loyalty' can indeed be the result of habit formation.[14]

Instead of focusing solely on higher market penetration rates, many high-penetration brands are now using advertising campaigns to encourage their loyal consumers to use the brand more frequently, as well as suggesting new ways to use the brand or new situations in which it can be consumed. The more frequent use of a brand may be a much more cost-effective way to build sales. Recent publications have therefore argued that when dealing with brands with a high degree of market penetration, consumption intentions are more likely to capture consumption-related responses (and success of a campaign) than attitudes towards the brand or purchase intentions. Volume estimates would then best approximate the actual consumption of heavy users and likelihood estimates are best used with light users or with infrequently consumed brands.[15]

Of course, not all communications objectives should be present in a promotional plan or campaign. A marketer should choose which of the above goals is most appropriate in the market and communications situation. Marketers will therefore need a clear view based on situation analysis and prior research among the target audience to decide which goals a campaign should focus upon. If awareness levels are low, they should focus on that goal; if preference is a problem, the campaign should stress liking. Brand awareness and brand attitude will always be part of the goals, as both effects should be maintained in every promotional campaign. As these objectives should be quantified to make them measurable, marketing communications objectives could be: to increase the percentage of unaided recall or aided recognition among the target group; to increase the number of target consumers preferring the brand above the competitive brands; to stimulate current buyers to stay loyal and purchase the products again or buy them more frequently; and to encourage non-buyers to try the brand for the first time. The number of people in each step of the hierarchy of objectives can be expected to decrease, as is illustrated in Figure 5.3.[16]

Figure 5.3 Percentage of the target group in each stage of the DAGMAR model

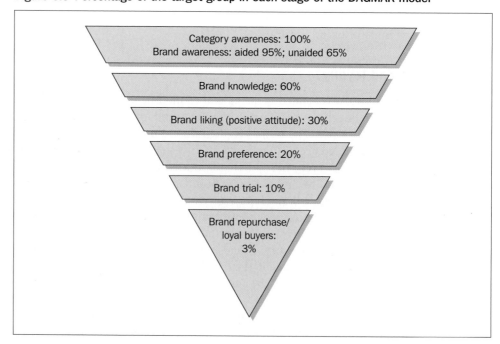

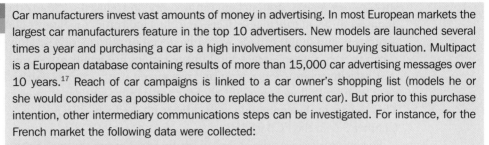

Car manufacturers invest vast amounts of money in advertising. In most European markets the largest car manufacturers feature in the top 10 advertisers. New models are launched several times a year and purchasing a car is a high involvement consumer buying situation. Multipact is a European database containing results of more than 15,000 car advertising messages over 10 years.[17] Reach of car campaigns is linked to a car owner's shopping list (models he or she would consider as a possible choice to replace the current car). But prior to this purchase intention, other intermediary communications steps can be investigated. For instance, for the French market the following data were collected:

- Average number of car models named spontaneously: 9.3.
- Average number of models respondents consider to be 'familiar': 3.6.
- Average number of models respondents claim they might be willing to buy: 3.5.
- Average number of models respondents actually intend to buy: 1.7.

The first objective of car advertising is to include the brand or model name in the 9.3 models that are spontaneously recalled. Afterwards it should push the model through the funnel to be the number one preferred brand or model. First of all, car advertising should be noticed by the consumers: the car ad should get their attention (recognition or recall) and the brand should be correctly attributed to the ad (make and model identification). Some of the well-perceived messages contribute to the purchase intention and others do not. This is reflected in persuasion scores (the ability to amend the shopping list). In the table below the recognition and correct brand identification scores for different European countries, based on the 1994 trackings, are presented.

Perception scores	France	Germany	Italy	Spain	UK
Recognition:					
Minimum	27	11	12	13	21
Maximum	78	76	95	92	82
Average	38	34	46	50	25
Standard deviation	19.5	17.2	18.1	21.8	22.5
Brand identification:					
Minimum	3	4	3	3	5
Maximum	75	72	92	88	65
Average	24	28	37	36	20
Standard deviation	18.6	17	20	21.4	15.9

Reproduced with permission of Esomar. © 2000 Esomar.

It is clear that the ability of campaigns to draw the attention of car owners, to convey the car model identity or to move buyers' choices is very much dispersed (high standard deviations) in all European countries. Moreover, the correlation between perception scores and persuasion scores are very low, which implies that good visibility is not necessarily the same as good performance on persuasion criteria.

The DAGMAR model has the merit that, instead of sales goals which are hard to correlate with communications expenditures, other quantifiable measures for effectiveness, such as awareness and image ratings, are introduced. These other measures are assumed to be intermediate effects, and thus indicators for future sales. An increase in awareness and brand ratings would be ahead of sales increases. However, in practice it can be seen that awareness and image ratings are highly associated with usage, but that sales fluctuate sooner than awareness and image ratings. Attitude changes were even found to follow behaviour changes and can be considered to be caused by them.[18] This change in the communications effects hierarchy has been extensively described in Chapter 3 (e.g. the FCB grid).

Further criticism of the so-called traditional 'strong theory of communications', as presented in the DAGMAR model, was formulated by Ehrenberg.[19] He states that there is no evidence that consumers experience a strong desire or conviction before they purchase a product or a service. The traditional model is a conversion model, i.e. turning non-users into users, whereas advertising is directed at experienced consumers. Jones[20] and Ehrenberg present an alternative 'weak theory of marketing communications': the ATR model (Awareness → Trial → Reinforcement). Marketing communications first arouse awareness, then induce consumers towards a first trial purchase and then reassure and reinforce those users after their first purchase. According to Ehrenberg, involvement is basically product involvement and very rarely brand involvement. Consequently, the goal of marketing communications is to create or recreate brand awareness and to nudge brand choice during purchases. Marketing communications is almost never directed to so-called virgin non-users as is implied in the DAGMAR model, but rather to consumers with prior experience of different brands. This is also true in the case of price promotions. Most buyers have already bought the brand before. Even when new or unfamiliar brands are promoted, they are rarely chosen.[21]

Stages in the product life cycle and marketing communications objectives[22]

The choice of the most appropriate communications goals depends on a number of factors that originate in the marketing strategy and the situation analysis. One of the more important factors in choosing objectives is the phase of the life cycle of a brand or product. In this section different strategies for different life stages are explored. They are summarised in Figure 5.4.

Introduction

A company that is marketing a completely new product will have to develop the market. Consumers will have to learn what the new product is about: which needs will be fulfilled by the product and what the differences are compared to the products the consumers were used to before the innovation or launch of the new product or brand. The major communications objectives in this market situation will be creating category need (explaining which needs are better fulfilled with the innovation), brand awareness and brand knowledge. With daily consumed goods consumers will have to be persuaded to try the new product. The communications strategy has to stress the basic selling points, i.e. the central functional advantages of the products.

Figure 5.4 Stages in the product life cycle and communications objectives

Stage	Introduction	Growth	Marketing	Decline	Time
Marketing communications objectives	Category need Brand awareness Brand knowledge Brand attitude	Brand attitude Brand preference	Top-of-mind awareness Brand attitude Brand loyalty Customer satisfaction	Purchase New target groups	

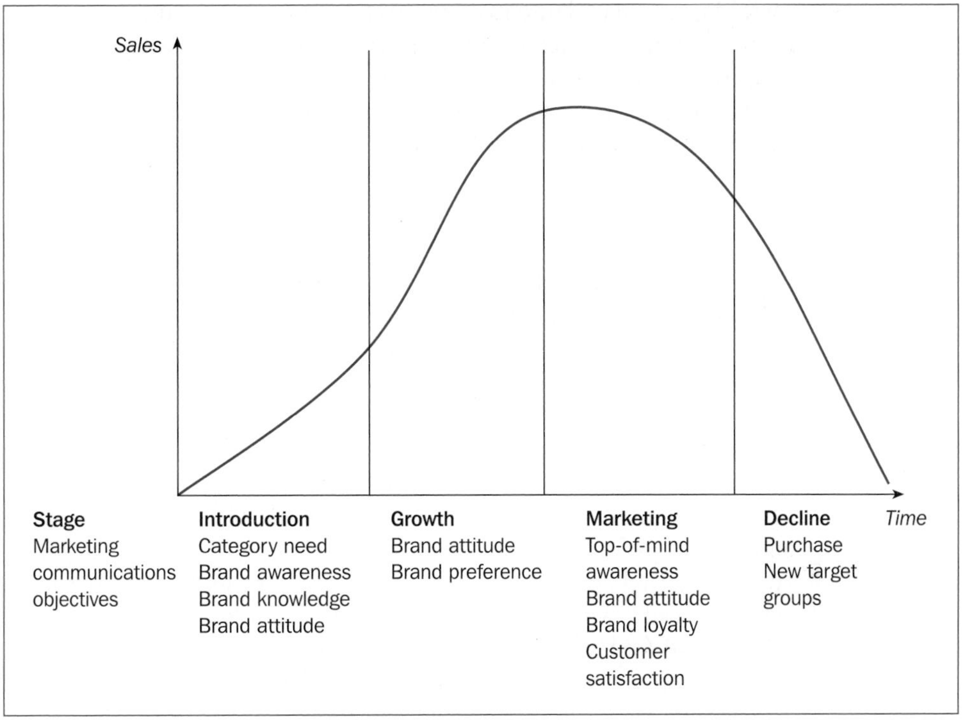

Most introductions are new brand launches rather than real product innovations. Evidently, in this case it is not necessary to communicate the central functional product features as consumers are aware of them from their experience with other brands. Goals are to create brand awareness and support psycho-social brand image connotations. This is done by associating a brand with a certain projected lifestyle. When Nivea first launched the colour cosmetic sub-brand Nivea Beauté onto the European market in 1997, the objective was to utilise the Nivea core competencies of skin-care expertise and emotional values to build a care-based decorative cosmetic brand focussing on products offering gentle formulas and classic colours in the segments eye, nail, lip and face. By 2000 stronger focus had to be placed on category-specific drivers such as modernity, new colours, fashion trends and innovative products to cope with the continued pressure from local competitors, global heavyweight L'Oréal Perfection and the US number one brand Maybelline, using heavy advertising investments to support its global rollout after merging with Jade (Germany, Austria and Switzerland) and Gemey (France and Belgium). Apart from television ads spreading the 'the most beautiful me' message, the print communication was especially important in demonstrating colour and fashion competence. In Germany and France, Nivea Beauté was the only brand in 2000 notably to improve brand image values on all levels. Not only the core Nivea values but also category drivers such as 'colours are modern and up to date' saw improvements. Brand likeability, brand usage and brand awareness also improved after the campaign.[23] A study[24] on what kinds of communications stimulate sales of new products came up with four factors. It should be clearly communicated that it is a new product and is thus different from other products. This difference should be specifically linked to the category such as 'the refreshing soft drink' or 'the strongest mint'. Third, differences in characteristics are not enough; they should be translated into real benefits for the consumer and communicated in that way. The last important factor is the support given to that beneficial point of difference. Some objective endorsements should give consumers the reason why a certain claim should be believed. Typical endorsements are demonstrations, scientific evidence, celebrity endorsements, testimonials of experts or 'normal' users in a slice-of-life setting.

Growth

In the growth stage a different situation leads to other strategies. Consumers are aware of the brand, the product and the most important characteristics and features. Other brands have entered the market with a comparable offer. Communications strategies in this stage of the product life cycle will be aimed at defending the brand's position against possible competitive attacks. Marketers will have to create brand preference by emphasising the right product features and benefits to differentiate the brand from competitors and position it as unique.

The VW Sharan was the market leader in the MPV (multi-purpose vehicle) segment until it was overtaken by its identical twin the Ford Galaxy in 2000. In May 2000 both models were relaunched although there weren't any technological benefits in favour of the higher-priced VW Sharan. In Hungary VW Sharan's group cousin Seat Alhambra led the market and the VW Sharan was challenged by the Nissan Serena. In the Czech Republic the VW Sharan was market leader, followed by the Seat Alhambra until in January 2000, the Mazda MPV was relaunched and took over the lead. The challenge for the VW Sharan was to compete against its by far less expensive and, in some cases, identical rivals in very price-sensitive markets. The VW Sharan opted for a strongly emotional positioning that goes back to its origins: an active family car. While competition was communicating alternative spheres for use such as leisure, business and transportation, the VW Sharan focussed on the most important buyers, families, by using analogies from the animal world to visualise the various features of the car: strength, comfort, safety, etc. As a result, in Germany in February 2001 the VW Sharan was able to boost its share of the segment from 19% to 28.5%, recapturing market leadership from the Ford Galaxy. In Hungary the VW Sharan obtained a share of 35.5% in March 2001, almost identical to the Seat Alhambra lead position, and in the Czech Republic the rapidly declining VW Sharan was able to catch up with Mazda MPV sales.[25]

Maturity

A brand in the mature stage of its life cycle has to cope with strong competition on a market that is scarcely growing. This implies that an increase in the return of one manufacturer will be reflected in a decrease in a competitor's revenues. Communications strategies will focus on increasing the brand loyalty of consumers. Customers should be induced to be less open to the advantages of competing brands. There are six possible communications objectives in this particular PLC stage:

- high spontaneous brand awareness, top-of-mind awareness;
- claim a clear and unique brand benefit, a characteristic on which the brand is better than competing brands;

- if there are none or only small product differences, stressing a lower price might be a good strategy;
- get the attention by offering small product innovations;
- reinforce the psycho-social meaning for product categories such as cigarettes, beer and coffee. These brands differ very little in functional characteristics but the experience of the brands by its consumer groups might be very different. The strategy of these brands is positioning by supporting the transformational meaning of a brand;
- communications strategies could also be more defensive in this stage of the PLC. Current customers should be reassured of their choice and their positive experience and satisfaction of the brand.

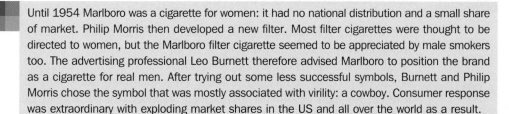

Until 1954 Marlboro was a cigarette for women: it had no national distribution and a small share of market. Philip Morris then developed a new filter. Most filter cigarettes were thought to be directed to women, but the Marlboro filter cigarette seemed to be appreciated by male smokers too. The advertising professional Leo Burnett therefore advised Marlboro to position the brand as a cigarette for real men. After trying out some less successful symbols, Burnett and Philip Morris chose the symbol that was mostly associated with virility: a cowboy. Consumer response was extraordinary with exploding market shares in the US and all over the world as a result.

Decline

When manufacturers are confronted with declining products or brands and decide to milk or harvest the brand, they will probably turn to sales promotions such as prizes and lotteries. If they decide to renew the life of the declining product or brand (and believe in life-cycle stretching), they can use the following strategies:

- communicate an important product adaptation or change;
- draw attention to new applications or moments of use (e.g. beer as a recipe ingredient instead of as a drink);
- increase the frequency of use;
- attract new target groups (e.g. Bacardi Breezer for youngsters).

Coral (Robijn in the Netherlands) is a light-duty detergent brand, long established in Germany, The Netherlands, Austria, Belgium, France, Switzerland and more recently in Sweden, Finland and Norway. Germany and The Netherlands represent two-thirds of global sales. Coral had a stable market share over time and nothing had been done to create a dynamic over the last decade, resulting in a drastically ageing consumer profile, with a core group of people of 50 years and over. To ensure a future for the brand, Coral had to recruit, and create a strong bond with, young European women of between 25 and 35 years old. This target group has absolutely no interest in washing, as they are certainly not housewives. Coral had to find another value that would speak emotionally to this young target group. Research showed Lever Fabergé, the company behind Coral, that clothes reflect personality, self-expression and self-confidence to young women. Hence, taking care of clothes is taking care of themselves. As black and dark clothes represent one-third of a modern woman's wardrobe, Coral decided to launch the first washing specialist for black clothes: Coral Black Velvet. In this way Coral was not a detergent anymore, but an essential fashion accessory helping young women to take care of their precious clothes. In order to demonstrate that Coral Black Velvet could be part of the strong emotional relationship between clothes and women, Lever used a media strategy that created contacts in locations where young women care about clothes, appearance and fashion: women's magazines, parties, fashion shows and bars. In Germany Corals share of market moved from 3.8% to 6.2% in six months; in the Netherlands Robijn moved from a share of 9.6% to 14.2% in the same period. Coral Black Velvet was such a success in the fabrics market that the German market now has six me-toos.[26]

Consumer choice situations and marketing communications objectives[27]

The effectiveness of communications goals may be determined not only by the product or brand life cycle, but also by the consumer choice situation. In Figure 5.5, six important variables affecting the consumer choice situation are shown. First, this is determined by the choice process a consumer follows. This situational characteristic is, for instance, different for high versus low-involvement products. In the former case, an extended choice process with a longer orientation and information processing phase is typical. Influencing consumers in this process and consequently communicating with them will also differ in these different situations.

Consumer characteristics are, for instance, experiences, knowledge and socio-economic characteristics. Consumer–product relationships have to do with involvement from low to extremely high, and routine purchases versus intensively considered purchases. The speed, frequency and modalities of choice, from often and superficial to once in a while and attentive, are elements of the choice process. Characteristics of the outlet or point of purchase (shop, home, office) are important, as well as advice involved with the purchase: is there any kind of personal advice (from a salesperson, friends, family, neighbours) involved with the purchase process? Finally, product characteristics, such

Figure 5.5 Factors affecting the consumer choice situation

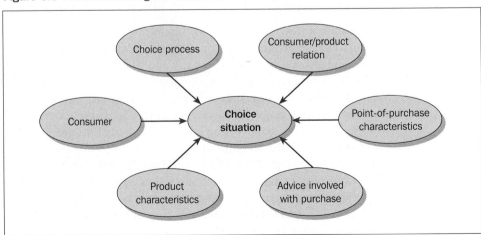

as articles bought daily, known brands or speciality goods, can have an impact. Based on these six groups of variables, a number of frequently occurring choice situations as well as their impact on the communications goal-setting can be described.

- *Standard mass products.* Fast-moving consumer goods, such as detergents and food products, are typically low-involvement situations in which mass communications focus on building brand awareness and brand knowledge. Generating trial and routine repeat purchases is also important.

- *Standard services.* Services targeted at a broad mass target market, like restaurants, shoe repairers, hairdressers, etc. Building brand awareness and stimulating trial through price cuts and other actions are often used.

- *Mail order products.* Mass products like clothing and non-food interior articles for mass markets but ordered through mail and catalogue sales. The awareness of the company is important, but stimulating catalogue enquiries is the first goal. Once the catalogue is mailed, the catalogue itself will be the main communications tool. Sales depend on the quality of this catalogue.

- *Impulse products.* These are products that seduce the buyers into an impulse purchase. The consumers need not be convinced. Quite crucial is the confrontation of consumers with the product: out-of-stock situations should be avoided. After creating brand awareness, creating confrontations is the most essential communications goal.

- *Quality products.* Valuable quality products and brands for relatively small markets of categories such as garment, design products, cosmetics, shoes, accessories, etc. are bought for their quality, for aesthetic reasons and because they symbolise a certain lifestyle. As customers are more involved with this kind of product, the marketer should focus on creating and supporting brand awareness.

- *Quality services.* Complex or special services for relatively small markets include travel agencies, tax advisers, etc. In the introduction phase of a quality service, network relations are crucial. Many people buy a service after being advised by friends or relations. For retention, after-sales communications, such as direct marketing, are important.

- *International luxury products.* World-famous brands such as Chanel, Dior, Yves Saint Laurent, Gucci, Vuitton, etc. appeal to customers. Initially, word-of-mouth communications are important, and generating traffic in the special stores is crucial. Later, direct marketing becomes important.

- *Special niche products.* Brands and products for specific segments of people (children, the elderly, hobbyists, etc.) cannot be mass communicated because this strategy would lead to too much 'waste'. Special interest magazines and trade magazines offer an efficient way of creating brand awareness. Direct, personal contact is also very important.

- *Showroom products.* The main objective of the marketer is to attract people to the showroom. Building brand awareness and reputation is the first step; subsequently, invitations to the showroom are made. The sales team will then have the major part in the communications process, persuading visitors to buy the products.

- *Products with new techniques.* Products such as audio and video equipment with technical innovations are bought by early adopters. All the marketer has to do is introduce the new product lines and their propositions to interested people and attract them to the retail outlets.

- *Investment products.* For products that are bought once or twice in a lifetime only, such as houses, boats, university education, word-of-mouth communications and personal contacts and selling are far more important than mass communications.
- *Unsought products.* These are complex products and services such as insurances and maintenance services which are bought because they are imposed or because they are needed, not because people actually want them. The first objective is to explain the use of the products, to change the negative perceptions of consumers and to create confidence.

Corporate communications objectives

Like all other marketing plans, the corporate communications plan has to be embedded in a global industry analysis on the basis of which strategic priorities such as the positioning of the company have to be defined. As already mentioned in Chapter 1, the corporate identity will have to be based on the company history and the strategic priorities defined. In a communications audit (see Chapter 9) the image of the company is studied, as it exists in the mind of members of relevant target groups, and as it is perceived on the basis of the 'communications history' of the company. All forms of communication, styling and behaviour will have to be screened and tested with members of target groups to establish the multidimensional picture that people hold of the company. Based on this analysis, a dissonance or gap between the desired corporate identity and the existing attitude towards the company may become apparent. This gap is the starting point of the definition of the corporate communications campaign objectives. One important point of focus has to be noted. If the corporate image corresponds with reality, but not with the 'desired reality' (corporate identity), reality will have to be changed first and communicated afterwards, and not the other way around. A company that has a bad reputation as to its level of customer friendliness will have to improve that factor first, before communicating the improvement. The future image largely depends on the consistency between reality and behaviour on the one hand, and the corporate claims communicated on the other.

Depending on the strategic priorities and positioning, and the nature of the gap between identity and image, different corporate communications messages can be developed. A number of specific situations or objectives that call for specific types of messages are summarised in Figure 5.6.

When the objective is to improve internal corporate culture through internal communications, the focus will be on communicating whatever important aspect of strategy that is not adequately assimilated by the staff. In hierarchy-of-effect models of persuasion, awareness is the first step in developing a favourable attitude. Campaigns to develop a better awareness of the company's name and identity will often be the first necessary step in the development of a corporate image. Changes in the corporate structure or corporate strategy always call for intensified corporate communications. This is especially the case when the company's name is changed as a result of a change of ownership or a merger. Target groups have to be reassured that the same company is dealing with them, and have to get used to the new name.

In terms of corporate communications, integrating two companies is a complex situation. On the one hand, each of the companies has its own corporate culture and its

Figure 5.6 Corporate communications objectives

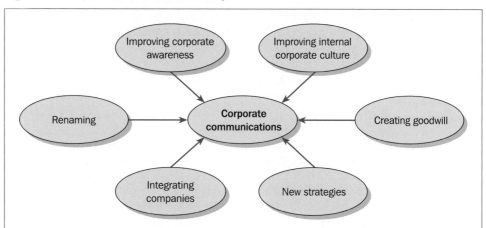

own target groups that are familiar with that particular identity but, on the other hand, there is the wish to integrate both companies into a new identity. Corporate communications will have to reassure target groups that the best of the two old companies is preserved, and that the integrated company will add something extra to the way in which business is done. Very often each company will bring its own brand range. As a result, integrated and new or renewed brand structures will have to be communicated too. Fundamental changes in strategic direction that have an impact on the relationship between the audiences and the company will have to be communicated, such as the decision to withdraw from a market, to focus on core activities, to lay off personnel, etc.

Last but not least, corporate communications messages can be aimed at laying the groundwork for a long-term, stable and favourable corporate image by creating goodwill or a positive effect for the company when target audiences are susceptible to it and no specific information needs are to be satisfied. This investment in goodwill is truly long-term image building.

By 31 December 2000 Accenture was required to cease using the Andersen Consulting name as a result of an arbitration against Andersen Worldwide and Arthur Andersen. On 1 January 2001 ('01/01/01' in the campaign) Accenture launched a $175 million global advertising campaign to communicate the birth of Accenture. It was the largest business-to-business rebranding and repositioning campaign in history. A multi-channel communications plan was put in place across 46 countries targeting the high-level business audience (CEOs, CFOs, CIOs, etc.) in global firms at home, at work and at leisure with the clear message that the firm was now called Accenture instead of Andersen Consulting.

The campaign ran in two phases. In the first phase advertising was designed to communicate the brand-new Accenture name. This part ran during January 2001. The second phase was the 'Now it gets interesting' advertising to convey the new positioning for Accenture and to transfer the positive brand equity that was built up under the Andersen Consulting name over to the new Accenture brand. This advertising campaign ran for the remainder of 2001 and into 2002. The main corporate communication objective was to register the new Accenture name in the minds of prospects. Accenture wanted to achieve 50% of the name recognition level that previously existed within six months of the name change. Furthermore the advertising was meant to establish a new positioning for Accenture by transferring the positive brand equity of the former name, the services and capabilities that Andersen offered, as well as the innovative, creative and forward thinking image. The main goal was thus to generate awareness of the new name and then position Accenture as the market maker, builder and architect of the evolving technology-enabled economy.

The core advertising message to attain these goals was: 'With its unmatched global business experience amplified by its extensive new technology resources and relationships, Accenture is uniquely positioned to help you realise emerging opportunities.' To get this message across Accenture developed a complete communications programme with heavy media weight to surround the target group at different possible contact points at work, home and at leisure. More than 3,000 TV commercials were broadcast across the five key European markets between January and March 2001. Space was bought in top newspapers and business journals in all markets; airport advertising was conducted in major international airports with a high business traveller concentration; print advertising was placed in leisure publications such as *Tiempo* and *Ronda Iberia* in Spain.

Apart from this traditional advertising, Accenture also did building and bus wraps in Paris, taxi wraps in London, Smart cars wraps in Germany and outdoor buys in Milan and Madrid. In addition, corporate sponsorships were employed such as the Davis Cup in Germany and the Williams Formula One Grand Prix Racing Team. An interactive campaign was developed to extend the brand message on-line by using banners, superstitials, microsites and wireless applications. An intensive PR campaign introduced the new Accenture name to the public. A promotional event in the UK dropped 20,000 copies of the *Financial Times* along with a voucher for a free cup of coffee at Starbucks.

Lastly, to reach the employees global webcasts were developed to get the information to every Accenture employee worldwide and a recruitment campaign was launched to make potential Accenture recruits aware of the name change and positioning. In 2001 Accenture achieved over 50% of the previous brand awareness in four out of the five key European countries and the advertising was also successful in generating recall of Accenture's breadth of services and in communicating a forward-looking and energetic brand image.[28]

Summary

A marketing communications campaign can have several objectives that are consistent with the stages in the consumer decision-making process: stimulating product category need, increasing brand awareness and brand knowledge, improving brand attitude or image, increasing purchase intention and facilitating purchases, and maximising customer satisfaction and brand loyalty. Different objectives will require a different communications mix. The objectives of a corporate communications campaign are partly different. They will focus on creating and maintaining goodwill in stakeholder target groups. The objectives of a communications campaign differ according to the stage in the product life cycle. While awareness-building is more important in the introduction and growth stages, brand image and brand preference-building will be crucial in the growth and the maturity stages, and purchase-directed objectives will prevail in the decline stage. On the basis of the consumer choice situation, twelve types of products can be distinguished for which marketing communications objectives are essentially different.

Review questions

1   Describe the various stages in the DAGMAR model. What is the consequence of this model for marketing communications objectives?

2   What are the characteristics of a good set of marketing communications objectives?

3   How does the definition of marketing objectives fit into the marketing communications plan?

4   In what circumstances is it useful to stress category needs and wants in marketing communications?

5   In what circumstances is brand recall rather than brand recognition the more important communications goal?

6   In what circumstances is the stimulation of purchase intention a good marketing communications objective?

7   What are the shortcomings of the DAGMAR model as a framework for marketing communications objectives?

8   To what extent should marketing communications objectives be adapted in the introduction, growth, maturity and decline stage of a product life cycle?

9   How can consumer choice situations influence communications objectives?

10 What corporate objectives can be distinguished?

Further reading

Ehrenberg, A.S.C., Hammond, K.A. and Goodhardt, G.J. (1992), 'The After-Effects of Large Consumer Promotions', *Journal of Advertising Research*, 34(4), 11–21.

Jones, D.B. (1994), 'Setting Promotional Goals: A Communication Relationship Model', *Journal of Consumer Marketing*, 11(1), 38–49.

Jones, J., Slater, J. and Clarck, H. (2003), *What's in a Name: Advertising and the Concept of Brands*. Armonk, NY: M.E. Sharpe.

Joyce, T. (1991), 'Models of the Advertising Process', *Marketing and Research Today*, 19(4), 205–13.

Percy, L., Rossiter, J. and Elliott, R. (2002), *Strategic Advertising Management*. Oxford: Oxford University Press.

Case 5

Dove – Campaign for real beauty

Unilever is one of the world's leading suppliers of fast-moving consumer goods across foods, home and personal product categories with a yearly turnover in 2005 of €39.7 billion. Unilever's portfolio includes some of the world's best-known brands and its operations are organised into two global divisions: Foods and Home and Personal Care. The latter includes global brands such as Dove, Lux, Omo and Surf. All these brands are about looking good, feeling good and getting more out of life.

Within the personal care business Unilever leads the global deodorants and skin cleansing markets and is in the top three daily hair care and mass-market skin care. Six global brands: Axe, Dove, Lux,

Pond's, Rexona and Sunsilk are the core of its business in these categories. Dove, Unilever's largest personal care brand, had grown from a mild soap bar in the US in 1957 to a full complement of products including shampoo, deodorant and a skin care range, available in more than 80 markets throughout the world today with a sales of over €2.5 billion a year.

Market situation

Dove's skin firming products makes skin more tight in so-called problem zones: hips, buttock and thighs. The 'skin firming' segment is a fast-growing segment in the skin care market. Dove introduced its skin firming lotion for the first time in 2002 in a market that was quite dominated by competitive market leaders. In 2004 the objective of Dove Europe was to increase the market share of its lotion and in that way participate more strongly in the skin firming segment growth. To support this re-launch of Dove's firming range two product line extensions (an anti-cellulite gel and firming shower gel) were put on the market next to the existing lotion.

Qualitative research in 2002 and 2003 had also taught Unilever that the marketing communications of the Dove brand were not obtaining the desired results. Following the traditional Dove product characteristics and claims (one-quarter moisturising cream), advertising up till then had been focusing on the rational and functional product features. This had strongly affected the brand knowledge and image of Dove, mainly perceived as a moisturiser with an image that was not emotionally defined or even suffered from rather negative associations of passive individual femininity for 'yesterday's women'. In short: following the five decades of being on the market and successive campaigns stressing the pH neutrality product benefit Dove had become a brand that was completely built on functional benefits without offering an emotional hook.

Target group

Most heavy users of skin firming products are women, who are also utilising other (normal, non-firming) body lotions. The penetration of (existing) skin firming products is above average in the 50+ age group, on average in the 40–49 age group and below average in the 30–39 age group. On the other hand qualitative research has found that women in their mid-thirties are confronted with the first signs of diminishing skin firmness and cellulite.

Communication strategy

A global study (named 'the real truth about beauty') was undertaken by Dove during the first firm skin campaign to better understand the everyday issues of women in regard to their own personal beauty. A total of 3,600 women in 11 countries including Argentina, Belgium, Brazil, Canada, France, Italy, Japan, The Netherlands, Portugal, the UK and US were interviewed, and the results were startling:

When women were asked if they were 'satisfied' with how they look:

■ Only 41% of women said they were 'satisfied' with their body weight and shape

■ Only 39% said they were 'satisfied' with their beauty

It got worse when asking women if they were 'very satisfied' with their appearance:

■ Only 13% of women were 'very satisfied' with their body weight and shape

■ Only 13% of women were 'very satisfied' with their beauty

The study also found that 68% of women strongly agreed that 'the media and advertisers set an unrealistic standard of beauty that most women can never achieve', while 47% strongly agreed that 'only the most physically attractive women are portrayed in popular culture'.

The study concluded that women are feeling disenfranchised by the beauty industry and feel pressured by it. Women are constantly told how they should look, dictated by a very narrow set of societal 'rules'. Many women were left feeling that they did not measure up to the ideals. Most of advertising in this segment shows young, skinny models with a wonderful firm skin and the message used is always the same: 'you can look perfect when you use this product'. Women worldwide were considering this promise in commercials as ridiculous and the physical perfection as unattainable since the models in the spots didn't look like they were in need of any lotion at all but rather needed something to eat. The underlying emotional effects of these product category messages were all quite patronising: 'you should be thin to be beautiful'. These global research findings initiated the brand and campaign strategy for the Dove firming product range: Dove would question the stereotype definition of beauty and the idea behind the Dove advertising campaign would be that women with a rounder curved, more female figure are beautiful and that beauty comes in all shapes, sizes and ages. This message was relevant for the skin firming products since it is precisely the rounder female body parts (belly, thighs and buttock) that are the ones that should be made more tight. The fact that the lotion is not only working for models but also for real women is also the best proof of quality for the product. Ogilvy Düsseldorf (Germany) was the advertising agency to take the lead in the European 'campaign for real beauty'.

Media strategy: to become talk of the town

For the advertising execution Ogilvy selected a number of diverse, real women (no models), asked them to use Dove's firming lotion, shot the results in a classic beauty shoot set-up and used the pictures without retouching or manipulating the images. Traditionally Dove's (and other beauty products) media strategy mainly consists of TV as the main campaign medium, supported by magazine print ads to extend the effects of the TV commercials. For the relaunch of the Dove skin firming products this strategy was completely knocked over: outdoor was used as the key medium to quickly convey the controversial Dove message, followed by 8- and 12-page bound inserts in leading beauty and style magazines. The 'making of' the photo shoot formed the basis of the documentary-style TV commercial that was only used to prolong the effect of the billboard and print campaign. The billboard featured six women of various body types confidently posing in underwear. The successor to this outdoor campaign to launch the firming skin range in 2004 took place in 2005 and used print ads and billboards showing non-models recruited from different walks of life asking the viewer to make a judgement about her looks. The ads presented viewers with a choice (tickboxes), effectively asking them to define beauty by choosing a response. In one ad featuring a 96-year-old African-American woman named Irene, Dove asks 'Wrinkled? Wonderful?' This follow-up 'campaign for real beauty' was meant to be an emotional brand umbrella campaign.

Both outdoor and print media also fitted with the PR strategy which was the most important part of the communications mix. Before the campaign launch the press was targeted with background and motives of the campaign as well as the result of the global survey on beauty that Unilever and Dove had commissioned. The omnipresent outdoor posters in the streets were a good motive for journalists to write about the Dove campaign. In the UK, the campaign had massive coverage on three TV networks, 14 radio stations, 23 newspapers and nine internet sites. In total, a €4.6 million-worth of media was generated by press coverage alone. In Germany, the campaign received an additional 475 million contacts through 16 TV reports, seven radio reports, 58 articles in printed media and 35 online articles. In France, over 33 articles featured the campaign over a six-month period.

The campaign also received significant media exposure in The Netherlands and in Belgium. It sparked a debate on how beauty is portrayed in the media. The campaign with the 96-year-old lady did also receive a lot of press coverage with more than 170 pieces of editorial ranging from a four-page feature in *Marie Claire* (a women's magazine) to a double page in the *Daily Mail*.

Integral to the follow-up campaign in 2005 was the creation of the website, campaignforrealbeauty.com. The site uses animated images of real women to pose a beauty question, allowing consumers to choose between two possible responses, one more in tune with current stereotypes, the other challenging them. Users see their vote counted instantly in the global debate before being guided through to discussion boards where they can state their views and engage other users with new questions and opinions. On the site, consumers can also view the latest advertising, which communicates Dove's point of view in other beauty categories such as hair care. The aim is for a woman to reassess the beauty in her hair and realise beauty lies in what she has, rather than what she doesn't have. Consumers spend nearly six minutes on the site, and view an average of seven pages. Consumers are not only voting, but taking part in the debate. In 2005, the website – campaignforrealbeauty.com – was rolling out across 16 markets in Europe. The site enables Dove to provide a forum for their global debate – a place for people to connect and express their views on beauty stereotypes.

Results

The business results for the firming range surpassed all expectations, with firming lotion sales exceeding forecast by 110% in western Europe (June 2004). From 2003 to 2004 the return of the total Dove firming product line increased by 77% from 5.6 million to 9.9 million Euro and the volume market share of Dove went up from about 10% in 2003 to 16% at the end of October 2004. Unilever was also able

Case Figure 5.1 Evolution of Dove's market share in Germany

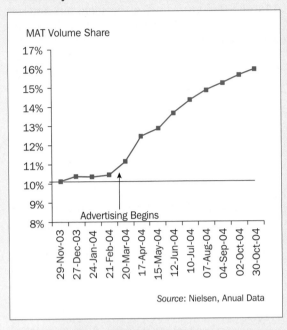

Source: Nielsen, Anual Data

Case Figure 5.2 Dove's beneficial brand association

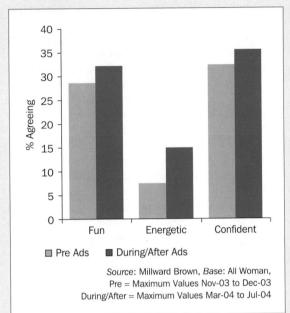

Source: Millward Brown, *Base*: All Woman,
Pre = Maximum Values Nov-03 to Dec-03
During/After = Maximum Values Mar-04 to Jul-04

to link increased market share to the starting date of the new campaign (beginning of March 2004) (see chart 1). Moreover the more emotional brand associations such as fun, energetic and confident all improved strongly (see chart 2). Dove firming body variants are now bigger than lotion or milk variants. The campaign has won different advertising awards such as a Golden Euro-Effie in 2005 and a bronze medallion on the AME (Advertising Marketing Effectiveness) Awards in New York in 2006.

The next step

There is a wealth of other initiatives being undertaken by Dove that demonstrate how passionate the company is about achieving its mission. Here are just a few:

The Dove Self-Esteem Fund. Too many girls develop low self-esteem related to hang-ups about looks, and consequently fail to reach their full potential later in life. The Dove Self-Esteem Fund has been created as an agent of change to educate girls and inspire them with a wider definition of beauty. Funds raised by Dove will be donated to local cause partners such as the National Eating Disorder Information Centre (NEDIC), Girl Scouts (uniquely ME!), etc.

Body Talk. This is a programme to inform and educate young schoolgirls about perceptions of beauty, helping boost their self-esteem. The longer-term goal is to put self-esteem on the curriculum of schools worldwide.

Beyond Compare. This is an international photography exhibit featuring the work of female photographers, capturing and expressing their views on beauty. The photographers were asked to donate their portraits to Dove, for which Dove made a contribution to NEDIC. The director of NEDIC Canada is a key spokesperson.

Questions

1 To reach the coverage (reach) goals of marketing communications, a good target group definition is essential. Describe the target group Unilever should aim for with its Dove skin firming product range? Should they focus on existing users of skin firming products or not?

2 At which stage in the product life cycle was the Dove brand in 2003? Which communications objectives are relevant in that stage? Which objective did Dove choose with the 'campaign for real beauty'? Was that consistent with the product life cycle stage of Dove?

3 Imagine you were responsible to launch Dove's skin firming range in your country (make an abstract of the

current market position and suppose Dove has to enter your local market). Which of the nine communication goals would you include in your marketing communications plan?

4 What do you think is more relevant for the Dove brand: brand recognition or brand recall? Why?

5 Which consumer choice situation is applicable to skin care products? What is the influence of this situation on the communication objectives for Dove?

6 Knowing that Dove's Campaign for Real Beauty is all about real women, diversity, authenticity and feeling good, what could be creative ideas for a new campaign? Think of ideas that can bring in a local touch (in your home country).

Sources: Interview with Wim Petermans, senior brand manager Dove Belgium, 13 February 2006 (Unilever Brussels); 'Keine Models – aber straffe Kurven', Euro-Effie case 2005; 'How real curves can grow your brand', Inge Selawry (OgilvyOne worldwide – Copenhagen) published on ogilvy.com; unilever.com – section About Unilever: corporate information.

References

1 Colley, R.H. (1961), *Defining Advertising Goals for Measured Advertising Results*. New York: Association of National Advertisers.

2 Jones, D.B. (1994), 'Setting Promotional Goals: A Communication Relationship Model', *Journal of Consumer Marketing*, 11(1), 38–49.

3 Pickton, D. and Broderick, A. (2001), *Integrated Marketing Communications*. Essex: Financial Times Prentice Hall.

4 Rossiter, J.R. and Percy, L. (1997), *Advertising Communication and Promotion Management*. Sydney: McGraw-Hill.

5 Hefflin, D.T.A. and Haygood, R.C. (1985), 'Effects of Scheduling on Retention of Advertising Messages', *Journal of Advertising*, 14(2), 41–7.

6 Euro Effie, (2001).

7 Rossiter, J.R. and Percy, L. (1997), *Advrtising Communication and Promotion Management*. Sydney: McGraw-Hill.

8 Euro Effie, (2001).

9 Rossiter, J.R. and Percy, L. (1997), *Advertising Communication and Promotion Management*. Sydney: McGraw-Hill.

10 www.jointogether.org

11 Rossiter, J.R. and Percy, L. (1997), *Advertising Communication and Promotion Management*. Sydney: McGraw-Hill.

12 Rossiter, J.R. and Percy, L. (1997), *Advertising Communication and Promotion Management*. Sydney: McGraw-Hill.

13 Euro Effie, (2001).

14 Franzen, G. (1998), *Merken en Reclame (Brands and Advertising)*. Kluwer Bedrijfsinformatie.

15 Wansink, B. and Ray, M. (2000), 'Estimating an Advertisement's Impact on One's Consumption of a Brand', *Journal of Advertising Research*, November/December, 106–13.

16 Belch, G.E. and Belch, M.E. (1998), *Advertising and Promotion: An Integrated Marketing Communication Perspective*. New York: McGraw-Hill.

17 Brulé, M. and Saporta, G. (1995), 'How Car Advertising Works', *Seminars on Advertising, Sponsorship and Promotions: Understanding and Measuring the Effectiveness of Commercial Communication*. Madrid: ESOMAR, 27–44.

18 Joyce, T. (1991), 'Models of the Advertising Process', *Marketing and Research Today*, 19(4), 205–13.

19 Ehrenberg, A.S.C. (1992), 'Comments on How Advertising Works', *Marketing and Research Today*, 20(3), 167–9.

20 Jones, J.P. (1991), 'Over-Promise and Under-Delivery', *Marketing and Research Today*, 19(40), 195–203.

21 Ehrenberg, A.S.C., Hammond, K.A. and Goodhardt, G.J. (1992), 'The After Effects of Large Consumer Promotions', *Journal of Advertising Research*, 34(4), 11–21.

22 Floor, K. and Van Raaij, F. (1993), *Marketingcommunicatiestrategie (Marketing Communications Strategy)*. Houten: Stenfert Kroese.

23 Euro Effie, (2001).

24 Andrews, K. (1986), 'Communication Imperatives for New Products', *Journal of Advertising Research*, 26(5), 29–32.

25 Euro Effie, (2001).

26 Euro Effie, (2001).

27 Koopmans, A.J., Stoevelaar, A.I. and Holzhauer, F.F.O. (1994) 'Voorwaarden voor Effectieve Marketingcommunicatie' ('Conditions for Effective Marketing Communication'), *Tijdschrift voor Marketing*, (October), 32–5.

28 Euro Effie, (2001).

Chapter 6
Budgets

Chapter outline

How communications budgets affect sales

Communications budgeting methods

Factors influencing budgets

Budgeting for new brands or products

Chapter objectives

This chapter will help you to:

- Understand how communications budgets may influence communications effectiveness
- Get an overview of theoretical and practical marketing communications budgeting methods
- Optimise share-of-voice decisions
- Identify factors that influence budgeting decisions
- Decide upon a communications budget for a new product or brand

Introduction

In this era of globalising, scaling-up and increasing competition, companies are continuously looking for new ways to economise. Restructuring and rationalisation have dominated companies' policies during the recession years of the new millennium. Costs were cut dramatically in areas such as employment and production. Companies tend to save most in those expenses that may be influenced in the short term. Hence, communications budgets are often first in line to be reviewed. The importance of the communications budget and the consequences of changes in this budget on a company's results are regularly marginalised or neglected. However, the communications budget level is one of the determinants of the communications mix effectiveness and thus of company sales and profits. Many researchers, academics and practitioners have been confronted with the difficulty of assessing the appropriate budgets for communications campaigns. Since returns are hard to identify, allocation of funds for promotion is one of the primary problems and strategic issues facing a marketer. This chapter discusses the elements a marketer should consider when making budget allocations, and offers some insights into the relation between communications intensity and communications effectiveness.

Deciding on the communications budget is not a one-off activity and certainly does not come at the end of the marketing communications planning cycle. The financial resources of a company or brand influence the communications programme and plans should be continuously assessed against financial feasibility at all stages in the planning process.

There is no ideal formula for making the best budgeting decision. Deciding on the budget requires experience and judgement. Therefore, the budgeting process should be well considered and based on concrete marketing and communications objectives defined in the communications plan. These goals, together with knowledge of past budgets and their effectiveness and competitive actions, will be an important input for the rest of the budgeting process. The second step is to apply one of the budgeting methods discussed in the next section. Using more than one method could help a marketer set minimum and maximum budgets which will be a guide to the rest of the process, such as planning concrete actions. The last step is to evaluate and possibly revise the budget and objectives, and adapt them to specific circumstances.[1] It is better to scale down the objectives (for instance, to reach a smaller target in a more effective way than was planned) than to try to reach the same objectives with a smaller budget. Finally, budgeting decisions should always take into account the long- and short-term effects of communications efforts on sales and profits.

How the communications budget affects sales

To be able to assess the size of the budget, it is important to understand how communications efforts influence sales. Sales response models depict the relationship between these two factors. In Figure 6.1, a concave sales response model is shown. In this model it is hypothesised that sales behave in a microeconomic way, following the law of diminishing returns: the incremental value of added communications expenditures decreases. An explanation for this relation is that, once every potential buyer is reached

Figure 6.1 Concave sales response model

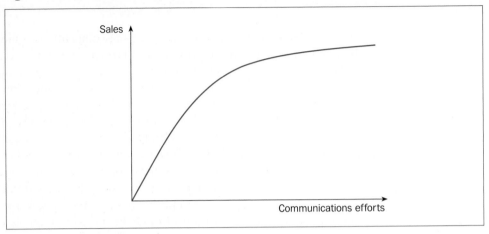

with the communications mix, he or she either will or will not buy, and beyond that optimal point prolonged communications will not change the non-buyers' mind. This model suggests that smaller budgets may be as effective as much bigger ones.[2]

Another way to model sales responses to communications efforts is the S-shaped relation (Figure 6.2). This model assumes that initially, when the level of effort is low, there is no communications effect at all. Even if communications effort is zero, there will be a certain level of sales, and a minimum investment is needed to enjoy any results of the communications programme and to increase sales. When that level is reached, sales will start to increase with incremental communications expenditures. The higher the investments, the greater the additional sales. At point A increased investments start to lead to smaller changes in sales. It is impossible, even with very high communications investments, to exceed a certain saturation level of sales. This is due to the market, and the cultural and competitive environment. Exorbitant communications investments may even lead to negative effects, such as irritation and consumer resistance.[3]

Figure 6.2 The S-shaped sales response model

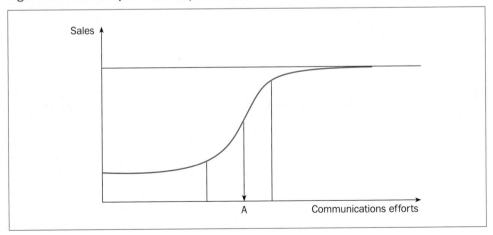

Estimating the relationship between the communications budget or effort and sales or market share is not easy. First of all, marketing communications are not the only marketing mix instrument influencing sales. Prices, product line decisions and changes in the distribution strategy will also influence sales. Furthermore, an effective marketing mix implies that synergy and interaction exist between the various marketing tools. In a well-designed marketing plan each tool reinforces the other. A communications plan may lead to better results if the distribution strategy is optimised or the price is lowered. A rearrangement of the product line may result in more effective communications, etc. As a result of this interaction, it is very difficult to isolate the effect of the communications budget on commercial results. Furthermore, sales response models do not take the effect of competitive actions and environmental factors into account.

Finally, and at least as importantly, communications efforts may have both an immediate short-term and a long-term effect on sales and market share. Traditional theories consider communications as a long-term investment in goodwill.[4] Cumulative investments are needed to lead to sales returns, and the long-term effects of communications efforts are much higher than the short-term effects.[5]

This traditional view is challenged by John Philip Jones,[6] who proposes a controversial theory on the short-term effects of advertising, claiming that paradigms stating that sales are mainly influenced by accumulated advertising campaigns of the past are mistaken. He tried to prove that immediate communications effects on sales exist. According to Jones the whole idea of long-term effects was due to a lack of scanner data. All other advertising testing methods were too irregular and too slow to discover short-term effects. Fluctuations in two-monthly data were explained as seasonal effects. Promotion effects, on the other hand, were traceable and thus researchers deduced that promotions had short-term effects and advertising long-term effects. This belief had serious repercussions on the ratio of advertising to promotions, because marketers confronted with recession and mature markets chose short-term immediate effects on sales instead of long-term image-building advertising. John Philip Jones used single-source data[7] relating advertising exposure (a test group with ad confrontation and a control group without ad exposure based on television viewing behaviour tracking) with scanner data of the same test subjects. Differences in purchases between the two groups were considered to be a measurement of ad effectiveness.

In the survey there were 142 brands, of which 78 were advertised. Calculations were made of 110,000 observations. Jones introduced a new measurement tool called STAS (Short Term Advertising Strength). The baseline STAS for brand X is the share of brand X in the budget of families who have not seen an ad for brand X in a seven-day period before purchase. Jones then calculated the share of brand X in the budget of families who were exposed to an ad at least once during the same period. This is called 'stimulated STAS'. The difference between baseline STAS and stimulated STAS is the 'STAS differential', expressing the immediate sales-generating effect of an ad campaign. STAS is calculated as an index by multiplying the ratio stimulated STAS/baseline STAS by 100. A brand with a market share of 6% without advertising and a share of 9% after one week of advertising had a STAS (differential) of $9/6 \times 100 = 150$.[8] Based on these calculations Jones discovered that 70% of all ad campaigns were able to generate immediate advertising effects. Mostly these effects were small and temporary. When looking at the distribution in deciles of differential scores, 20% had good differential scores, 30% on average a positive score, 30% had no definite positive or negative score and 20% had a negative score and were not effective in beating competing ad campaigns. Only 46% of brands created a long-term effect, defined as an increase in market share compared to that of the previous year. Jones concluded that when a brand is not able to hold its STAS differ-ential constant, this is often caused by lack of continuity in its advertising campaigns.

He also came to the rather surprising conclusion that the first exposure of an ad causes the largest part of sales returns, and that additional exposures will only lead to small effects on sales. The sales response curve would then be a concave degressive function (Figure 6.1).[9] The most effective frequency of an ad campaign according to Jones is one single exposure.

Jones believes that long-term effects will only come about when an ad campaign is also effective in the short term and does not believe in the sleeper effects of marketing communications. This statement is radically opposed to the widespread belief that a higher ad frequency is needed to gain any effects on sales. Therefore, Jones's statements on short-term communications effects are very controversial, and may be an overreaction to the widespread belief that there are mainly carry-over effects of communications efforts. In reality, both short-term and long-term effects are important.[10]

A frequently used and simple sales response model, taking long-term and short-term effects into account, is the following (numbers are exemplary):

$$S_t = 250 + 1.4A_t + 0.6S_{t-1}$$

where: S_t = sales in period t
        S_{t-1} = sales in period t–1
        A_t = advertising in period t
        250 = constant term expressing that even if there was no advertising at all in period t or in the past, sales would still be €250

The short-term effect of advertising is the coefficient of A_t. Every €1,000 invested in advertising results in €1,400 extra sales. The coefficient of S_{t-1} summarises the effect of all advertising efforts in the past. The long-term effect of advertising on sales is calculated as: 1.4/(1 – 0.6) = 3.5. This means that, in the long run, every €1,000 invested in advertising results in 3,500 extra sales.

Communications budgeting methods

In Table 6.1, the various communications budgeting methods are shown.

Table 6.1 **Communications budgeting methods**

- Marginal analysis
- Inertia
- Arbitrary allocation
- Affordability
- Percentage of sales
- Competitive parity
- Objective and task

Marginal analysis

The basic principle of marginal analysis is quite obvious: to invest resources as long as extra expenses are compensated by higher extra returns. Marketers should invest in promotional or communications efforts as long as their marginal revenue exceeds the marginal communications cost (optimum point indicated in Figure 6.3). Profit is calculated as the difference between gross margin and communications expenditures. It is clear that sales and gross margin will increase with higher communications efforts, but will level off, which leads to lower profits and eventually loss. This analysis has the advantage of estimating the effect of advertising on profits, and derives a normative rule of optimal advertising efforts. However, the analysis remains largely theoretical because of the problems involved in estimating the sales response relation. As a result, marginal analysis is seldomly used as a practical budgeting method.[11]

In addition to the theoretical marginal approach there are a number of techniques that are relatively easy to use without requiring difficult calculations. Some of the techniques that practitioners commonly use when developing communications budgets are the following.

Figure 6.3 The marginal analysis

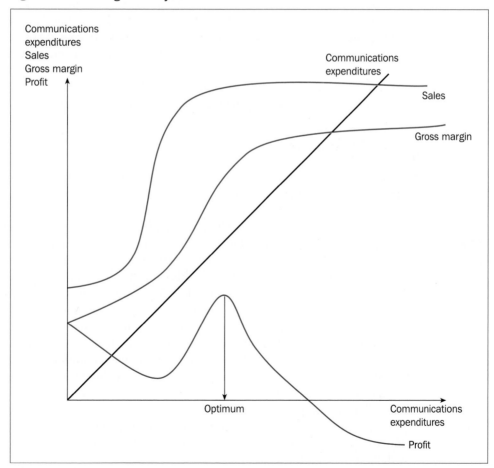

Inertia

The inertia method is nothing more than keeping budgets constant year on year, while ignoring the market, competitive actions or consumer opportunities. Needless to say, this is not a very strategic method.

Arbitrary allocation

Again, this is one of the most simple of all budgeting methods, but also one of the least appropriate. Whatever the general manager or managing director decides will be implemented. This very subjective way of deciding how to spend promotional funds does, of course, lack critical analysis and overall strategy. The technique is mostly used by small companies where the managing director's personal preferences (e.g. sponsoring a golf event) and contacts overrule more strategic processes that take the marketing and competitive environment and customer wants into account.

Affordability method

In this method 'leftover' resources, after all input costs (i.e. human resources, operational and financial costs), are invested in communications. This method is often used in small and medium enterprises. Marketing communications are considered to be a pure cost rather than an investment and are mostly not part of the strategic plan, nor are any concrete communications goals defined. As a result, it is a technique without any focus on strategic market or brand issues. This approach will never lead to optimal budgeting, since some opportunities will be lost because of lack of investment-proneness.

Percentage of sales

In this technique, budgets are defined as a percentage of the projected sales of the next year. An alternative to this technique is to take the communications outlays of the past year as a basis and then add a certain percentage, based on the projected sales growth of the following year. These techniques are very popular in many companies thanks to their ease of use. The percentages used by companies differ. Some sources indicate that they fluctuate around an average of 5%.[12] Other authors speak of percentages between 0.5% and 10%.[13] Although they are commonly used, and like the affordablity method ensure that costs do not threaten profits, these budgeting methods have some notable disadvantages. The percentage of sales method could lead to overspending in markets in which these kinds of investments are not needed and at the same time communications budgets might be too small where they might have had a major impact. Decreasing returns of sales will lead to smaller communications budgets, which will certainly not help to change the negative sales evolution. Communications budgets should not be the result of sales but rather should create demand and thus push up sales. This technique also defends the theoretical insight that sales are dominated by communications investments and that other marketing mix elements do not have an impact on sales. This technique does not consider any potential sales growth areas and will limit sales performance.

Another common way of using the percentage of sales method is to take the sales of the past year instead of projected sales, but that is even worse. This method uses past performance as a *ceteris paribus* situation. Therefore, it is unlikely that the company will make progress (unless a lucky wind changes the competitive environment or consumer demands in the right direction).

A last variant of this method is to take a percentage of profits instead of sales. This has the same disadvantages as an existing brand might need less advertising than a recently launched brand which is not making any profit at all during the first year. Losses will lead to cancelling communications budgets and thus to abandoning all hope instead of investing in brand communications to make them profitable again.

Competitive parity

Competitive parity means that companies look at the amount of money competitors spend on communications and then copy their budgets. The logic of this method lies in the fact that the collective behaviour of a market will not skew much of the budget optimum. The advantage of this method is that the market will not be destabilised by overinvestments or extremely low promotional budgets. This method is often used in fast-moving consumer goods where sales are believed to be highly influenced by advertising and communications spendings.

Nevertheless, the theoretical basis of this method has some disadvantages. The underlying assumption is again that promotional spendings are the only variable that influences sales. Furthermore, a company assumes that the competitor's communications budget was set in an effective and efficient way. Lastly, this method implies that resources, operational methods, opportunities and objectives of competitors used as a benchmark are exactly the same as those of our company. These are three quite dangerous assumptions. Companies may have other market definitions or other targets, leading to other activities and products in other stages of their life cycle which makes comparisons a difficult and unreliable technique for financial decisions. The parity method is also based on historical data and not on competitors' plans for the future. Believing that competitors will adhere every year to the same communications efforts is probably not the best analytical way to make marketing plans.

Some researchers have developed paradigms that are of practical use to marketers wanting to assess the effects of their share of voice (SOV) on their share of market (SOM). Share of voice is calculated as the ratio of own communications investments divided by the communications investments of all market players. A study on the impact of advertising of competitors with comparable products on market share, not taking the advertising quality or any formal or content characteristics of advertising into account, came to the following conclusions.[14] Ad spendings will only influence market share (SOM) when there is a different advertising intensity over a long period. Marginal budget changes do not affect SOM. If competitors aggressively augment their communications budgets, this can be countered by following with increasing communications expenditure. If, however, there is no reaction to this attack, the increase in share of voice will lead to a higher SOM. This means that market leaders will have to track the expenditures of competitors and react to changes to prevent them from gaining market share.

The largest and smallest player in the market, as shown in Figure 6.4, are located above the 45° line. This means that their SOV is smaller than their SOM. The follower in a market is located in a position where it has a higher SOV than market share. Leaders enjoy economies of scale and have a smaller advertising cost per unit. The smallest players should focus on niches because they do not have the resources to compete with the leader and are only profitable if they concentrate on specific niches and forget growth ambitions. If followers want to increase their market share, they will have to increase their SOV above their SOM. This will put pressure on their profitability, which could be dangerous for their competitive positions. This is why stuck-in-the-middle positions are very difficult to hold and market consolidation will lead to two or three large leaders, like Coca-Cola and Pepsi in the cola market. These leaders will have to compete with local or national strong brands (niche players). A market will stay in equilibrium as long as the market leaders keep their SOV within a certain range. Market shares and positions will only change with a minimum of 20 or 30 percentage points differences in SOV.

In Figure 6.5 a matrix is proposed with strategic recommendations for communications budgets in different market situations.

The relation between SOV and SOM in different market situations was also studied by John Philip Jones.[15] Brands with a higher SOM than SOV are called profit-taking brands. Brands with the opposite relation are investment brands. In his study in 23 countries, data on 1,096 brands in repeat-purchase packaged goods markets were collected (Table 6.2).

In Table 6.2 it can be seen that the percentage of profit-takers among brands with a small market share is low. The higher the market share, the more profit-taking brands will appear: 59% of brands with a market share of 16% or more have a share of voice that is lower than their share of market. Some explanations can be offered to explain

Figure 6.4 Relation between SOM and SOV in market dynamics

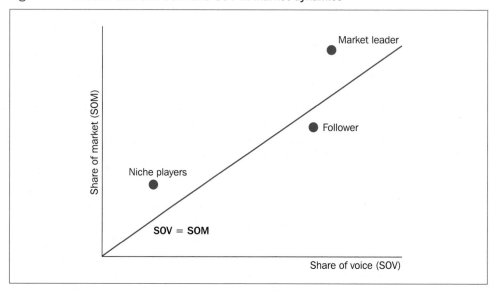

Based on: Schroer, J.C. (1990), 'Ad Spending: Growing Market Share', *Harvard Business Review*, 68(1), 44–8. Reproduced with permission of Harvard Business School Publishing.

Figure 6.5 SOV effect and strategies for different market positions

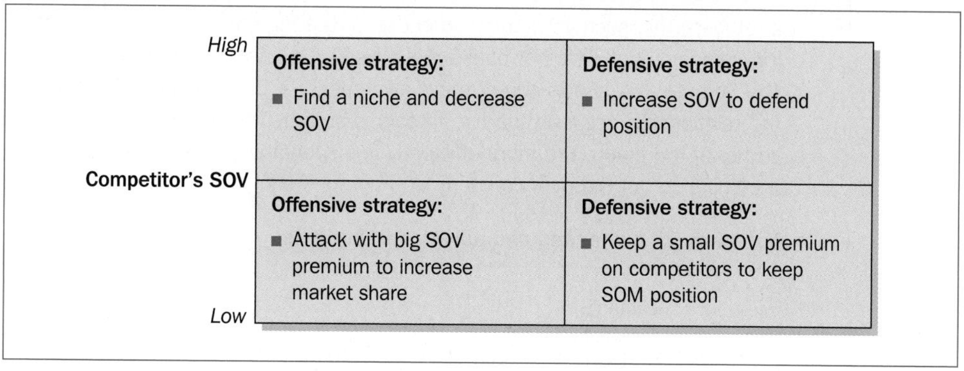

	Offensive strategy: ■ Find a niche and decrease SOV	Defensive strategy: ■ Increase SOV to defend position
High		
Competitor's SOV		
Low	Offensive strategy: ■ Attack with big SOV premium to increase market share	Defensive strategy: ■ Keep a small SOV premium on competitors to keep SOM position

Based on: Schroer, J.C. (1990), 'Ad Spending: Growing Market Share', *Harvard Business Review*, 68(1), 44–8. Reproduced with permission of Harvard Business School Publishing.

Table 6.2 The relation between share of voice and share of market

	All brands	Profit-taking brands % in total	Investment brands % in total
Total	1,096	44	56
SOM 3% and less	224	27	73
SOM 4%–6%	218	37	63
SOM 7%–9%	153	41	59
SOM 10%–12%	112	45	55
SOM 13%–15%	77	56	44
SOM 16% and more	312	59	41

Based on: Jones, J.P. (1990), 'Ad Spending: Maintaining Market Share', *Harvard Business Review*, 68(1), 38–43. Reproduced with permission of Harvard Business School Publishing.

this phenomenon. Small brands have to invest in communications to create brand awareness. Larger and usually older brands are often being 'harvested'. Communications budgets are cut in order to make the brand more profitable. Among brands with market shares larger than 13% harvesting could be a valid explanation for their profit-taking status. Twenty-eight per cent of profit-taking brands are able to charge a price premium and two-thirds of profit-takers are able to gain market share. Economies of scale in advertising are explained by Jones as a tendency for popular brands to benefit from above-average purchase and repurchase frequency. He calls this phenomenon 'penetration supercharge' and illustrates his theory with Unilever's Lux brand. Lux is sold in 30 countries and has an average market share of 17% and an average share of voice of 14%. Unilever is able to keep the market share stable and occasionally enjoys sales increases. In some markets Lux tried to economise by lowering SOV. In markets where the SOV was below 12%, SOM began to fragment. The conclusion is that the underinvestment barrier is 5% (17% − 12%).

The relation between SOM and SOV provides an objective tool for companies to compare their communications spend with the budgets of other players in the market. This allows marketers to make a better analysis. The average SOV helps to estimate the maximum underinvestment big brands can afford without losing too much of their market position.

Besides sales effects, the result of the marketing communications effort can also be measured in other terms, such as brand awareness. In the following graph the efficiency of the advertising campaigns of different banks is analysed. On the horizontal axis budgets are measured. The vertical axis shows top-of-mind awareness of bank names. For two consecutive years, the relationship between the two factors is shown. The more a bank moves to the upper left corner of the graph, the more efficiently it is spending its resources. The analysis also permits a comparison of the own company with competitors.

Top-of-mind awareness and advertising budgets

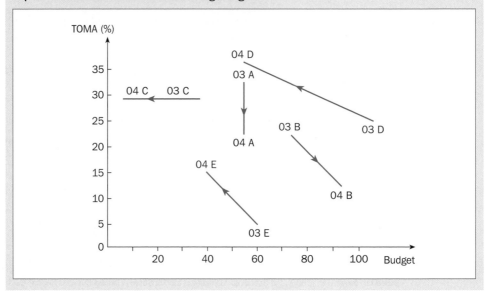

Objective and task method

This method is one of the least arbitrary methods which makes it a difficult technique to use. It differs from the other methods in that it starts from communications objectives and the resources that are needed to reach these planned goals. All needed investments are then added and this will lead to the overall communications budget. It requires more strategic planning and investment analysis and is therefore clearly superior to all the other methods. Moreover, budgets can be evaluated each year and this feedback will lead to improved decision-making and more efficient budgeting in the future. The difficulty in this method lies in the estimation of profit impacts of different communications actions and tactics. Therefore it is of the utmost importance that historical data on, for instance, sales promotion responses in each market are stored. But estimating all costs of every action needs some effort and often the final costs of an action are difficult to foresee.[16]

Table 6.3 shows the three most frequently used budgeting methods in the US.[17] Percentage of sales is the most commonly used communications budgeting technique. It is likely that variants such as percentage on last year's returns and percentage on profits are also commonly used. Spending what is left after all other costs are covered is also popular and the arbitrary method is frequently used in smaller companies and business-to-business contexts. A survey by Belgian Business & Industry revealed that 40% of

Table 6.3 Budgeting methods most often used in the US

Budgeting method	Consumer goods	Business-to-business
1 % of expected sales	50%	28%
2 Affordability method	30%	26%
3 Arbitrary method	12%	34%

Based on: Sissors, J.Z. and Surmanek, J. (1986), *Advertising Media Planning*. Lincolnwood, IL: NTC Business Books.

all business-to-business companies had no preset communications budget: funds were allocated according to needs. Eighteen per cent said they had a budget, but admitted that the funds weren't allocated to specific tasks and objectives.

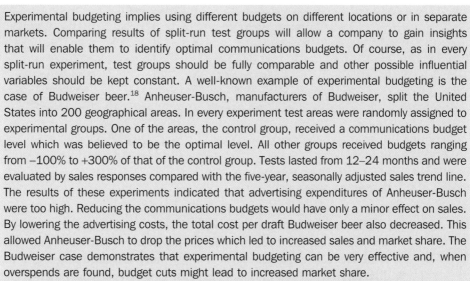

Experimental budgeting implies using different budgets on different locations or in separate markets. Comparing results of split-run test groups will allow a company to gain insights that will enable them to identify optimal communications budgets. Of course, as in every split-run experiment, test groups should be fully comparable and other possible influential variables should be kept constant. A well-known example of experimental budgeting is the case of Budweiser beer.[18] Anheuser-Busch, manufacturers of Budweiser, split the United States into 200 geographical areas. In every experiment test areas were randomly assigned to experimental groups. One of the areas, the control group, received a communications budget level which was believed to be the optimal level. All other groups received budgets ranging from −100% to +300% of that of the control group. Tests lasted from 12–24 months and were evaluated by sales responses compared with the five-year, seasonally adjusted sales trend line. The results of these experiments indicated that advertising expenditures of Anheuser-Busch were too high. Reducing the communications budgets would have only a minor effect on sales. By lowering the advertising costs, the total cost per draft Budweiser beer also decreased. This allowed Anheuser-Busch to drop the prices which led to increased sales and market share. The Budweiser case demonstrates that experimental budgeting can be very effective and, when overspends are found, budget cuts might lead to increased market share.

However, there are some fundamental disadvantages with this method. First, experiments tend to be expensive. To test different budget levels it would be necessary to assign an amount of non-optimal budgets. High budgets will lead to a spill of resources and low budgets could affect market positions. Moreover, experiments and the data-gathering process require additional investments. When cutting costs through reducing the number of test groups and/or the test period, less accurate and thus less reliable results will be achieved. A second disadvantage is that experiments are hard to control and that uncontrollable factors such as competitive actions, distribution influences, etc. are likely to skew the experimental settings. It is also very difficult to reach each of the test groups with different isolated communications channels, and when regional media are used communications impacts might not be comparable with the traditional national media coverage.

Factors influencing budgets

A number of factors may influence the budgeting decision or may call for budget adjustments.[19] They are summarised in Figure 6.6.

Figure 6.6 Factors influencing communications budgets

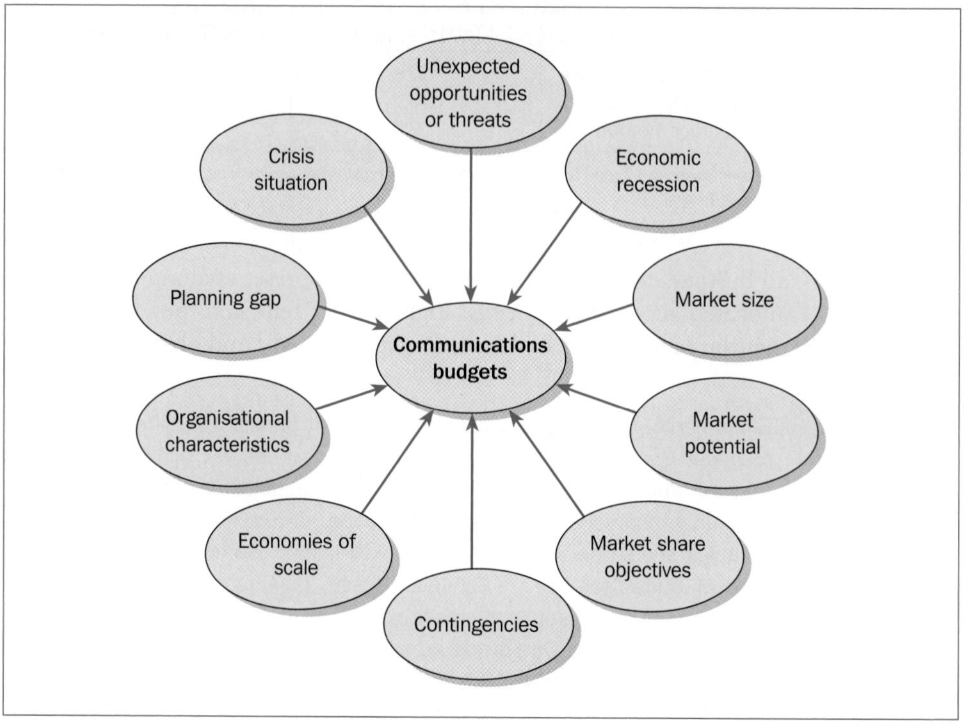

Based on: Belch, G.E. and Belch M.A. (1998), *Advertising and Promotion. An Integrated Marketing Communication Perspective.* New York: Irwin/McGraw-Hill.

The smaller the targeted markets, the easier it is to reach the targets in a cost-efficient way. Spending too much in small markets leads to saturation and overspends are likely to be ineffective. Larger markets imply more dispersed target groups which are more difficult to reach and thus more expensive. When particular markets have higher potential, it may be a good idea to allocate more money to these specific markets. Brands with smaller market shares and new brands require a high communications budget, larger well-established brands and 'harvested' brands in the maturity stage of their life cycle could do with a lower allocation of communications funds.

Some studies[20] show that companies and brands with larger market shares have an advantage in communications costs (such as better media space buying, synergy between different communications mix elements on different company brands, better media rental rates and lower production costs) and can thus spend less money on promotional activities while having the same or even better sales. However, other research[21] claims that there is no evidence that larger companies are able to support their brands with lower advertising costs than smaller ones. A number of organisational factors that have a potential influence on the budgeting decision can be identified:[22] the organisational structure (centralised vs decentralised, formalisation and complexity), the use of experts such as consultants, the organisational hierarchy, preferences and experiences of decision-makers and decision-influencers, and pressure on management to reach certain budgets.

Sometimes it is necessary to make adjustments to the planned budgets during the year or during the communications campaign. If sales and profits lag behind projected and budgeted figures (planning gap), cutting communications efforts is often the easiest and fastest way to increase profits. Of course, this will only have an immediate effect in the short term. In the long run this might lead to eroding competitive edges and market and brand positions. Crisis situations such as troubles with production or distribution might need exceptional investments in public relations and crisis communications. Other internal occurrences such as financial scandals, strikes, ecological catastrophes, etc. might also demand budget adjustments.

Unexpected opportunities or threats in the market might change strategic plans and communications budgets, as well as unexpected moves by competitors, new legislation, new media and changes in media costs.

Economic recessions will often have serious consequences for communications budgets. Consumers spend less money and shrinking markets mean stronger competitive battles in which price is a commonly used weapon. Companies may react in one or two ways with regard to their promotional spending. Some try to economise in every way possible. A substantial amount of all costs are fixed and cannot be lowered in the short term. Most companies are attracted by a budget that is quite easy to bring down: the communications budget. Other companies react by increasing their budget, believing that extra investment will drive sales up. A crisis is regarded as the ideal moment to establish their position. This is called anti-cycle budgeting. Market share is gained during recessions and then defended in periods of a booming economy. Some multinationals such as PepsiCo, Coca-Cola, General Mills, Kellogg's and Procter & Gamble have a strong belief in long-term investments in marketing communications.

Some companies prepare contingency budgets. These are reserve budgets provided for financing quick management actions as necessary. These crisis actions are planned in so-called contingency plans. They stipulate which actions must be taken when, for instance, when significant drops in sales occur or when an important competitor switches to aggressive promotional actions or launches a new product. Reaction time will be substantially lower in such cases when all appropriate actions and budgeting have been foreseen.

Budgeting for new brands or products

Although budgeting for existing brands in established product categories is the most common task for marketers, often they are confronted with the problem of budgeting for a brand or product launch. This is even more difficult than the former. Historical data on the budget settings that have been successful are not available and consequently easy-to-use schemes as discussed above are not appropriate for estimating required budgets.[23]

The primary budgeting method for launching new brands or products should be the objective-and-task method. But given the uncertainty and lack of historical data, this is not only a difficult budgeting method but also one that is not risk free. Therefore, other methods are good back-ups to compare estimations made earlier. A marketer may, for instance, examine the industry advertising-to-sales (A/S) ratio (advertising intensity) for the market in which a brand is to be launched. He may decide to set a budget that is higher than the industry average in order to make an impact. Doubling the A/S ratio is considered a safe guideline for the first year of introduction. In the second year overspending the ratio by 50% should do. Of course, it could be even more informative to make comparisons with particular competing brands or products.

Peckham, a consultant with AC Nielsen, developed a rule of thumb for new fast-moving consumer good brands.[24] Peckham's 1.5 rule recommends setting the SOV of the brand to be launched at 1.5 times the desired SOM at the end of the brand's first two years. A limitation of Peckham's rule is that it is only applicable in markets or product categories for which there is a strong correlation between SOV and SOM. A study of 638 firms across 20 industries[25] found a strong relationship between SOV and SOM across a broad range of industries for consumer as well as industrial products.

It is quite easy to calculate share of voice once the industry communications budgets are known, but to estimate target market shares, the brand's order of entry on a market should be studied.[26] In almost all markets a brand's competitive advantage is determined by the order of entry on a market. Pioneer brands often enjoy market share leadership, the second brand gets the second largest market share, etc.[27] The market share of a brand entering a category is on average 0.71 times the share of the previous entrant, although for frequently purchased (fast moving) consumer products it is 0.92.[28] Overcoming this order-of-entry effect by later entrants is difficult and can only be achieved when introducing a product of superior quality, by spending a lot more on advertising or by making advertising of better quality. Quality of advertising – that is, advertising that gets better results in getting the message across and creating better awareness, being more persuasive or getting higher purchase intentions or sales results – depends on the creative work of advertising agencies and the media planning job of media agencies. These factors have not been considered in this chapter but are, of course, of huge importance and influence the effectiveness and consequently the needed budget. However, according to some studies,[29] in about 76% of all product categories order-of-entry advantages in market share are never overcome.

Summary

Sales response models have been developed to describe the relationship between communications budgets and communications effects. However, the extent to which sales respond to advertising depends on a number of other factors, such as the product range, price and distribution strategies, the marketing environment and the competition. As a result, it is very difficult to decide on communications budgets on the basis of these models because the effects of communications efforts on sales cannot be isolated. Furthermore, traditionally, advertising is assumed to affect sales only in the long run (although this point of view is radically contradicted by the works of Jones), which makes it even harder to decide on budgets in terms of effectiveness. Therefore, companies often resort to more practical and easier, but not very relevant, budgeting methods such as inertia, arbitrary allocation, affordability and percentage of sales. In the objectives and task method, the communications needs are assessed, after which a task-related budget is defined. In the competitive parity method, companies analyse their market position and decide on their share of voice accordingly. Communications budgets are influenced by multiple factors, such as a crisis situation, contingencies, unexpected opportunities, economic recessions and other market and company factors, and companies should always be alert and prepared to adapt budgets to changing situations.

Review questions

1 What is a sales response model and why is it not easy to estimate it?

2 Discuss Jones's theory on the short-term and long-term relationship between advertising budgets and sales.

3 Discuss the various communications budgeting methods that are frequently used by practitioners.

4 What is the relationship between share of voice and share of market, and how does it affect budgeting?

5 What are the factors that influence the budgeting decision?

6 How should the communications budget for a new product launch be determined?

Further reading

Butherfield, L. (2003), *AdValue*. New York: Butterworth-Heinemann.

Dekimpe, M.G. and Hanssens, D.M. (1995), 'The Persistence of Marketing Effects on Sales', *Marketing Science*, 14(1), 1–21.

Jones, J.P. (2001), *Ultimate Secrets of Advertising*. London: Sage Publications.

Jones, J.P. and Slater, J.S. (2003), *What's In a Name? Advertising and the Concept of Brands*. Armonk, NY: M.E. Sharpe.

Case 6

Budgeting in the automobile industry

While analysts pointed to a stable situation for the world automotive industry in general, Western Europe clearly experienced recessive trends in its motor vehicle market during the year 2002. This reflected the rather weak performance of the European economy. The European Commission's consumer confidence indicator decreased in December 2002 for the third consecutive month and was at its lowest level for about six years. This was due to the deterioration of consumers' expectations about the general economic situation and the job market in particular.

The year 2002 ended with a total of 14.4 million passenger cars registered in Western Europe, reflecting a decrease of 2.9% compared to 2001. This slowdown came about despite the surge of auto sales that took place in December 2002, in particular in The Netherlands, Ireland and Italy. Looking at annual figures in detail, five countries posted increases, namely Denmark (+15.3%), Finland (+7%), the UK (+4.3%), Sweden (+3.2%) and Luxembourg (+1.4). All other

countries recorded decreases ranging from −11.4% in Portugal to −2.6% in Germany. Despite financial incentives, the Italian market experienced a fall of −6% on 2001 levels. While Germany also saw a decline in passenger car registrations, it remained the biggest individual European automotive market, accounting for about 23% of total registrations in the EU15.

Concerning market share figures, German and Japanese group brands had generally retained their position on the European market, while Italian and Korean makes had a marked decline in market share. In terms of new passenger car registration specifications, the diesel boom continues in Western Europe. The share of diesel-powered cars out of total new registrations rose from 36.6% in 2001 to 40.9% in 2002 (5.8 million units). As for new passenger car registrations by market segment, the highest share remains in the so-called 'small' segment, followed by the 'lower medium' segment. The 4 × 4 segments enjoyed a small increase in demand, accounting for

5.24% of new registrations in 2002 compared to 4.6% in 2001. Production of motor vehicles in Western Europe fell in parallel with the fall in demand. Latest figures from the CCFA (Comité des Constructeurs Français d'Automobiles – French Carmaking Association) indicate that production of passenger cars reached 14,810,460 units in 2002, a decrease of 1% compared to 2001.

In 2002 Belgium assembled 876,858 private vehicles for export. The figure has been decreasing for some years (for instance –22% compared to 1995). The main export countries for cars assembled in Belgium were Germany (17.6%), the UK (13.8%), Spain (11.2%) and France (8.8%).

In 2000 Belgian households spent 11.6% of their annual household budget on the purchase (4.8%) and use (6.8%) of their own transportation vehicles. At the end of 2002 Belgium had 4,724,856 passenger cars of which 55% ran on petrol, 43.4% on diesel and 1.2% on LPG. Petrol is becoming less popular as 64% of newly registered cars in 2002 had diesel engines compared to the 35.7% petrol registrations.

The smallest engines (less than 1399cc) are also losing popularity and account for 23% of new cars compared to 31% in 1995.

Evolution of number of new passenger cars in Belgium

In 2002 a total of 472,630 new passenger cars were registered in Belgium: 40% were German car brands, 33% French and 11% Japanese. Italian makes represented 5% of the market of new cars and Swedish 3%. German brands were maintaining their strong market position, although in 1997 their share was even higher (46%), while French car makes were increasing their success (share of 24.5% in 1997). Japanese brands, on the other hand, were slightly losing their impact on the Belgian market (15.4% share in 1997). The average age of the Belgian passenger car is increasing: in 2002 it was 7 years, 7 months and 2 days, while in 1991 the average age was 6 years and 21 days.

Case Table 6.1 summarises the number of registrations of new private cars in Belgium for major brands in the period 1998–2002.

Case Table 6.1 Registration of new private cars in Belgium, 1998–2002

Make	1998	1999	2000	2001	2002
VW, Audi	77,802	85,413	85,238	79,672	67,726
Peugeot	38,320	47,416	54,093	53,089	53,360
Renault	48,968	52,565	57,336	61,705	51,423
Citroën	32,878	34,508	39,401	45,761	48,853
Opel	43,615	51,854	54,405	51,017	48,194
Ford	29,871	31,140	32,106	26,834	22,850
Toyota	24,525	22,768	22,641	19,883	24,860
Mercedes-Benz	17,560	21,353	22,993	23,131	23,940
Smart	–	978	2,118	2,054	2,161
BMW	15,841	18,048	20,714	20,960	18,962
Fiat	15,895	16,085	19,422	14,461	14,750
Seat	10,444	11,944	13,831	12,008	10,512
Saab	2,947	2,607	2,966	2,426	2,548
Volvo	11,969	11,289	10,379	9,966	9,991
Lancia	2,535	2,875	3,693	2,489	1,176
Alfa Romeo	6,172	7,152	8,533	8,911	8,064
Nissan	14,334	11,821	10,903	8,990	7,205
Honda	6,644	6,187	5,203	3,224	3,605
Hyundai	3,548	4,393	4,910	4,471	6,342
Daewoo	4,228	4,934	7,030	3,197	3,213
Mazda	7,748	8,368	7,275	4,126	4,615
Mitsubishi	11,293	11,291	8,788	5,604	3,980
Suzuki	5,747	6,312	5,410	4,345	3,974
Skoda	3,892	4,360	5,325	7,198	6,462
Others	26,948	28,542	26,927	24,257	23,864
Total market sales	**463,724**	**504,203**	**531,640**	**499,779**	**472,630**

Evolution of advertising budgets of car brands in Belgium

The car industry is one of the largest advertising spenders in Belgium, together with government, financial services (banking and insurance), telecom, retail distribution and fast-moving consumer goods. Case Table 6.2 gives an overview of total advertising budgets spent by the major car makes in Belgium. They are an aggregation of all traditional above-the-line media: TV, radio, magazines, newspapers, billboards and cinema advertising.

Questions

1 Using Case Tables 6.1 and 6.2, carry out a share of voice/share of market analysis of the automobile industry for 1998, 2000 and 2002. Indicate the profit-taking car makes and the investment makes for each

year. Do they match the leaders and followers in this market?

2 Study the figures of Swedish car manufacturers Saab and Volvo. What budgeting method would you assume they are using: a percentage of sales method or a competitive parity method? Why do you think this?

3 Suppose you want to launch the Smart brand on the Belgian market. Your goal is to capture a market share of 1% by the year 2002. What budget would you suggest to reach this goal? Consider two methods: the A/S ratio method on the one hand and the Law of Peckham on the other.

4 What factors might influence advertising budgets in the car industry?

Sources: ACEA economic outlook 2003, www.acea.be; Febiac, www.febiac.be, 2003; NIS, Vervoer 2003; OMD, 2003 based on MDB/CIM figures. Thanks to Dimitri De Lauw, strategic planner of VVL/BBDO for providing advertising budgets of the car industry.

Case Table 6.2 Advertising budgets per year (all media) in Belgium, 1998–2002 (€)

Make	1998	1999	2000	2001	2002
VW, Audi	15,809,170.35	20,656,093.90	18,656,745.01	21,807,961.13	20,044,759.61
Peugeot	10,888,469.30	10,105,524.48	8,524,046.24	9,129,936.45	6,276,534.71
Renault	17,591,736.11	17,934,047.18	17,819,656.61	16,232,637.81	19,188,633.74
Citroën	9,955,551.87	9,375,897.29	11,086,149.13	12,198,320.66	13,017,747.55
Opel	14,907,251.89	12,887,025.55	10,980,162.18	9,163,331.29	10,844,352.62
Ford	8,516,837.41	10,393,582.90	11,545,233.64	13,376,451.02	12,010,710.22
Toyota	9,847,257.74	8,201,152.66	10,621,321.61	8,332,861.58	10,008,409.60
Mercedes-Benz	6,940,913.10	5,560,698.14	8,399,114.65	9,517,310.76	12,191,168.81
Smart	3,123,118.59	2,783,227.05	1,582,280.81	1,616,182.46	1,460,899.11
BMW	5,032,418.82	6,095,307.88	6,184,385.56	6,621,779.61	7,189,418.45
Fiat	5,327,047.86	8,847,812.11	12,557,700.37	9,635,783.89	9,891,849.47
Seat	2,150,855.45	2,112,097.45	2,086,490.08	2,903,379.88	2,128,023.85
Saab	1,655,003.19	1,402,388.78	1,528,974.49	1,603,025.56	1,428,475.97
Volvo	3,897,299.15	4,839,459.85	5,571,333.04	2,070,494.60	3,015,340.12
Lancia	2,631,209.41	4,068,658.05	4,047,285.00	2,634,802.10	1,519,265.21
Alfa Romeo	3,047,275.74	3,431,974.87	4,454,473.31	4,282,977.24	5,025,305.25
Nissan	6,683,893.41	8,727,066.90	6,780,205.59	2,684,917.56	2,724,271.07
Honda	3,806,397.48	3,589,412.82	3,383,812.76	4,147,024.46	5,201,614.72
Hyundai	2,719,035.53	3,548,823.18	4,196,364.26	5,879,133.11	3,223,323.62
Daewoo	2,101,593.31	5,461,256.00	5,516,252.30	2,087,685.89	924,195.05
Mazda	4,709,351.67	4,273,819.94	3,516,591.18	171,247.30	2,496,149.14
Mitsubishi	6,437,979.05	6,814,626.93	4,254,547.97	3,271,787.78	3,573,022.81
Suzuki	2,320,588.39	2,308,655.19	2,486,431.69	1,389,115.14	1,768,284.50
Skoda	1,131,465.31	1,897,709.86	3,593,035.70	4,165,299.34	3,753,867.50
Others	10,385,608.41	12,246,897.46	13,167,123.96	14,286,180.37	17,857,026.20
Total market advertising	**161,617,328.54**	**177,563,216.42**	**182,539,717.14**	**169,209,626.99**	**176,762,548.90**

References

1 Bovée, C.L., Thill, J.V., Dovel, G.P. and Wood, M.B. (1995), *Advertising Excellence*. New York: McGraw-Hill.

2 Arndt, J. and Simon, J. (1983), 'Advertising and Economies of Scale: Critical Comments on the Evidence', *Journal of Industrial Economics*, 32(2), 229–41.

3 Longman, K.A. (1971), *Advertising*. New York: Harcourt Brace Jovanovich.

4 Jegers, M. and De Pelsmacker, P. (1990), 'The Optimal Level of Advertising, Considering Advertising as an Investment in Goodwill', *Ekonomicko Matematicky Obzor (Review of Econometrics)*, 26(2), 153–63.

5 Aaker, D.A., Batra, R. and Myers, J.G. (1987), *Advertising Management*. Englewood Cliffs, NJ: Prentice Hall.

6 Jones, J.P. (1995), *When Ads Work: New Proof that Advertising Triggers Sales*. New York: The Free Press/Lexicon Books.

7 Jones, J.P. (1995), Editorial, *Harvard Business Review* (Jan.–Feb.), 53–66.

8 François, J. (1996), 'Forecasting Effect of Advertising on Sales: Reporting on a Large-scale US Research', *Media Line News*.

9 McDonald, C. (1995), 'Advertising Response Functions, What are They, What do They Mean, and How Should we Use Them?', *Admap* (April), 10.

10 Dekimpe, M.G. and Hanssens, D.M. (1995), 'The Persistence of Marketing Effects on Sales', *Marketing Science*, 14(1), 1–21.

11 Belch, G.E. and Belch, M.A. (1998), *Advertising and Promotion. An Integrated Marketing Communication Perspective*. New York: Irwin/McGraw-Hill.

12 Aaker, D.A., Batra, R. and Myers, J.G. (1987), *Advertising Management*. Englewood Cliffs, NJ: Prentice Hall.

13 Kaynak, E. (1989), *The Management of International Advertising. A Handbook and Guide for Professionals*. New York: Quorum Books.

14 Schroer, J.C. (1990), 'Ad Spending: Growing Market Share', *Harvard Business Review*, 68(1), 44–8.

15 Based on Jones, J.P. (1990), 'Ad Spending: Maintaining Market Share', *Harvard Business Review*, 68(1), 38–43.

16 Fill, C. (1995), *Marketing Communication. Frameworks, Theories and Applications*. London: Prentice Hall.

17 Sissors, J.Z. and Surmanek, J. (1986), *Advertising Media Planning*. Lincolnwood, IL: NTC Business Books.

18 Aaker, D.A., Batra, R. and Myers, J.G. (1987), *Advertising Management*. Englewood Cliffs NJ: Prentice Hall.

19 Belch, G.E. and Belch, M.A. (1998), *Advertising and Promotion. An Integrated Marketing Communication Perspective*. New York: Irwin/McGraw-Hill.

20 Brown, R.S. (1978), 'Estimating Advantages to Large Scale Advertising', *Review of Economics and Statistics*, 60, 428–37.

21 Boyer, K.D. and Lancaster, K.M. (1986), 'Are There Scale Economies in Advertising?', *Journal of Business*, 59(3), 509–26.

22 Low, G.S. and Mohr, J.J. (1991), 'The Budget Allocation between Advertising and Sales Promotion: Understanding the Decision Process', *AMA Educators' Proceedings*. Chicago, 448–57.

23 Rossiter, J.R. and Percy, L. (1998), *Advertising Communication and Promotion Management*. Sydney: McGraw-Hill.

24 Peckham, J.O. (1981), *The Wheel of Marketing*. Scarsdale, NY: self-published.

25 Simon, C.J. and Sullivan, M.M. (1993), 'The Measurement and Determinants of Equity: A Financial Approach', *Marketing Science*, 12(1), 28–52.

26 Rossiter, J.R. and Percy, L. (1998), *Advertising Communication and Promotion Management*. Sydney: McGraw-Hill.

27 Parry, M. and Bass, F.M. (1990), 'When to Lead or Follow? It Depends', *Marketing Letters*, 1(3), 187–98.

28 Urban, G., Carter, T., Gaskin, S. and Mucha, Z. (1986), 'Market Share Rewards to Pioneering Brands: An Empirical Analysis and Stratgeic Implications', *Management Science*, 32(6), 645–59.

29 Buzell, R.D. (1981), 'Are There Natural Market Structures?', *Journal of Marketing*, 45(1), 42–51.

Chapter 7
Advertising

Chapter outline

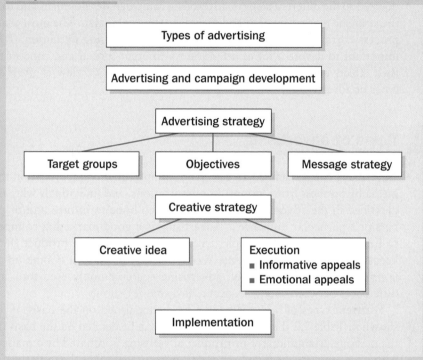

Chapter objectives

This chapter will help you to:

- Distinguish the various stages in advertising campaign development
- Learn about the information that is needed about the target groups of an advertising campaign
- Understand the various objectives of an advertising campaign and the characteristics of a good set of objectives
- Understand the importance of creativity in advertising
- Evaluate the effectiveness of various execution strategies for rational appeals
- Understand the effectiveness of emotional execution strategies such as humour, eroticism and warmth

Introduction

Advertising is one of the oldest, most visible and most important instruments of the marketing communications mix. Large sums of money are spent on advertising, and no other marketing phenomenon is subject to so much public debate and controversy. Huge amounts of research are devoted to the question of what makes advertising effective and to the role of advertising characteristics on its effectiveness.

As is the case with other communications instruments, special attention has to be devoted to the different steps in advertising campaign development and to the fit between the strategic marketing plan and the advertising campaign. The most crucial step in this process is translating the creative idea in an advertising execution. To this end, it is important to devote a lot of attention to different formal and content techniques and their effectiveness in advertising. But first of all, an overview is given of the different types of advertising.

Types of advertising

Advertising can be defined as any 'paid, nonpersonal communication through various media by business firms, nonprofit organizations, and individuals who are in some way identified in the advertising message and who hope to inform and/or persuade members of a particular audience'.[1] Advertising is a good marketing communications tool to inform and persuade people, irrespective of whether a product (Fitness of Nestlé keeps you slim), a service (Avis: We try harder) or an idea (Come up against cancer) is promoted. Not surprisingly, advertising is a commonly used tool, although major differences between countries occur, as Table 7.1 shows.

Different types of advertising can be distinguished on the basis of four criteria, as shown in Table 7.2. First of all, advertising can be defined on the basis of the sender of the message. Manufacturer or product advertising is initiated by a manufacturing company that promotes its own brands. If a government takes the initiative for a campaign, this is called collective advertising. Retail organisations also advertise. Sometimes two manufacturer companies, or a retailer and a manufacturer, jointly develop an advertising campaign. This is called co-operative advertising. Besides goods and services, ideas can be promoted, mostly by not-for-profit organisations.

The intended receiver of the advertising message can be either a private end-consumer or another company. In the latter case, the company may buy the products to use in its own production process (industrial advertising), or buy the products to resell them (trade advertising). Business-to-business communications are covered in Chapter 18.

Different types of advertising can also be distinguished according to the type of message conveyed. The difference between advertising focussed on informational and transformational consumer motives was explained in Chapter 3. Institutional advertising is the term used to describe government campaigns. Selective advertising campaigns try to promote a specific brand, while a generic campaign promotes a whole product category, such as Dutch cheese, British beef or French wine. Theme advertising attempts to build a reservoir of goodwill for a brand or a product. Action advertising tries to stimulate consumers to buy a product immediately. Often, the latter is used in support of a sales promotion campaign.

Table 7.1 Advertising expenditures, 2004

Country	Ad spendings	Ad spendings per capita	Rank	Ad spendings (% GDP)
Italy	25,625	460.1	1	1.97
Norway	1,965	429.3	2	1.02
US	120,977	412.9	3	1.38
Iceland	115	395.9	4	1.28
Switzerland	2,365	323.2	5	0.86
Sweden	2,806	312.6	6	1.04
Spain	12,500	296.2	7	1.68
Ireland	1,156	290.5	8	0.86
Netherlands, The	4,468	275.9	9	0.98
France	16,366	265.3	10	1.05
Portugal	2,648	255.7	11	2.01
Denmark	1,280	237.1	12	0.70
Austria	1,908	236.9	13	0.87
Germany	17,407	210.9	14	0.82
Finland	1,079	206.7	15	0.75
Belgium	2,137	206.4	16	0.80
UK	11,987	202.4	17	1.55
Greece	2,131	194.4	18	1.40
Luxembourg	87	194.1	19	0.37
Slovenia	277	141.0	20	1.16
Hongary	1,412	139.6	21	2.00
Russia	9,473	65.2	22	2.47
Poland	2,410	63.1	23	1.41

Source: IP Peaktime, Television Key Facts 2004 (www.ipb.be).

Table 7.2 Types of advertising

Sender	Message
■ Manufacturer	■ Informational
■ Collective	■ Transformational
■ Retailer	■ Institutional
■ Co-operative	■ Selective vs generic
■ Idea	■ Theme vs action
Receiver	**Media**
■ Consumer	■ Audiovisual
■ Business-to-business	■ Print
– industrial	■ Point-of-purchase
– trade	■ Direct

Finally, different types of campaigns can be distinguished on the basis of the medium in which the ad is placed. Two main categories of traditional or above-the-line advertising can be distinguished: audiovisual and print. Other forms of advertising, such as in-store communications (Chapter 14) and direct advertising (Chapter 13), are called below-the-line.

Campaign development

Developing an advertising campaign, like any other communications plan, consists of a sequence of steps (Figure 7.1).[2] The starting point is the marketing strategy, on the basis of which a specific advertising strategy needs to be developed. The three main points in the advertising strategy are: the target group (to or with whom are we going to communicate?), the advertising objectives (why are we going to communicate or what are we trying to reach?) and the message strategy (what are we going to communicate?). The most difficult step is translating the advertising strategy into a creative strategy or, in other words, going from 'what to say' to 'how to say it'. Afterwards the media strategy is developed. The different ideas will be evaluated on the basis of the creative brief and objectives stated, and the winning idea will be produced and implemented. In the process the ads in the campaign may be tested, and often the effectiveness will be assessed after the campaign. Target groups, objectives, media planning and campaign testing are discussed in Chapters 4, 5, 8 and 9 respectively.

Figure 7.1 Stages in campaign development

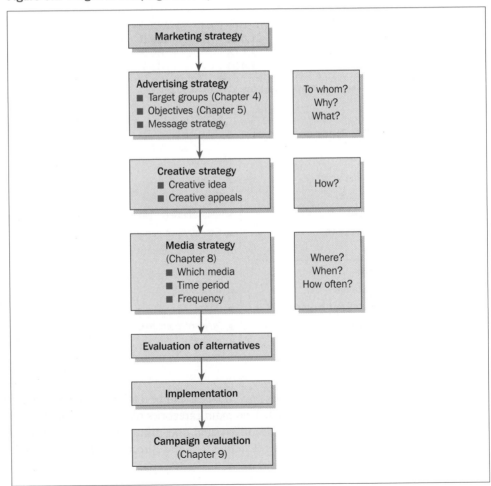

Message strategy

What are we going to say to the consumers? The message strategy or advertising platform is a very important element of advertising strategy since it has to convince consumers. They have to know why they should buy the product, to learn in what way it is special, how it is beneficial or advantageous for them, how it can help them, what characteristics it has or what benefits, value it offers, etc. In order to answer the question 'what to communicate?' the advertiser has to know and understand the target group very well: he or she has to know what the product can do for the target group, what the product can mean to them and how the product can help the consumers to reach their goals. Indeed, advertising can only be effective if it benefits the consumer. Therefore, the message cannot be focussed on seller-objectives, but has to start from the target consumers' motives.[3] Some customers see a car just as a functional vehicle, a means of getting them from A to B. This target group can perhaps be convinced by communicating the brand's attributes (airbag, engine, etc.) or benefits (reliability, safety, etc.). Other customers do not want to buy a car, they want to buy an image, a status. Obviously, communications to the latter group should be different from those to the former group. Communicating a lifestyle, an image or a product's identity might be more suitable than telling customers about attributes or benefits.

Knowing the problems, preferences and aspirations of the target group may be essential for deciding on the right message.

Advertising to specific target groups: kids and teens and senior citizens

Both kids and teens and senior citizens require a specific advertising approach (see Plate 9). The table below outlines some dos and don'ts.

Advertising do's and don'ts

Kids and teens		Senior citizens	
Dos	Don'ts	Dos	Don'ts
1 Tell a basic story	1 Long dialogues	1 Positive message	1 Remind of getting older
2 Entertain kids	2 Complex messages	2 Inter-generational approach	2 Use senior positioning
3 Surprise kids	3 Imitate kids' talk	3 Focus on cognitive age	3 Age labels
4 Use older models	4 Patronise	4 Promote benefits to overcome guilt	4 Make long story short
5 Remember mum and dad	5 Execution mistakes	5 Use symbols of their youth	5 Take physical consequences of getting older into account

Kids and teens want to hear a basic story (a product is a solution for a problem or a reward for good behaviour), but not a long dialogue or complex message. Children want to be entertained and surprised. They continually look for new experiences and details, and like the use of music, humour, animation, colours, jingles, games, puzzles, etc. Although they do like catchy slogans and are fond of slang and kids' talk, it is better for an advertiser to avoid using it since by the time you discover their sayings they are already out of date. The aspirational age of children is about four years older than they actually are, therefore it is better to cast older children to avoid reactions like 'This is not for me, this if for babies'. Kids hate being patronised, so do not pretend to be one of them or to know better than them. Although you want children to be fond of your brand, it is usually the parents who have to buy it. Therefore, make sure that your appeal is also attractive to parents by mentioning arguments pertaining to health, durability, lifetime value, values, etc. Finally, try to avoid 'wrong executions' such as showing children who are too young or the wrong gender (remember that boys have difficulty identifying with girl characters while girls can identify with both boys and girls) and not using enough visuals (children listen with their eyes!).[4]

Senior citizens represent a group that accounts for 80% of personal wealth and about 40% of consumer spending. Since 80% of consumers over the age of 50 perceive contemporary advertising as irrelevant to them, it is about time to take their needs and motivations into account.[5] Senior citizens know they are getting older and that this will bring inconveniences; they do not want advertising to remind them of this or to confront them with these negative life aspects. Rather, focus on what the product can do for them, what the main benefits are. Another possibility is to stress positive aspects of getting older such as friendships, children and grandchildren, a good financial position, wisdom and experience.[6] An inter-generational approach may tap into these perfectly, such as featuring grandparents enjoying a certain product or service with the rest of the family,[7] certainly much better than using a senior positioning. Seniors are not looking for a product 'ideal for seniors' because they still want to belong to society and do not want to form an isolated group, or as Ahmad put it: 'Older consumers like to be respected as people and not because they are old in terms of chronological age.'[8] Moreover, many seniors do not feel old (actually, at an age of 55 they feel about eight years younger than they are) and do not want to be addressed as old or senior citizens, certainly not if they have not reached the age of 65 yet. Unfortunately, in practice the age of 50 or 55 is often chosen as the boundary.[9] European seniors have lived through war situations and recessions and know what poverty and scarcity mean. As a consequence, many of them still feel guilty about spending money. Therefore, advertising should try to take away the feeling of being thrifty by providing them with good reasons to buy. Many senior citizens are rather critical and want objective, extended information and compelling reasons why they should buy the brand.[10] As mentioned in Chapter 3, nostalgic appeals showing symbols, heroes, music groups, etc. from the seniors' youth can be very powerful. Finally, although seniors do not like to admit it, they do encounter problems when ageing, for example sight and hearing problems. Therefore, it is better to use high contrast levels between text and background, a serif font not smaller than 10 points, and to use slower-paced TV and radio commercials, in which background noise is avoided.[11]

Furthermore, it is important not to confuse consumers. Therefore, most companies stick to promoting one unique benefit of their brand, which can be functional or non-functional. A functional benefit, also called a unique selling proposition (USP), usually refers to functional superiority in the sense that the brand offers the best quality, the best service, the lowest price, the most advanced technology. For example, Gillette is 'the best a man can get', there is 'no better washing machine' than Mièle, Lee Casuals 'make any situation comfortable', Philips 'makes things better', Durex Avanti 'gives the most natural feeling', no card is more accepted than MasterCard, etc. A non-functional benefit usually reflects a unique psychological association to consumers and is referred to as an emotional selling proposition (ESP).[12] Dune of Dior is the essence of freedom, you buy L'Oréal because 'you are worth it', you buy your girlfriend a Chaumet watch because 'chaque instant est une émotion' (every moment is an emotion). Other examples of brands that are promoted on the basis of non-functional benefits include Porsche, Rodania, Rolls-Royce, Louis Vuitton, and Van Cleef & Arpels.

In order to know which USP or ESP to go for, the advertiser needs to have a clear consumer insight. These are often revealed by qualitative research. For example, for Kraft a consumer insight was that mothers would not buy Lunchables for their kids because it is convenient (they do not have to prepare sandwiches in the morning, etc.), but they could be convinced if it made them feel like a good mother. Therefore, a child in the Lunchables commercial says 'Yes, yes, thank you Mama' when he discovers his mother gave him Luncheables for lunch instead of ordinary sandwiches. The Luxembourg fixed-line operator, TELE2 AB, was well aware of the fact that heavy phone users are sensitive about the cost the telephone represents in their monthly household budget. These heavy users would love to call more if they did not have to worry about the cost. Therefore, TELE2 positions itself on the promise of providing the 'best price offer' and the 'most simple and clear offer'. A pan-European campaign with the slogan 'TELE2, simply phone for less' proved to be very successful in France, Germany, Italy, Austria, Switzerland and Holland.[13]

Advertising to children and obesity

It is estimated that in the US the average child sees more than 40,000 television commercials a year and that advertisers spend more than $12 billion per year to target the youth market.[14] This is attributed to the strong contribution of children to the consumer economy. McNeal (1998)[15] estimated that children aged 14 years old and under make $24 billion in direct purchases and influence $190 billion in family purchases. Ads for food during children programmes are estimated to be 37% of all ads in the US and 49% in the UK.[16] Furthermore, Lyna (2005)[17] claims that 97.5% of all food commercials appearing on weekend morning TV and 78.3% of weekend programming are for unhealthy foods.

There is a widespread criticism that kids are targeted in relentless ways by food and drinks companies.[18] Therefore, food advertising to children may be contributing to the increase in childhood obesity by promoting unhealthy foods (especially sugary cereals, sweets, fast food restaurants). In many countries obesity is a serious and increasing health problem. It is estimated that obesity accounts for $40 billion of treatment costs a year.[19] However, obesity is a multifactor phenomenon. A sedentary lifestyle and lack of physical activity (the 'couch potato' effect), family eating habits and attitudes towards (fat) food, genetic predisposition, peer pressure, quality of life, in-school food service, nearby retail outlets, socio-economic status, television viewing and advertising have all been suggested to be determining factors of obesity.[20] The empirical evidence for the link between obesity and television viewing and advertising is mixed at best.[21] Eagle, Bulmer and Hawkins (2003) and Eagle et al. (2004b)[22] state that TV viewing is correlated with obesity only to the extent that viewing may replace more active pastimes. Vandewater, Shim and Caplovitz (2004)[23] in their study of 2,831 children aged 1–12 concluded that television viewing had no effect on obesity (measured as BMI) and television viewing, and other studies also found only a weak link between television viewing and obesity.[24] However, food advertising on television has been partially held responsible for what has been called the 'obesity epidemic'.

Creative idea

Before an advertising agency can start thinking of a creative strategy, the advertiser must give them a creative brief. The necessary elements of a creative brief are summarised in Figure 7.2. The creative brief or the document that forms the starting point for the advertising agency should contain not only information on the target group, advertising objectives and message strategy, but also provide sufficient information concerning the background of the company, the product, the market and the competitors. This implies information concerning the past, present and future in order to give the agency as accurate a view of the brand and its environment as possible. Some examples of necessary elements are the long-term company and brand strategy, past, current and desired positioning, former advertising campaigns, message strategies and execution styles, desired media, available budget, and timing of the different steps (creative idea, execution strategies, campaign running, etc.).

The first step of the creative strategy is to develop a creative idea. But what is a creative idea? It is hard to give an accurate definition, but let's consider some attempts. A creative idea can be defined as an 'original and imaginative thought designed to produce goal-directed and problem-solving advertisements and commercials'.[25] According to others, a creative advertising idea has to be attention-grabbing and should work as a catalyst in the sense that it should create a 'chemical reaction' of immediately understanding the brand's position.[26] According to the jazz musician Charlie Mingus, 'Creativity is more than just being different. Everybody can play weird, that's easy. What's hard is to be as simple as Bach. Making the simple complicated is commonplace, making the complicated simple, awesomely simple, that's creativity.'[27] In essence, a creative idea seems to boil down to a proposition which makes it possible to communicate a brand's position in an original, attention-getting, but easy-to-catch way. Several researchers

Figure 7.2 The creative brief

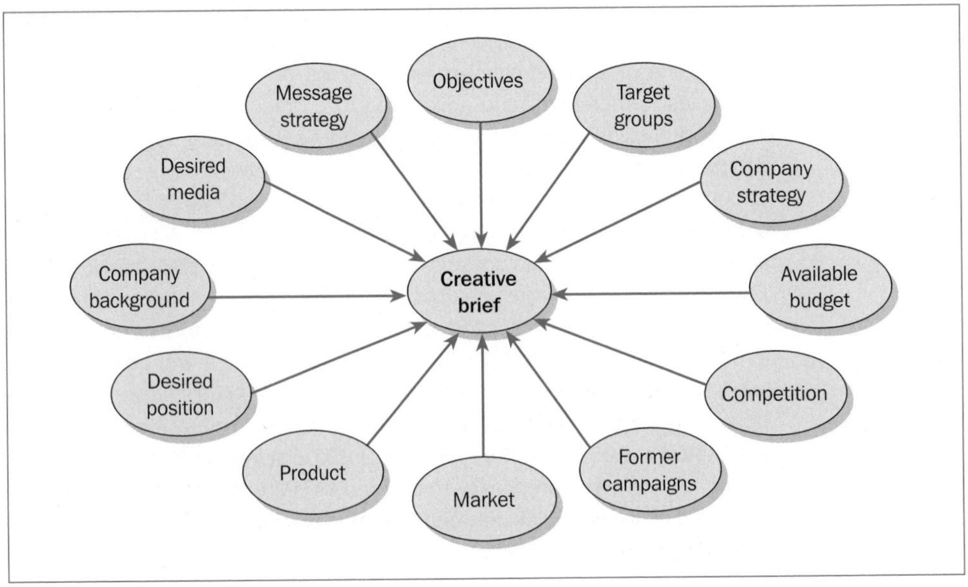

argue that creativity probably is the most important aspect of advertising.[28] An expert panel even held the opinion that 'the selling power of a creative idea can exceed that of an ordinary idea by a multiple of 10' (see Plate 9).[29]

A few examples may clarify what is meant by creative advertising ideas.

- Miller beer has a screw cap instead of a crown cap. Miller promoted its beer in TV commercials with the slogan 'twist to open', showing a fat man in his underwear twisting in front of his bottle of Miller beer, pausing a moment to see whether his bottle had opened, and then starting to twist again.

- Volkswagen promoted its Beetle with the slogan 'think small', turning the small size into a competitive advantage, just as Smart tried to do with 'reduce to the max'. Nissan did the opposite, promoting its new pick-up using print ads and billboards. To stress the size of the pick-up, a countryside picture features a man and, no, not his dog, but his hippopotamus playing with a stick. The baseline reads 'Think Bigger'. Nissan won a Gold Clio Award for this campaign.

- To make clear to the Spanish audience that children should watch less TV and play more, an ad was run in which a little boy is shown watching TV while his dog is watching him. After having waited a while to get a bit of attention, the dog turns away and starts packing its bags. With the bag in its mouth, the dog waits a few minutes in front of the boy, but when the boy does not even look up, the dog sadly leaves.

- Oslo Sporveier wanted to encourage existing users to use public transport more often, as well as encourage new users to take up the habit of using public transport. To reach these objectives, public transport had to be made easier since at that time tickets could be purchased only at one place. Therefore, Oslo Sporveier started to sell season tickets through newsagents. The communications campaign promoting this season ticket featured a ticket collector on a bus. A smug-looking, self-satisfied woman holds her ticket ready for the collector. Just before the collector arrives, a punk seated next to the woman grabs the ticket, eats it, and then shows his season ticket to the collector. The pay-off slogan reads 'Smart people buy season tickets – not single tickets'.[30]

- British Coal wanted to stop the decline in the use of coal as a heating fuel. In order to avoid the negative associations with coal, it was decided to concentrate on the sensual qualities of a lit fire. The ad shows a bulldog walking into a room and lying down by a roaring fire. Next, a cat follows, sits next to the dog and starts licking its ear. Finally, a mouse comes in, sits next to the cat and the two touch noses. In the background Shirelles' song 'Will you still love me tomorrow?' plays. The final frame says 'Now you know what people see in a real fire'.[31]

- Nicorette, a product to help smokers give up the smoking habit, received a Silver Euro Effie for its Beat Cigarettes campaign. Instead of showing quitters suffering cravings, they were shown beating a giant cigarette. In some ads the giant cigarette represented a boxing-ball; in others it was used as a battering-ram. All ads showed happy quitters in a humorous setting, while the baseline 'Beat cigarettes one at a time. You're twice as likely to succeed with Nicorette' summed it all up (see Plate 17).[32]

- Frisk Mints received a gold Clio award for its campaign in which an imbecilic-looking guy is brought into a laboratory to test his response latency. In the laboratory, a real horse and a fictitious horse played by humans is shown. The imbecile first has to eat a Frisk and is then asked to distinguish between the real horse and the fictitious horse by pushing a button. Amazingly he succeeds in pressing the right button, after which the slogan 'Frisk sharpens you up' appears.[33]

Besides the need for a creative idea to develop effective advertising, one can question how creative the ad itself has to be. Indirect evidence of the belief in the success of creative ads might be the fact that advertising seems to be more creative than a few decades ago.[34] However, attention-grabbing, originality and imagination do not suffice. In the end advertising must help to accomplish marketing objectives. The few existing studies do not convey consistent results. One study[35] claims creativity has a positive impact on ad likeability, but other studies could not find a relation between ad creativity on the one hand and the attitude towards the ad, brand attitude, purchase contention or firm profitability on the other.[36] Although it is clear that a creative idea is needed to express a brand's positioning statement attractively, the question remains as to how creative the ad itself should be, and whether the average consumer holds a similar opinion on what constitutes a creative ad to that of creative directors. It would not be the first time that consumers rank commercials differently to creative directors. The latter are often quite surprised that the public do not select the ads perceived as most creative by themselves. The foregoing illustrates that more research is called for to find out how important creativity is in the eyes of the consumers and what creativity means to them.

The relationship between winning a Clio Award and firm profitability

Measuring the return on investment of advertising campaigns is a long-standing issue with marketing professionals. A clear link between advertising expenditures and financial performance is often difficult to establish. Taking it one step further, although there is the common belief that advertising creativity is an essential element of advertising success, the link between creativity in advertising and advertising effectiveness is not an obvious one. The evidence of an impact of creative advertising on the bottom line of companies is anecdotal at best. In the US the Clio Awards recognise advertising excellence worldwide in mass media, integrated media, design and the internet. The campaigns are judged by a jury of industry experts. Many thousands of campaigns are submitted each year. The winners are made public during an awards ceremony lasting three days. It can be assumed that winning a Clio signals a firm's quality, effectiveness and innovativeness in advertising, and that this information reaches all the stakeholders quickly. In a study of 126 Clio Award winning companies that were also traded on the New York Stock Exchange, the relationship between winning Clio Awards and the evolution of stock price was examined. The general conclusion of the study was that, in terms of adding value to the winning firms, Clio Awards did not seem to generate any substantial attention from the investment community. The only exception were the group of 16 food advertisers for which a cumulative excess return of 2% was measured. Surprisingly, some of the results seem to indicate that winning an award affects stock prices negatively, for instance for retailers and manufacturers. This may reflect the financial market's bias against perceived overspending on advertising, or even the prejudice that spending too much on advertising is wasteful. The study illustrates that establishing a relationship between advertising efforts, let alone creative ones, and financial results is not obvious.

Sources: Tippins, M.J. and Kunkel, R.A. (2006): Winning a Clio Award and its relationship to firm profitability', *Journal of Marketing Communications*, 12(1), 1–14.

Creative appeals

In trying to generate the established advertising objectives, agencies or creatives can use a multitude of appeals, formats and execution strategies to express or translate their creative idea.[37] Broadly speaking, two different types of creative appeals can be distinguished: rational appeals and emotional appeals. Emotional appeals are advertisements whose main purpose is to elicit affective responses and to convey an image. Rational appeals, on the other hand, contain features, practical details and verifiable, factually relevant cues that can serve as evaluative criteria. Referring to the difference between action and image communications as discussed in Chapter 1, many image communications make use of emotional appeals, while most action communications use rational appeals. However, mixed appeals also exist, employing both rational and emotional elements. Both for emotional and rational appeals, different formats or execution strategies and different types of endorsers can be used (see Table 7.3). Also, it has to be added here that several of the formats that can be used for rational appeals could just as well be used for emotional appeals, although they are discussed only once. For example, a comparative ad can be purely factual describing own and competitive prices, but could also be humorous such as Virgin Atlantic's campaign featuring large billboards in airports with the message 'Enjoy your overpriced flight' (see Plate 12).

Table 7.3 Creative advertising appeals, advertising formats and endorsers

Rational appeals	Emotional appeals
■ Talking head	■ Humour
■ Demonstration	■ Fear
■ Problem solution	■ Warmth
■ Testimonial	■ Eroticism
■ Slice of life	■ Music
■ Dramatisation	■ Etc.
■ Comparative ads	
■ Etc.	
Endorsers	
■ Expert endorsement	
■ Celebrity endorsement	

Rational appeals

Rational ads may contain one or several information cues. The most widely used classification system of information cues is the one presented in Table 7.4, which has been applied in more than 60 studies.[38] The classification consists of 14 different types of information.

Abernethy and Franke performed a meta-analysis on 59 studies in 24 different countries, including the US, most Western countries and the Pacific Rim, in which this classification

Table 7.4 Resnik and Stern's information classification

■ Price	■ Special offers	■ Safety
■ Quality	■ Taste	■ Independent research
■ Performance	■ Nutrition	■ Company research
■ Components	■ Packaging	■ New ideas
■ Availability	■ Warranties	

Based on: Abernethy, A.M. and Franke, G.R. (1996), 'The Information Content of Advertising: A Meta-Analysis', *Journal of Advertising*, 25(2), 1–17.

had been used, and revealed the following.[39] The mean number of information cues (over the different countries and over different media) is 2.04, and the cues most frequently used are performance (in 43% of the cases), availability (37%), components (33%), price (25%), quality (19%) and special offers (13%) (Figure 7.3).

As could be expected, ads for durable goods contain significantly more information cues than ads for non-durable goods (2.7 versus 2.0). Ads in developed countries (US, Canada, Southern and Western Europe, Japan, Australia, New Zealand) are more informative than ads in less developed countries (China, Taiwan, South Korea, India, Saudi Arabia, parts of Latin America). Another study showed that rational appeals are more effective than emotional appeals when a product is new to the market, while the opposite holds true in markets in which consumers are already very familiar with the product.[40] Moreover, ads for intangible products (e.g. services) contain more information cues than for tangible products. The same conclusion holds for low as compared to high competitive markets.[41] Finally, the level of information varies between different advertising media (see also Chapter 8).

Turning to the advertising formats noted in Table 7.3, a **talking head** refers to an ad in which the characters tell a story in their own words: monologue, dialogue or interview techniques could be used.

Figure 7.3 Most frequently used information cues in advertising

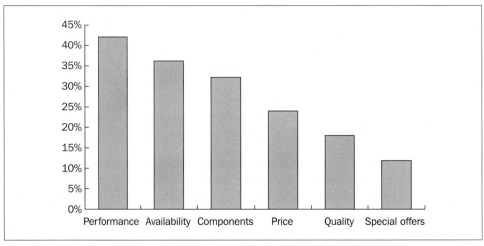

Based on: Abernethy, A.M. and Franke, G.R. (1996), 'The Information Content of Advertising: A Meta-Analysis', *Journal of Advertising*, 25(2), 1–17.

In a demonstration consumers are shown how a product works. It is an easy way to focus on product attributes, tell about the benefits and product uses while demonstrating the product. For example, when Febreze was launched in Europe, ads showed consumers that the product could be used for preventing disturbing odours in clothes, sofas, curtains, cars, etc.

A **problem solution** shows how a problem can be solved or avoided. Problem solution is often combined with a fear appeal showing consumers what happens if the brand is not used.[42] For example, the ads for Head & Shoulders feature an elegant-looking business professional wearing a nice dark suit. Unfortunately he has a dandruff problem which clearly shows on the suit. Head & Shoulders can solve this problem.

A **testimonial** features ordinary people saying how good a product is. Typical products which are advertised in this way are detergents: 'I really was amazed, my clothes have never been so white'. SlimFast ('You really can') also used ads featuring local testimonials of how much weight people lost to introduce or relaunch the brand in the UK, Germany, France and the Netherlands.[43] Testimonials are often effective because they rely on the positive membership reference group effect. However, one should think twice when considering this advertising technique since research shows that testimonials often lead to irritation in consumers.[44]

Reaching the consumer with new advertising media

Advertising professionals try to break through the advertising clutter by trying to find ever more creative channels to reach their target audience:

In the UK a campaign was launched for a new videogame by using 'bleeding' busstop posters. For a full week a red blood-like fluid was dripping out of the posters, generated by an ink cartridge that was built into the ad. The campaign generated a lot of 'rumour around the brand'. The agency did clean the sidewalks afterwards.

A US advertising agency pays people $19.50 to walk around with an advertising message on their forehead five days in a row and three hours per day. The message is tattooed on the forehead with vegetable ink, and disappears by itself after one week. The concept is called Fan Branding or Headvertising, and has already been used by, amongst others, Dunkin Donuts and the British television channel CNX.

The Belgian agency Rapid-Affichage writes advertising messages on sidewalks in fluorescent paint. For instance, at the entrance of a music store, visitors can read: 'Soulwax. Nite Versions. Out now'. Some public authorities don't like the idea, because they consider it as 'damaging the public domain', but the company meticulously removes all traces after the campaign period.

The American company Convex Group patented LidRock, a system to attach CD-roms or DVDs to the lid of cardboard cups in fast food restaurants, cinemas, sport stadiums, and amusement parks. The lid is adjusted to allow the CD to be clicked on it. The market potential is enormous. In 2005 in North America 634 drinks were sold every second.

Destroying or damaging bank notes is not allowed in the US, but attaching removable stickers on it is allowed. That's all it takes to create a new advertising medium. Research showed that 95% of consumers noticed the message on their bank notes, and 56% did not remove it, thus generating extra exposure with other consumers.

The Belgian company Activemedia invented a wheel cover that does not turn along with the wheel when the car is moving. For €150, your message is attached to the four wheels of one of the hundreds of cooperating Antwerp taxis.

Source: Bizz, March 2004, 34–5, *De Morgen*, 8 December 2005.

Slice-of-life ads feature the product being used in a real-life setting, which usually involves solving a problem. The effectiveness of this type of ad is attributed to the fact that the product is shown in a real-life context the target group can relate to. An example would be a family putting picnic hampers, blankets, toys, etc., in their new Mercedes space van to go out for a picnic on a Sunday afternoon. Another example shows a boy playing soccer with his friends, then he comes home with his clothes so dirty you think they will never get clean again. Fortunately, the boy's mother has Dreft which cleans the clothes without a problem. Although slice-of-life is used quite often, research shows that such ads are more likely to cause irritation.[45]

A dramatisation is rather similar to a slice-of-life. Both first present a problem and afterwards the solution, but a dramatisation builds suspense and leads consumers to a climax. The difference between a slice-of-life, and for that matter a drama (which just tells a story), and a dramatisation lies in the intensity. The Alldays Tanga campaign is an example of a dramatisation. A young woman is dancing on a stage amidst a large crowd, wearing extremely close-fitting clothes. Suddenly, in front of everyone, her panty liner gets dislodged, causing her a lot of embarrassment while other girls make fun of her. The spot ends showing several other girls dancing without any worries. The solution becomes obvious in the base line 'Should've worn ALLDAYS TANGA'.[46]

Comparative advertising can be used as a means to differentiate a brand from a competitor. A direct comparative ad explicitly names the comparison brand (often a well-known competitive brand) and claims that the comparison brand is inferior to the advertised brand with respect to a specific attribute. An indirect comparative ad does not explicitly mention a comparison brand, but argues to be superior on a certain attribute compared to other brands ('Gillette, the best a man can get'). Up to now, directly comparative advertising was an American phenomenon. However, the European Commission has decided to allow comparative advertising in certain circumstances. The question remains how Europeans will react to this form of advertising. A 1998 study points out that consumers in countries in which comparative advertising is not allowed, or is used infrequently, have a much more negative attitude towards comparative ads than American consumers.[47] Taylor Nelson Sofres found in 2001 that two-thirds of UK consumers find comparable ads unacceptable; women were most opposed and youngsters between 16 and 24 minded least that brands criticise competitors.[48] Research in France in 2002 showed that direct comparative ads led to more positive brand attitudes than indirect or non-comparative ads.[49] However, French advertisers remain unconvinced of the effectiveness of comparative advertising on French consumers and do not intend to use it more often in the future.[50] Also in Spain comparative advertising does not seem to be well received. A study in 2003 revealed that the more intense the comparative claim was, the less consumers believed the propositions, the more counterarguments were formed, and the more negative attitudes and brand intentions became.[51] This seems to suggest that advertisers should be careful with using this technique in Europe.

Are comparative ads more effective than non-comparative ads? A short review of research results reveals the following.

The advantages and disadvantages of comparative advertising

Advantages	Disadvantages
More attention	Less credible
Better brand and message awareness	Comparison of similar brands confuses people
More elaborate processing	Less favourable attitude towards the ad
Association with comparison brand	Possibility of increasing brand confusion
Differentiation	Possibility of aggressive media wars
More favourable attitude towards the brand	Costs due to law cases, . . .
Purchase behaviour more likely	

Consumers seem to devote more attention to a comparative than to a non-comparative ad. The reason is that since at least two brands are being compared, the ad is relevant to more consumers (users of both the sponsored and comparison brand).[52] Because of more attention, comparative ads lead to a better message and brand awareness, evoke more cognitive responses, and as a consequence enhance a more central communications processing.[53] However, it should be noted that consumers perceive comparative advertising as less credible.[54] Concerning product positioning, positive effects can be observed. With new brand introductions, advertisers often stress the superiority of the new brand over a more familiar competitor on a typical attribute. By doing so, two desirable goals seem to be reached: (1) the new product is associated with the comparison brand and, as a consequence, more easily included in the consideration set of the target consumers; (2) the brand advertised is different from, and is more likely to be preferred to, the comparison brand.[55]

The attitude towards the brand usually is positively influenced by comparative ads, while the contrary holds for the attitude towards the ad.[56] The latter is perceived to be less personal, less friendly and amusing, less honest and more aggressive.[57] Although conative or behavioural effects have not been extensively studied, it seems that comparative ads have a positive influence on purchase intention.[58] Furthermore, comparative as opposed to non-comparative ads seem to enhance purchase behaviour, as indicated by coupon redemption.[59]

Although the balance of advantages and disadvantages turns out to be in favour of comparative advertising, one should also take into account the following threats. The use of comparative advertising may lead to aggressive, competitive media wars when the comparison brand feels attacked (the so-called boomerang effect). Furthermore, comparative advertising may be misleading and confusing for consumers.[60] One should try to avoid promoting a competitive brand. This occurs when, as a result of the ad, the consumer wrongly thinks the ad sponsor is the comparison brand. Costs may also rise because of law suits, etc. Finally, remember that comparative ads are not appreciated to the same extent in different cultures and countries. The findings reported in US studies may not hold at all for Europe, Asia, etc.

Emotional appeals

Emotional advertising refers to advertising that tries to evoke emotions in consumers rather than to make consumers think. Emotional ads mainly consist of non-verbal elements such as images and emotional stimuli. It should be clear that there is a difference between the intended emotional content of a stimulus, or the emotional technique used, and the emotions experienced by a consumer as a result of being exposed to an ad. Emotional appeals do not necessarily evoke emotions in all people, although they are designed to do so.

Humour

Humorous advertising can be defined as an appeal created with the intent to make people laugh, irrespective of the fact that the humour is successful (people indeed perceive the ad as humorous) or unsuccessful (people do not think the ad is funny). Humour seems to be one of the most frequently used emotional techniques throughout the world. A survey in 1992 in 33 countries revealed that approximately 35% of all magazine and outdoor advertising contained humour. No significant differences could be detected between the different countries, nor between the two media.[61]

Are humorous appeals effective? No doubt most people appreciate a good joke, but can humorous ads convey a brand message? Or does it leave people remembering the joke, but neither the brand nor the brand message? Can humour be used for 'serious' products, or does a humorous approach make a clown of the advertising company? Humour seems to raise a lot of questions, and unfortunately not a lot of straight answers can be given. Humour has been studied by many researchers, and overall there is only one aspect on which agreement between the researchers can be found: humour attracts attention.[62] However, the question remains to what extent humour also attracts attention to the brand. As far as recall and recognition, creating positive ad and brand attitudes and increasing purchase intention are concerned, no conclusive results can be drawn.[63] This can partly be explained by several moderating variables (Figure 7.4).

Different types of humour exist, for example cognitive humour (see Plate 14). In this case there is an incongruity, an unexpected element as a result of which the consumer has to follow different lines of reasoning to solve the incongruity;[64] for example, the latest Amstel Light beer ad shows products that normally belong in the refrigerator in an unexpected spot because Amstel Light has taken their place in the refrigerator. One example features a woman who is sleeping in bed. When she wakes up and turns on the

Figure 7.4 Moderating variables affecting the effectiveness of humour in advertising

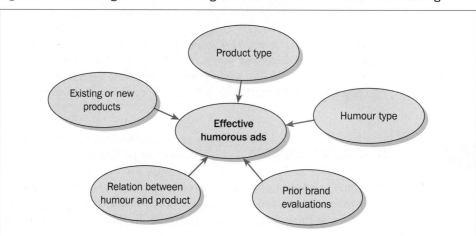

light, she screams when she finds a plate of meatloaf next to her in bed. The next scene shows the refrigerator where a 12-pack of Amstel Light is jammed into the meatloaf's position.[65] There is also sentimental humour, for example, a little kitten that tries to catch the ball in a football game on TV, a satire, meant to be funny and insulting at the same time, sexual humour, making fun of the other sex, etc. The different types of humour are appreciated by the target consumers to a different extent leading to different communications effects. While sentimental humour is quite innocent, satire or sexual humour is more aggressive, and not surprisingly not everyone finds the latter types of humour funny.

The effectiveness of humour also depends on the product type. The prevailing opinion seems to be that humour is more appropriate for low than for high-involvement products, and for transformational rather than for informational products and that humour, in any case, should be avoided for high-involvement/informational products, such as banking and insurance.[66]

In general, humour seems to be more effective for existing and familiar brands than for new and unfamiliar brands.[67] In other words, building brand awareness is more difficult by using humour, since the humour might gain too much attention, leading to inferior brand attention. Humour that is in one way or another related to the product is more effective than unrelated humour. Finally, humour may have a detrimental effect when prior brand evaluations are negative.[68] In other words, if you are convinced that Lion tastes awful and sticks to your teeth, you are more likely to think that the company wants to be funny, but is not funny at all, while a positive brand attitude leads to more tolerance and acceptance.

Eroticism

Defined very broadly, an ad can be classified as erotic if one or more of the following elements are present: partial or complete nudity, physical contact between two adults, sexy or provocatively dressed person(s), provocative or seductive facial expression, and suggestive words or sexually laden music, etc. Although some people seem convinced that eroticism is being used more and more in European advertising, content analyses show that this is only in the eyes of the beholder.[69] (See Plate 16.)

How effective is an ad showing a seductive Claudia Schiffer in front of the Citroën Xsara, the erotic style of the Martini campaigns, the nude Sophie Dahl for Opium or the full-frontal nude model for Yves Saint Laurent's scent H7? As was the case with humour, no clear guidelines can be provided for the use of eroticism. However, an indisputable conclusion is that eroticism attracts attention, even to the extent that more car accidents occur near erotic billboards.[70] One may wonder, though, whether any attention is directed at the brand or the brand message. Indeed, most researchers agree that eroticism reduces brand and message recall.[71] Another negative aspect on which most researchers agree is that eroticism has a negative impact on the image of the advertiser.[72] For other communications objectives such as the attitude towards the ad or the brand, and purchase intention, mixed research results have been reported.[73]

An explanation can perhaps be found in a number of moderating factors. For instance, the more intense the eroticism or, in other words, the more overt the sex appeal in the form of nudity or suggestion of sexual intercourse, the more negative the responses to the ad become.[74] However, a recent study for suntan lotion found exactly the opposite, suggesting that advertisers would do better opting for 'the full monty' rather than for partial nudity.[75] Perhaps this result can be explained by the product promoted, namely suntan lotion. Previous research results reveal that the more the erotic appeal is related to the product, the more positive the responses to it become.[76] In other words, functional products such as underwear, bath foam, shower cream, etc. and romantic products such as perfume, aftershave, alcohol, cosmetics, etc. are expected to benefit more from an erotic appeal than other product categories such as coffee, a lawn mower, or a lathe, etc. Notwithstanding the foregoing, a recent study in which the effectiveness of eroticism for social marketing topics (as diverse as eating healthily, public library and museum attendance, HIV/AIDS prevention, etc.) was tested showed that sexual appeals were more persuasive than matched non-sexual appeals.[77] So for this variable research results are also inconclusive.

Which target group can most effectively be addressed with an erotic appeal? Research shows that men respond significantly more positively to eroticism than women.[78] However, in most of the studies ads with seductive or naked women were used. Handsome men as product endorsers might have completely altered the picture. In fact, lately more and more advertisers are using men as sex objects to please women. Examples are the Cola Light 11.30 break commercial, the Australian ad for Underdaks men's underwear in which two female airport officers have a man stripped to his underwear by sounding a false alarm each time he passes through the control gate, the Gini ad in which a female passionately grabs a guy, starts opening the buttons of his shirt, unhooks his belt, pulls the belt out of his trousers and . . . uses the belt to open her bottle of Gini.

To conclude, among marketing practitioners there seems to be agreement that sex sells, but some are wondering for how much longer. According to them sex is becoming a commodity that is no longer able to shock or convey indulgent sensuality.[79]

Warmth

Warm appeals can be described as advertising that consists of elements evoking mild, positive feelings such as love, friendship, cosiness, affection and empathy. Although warmth now seems to be used less than it was a few decades ago, it is still a frequently used emotional technique.[80] Is this frequent use of warmth justified? The answer is clearly, yes. Although mixed results have been reported as to the effect of warmth on message and brand recall and recognition, warmth leads to more positive affective responses, less negative feelings such as irritation, a more positive attitude towards the ad and towards the brand, and sometimes an enhanced purchase intention.[81] Target groups most responsive to warm appeals are females, emotional individuals and individuals with a lot of cognitive empathy (meaning that they can understand the situation of others).[82]

Fear

A fear appeal refers the consumer to a certain type of risk he or she might be exposed to and which he or she usually can reduce by buying (e.g. an insurance) or not buying (e.g. not drinking when driving) the product advertised. Typical risks that might be used in a fear appeal are:[83]

- *Physical*: the risk of bodily harm, which is often used for burglar alarms, toothpaste, analgesics, etc. An example would be 'When are you going to install an alarm? After they break in?'.

- *Social*: the risk of being socially ostracised, often used for deodorants, dandruff shampoo, mouth wash, etc.

- *Time*: the risk of spending a lot of time on an unpleasant activity while the activity can be performed in less time. During the introduction period of dishwashers, messages frequently read 'Do you realise that most people spend X years of their life washing the dishes?'.

- *Product performance*: the risk that competitive brands do not perform adequately. Dyson vacuum cleaners are promoted as having no bag, which makes them the only cleaner to maintain 100% suction, 100% of the time.

- *Financial*: the risk of losing a lot of money, typically used by insurance companies.

- *Opportunity loss*: pointing out to consumers that they run the risk of missing a special opportunity if they do not act right away. For example, the Belgian mobile phone provider Proximus ran a campaign with the following message: 'Subscribe now to Proximus, and pay nothing until April'.

Are fear appeals effective? Most studies point in an affirmative direction. Several studies confirm that fear appeals are capable of sensitising people to threats and of changing their behaviour.[84] For example, a recent study shows that fear appeals succeed in lowering alcohol consumption in students.[85] An unresolved question, however, is how intense fear appeals should be.

The alleged inverted U-shape of fear appeals

Is there an optimal intensity in fear appeal? Some researchers claim an inverted U-shaped relation between fear level and attitude enhancement. If the intensity level of the fear appeal becomes too high, consumers will be too frightened, and as a consequence will try to avoid the ad instead of following the recommendations proposed.[86] Other researchers argue that an approximately linear relationship between the level of fear and persuasion can be observed, and that no evidence can be found of the so-called boomerang effect.[87] The latter view was recently confirmed in a meta-analysis.[88] Furthermore, it is suggested that one should not investigate the different levels of the fear appeal in the ad, which is actually a representation of a threat, but look at the level of fear experienced by the consumers, or in other words, look at how different people respond to the ad.[89] It may indeed be impossible to reach the whole target group by means of one specific fear appeal. Different consumers fear different threats and an objectively high level of fear appeal might not induce any fear in certain consumers because they do not perceive it as a threat to them. LaTour and Henthorne give the following example: an ad showing a person undergoing a lung cancer operation might not evoke fear in teenagers because they think that they are immortal and that they can smoke without getting lung cancer. An optimal threat to persuade teens to stop smoking would rather be an ad showing that teens who smoke have trouble finding a date. For adults an optimal threat might be to point to the fact that their children are very likely to take up the smoking habit as well.

On the one hand, different people seem to be sensitive to different threats, and on the other hand, different people seem to cope differently with fear appeals representing a threat for them. In this respect, the individual differences variable, sensation seeking, has been proved to play an important role. Not only do high and low sensation seekers differ in their behaviour, they also differ in their responses to fear appeals. High as compared to low sensation seekers are, for example, four times more likely to use marijuana, seven times more likely to use cocaine, and twice as likely to drink alcohol, and they view these habits favourably. Furthermore, they feel to a greater extent immortal, react negatively to anti-drug messages, and as a consequence are much harder to persuade by means of a fear appeal.[90] Besides personality traits such as sensation seeking, no doubt consumer motives, goals and culture play an important role. One study showed that fear appeals stressing a threat to the family evoked more fear in individuals belonging to a collectivistic than an individualistic society, while the opposite was found for a fear appeal focussing on a threat to the individual.[91] Once more, this example illustrates the importance of carefully studying the characteristics of the target group.

Music

Who has not caught themselves singing an ad jingle? – '. . . whenever there is fun, there is always Coca-Cola', 'I feel cointreau tonight', etc. or thinking about one of the songs used in a commercial? For example, Celine Dion's 'I Drove All Night' for DaimlerChrysler, Steppenwolf's 'Born to Be Wild' in the Ford Cougar ad, 'L'air du Temps' for the champagne brand Bernard Massard, Marvin Gaye's 'I Heard it through the Grapevine' in the California Raisin ad, etc. Music is extensively used in TV and radio commercials. For example, a study found that 84.5% of US commercials and 94.3% of the ads in the Dominican Republic contained music.[92]

The major reasons why advertisers make use of music is because they believe that mucic can gain attention, create a mood, a sense of relaxation or can set an emotional tone that enhances product evaluations and facilitates message acceptance, send a brand message and convey a unique selling point, signal a certain lifestyle and build a brand personality, and communicate cultural values.[93]

Although there seems to be general agreement that the right music may have a significant impact on an ad's effectiveness, not much empirical evidence exists to support this claim. The only point of agreement seems to be that music induces more positive feelings.[94] As far as brand recall is concerned, for example, one could expect that jingles may have a positive influence because by singing the jingle yourself afterwards, you actually rehearse the brand name and brand message over and over again. However, empirical studies show mixed results: sometimes music seems to have a positive effect, sometimes a negative effect and sometimes no effect at all on ad recall.[95] Regarding behavioural consequences, Gorn[96] demonstrated experimentally that consumers were more likely to choose a specific colour of pen if they had been exposed to an ad in which that pen had been paired with pleasant rather than unpleasant music. Other researchers were not able to replicate his findings, however.[97]

Two moderating variables may partly account for these contradictory results.[98] The effectiveness of music may depend on the attention-gaining value referring to the arousal or activation potential of the musical sound. Fast, loud music, for example, can be expected to have a higher attention-gaining value and therefore a higher message reception than slow, soft music. A second factor is the music/message congruence, referring to the extent that the music and the ad copy convey the same message. Incongruence may lead to distraction from, instead of attention to, the brand message.

Endorsers

Experts can be used to demonstrate the quality or high technology of a product. For example, toothpaste brands are often promoted by means of someone in a white lab coat to infer a dentist's opinion. The effectiveness of this type of ad is assumed to be based on the perceived credibility of the experts' judgement.[99] In contrast with testimonials, expert endorsements do not seem to be perceived as irritating. On the contrary, one study even suggests experts evoke more positive affective responses.[100]

Celebrities can also be used to endorse a product. Their effectiveness is based on the 'aspiration group' effect. Examples of celebrity endorsement are Pamela Anderson for Pizza Hut, Naomi Campbell for the milk campaign, Justine Henin for Danette of Danone, Claudia Schiffer for Citroën, Rowan Atkinson for Barclaycard, etc. (See Plate 10.)

As is obvious, celebrities are used extensively. For example, one in four ads in the US and one in five UK campaigns feature celebrities.[101] But how effective are celebrity endorsements? They certainly attract a lot of attention, not only from the target group, but also from the media. The latter is very interesting since it can give rise to free publicity. For example, when the 'Won't Kiss Off Test' campaign for Revlon's Colorstay Lipsticks was launched, Cindy Crawford kissed reporters, leading to massive free publicity.[102] Moreover, several studies have shown that celebrities can have a direct positive impact on ad likeability and also an indirect effect on brand attitude and purchase intentions.[103] For instance, the management of Pepsi attributes its 8% increase in sales in 1984 to the Michael Jackson endorsement, while the Spice Girls were good for a 2% global market share increase in 1997.[104] However, not all celebrities are effective for all products or all situations. Several factors play a role.[105] According to the Source Credibility Model, the celebrity should be credible in the sense that he or she has expertise and is trustworthy. The trustworthiness of an endorser is defined as the degree to which the endorser is perceived to be honest and believable. Eric Cantona has proved that he has mastered how to play soccer, which makes him highly credible for promoting soccer shoes and sports wear. In a study in which both an actor and an athlete promote a candy bar and an energy bar, it was found that the ad featuring the athlete was more effective when an energy bar was promoted, while the type of endorser did not matter for the candy bar.[106]

Besides credibility, attractiveness may also be important. According to the Source Attractiveness Model, attractiveness refers in this context to the degree that the celebrity is known (awareness and familiarity), is physically perceived to be attractive and is liked by the target group. Although all adults agree that Sean Connery is a great movie star, Leonardo DiCaprio will no doubt have more impact on teenagers. Several studies found support for this model, although a recent study warns that one should be cautious about using highly attractive models. Using very thin models, for example, may reduce the self-image of the target group and evoke negative feelings both towards the celebrity and the product.[107]

Finally, as is summarised in the Product Match-Up Hypothesis, there should be an appropriate fit between the endorser's image, personality, lifestyle, etc. and the product advertised. In this respect, it should be added that the behaviour of the celebrity may turn against a brand he or she is associated with. Cantona, for example, was prosecuted for kicking a soccer fan. Although this could have been a disaster for Nike, the company cleverly managed the problem and even succeeded in turning it to an advantage by starting to sell sports wear showing the word 'punished'. Youngsters who like rebels, and who still admire Cantona for his soccer skills, were extremely fond of these shirts. The potential risk of negative celebrity information is expected to be especially great for new or unfamiliar brands for which the celebrity is the primary cue on which consumers base their brand evaluations (see Plate 11).[108]

Campaign implementation

After advertising agencies have come up with creative and executional ideas, the advertiser has to evaluate the different alternatives on the basis of the creative brief. This means that the idea ultimately chosen needs to be suited and appealing to the target group, be capable of reaching the advertising objectives, be a kind of catalyst, making the brand's position immediately clear in a simple, eye-catching manner. The idea must also fit with the company's and brand's long-term strategy and with previous campaigns. It has to be adaptable to the different media to be used, and financially implementable within the given advertising budget and within the given time limits.

When agreement is reached on the creative idea to be used for the different media, the advertisements need to be produced. Since advertisement production needs special skills, this job is typically carried out by technical experts. Photography, typography and sound recording needs to be well thought through, so that headline, baseline, copy, background music, packshots, presenters, characters, the set, etc. form an integrated and consistent advertisement. As soon as the advertiser approves of the advertisement proposal, the advertisements are produced and handed over to the media.

After the campaign has run, it has to be evaluated on its effectiveness. In order to be able to do this, it is very important to have clear, measurable objectives at the beginning of the campaign development process, as well as accurate data of the situation prior to the campaign launch. The important aspect of media planning is discussed in the next chapter. Advertising research is extensively covered in Chapter 9.

Integrating advertising in IMC

Advertising as the classic instrument to reach a large audience and as one of the most flexible communication tools, is the obvious channel to support and supplement other communication efforts. Advertising can be used to reinforce sponsorship campaigns, by using events and celebrities in advertising, by capitalising on product placement in movies and television programmes, or by pointing out the corporate social responsibility efforts of the company. Advertising can also be used to monopolising the broadcast of the sponsored event. Shareholder meetings, points-of-view on societal issues and press releases can be referred to in advertising campaigns. Sales promotions can be announced in ads, and ads can build traffic for in-store and promotion campaigns. The latter can be reinforced by referring to the ads on the shop floor ('as seen on television'). Off-line advertising can be used to build traffic to websites and as an introduction to interactive advertising formats. In general, advertising can be used to build the necessary awareness and brand image to provide the fertile soil for other communication efforts.

Summary

Advertising is any paid, non-personal communication through various media by an identified company. It is one of the most visible tools of the communications mix. Advertising campaign development consists of a number of stages. First, advertising strategy has to be decided on: Who are the target groups of the campaign, what are the objectives, and what messages are going to be conveyed? At the very core of the advertising process is the development of a creative idea. Companies have to write a creative brief before the advertising agency can start to do its job. Creativity is hard to describe, but bringing the message in an original, novel and appealing way comes close. In general, two broad types of creative appeals, rational and emotional appeals, can be used to develop a campaign, although mixed forms also exist. Emotional appeals are advertisements whose main purpose is to elicit affective responses and to convey an image. Rational appeals, on the other hand, contain information cues such as price, value, quality, performance, components, availability, taste, warranties, new ideas, etc. For both rational and emotional appeals different formats or execution strategies can be used. Rational appeals may, for instance, make use of a talking head, a demonstration, a problem solution, a testimonial, a slice-of-life, a drama or a (direct or indirect) comparison with competitors. Emotional appeals may be based on humour, fear, warmth, eroticism, music or the like. Rational and emotional appeals may further feature different types of endorsers: ordinary people, experts or celebrities. None of the execution strategies work in all situations and for all target groups; for example, although everyone agrees that emotional techniques are capable of attracting attention, it is by no means certain that they get the message across in the manner intended. Therefore caution should be taken to select the right technique.

Review questions

1 What are the various stages in advertising campaign development?

2 Is creativity in advertising important?

3 What are the necessary elements in a creative brief?

4 What are the most frequently used execution strategies for rational appeals and why are they supposed to be effective?

5 What are the advantages and disadvantages of comparative advertising?

6 Are humorous advertising appeals effective? What about erotic ones?

7 To what extent are fear appeals effective advertising techniques?

8 On the basis of what criteria would you select a celebrity?

Further reading

Arens, W.F. (2006), *Contemporary Advertising*, 10th edn. New York, NY: McGraw-Hill/Irwin Publishing.

Belch, M. and Belch, G. (2004) *Introduction to Advertising and Promotion: An Integrated Marketing Communications Perspective*, 6th edn. New York, NY: McGraw-Hill.

Cappo, J. (2003), *The Future of Advertising*. New York, NY: McGraw-Hill.

Journal of Advertising

Journal of Advertising Research

Journal of Marketing Communications

O'Guinn, T., Allen, C.T. and Semenik, R.J. (2006), *Advertising and Integrated Brand Promotion*, 4th edn, Mason, OH: Thomson/South-Western.

Case 7

Launching the Citroën Xsara Picasso and relaunching the Volkswagen Sharan

By the year 2000, the market segment of so-called small MPVs (multi-purpose vehicles) had grown considerably and was already well established. The annual growth of sales in Europe was 1.3% in 1997 and 6% in 2000. The European car market is fiercely competitive and the competition in the MPV market segment has intensified. All across Europe the major car manufacturers have introduced their own version of the MPV: VW Sharan, Ford Galaxy, Seat Alhambra, Mazda MPV, Nissan Serena, Renault Espace, Peugeot 806, Citroën Xsara Picasso . . . The levels of advertising expenditure and the resulting levels of advertising clutter are very high. In 2000, one of the already well-established MPVs was the Volkswagen Sharan. Faced with increasing competition, which had led to losing its market leader position, Volkswagen decided to relaunch the model in May 2000. The Citroën Xsara Picasso was a latecomer into this market; it was launched in January 2000. Both car models are sold all across Europe. This case focusses on the campaigns in a number of selected European countries.

Citroën Xsara Picasso

Advertising objectives, creative strategy and media strategy

In January 2000 the Xsara Picasso was launched by means of a global campaign in 41 countries worldwide, including 17 European countries. The main objectives of the campaign were as follows:

- To build a global campaign with advertising recognition and correct attribution above market average.

- To gain rapid awareness and desirability for the Xsara Picasso, and to attract younger and more family-oriented customers. The aim was to have a strong communication return on investments: to be the number two brand in product awareness within a year of launch.

- To rapidly build market share.

The Xsara Picasso is the first mass-produced car to carry the name of a famous painter. The invention of the product name was at the very heart of the creative strategy. From European research Citroën learned that customers attach a lot of importance to the 'badge' effect. A well-chosen name, and a communications campaign that links the values associated with this name to the values associated with the Citroën Xsara brand, can lead to rapid awareness and distinctiveness. Therefore, the creative strategy, developed by Euro RSCG Works, builds on the spirit of Picasso, using the concept 'Citroën Xsara Picasso, free your mind', making the car both distinctive and aspirational. The campaign did not focus at all on product attributes. At the same time, the campaign was placed in a familiar car environment, i.e. the car factory. The core element of the creative strategy was the 'Robot' television campaign, focussing around the name and the spirit of the new car. Robots in a car factory make a Picasso-like painting on a semi-finished Xsara Picasso. When they hear a noise, they rapidly clean the car and replace the drawing with the signature of Picasso (see Plate 15). Television was chosen as a primary campaign medium to clearly position the Xsara Picasso as a major challenger to the competition. Share of voice levels were reasonable,

Case Table 7.1 Share of voice of the Xsara Picasso campaign and its main competitors 2000 (%)

	Germany	France	UK	Spain	Italy
Xsara Picasso	2.0	3.5	2.5	1.8	2.2
Main competitor	3.0	2.5	4.6	2.8	3.0

and in many countries close to those of the market leader (see Case Table 7.1). A print campaign (magazines and newspapers) was also developed to provide more rational product information and posters and other point-of-sale materials were developed in synergy with the other campaign materials.

Campaign results

The campaign was among the best five tested by IPSOS since 1981. With 63% advertising recognition, the television campaign obtained the best IPSOS impact score in France ever, five times above the general average and 50% over the second score in all sections. In Case Figure 7.1, the correct attribution and the percentage of people liking the campaign of the Xsara Picasso campaign is compared with the average correct attribution and likeability scores of the foreign MPV car campaigns in five European countries. The correct attribution of the Xsara Picasso campaign is well above average in all five countries, and so are the likeability scores in at least three out

of five countries. In Case Figure 7.2 the evolution of the prompted product awareness of the Xsara Picasso and its two major competitors in France is shown over the period November 1999 to March 2001. The Xsara Picasso occupies the second place, and has rapidly built awareness to levels close to those of the mental market leader.

A year and a half after its launch, the Xsara Picasso occupied the first position in the compact people carrier market segment in the UK with 29% market share, and in Spain with 24% market share. In France it occupies the second place with 28% market share.

The campaign has won various awards around the world. It won the Jury Grand Prize and the prize for the Best European Campaign at the European Automobile Film Festival 2000, the Best Brand Strategy at the Grand Prix Pubblicita 2000 in Italy, and the Grand Prize for Best Car Advertising Film at the Poznan Car Salon in Poland. In 2001 it won a silver Euro Effie award for its results in 2000.

Case Figure 7.1 Attribution and likeability scores of the Citroën Xsara campaign (%)

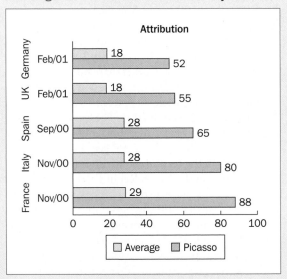

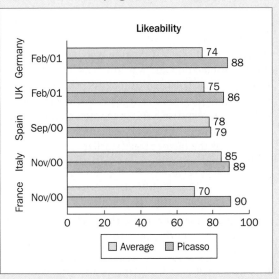

Case Figure 7.2 Prompted product awareness of the Citroën Xsara and its main competitors in France (%)

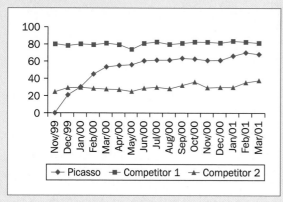

Volkswagen Sharan

The data in this section describe the situation, and the campaign details and results in three central European countries, i.e. Germany, Hungary and the Czech Republic. In Germany the Volkswagen Sharan was the market leader until it was overtaken by its identical twin, the Ford Galaxy, in early 2000. In Hungary the Seat Alhambra (Seat is a part of the Volkswagen group) was the market leader, and the Volkswagen Sharan was challenged for second place by the Nissan Serena. In the Czech Republic, the Volkswagen Sharan was market leader, followed by the Seat Alhambra, until it was overtaken by the relaunched Mazda in January 2000. All other competitors were also suffering.

Advertising objectives, creative strategy and media strategy

In early 2000 the VW Sharan was suffering from intense competition and was losing its leading market position. The challenge was to retake the lead against competitors that were in some cases identical, were often far less expensive and in markets that were very price-sensitive by means of a relaunch of the model. Germany is the major target market.

The advertising objectives were defined as follows:

- *Germany*: to recapture market leadership in the MPV segment within six months.
- *Hungary*: to catch up with the Seat Alhambra within six months, and to stop the rise of the Nissan Serena.
- *Czech Republic*: to recapture market leadership in the MPV segment within six months.

The original idea for MPVs was the 'active' family car. Gradually, MPVs have positioned themselves away from this original idea by emphasising other areas of use, such as leisure, business vehicle, transporting bulky loads, etc. The Sharan wanted to position the car 'back to its origins'. It wanted to become 'the family car in Europe'. This positioning should bring the car closer to what were still the most important buyers: families. Since the VW Sharan was much more expensive than its major, often identical, competitors, it could only be successful with a strong emotional positioning strategy. Apart from small children, animals were considered the best guarantee for high emotionalisation. They can arouse parently feelings in potential customers. Furthermore, the animal world offers a wealth of opportunities to visualise the strong points of the Sharan, such as strength, comfort, safety, etc. The 'Safari' campaign shows different animals and their babies in connection with the VW Sharan.

Television and cinema were used as the prime media. They are the most supportive for emotionalising campaigns aimed at a large family audience. Often the commercials were embedded in animal and other family-oriented programmes. Double- and single-page ads in consumer magazines supported the emotionalising positioning, supplementing it with rational product attribute arguments. Traffic at the dealership was enhanced by similar advertisements targeted at the trade channel. The campaign was launched in May 2000.

Campaign results

By September 2000, the VW Sharan was market leader in Germany again. In four months it increased its market share from 19% in April to 24%, overtaking the Ford Galaxy. By February 2001 the Sharan managed to increase its market share further to 28.5% (Case Figure 7.3). In Hungary, the VW Sharan more than doubled its market share from 14.9% in August 2000 to 35.3% in March 2001. The car almost closed the gap with the Seat Alhambra, and displaced the Nissan Serena from third to last position (Case Figure 7.4). In the second month after the roll-out of the campaign in the Czech Republic, the VW Sharan managed to sell twice as many cars as its main competitor, the Mazda MPV. In November, three months after the roll-out of the campaign, the VW had overtaken the Mazda (Case Figure 7.5).

The Volkswagen Sharan campaign was rewarded with a silver Euro Effie in 2001 for its effectiveness in 2000.

Case Figure 7.3 Market share of the VW Sharan and its competitors in Germany (%)

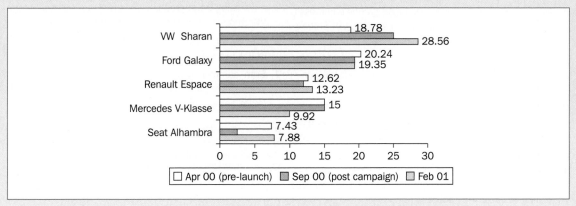

Case Figure 7.4 Market share of the VW Sharan and its competitors in Hungary (%)

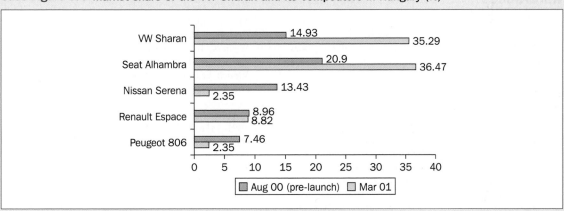

Case Figure 7.5 Market share of the VW Sharan and its competitors in the Czech Republic (%)

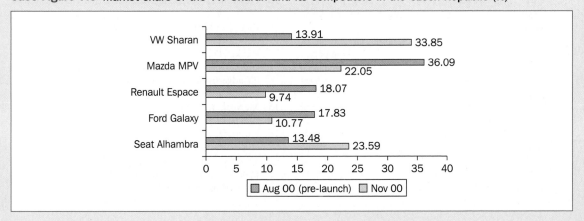

Questions

1 What were the main objectives, target groups and message strategies of the Xsara Picasso and the VW Sharan campaigns? Are they relevant and meaningful?

2 Compare the creative strategies of the Xsara Picasso and the VW Sharan. What do you think about the positioning strategies of the two car models?

3 Compare the execution strategies that were used in the two campaigns. What emotional and informational elements were used? Do you think they made the correct choices?

4 How can the competitors of the Xsara Picasso and the VW Sharan react? Which communications and creative strategies could they adopt?

5 Would the use of humour, eroticism or comparative advertising be appropriate for the Xsara Picasso or the VW Sharan, or any of their competitors?

6 Do you think the appropriate media strategy was used in the two campaigns?

7 Both campaigns appear to have been successful. Do you believe that the effectiveness claims made are legitimate and credible?

Based on: Euro Effie 2001 – efficiency in advertising 2001, Berlin, Gesamtverband Werbeagenturen GWA e.V; *See also:* www.citroen.com and country-specific Citroën sites; www.volkswagen.de and country-specific Volkswagen sites.

References

1 Bennett, P.D. (1995), *Dictionary of Marketing Terms.* Chicago: American Marketing Association.

2 Many organisations offer software to help companies to plan their advertising campaigns. See, for instance www.paloalto.com.

3 Mitchell, A. (2001), 'Why the Old Advertising Model is Breaking Down', *Marketing Week*, 29 March, 34–35.

4 Geuens, M., De Pelsmacker, P. and Mast, G. (2003), 'Family Structure as a Moderator of Parent–Child Communication about Consumption', *International Journal of Advertising and Marketing to Children*, 4(1), 1–6; Roedder John, D. (1999), 'Consumer Socialization of Children: A Retrospective Look at Twenty-five Years of Research', *Journal of Consumer Research*, 26(3), 183–213; McNeal, J.U. (1999), *Kids Market: Myths and Realities*, Ithaca, NY: Paramount Market; Gunter, B. and Furnham, A. (1998), *Children as Consumers. A Psychological Analysis of the Young People's Market*, London: Routledge; Acuff, D.S. (1997), *What Kids Buy and Why. The Psychology of Marketing to Kids*, New York: The Free Press.

5 Clegg, A. (2006), Mining the Golden Years, 24 April, www.brandchannel.com.

6 Weijters B. and Geuens, M. (2003), 'Evaluation of Age-Related Labels by Senior Citizens', Working paper, Vlerick Leuven Gent Management School; Young, G. (2002), 'Ageing and the UK economy', *Bank of England Quarterly Bulletin*, 42(3), 285–92.

7 Walker, M.M. and Macklin, M.C. (1992), 'The Use of Role Modeling in Targeting Advertising to Grandparents', *Journal of Advertising Research*, 32(4), 37–45.

8 Ahmad, R. (2002), 'The Older Ageing Consumers in the UK: Are They Really that Different?' *International Journal of Market Research*, 44(3), 337–60; Moschis, G.P. and Mathur, A. (1997), 'Targeting the Mature Market: Opportunities and Challenges', *Journal of Consumer Marketing*, 14(4), 282–93.

9 Weyters, B. and Geuens, M. (2003), 'Evaluation of Age-Related Labels by Senior Citizens', Working Paper, Vlerick Leuven Gent Management School; Szmigin, I. and Carrigan, M. (2001), 'Time, Consumption and the Older Consumer: An Interpretive Study of the Cognitively Young', *Psychology & Marketing*, 18(10), 1091–1116; Barak, B., Mathur, A., Lee, K. and Zhang, Y. (2001), 'Perceptions of Age-Identity: A Cross-Cultural Inner-Age Exploration', *Psychology & Marketing*, 18(10), 1003–30.

10 Lewis, H.G. (1996), *Silver Linings: Selling to the Expanding Motive Market*. New York: Bonus Books.

11 Lumpkin, J.R. (1989), *Direct Marketing, Direct Selling, and the Mature Consumer: A Research Study*. Westpoint, CT: Quorum Books.

12 Kotler, P., Armstrong, G., Saunders, J. and Wong, V. (2001), *Principles of Marketing, European Edition*. London: Prentice Hall Europe.

13 Euro Effie (2001), Berlin: Gesamtverband Werbeagenturen GWA e.V.

14 Rice, F. (2001, 2) 'Superstars of spending: Marketers clamor for kids', *Advertising Age*, 1 February, S1; Kunkel, D., Wilcox, B.L., Cantor, J., Palmer, E., Linn, S. and Dowrick, P. (2004) Report of the APA Task Force on advertising to children. Retrieved 7 October 2005 from http://www.apa.org/releases/childrenads.pdf.

15 McNeal, J. (1998) 'Tapping the three kids' markets', *American Demographics*, 20(4), 37–41.

16 Furnham, A., Abramski, S. and Gunter, B. (1997) 'A cross-cultural content analysis of children's television advertisements', *Sex Roles*, 37, 91–9.

17 Lyna, A. (2005) TV confuses children about which foods are healthy, new study finds. University of Illinois at

Urbana-Champaign News release (6 June 2005). Retrieved 28 July 2005, from http://www.news.uiuc.edu/news/05/0606kidfood.htm.

18 Bijmolt, T.H.A., Claassen, W. and Brus, B. (1998) 'Children's understanding of TV advertising: Effects of age, gender and parental influence', *Journal of Consumer Policy*, 21(2), 171–94; Clarke, B. (2003) 'The complex issue of food, advertising, and child health', *International Journal of Advertising and Marketing to Children*, 5(1), 11–16; Clarke, B. (2005) 'Responsible marketing,' *Young Consumers*, 6(4), 3–4.

19 Eagle, L.C., Bulmer, S.L., de Bruin, A.M. and Kitchen, P.J. (2004a) 'Exploring the link between obesity and advertising in New Zealand,' *Journal of Marketing Communications*, 10(1), 49–67.

20 Lvovich, S. (2003) 'Advertising and obesity: the research evidence', *International Journal of Advertising and Marketing to Children*, 4 (January/March), 35–40; Young, B. (2003) 'Does food advertising make children obese?', *International Journal of Advertising and Marketing to Children*, 4 (April/June), 19–26; Eagle, L.C., Bulmer, S.L., de Bruin, A.M. and Kitchen, P.J. (2004a) 'Exploring the link between obesity and advertising in New Zealand', *Journal of Marketing Communications*, 10(1), 49–67.

21 Vandewater, E.A., Shim, M. and Caplovitz, A.G. (2004) 'Linking obesity and activity level with children's television and video game use', *Journal of Adolescence*, 27, 71–85.

22 Eagle, L.C., Bulmer, S.L. and Hawkins, J.C. (2003) The 'obesity epidemic': Complex causes, controversial cures – Implications for marketing communication. Auckland, Massey University: Technical report, 3 March; Eagle, L.C., Bulmer, S.L., Kitchen, P.J. and Hawkins, J.C. (2004b) 'Complex and controversial causes for the "obesity epidemic": The role of marketing communications', *International Journal of Medical Marketing*, 4(3), 271–87.

23 Vandewater, E.A., Shim, M. and Caplovitz, A.G. (2004) 'Linking obesity and activity level with children's television and video game use', *Journal of Adolescence*, 27, 71–85.

24 Clarke, B. (2003) 'The complex issue of food, advertising, and child health' *International Journal of Advertising and Marketing to Children*, 5(1), 11–16; Young, B. (2005) 'The obesity epidemic reviewed', *Young Consumers*, 6(3), 50–5.

25 Reid, L.N., King, K. and DeLorme, D.E. (1998), 'Top-Level Agency Creatives Look at Advertising Creativity Then and Now', *Journal of Advertising*, 27(2), 1–15.

26 Rossiter, J.R. and Percy, L. (2000), *Advertising Communication and Promotion Management*. New York: McGraw-Hill.

27 Centlivre, L. (1988), 'A Peek at the Creatives of the '90s', *Advertising Age*, 18 January, 62.

28 Otnes, C., Oviatt, A.A. and Treise, D.M. (1995), 'Views on Advertising Curricula from Experienced Creatives', *Journalism Educator*, 49 (Winter), 21–30.

29 *Management and Advertising Problems in the Advertiser–Agency Relationship* (1985). New York: Association of National Advertisers.

30 Ind, N. (1993), *Great Advertising Campaigns. How they Achieve Both Creative and Business Objectives*. London: Kogan Page.

31 Ind, N. (1993), *Great Advertising Campaigns. How they Achieve Both Creative and Business Objectives*. London: Kogan Page.

32 Euro Effie (2001), Berlin: Gesamtverband Werbeagenturen GWA e.V.

33 Anonymous (2003), 'Belgisch Regisseursduo Gooit Hoge Ogen op Amerikaans Reclamefestival' ('Belgian Producers Amaze at American Advertising Awards'), *De Morgen*, 22 May 2003.

34 Reid, L.N., King, K. and DeLorme, D.E. (1998), 'Top-Level Agency Creatives Look at Advertising Creativity Then and Now', *Journal of Advertising*, 27(2), 1–15.

35 Leather, P., MacKechnie, S. and Amirkhanian, M. (1994), 'The Importance of Likeability as a Measure of Television Advertising Effectiveness', *International Journal of Advertising*, 13(3), 265–80.

36 Biel, A.L. and Bridgwater, C.A. (1990), 'Attributes of likeable television commercials', *Advances in Consumer Research*, 11, 4–10; De Pelsmacker, P. and Van den Bergh, J. (1998), 'Ad content, product category, campaign weight and irritation. A study of 226 TV commercials', *Journal of International Consumer Marketing*, 10(4), 5–27; Till, B.D. and Baack, D.W. (2005), 'Recall and persuasion. Does creative advertising matter?', *Journal of Advertising*, 34(3), 47–57; Tippens, M.J. and Kunkel, R.A. (2006), 'Winning a Clio Award and its relationship to profitability', *Journal of Marketing Communications*, 12(1), 1–14.

37 De Pelsmacker, P., Decock, B. and Geuens, M. (1998), 'Advertising Characteristics and the Attitude Towards the Ad – A Study of 100 Likeable TV Commercials', *Marketing and Research Today*, 27(4), 166–79.

38 Abernethy, A.M. and Franke, G.R. (1996), 'The Information Content of Advertising: A Meta-Analysis', *Journal of Advertising*, 25(2), 1–17.

39 Abernethy, A.M. and Franke, G.R. (1996), 'The Information Content of Advertising: A Meta-Analysis', *Journal of Advertising*, 25(2), 1–17.

40 Chandy, R.K., Tellis, G.J., MacInnis, D.J. and Thaivanich, P. (2001), 'What to Say When: Advertising Appeals in Evolving Markets', *Journal of Marketing Research*, 38(4), 399–414.

41 Pickett, G.M., Grove, S.J. and Laband, D.N. (2001), 'The Impact of Product Type and Parity on the Informational Content of Advertising', *Journal of Market Theory and Practice*, 9(3), 32–43.

42 Brassington, B. and Pettitt, S. (2003), *Principles of Marketing, 3rd Edition*. Edinburgh Gate, Harlow: Pearson Education.

43 Ball, D. (2003), 'Unilever Sees Hefty Profit in SlimFast', *Wall Street Journal*, 23 April.

44 De Pelsmacker, P. and Van den Bergh, J. (1998), 'Ad Content, Product Category, Campaign Weight and Irritation. A Study of 226 TV Commercials', *Journal of International Consumer Marketing*, 10(4), 5–27; Aaker, D.A. and Bruzzone, D.E. (1985), 'Causes of Irritation in Advertising', *Journal of Marketing*, 49 (Spring), 47–57.

45 De Pelsmacker, P. and Van den Bergh, J. (1998), 'Ad Content, Product Category, Campaign Weight and Irritation. A Study of 226 TV Commercials', *Journal of International Consumer Marketing*, 10(4), 5–27; Aaker, D.A. and Bruzzone, D.E. (1985), 'Causes of Irritation in Advertising', *Journal of Marketing*, 49 (Spring), 47–57.

46 Euro Effie (2001), Berlin: Gesamtverband Werbeagenturen GWA e.V.

47 Donthu, N. (1998), 'A Cross-Country Investigation of Recall and Attitude Toward Comparative Advertising', *Journal of Advertising*, 27(2), 111–22.

48 Brabbs, C. (2001), 'Two-thirds Find Comparative Ads "Unacceptable"', *Marketing*, 20 September, 4.

49 Dianoux, C. and Herrmann, J.L. (2001), 'The Influence of Comparative Advertising on Memorization and Attitudes: Experimentation in the French Context', *Recherche et Applications en Marketing*, 16(2).

50 Dianoux, C. (2002), 'What is the Future for Comparative Advertising in France?', *Décisions Marketing*, 25 (Janvier–Mars), 93.

51 del Barrio-Garcia, S. and Luque-Martinez, T. (2003), 'Modelling Consumer Response to Differing Levels of Comparative Advertising', *European Journal of Marketing*, 37(1), 256–74.

52 Grewal, D., Kavanoor, S., Fern, E., Costley, C. and Barnes, J. (1997), 'Comparative Versus Non-Comparative Advertising: A Meta-Analysis', *Journal of Marketing*, 61(4), 1–15; Barry, T. (1993), 'Comparative Advertising: What Have We Learned in Two Decades?', *Journal of Advertising Research*, 33(2), 19–27.

53 Putrevu, S. and Lord, K. (1994), 'Comparative and Non-Comparative Advertising: Attitudinal Effects Under Cognitive and Affective Involvement Conditions', *Journal of Advertising*, 23(2), 77–90.

54 Grewal, D., Kavanoor, S., Fern, E., Costley, C. and Barnes, J. (1997), 'Comparative Versus Non-Comparative Advertising: A Meta-Analysis', *Journal of Marketing*, 61(4), 1–15.

55 Pechmann, C. and Ratneshwar, S. (1991), 'The Use of Comparative Advertising for Brand Positioning: Association Versus Differentiation', *Journal of Consumer Research*, 18(2), 145–60.

56 De Pelsmacker, P., Van den Bergh, J. and Anckaert, P. (1998), *Vergelijkende Reclame: Een Literatuurstudie (Comparative Advertising: Review of the Literature)*. Research report, Marketing Communication Research Centre, Ghent: De Vlerick School voor Management.

57 Droge, C. (1989), 'Shaping the Route to Attitude Change: Central versus Peripheral Processing Through Comparative versus Non-Comparative Advertising', *Journal of Marketing Research*, 26 (May), 193–204.

58 Droge, C. (1989), 'Shaping the Route to Attitude Change: Central versus Peripheral Processing Through Comparative versus Non-Comparative Advertising', *Journal of Marketing Research*, 26 (May), 193–204.

59 Swinyard, W. (1981), 'The Interaction Between Comparative Advertising and Copy Claim Variation', *Journal of Marketing Research*, 18 (May), 175–86.

60 Pechmann, C. and Stewart, D. (1990), 'The Effects of Comparative Advertisements on Attention, Memory, and Purchase Intentions', *Journal of Consumer Research*, 17(2), 180–91.

61 McCullough, L.S. (1992), *The Use of Humor in International Print Advertising: A Content Analysis*. Working paper, Miami University.

62 Weinberger, M.G. and Gulas, C.S. (1992), 'The Impact of Humor in Advertising – A Review', *Journal of Advertising*, 21(4), 35–59.

63 Geuens, M. and De Pelsmacker, P. (2002), 'The Moderating Role of Need for Cognition on Responses to Humorous Appeals', in Broniarczyk, S. and Nakamoto, K. (eds), *Advances in Consumer Research*, Provo, UT: Association for Consumer Research, 29, 50–56.

64 For a typology of humour types, see Speck, P.S. (1991), 'The Humorous Message Taxonomy: A Framework for the Study of Humorous Ads', *Current Issues and Research in Advertising*, 1–44.

65 Beirne, M. (2003), 'Heineken's Headlines are Humorous, but Amstel Light Spots are a Scream', *Brandweek*, 44(19), 8.

66 Spotts, H.E., Weinberger, M.G. and Parsons, A.M. (1997), 'Assessing the Use and Impact of Humor on Advertising Effectiveness', *Journal of Advertising*, 26(3), 17–32.

67 Weinberger, M.G. and Gulas, C.S. (1992), 'The Impact of Humor in Advertising – A Review', *Journal of Advertising*, 21(4), 35–59.

68 Chattopadhyay, A. and Basu, K. (1990), 'Humor in Advertising: The Moderating Role of Prior Brand Evaluation', *Journal of Marketing Research*, 27, 466–76.

69 De Pelsmacker, P. and Geuens, M. (1997), 'Emotional Appeals and Information Cues in Belgian Magazine Advertisements', *International Journal of Advertising*, 16(2), 123–47.

70 Anonymous (2001), 'Sexy Vrouwelijk Strijkerskwartet Zorgt voor Mannelijke Blikschade' ('Sexy Female Musicians Cause Male Car Accidents'), *De Morgen*, 6 April 2001.

71 De Pelsmacker, P. and Geuens, M. (1996), 'The Communication Effects of Warmth, Eroticism and Humour in Alcohol Advertisements', *Journal of Marketing Communication*, 2(4), 247–62.

72 Ford, J.B., LaTour, M.S. and Lundstrom, W.J. (1993), 'Contemporary Women's Evaluations of Female Sex Roles in Advertising', *Journal of Consumer Marketing*, 8(1), 15–28.

73 De Pelsmacker, P. and Geuens, M. (1996), 'The Communication Effects of Warmth, Eroticism and Humour

in Alcohol Advertisements', *Journal of Marketing Communication*, 2(4), 247–62.

74 Smith, S.M., Haughtvedt, C.P. and Jadrich, J.M. (1995), 'Understanding Responses to Sex Appeals in Advertising: An Individual Difference Approach', *Advances in Consumer Research*, 22, 735–9.

75 Dudley, S.C. (1999), 'Consumer Attitudes toward Nudity in Advertising', *Journal of Marketing Theory and Practice*, 7(4), 89–96.

76 Geuens, M. (1997), 'Erotische Reclame: Een Effectieve Strategie?' ('Erotic Advertising: An Effective Strategy?'), *Tijdschrift voor Economie en Management*, 42(1), 57–79.

77 Reichert, T., Heckler, S.E. and Jackson, S. (2001), 'The Effects of Sexual Social Marketing Appeals on Cognitive Processing and Persuasion', *Journal of Advertising*, 30(1), 13–27.

78 De Pelsmacker, P. and Geuens, M. (1996), 'The Communication Effects of Warmth, Eroticism and Humour in Alcohol Advertisements', *Journal of Marketing Communication*, 2(4), 247–62.

79 Benady, D. (2002), 'Playing the Game', *Marketing Week*, July 25, 24–27.

80 De Pelsmacker, P. and Geuens, M. (1997), 'Emotional Appeals and Information Cues in Belgian Magazine Advertisements', *International Journal of Advertising*, 16(2), 123–47.

81 De Pelsmacker, P. and Geuens, M. (1998), 'Different Markets, Different Communication Strategies? A Comparative Study of the Communication Effects of Different Types of Alcohol Ads in Belgium and Poland', *International Marketing Review*, 15(4), 277–90; De Pelsmacker, P. and Geuens, M. (1996), 'The Communication Effects of Warmth, Eroticism and Humour in Alcohol Advertisements', *Journal of Marketing Communication*, 2(4), 247–62; Geuens, M. and De Pelsmacker, P. (1998), 'Feelings Evoked by Warmth, Eroticism and Humour in Alcohol Advertisements', *AMS Review*, www.ams.com; De Pelsmacker, P. and Van den Bergh, J. (1998), 'Ad Content, Product Category, Campaign Weight and Irritation. A Study of 226 TV Commercials', *Journal of International Consumer Marketing*, 10(4), 5–27.

82 Geuens, M. and De Pelsmacker, P. (1999), 'Individual Differences and the Communication Effects of Different Types of Emotional Stimuli: Exploring the Role of Affect Intensity', *Psychology and Marketing*, 16(3), 195–209.

83 Mowen, J.C. (1993), *Consumer Behavior*. New York: Macmillan.

84 Stephenson, M.T. and Witte, K. (2001), 'Creating Fear in a Risky World', in Rice, R. and Atkin, C.K. *Public Communication Campaigns*, Thousand Oaks: Sage, 88–102.

85 Moscato, S., Black, D.R., Blue, C.L., Mattson, M., Galer-Unti, R.A. and Coster, D.C. (2001), 'Evaluating a Fear Appeal Message to Reduce Alcohol Use among "Greeks"', *American Journal of Health Behavior*, 25(5), 481–91.

86 Keller, P.A. and Block, L.G. (1996), 'Increasing the Persuasiveness of Fear Appeals: The Effect of Arousal and Elaboration', *Journal of Consumer Research*, 22(4), 448–59.

87 LaTour, M.S., Snipes, R.L. and Bliss, S.J. (1996), 'Don't Be Afraid to Use Fear Appeals: An Experimental Study', *Journal of Advertising Research*, 36(2), 59–76.

88 Witte, K. and Allen, M. (2000), 'A Meta-Analysis for Fear Appeals: Implications for Effective Public Health Campaigns', *Health Education and Behavior*, 27, 591–615.

89 LaTour, M.S. and Rotfeld, H.J. (1997), 'There Are Threats and (Maybe) Fear-Caused Arousal: Theory and Confusions of Appeals to Fear and Fear Arousal Itself', *Journal of Advertising*, 26(3), 45–59.

90 Schoenbachler, D.D. and Whittler, T.E. (1996), 'Adolescent Processing of Social and Physical Threat Communication', *Journal of Advertising*, 25(4), 37–54.

91 Murray Johnson, L., Witte, K., Liu, W.Y., Hubbell, A.P., Sampson, J. and Morrison, K. (2001), 'Addressing Cultural Orientations in Fear Appeals: Promoting AIDS-protective Behaviors among Mexican Immigrants and African American Adolescents and American and Taiwanese College Students', *Journal of Health Communication*, 6(4), 335–58.

92 Murray, N.M., Murray, S.B. (1996), 'Music and Lyrics in Commercials: A Cross-Cultural Comparison Between Commercials Run in the Dominican Republic and in the United States', *Journal of Advertising*, 25(2), 51–63.

93 Braithwaite, A. and Ware, R. (1997), 'The Role of Music in Advertising', *Admap*, (July/August), 44–7; Alpert, J.I. and Alpert, M.I. (1990), 'Music Influences on Mood and Purchase Intentions', *Psychology and Marketing*, 7(2), 109–33; Bruner, G.C. (1990), 'Music, Mood and Marketing', *Journal of Marketing*, 54(4), 94–104.

94 De Pelsmacker, P. and Van den Bergh, J. (1998), 'Ad Content, Product Category, Campaign Weight and Irritation. A Study of 226 TV Commercials', *Journal of International Consumer Marketing*, 10(4), 5–27.

95 Walker, D. and von Gonten, M.F. (1989), 'Explaining Related Recall: New Answers From a Better Model', *Journal of Advertising Research*, 29(30), 11–21.

96 Gorn, G.J. (1982), 'The Effects of Music in Advertising on Choice Behavior: A Classical Conditioning Approach', *Journal of Marketing*, 46(4), 94–101.

97 Kellaris, J.J. and Cox, A.D. (1989), 'The Effects of Background Music in Advertising: A Reassessment', *Journal of Consumer Research*, 16(1), 113–18.

98 Kellaris, J.J., Cox, A.D. and Cox, D. (1993), 'The Effect of Background Music on Ad Processing: A Contingency Explanation', *Journal of Marketing*, 57(4), 114–25; MacInnis, D.J. and Park, C.W. (1991), 'The Differential Role of the Characteristics of Music on High and Low Involvement Consumers' Processing of Ads', *Journal of Consumer Research*, 18 (September), 161–73; Anand, P. and Sternthal, B. (1990), 'Ease of Message Processing as a Moderator of Repetition Effects in Advertising',

Journal of Marketing Research, 27 (August), 345–53.

99 Wang, A. (2005), 'The effects of expert and consumer endorsements on audience response', *Journal of Advertising Research*, 45 (Dec.), 402–12.

100 Aaker, D.A. and Bruzzone, D.E. (1985), 'Causes of Irritation in Advertising', *Journal of Marketing*, 49 (Spring), 47–57.

101 Erdogan, Z., Baker, M.J. and Tagg, S. (2001), 'Selecting Celebrity Endorsers: The Practitioner's Perspective', *Journal of Advertising Research*, 41(3), 39–48.

102 Erdogan, Z., Baker, M.J. and Tagg, S. (2001), 'Selecting Celebrity Endorsers: The Practitioner's Perspective', *Journal of Advertising Research*, 41(3), 39–48.

103 Lafferty, B.A., Goldsmith, R.E. and Newell, S.J. (2002), 'The Dual Credibility Model: The Influence of Corporate and Endorser Credibility on Attitudes and Purchase Intentions', *Journal of Marketing Theory and Practice*, 10(3), 1–12.

104 Erdogan, B.Z. (1999), 'Celebrity Endorsements: A Literature Review', *Journal of Marketing Management*, 15(4), 291–314.

105 Erdogan, Z., Baker, M.J. and Tagg, S. (2001), 'Selecting Celebrity Endorsers: The Practitioner's Perspective', *Journal of Advertising Research*, 41(3), 39–48.

106 Till, B.D. and Busler, M. (2000), 'The Match-Up Hypothesis: Physical Attractiveness, Expertise, and the Role of Fit on Brand Attitude, Purchase Intent and Brand Beliefs', *Journal of Advertising*, 29(3), 1–13.

107 Bower, A.B. (2001), 'Highly Attractive Models in Advertising and the Women Who Loathe Them: The Implications of Negative Affect for Spokesperson Effectiveness', *Journal of Advertising*, 30(3), 51–63.

108 Till, B.D. and Shimp, T.A. (1998), 'Endorsers in Advertising: The Case of Negative Celebrity Information', *Journal of Advertising*, 27(1), 67–82.

Chapter 8

Media planning

Chapter outline

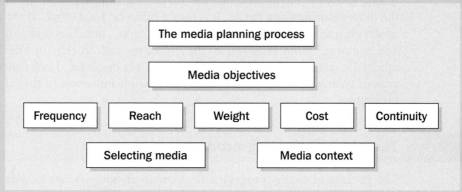

- The media planning process
- Media objectives
- Frequency
- Reach
- Weight
- Cost
- Continuity
- Selecting media
- Media context

Chapter objectives

This chapter will help you to:

- Distinguish the various steps in the media planning process
- Understand the technical details of media objectives, such as frequency, reach, weight, continuity and cost
- Learn on the basis of which criteria the media mix can be composed
- Understand the advantages and disadvantages of the different advertising media
- Get an overview of the criteria to be used in media planning
- Understand the importance of media context for advertising effectiveness

Introduction

Media planning is receiving more and more attention. This is not surprising since the cost of buying advertising time and space makes up 80%–90% of the advertising budget.[1] The latter also explains the recent attention paid to integrated marketing communications, the purpose of which is to use all advertising media, as well as other communications tools, as effectively and efficiently as possible. Attention is paid to each of the different steps in a media plan. Media planning is not just a matter of selecting the appropriate media, given the target group of the advertising campaign and the characteristics of the different advertising media. It is also a technical issue in which the components of media objectives (such as frequency, reach, weight, continuity and cost) are calculated and compared. Both technical media objectives and criteria for selecting the media mix and characteristics of the different media are discussed. Furthermore, the importance of creativity in the use of media and possible influences of the media context are highlighted.

The media planning process

The purpose of media planning is to draw up an adequate media plan. A media plan can be defined as a document specifying which media and vehicles will be purchased when, at what price and with what expected results. It includes such things as flow charts, the names of specific magazines, reach and frequency estimates, and budgets.[2] Creating a media plan is a process which consists of different steps (Figure 8.1).

Just as an environmental analysis is necessary to formulate the marketing strategy and to create a marketing plan, the communications environment needs to be screened to formulate a media plan. First of all, media planners should be acquainted with all regulations and legal aspects, as well as with local habits. Is TV advertising allowed, do people watch predominantly TV, read magazines or listen to the radio, etc.? In

Figure 8.1 **Steps in media planning**

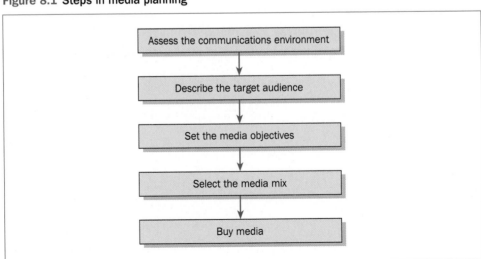

Chapter 19 examples will be given on what is and what is not allowed in different European countries.

Second, media planners should be able to judge the communications efforts of the competition. In this respect, the following elements are important:[3]

■ Category spending: What is the advertising spending in the product category, and how has it evolved over the last five years? Did category spending increase, decrease or remain stable?

■ Share of voice: What is the relative advertising spending of the different competitive brands in the product category? Share of voice (SOV) is calculated by dividing a particular brand's advertising spending by the total category spending. Besides the share of voice, one should also investigate the share of market (SOM) and how share of voice relates to share of market. Some researchers assume that share of market follows share of voice, while others argue that the share of market should always be smaller than the share of voice in order to be able to maintain growth (see also Chapter 6 on budgets).

■ Media mix: Identify how each competitor divides its advertising spending across the different media and analyse the trend in media mix composition. Table 8.1 shows the media mix and SOV for petroleum companies in Luxembourg.

Target groups were extensively discussed in Chapter 4. Although all segmentation variables mentioned there remain valid, a variable that needs special attention at this stage is the media behaviour of the target audience. Do the target consumers listen to the radio or watch TV, and if so, which programmes do they listen to or watch, at what time, and on which days? Do the target consumers read newspapers or magazines, and if so, which ones do they read? Do the target consumers use electronic media, do they often go the cinema, etc.? This information is indispensable.

Table 8.1 Advertising spend of petroleum companies in Luxembourg 2002 (€)

	Weekly magazines	Other Magazines	Newspapers	Radio	TV	Total	SOV (%)
ARAL	12,538	37,692	23,676	5,783		79,688	29.8
BP Luxembourg			594			594	0.2
DEA		864				864	0.3
Esso Luxembourg	135	22,513			948	23,596	8.8
Kuwait Petroleum	10,901	350	44,932	9,490		65,673	24.5
Shell Luxembourg	7,724	883	2,088	21,890	44,334	76,919	28.7
Texaco	314	577	82			972	0.4
TotalFina	7,293	1,939	805	9,490		19,528	7.3
Total	38,904	64,818	73,125	46,655	44,334	267,835	100

Source: VVL/BBDO Belgium.

Media objectives

Media objectives are derived from the communications objectives, and ought to be concrete, measurable and realistic. Media objectives usually are formulated in terms of the characteristics shown in Figure 8.2.

Figure 8.2 Media objectives

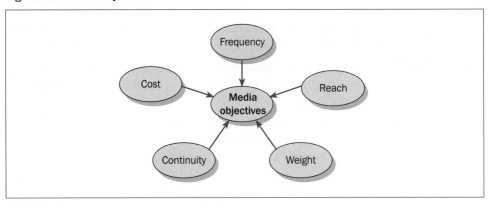

Frequency

Frequency indicates how many times a consumer of the target group, on average, is expected to be exposed to the advertiser's message within a specified time period. It is important to know that frequency is estimated on the basis of the number of times one could be exposed to the media vehicle, and not to the message itself. For example, if a consumer has a newspaper subscription and a certain campaign has one ad a week for six weeks in that newspaper, we could expect that the particular consumer will be exposed to the advertisement six times during the six-week period. However, if the consumer does not always read the full newspaper and occasionally omits the pages in which the ad appears, the actual number of times he or she will be exposed to the message will be lower than six.

When deciding on the objective of how many times the target group has to be reached, a first question that arises is how often should a consumer be exposed to a message for it to be effective? And how does a consumer respond to frequent exposures to the same message? Research shows that advertising repetition initially increases learning, but may lead to boredom and irritation later.[4] According to the two-factor model, an inverted-U relationship exists between the level of exposure on the one hand, and advertising effectiveness (cognitive responses, attitudes, purchase) on the other (Figure 8.3). Wear-in and wear-out effects explain the nature of this relationship.[5] At low levels of exposure, consumers develop rather negative responses (e.g. counterarguments) due to the novelty of the stimulus. After a few exposures, the reaction becomes more positive. This is referred to as wear-in. More frequent exposures again lead to more negative responses, a phenomenon called wear-out. Negative responses, such as irritation, can be expected to be the highest both at low and high exposure levels, while positive responses are optimal at intermediate exposure levels. One way to counter or delay the wear-out effect is to make minor changes to the ad so that the consumer is not exposed to the same ad over and over again or to use executional cues that evoke positive emotional responses.[6] A recent study shows that in cases where consumers process messages in a superficial or shallow way (for example, when they are hardly aware of the fact that there is an ad), wear-out may not occur at all.[7]

Figure 8.3 Ad frequency and ad effectiveness

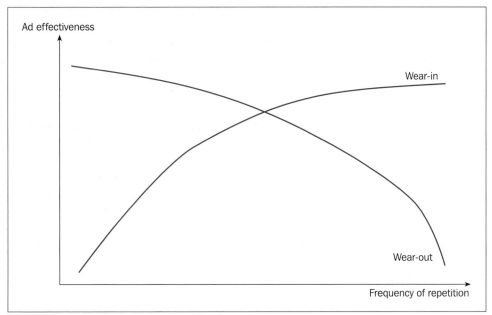

Another way of thinking about advertising repetition is comprised in the economic signalling theory which assumes that consumers take advertising repetition as a signal of the quality of a brand. In this view, higher advertising costs signal greater manufacturer effort and higher manufacturer confidence and trust in quality.[8] In other words, consumers think that if a manufacturer is willing to spend a lot of money on advertising, they must be convinced they will get it back in the long run. The latter is only possible if consumers not only try, but also repurchase the product, which can only occur with a high-quality product. However, at extremely high levels of repetition, consumers find the advertising expenses excessive. At that point people think something must be wrong and perceptions about the advertising company as well as about the quality level of the brand detoriate. It is interesting to note that the attitude towards the ad seems to wear out more quickly than the perception of brand quality.[9] In this sense repetition beyond ad wear-out can make sense.

In conclusion, several reasons have been reported in the literature as to why a high (but not excessive) repetition level of advertising might be beneficial:

- It makes the message more memorable and raises brand recall.[10]
- It makes attitudes more accessible and raises consumers' confidence in their attitudes,[11] making them more resistant to attitude change and brand switching.
- It increases the believability of the ad claims.[12]
- It leads to a greater top-of-mind brand awareness.[13]
- It functions as a signal or cue for brand quality.[14]

However, the difficulty remains to determine the optimal frequency level, which is inevitably linked to the advertising objective, the type of message used, media clutter, the product category, the competition level, the target group and the media used. Controversy also exists concerning the frequency level that is sufficient to evoke the intended response in the consumer. This frequency level is also referred to as the motivational frequency or the effective frequency, defined as 'the minimum number of exposures, within a purchase cycle, considered necessary to motivate the average prospect in the target audience to accomplish an advertising objective'.[15] Some researchers think one exposure is sufficient, while others assume an effective frequency of at least three.[16] One exposure may be sufficient if you reach the consumer at the right moment, with the right message. For example, a consumer is driving home from work and a little stone makes the car window burst. One advertisement for Car Glass mentioning that it repairs car windows 24 hours a day may be very effective at that moment. On the other hand, a consumer may need to see a yoghurt ad 15 times before it becomes effective. Moreover, two exposures may be sufficient for market leadership or an established brand image, while at least four might be necessary for new campaigns targeted at infrequent users, if the objective is to increase the usage of a product or when medium clutter is high.[17] In other words, situational variables play an important role.

Is advertising money efficiently used?[18]

Given the large amount of money that is annually spent on advertising, the question of possible inefficiency in the use of advertising money is a very relevant one. However, it is not so easy to measure such efficiency or inefficiency and the resulting loss of sales as a consequence of an inefficient use of advertising money. Measuring, minimising inputs, maximising outputs and benchmarking are vital to detect and correct problems. Defining efficiency as the ratio between outputs (sales attributed to advertising) and inputs (advertising media expenditures), a recent study used data envelopment analysis (DEA) to evaluate and benchmark the efficiency of the top 47 US advertisers' ad expenditures in print (magazines and newspapers), broadcast (television and radio) and the internet. The advantage of DEA is that it can handle multiple inputs and multiple outputs, and that it is capable of calculating the efficiency of the 47 advertisers relative to each other. The results showed several clear inefficiencies. More specifically, 34 of the 47 advertisers appeared to be inefficient in their ad expenditures and they were least efficient with internet advertising. As compared to the other advertisers, Federated Department Stores, for example, would have to reduce print media investments by $2.3 billion, broadcast media expenditures by $68 million and internet ad spending by $7 million to become an efficient advertiser. John Wanamaker's famous saying: 'Half of every dollar spent on advertising is wasted; the problem is I just don't know which half', could well be true. The good news is that with recent techniques such as DEA, advertisers can get an idea of which part they need to cut down.

One technique to judge the effectiveness of media is the β-coefficient analysis, developed by Morgensztern, in which the relationship between the number of exposures and the degree of memorisation (i.e. the percentage of the target group that remembers the ad) is analysed. The mathematical form of the β-coefficient model is as follows:

$$M_n = 1 - (1 - \beta)^n$$

where: M_n = memorisation after n exposures
  β: medium-specific memorisation rate

Figure 8.4 illustrates the evolution of memorisation, given a β-coefficient of 12%. As the figure illustrates, total recall increases decreasingly in function of exposure.

The β-analysis takes into account that memorisation of a message depends on the medium used. It is assumed that each exposure is able to make a constant percentage (β) of the consumers who previously could not remember the message of a campaign actually remember the message. Table 8.2 gives a few examples of media and their β-coefficients while Figure 8.5 shows the relation between the number of exposures and the memorisation rate for different media. Cinema advertising is by far the most effective medium to make people memorise your advertising message, while outdoor seems to be the least effective. Applying the formula shown above suggests that the number of people who have memorised a message after three exposures is 97.3% for cinema advertising, but only 27.1% for daily papers.

Morgensztern not only developed different β-coefficients for different media, he also used these coefficients to suggest the minimum and maximum number of exposures for

Figure 8.4 The β-coefficient: exposure and memorisation

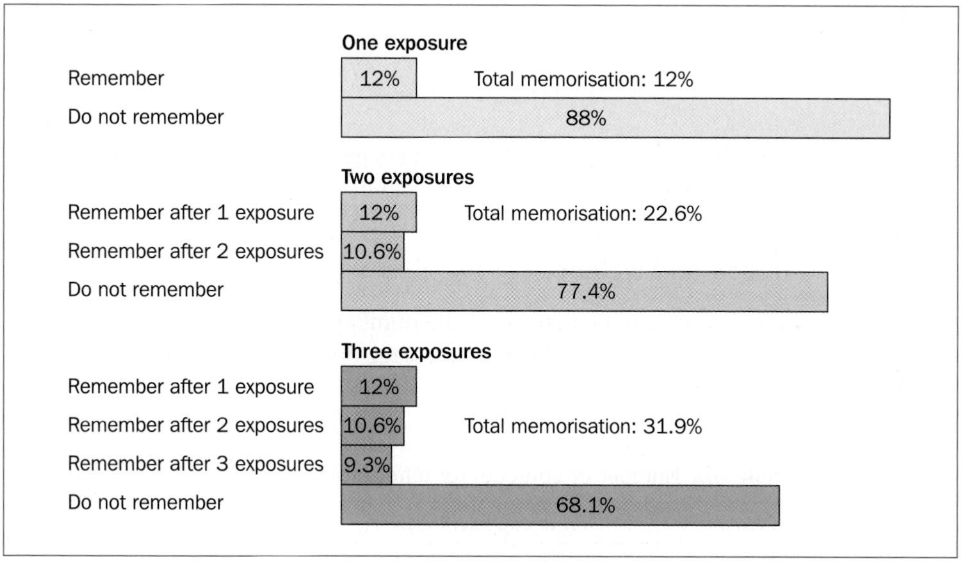

Table 8.2 β-coefficients for different media

Medium	β-coefficient
Cinema	70%
Magazines	10%
Daily papers	10%
TV	15%
Radio	5%
Outdoor	2%

Source: Quattro Saatchi, Brussels, Belgium (2003).

Figure 8.5 The relation between exposures and memorisation for different media

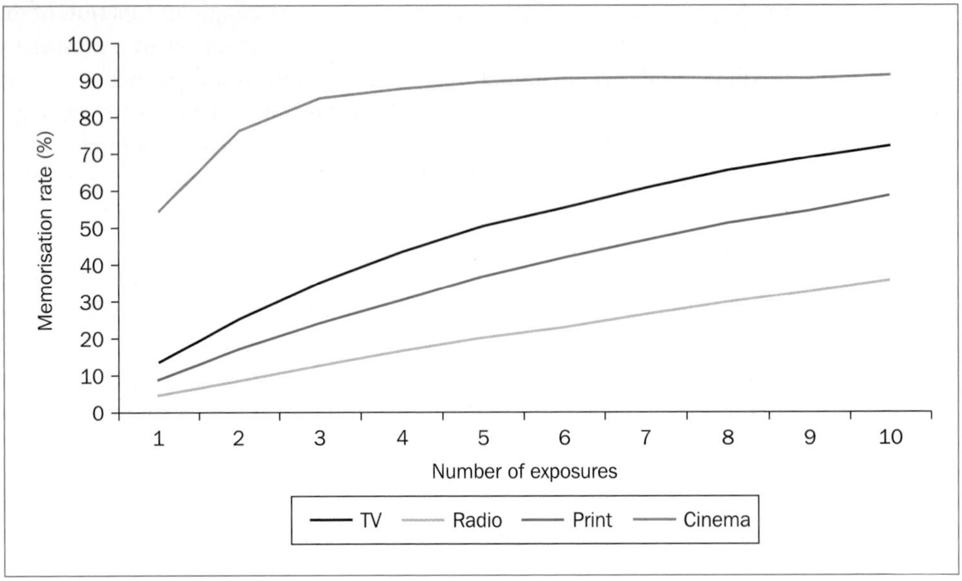

Source: JFC Informatique & média, Paris, France (2003). Reproduced with permission.

the different media in order for a message to be effective. Table 8.3 shows the suggested number of contacts.

Reach and weight

Total reach can be defined as the number or percentage of people who are expected to be exposed to the advertiser's message during a specified period.

Table 8.3 Number of contacts for different media

Medium	Not enough contacts	Too many contacts	Suggested contacts
Radio	4	15	5–14
Press	3	10	4–9
Television	2	7	3–6
Cinema	1	3	2

Source: Quattro Saatchi, Brussels, Belgium (2003).

Audience shares of the leading European channels

Total reach refers to the audience you can expect to reach with a certain medium. The following table shows the TV channels with the highest share of the adult population for the different European countries.[19]

▶

Audience shares of the leading European channels

Country	Channel	Reach	Country	Channel	Reach
Austria	ORF 2	29.8	Luxembourg	RTL Télé Letzebuerg	52.9
Belarus	ONT	52.8	Macedonia	A 1	28.9
Belgium N	TV1	29.2	Netherlands, The	RTL4	16.8
Belgium S	RTL TVI	23.2	Norway	NRK1	40.2
Bulgaria	BTV	37.9	Poland	TVP 1	25.8
Croatia	HTV 1	43.8	Portugal	SIC	29.3
Czech Rep	Nova	43.4	Romania	Romania 1	28.4
Denmark	TV2	36.2	Russia	PERVY	26.8
			Serbia and		
Estonia	TV3	22.1	Montenegro	PINK	21.2
Finland	MTV3	38.1	Slovakia	Markiza	45.9
France	TF1	30.6	Slovenia	POP TV	29.0
Germany	RTL	15.0	Spain	TVE 1	24.0
Greece	Antenna	22.5	Sweden	TV4	25.6
Hungary	RTL KLUB	29.5	Switzerland F	TSR 1	25.8
Iceland	RUV	42.7	Switzerland G	SF 1	24.8
Ireland	RTE 1	27.4	Switzerland I	TSI 1	26.7
Italy	RAI 1	24.2	Turkey	KANAL D	15.0
Latvia	LNT	22.2	Ukraine	INTER	29.3
Lithuania	LNK	27.0	United Kingdom	BBC 1	26.3

Whether these channels are the best to include in the media plan depends on the target group. If your target group consists of children and teens, an ad on a youth channel may be more efficient than the leading channels shown in the table. Moreover, some of these channels are public channels which do not take advertising. In this case, companies are obliged to look for other options.

The difference between total and useful reach is important. The latter is usually referred to as reach. Reach is not about how many consumers will probably see the message, but how many consumers from the target group are likely to see the message. As was the case for frequency, only exposure to the media vehicle can be estimated, not to the message itself. Furthermore, one should realise that, although total reach may be higher for a TV campaign, useful reach may be higher for a campaign in specialised magazines. Even within the same medium, total and useful reach can differ enormously for different media vehicles. For instance, for a target group of youngsters aged between 3 and 14 years, the reach shown in Table 8.4 can be obtained with an ad on the Swedish TV channels SVT1 and SVT2.

When the same message comes in different media or multiple times in the same vehicle, a distinction can be made between gross reach and reach. As illustrated in Figure 8.6,

Table 8.4 Example of reach by medium

	Total reach (thousands)	(Useful) reach (thousands)	(Useful) reach (%)
SVT1	2,193	409	30.9%
SVT2	1,234	69	5.2%

Based on: IP Peaktime (2004), *Television 2004. European Key Factors*. Neuilly-sur-Seine, Cedex, Brussels: IP.

Figure 8.6 Gross reach and reach

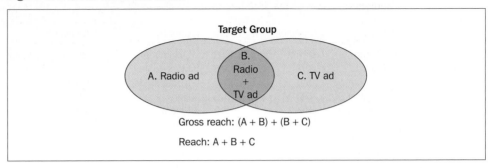

gross reach is the sum of the number of people each individual medium reaches, regardless of how many times an individual is reached. In other words, a person who is reached by medium x and medium y counts as two. Reach is the sum of all people reached at least once (a person reached by x and y counts as one). In other words, reach equals gross reach minus the duplicated audience. Gross reach, expressed as a percentage of the target group, is referred to as gross rating points (GRPs). The weight of a campaign is typically expressed by GRPs. For example, an objective of Gatorade could be to realize a total of 400 GRPs in a month for a target group of sports people. These GRPs can be realised by means of different media and different media vehicles.

A measure often used by media planners is opportunity to see (OTS). OTS is defined as the average probability of exposure that an average target consumer has. It is calculated by dividing gross reach by reach. For instance, suppose that Bacardi Breezer wants to reach the adult Polish population. Reach of an ad during the break of the daily soap *Clan* on the Polish TV channel TVP1 is 57.2%, of an ad during the break of the daily soap '*L*' *like love* on TVP2 is 51.5%, of an ad on Polskie Radio is 17.3%, and of an ad on Radio RMF FM is 22.6%.[20] A four-week campaign consisting of four ads during the *Clan* and *For Better or for Worse* programmes, six ads on Polskie Radio and eight ads on radio RMF FM results in 719.4 GRPs. To compute reach, we cannot just add the reach of the four vehicles since we can expect that some people will watch several channels or watch TV and listen to the radio. Assume therefore that reach is not 100% but 65%. In this case, OTS would be 11.1 (GRPs divided by reach in percentage, or 719.4 divided by 65). To come back to gross rating points, the latter means that GRPs can actually be calculated in two different ways:

■ By multiplying reach (in percentage) and frequency for the different media vehicles used:

$$GRP = \sum_{i=1}^{n} (f_i \times r_i)$$

where: n = number of media vehicles
f$_i$ = frequency of media vehicle i
r$_i$ = percentage reach of media vehicle i

■ By multiplying reach (in percentage) and opportunity to see:

$$GRP = Reach \times OTS$$

where: reach = audience across different media vehicles minus duplicated audience

Effective reach is the number of target consumers who are expected to be exposed to the advertiser's message at an effective frequency level. Suppose an advertising campaign reached 60% of its target consumers with the frequencies reported in Table 8.5. If the consumer needs to be exposed at least three times to be effective, then the effective reach is 24.0% (11.5% + 6.0% + 3.5% + 1.8% + 1.2%).

Table 8.5 Reach and frequency distribution

Exposures	Reach
1	20.0%
2	16.0%
3	11.5%
4	6.0%
5	3.5%
6	1.8%
7	1.2%

Calculating gross reach, OTS and effective gross reach

A company defines its target group as all males between 30 and 40. The total size of the target group is 10 million consumers. The company plans a newspaper campaign. The newspaper has a total readership of 18 million and a useful readership of 5 million. Ten ads are placed in the newspaper. The table below gives the distribution of percentage reach in function of the exposure frequency.

The reach of the campaign is 5 million or 50% of the target group. The weight of the campaign is 238 GRP ($5 \times 1 + 6 \times 2 + 3 \times 3 + 9 \times 4 + 8 \times 5 + 7 \times 6 + 6 \times 7 + 3 \times 8 + 2 \times 9 + 1 \times 10$). As a result, the gross reach is 23.8 million exposures (238% × 10 million). Opportunity to see is 4.76 (238/50 or 23.8/5). Effective rating points (ERP), or effective gross reach, defined as at least 3 exposures, is 221 GRPs.

Frequency	Newspaper reach (% of target group)
1	5
2	6
3	3
4	9
5	8
6	7
7	6
8	3
9	2
10	1

Continuity

Concerning campaign continuity, advertisers have three possibilities: a continuous, a pulsing or a flighting schedule:

■ A continuous schedule means that the advertiser spends a continuous amount of money throughout the whole campaign period (Figure 8.7). However, since most companies have budget constraints, a continuous schedule might result in too low expenditures per period to be effective.

■ A pulsing schedule indicates that a certain level of advertising takes place during the whole campaign period, but during particular periods higher advertising levels are used (Figure 8.8).

■ A flighting schedule is used when advertising is concentrated in only a few periods and not during the whole campaign period (Figure 8.9). This might be preferred due to budget contraints, for example. In other words, during some months no advertising takes place in order to be able to spend higher levels during peak demand months.

As mentioned before, some researchers argue that the most important thing is to reach consumers near the point of purchase. Jones[21] suggests that one exposure is sufficient and may have a much greater influence than frequent exposures. According to him, trying to reach as many people in the target group within the period near their purchasing is more effective than trying to reach a particular segment more frequently during the same time period. Ephron[22] shares this view and compares being off-air, as is the case with a flighting schedule, with being out-of-stock at the sales point. According to him, you reach this week's buyers with this week's advertising, and next week's buyers only with next week's advertising, and not with this week's advertising. Also, a recent study investigating the impact of 1,482 radio commercials reveals that media consistency and spending the advertising budget in complementary media and radio channels, i.e. focusing on reach rather than frequency of exposure (and, as a consequence, using a continuous rather than a flighting or pulsing schedule), is an important explanatory factor for both ad and brand recognition.[23] Others argue that both reach and frequency remain important.[24] When the purpose of advertising is to give information, frequent

Figure 8.7 Continuous advertising

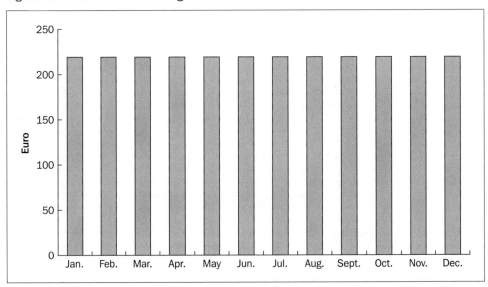

Figure 8.8 Pulsing advertising

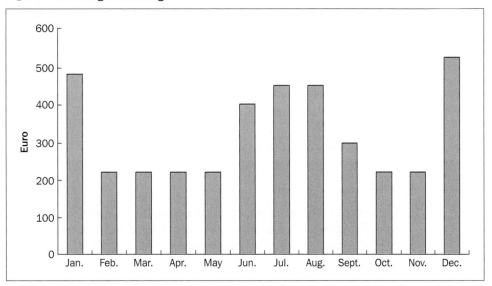

Figure 8.9 Flighting advertising

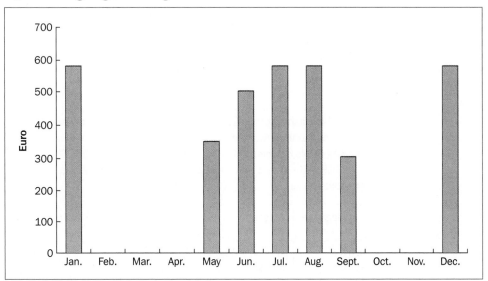

exposure can be important; when the objective of advertising is to remind people (e.g. in the case of mature products), one exposure may be enough.[25] But even in the latter case, a positive effect of frequent exposure can be measured.[26] Moreover, it cannot be stressed enough that a drop in ad spending during recessions is not a wise decision. More and more studies find strong support for the argument that recessions provide special opportunities for maximising the benefit of advertising euros.[27]

Another aspect worth considering when deciding on whether to use a continuous, pulsing or flighting schedule, is how long people remember the message. Too much focus on a certain period of time without any repetitions during the rest of the year can be detrimental, since people easily forget the communication they have been exposed to.

Two scheduling tactics worth mentioning are double-spotting and roadblocking.[28] With double-spotting, two spots are placed within the same programme to increase the likelihood of obtaining the effective frequency. Roadblocking refers to placing the same ad across many channels at the same time. In this case, reach can be seriously increased since everyone watching television at, for example, 9 p.m., will be confronted with the ad. Moreover, it is also a partial solution to the zapping phenomenon since even zapping will not help consumers to avoid the ad.

Cost

The cost of a medium is usually expressed as the cost per thousand (CPT), meaning the cost of reaching 1,000 people. Cost per thousand (CPT) is usually referred to as CPM, the 'M' referring to the Roman symbol for thousand, CPM is calculated by dividing the cost of the medium (the air cost of a 15- or 30-second commercial, the cost of a one-page magazine ad, etc.) by the medium's audience. More interesting to know is the cost per thousand people of your target market, also represented by CPM-TM. In this case, the cost of the medium has to be divided by the reach.

$$CPM = \frac{\text{Cost of the medium}}{\text{Total reach}} \times 1{,}000$$

$$CPM\text{-}TM = \frac{\text{Cost of the medium}}{\text{Reach}} \times 1{,}000$$

Suppose an Irish fashion chain wants to reach young females (between 16 and 30 years of age). An ad is inserted in three women's magazines, in a TV guide and in a special interest magazine. The following CPMs can be calculated. Although the CPM for *RTE Guide* is the lowest, calculation of the CPM-TM shows that for reaching the young female audience, *Woman's Way* may be more cost efficient.

Type of magazine	Magazine	Cost (I£)	Total reach (000s)	CPM	(Useful) reach	CPM-TM
Women's magazines	Woman's Way	3,250	230	14.13	115	28.26
	Image	1,995	116	17.19	58	34.39
	U	1,800	106	16.98	53	33.96
TV guide	RTE Guide	3,900	585	6.67	117	33.33
Special interest	Hot Press	2,260	44	51.36	7	322.8

As was the case with the other concepts, only taking CPM and CPM-TM into account can lead to major errors. CPM and/or CPM-TM may be low just because the medium vehicle is very cheap and does not reach the target medium in an effective way. Using billboards near small roads does not cost a lot, but only a very small percentage of the target audience may be reached.

Selecting media

There is a difference between media and vehicles. Advertising media refer to types of communications channels that can distribute a message. Examples are newspapers, magazines, TV, etc. On the other hand, vehicles are particular programmes, magazines, etc., such as *The Simpsons*, *The Osbournes*, *Pop Idol*, *Cosmopolitan*, *Star*, etc. This section is mainly devoted to media, and not so much to specific vehicles.

The percentages presented in Figure 8.10 reveal that TV is the medium to which most of the advertising spendings are devoted, followed by newspapers, magazines and radio. Magazine advertising is much more important in Europe than in the US, while

Figure 8.10a Percentage spend on advertising media in the European Union

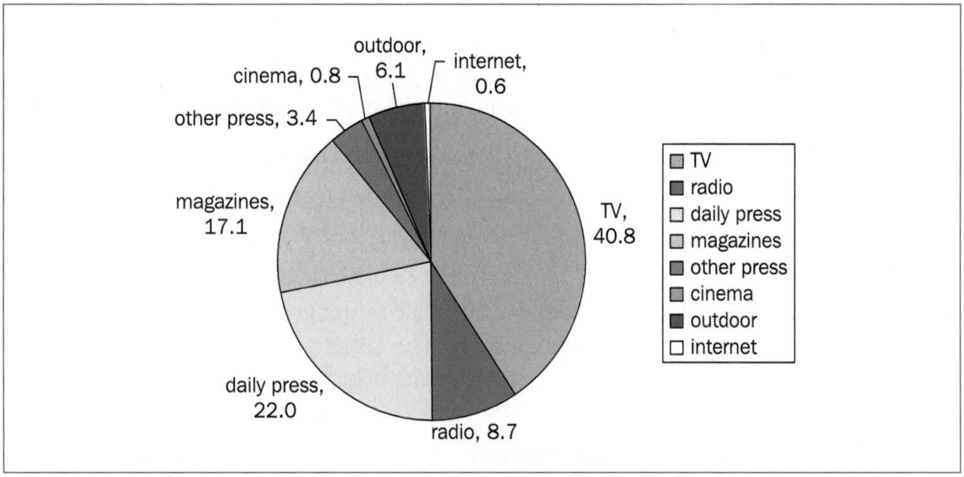

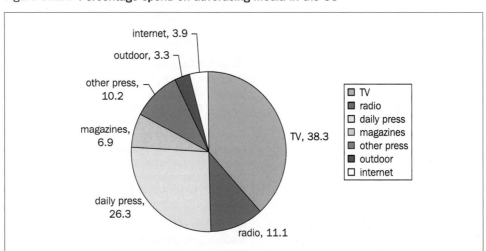

Based on: IP Peaktime (2004), Television 2004. European Key Factors. Neuilly-sur-Seine, Cedex, Brussels: IP.

Figure 8.10b Percentage spend on advertising media in the US

Based on: Ad Age Fact Pack, February 2006, Crain Communications Inc. (http://www.adage.com)

radio, other press and internet ad spendings are higher in the US than in Europe. Outdoor is again more used in the EU than in the US.

Media mix criteria

Before deciding which media will and will not be included in the media mix, the different media should be evaluated on several criteria. These criteria can be categorised in quantitative, qualitative and technical criteria. Table 8.6 gives an overview of several potential criteria.

Quantitative criteria deal with factors such as how many people can be reached, how often and how quickly the target group can be reached, whether the advertising message can be adapted for different geographic regions, whether the medium is more effective during certain periods of the year than during others, and how selective the advertising medium is.

Medium selectivity refers to the extent that a medium is directed towards the target group. Medium selectivity can be represented by a selectivity index showing how well the target group is represented in the medium reach, relative to the universe:[29]

$$\text{Selectivity index} = \frac{\% \text{ of the target group in total reach}}{\% \text{ of the target group in the universe}} \times 100$$

Selectivity index < 100: The target group is under-represented;
The vehicle is not selective on the target group
Selectivity index = 100: The target group is proportionally represented
Selectivity index > 100: The target group is over-represented;
The vehicle is selective on the target group

Table 8.6 Mixed media criteria

Quantitative criteria	Reach Frequency Selectivity Geographic flexibility Speed of reach (delayed or not) Message life Seasonal influence
Qualitative criteria	Image-building capability Emotional impact Medium involvement Active or passive medium Attention devoted to the medium Quality of reproduction Adding value to the message (by means of the context) Amount of information that can be conveyed Demonstration capability Extent of memorisation of the message (β-coefficient) Clutter
Technical criteria	Production cost Media buying characteristics (lead time, cancellation, etc.) Media availability

Qualitative criteria to evaluate different media are the extent to which the medium is capable of building a brand image and a brand personality, the impact the medium has on the audience, how involved the audience is with the medium, and as a consequence whether the audience is active or passive and whether the audience pays a lot or only minor attention to the messages conveyed by the medium. Qualitative criteria are also about whether or not the vehicle can add value to the brand or product due to the context in which the brand or product is shown (see also further in this chapter), whether or not the quality of reproduction is sufficiently high, how much and what type of information can be conveyed to the consumer (e.g. can the use and customer friendliness of the product be demonstrated?), how many exposures are needed to make consumers remember the message (β-coefficient) and whether or not the medium is characterised by a lot of advertising clutter resulting in a need for more exposures to become reasonably effective.

Calculating medium selectivity

Consider the Danish TV channels TV2 and ZULU. How selective are they for a target group consisting of young adults aged between 12 and 30?

Media vehicle	Population size young adults (12–30) (000s)	% young adults (12–30) of total TV population	Reach for young adults (12–30) (%)	% of young adults in total reach	Selectivity index (column 5/ column 3)
TV2	1,240	23.0	32.2	22.6	98.3
Zulu	1,240	23.0	3.8	45.2	196.5

Based on: IP Peaktime (2004), *Television 2004. European Key Factors*. Neuilly-sur-Seine, Cedex, Brussels: IP.

TV2 reaches 32.2% of the youngsters and Zulu only 3.8%. However, Zulu appears to be very selective for the target group of youngsters while TV2 is not. The latter can be explained as follows: TV2 has a large audience and although almost one in three youngsters watch this channel, other age groups are better represented. Zulu, on the other hand, has a very limited audience and although it reaches only 3.8% of the youngsters, youngsters are the age group that is most represented in Zulu's audience.

Technical criteria refer to the production costs of the message, often expressed as CPM or CPM-TM, the convenience or problems related to media buying (is it difficult to book media time or space, how long in advance do you have to book media time in order to be sure that you can distribute your message, can this media time or space be cancelled and if so, how long in advance, etc.?). Another criterion is media availability or what the penetration rate of the medium among the population is. If people do not own a TV or a radio, or never buy a newspaper, it is no use spending a lot of money advertising in these media.

Every vehicle has its own audience which forms a market. The seller tries to sell the vehicle by claiming that the vehicle audience (e.g. people who read the *Financial Times*) consists of a relatively high number of people with buying power, although he also has the responsibility of giving the buyer an accurate overview of what the audience looks like. The buyer's task is to find out whether or not the vehicle audience matches the target group or whether or not the target group is sufficiently represented in the vehicle audience. Every vehicle is also related to its medium and inherits the characteristics associated with the medium. Therefore, the starting point for discussing the medium can be the advantages and disadvantages of each medium (see below). However, buyer and seller must go further than that and try to form a clear picture of the medium's social role and expression capacity.

Knowing that the target group reads magazines every week is not sufficient; you need to know which magazines they read. If your target audience likes to watch TV which channels do they watch, at what time of the day do they watch, which programmes do they select, etc.? The different vehicles should be compared with each other within the same medium, between the different media and in relation to the target audience. The price must be understood in terms of value and not in terms of cost. Therefore comparisons are made to direct (other vehicles within the same medium) and indirect (vehicles within other media) competitors.

Care must be taken that media planning is more than just selecting the vehicles with the most promising results. The different media and vehicles must be considered in conjunction with each other. Is it wise, for instance, to plan the television campaign after the radio campaign, or vice versa? Is it better first to explain the message in more detail in magazines before the out-of-home campaign starts? How important is it to have several TV commercials during prime time in the first week of the launch of a new product? Research on β-coefficient issues is very important to get some insight into the consequences of planning one medium before the other, or to decrease the GRPs of radio to the advantage of television. Furthermore, for a media planner, media consumption should be far more important than GRP cost. The most important questions are: Which radio channel does a target consumer listen to in the morning? Which billboards does he or she come across on the way to work? Which magazines or newspapers are read in the evening? Which TV programmes are watched in the evening? Which events that can be sponsored does the target consumer go to? etc. In Table 8.7 an example is given of a preparatory analysis for a media plan. The different advertising media are listed. The use, advantages and disadvantages of these media will now be discussed in more detail.

Outdoor

Outdoor advertising consists of media such as billboards, but also transit media in the form of messages on buses, trams, in stations, etc. Outdoor advertising has the advantage of reaching a lot of people. As a consequence, effective reach can be very high (see Plate 18). Not only reach, but also frequency can be quite high. The lifetime of a message is very long, and the same message can be seen over and over again. For instance, on the way to school or office you might encouter the Nokia message of 'connecting people' every day. Or you might see a bus or tram with the announcement of the film *The Matrix Reloaded* over and over again. The time period to reach the audience is very short and the costs are moderate. For certain types of billboards there is the obligation to work nationally, but for others a regional approach is obtainable.

However, people do not feel highly involved in billboards or transit advertising and usually do not pay a lot of attention to it. Furthermore, only a limited amount of information can be conveyed. Targeting or selective reach is not possible, since all kinds of people will see the messages. Usually, there is no context that can add value to the message.

Table 8.7 Advertising media and media planning criteria

Criteria	Importance	Daily papers	Magazines				Billboards		Cinema	Radio		TV		Transit
			General interest	Specialised	Women	Men	City	Other		Local	National	Local	National	
Quantitative														
Reach*	++	+	+	0	+	+	+	0	0	0	+	+	+	+
Frequency	+	–	0	0	0	0	+	+	–	–	–	–	–	+
Selectivity**	++	0	+	+	+	+	+	0	+	+	0	–	–	–
Geographic flexibility	+	+	–	–	–	–	+	0	+	+	–	+	–	+
Speed of reach	+	+	0	0	0	0	+	+	+	+	+	+	+	+
Message life	+	0	+	+	+	+	+	+	–	–	–	–	–	+
Seasonal influence	+	+	+	+	+	+	+	+	0	+	+	–	–	+
Qualitative														
Stage building	++	+	+	+	+	+	+	+	+	0	+	0	+	0
Impact (emotional or formational)	++	+	0	+	0	0	–	–	++	0	0	+	++	0
Involvement	+	+	0	+	0	0	–	–	+	0	0	+	+	–
Attention	++	+	0	+	0	0	–	–	+	0	0	+	+	0
Active medium	+	+	0	+	+	+	0	0	+	–	–	–	–	–
Adding value	+	0	0	0	0	0	0	0	+	0	0	+	+	0
Quality of reproduction	++	0	+	+	+	+	+	+	+	0	+	+	+	+
Amount of information	+	+	+	+	+	+	–	–	0	0	0	0	0	–
β-coefficient	+	+	+	+	+	+	–	–	++	0	0	+	+	–
Clutter	++	–	–	–	–	–	–	–	–	0	–	+	+	–
Technical														
CPM	+	+	+	+	+	+	+	+	–	+	0	–	–	+
Flexibility in buying***	+	+	+	+	+	+	+	+	+	+	+	+	+	+

* x < 30%: –   30% ≤ x < 60%: 0   x ≥ 60%: +
** x < 100: –   100 ≤ x < 110: 0   x ≥ 110: +
*** Differs for different countries

Grolsch: Using outdoor to shine a light on sales promotions

In November 2001 the beer brand, Grolsch, ran an integrated marketing communications campaign in the Netherlands. The objective of the campaign was to increase home consumption of Grolsch in men aged between 20 and 34. To reach this objective a sales promotion ran during three weeks (weeks 47, 48 and 49) consisting of a free lamp for every skeleton case of Grolsch beer purchased. The sales promotion was supported by point-of-purchase material, information on the website, TV advertising, an ad in a regional newspaper and an outdoor Abribus campaign. The Abribus campaign ran for one week in the middle of the sales promotion campaign (week 48). During this week, media investments in the product category amounted

▶

to €1.3 million, with following shares of voice: Heineken 30%, Grolsch 25%, Amstel 13%, Brand 10%, Bavaria 3% and another six competitors 19%. Heineken, Grolsch and Amstel are also the largest players in the Dutch beer market, each enjoying a brand awareness of over 97%. Did the outdoor campaign reach its objectives? It sure did. Comparing top-of-mind awareness for Grolsch at the beginning of week 48 and at the end of week 48 showed an increase from 25% to 31%. The spontaneous awareness of the sales promotion doubled from 15% to 30%. Total awareness of the promotion amounted to 37%, while awareness in the target group reached 46%. As source of the sales promotion awareness, 41.3% of the respondents mentioned outdoor advertising, 46.0% in-store communication and 23.8% TV advertising. Intention to buy Grolsch during the promotion action did not increase though.[30]

Magazines

Magazines have the advantage that a large audience can be reached. Furthermore, special interest magazines or magazines directed at a specific target group, such as females or youngsters, create the possibility of a selective approach for different target groups. Depending on the type of magazine, a high-quality context can be offered, making it a good medium for image building (e.g. *Vogue*). Special interest magazines, such as computer magazines, also have the advantage of inducing a high involvement level and being perceived as highly credible, adding a certain value to the inserted ads. For magazines in general the quality of reproduction is high and a lot of information can be distributed. The message life is relatively long, people can process the messages at their own pace, and the same message or ad may be seen several times, since it is very likely that a reader does not read the magazine only once, but rather takes it up several times before he or she disposes of it.

Major disadvantages are that it is a rather slow medium, which leads to a delay in reach. People can buy a monthly magazine this week, but not read it for the next two weeks. Furthermore, the medium is not so flexible in the sense that last-minute changes are not tolerated and regional versions are impossible. Some magazines also suffer from high clutter, rendering an advertising message less effective.

Newspapers

The major advantage of newspapers is the number of people that can be reached in a very short period of time. Furthermore, it is a flexible medium in the sense that last-minute changes are possible in case the company's needs change or when the company wants to take advantage of, or make use of, recent events. Ads referring to recent events are called 'top topicals' and usually can count on more attention. The readers are usually highly involved in their newspaper, and the objective, informational context makes newspapers a credible medium with a high impact, not only for ads, but also for PR messages. Newspapers also provide the possibility of working region-ally. In contrast with several other media, newspapers can convey large amounts of information.

Disadvantages of newspapers are the limited selectivity of the medium and the low quality of reproduction. Furthermore, it is a transient medium in the sense that the message has a very short life since a newspaper lasts only one day.

Compaq wins award for best use of newspapers

In 2002 Compaq won an award for best use of newspapers. Full-page newspaper ads were created that resembled actual news reports. The ads contained testimonials from leading businesses and governments indicating that Compaq had never been more dependable. For example, one of the headlines read 'Hong Kong SAR: Government Teams with Compaq to Deliver Online Public Services to Hong Kong Citizens'. Moreover, in some newspapers Compaq had fixed positionings on a certain day of the week, always featuring the same headline, for example 'BT: Business Tuesday from Compaq'. In the first instance, Compaq wanted to go for business magazines and information-technology trade magazines. In the end it chose newspapers because of their 'credibility and immediacy'.[31]

Door-to-door

Door-to-door advertising periodic publications (once a week, once a month, etc.) are distributed locally and free of charge. Advertisers in this medium are usually local merchandisers or local service organisations. Door-to-door publications have the advantage of being geographically flexible and of obtaining a fairly high reach. Furthermore, the medium provides the opportunity to deliver a lot of information at a fairly low cost. The promotional context in which the message appears may be useful for reaching consumers interested in promotional offers.

Limitations are that the medium is not at all selective and people may only be marginally involved in door-to-door publications and may not pay much attention unless they are interested in certain promotions. Furthermore, the quality of reproductions is often doubtful. Because of the overload of such publications, people often react negatively to this form of irresponsible use of paper and 'environmental pollution', and more and more people are putting a note on their mailbox stating 'no advertising please'.

Television

A clear advantage of television is the communication power of an audiovisual message which, in general, leads to a fairly high (especially emotional) impact. Television is a passive medium, making it ideal for transferring a brand image or brand personality. The context surrounding the message can also add value to the message by inducing in the audience a certain mood (e.g. by the programme or movie during which the message is shown). Furthermore, a lot of people can be reached in a fairly short period of time. Local TV makes it possible to exert a regional approach. Research on viewing habits reveals that different personalities and people with different life-styles watch different programmes, creating the possibility of using TV as a selective medium.

Major drawbacks are the high production costs that are involved and the fact that it is not always possible to direct a message at a selective target group. Often, a lot of occasional viewers are reached, which results in a low effective reach. Furthermore, the lifetime of a message is extremely short: 15 or 30 seconds pass very quickly and often nothing is left of the message afterwards. Increasing advertising clutter further impedes the effectiveness of messages, making more exposures a necessity, which adds to total costs. Television also has a seasonal influence. During the summer more people spend time outdoors instead of spending their evenings in front of the television screen. In other words, during winter a TV commercial will reach a greater audience than in the summer.

Can advertising reach the whole target group?

Advertising clutter is becoming a real problem.[32] Before you can convince consumers to buy, you have to build a brand. To build a brand, you need to create awareness. To create awareness, you need to attract attention. To attract attention, you have to find a way to break through the massive amount of other messages known as advertising clutter. One way to do this is to create original ads. Although this has been a long-held conviction by copywriters and art directors, only recently has the power of original ads to attract attention been empirically demonstrated.[33] Several advertisers do not opt for originality but react to the increasing clutter by outspending their competitors and launching even more ads. The result of all this is that in the UK, on television alone, 17,278,730 ads were broadcast in 2004, in Spain 2,601,972 were broadcast, in Germany 1,255,084, in France 2,002,739 and in Italy 1,415,507.[34] Not surprisingly, consumers are not too keen on this and some of them start rejecting advertisements. A segmentation that seems to enjoy some consistency across studies classifies TV viewers into 'acceptors', 'rejectors', 'players' and 'uninvolved' on the basis of their answers to statements such as:[35]

1 I find TV advertising interesting and quite often it gives me something to talk about.

2 Nearly all TV advertising annoys me.

3 I find some TV advertising is OK but I think quite a lot of it is devious.

4 Quite often I find TV advertising more entertaining than the programmes.

Studies in 1996 and 2001 describe these segments as follows: *Players* form the largest group (between 35% and 50%) and want to be entertained and challenged. They do not have a negative attitude towards advertising as long as it is good advertising. *Acceptors* (between 19% and 22%) think TV advertising is interesting, moderately entertaining and rarely annoying. *Uninvolved* (between 11% and 23%) do not think TV advertising can be considered as interesting, entertaining or involving. *Rejecters* (20%) feel TV advertising is annoying, is not interesting or entertaining at all and is often devious.[36] Unfortunately, the latter group is an interesting target group for marketers since they seem to have considerable spending power. Are TV rejectors a lost group for advertising? For TV advertising: yes. For advertising in other media: no. Indeed, 56% of the TV rejectors and 60% of the TV uninvolved appear to be acceptors or players for press advertising, while 38% of TV rejectors and 46% of TV uninvolved are acceptors or players for radio advertising.[37] Therefore, an easy solution seems to be combining TV advertising with other media such as press and/or radio.

Cinema

As is the case with television, cinema benefits from the audiovisuality of the message, leaving a greater impact on the audience. The impact of cinema advertising is even increased by the fact that the audience pays much more attention to the message than in any other circumstances, while distraction is less likely to occur. The surroundings and context further add to the value of the message, because of the mood and expectations of the audience. As will be discussed later in this chapter, a positive mood can lead a viewer to process all incoming information more positively than when the viewer is in a neutral or a negative mood. Going to the cinema is fun, people have a lot of expectations and are, in a sense, quite excited. This can lead to more positive processing of the advertising messages. Another important advantage of cinema advertising is the fact that this medium is fairly selective to a young and upmarket audience. Furthermore, this audience seems to like cinema advertising, and considers it as a part of their cinema visit that cannot be missed.[38]

The disadvantages are that the potential reach is limited, and that the speed and the frequency of reaching the audience is very slow. The lifetime of a message is very short. Furthermore, relatively high production costs are encountered.

Radio

The major benefit of radio advertising is that potentially a lot of people can be reached. Furthermore, the production costs are low and radio is a very dynamic medium. Different people (not only in terms of demographic characteristcs, but also in terms of lifestyle, etc.) seem to listen to different radio stations, making it a selective medium to target a specific consumer group.

Limitations are that the lifetime of a message is very short and that people use the radio as background noise. The latter means that the potential attention that will be paid to a message is fairly low.

Who is willing to listen, pays less[39]

A review of 50 year's research on radio advertising, reveals the following:

- The impact of a euro invested in advertising is larger for radio than for TV advertising.
- Recall of radio commercials is higher when consumers hear the ad while in their cars.
- A good radio commercial is more effective than an average TV commercial.
- Longer radio spots are more effective than short ones.
- A good radio commercial mentions the brand several times and mentions the brand at the beginning of the spot.
- A radio spot is most effective when it is broadcast at the beginning of a short commercial break before or after a news bulletin.
- Transferring 10% of the advertising budget from television to radio may increase the impact of the campaign by 15%.

For many years quantitative criteria such as reach, frequency, CPT, etc. have dominated media planning. Recently, more and more media planners are convinced of the importance of qualitative criteria such as the context, capacity of image building, creativity, etc. Creativity is very important because several media have become increasingly cluttered. Some advertisers succeed in running a very effective and efficient advertising campaign with relatively low costs thanks to creative use of the different media. Some examples are the following:

▶

- Several years ago the newly launched Fiat Regata was promoted by attaching a life-size car to a billboard. In the press consumers were encouraged to walk near these billboards while filling out questions for a contest. The campaign received media exposure in the press worth five times more than the actual media investment.[40]

- In 1992 every time someone passed a tram shelter with a promotion for 3 Suisses, the billboard began to sing a Jacques Dutronc song 'J'aime les filles dans les abribus, j'aime les filles qu'on croise dans les trams . . .' (I love the girls in bus shelters, I love the girls I encounter on the tram). The campaign ran for seven days and was a huge success. It is said that some people were so surprised that they even forgot to get on the tram.[41]

- In Denmark Carlsberg used an Abribus campaign in 2003 where the ad looked different during daytime than at night-time. During the day a pint of Carlsberg was shown on a black background. The pint itself was 80% filled with white foam. At night-time, the same ad on the same black background was shown, but the pint was now 80% filled with the gold Carlsberg beer.[42]

- In 2002 Virgin Express used a similar approach with newspaper ads. To promote the air-line company, a full-page ad was created with different fictitious news reports. All reports mentioned the low attendance on occasions where normally many people are present. Headlines ran as follows: 'Problem of the traffic jams finally solved. Highways empty, except in the neighbourhood of the airport', 'Major peace manifestation attracts only 7 participants', 'Nobody attends erotica fair', 'Sudden idling swept our cities', and 'Members of Parliament play truant as never before'. In the middle of the page readers found the explanation for the situation: Virgin Express' extremely low fares to attractive cities such as Madrid, Milan, Nice, Rome, Athens, Barcelona, Lisbon, etc.[43]

- In 2002 Procter & Gamble's antidandruff shampoo, Head & Shoulders, was promoted by means of fragrance-emitting ads on bus shelters. The posters showed a happy young lady with the wind in her hair inviting consumers to press a button to dispense the scent of new citrus fresh.[44] By 2003 scent advertising is used more and more. In the Netherlands, the advertising agency Senta is completely devoted to scent advertising. It ran a magazine campaign for the fabric softener Robijn (also known as Snuggle and Cocolino). When con-sumers rubbed the ink, the scent was released. About 80% of readers noticed the ad and also seemed to remember it.[45]

- Marketers also invent new media. In 2003 a London ad agency recruited university students to wear brand logos on their foreheads, turning their heads into living billboards. In exchange for wearing these ads in public places for three or four hours, students received about €6.5 an hour.[46]

Media context

Advertising always forms part of a surrounding context. An advertising context con-sists of the receiver context and the medium context.[47] The receiver context refers to the situational circumstances in which a person is exposed to an advertisement (e.g. at home, in the company of friends, on one's way to work, when one is in a bad mood, etc.). The importance of the receiver's context (especially the psychological state) was dealt with in Chapter 3. The medium context is the topic of this section and

Table 8.8 Impact of media context variables

Media context variable	Impact on ad effectiveness
Objective context variables	
■ Medium itself	Context effects more pronounced for TV
■ Vehicle content	Violence, humour and sex have a negative impact
■ Media clutter in vehicle	The more clutter, the less positive ad results
■ Type of ad block	Context effects more pronounced for interrupting than shoulder blocks
■ Sequence within ad block	Primacy and recency effects
■ Congruence between context and ad	Product involvement (PI) moderates impact: for low PI congruency is best, for high PI contrast is best
Subjective context variables	
■ Intensity of response	Mixed results, balance in direction of higher intensity, better ad results
■ Valence of response	Positive valenced context improves ad effectiveness

Based on: Moorman, M. (2003), *Context Considered. The Relationship Between Media Environments and Advertising Effects*, Doctoral Dissertation. Universiteit van Amsterdam, the Netherlands.

refers to characteristics of the content of the medium in which an ad is inserted, as they are perceived by the individuals who are exposed to the ad.[48] TV commercials appear before, after or between TV programmes or other commercials, magazine or newspaper ads are inserted between articles, billboards are placed on the wall of a building or in a bus shelter, transit advertising forms part of the bus, tram, etc. Several studies indicate that the media context has an influence on how people perceive, interpret and process an advertising message. Since the effectiveness of the same ad may depend on the context surrounding the ad, it is useful for the advertiser to get a clearer view on what these context effects might look like.

The conclusions outlined in Table 8.8 are made on the basis of an extensive literature review.[49]

Context effects seem to be more prevalent in one medium than another. Although most studies so far focus on TV, there seems to be some evidence that context variables matter more in a TV than in a print environment.[50]

Besides the medium, the content of the medium vehicle also plays a role. Concerning how interesting and involving a programme is, a recent study found that violent and sexual programmes, as compared to neutral programmes, impair TV viewers' memory for television ads.[51] This was found to be the case for males and females, for all age groups and for people who like and dislike programmes containing violence and sex. One possible explanation for this finding is that sex and violence attract so much attention that there is not enough processing capacity left to process the embedded ads. Another explanation is that sexual and violent programmes evoke sexual and violent thoughts. Being occupied with thinking about sex and violence, consumers' memory for commercials could be seriously reduced. A similar conclusion also seems to hold for humorous programmes, although in the past comedies have been shown to lead to a higher ad recall than news or dramas.

Buzz marketing

Consumers pay less attention to mass media and mass media advertising. Moreover, traditional advertising is no longer as credible as it used to be. People know the tricks of the trade by now. Word-of-mouth has always been important in steering the behaviour of people, but it has become increasingly important also in people's buying behaviour. More than two-thirds of all consumer buying behaviour is influenced by word-of-mouth advertising.[52] Advertisers and advertising agencies have reacted by means of 'hiding' commercial messages in media content. Product placement in movies and shows on television is one example. And even in books this is practiced: Fay Weldon got a lot of criticism because she was paid to mention the luxury brand Bulgari in one of her books. But of course, people notice these tactics, and some of them will probably feel cheated and will not regard it as the honest communication they prefer.

People look for others they can relate and aspire to. Traditionally, media figures, celebrities, sports heroes, etc. play an important role in commercial communication. But recently, consumers seem to relate more to 'ordinary' people than to celebrities. This is the origin of buzz marketing. The essence of buzz marketing is the fact that the spontaneous networks that make up our society constitute the most effective way to meaningfully reach people and influence consumers. Buzz marketing is aimed at spreading the message through the personal network of consumers. It is 'organised-word-of-mouth'. Buzz marketing works on the basis of the principle 'give them something to talk about'. It works on the basis of individuals who like to receive messages and like to spread the word. The leaders of the process are called 'alphas', the followers are 'bees'. What do people want to talk about? Here are the six magic buttons of buzz marketing:

- Play with taboos: intimacies, sex . . .
- Talk about the extraordinary
- Look for the unusual, but keep the link with the brand
- Give people something to laugh about, that makes them enjoy and talk about it to others
- Bring a story with a special angle
- Keep it 'secret', people like to talk about secrets.

Buzz is not something that just happens to companies; it can be organised. A typical example of buzz marketing is blogging (weblogging), individuals who give their opinion in real-time on internet diaries. Blogs are important for companies: they are an invaluable source of information, give reliable feedback on company activities, they are often an outlet for satisfied as well as dissatisfied customers, they constitute a reality check of marketing plans, and they enable companies to reach a relevant public. But buzz marketing can also be organised off-line. Watch out if someone offers you a fancy drink in a trendy bar. There is a good chance that they are paid by the manufacturer. This technique is called 'Roach bait'. By means of 'product seeding' a manufacturer sends samples of a new product to 'ideal consumers' who then talk about it to their friends.

Is buzz marketing ordinary 'push and cheat' marketing? Some forms may come close to the old push techniques, but others such as organising blogs and starting viral marketing (using networks to spread advertising messages on the internet) require a completely different and much more credible way of communicating with target groups than before. In its true form, buzz marketing is the ultimate example of pull communication.

As discussed earlier, advertising clutter has increased significantly in most media. A problem is that due to this enormous clutter, advertisements become less effective. The more clutter, the lower the motivation and opportunity to pay attention to an ad. Too many marketing messages compete for the attention of the consumer. As a consequence, less attention will be devoted to individual ads.[53]

Concerning ad blocks, a distinction can be made between interrupting blocks (a commercial block in the middle of the programme) or shoulder blocks (a commercial block between two different programmes). Although some researchers hypothesise that commercials in interrupting blocks are less effective because viewers do not want to be disturbed at that moment, this does not seem to be true. Intense and positive responses towards the context carry over more easily to ads in an interrupting break than in a shoulder break. An explanation for the latter is that during the programme viewers experience more arousal and interest than between programmes.[54]

As for the sequence within a block, the earlier an ad appears in the block, the higher the motivation to pay attention to the ad and process the information. Furthermore, the placement of an ad also determines the opportunity to pay attention to it. The primacy effect, suggesting that ads that come early in a magazine or early in a sequence of TV commercials are more effective, has been confirmed on several occasions.[55] However, for TV advertising the last position can also be beneficial since the consumer has more time to process the ad due to the fact that it is not followed by another ad, but by a short silence.[56] Because of inherent characteristics of the medium, certain places can raise the opportunity to pay attention; for example, the upper left corner of a magazine (people normally start reading from the left to the right), the right page (this is the flat page when a magazine is open) or the cover page.[57]

Studies on the impact of media style–ad style congruency are scarce and reveal contradictory conclusions. Some researchers claim that the better the fit between the ad and the media context, the more motivated consumers will be to process the ad and the easier this job will be for them. A computer ad inserted in a computer magazine, for instance, increases the likelihood that the reader wants to pay attention and is willing to process the ad, since the computer magazine makes the need for a computer or information on computers more salient and this evoked need stimulates the motivation to pay attention to stimuli that are relevant to the need. Similarly, people reading a magazine that evokes transformational needs, such as a beauty magazine, are more likely to look for transformational cues in ads, such as the attractiveness of the hair after using a certain shampoo, while reading a health magazine is more likely to make people pay attention to cues such as the revitalisation of damaged hair.[58] Also, contexts evoking the same feeling as the ad appear to enhance ad responses as compared to contexts evoking a different feeling.[59] According to the priming principle, an ad can be interpreted on the basis of schemas (knowledge structures) activated or primed by the context.[60] Congruency between the ad and the context means that the ad can be more easily interpreted since the relevant knowledge structures are already activated. However, some studies found no effects or even a positive impact associated with placing an ad in a style that is incongruent with the media context. This relation between ad-context congruency and ad effectiveness can be explained as follows: the novelty of the ad or the unexpectedness of the information given its context increases the attention to the ad because consumers see the ad as innovative and interesting. How can the contradictory results be explained and what should an advertiser go for: a context-congruent or a context-incongruent ad? The solution can be found in moderator variables. Apparently, people react differently depending on how involved they are with the product category.[61] When product involvement is low, consumers go for the peripheral route of processing and it helps them that context and ad style are congruent. On the other hand, when product involvement is high, they are more likely to follow the central route. In this case, they are willing to expend more cognitive resources and they seem to appreciate a context-incongruent ad more.

Concerning the intensity of context responses, two opposing views are held. Some claim that the more intense context responses are, the less capacity will be left for consumers to process the ad. As a consequence, less attention will be paid to the ad and the ad will be less effective. An exciting context inducing high arousal in respondents has been shown to lead to less positive ad responses than a romantic or cosy context which induced a significantly lower arousal level.[62] However, other researchers claim that the more intense consumer responses to the context are, the more attentive and aroused they are, and as a result the better the ads will be processed. Research results are mixed, but the majority of the findings point in the direction of a positive impact of intensity of context responses on attitudes and purchase intention.[63] Besides the intensity, the valence of context-induced responses (whether they are positive or negative) may also matter.[64] Some researchers suggest that a context that evokes a positive mood induces less elaborate processing of embedded ads and a less positive attitude towards the ad. Two theories try to explain this.[65] According to the cognitive capacity theory, a positive mood activates a whole bunch of information in memory that limits the consumer's processing of incoming information. A second theory proposes that when people are in a positive mood, they try to keep this mood and as a consequence avoid all stimuli (such as ads) that could alter this situation. The opposite can be expected when they are in a neutral or a bad mood. On the other hand, there is also evidence that people who are in a good mood evaluate ads more positively and are more capable of, and willing to, process ad-related information. This can be explained by affect transfer (see Chapter 3) by means of which the positive evaluation of the context is transferred (or misattributed) to the ad. However, the majority of the studies investigating the impact of context-induced mood on embedded ads find that emotional responses to the context indeed carry over to the ad, but not to the brand.[66]

'The medium is the message'[67]

Instead of facilitating or inhibiting consumers' processing of advertising messages, the medium itself can also be the message. A recent study investigated the impact of creative media choice. In this study creative media choice refers to the fact that the brand logo and slogan are shown, but that brand associations are primed by the medium and as a consequence implicitly instead of explicitly communicated. Advantages of creative medium choice could be that

1　The ad context is intentionally rather than incidentally processed

2　The distinctiveness of the medium increases the transfer from associations from the medium to the brand

3　The indirect approach creates less negative cognitive responses and enhances ad credibility and attitudes.

▶

In the study two products were investigated: an insurance company and an energy drink. The insurance company was promoted either on an egg or in a traditional newspaper. An egg was chosen because of its protective shell and the fact that it is a fragile and easily breakable product. The energy drink was promoted either on an elevator or in a traditional newspaper. An elevator was chosen because it is powerful, moves quickly and reminds people of the energy that is needed to walk up or down the stairs. About 600 students participated in the experiment. Results confirmed the hypotheses: the creative media enhanced the brand associations more than did the traditional medium (newspaper). Moreover, the creative media increased ad credibility significantly and induced significantly more positive ad and brand attitudes as compared to the traditional medium.

Summary

In media planning the decision is taken what media and vehicles will be purchased, at what time and at what price. Media planning consists of a number of steps. After assessing the communications environment and describing the target audience, media objectives have to be set, and media vehicles have to be selected and bought. Media objectives refer to criteria, such as the frequency with which the target group has to be exposed to the message, and the reach or weight of a campaign, i.e. the number of desired contacts with the target group. Furthermore, the continuity or schedule of the campaign has to be decided on, and media costs have to be taken into account. Media selection is based on quantitative criteria, such as frequency, reach and seasonal influences, but also on qualitative criteria, such as image-building capacity, emotional impact, demonstration capacity and quality of reproduction. Technical criteria, such as production costs and media buying characteristics, also have to be taken into account. Each type of advertising medium (newspapers, magazines, television, radio, etc.) has its advantages and disadvantages. Furthermore, the media context can have a considerable impact on advertising effectiveness. The role of mood and compatibility of media and advertisements appear to be important.

Review questions

1 What are the various steps in the media planning process?

2 How does ad message repetition affect advertising effectiveness?

3 How can the β-coefficient analysis be used to optimise message repetition?

4 What is the relationship between reach, gross and effective reach, opportunity to see, and gross and effective rating points?

5 How can media scheduling or continuity affect advertising effectiveness?

6 On the basis of which criteria should a media plan be composed?

7 What are the main advantages and disadvantages of print and audiovisual media?

8 Why is cinema advertising effective?

Further reading

Sissors, J. and Baron, R. (2002), *Advertising Media Planning*. McGraw-Hill.

Jones, J.P. (2002), *The Ultimate Secrets of Advertising*. Sage Publications.

Katz, H.A. (2003), *The Media Handbook: A Complete Guide to Advertising Media Selection, Planning, Research and Buying*. Lawrence Erlbaum Associates.

Rossiter, J.R. and Danaker, P.J. (1998), *Advanced Media Planning*. Kluwer Academic Publishers.

Case 8

Relaunching Nizoral in Russia

The Russian economic, advertising and media context

The economic development of Russia in the past decade has experienced ups and downs. For instance, during the recession of 1998 and 1999, the Gross Domestic Product decreased by 35% and 53% respectively, and in 1998 capital investment in the Russian economy diminished by more than 70% compared to 1997. Inflation skyrocketed in 1998 and 1999, with inflation rates of 84% and 36.5%. From 2000 onwards, the economic situation has improved considerably. The growth of GDP was 22% in 2001 and 10% in 2002. During the same years, capital investment was increased by 28% and 8%. Inflation was down to 14% in 2002, and the rate of unemployment was 8.2%. Russia is a large country with a population of about 145 million (2001), more than 70% of which live in cities. Of these cities, Moscow and, to a far lesser extent, St Petersburg represent the economic heart of the country. The Buying Power Index (BPI), measured as a weighted average of the population share, consumer spends and share in national turnover of each city is 21 for Moscow, 4 for St Petersburg and less than 1 for practically all other cities. The BPI of Moscow is 20% higher than the other 20 largest cities of Russia, St Petersburg included, taken together. Needless to say that, in these circumstances, any marketing campaign will have to focus heavily on the Moscow region.

Total ad spends in Russia were US$2,320 million in 2001, i.e. approximately US$16 per capita. They increase substantially every year. Television has a relatively stable market share of about 30%, print has a market share that has been decreasing slightly over the past few years, amounting to 27% in 2001.

The share of outdoor advertising is increasing and equalled 16% in 2001. Radio has 3% market share, and direct marketing 6%. Top advertisers during the first half of 2002 were, amongst others, Procter & Gamble, Unilever, Nestlé, Mars, Henkel, Wrigley, Danone, Pepsico, Beiersdorf and Coca-Cola.

Nearly every Russian household has a television set. The top eight television channels attract more than 80% of the TV advertising investments. There are three national channels, ORT, RTR and NTV. They have a daily reach of 60%, 55% and 45% of the Russian population respectively. Their share of audience is approximately 30%, 20% and 15%, and they attract 32%, 25% and 26% of the ad spends on television in Russia. For each channel the list price per GRP is approximately the same, about US$2,800 per 30-second spot, and so is their cost per thousand (CPM) of approximately US$5.5. Various types of Russian magazines can be distinguished: magazines for business managers, parents with young kids, teens and young adults (16–25), male adults and female adults (25–45 years old), and general interest magazines. The readership of these magazines differs from one title to another, and so does the CPM. The latter ranges from as low as US$27 to as high as US$550. The 10 largest newspapers reach a daily audience of about 23% of the Russian population. There are numerous radio stations in Russia, the majority of which are very focussed on a specific region and/or target group. The three largest national radio channels each reach about 18% of the population. Outdoor advertising is increasing, both in number of sites and in budgets. Tobacco brands constitute a major part of the investments in outdoor advertising.

The advertising and media briefing for Nizoral

Nizoral is a medicated antidandruff shampoo that is globally marketed by the pharmaceutical company Janssen-Cilag and its subsidiaries. Traditionally, Nizoral has tried to attract a mass market of consumers. As such it has a number of direct competitors in the inner market of pharmacy products (Freederm, Skin-cap, Vichy) and indirect competitors in the mass market of supermarket products (Head & Shoulders, Fructis, Schauma, Timotei, etc.). Case Figure 8.1 illustrates the reach and frequency of earlier campaigns of Nizoral and some of its competitors.

The new marketing target group for the relaunch of Nizoral in 2003 has been defined as people concerned about dandruff, who regard it as a medical problem and seek a really effective, medical solution – people aiming for a high-quality, healthy and modern lifestyle. They choose only original products and the best quality: 'exclusive – really the only one that is effective'. An overview of the old and new positioning strategies is presented in Case Table 8.1. The marketing objectives of the 2003 relaunch were to reposition the brand and focus more heavily on the core market of Nizoral, those people who are seeking a high-quality medicated solution for their dandruff problem, to recruit new patients in the medicated segment and to protect existing users and market share. The objectives of the communications campaign were to explain the new positioning and benefits of the product, to

Case Figure 8.1 Reach and frequency of advertising campaigns of Nizoral and its competitors

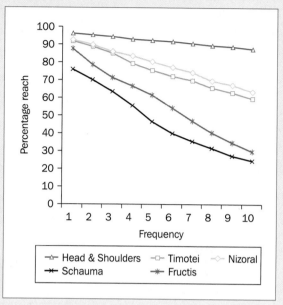

reinforce the medical image of the brand and to justify its higher price.

Janssen-Cilag Russia specified the media planning tasks as follows:

- To create an effective and cost-effective communications mix.

Case Table 8.1 The old and new positioning strategies of Nizoral

	Target	Competitive framework	Rational benefit	Emotional benefit	Reason why	Brand character/ personality
Old	All antidandruff shampoo users Income average+	All antidandruff shampoos (Head & Shoulders, Schauma, Pantene Pro-V)	The most cost-effective medicated antidandruff shampoo (calendar)	Soft medicated shampoo (association with nature – green trees – beauty and health)	Impact on cause of dandruff Long-term effect (two weeks)	Soft, reliable care
New	Only medicated shampoo users Income average+	Medicated shampoos (Freederm, Skin-cap)	The only really effective antidandruff treatment	Luxurious, high-quality, healthy lifestyle	Contains medicine acting on cause of dandruff Recommended by specialists (pharmacists, dermatologists)	Brings the most valuable benefit to life

- To identify the most relevant communications channels for the target audience.
- To provide maximum reach of effective frequency of the target audience.
- To provide a cost-effective reach of the target groups.

The target group of the campaign was described as people between 25 and 55 years old, of both sexes, but women in particular, with a monthly income of at least US$200, and predominantly highly educated.

The start of the campaign was planned in February 2003, and the total budget, all included, was US$800,000. A number of media agencies were asked to propose a media plan for this campaign. The proposal of First Media, one of the largest media planning agencies in Russia, is presented in the next section.

The media plan of First Media

The target group, as defined by Janssen-Cilag's Nizoral brand management, is of course the starting point of the media planning process: men and women aged between 25 and 55, with monthly income of at least US$200, and mostly with a higher income. Special emphasis should be put on frequent users of anti-dandruff shampoo, frequent users of medical shampoo and current users of Nizoral. In Case Figure 8.2, the

Case Figure 8.2 Demographic and behavioural definition of the target groups of the Nizoral campaign

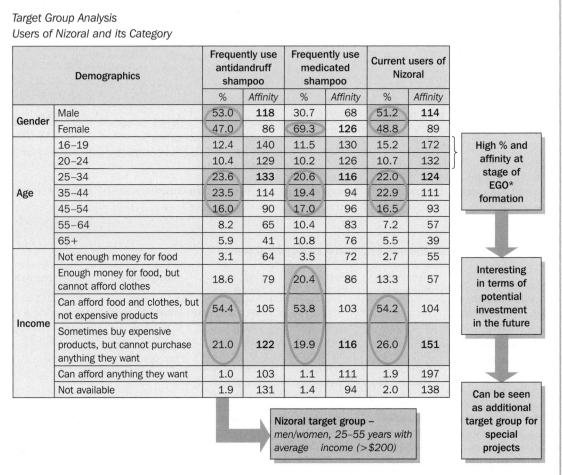

Target Group Analysis
Users of Nizoral and its Category

Demographics		Frequently use antidandruff shampoo		Frequently use medicated shampoo		Current users of Nizoral	
		%	Affinity	%	Affinity	%	Affinity
Gender	Male	53.0	118	30.7	68	51.2	114
	Female	47.0	86	69.3	126	48.8	89
Age	16–19	12.4	140	11.5	130	15.2	172
	20–24	10.4	129	10.2	126	10.7	132
	25–34	23.6	133	20.6	116	22.0	124
	35–44	23.5	114	19.4	94	22.9	111
	45–54	16.0	90	17.0	96	16.5	93
	55–64	8.2	65	10.4	83	7.2	57
	65+	5.9	41	10.8	76	5.5	39
Income	Not enough money for food	3.1	64	3.5	72	2.7	55
	Enough money for food, but cannot afford clothes	18.6	79	20.4	86	13.3	57
	Can afford food and clothes, but not expensive products	54.4	105	53.8	103	54.2	104
	Sometimes buy expensive products, but cannot purchase anything they want	21.0	122	19.9	116	26.0	151
	Can afford anything they want	1.0	103	1.1	111	1.9	197
	Not available	1.9	131	1.4	94	2.0	138

High % and affinity at stage of EGO* formation

Interesting in terms of potential investment in the future

Can be seen as additional target group for special projects

Nizoral target group –
men/women, 25–55 years with average income (>$200)

* EGO = a kind of lifestyle/personality variable that is measured in a large Russian media planning study.

Source: Gallup M'Index 2002/2.

demographic criteria as defined by Janssen-Cilag are combined with these user criteria to give a broader picture of the target groups. The affinity index represents the involvement of the various segments in the product category. However, according to First Media, the target group of the campaign cannot be defined on the basis of demographics and buying behaviour alone. The basic positioning of Nizoral is that dandruff is a disease that requires a special medical solution, and that Nizoral is the only product for those who recognise the problem sufficiently and want to get the best solution. Therefore, lifestyle and value considerations of the target groups should also be considered. On the basis of a psychographic analysis of the current and future target groups, First Media comes to the conclusion that the current consumers are mainly imprudent innovators and individualists that are ready to accept risks in buying new products. The basic psychographic characteristic of the new target consumers is, according to the agency, egocentrism: Nizoral should be targeted at independent and loyal consumers who are inclined towards a well-considered choice of the best solution for them on the market.

Based on this analysis, a media plan is composed. At first an analysis is made of the communications objectives, the consumer response sought, the target groups and the appropriate media types to support these objectives. The basis of this decision is an assessment of various media types. This analysis is based on a number of criteria. An importance weight is attached to each criterion, and each medium receives a score on each criterion. In Case Figure 8.3, an overview is given of the resulting 'value' of each medium type, i.e. the overall weighted average of importance and performance scores. Case Figure 8.4 gives an overview of the perceived quality and use of different media types in the mind of the target group. Given the target groups of the campaign and the value and (perceived) characteristics of different types of media, the agency translates the communications objectives of the campaign to media solutions and to specific selected media types (Case Figure 8.5).

The agency then analyses the characteristics of specific television channels, magazines and newspapers to see whether they can reach the target groups effectively and efficiently. In Case Figure 8.6 the viewing share of the eight largest television channels is shown. On the basis of this analysis the agency proposes a television rating point (TRP) mix of 55% ORT and 45% RTR. Magazines and newspapers are used as supplementary media for

Case Figure 8.3 Value of media types

Available Media
Medium Value

Criteria	Weight	National TV Score	National TV Result	Regional TV Score	Regional TV Result	Magazines Score	Magazines Result	Newspapers Score	Newspapers Result	Radio Score	Radio Result	Outdoor Score	Outdoor Result	Cinema Score	Cinema Result	Internet Score	Internet Result
Reach-building potential	4	5	20	5	20	3	12	3	12	4	16	2	8	1	4	1	5
Geographic focus	4	1	4	4	16	2	8	3	12	4	16	5	20	5	20	1	1
Psychographic focus	4	4	16	4	16	5	20	5	20	3	12	1	4	2	8	2	8
Cost-efficiency	4	5	20	5	20	3	12	4	16	4	16	2	8	1	4	1	5
Frequency-building potential	2	4	8	5	10	3	6	3	6	5	10	2	4	1	2	2	8
Demographic focus	2	5	10	5	10	4	8	3	6	3	6	1	2	2	4	2	10
Visualisation	2	5	10	5	10	4	8	2	4	1	2	3	6	2	4	2	10
Detailed message	1	2	2	2	2	4	4	5	5	3	3	1	1	2	2	4	8
Prestige, image	1	5	5	5	5	4	4	3	3	3	3	2	2	2	2	1	5
Affordability	1	1	1	3	3	2	2	3	3	5	5	1	1	4	4	5	5
Totals:		37	96	43	112	34	84	34	87	35	89	20	56	22	54	21	65

Medium value

Weighted medium value

Case Figure 8.4 Perceived characteristics and use of media types by the target group

Available Media
Candidate Vehicles in the Minds of TG

Men/women, 25–54 years, average + income

Type of ad	Notice		Trust		Use	
	%	Affinity	%	Affinity	%	Affinity
Newspaper ads	47.9	112	24.3	114	25.4	122
TV ads	58.0	107	19.4	106	18.3	112
Magazine ads	26.7	114	11.7	118	8.0	125
Radio ads	26.2	100	8.9	96	6.2	101
Ads in shop windows	18.6	114	6.0	116	3.9	116
Billboard ads	23.2	115	5.1	123	3.3	120
Direct mail sent to home	14.7	114	5.0	120	5.0	131
Ads on buses, trolleys and trams	22.3	111	3.0	103	2.0	116
Metro car ads	12.2	122	2.6	141	1.9	150
Direct mail sent to office	5.7	145	2.5	145	2.0	156
Advertising agents	5.1	112	2.5	107	2.6	125
Metro station ads	10.5	127	1.7	127	0.8	119
Internet ads	4.4	112	1.5	103	1.8	121
Roof ads	5.9	121	0.6	105	0.5	121

Source: Gallup M'Index 2002/2.

different reasons. Magazines are good media to build brand image and to carry over emotional messages and benefits, and to strengthen the emotional bond with the brand. On the other hand, newspapers are good media to objectively and rationally explain the details of the dandruff problem and the advantages of the Nizoral brand, and to persuade consumers. In Case Figures 8.7 and 8.8 the characteristics of a number of magazines and newspapers are highlighted: percentage coverage of the target group, the affinity of the readers with the medium and their score on the 'egocentric' lifestyle values judged to be important in this campaign. The selection of the print media is based on the maximum coverage of the target group, with special emphasis on Moscow (7 Day, Cosmopolitan, AIF), maximum correspondence to the demographic and psychographic profile of the target group, and the support to the image of the brand (Men's Health, GEO). On the basis of these considerations, First Media proposes a print media plan (Case Figure 8.9) and a total media plan and budget (Case Figure 8.10).

Case Figure 8.5 Communications objectives, media solutions and selected media types

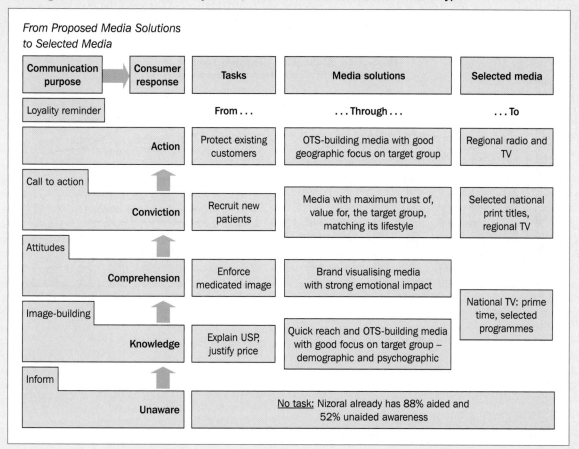

From Proposed Media Solutions to Selected Media

Communication purpose	Consumer response	Tasks	Media solutions	Selected media
Loyalty reminder		From...	...Through...	...To
	Action	Protect existing customers	OTS-building media with good geographic focus on target group	Regional radio and TV
Call to action	Conviction	Recruit new patients	Media with maximum trust of, value for, the target group, matching its lifestyle	Selected national print titles, regional TV
Attitudes	Comprehension	Enforce medicated image	Brand visualising media with strong emotional impact	
Image-building	Knowledge	Explain USP, justify price	Quick reach and OTS-building media with good focus on target group – demographic and psychographic	National TV: prime time, selected programmes
Inform	Unaware		No task: Nizoral already has 88% aided and 52% unaided awareness	

Case Figure 8.6 Viewing share of television channels

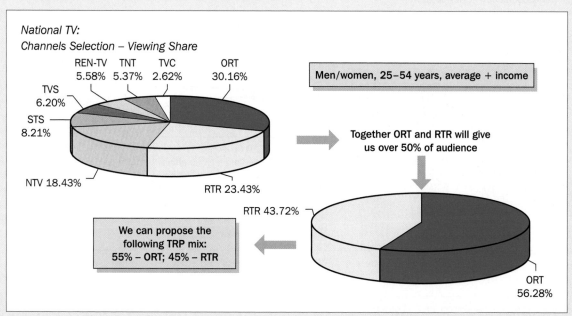

National TV:
Channels Selection – Viewing Share

REN-TV 5.58%   TNT 5.37%   TVC 2.62%   ORT 30.16%
TVS 6.20%
STS 8.21%
NTV 18.43%
RTR 23.43%

Men/women, 25–54 years, average + income

Together ORT and RTR will give us over 50% of audience

RTR 43.72%
ORT 56.28%

We can propose the following TRP mix: 55% – ORT; 45% – RTR

Source: Gallup TV – Russia.

Case Figure 8.7 Characteristics of magazines

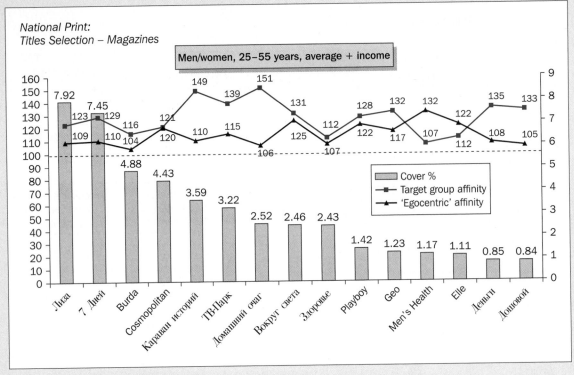

National Print:
Titles Selection – Magazines

Men/women, 25–55 years, average + income

Source: Gallup NRS July–October 2002, Media Ego.

Case Figure 8.8 Characteristics of newspapers

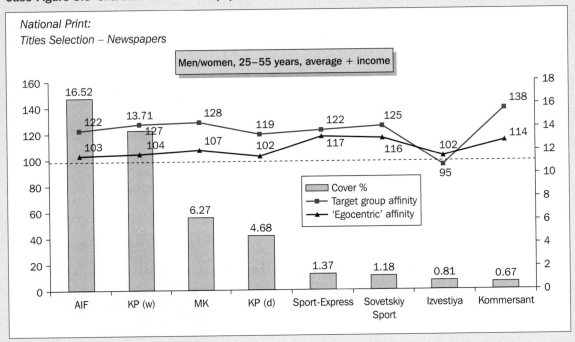

National Print:
Titles Selection – Newspapers

Men/women, 25–55 years, average + income

Source: Gallup NRS July–October 2002, Media Ego.

Case Figure 8.9 Print media plan

Print
Proposed Media Plan

DETAILED PRINT PLAN 2003

Date: December 9 2002

CLIENT: Janssen Cilag   COUNTRY: RUSSIA

PRODUCT: Nizoral   TARGET GROUP: Men/women, 25–55 years, average + income

BUDGET (USD) 149 928

		Total No INS	Insertion Cost	Gross Cost	Disc. %	Client Net	AC %	Client Net-Net	VAT 20%	CNN Incl. VAT
Men's Health	1/1 4c	3	9,900	29,700	23.53	22,712	15	19,305	20	23,166
Cosmopolitan	1/1 4c	3	18,600	55,800	17.65	45,953	15	39,060	20	46,872
7 Day	1/2 4c	3	12,500	37,500	8.24	34,412	15	29,250	20	35,100
AIF	2/10 2c	5	5,741	28,707	13.00	24,975	0	24,975	20	29,970
GEO	1/1 4c	2	9,500	19,000	23.53	14,529	15	12,350	20	14,820
		16	85,500		68,665		58,365		149,928

TWIGA fee (0% on CNN):

Media Budget USD: 149,928

Total Budget USD: 149,928

Case Figure 8.10 Media plan and budget

*National Campaign
Summary*

National Campaign			Jan	Feb	Mar	Apr	May	Jun	Jul	Aug	Sep	Oct	Nov	Dec
TV	Budget, $	$337,000		$104,500	$111,500							$121,000		
	TRPs	466		160	153							153		
	Spots	64		22	21							21		
Print	Budget, $	$149,928						$149,928						
	Insertions	16						16						

To be topped up with Regional Campaign

Questions

1 What do you think about the media target group definition of Media First? Is it consistent with the marketing and communications brief of Janssen-Cilag?

2 Do you think that the assessments of the different types of media in Case Figure 8.3 and the target group's appreciation of these media is correct? Would this appreciation be different in your country? Would it be fundamentally different in other segments of the population?

3 Is the translation of communications targets to media solutions and media types in Case Figure 8.5 correct? Could there have been other good solutions (other types of media)?

4 Do you think it is a good idea to split the TV budget between ORT and RTR, and to leave out NTV? Why or why not?

5 Based on the information in Case Figures 8.7 and 8.8, and using the various criteria to compose a media mix, do you think that the print media choice is appropriate?

6 What type of continuity scheme is used for the print campaign?

7 Do you think the media objectives (reach, frequency, weight, continuity, cost) of the campaign are reached?

Based on: Russian State Committee on Statistics, Central Bank of Russia, Russian Association of Ad Agencies, First Media, Taylor Nelson Sofres, Gallup Russia, Gallup M'Index 2002/2; see also: www.nizoral.com, www.janssen-cilag.com and country-specific sites.

References

1 Donnelly, W.J. (1996), *Planning Media, Strategy and Imagination*. Upper Saddle River, NJ: Prentice Hall.

2 Donnelly, W.J. (1996), *Planning Media, Strategy and Imagination*. Upper Saddle River, NJ: Prentice Hall.

3 Donnelly, W.J. (1996), *Planning Media, Strategy and Imagination*. Upper Saddle River, NJ: Prentice Hall.

4 Nordhielm, C.L. (2002), 'The Influence of Level of Processing on Advertising Repetition Effects', *Journal of Consumer Research*, 29 (December), 371–82.

5 Pechman, C. and Stewart, D.W. (1989), 'Advertising Repetition: A Critical Review of Wearin and Wearout', *Current Issues and Research in Advertising*, 12, 285–330.

6 MacInnis, D.J., Rao, A.G. and Weiss, A.M. (2002), 'Assessing When Increased Media Weight of Real-World Advertisements Helps Sales', *Journal of Marketing Research*, 39 (November), 391–407.

7 Nordhielm, C.L. (2002), 'The Influence of Level of Processing on Advertising Repetition Effects', *Journal of Consumer Research*, 29 (December), 371–82.

8 Kirmani, A. (1997), 'Advertising Repetition as a Signal of Quality: If It's Advertised so Much, Something Must Be Wrong', *Journal of Advertising*, 26(3), 77–86.

9 Kirmani, A. (1997), 'Advertising Repetition as a Signal of Quality: If it's Advertised so Much, Something Must Be Wrong', *Journal of Advertising*, 26(3), 77–86.

10 Newell, S.J. and Henderson, K.V. (1998), 'Super Bowl Advertising: Field Testing the Importance of Advertisement Frequency, Length and Placement on Recall', *Journal of Marketing Communication*, 4(4), 237–48.

11 Berger, I.E. and Mitchell, A.A. (1989), 'The Effect of Advertising on Ad Accessibility, Attitude Confidence, and the Attitude–Behavior Relationship', *Journal of Consumer Research*, 16 (December), 269–79.

12 Hawkins, S.A. and Hoch, S.J. (1992), 'Low Involvement Learning: Memory Without Evaluation', *Journal of Consumer Research*, 19 (September), 212–25.

13 D'Sousa, G. and Rao, R.C. (1995), 'Can Repeating an Advertisement More Frequently than the Competition Affect Brand Preference in a Mature Market?', *Journal of Marketing*, 59, 32–42.

14 Kirmani, A. (1997), 'Advertising Repetition as a Signal of Quality: If it's Advertised so Much, Something Must Be Wrong', *Journal of Advertising*, 26(3), 77–86; Nelson, P. (1974), 'Advertising as Information', *Journal of Political Economy*, 82(4), 729–54.

15 Donnelly, W.J. (1996), *Planning Media, Strategy and Imagination*. Upper Saddle River, NJ: Prentice Hall.

16 Katz, H. (2003), *The Media Handbook*. Mahwah, NJ: Lawrence Erlbaum Associates.

17 Donnelly, W.J. (1996), *Planning Media, Strategy and Imagination*. Upper Saddle River, NJ: Prentice Hall.

18 Cheong, Y. and Leckenby, J.D. (2006), An evaluation of advertising media spending efficiency using data envelopment analysis. Paper presented to the 2006 Conference of the American Academy of Advertising.

19 IP Peaktime (2004), *Television 2002. European Key Factors*. Neuilly-sur-Seine, Cedex, Brussels: IP.

20 IP Peaktime (2004), *Television 2002. European Key Factors*. Neuilly-sur-Seine, Cedex, Brussels: IP; IP Peaktime (2002), *Radio 2002. European Key Factors*. Neuilly-sur-Seine, Cedex, Brussels: IP.

21 Jones, J.P. (2002), *The Ultimate Secrets of Advertising*. Sage Publications.

22 Ephron, E. (1995), 'More Weeks, Less Weight: The Self-Space Model of Advertising', *Journal of Advertising Research*, 35(3) (May/June), 18–23.

23 De Pelsmacker, P., Geuens, M. and Vermeer I. (2004), 'The importance of media planning, ad likeability and brand position on ad and brand recognition in radio spots', *International Journal of Market Research*, 46(4), 465–77.

24 McDonald, C. (1997), 'From "Frequency" to "Continuity" – is it a New Dawn?' *Journal of Advertising Research*, 37(4), 21–25.

25 Newell, S.J. and Henderson, K.V. (1998), 'Super Bowl Advertising: Field-testing the Importance of Advertising Frequency, Length and Placement on Recall', *Journal of*

Marketing Communications, 4(3), 237–48; D'Souza, G. and Rao, R.C. (1995), 'Can Repeating an Advertisement more Frequently than the Competition Affect Brand Preference in a Mature Market?' *Journal of Marketing*, 59 (April), 32–42.

26 Katz, H. (2003), *The Media Handbook*. Mahwah, NJ: Lawrence Erlbaum Associates.

27 Kamber, T. (2002), 'The Brand Manager's Dilemma: Understanding How Advertising Expenditures Affect Sales Growth during a Recession', *Brand Management*, 10, 2, 106–20.

28 Katz, H. (2003), *The Media Handbook*. Mahwah, NJ: Lawrence Erlbaum Associates.

29 De Landtsheer, D., Van Rensbergen, N. and Van Roy, T. (2001), Mediaplanning, Begrijpen en Benutten (Mediaplanning: Understanding and Using), Mechelen: Koncept.

30 www.jcdecaux.nl

31 Case, T. (2002), 'Media Plan of the Year', *Adweek*, 43(25), 34–36.

32 Ritson, M. (2003), 'Marketers Need to Find a Way to Control the Contagion of Clutter', *Marketing*, 6 March, 16.

33 Pieters, R., Warlop, L. and Wedel, M. (2002), 'Breaking Through the Clutter: Benefits of Advertisement Originality and Familiarity for Brand Attention and Memory', *Management Science*, 48(6), 765–81.

34 IP Peaktime (2004), *Television 2002. European Key Factors*. Neuilly-sur-Seine, Cedex, Brussels: IP.

35 Bond, G. and Brace, I. (1997), 'Segmenting by Attitudes to TV Advertising – Eye Opener or Blind Alley?', *Journal of the Market Research Society*, 39(3), 481–508.

36 Brace, I., Edwards, L. and Nancarrow, C. (2002), 'I Hear You Knocking . . . Can Advertising Reach Everybody in the Target Audience?', *International Journal of Market Research*, 44(2), 193–211.

37 Brace, I., Edwards, L. and Nancarrow, C. (2002), 'I Hear You Knocking . . . Can Advertising Reach Everybody in the Target Audience?', *International Journal of Market Research*, 44(2), 193–211.

38 Magiera, M. (1989), Advertisers Crowd onto the Big Screen, *Advertising Age*, 60(40), 14–15.

39 www.radioadlab.com

40+41 Van Zeebroeck, T. (1996), *Media Creativiteit (Media Creativity)*. Antwerp: MIM Standaard Uitgevery.

42 www.afajcdecaux.dk

43 *De Morgen*, 11 May 2002.

44 White, E. (2002), 'Advertisers Hope Fragrant Posters Are Nothing to Sniff At – Firms Target UK Consumers With Ads That Sing and Spray', *Wall Street Journal*, 10 October.

45 Smets, F. (2003), 'De Geur als Wapen' ('Scent as a Weapon'), *De Morgen*, 22 March.

46 White, E. (2003), 'In-Your-Face Marketing: Ad Agency Rents Foreheads', *Wall Street Journal*, 11 February.

47 Moorman, M. (2003), *Context Considered. The Relationship Between Media Environments and Advertising Effects*, Doctoral Dissertation. Universiteit van Amsterdam, the Netherlands.

48 De Pelsmacker, P., Geuens, M. and Anckaert, P. (2002), 'Media Context and Advertising Effectiveness. The Role of

Context Appreciation and Context-Ad Similarity', *Journal of Advertising*, 31(2), 49–61.

49 Moorman, M. (2003), *Context Considered. The Relationship Between Media Environments and Advertising Effects*, Doctoral Dissertation. Universiteit van Amsterdam, the Netherlands.

50 De Pelsmacker, P., Geuens, M. and Anckaert, P. (2002), 'Media Context and Advertising Effectiveness. The Role of Context Appreciation and Context-Ad Similarity', *Journal of Advertising*, 31(2), 49–61.

51 Bushman, B.J. and Bonacci, A.M. (2002), 'Violence and Sex Impair Memory for Television Ads', *Journal of Applied Psychology*, 87(3), 557–64.

52 Mees, M. (2006), Buzz marketing or bullshit marketing, *Management Jaarboek*, forthcoming.

53 Ha, L. (1996), 'Observations: Advertising Clutter in Consumer Magazines: Dimensions and Effects', *Journal of Advertising Research*, 36(4), 76–81.

54 Moorman, M. (2003), *Context Considered. The Relationship Between Media Environments and Advertising Effects*, Doctoral Dissertation. Universiteit van Amsterdam, the Netherlands.

55 Finn, A. (1988), 'Print Ad Recognition Readership Scores: An Information Processing Perspective', *Journal of Marketing Research*, 25 (May), 168–77; Pieters, R. and de Klerk-Warmerdam, M. (1993), 'Duration, Serial Position and Competitive Clutter Effects on the Memory for Television Advertising', in Chias, I.J. and Sureda, J. (eds), *Marketing for the New Europe: Dealing with Complexity, Proceedings of the 22nd Annual Conference of the European Marketing Academy*, Barcelona, 59–68.

56 Olson, D. (1994), 'The Sounds of Silence: Functions and Use of Silence in Television Advertising', *Journal of Advertising Research* (Sept./Oct.), 89–95.

57 Janiszewski, C. (1990), 'The Influence of Print Advertisement Organization on Affect Toward a Brand Name', *Journal of Consumer Research*, 17, 53–65; Finn, A. (1988), 'Print Ad Recognition Readership Scores: An Information

Processing Perspective', *Journal of Marketing Research*, 25 (May), 168–77.

58 Park, C. and Young, M. (1986), 'Consumer Response to Television Commercials: The Impact of Involvement and Background Music on Brand Attitude Formation', *Journal of Marketing Research*, 23 (Feb.), 11–24.

59 Faseur, T. and Geuens, M. (2006), 'Different positive feelings leading to different ad evaluations: the case of cosiness, excitement and romance', *Journal of Advertising*, 35 (forthcoming).

60 Yi, Y. (1993), 'Contextual Priming Effects in Print Advertisements: The Moderating Role of Prior Knowledge', *Journal of Advertising*, 22 (1 March), 1–10.

61 De Pelsmacker, P., Geuens, M. and Anckaert, P. (2002), 'Media Context and Advertising Effectiveness. The Role of Context Appreciation and Context-Ad Similarity', *Journal of Advertising*, 31(2), 49–61.

62 Faseur, T. and Geuens, M. (2006), 'Different positive feelings leading to different ad evaluations: the case of cosiness, excitement and romance', *Journal of Advertising*, 35 (forthcoming).

63 Moorman, M. (2003), *Context Considered. The Relationship Between Media Environments and Advertising Effects*, Doctoral Dissertation. Universiteit van Amsterdam, the Netherlands.

64 De Pelsmacker, P., Geuens, M. and Anckaert, P. (2002), 'Media Context and Advertising Effectiveness. The Role of Context Appreciation and Context-Ad Similarity', *Journal of Advertising*, 31(2), 49–61.

65 Lee, A. and Sternthal, B. (1999), 'The Effects of Positive Mood on Memory', *Journal of Consumer Research*, 26, 115–127.

66 Moorman, M. (2003), *Context Considered. The Relationship Between Media Environments and Advertising Effects*, Doctoral Dissertation. Universiteit van Amsterdam, the Netherlands.

67 Dahlén, M. (2005), 'The medium as a contextual cue. Effects of creative media choice', *Journal of Advertising*, 34(3), 89–98.

Chapter 9
Advertising research

Chapter outline

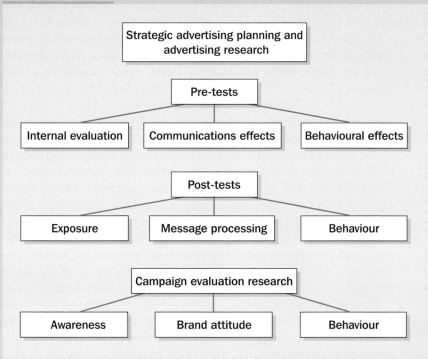

Chapter objectives

This chapter will help you to:

- Carry out strategic communications research in preparation of a communications campaign
- Understand the objectives, techniques and limitations of pre-testing advertising campaigns
- Understand the objectives, techniques and limitations of post-testing advertising campaigns
- Learn the techniques and procedures of advertising campaign evaluation research

Introduction

Advertising research is not always supported by those who are involved in the communications process. Creative professionals, for instance, are inclined to perceive research efforts as a potential threat and limitation to their creativity. Moreover, many marketing managers and other communications professionals believe that research cannot replace experience and intuition, and therefore is a waste of time and money. Finally, there is a widespread belief that the effects of communications efforts cannot be measured validly, and therefore one should not even try to do so. As in all prejudices, there is a core of truth, and a lot of ego defence and/or misunderstanding.

Obviously, advertising research should not lead to a situation in which all creativity is stifled, but should lead to more relevant, functional and, therefore, more effective creativity. Furthermore, research can never replace marketing knowledge, and even intuition, but should rather serve as an eye-opener and a correction to the 'marketing myopia' that is often mistakenly called 'experience'. There is more truth in the belief about the problem of measuring the effectiveness of communication efforts. Their effect on sales, market share or profits often cannot be isolated, and the commercial payoff of marketing communications is only visible after a certain period of time. Therefore, in advertising research, very often 'intermediate' effects, such as brand awareness, brand knowledge, attitude, preference or purchase intention, are measured, and they are assumed to be predictors of commercial success. In previous chapters it has been established, though, that positive intermediate effects are not always good predictors of commercial results. Nevertheless, the measurement of intermediate effects is frequently used in advertising research. In spite of these fundamental caveats, it is still worthwhile carrying it out. Like all research, it avoids mistakes or allows the communications manager to control the process and to adapt strategies whenever necessary.

Most of the research techniques discussed in this chapter have been developed for, and used in, an advertising context. Four basic types of advertising research will be discussed: preliminary or strategic communications research, pre-testing, post-testing and campaign evaluation research. Most of the techniques discussed can easily be transferred to other communications tools, such as public relations or in-store communications. In the chapters on specific communications instruments such as sales promotions, direct and interactive marketing and sponsorship, some specific research techniques to measure the effectiveness of these tools will be highlighted.

Strategic advertising planning and the role of research

Advertising research is used to improve decision-making in each stage of the advertising planning process. The various types of advertising research can therefore be linked to the stages in this process. This is illustrated in Figure 9.1. The starting point of a good advertising plan is a situation analysis or strategic research, on which the strategy can be built. On the basis of this research, objectives and target groups can be defined, and message and creative strategies can be developed. Following the development of an advertising strategy, a number of advertising tools (print advertisements, television spots, posters, etc.) will be developed and tested. This process is called pre-testing. After

Figure 9.1 Stages in the development of an advertising campaign and the role of advertising and advertising research

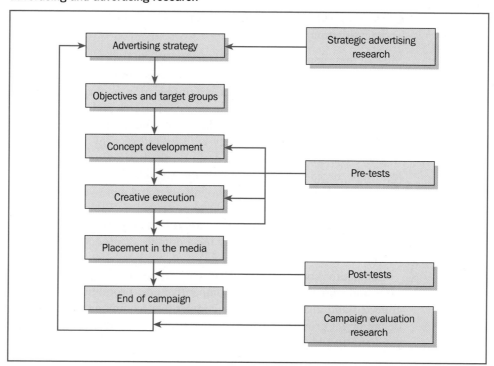

the development of the campaign, it is placed in the media. The impact of each of the tools can be assessed in post-tests. Finally, the results of the whole campaign can be compared with its objectives in campaign evaluation research. The results of the latter can serve as input for the development of subsequent advertising campaigns.

Strategic advertising research

Marketing communications, as one of the instruments of the marketing mix, have to be embedded in the overall marketing strategy of the company. Therefore, it has to be consistent with the overall marketing objectives, it has to be aimed at the desired market segments, and it should reflect the positioning strategy defined. Strategic communications research, and more particularly strategic advertising research, will therefore partially overlap with strategic marketing research. Although it is a frequently neglected research task, it is of extreme importance, since it enables the communications manager to establish a solid base on which the communications strategy can be built. Given the integrated nature of marketing communications, strategic research cannot be confined to advertising, but should cover the whole range of communications tools. Elements that have to be studied and prepared in this stage are:

■ *Product*: what are its unique strengths and weaknesses, what is the unique selling proposition to be advanced, what is the advertising platform, i.e. the arguments with which to convince the target group, etc.?

- *Market*: market size evolution, market shares, market segments, competitors' strategies, consumer characteristics and behaviour, etc.?
- *Environment*: what are the legal restrictions, cultural and political trends, the economic situation, etc.?

Most of these issues can be studied on the basis of desk research and/or qualitative interviews. Apart from that, more specific analyses can be carried out to prepare the communications strategy, such as the communications audit, competitor communications strategy research, communications content research and management judgement tests.

In a communications audit all forms of internal and external communications are studied to assess their consistency with overall strategy, as well as their internal consistency. The audit can be carried out on the basis of an internal analysis, but should ideally be based on research with the various audiences and target groups of the company to determine the impact of all overt and non-overt communications. A framework for a communications audit is presented in Table 9.1. The consistency of the communications mix in this table should be assessed both vertically and horizontally, and the communications strategy for a number of products and/or instruments can be based on the results of this analysis.

Competitor communications strategy research is largely similar to the communications audit for the company. Competitive ads, promotions, PR material, etc. can be collected and analysed to judge competitive (communications) strategies in order to define target groups and positioning strategies more clearly for the company's own products. In addition, competitive media strategies and media mixes can be studied, not to copy them, but to get an idea of the competitors' communications budgets and shares of voice, target groups, positioning and communications strategies.

Communications content research is used to help communications creatives generate ideas about the content of new communications stimuli. When a new campaign is to be launched, brainstorming sessions can be organised, involving creatives, advertisers and consumers. Thought-starter lists, in which a multitude of potential benefits of the product are listed, may also be used to get the process underway. Finally, famous advertising gurus have issued their own sets of execution guidelines to be implemented in effective advertising. However, not only do they conflict in a number of ways, but

Table 9.1 The communications audit

	Product A	Product B	Product C	Corporate
TV advertising				
Newspaper advertising				
Magazine advertising				
Sales promotions				
Direct mail				
In-store communications				
Front desk staff				
Public relations material				
Publicity				
Sponsorship				

they are also far too general to be implementable in each advertising strategy. The worst thing about these guidelines is that they lead to similar advertising executions and suffocate creative input.

If the advertising creative has too many ideas, they will have to be screened before including them in a campaign. These ideas can refer to headlines, slogans, illustrations, pictures, benefits (stated in different ways), endorsers, situations, advertising styles, etc. A sample of the target audience can be selected, and the various elements of the communications execution can be tested. The participants can be asked to order the headlines in terms of how convincing they are, the benefits in terms of their strength, the endorsers in terms of their likeability or similarity to themselves, etc., or they can be asked to rate each alternative on a scale. This *a priori* procedure is sometimes referred to as the Q-sort procedure.[1] It bears a lot of resemblance to the direct opinion measurement method in ad pre-testing (see below), but it is used before actual rough ad conception. Finally, in a **management judgement test** the ad execution proposals are presented to a jury of advertising managers, to check whether all the crucial elements of the strategic brief are correctly represented in the execution elements proposed. Again, this test bears a lot of resemblance to the internal analysis discussed in the pre-testing section.

Pre-testing of advertising

In a pre-test, advertising stimuli are tested before the ad appears in the media. The general purpose is to test an ad or different ads to assess whether or not they can achieve the purpose for which they are designed. The problems for which pre-testing can provide an answer are shown in Figure 9.2.

Often different concepts or executions of a new campaign are developed. Pre-testing helps with selecting the most effective one. As a final check a number of characteristics of a finished stimulus can be tested before media placement. As discussed before, consumers are assumed to go through a number of persuasion stages before buying a product or becoming loyal to a brand. Advertising, and communications in general, should serve as a guide to accompany the potential consumers through these stages. To that end,

Figure 9.2 Objectives of pre-testing

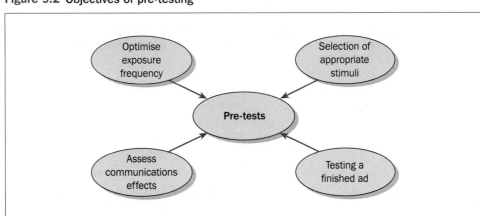

communications stimuli should generate a number of intermediate processes or communications effects, such as creating attention, carrying over information, evoking acceptance of the message, credibility, positive affective reactions about the ad and the brand, and purchase intention. In a pre-test the extent to which these intermediate effects are generated can be tested. Often, a campaign consists of a number of similar ads, i.e. different executions of the same basic communications strategy. Different executions are often used to keep the attention to the campaign alive by altering the format of the ad. Evidently, not all formats are equally appealing. A pre-test can help in establishing the extent to which some executions are more effective than others, and thus assist in deciding upon the frequency of placement of the various ads.

Three basic categories of ad pre-tests can be distinguished (Figure 9.3): a number of desirable characteristics can be tested internally, and samples of consumers can be used to test the communications or intermediate effects, or to test behavioural effects.

A campaign can be tested internally by the advertising agency and/or the advertiser by means of a checklist or readability analysis. Checklists are used to make sure that nothing important is missing, and that the ad is appealing, powerful and 'on strategy'. In Table 9.2 an example of a checklist for internal evaluation is given. Every ad can be qualitatively judged on each criterion. Obviously, not every criterion will be equally important for every campaign. For instance, the number of times the brand name is mentioned may not be important at all in an image campaign, and in a provocative campaign 'likeability' may not be all that important.[2]

Another type of internal test is the readability analysis. Good advertising copy is simple and easy to understand, especially since members of the target group are often paying only marginal attention to the text in an ad. This implies that advertising copy should be understood 'at first glance'. Several methods have been developed to test this 'readability'. For instance, a number of words in the text (e.g. every sixth word) can be removed, and a sample of consumers can be asked to fill in the missing words. The number of correctly reproduced words is an indication of the readability of the text.

Figure 9.3 Pre-testing techniques

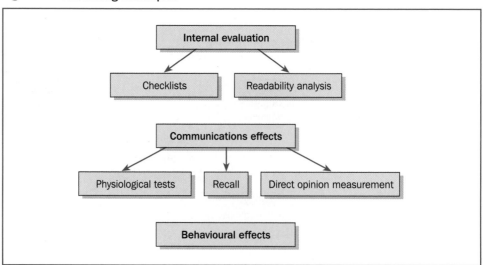

Table 9.2 A checklist for qualitative internal ad pre-testing

- Is the ad appealing at first sight?
- Does the ad have impact, 'standout', 'stopping power'?
- Is the ad 'on strategy', i.e. consistent with the briefing?
- Is the essential selling proposition mentioned frequently enough?
- Is there a benefit-oriented headline?
- Is the brand name mentioned often enough?
- How appropriate and credible are the images, the characters, the storyline, etc.?
- What is the visual impression, is the ad likeable, is it pleasing aesthetically?
- Are headlines, captions and body copy consistent?
- Does the text tell the same story as the visual elements: is the ad cohesive?
- Is the product shown appropriately?
- Does the relative importance of the logo, brand name, slogan, pack shot in the ad correctly reflect their relative importance?
- What seems to be the intended message of the ad, and is it consistent with the objectives of the campaign?

Partly based on: Pickton, D. and Broderick, A. (2001), *Integrated Marketing Communications*. Harlow: Financial Times/ Prentice Hall.

Another technique is the Reading Ease (RE) formula of Flesch-Douma.[3] In this formula RE is defined as depending on the length of words and sentences:

$$RE = 206.8 - 0.77wl - 0.93sl$$

where: wl = number of syllables per 100 words
sl = average number of words per sentence

A score between 0 and 30 means that the text is very difficult to read. A score close to 100 means that the text is very easy to understand. Research indicates that easy-to-read copy contains short sentences with short, concrete and familiar words, and lots of personal references.[4]

Communications or intermediate effects are measured in a sample of customers of the target group. The distinction can be made between physiological tests, recall tests, direct and indirect opinion measurement.

In a physiological test the reaction of the body to advertising stimuli is measured. Two types of physiological measurement can be carried out. The first involves the measurement of arousal, i.e. the activation of the nervous system, which is merely an indication of the intensity of the evoked affect by an ad. However, arousal measurement does not allow an assessment of the direction (positive or negative) of the affect, but is an indication of the primary affective reaction, which is assumed to trigger further processing of the ad.[5] Several techniques are used under very strict experimental conditions. For instance, the higher the arousal, the more the pupil of the eye dilates. Pupil dilation measurement is therefore used to assess the amount of arousal during, for instance, a television commercial. Another measure is the galvanic skin response. In this method, the varying humidity of the skin is measured by means of an electric current, on the basis of which the amount of arousal can be assessed. Other arousal measurement techniques are heartbeat and voice pitch analysis and electroencephalography. Most of these techniques are complicated and expensive, while the results are often difficult to interpret. Therefore, they are not frequently used.

Measuring attitudes indirectly: The Implicit Association Test

When social desirability limits the validity of explicit attitude measurement, implicit or indirect methods can be used. They measure a person's attitude without asking him or her for an explicit opinion. Implicit attitude measurements can to a certain extent predict behaviour that is spontaneous or uncontrolled. The Implicit Association Test (IAT) is an implicit attitude measurement technique that is based on the ease with which people make associations between attributes and target concepts. Images, words, logos, colours, etc. can be used as target concepts, while adjectives and nouns can be used as attributes, for instance likeable, dirty, etc. In the IAT people are asked to react as quickly as possible to a series of target concepts and attributes. If a person spontaneously and easily links a concept to an attribute, the speed with which he reacts to a combination will be higher. The opposite can be expected if the combination between the concept and attribute is less obvious or even appears contradictory to the individual. A careful analysis of reaction times provides insights into the attitude of individuals towards concepts and characteristics of these concepts. The IAT can be used to measure the reaction of individuals towards stimuli that may contain sensitive elements, or to test ads for sensitive products or issues, such as environmentally friendly buying behaviour, male/female stereotypes, hidden attitudes, racism, etc.[6] The results can be used to adapt elements of the creative execution of the ad, such as the models or arguments used, the combination between slogans and pictures, the type of appeal, etc.

For an advertisement to be effective, it has at least to be noted, and a minimum of information has to be carried over. The second type of physiological measurement tries to measure the potential of an ad to be seen. By means of a tachistoscope, print ads can be shown during a very short period of time. After exposure, the subject is asked to reproduce as many ad elements as possible. The element that is most recognised after the shortest exposure time is supposed to be the most effective one. Eye camera research[7] measures eye movements as a subject looks at a print ad or a television commercial. This technique registers what is looked at and for how long, and can be used to improve the structure or layout of an ad. It can also be used to test in-store communications tools and sponsorship activities.

In recall tests, such as the portfolio test, the extent to which an individual recalls a new ad or a new execution amidst existing ads is tested. The ad to be tested is put in a portfolio, together with the other ads. The subject is asked to look at the ads, and some time later (20 or 30 minutes), the recall test takes place. The subject has to name the ads and the brands, as well as the content of the ad that he or she can remember. Ads that are more frequently recognised are assumed to have drawn the attention better, and therefore are better ads.

Recall tests have a number of severe limitations. First of all, more than anything else, the memory of the individual as such is tested. People with a good memory will recall more ads and more of the content of the ads. This does not necessarily mean that the ads tested are good ones. Furthermore, product category involvement plays an important role. The more one is interested in a certain product (because one is planning to buy it in the near future, for instance), the more attention is paid to the ad, and the

Eye movement research: which part of the ad stands out?

MARKETS

HORIZONTAL TEXT: 20%

x 1.0

VERTICAL

IKEA – AD: SLOGAN PART 1: 60%

x 1.2

SLOGAN PART 2: 60%

x 1.2

LAMP
495 – BEF
30%
x = 1.3

WOMEN: 40%
x 1.3

MAN: 50%
x 1.0

PILLOW: 30%
x 1.0

BED: 60%
x 1.0

BLACK RECTANGLE: 30%
x 1.7

LAMP 1,100 – BEF
30%
x 1.0

LAMP
595 – BEF
40%
x 1.0

LAMP
2,100 – BEF
20%
x 1.0

LAMP 1,300 BEF
x 1.0
30%

LAMP 95 – BEF

30%
x 1.0

LAMP
3,850 BEF –

10%
x 1.0

LAMP
560 – BEF
20%
x 1.0

LAMP
12 – BEF
20%
x 1.0

SMALL TEXT   PART 1   PART 2   PART 3
               10%   10%   10%
               x 1.0   x 1.0   x 1.0

BRAND NAME
10%
x 1.0

SLOGAN   10% x   1.0

CITIES   0% x 0.0

The diagram opposite is an example of the result of an eye camera test of an Ikea advertisement in a newspaper.[8] The percentages represent the relative number of people in the sample that have noticed that part of the ad, 'noticed' meaning having had a fixation of the eye to that part of the ad. The second indication (x) refers to the average number of times the respondents in the sample fixated their eyes to that part of the ad (x = 2 meaning that, on average, each person paid attention twice to that part of the ad).

better it is recalled. Finally, very often the recall test is carried out very briefly after the exposure. The subject does not really have time to forget the ad. Ideally, the time between the exposure and the recall test should be as long as the time between the exposure and the buying situation in real life, but this can hardly be organised in a controlled experiment like the portfolio test.

In direct opinion measurement, a jury of customers is exposed to a number of ads, and they are asked to rate the ads on a number of characteristics. Most of the standardised ad testing procedures of advertising agencies, which enable them to compare test results over time, are of this type. Ad elements that can be tested are: clarity, novelty, evoked feelings, evoked attitude towards the ad and the brand, interest, quality of the information, the extent to which an ad induces the person to buy the product, etc.[9]

Direct opinion measurement of the attitude towards the ad

Many ad testing scales have been developed. Most of them test at least three dimensions by means of various items each: the affective reaction, the perception of informativeness, and the clarity of the ad. In the following scale, for instance, all statements have to be scored on 5- or 7-category scales (completely disagree – completely agree).

This ad appeals to me.

This ad gives useful information.

This ad is interesting.

This ad is beautiful.

This ad is believable.

This ad draws the attention.

This ad tells me something new.

This ad fits the brand.

This ad is boring.

This ad gives me a positive impression of the brand.

It is clear what this ad tries to say.

It is not immediately clear who the sender of the message is.

The baseline is easy to understand.

You have to look at the ad a long time before you understand what it is about.

This ad is confusing.

This ad is remarkable.

I think this ad is well made.

I think this ad is original.

The subject may be asked to rate each ad on a number of scales, to order them on the basis of a number of criteria, or to pairwise compare them on the basis of these criteria. The most important disadvantage of the direct rating method is that individuals are exposed to ads in a very unnatural environment. Therefore, they may be inclined to approach the ads too rationally compared to a real-life situation of ad exposure. They may even start to act and rate as 'instant experts', i.e. rating the ads from a professional advertiser's point of view, as they perceive it. This phenomenon is also known as the 'consumer jury effect'.

A pre-test for a bank commercial

A campaign can be pre-tested and subsequently adapted to the desired profile. In the following test this procedure is carried out for a bank commercial. A consumer jury is randomly selected and assembled in a room. A video is shown with a new commercial for the bank. After registering a number of characteristics of the respondents (age, income, gender, education, profession, clientship of banks, etc.), the following questions are asked.

We talked to a number of people about this video. In that way we obtained a number of words by means of which they described it. We will read each pair of words. Please indicate each time which word of the pair you think adequately describes the video.

I think this video is rather:

- dynamic – calm
- controlled – spontaneous
- boring – exciting
- mainstream – exclusive
- entertaining – informative
- conservative – new
- family-oriented – businesslike

May we first know what your ideal bank is: . . . .

We also talked to a number of people about banks. Again, we obtained a number of words by means of which they described banks. We will again read these words pairwise. Please indicate which one of the two is most appropriate to describe your ideal bank.

My ideal bank is:

- dynamic – calm
- traditional – progressive
- specialised – general
- family-oriented – businesslike
- exclusive – mainstream
- . . .

On the basis of the differences in scores between the perception of the video and of the ideal bank of a particular target group, some characteristics of the campaign can be adapted and, if considered necessary, the campaign can be retested.

An example of an indirect opinion test is the theatre test. A group of test subjects is invited to a theatre to view a pilot programme of a new television show. On arrival, they are invited to choose a present from a number of available items (competitive products in the same product category). If the product tested is too expensive, a lottery is organised and subjects are asked to indicate what product they would choose should they win. After viewing the programme, in which the ad to be tested is also shown, the participants are asked to make their choice again, as an extra award or because 'we made a mistake the first time'. The difference between what participants choose before and after the programme is attributed to the effect of the ad tested. Apart from being expensive, this test is potentially invalid, given the unrealistic situation of the measurement and the fact that participants know they are being tested.

Finally, behaviour tests try to measure actual behaviour, as opposed to recall, arousal or attitudes. Apart from actual buying behaviour, the response to a direct response television commercial, to a direct mailing or to a direct response print ad can be measured. In a trailer test or coupon stimulated purchasing test, respondents are randomly recruited in an experimental and a control group. The members of the first group are shown a commercial that is being tested in a trailer in a supermarket car park. The control group has to answer a number of questions without being exposed to the commercial. Several experimental groups can be formed if different commercials have to be tested. Both groups receive a number of coupons as a reward for their co-operation. An individualised store card registers the items purchased. Ad effectiveness is measured by means of differences in redemption between the various coupons. Again, the participants know that they are being tested, and this might influence their buying behaviour.

A second example of a behaviour test is the split scan procedure, in which the split cable and scanner technology are combined to generate data on the effectiveness of advertising campaigns. In a split scan procedure television viewing behaviour of a panel of consumers is measured by means of a telemetric device. All members of the panel also receive a store card. The split cable technology allows different random groups of panel members to be exposed to different campaigns. By means of a store card, the actual purchase of the panel members can be measured, and in that way the effectiveness of the different commercials can be assessed. The split scan technology is very promising, because the actual behaviour can be measured of the same consumers that were exposed to the different ads in a controlled way (single source data). Furthermore, other parameters can be manipulated or controlled, such as the frequency of exposure and the exposure of specific target groups.[10]

Although pre-testing procedures are very valuable, they have some limitations that should be taken into account when interpreting their results (Figure 9.4). A pre-test

Figure 9.4 Limitations of pre-testing

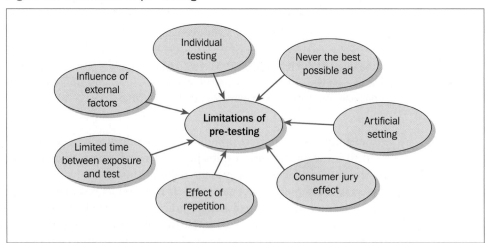

only offers the opportunity of selecting the best ad out of a series of ads tested. A pre-test will never lead to the best possible ad, but only to the best ad, given the executions tested. In that respect, pre-testing is only 'a guide to better advertising'. Pre-testing is only useful when the ads are tested in an individual interviewing procedure. Since ads are processed individually, they should also be tested individually, and not in a group setting in which the influence of the other members of the group invalidates the test rather than being synergetic. Most pre-tests take place in an experimental setting. Consumers may behave differently when exposed to an ad in a real-life situation. Some pre-test methods, especially the explicit ones such as the direct rating method, are susceptible to consumer jury effects. In most pre-tests the influence of external factors such as competitive action on the effectiveness of the ad is not measured. Often the effectiveness of the ad is measured almost immediately after exposure. The effect of the elapse of time on ad effectiveness is not assessed. Except for procedures like the split-scan method, the effect of repetition or frequency of exposure on ad effectiveness cannot be assessed.

Pre-testing a new campaign for a sauce mix

In a pre-test a number of elements can be measured that are considered to be important for the success of the campaign. However, before any judgement on the appropriateness of the campaign can be made, the results of the pre-tests should be benchmarked against other relevant campaigns. In the table below, the pre-test results of a new campaign for a prepacked sauce are given. Criteria such as attention, branding, communication, rational response and persuasion aspects are measured. The comparison is made between the new campaign and the average pre-test results of the same campaign in different countries, the average results of all other tested campaigns in the same country, and of all other food campaigns in this country. Furthermore, the pre-test results are benchmarked against normative action standards or pre-test objectives.

Pre-test scores of new campaign and benchmark campaigns for key criteria

		New campaign	Index against country average	Action standards	Country of campaign average	Country of campaign average food
Attention	Active	3.98	99	105	3.83	3.66
	Enjoyment	3.99	109	105	3.64	3.69
Branding	Brand linkage	4.18	109	110	3.90	3.88
Communication	Ease of understanding	3.73			3.65	3.70
	Specific criteria:					
	– Are practical to use	81%				
	– Have a very good taste	58%				
	– Are very good in quality	49%				
	– Are disposable in a large range of variety	71%				
	– Offer you something really new	63%				
Rational response	New information	3.15			2.59	2.67
	Different	3.23			3.15	3.30
	Relevant	3.06			2.85	3.02
	Believable	4.05			3.66	3.79
	Didn't tell you enough	2.89			2.88	2.89
Persuasion	Persuaded me	25%	120	110	12	

Post-testing of advertising

A post-test is a test of the effectiveness of a single ad after placement in the media. Post-tests are only meaningful if there is a before measurement or a control measurement as a benchmark. Three types of post-tests can be distinguished (Figure 9.5): measurement of exposure, communications effect tests and measurement of behaviour.

First of all, the extent to which an ad has reached its audience can be measured. Net reach, GRP, OTS and other exposure measures can be calculated. Normally, this type of effectiveness measurement is not only done after media placement, but also as a part of the media planning effort. Similarly, the amount of publicity generated in the press or sponsorship exposure can also be measured and expressed in terms of reach or GRP.

In measuring the communications or message processing effects of an ad, two types of tests are used: recall and recognition tests. A recognition test is a very obvious effectiveness test. A sample of ads are presented to a consumer, who is asked to indicate whether he or she recognises the ad or not. The underlying assumption is that ads can only be effective when they are at least noted. A well-known recognition test procedure for print ads is the Starch method. Some 75,000 advertisements in 1,000 issues of magazines and newspapers are assessed each year, using 100,000 personal interviews.[11] Consumers who say they have read a specific issue in a magazine are interviewed at home. The magazine is opened at a random page, and for each ad a number of questions are asked. The procedure leads to four percentage scores for each ad:

- *Non-readers*: the percentage of people who do not remember having seen the ad.
- *Noted*: the percentage of readers that claim to have seen the ad.
- *Seen/associated*: the percentage of readers that claim to have read the product and brand name.
- *Read most*: the percentage of readers that claim to have read at least half the ad.

Obviously the Starch test is very susceptible to the test subject's honesty. However, research reveals that high 'noted' scores are positively correlated with a positive attitude towards the brand ($r = 0.43$) and a positive intention to buy ($r = 0.52$).[12]

Figure 9.5 Post-testing techniques

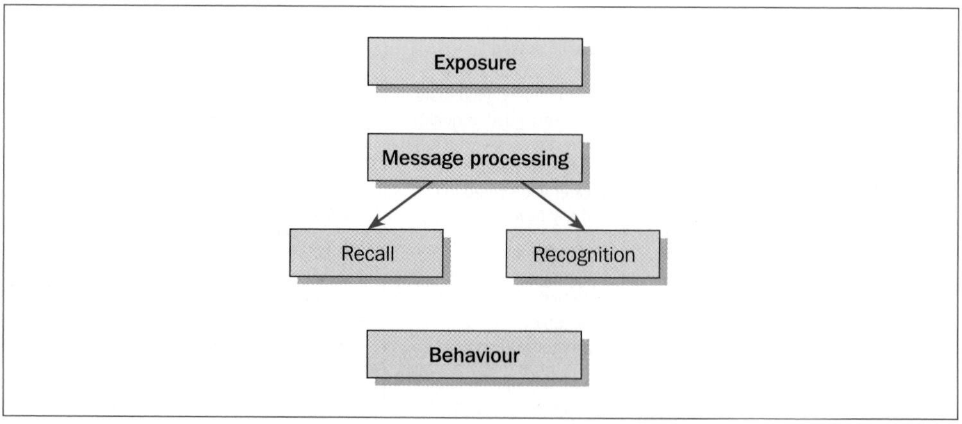

In a masked identification test, part of a print ad, usually the brand name, is covered. The subject is asked if he or she recognises the ad, and if he or she knows what brand it is for. Recognition and correct attribution scores can then be calculated. Obviously, brand confusion can be measured too. The combination of recognition and correct attribution scores leads to the useful score: the percentage of the consumer sample that both recognised the ad and attributed it correctly to the brand advertised. In Figure 9.6, an example of the results of a masked identification test of a billboard ad for a new car are shown, together with the results of a number of categories of control ads.

A second type of communications effect measurement is the recall test. In an unaided recall test consumers have to indicate which ads they remember having seen, in a specific magazine, on television or on billboards. In an aided recall test the consumer's memory is helped by means of clues such as: what car ads did you see on television yesterday? As such, the masked identification test can be regarded as an aided recall test. Unaided recall scores are usually lower than aided recall scores, which in turn are lower than recognition scores. Therefore they cannot be compared.

A well-known recall test is the Gallup-Robinson Impact test for print ads. First, the respondents have to read a magazine at home. The following day the respondents are called and asked to recall as many ads as they can. After that a number of questions about the content of the ads are asked. The Gallup-Robinson procedure leads to three indicators of advertising effectiveness:[13]

- *Proved name registration*: the percentage of subjects that remember an ad without having seen it during the test.

- *Idea penetration*: the extent to which subjects have understood the main idea in the ad.

- *Conviction*: the percentage of subjects that want to buy or use the product.

Another well-known recall test, used for audiovisual ads, is the Day After Recall (DAR) test. In this telephone interview procedure, a number of consumers are called. They are asked to indicate which ads they saw on television or heard on the radio the day before, within a certain product category. In the second stage, brand names are

Figure 9.6 Masked identification test

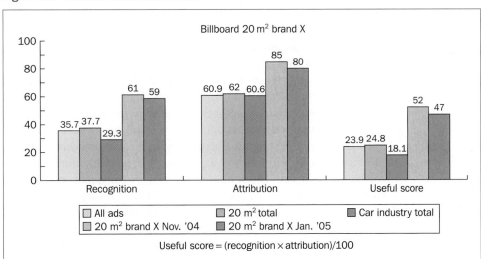

Useful score = (recognition × attribution)/100

mentioned, and the respondent has to indicate if he or she remembers having seen or heard an ad for the brand. Additionally, a number of questions about the ad content are asked. The resulting percentages of correct recall are always compared with some kind of benchmark such as all commercials within the same product category, or all commercials of the day before. In the triple association test a product category and a selling proposition are given, and the respondent has to indicate a brand name, e.g. 'What brand of petrol puts a tiger in your tank?'

Finally, the effect of an ad can be tested by means of behavioural measures. Especially in the case of direct response advertisements, the number of people calling a free telephone number announced in the ad, sending back a coupon or actually buying the product can be considered a measure of the effectiveness of the ad.

Measuring website visiting behaviour

Every time a visitor clicks on a website link or interacts with a website, the web server automatically keeps track of a number of data in so-called *log files*. Most servers generate four types of log files. The *access log file* keeps track of the file names that are downloaded, the IP address of the client server that requested the file, and an indication of time. The *agent log file* registers which browser is being used by which visitor's server for every visit to the site. The *referrer log file* registers the pages that were visited before the visitor landed on our web page. The *error log file* keeps track of errors that occurred during the process. The log files give information such as the number of 'hits' (downloaded files), the point in time at which files were downloaded, the number of bytes transferred, the domains from which the visitor arrived (internet service providers, proxy servers, firewalls), and the browsers used. A number of software instruments, such as Nedstat and WebTrends, have been developed to efficiently analyse and summarise this enormous data stream. Also data-mining software is used to find meaningful patterns in the large amount of data on website visiting behaviour. Log files have an important limitation. They cannot identify individual users. Therefore, log file data are often supplemented with *cookies*, a piece of software that is planted in the system of the website visitor and allows web servers to register and keep track of the revisit behaviour of visitors. The visiting of advertisements on websites (banners, buttons) can be assessed by means of *click-through rates*. Most click-throughs result in a transfer of the visitor to the advertiser's website. A click-through is the virtual counterpart of a response of an individual to a direct mailing.[14]

Recall and recognition tests are useful and easy to carry out, but they have a number of severe limitations (Figure 9.7). In recognition tests, consumers can say what they like, they can lie, exaggerate or guess. This makes the results of recognition tests far from reliable. An ad that is part of a campaign of similar ads will be more easily recognised or recalled. In these circumstances it is very hard to isolate the effect of one single ad. The underlying assumption that recognition or recall of the ad eventually leads to buying the product may be erroneous. Recognising or recalling marketing communications may be a necessary condition to buy a product, but certainly not a sufficient one. Product involvement influences the results of the test. A consumer who is very interested in a certain product category will perform better in recognising ads for this product category. This does not imply anything about the effectiveness of that specific ad. Recall scores are very dependent on the time elapsed between exposure and recall measurement. Recall scores are nearly 100% immediately after exposure, but studies indicate that they drop to about 25% one day after, and to about 10% two days after exposure.[15] Rational mass appeals are recalled better than complex and/or emotional appeals, certainly after

Figure 9.7 Limitations of post-testing

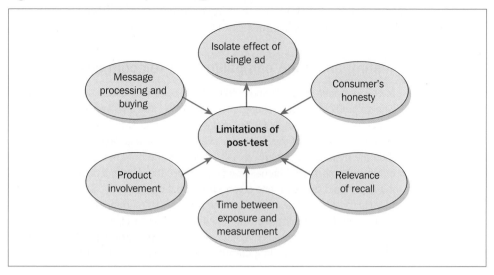

one exposure. Recall is in a number of cases an irrelevant indication of advertising effectiveness. The only thing recall tests measure is whether the ad has been able to draw attention. Especially in cases in which it is sufficient for a consumer to recognise a picture or a brand in a shop to be inclined to buy the product, recognition tests are a much more valid and relevant measure of ad effectiveness than recall measurements.

Advertising campaign evaluation research

Contrary to post-tests in which the effectiveness of only one ad is assessed, campaign evaluation research focusses on the effectiveness of a whole advertising campaign. Campaign evaluation research tends to become increasingly more relevant than post-tests. Integrated marketing communications imply that it is very difficult or even irrelevant to assess the effects of one single medium or ad. Rather, the effects of the whole communications mix should be assessed.

In campaign evaluation tests, not ad-related responses, but brand-related effectiveness measures are focused on. As in post-tests, a before or control measurement is necessary to assess adequately the effect of a particular campaign. Again, communications effects as well as behaviour effects can be measured.

Communications effects measurements can be structured following the hierarchy-of-effects logic: awareness, knowledge, attitude and intention to buy. Top-of-mind awareness (TOMA) measurement is an unaided awareness telephone test in which the consumer is asked which brand of a specific product category is the first one that comes to mind. Subsequently, the consumer is asked if he or she can name other brands in the same product category (again unaided awareness). Finally, a number of brands are mentioned, and the consumer has to indicate the ones he or she knows (aided awareness). The advertising campaign is not mentioned, but by comparing the awareness before and after a campaign, its effect on brand awareness can be assessed. Furthermore, brand awareness rates of competitive products are also measured, and can serve as a control measurement or benchmark.

Also attitude change or the change of the brand's image can be measured. Often a campaign aims at changing the target group's opinion about certain aspects or attributes of a brand. Scale techniques can be used to measure this change in image components.

Testing an image campaign for a telecom operator

In one European country[16] the mobile phone operator market is dominated by three competitors who's combined market share is almost 100%. The two largest companies have a combined market share of about 90%. The market splits into two important segments, i.e. prepaid and post-paid. In terms of the number of clients, the pre-paid segment has grown much more rapidly than the post-paid segment. Initially, 100% of the market was post-paid. By 2002, two-thirds of the customers used prepaid cards. In 1996, the market leader had a relatively weak position in the pre-paid segment, and a very strong post-paid position. An image campaign was launched to build top-of-mind awareness, brand preference, emotional bonding and trust. Reliability and superior product quality (network, sound, number of clients, etc.) were stressed. Throughout the campaign, the campaign results were monitored. Chart 1 shows top-of-mind brand awareness of the three competing brands; in Chart 2 brand preference evolution is shown.

Chart 1 Top-of-mind brand awareness

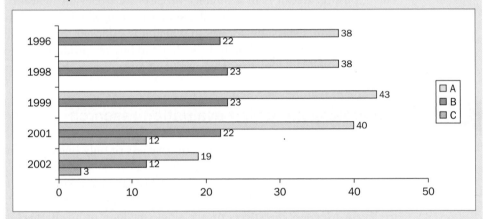

Chart 2 Brand preference

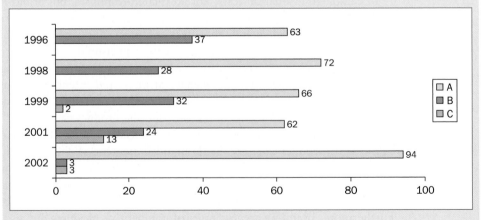

In Chart 3 the score of the market leader on a number of image attributes is given. The market leader has a better image on all criteria measured.

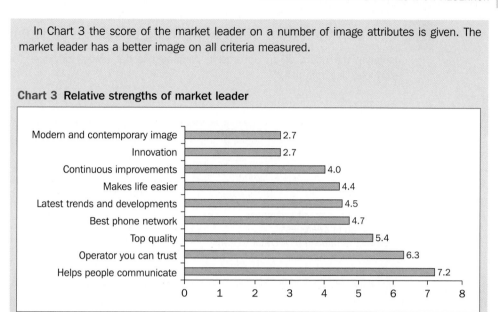

Chart 3 Relative strengths of market leader

Modern and contemporary image: 2.7
Innovation: 2.7
Continuous improvements: 4.0
Makes life easier: 4.4
Latest trends and developments: 4.5
Best phone network: 4.7
Top quality: 5.4
Operator you can trust: 6.3
Helps people communicate: 7.2

Finally, the communications effect of a campaign can be measured on the basis of the intention to buy of a target group of consumers. It is important that the question on the purchase intention is related to the near future or the next purchase, e.g.: 'The next time you buy coffee, what is the chance that you will buy brand X (as a percentage, or on a ten-point scale)?'

Most of the communications effect measurements are frequently used in tracking studies, in which comparable (random) samples of consumers are asked a standardised set of questions at regular intervals (e.g. every three months). As a result, the position of a brand and competing products can be tracked over time, and effects of subsequent campaigns can be assessed. As in all before–after measurements, problems of interpretation arise. The effect of a campaign cannot always be isolated. A deteriorating image, for instance, may be the result of, amongst others, a bad campaign, a price increase, bad publicity, competitors' actions, an inappropriate sales promotion campaign or a bad distribution strategy. Furthermore, the effect of advertising campaigns may only become visible after some time. The performance of a brand immediately after the campaign may therefore underestimate its true impact in the long run.

Obviously, the ultimate objective of an advertising campaign is to make people buy the product and eventually make a (better) profit. In behaviour tests the relation between advertising and buying behaviour is directly studied. Various behavioural measures of ad effectiveness can be distinguished, the most obvious ones being sales and market share evolution. Again, as in all campaign evaluation measurements, it should be noted that the evolution of market share and sales may be attributable to other marketing mix instruments than advertising. The effect of an advertising campaign cannot always be isolated easily.

How can the effect of an advertising campaign be isolated?

Isolating the effect of an advertising campaign is not always obvious. The following two examples illustrate this.[17]

Example 1

A small bank advertised a savings account with an interest rate that was twice that of the interest rates of the major banks at the time. The campaign results (campaign in Year 1 and Year 2) were the following:

	Year 1	Year 2	Year 3
Spontaneous brand awareness	7%	9%	10%
Aided brand awareness	45%	47%	66%
Correct attribution of account to bank	9%	36%	55%

The following chart indicates the evolution of the number of account holders, as well as the advertising periods.

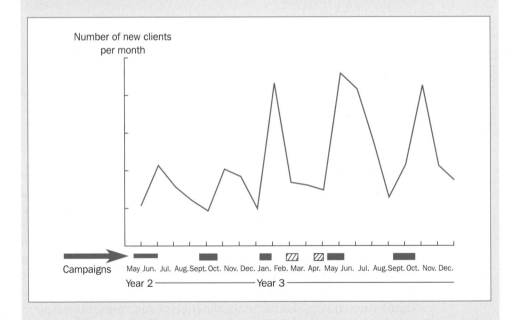

On the basis of the communications effects, the communications campaign seems to have been successful. Obviously, the number of clients increased substantially each time an advertising wave took place. The question is: is this increase attributable to the advertising effort or to the intrinsic attractiveness of the product, i.e. the high interest rate, that is simply communicated to the target audience?

Example 2

A chain of do-it-yourself supermarkets launched a radio advertising campaign. The commercial results of the supermarkets look as follows (campaign in Year 2, Year 3 and Year 4):

	Year 1	Year 2	Year 3	Year 4
Sales	100	139	188	224
Annual growth of sales		+39%	+36%	+19%
Number of transactions	100	130	171	194
Ticket size	100	107	110	116

At first sight, this seems to be an impressive result. However, when a correction is made for the expansion of the number of supermarkets that increased in the period under consideration, the following picture emerges.

	Year 1	Year 2	Year 3	Year 4
Sales	100	131	159	183
Annual growth of sales		+31%	+21%	+15%
Number of transactions	100	128	165	189
Ticket size	100	106	110	118

The result still looks impressive, but not as impressive as the first set of figures in which the effect of a larger distribution network was included.

Apart from changes in sales, more specific behavioural effects can be measured, such as trial purchases and the degree of adoption of, or loyalty to, a brand.

The 'awareness–trial–retention' framework

An analysis combining awareness and behavioural measures to assess the effectiveness of advertising campaigns is the following. Three indicators are measured:

AR = AW/TG
TR = T/AW
ADR = A/T

AR awareness rate
AW number of target group members that are aware of the brand
TG number of people in the target group
TR trial rate
T number of target group members that have purchased the brand at least once during a given period
ADR adoption rate
A number of people that have purchased the brand at least a specific number of times during the same period

Evidently, the period under study and the number of times a consumer has to have purchased the product to be called a loyal consumer have to be determined in advance, and will depend upon the product category studied.

Suppose that for two competing brands the following results have been obtained after an advertising campaign:

▶

	Brand A	Brand B
Awareness rate	70%	20%
Trial rate	40%	20%
Adoption rate	10%	70%

Obviously, the commercial end-result is the same for both brands: 2.8% of the target group have become loyal to the brand. However, the three indicators show a more differentiated picture. Brand B was not very successful in building awareness and trial. One might say that the advertising campaign was not very effective. On the other hand, the marketing strategy seems to be on target: most people who have tried the product have become loyal to it. Brand A has had a successful advertising campaign, but something seems to be wrong with the rest of the marketing strategy. Maybe the product is of bad quality, the price may be too high or the distribution strategy inappropriate. It could also be that the product is a luxury item, for which in the short run trial is more important than repeat purchase.

Most of the aforementioned measures of communications results are effectiveness measures, while marketers will also be interested in efficiency measurement, i.e. the extent to which the investment in an advertising campaign has had a commercial result. More specifically, marketers might want to know how many sales for every pound (or euro, or dollar) spent on communications has resulted. Over a longer period of time, data could be collected on advertising budgets and sales per time unit (three months, a year, etc.), and the relationship between the two may be estimated. This could result in the following:

$$S = 1.5 + 0.2 \times A$$

where: S = sales in € million
A = advertising in € million

The conclusion would be that, over time, every euro invested in advertising has resulted in 0.2 euros of extra sales. Additionally, the cost function of the company may be modelled, in order to be able to calculate the profitability of the advertising efforts. However, advertising efforts usually have carry-over effects: the efforts of today do not lead to extra sales during the same period only, but also to extra commercial results in future periods. This effect may be modelled as follows:

$$S(t) = 1.5 + 0.2 \times A(t) + 0.8 \times S(t-1)$$

where: S(t) = sales in period t
A(t) = advertising investments in period t
S(t − 1) = sales in period t − 1

The coefficient of S(t − 1) represents the effect of advertising investments in the past on this period's sales. This effect is assumed to decrease over time. The long-term effect of advertising can in this example be calculated as: 0.2/0.8 = 0.25. This implies that, in the long run, every euro invested in advertising leads to an increase in sales of 0.25. The short-term effect of advertising on sales in the same period is only 0.20.

Evidently, life is not so simple. First, sales are influenced by more than communications alone, so the model will have to be extended. Additionally, the competitors' efforts will have to be taken into consideration too. Consequently, estimating the profitability of advertising investments is a complicated task.[18]

Summary

Advertising campaigns can only be effective if they are accompanied by a well-structured research plan. Research can support the advertising activity in four stages of the advertising process. In strategic advertising research the advertising campaign is prepared by studying the marketing strategy, the competitive situation and the competitive environment it has to be embedded in. Techniques, such as the communications audit, competitor communications strategy research and communications content research are being used in this stage. During development of the advertising campaign, and before it appears in the media, the ads can be pre-tested. The major advantage of pre-testing is that it is a guide to better advertising. However, due to all kinds of limitations and the shortcomings of most of the techniques used, it can never lead to the best possible ad. Techniques used in pre-testing can be internal, such as the readability analysis, or external (with consumers), such as physiological tests, recall tests and direct or indirect opinion measurement. After a specific advertisement has been placed in the media, post-tests can be carried out, such as exposure, recall and recognition tests, and behavioural measures. Well known test procedures, such as the Starch test, the Gallup-Robinson impact test and the Day After Recall tests are used in post-testing. Not just a single ad can be tested, but a whole campaign. Campaign evaluation tests focus on the brand-related effects of the campaign, such as brand recall and recognition, attitude towards the brand, purchase intention and, most importantly, behavioural or commercial measures, such as trial, repeat purchase, loyalty, sales and market share.

Review questions

1 What are the major techniques used in strategic communications research?

2 Discuss ad pre-testing techniques. What are the objectives and limitations of these measurement procedures?

3 Discuss ad post-testing techniques. What are the objectives and limitations of post-testing?

4 What measures of brand-related campaign evaluation techniques can be used?

5 How can advertising efficiency be measured? Why is it so difficult to judge the effectiveness and efficiency of an advertising campaign?

Further reading

Aaker, D., Kumar, V. and Day, G.S. (2001), *Marketing Research*. New York: John Wiley & Sons.

Malhotra, N. (1999), *Marketing Research, an Applied Orientation*. Upper Saddle River, NJ: Prentice-Hall.

McDonald, C. and Vangelder, P. (1998), *ESOMAR Handbook of Market and Opinion Research*. Amsterdam: ESOMAR.

Case 9

Building added brand value for Smiths and transferring it to Lay's

The in-home snacking market

In Belgium, potato crisps are primarily eaten at home: 60% of crisp consumption is at home, after 6 p.m. In the 1980s and 1990s the in-home snacking market became increasingly competitive. Variation is an important driver in this product category. New competitors and appealing product concepts have emerged. As a result of the trend towards more healthy food, vegetables, cheese, olives, etc. have also become a part of the evening snacking habit. In Case Figure 9.1 the structure of the snacking market is presented. All potato crisp brands have basically the same product range, flat crisps and ribbed crisps, and they all have the same 'success flavours': salt, pepper, and pickles.

A commodity product, dominated by private labels

Case Table 9.1 shows the market share of the two most important manufacturer brands on the Belgian market and of the private label brands. Because of the price premium, Smiths (a FritoLay brand) is the market leader in value. Compared with some of the new successful products, the consumer perceives potato crisps as a low added-value product. Attempts

to launch new crisp concepts in 1996 and 1997 failed. The consumer does not see the difference between the quality of manufacturer brands and private labels, and consequently is not prepared to pay more for a manufacturer brand. In 1995 only 16% of consumers agreed with the statement that Smiths crisps were worth paying more for, and only 12% that Croky chips were worth paying extra for. Marketing efforts traditionally focus upon sales promotions, but the production volume of Smiths has remained relatively stable over time. Between 1982 and 1997, the volume has only increased by 28%.

Case Table 9.1 Market shares on the salty crisps market in Belgium, 1997

	Share of market (% volume)	Share of market (% value)
Smiths	28.8	38.1
Croky	23.5	29.7
Private labels	41.4	25.1
Other	6.4	7.1

Case Figure 9.1 The snacking market

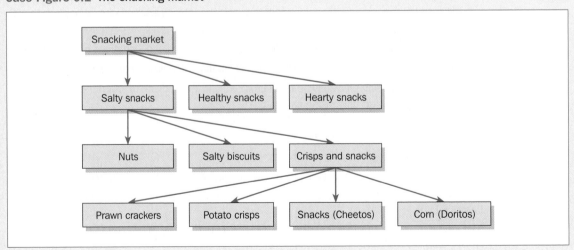

Building brand awareness, image, sales and market share

From 1998 onwards the Smiths brand has been supported by an image campaign, aimed at building brand awareness and brand preference, and stressing image components such as fun, modern, popular, irresistible, high quality, dynamic, and worth paying extra for. A series of humorous television and cinema spots was created. The ultimate goal was to strengthen the position of Smiths as a market leader. In 2000 it was decided to change the brand name to Lay's. From the beginning of 2001 onwards, this re-branding decision was implemented, and the objective was to carry over the Smiths brand awareness and brand image to Lay's.

The communications objectives were as follows:

- Increase the relevant image parameters by 50% compared with 1995. Two types of image parameters were discerned:
  - *Expressive*: fun to eat, modern and popular brand
  - *Instrumental*: high quality, worth paying more for.
- The image gap with Croky should increase substantially.
- The day-after recall of each spot should score above product category mean.
- By the end of 2001 the aided brand awareness of Lay's should be at least at the same level as Smiths was at the end of 2000.

The commercial objectives can be summarised as follows:

- To increase volume market share to 35%, implying a growth of sales of 25%, and retain the market share after re-branding.
- To increase the market share gap with Croky.

Case Table 9.2 Market shares of Smiths/Lay's and its competitors

	Market share in volume (%)				
	1997	*1998*	*1999*	*2000*	*2001*
Smiths/Lay's	28.7	30.7	35.5	36.3	39.6
Croky	23.5	19.6	17.0	15.9	12.8
Private labels	41.4	44.3	42.4	43.1	42.6
Other	6.4	5.4	5.1	4.7	5.0

- To stop the private label growth.
- The increased sales should not be the result of price cuts and promotions; volume and value growth should increase to the same extent.

All of these objectives should be reached by the end of 2001.

Results

In Case Tables 9.2 and 9.3 the commercial results are shown. In Case Table 9.2 market shares are presented. Case Table 9.3 shows the evolution of volume and value growth of both the total market and Smiths/Lay's. Not only did Smiths reach its objectives, it also claims that the whole product category revived as a result of the campaign. In Case Table 9.4, day-after recall results are shown of the various television spots. In Case Table 9.5 the evolution of brand awareness is shown, and Case Table 9.6 presents the evolution of the image of Smiths/Lay's compared with the second largest manufacturer brand, Croky.

The marketing management of the brand claims that these results should be exclusively attributed to the advertising campaign. There were no price changes during the campaign; the promotional activity remained the same (one sales promotion campaign

Case Table 9.3 Volume and value growth of total market and Smiths/Lay's

	Index volume growth		Index value growth	
Year	*Market vs 1997*	*Smiths/Lay's vs 1997*	*Market vs 1997*	*Smiths/Lay's vs 1997*
1997	100	100	100	100
1998	107	114	108	115
1999	107	133	113	135
2000	114	144	121	142
2001	126	174	137	177

Case Table 9.4 Day-after recall of Smiths/Lay's television spots and attitude towards the ad

Percentage of people:					
	Objective	Spot 1	Spot 2	Spot 3	Spot 4
Useful score (ad recognition and correct attribution of brand to ad)	30.2	35.0	34.0	32.0	31.0
Likeability	50.0	74.0	53.0	59.0	54.0
Percentage of people agreeing:					
	1995	Objective	Lay's 2001	Croky 2001	Gap
Makes good ads	7	Not given	42	14	28

Case Table 9.5 Evolution of brand awareness of Smiths/Lay's, end 2001

	Objective (%)	Result (%)
Top-of-mind	Not given	16.0
Unaided	53.0	50.1
Aided	85.0	97.7

per year); the R&D strategy did not change; the distribution coverage remained the same. The difference was made as a result of active brand-building by means of an image advertising campaign. Smiths/Lay's won a bronze Effie Award in Belgium in 2002.

Questions

1 Would you say Smiths did enough strategic communications research upon which to build its advertising strategy? If not, what other information could have been useful to prepare its campaign?

2 No pre-test research results are reported. If you were asked to conduct pre-tests, what types of pre-tests would you use, and what would you try to find out?

3 Do you think that the post-tests that Smiths conducted are appropriate? What do you think of the recall and attribution results that are reported? What else could have been measured?

4 Are the campaign evaluation tests appropriate? Should they have focussed on other types of tests or questions? If yes, which ones?

5 Have the objectives of the campaign been met? Are the results of the campaign impressive in all respects? If the latter is not the case, what could be the reason?

Based on: Effie Book Belgium 2002, AC Nielsen Scantrack, Research & Marketing, CBEM.

Case Table 9.6 The evolution of the brand image of Smiths/Lay's and Croky

Percentage of people agreeing					
	1995	Objective	Lay's 2001	Croky 2001	Gap
Expressive:					
Fun to eat	40	60	45	24	21
Modern brand	30	45	59	29	30
Popular brand	41	61	62	24	38
One of my favourites	28	42	53	30	23
Instrumental:					
High quality	48	72	74	42	32
Worth paying more for	16	24	50	22	28

References

1 Rossiter, J.R. and Percy, L. (1987), *Advertising and Promotion Management*. New York: McGraw-Hill.

2 Pickton, D. and Broderick, A. (2001), *Integrated Marketing Communications*. Harlow: Financial Times/Prentice Hall.

3 Ferrée, H. (1989), *Groot Inspiratieboek voor Creatieve Reclame (Great Inspiration Book for Creative Advertising)*. Deventer: Kluwer Bedrijfswetenschappen.

4 Fill, C. (2002), *Marketing Communications: Contexts, Strategies and Applications*. Harlow: Financial Times/ Prentice Hall.

5 van Raaij, F.W. (1989), 'How Consumers React to Advertising', *International Journal of Advertising*, 8(3).

6 See also: de Houwer, J. (2001), 'A Structural and Process Analysis of the Implicit Association Test', *Journal of Experimental Social Psychology*, 37, 443–51; Maison, D. (2002), 'Using the Implicit Association Test to Study the Relation Between Consumers' Implicit Attitudes and Product Usage', *Asia Pacific Advances in Consumer Research*, 5; Vantomme, D., Geuens, M., De Pelsmacker, P. and De Houwer, J. (2005), 'Explicit and implicit determinants of fair-trade buying behaviour', *Advances in Consumer Research*, forthcoming; Vantomme, D., Geuens, M., De Houwer, J. and De Pelsmacker, P. (2005), 'Implicit attitudes toward green consumer behaviour', *Psychologica Belgica*, 25(4), 217–239.

7 For an overview of physiological tests; Hansen, F. (1998), 'Advertising Research: Testing Communication Effects', in McDonald, C. and Vangelder, P. (eds), *ESOMAR Handbook of Market and Opinion Research*. Amsterdam; ESOMAR, 653–724.

8 Rogil Field Research (1988), *De Plaats van de Advertentie in het Nieuwsblad (The Place of the Advertisement in Het Nieuwsblad)*. Leuven: Rogil Field Research.

9 De Cock, B. and De Pelsmacker, P. (2001), 'Emotions Matter', in *ESOMAR, Excellence in International Research*. Amsterdam: ESOMAR, 63–88.

10 Aaker, D., Kumer, V. and Day, G. (2001), *Marketing Research*. New York: John Wiley & Sons.

11 Aaker, D., Kumer, V. and Day, G. (2001), *Marketing Research*. New York: John Wiley & Sons.

12 Zinkhan, G.M. and Gelb, B.D. (1986), 'What Starch Scores Predict', *Journal of Advertising Research*, 26(4), 23–6.

13 Duncan, T. (2002), *IMC. Using Advertising and Promotion to Build Brands*. Boston: McGraw-Hill/Irwin.

14 De Pelsmacker, P. and Van Kenhove, P. (2005), *Marktonderzoek. Methoden en Toepassingen (Marketing Research. Methods and Applications)*. Amsterdam: Pearson Education Benelux Insites, (2002), www.insites.be; Stout, R. (1997), *Web Sites Stats: Tracking Hits and Analysing Traffic*. Berkeley, CA: McGraw-Hill.

15 Rossiter, J.R. and Percy, L. (1987), *Advertising and Promotion Management*. New York: McGraw-Hill.

16 Due to confidentiality requirements, the country and companies involved are not given.

17 Due to confidentiality requirements, the names of the bank and supermarket are not given.

18 For modelling approaches in advertising research: Leeflang, P., Wittink, D., Wedel, M. and Naert, P. (2000), *Building Models for Marketing Decisions*. Boston: Kluwer Academic Publishers; Hanssens, D.M. Parsons, L.F. and Schultz, R.L. (2001), *Market Response Models. Econometric and Time Series Analysis*. Norwell, MA: Kluwer Academic Publishers.

Chapter 10
Public relations

Chapter outline

```
              ┌─────────────────────────────┐
              │   Public relations as a     │
              │    communications tool      │
              └─────────────────────────────┘

┌─────────────────────┐         ┌─────────────────────┐
│    Target groups    │         │ Objectives and tasks│
└─────────────────────┘         └─────────────────────┘

              ┌─────────────────────────────┐
              │  Instruments and channels   │
              └─────────────────────────────┘

              ┌─────────────────────────────┐
              │           Budgets           │
              └─────────────────────────────┘

              ┌─────────────────────────────┐
              │   Measuring effectiveness   │
              └─────────────────────────────┘

              ┌─────────────────────────────┐
              │    Crisis communications    │
              └─────────────────────────────┘
```

Chapter objectives

This chapter will help you to:

- Understand the difference between public relations and marketing communications, and the role of public relations in the company's communications effort
- Get an idea of the strengths and weaknesses of public relations, and the challenges it faces
- Distinguish the various target groups, objectives and tasks of public relations
- Get an overview of the instruments and channels used by public relations
- Learn about the nuts and bolts of good media relations
- Distinguish a number of public relations budgeting techniques
- Learn how to measure public relations effectiveness
- Communicate in times of crisis

Introduction

Traditionally, public relations (PR) is an activity which in most companies has been structurally separated from marketing communications. It originated in the function of 'press agent', the main activity of whom was to bridge the gap between the company's point of view and media coverage of the company's activities. Gradually, press agents became a vital part of the company's communications efforts targeted at various publics or stakeholders, and the activity of 'press relations' evolved into the 'public relations' function. Staying in touch and creating goodwill with all types of audiences has become an extremely sophisticated and complex task. This is illustrated by the fact that in most companies the PR function directly reports to the chief executive officer (CEO). But not only the type and number of target groups of public relations are different from marketing communications, the nature of the objectives is quite specific, as well as the tools and instruments used, although some of the latter are similar to those used in marketing communications. All in all, it is fair to say that public relations is more complex than marketing communications, due to the variety of objectives and target groups it has to take into account.

Public relations also plays a vital role in integrating the company's communications efforts (see also Chapter 1). Integrated communications at the corporate level imply the creation of synergies between all communications tools, especially marketing communications and corporate communications. Public relations is a very important component of the latter.

Public relations as a communications tool

There are different definitions of public relations, which all stress one or more important aspects of this communications tool. Essentially, public relations is a communications tool that is used to promote the goodwill of the firm as a whole.[1] It is the projection of the personality of the company, the management of reputation.[2] Public relations is the planned and sustained effort to establish and maintain good relationships, mutual understanding, sympathy and goodwill with secondary target groups, also called publics, audiences or stakeholders.[3] It is those efforts that identify and close the gap between how the organisation is seen by its key publics and how it would like to be seen.[4] Publicity is the term used to describe the free media coverage of news about the company or its products, often as a result of PR efforts.

Publics are groups of people that the company is not directly trying to sell products to (that is why they are called secondary target groups), but that are perceived as influencing opinions about the company. As such, publics can be considered as a component of the external company environment. The relations with these publics should be positive because they can be vital to the company's survival and success. Essential in most definitions of public relations is that it is a two-way form of communication: the company learns from its publics and conveys information to them. Furthermore, like any other communications activity, public relations should be a planned effort. It is also a major component of a successful integrated communications activity, since it covers a range of activities that can be linked to other elements of the communications mix,[5] such as:

- Creation and maintenance of corporate identity and image, by communicating the company's philosophy and mission through corporate advertising, open days, etc.;

- Improving the company's standing as a good corporate citizen, by means of activities such as arts and sports sponsorship or community programmes;

- Maintaining good relations with the media, both for disseminating good news and in times of crisis;

- Attendance at trade exhibitions and the organisation of contacts with suppliers and intermediaries;

- Looking after the internal communications, with the purpose of involving the employees in the stategic priorities of the company.

Public relations is different from marketing communications in a number of ways. Marketing communications tend to be commercial and short-term. Few marketers will jeopardise short-term benefits for the sake of long-term returns. Although public relations executives recognise the importance of customer satisfaction and profits, their main concern is the long-term goodwill towards, and reputation of, the company as a whole. They want people to respect their organisation. As a result, marketers will always have to keep PR people focussed on marketing objectives. On the other hand, public relations professionals will have to challenge marketing people in terms of the effects of their actions on a broader public. The role of PR people is to stress the importance of non-marketing audiences for the well-being of the company in the long run.[6] Good public relations lay the groundwork, create the platform for successful marketing communications. The relation between corporate and marketing reputation is illustrated by the fact that most people seem to believe that a company that has a good reputation would not sell bad products, that old-established companies make the best products, and that they would never buy products made by a company they have never heard of.

The privacy issue and two big brands

In March 2003 Benetton and Philips announced that Philips was going to help Benetton embed computer chips in the clothes it sells, enabling individual garments to be tracked, potentially beyond the point of sale. This initiative was announced at a time when the following things also happened:

- The US government confirmed that it was going to mine commercial databases for clues about terrorist organisations;

- The movie *Minority Report* with Tom Cruise featured talking billboards that track wherever you go;

- The US government threatened to block flights to America by European airlines that refuse to give the US government access to passenger lists;

- Surveys indicate that a majority of consumers do not believe commercial companies are handling personal information about their customers in a confidential way.

▶

Within two days a consumer privacy group was calling for an immediate worldwide boycott of Benetton. CASPIAN, Consumers Against Supermarket Privacy Invasion and Numbering, warned the public that Benetton could easily link the serial number in your sweater to credit card information, and that this information would be available to anyone with access to the Benetton database. A number of consumers expressed their concern about the initiative. A website calling for a Benetton boycott and posters featuring messages such as 'I'd rather go naked' quickly appeared. Less than three weeks later Benetton announced that it was 'reconsidering', and no chips were currently present in the garments produced. Philips removed all traces of the press release from its website. Companies should be increasingly aware of the perceptions of the general public, pressure group activities, and the potential damage to the image of the company that occurs as a result of PR initiatives that do not take major concerns of these publics into account.[7]

Although advertising, sales efforts, direct mailing on the one hand, and public relations – more specifically the publicity generated by PR activity – on the other, can both have a similar influence on the reputation of a company and its products, there are a number of important differences between the two types of instruments. As compared to marketing communications, public relations – and the resulting publicity – has a number of strengths and weaknesses. They are summarised in Figures 10.1 and 10.2.

PR targets important stakeholders and difficult-to-reach audiences such as opinion leaders, financial analysts and investors. Many of them are not interested in advertising or direct mailing, and even avoid it, or are very sceptical towards it.[8] Furthermore they are shielded from salespersons by their assistants. On the other hand, they are often interested in news and may be reached indirectly by the media exposure generated through PR activity. PR professionals can advise companies on important trends and on the consequences of corporate activities on marketing effectiveness. PR can present the company as a good citizen and as such contributes to the corporate image and reputation.

PR plays an important role in guiding the company through crises without too much damage to its reputation. Often, advertising and sales promotions are strictly regulated by governments. PR offers the opportunity of more message flexibility. PR is often relatively

Figure 10.1 Strengths of public relations

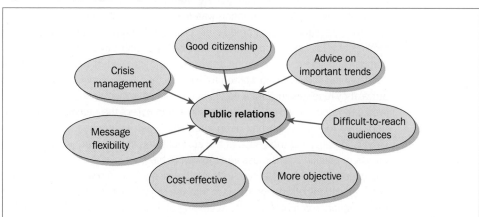

Figure 10.2 Weaknesses of public relations

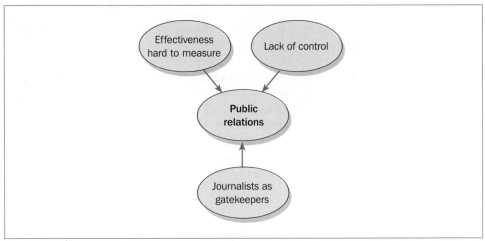

cost-effective because the media coverage generated is free. Getting media coverage often enables the company to reach a variety of audiences and a large number of people at a fraction of the cost that would have been required in an advertising campaign.

The most important advantage of PR and the resulting media exposure over marketing communications tools may be that the former is generally considered to be more objective and therefore more believable in the perception of the target groups. News is also generally more exciting, or is presented as such. Marketing communications, on the other hand, are paid for by the company, and the public are aware of that. This results in a certain cynicism about the bias in the message. As a result, PR is capable of breaking through the communications clutter more effectively.

Hitachi: corporate compassion

Three Japanese Hitachi engineers visiting a subsidiary in the US were killed and two were seriously injured when a truck accidentally drove into the restaurant where they were having dinner. Hitachi US responded quickly, formed a crisis management team and identified a crisis response leader. Information was released to employees and to the media as quickly as possible. The spokesman immediately expressed company concern for the victims and their families and for plant employees. He did not speculate about the causes of the accident. The company president was appropriately visible and involved. It was decided to invite everyone in the Japanese families who wanted to come to the US. According to Japanese tradition, on their arrival they received flowers. A day-long trip was organised to show the group how their relatives lived and where they died. They were allowed to collect the personal possessions of the victims from their rooms, which had been intentionally left untouched. A meeting was held with the lawyers investigating the cause of the accident. Internal communication was quick and overt by means of bulletin board messages, following the principle 'the more you try to hide, the worse things get'. The only false note in this otherwise well-organised and culturally fine-tuned crisis communications effort was the fact that the truck driver did not assume any responsibility for the accident, something that is, according to Japanese culture, incomprehensible.[9]

The major weakness of PR is the lack of control over the content of the press coverage of news releases. Evidently, the media have other priorities and other sources, and the published story may be quite different from the information disseminated by the PR department. The context and style of the original message may be substantially changed or completely lost. In advertising, for instance, the company has full control over the content of its communications. With PR, journalists act as gatekeepers: if a story is perceived as having not enough 'news value' it may not be published, especially in a period in which there is other important news to cover. The timing of ads and sales promotions are fully controlled by the company. The effectiveness of PR is hard to measure. Often, exposure measures, such as the amount of media coverage, are used, but they hardly say anything about the long-term effect of PR efforts on company good-will or sales. Measuring the effectiveness of advertising is often more straightforward.

Public relations is of growing importance for companies. In the US three out of four companies have a PR department. The number of people working in PR is estimated to be 145,000. The growth of the PR industry is estimated to be in double digits.[10] In recent years, the UK PR market has grown by approximately 20% per year.[11] There are a number of trends that make PR an increasingly important communications tool. At the same time PR faces a number of challenges (Figure 10.3).[12]

The maintenance of good employee relations is considered to be increasingly vital. This implies effective communications between management and employees. Corporate branding is of growing importance (see also Chapter 2). PR plays a crucial role in cor-porate communications and, consequently, corporate brand-building. Growing consumer awareness leads to a stronger involvement of the public in the activities of companies, thereby increasing the need for proactive PR activity and crisis management. More and more 'single-issue' publics, such as animal liberation groups and consumer and environmental pressure groups, that use confrontation as a tactic, are emerging, and are seriously challenging the PR skills of companies.[13]

Figure 10.3 Trends and challenges in public relations

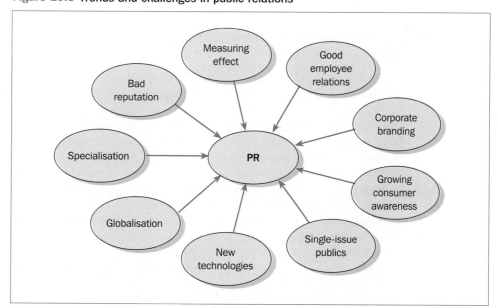

Recent events, such as the opening of Eastern Europe and the former Soviet Union, as well as the globalisation of marketing activities in general, have caused substantial changes in the marketing environment. Public relations is an important tool in gaining understanding of these changes, being aware of the influence of government regulations on marketing activity, and laying the groundwork for effective market entry. PR departments are increasingly confronted with the need to operate globally and draw up international PR campaigns. PR activity becomes increasingly specialised. In the past, PR firms tried to solve all the PR problems of a company. Nowadays there is a growing trend of specialisation and niching in the PR support that companies need and, as a result, in the way in which PR companies or departments have to organise themselves.

PR suffers from a bad reputation stemming from the era in which PR activity was mainly associated with press conferences, manipulating the media and fancy parties for stakeholders. And although PR professionals view their activities as having strategic and corporate impact, many marketers classify PR as little more than a tactical ingredient of the promotional mix.[14] Attracting and keeping high-quality personnel and improving the image of the PR profession have become priorities for PR executives and management in general. Measuring the effect of PR is a difficult task. PR departments will have to upgrade their function into a strategic tool for top management and, consequently, will have to develop the tools to prove their effectiveness in supporting the company's long-term profit base. PR, as with all other forms of marketing communications, will have to adapt to the opportunities and threats, and more generally the environment, created by new technologies such as business television, the internet and smart telephony.

Good public relations is based on a PR plan that contains the same fundamentals as any other communications plan. Target groups or audiences have to be defined, and the objectives and messages to be conveyed have to be determined. Communications channels, tools and instruments have to be put in place, and timing and a budget have to be decided on. The PR plan has to be implemented, and its effectiveness has to be measured. Different types of public relations can be defined. Depending on the type of PR, different target groups, objectives and tools can be distinguished.

International practices and trends in public relations evaluation practice

An on-line survey in September 2004 with 1,040 PR practitioners in 25 countries (mainly North America and the European Union) revealed the following trends. CEOs drive the demand for accurate measurement of PR results. However, most practitioners measure outputs rather than outcomes. When they do measure outcomes, the majority is restricted to media evaluation, internal reviews and benchmarks. Opinion surveying, although not often used, is regarded as the most effective outcome measurement tool. Dashboards and league tables were seen as the least effective. In internal communication, 23% of the respondents claim to work on instinct alone. Employee surveys and focus groups are considered most effective. Only 18% believe that meeting the budget of the PR campaign is a success criterion. The main barriers to measurement (mentioned by at least half of the respondents) are cost, time, lack of expertise and questionable value of results. The vast majority of respondents was interested in measuring the return on investment of PR efforts, though only 13% believed strongly in the possibility of measuring it. More than two-thirds of the respondents expressed the intention of measuring PR practices more in the future.

Source: Gaunt, R. and Wright, D. (2004). PR Measurement, available from: www.benchpoint.com/download.

Target groups, objectives and tasks

As indicated above, publics, audiences or stakeholders are groups of people or organisations to which the company is not directly selling products, but the favourable opinion of whom can be vital for the company in the long run. Depending on the type of audience, different types of public relations can be distinguished. They are summarised in Table 10.1.

The first important distinction that can be made is between corporate and marketing public relations. The main difference between the two is that corporate PR is mainly aimed at maintaining good relations and creating goodwill with all kinds of audiences who may be important for the company in the long run. In marketing PR the direct or indirect profitability of the PR activity is more important. Marketing PR is targeted at commercial stakeholders, such as distributors, suppliers, competitors and potential customers, and can be defined as being more in direct support of marketing communications. Evidently, in an environment of growing integrated communications, both types of PR will not be mutually exclusive, but will support one another.

The second important distinction is between internal and external corporate public relations. Internal PR is aimed at internal stakeholders, such as employees and their families and shareholders. The latter could also be defined as an internal financial audience. External PR – the oldest form of public relations activity – is directed towards various types of external target groups. Three important types of external corporate PR and PR target groups can be distinguished, i.e. public affairs, financial and media PR.

Apart from this typology, sometimes a distinction is made between direct and indirect PR. Direct PR activity is directly aimed at the stakeholders of interest, while indirect PR tries to reach them indirectly through other publics. In that respect, employees, consultants and especially the media can be considered as indirect PR audiences. Keeping good relations with the media, consultants and other opinion leaders is not important as such. It is because of their role as intermediate groups between the company and important 'end-audiences' that they are important PR target groups. It is no coincidence that media PR is the oldest and still a very important form of corporate public relations.

Although employees can be a direct target group of PR activity, they are an important intermediate public too, because they are often in close contact with other audiences such as the general public, the local community, suppliers and distributors, etc.

Table 10.1 Audiences of different types of public relations

Corporate				Marketing
Internal	External			
	Public Affairs	Financial	Media	
Employees	General public	Investors	Television	Suppliers
Families of	Local community	Bankers	Radio	Distributors
employees	Government	Consultants	Press	Competitors
Trade unions	Trade associations	Stock exchange	Trade press	Wholesalers
Shareholders	Pressure groups			Retailers

It is therefore vital that they are 'spreading the good news' about the company. Therefore, internal PR should create goodwill with the employees to motivate them to do so.

Finally, a specific type of PR activity is crisis management or crisis communications. It may involve different types of audiences, corporate and marketing, as well as internal and external. Crisis communications are covered in a separate section of this chapter.

Most public relations objectives relate to giving information, influencing opinion and building or sustaining attitudes and feelings. Only seldomly is PR directly aimed at changing behaviour. Although objectives can be similar across target groups, different emphasis can be put on different types of objectives, depending on the nature of the audience (Table 10.2).

Internal public relations

The main purpose of internal public relations is to inform employees about the company's strategic priorities, the role they are playing in them, and to motivate them to carry out these objectives. Internal communications start with building a corporate identity and motivating and training the company's own personnel to behave accordingly in their contacts with external audiences. This should be a continuous concern, as discussed in the Chapter 1 section on corporate communications. Additionally, employees should be informed about specific marketing actions or major decisions that affect them, to motivate them to accept the decisions and to co-operate in carrying them out. A bank that launches an advertising campaign to stress service quality should convince its own personnel to make the quality of service a priority in its day-to-day contacts with customers. Otherwise the whole advertising campaign may contrast badly with the actual behaviour of the employees, and may, as a result, be completely unbelievable.

Often the families of the personnel are also involved in the decisions taken, or in events that are employee-related. Organising open days and inviting friends and relatives of the personnel, for instance, may create a lot of goodwill and sympathy for the company with its employees.

Table 10.2 Public relations objectives and tasks

Corporate				Marketing
Internal	External			
	Public affairs	Financial	Media	

Information
Training
Motivation
Building corporate
  identity
	Impact of trends
	Public visibility
	Information
	Opinions
	Attitudes
	Corporate image
	Build goodwill
	Influence decisions
		Information
		Credibility
		Trust
			Information
			Opinions
			Corporate
			  image
			Goodwill
				Support marketing
				  agenda
				New products
				Sponsorship
				Events

KBC on-line: involving employees in an advertising campaign promoting on-line banking

KBC is one of the major Belgian banks. In 2000 it decided to launch an advertising campaign to stimulate on-line banking by switching regular customers to KBC-on-line, a service that is free of charge and by which KBC customers can carry out their banking activities electronically. The on-line activation is done during a visit to the bank office. The duration of the campaign was from early 2000 to February 2003. During the first stage of the campaign, awareness and interest was built with the slogan 'Always your banker at hand'. The second stage focussed upon the adoption of the new product: 'Don't be the last one to become a KBC on-liner'. During the last stage, the KBC on-line customer was reassured: 'Everything under control with KBC on-line'.

Especially during the early stages of the campaign, there was the risk that employees would not buy in to the on-line idea. They may have been offended by the fact that they would be replaced by a computer, and they may have feared that, in the long run, their jobs could become redundant. Therefore, KBC involved the employees in the campaign in different ways. In the first stage of the campaign, the focus was on the importance of the availability of the personal banker. In television spots, billboards and print ads, customers are shown in various circumstances, literally holding the hand of what appears to be their personal banker. The message is conveyed that on-line banking enables you to do your banking business wherever and whenever you want, but at the same time it stresses the point that human contact is indispensable. The mailings to customers were sent out from the local branches to increase the link between the bank office and its employees on the one hand, and the customers on the other. Each campaign stage and tool contained an opportunity (both for the employees and the customers) to engage in a personal conversation. All personnel received the campaign material six weeks before the start of the campaign so they could prepare themselves for an efficient personal follow-up to the mail. The campaign took into account the potential negative fallout of advertising campaigns on the motivation of the employees, and tried to integrate internal PR and external communication to avoid negative side effects. The campaign was a considerable success and won a Belgian Gold Effie Award in 2003.[15]

Public affairs

Public affairs is a management function directed towards the societal and political relations of the company. It is aimed at continuously studying trends and issues related to government decision-making and opinions and attitudes of the general public. Good contacts with the general public and the local community are a part of the public affairs activity. The handling of the sinking of the Brent Spar oil platform and the *Exxon Valdez* disaster are examples of events that required consistent PR activity to restore faith and goodwill with the general public or local communities. The support of good causes by a company are all aimed at restoring or maintaining goodwill with the general public. Public affairs also encompasses the relations with local, regional, national and international governments and regulatory bodies, as well as pressure groups of all kinds, such as ecological, ethnic, linguistic and consumer interest groups. It attempts to influence the decision-making of important stakeholders, or to respond to trends and changes in opinions and attitudes in such a way that the long-term goodwill of the company benefits from it. For instance, the World Federation of Advertisers (WFA) is an international lobbying group that tries to influence government regulations on promotional activity, and tries to monitor and/or counter the influence of pressure groups on behalf of the world advertising community.

Financial public relations

Financial audiences are those groups that are potential shareholders, investors or (potential) advisers to shareholders and investors, such as financial consultants and banks. They are vital for the establishment of the long-term money-raising potential of a company. A crucial objective towards these audiences is to build and maintain the confidence that is necessary to give the company an image of an interesting investment. The preparation and presentation of a sound financial report, the stock exchange introduction of a company, financial communications accompanying mergers and acquisitions are all examples of financial PR. The European cinema group Kinepolis, for instance, was able to attract massive numbers of new shareholders as a result of a successful introduction of the company's shares on the stock exchange.

Approaches to investor relations in the UK

An exploratory empirical investigation into the extent to which 18 British companies communicate with investor audiences, and who is responsible for these relations – the communications department or the investor relations department – concluded that the relationship with investors has become an important corporate communication task and plays a core role in the strategy of the corporation itself. All those interviewed confirmed that they were concerned with communicating with investor audiences. Half of them identified the institutional investor audience as very important, and 13 respondents identified shareholders as a key audience. Fifteen respondents indicated that investor relations had increased in importance over the last 10 years. Seven executives had established a separate investor relations department within the corporate communications division, two had arranged for investor relations to be handled by the corporate finance division, and two had the legal department handle investor relations. In the remaining seven companies, the communication executive handled investor relations. Fourteen respondents handed the task of communicating with investors to professional communication people. In general, the CEO and the financial director were not primarily involved in the communication function. Again 14 respondents use external consultants to assist them in their communications with investor audiences, half of which employed external consultants to handle all their communications with these publics. Most of them agreed that, especially in the relations with financial stakeholders, external consultants have a significant added value.[16]

Media public relations

Since the media are the most important intermediate public, developing and maintaining good contacts with radio, television and the (trade) press is often extremely important. All the objectives to be met by end publics are also important in media PR: to inform, build favourable attitudes, create a positive image and a reservoir of goodwill, and to ensure coverage of marketing-related news. Indirectly, media PR is aimed at generating favourable publicity about the company, its products and brands, and more generally all events and projects that support the image of the company and its marketing objectives.

Good media PR can result in positive comments during the introduction of a product, can create goodwill for the company's activities and can generate publicity for a range of organisational events, activities and sponsorship programmes. In the aftermath of the Class A moose test problems, Mercedes was able to neutralise the bad publicity quickly by means of careful PR campaigns directed at the specialised press. Obtaining media attention for sponsorship projects can generate publicity that is, in terms of media exposure, worth much more than the initial investment in the event. In times of crisis, the media are a crucial audience in order to avoid or neutralise negative 'fallout' from the event that caused the crisis. Bad handling of media relations caused the Perrier problem (benzene in Perrier mineral water) to evolve into a major wave of bad publicity that resulted in enormous image and commercial damage to the brand and the company.

Ariel and the Palestinians

'We cannot tolerate that, without our permission, political messages are linked with one of our products' was the official reaction of Procter & Gamble to a campaign run by the Palestine Action Platform. This pressure group launched a print advertising campaign in which a fist holds a bloodstained Palestinian shawl, accompanied by the slogan: 'How will Ariel get this clean?' The purpose of the campaign was to make the public aware of the Palestinian problem and the alleged role of the Israeli Prime Minister, Ariel Sharon, using Procter & Gamble's well-known brand of washing powder. The campaign appeared in national newspapers, and Procter & Gamble first sent friendly letters to the organisation and to the media, asking them to stop the campaign immediately. The action group was not impressed, and continued its campaign: 'It is obvious that only Mr Sharon is implied, not P&G'. Procter & Gamble then threatened to start legal action if the campaign was not stopped. The company stated that 'we as a company do not want to take a stand on the political situation in the Middle East. Therefore we do not tolerate that our brand name, for which we are responsible, is used in this manner.' By that time all major media had covered the dispute.[17] Eventually, the campaign was withdrawn. Sometimes companies are confronted with unexpected publicity that can damage their reputation or that of their brands. Fast and well-balanced PR activity is then called for.

Marketing public relations

Marketing PR is directly related to selling products and/or supporting brands. As such it is a part of marketing communications for which often product or brand managers are responsible. Marketing PR can be used to support the launch of a new product, for instance by inviting the trade press to test-drive a new car, or to see to it that a new CD gets enough 'airplay'. It can also be used to support and revive existing products, for instance by means of creating an event when the 50th shop is opened, or after the first 100,000 cars of a certain model have been sold. Sponsorship and special events can be used as PR tools to improve the relationship with suppliers and distributors, by offering free tickets for sports or arts events. Restaurants may invite journalists from the specialised press to encourage them to write a positive article, and as a result boost sales. All these examples illustrate that marketing PR is an activity that is largely integrated with both corporate PR and other tools of the communications mix.

Depending on the problem and the objective, publics will have to be divided into primary and secondary audiences. Public relations efforts will be more intense towards primary target groups. Launching a new product, for instance, will generally imply more efforts towards the marketing PR target groups, the media, and the general public than towards financial audiences or the government. Furthermore, an individual can belong to more than one public at a time. As a result, consistent PR communications across audiences is vital to avoid conveying contradictory messages to the same members of different publics.

Sales and marketing PR

The sales team can be motivated to feed the PR department with interesting stories that can be a starting point for marketing-derived and marketing supporting PR activity. The following sales events can be considered:[18]

- *Prestige orders.* These can be orders from famous companies or contracts relating to special projects that are themselves in the news;
- *Problem-solving orders.* Sales of products that have provided the solution for a particularly demanding need;
- *Added value contracts.* The product has made the life of customers and employees more agreeable;
- *Unusual orders.* Products used at famous locations or in places of interest;
- *Sympathetic associations.* Selling products in a situation of strong human interest appeal or related to a good cause of general interest.

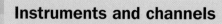

Instruments and channels

Public relations professionals use a multitude of instruments and channels to reach their objectives. The instruments used may be similar for different target groups and objectives, but some of them are specifically suited for specific target groups and objectives. In Table 10.3 a number of instruments and channels are summarised.

Internal public relations

A special category of PR tools and techniques are the ones used in internal PR. Internal PR should ideally be a two-way communications activity, in which mainly 'oral' communications techniques will be used. But other tools are of increasing importance.[19]

Personal and oral communications

Structured consultation is a crucial factor in internal PR. To count on a spontaneous and proactive attitude on the part of employees to enter a manager's office (even if the door is permanently open and the atmosphere is inviting) is insufficient. Two-way

Table 10.3 Public relations instruments and channels

Corporate				Marketing
Internal	External			
	Public affairs	Financial	Media	
Consultation	Corporate	Corporate	Press kit	Product
Open-door policies	advertising	advertising	Press release	placement
Internal presentations	Annual report	Annual report	Press	Product events
Training programmes	Corporate	Meetings	conference	Sponsorship
Team projects	events	Newsletters	Interviews	Meetings
Team meetings	Sponsorship		Video or	Newsletters
Social activities	Lobbying		radio news	
Direct mailing	Meetings		release	
Bulletin boards	Newsletters			
Newsletters or video	Flyers,			
Company television	brochures			
Annual reports				
Idea (suggestion)				
boxes				
Surveys				
House style material				

communication between managers and employees, and communication amongst employees should be properly organised. By means of internal presentations managers can clarify new strategic directions or important organisational changes and the role that employees play in effectuating them. Besides an obvious didactical purpose, training programmes (internally or externally) can enhance internal communications amongst employees because they provide the structured setting and the opportunity to communicate issues that are otherwise neglected. The same goes for team meetings, projects and social activities. An example of the latter are team-building activities, such as go-karting, paintball, exotic trips or survival weekends.

Communications through media

Direct mailing or internal e-mail can be an effective tool of internal communications. Bulletin boards, on the other hand, are not so effective. They are hardly noticed and people tend to walk past them without looking up. In-house newsletters are a frequently used tool and allow the diffusion of information of a less urgent nature. Company television narrowcast through television sets at places in the company that are frequented by a lot of people (restaurants, halls, etc.) are excellent means of rapid diffusion of essential information. Annual reports, both financial and social, can be distributed to all personnel. Pens, noteblocks, coffee cups, placemats, mousepads, etc. can support the logos or slogans of a major internal communications campaign.

Public affairs

The purpose of corporate advertising is to reinforce the attitudes towards the company and/or its products. This type of advertising is often mainly affective, and is seldom used to convey information or to elicit sales. It is mainly targeted at the general public or broad audiences. It is a PR tool that is often used to reinforce the corporate image. Companies also use different types of publications to inform publics and/or build a favourable image with target audiences: newsletters, flyers, brochures and annual reports. Corporate events sponsorship is used to enhance the corporate image. The latter technique is discussed in Chapter 11.

Lobbying is a word that is used to describe the activities that companies undertake to influence decisions of government bodies or the opinion of pressure groups in a positive direction. Lobbying implies giving information, negotiating, influencing complex decision-making units, and getting the best out of it for the company. Often, lobbying is done by specialised companies. It is an increasingly important business, in which a growing number of lobbyists are employed.

Agenda-setting as a PR tool

Most of what consumers and stakeholders know about companies and issues that surround them comes from the news media. There has been a tremendous growth in the volume of business news that appears in the media. The selection by journalists of the issues to cover or not to cover significantly influences the opinions and perceptions of the public. The specific ability to influence the salience of topics, attributes of these topics, and images among the public by making them salient in the media is called agenda-setting. Agenda-setting theory and research leads to the following 'rules'.[20]

- The amount of news about a company that appears in the news media is positively related to the public's awareness of the company;

- The amount of news coverage devoted to particular attributes of a company is positively related to the proportion of the public that defines the firm by those attributes: if a company mainly receives press coverage about its products, it will primarily be known through its products;

- The more positive (negative) that media coverage is for a particular attribute, the more positively (negatively) members of the public will perceive that attribute;

- The agenda of substantive and affective attributes associated with a company in business news coverage primes the public's attitude and opinion about the company: if the news coverage is positive (negative) about an important characteristic of the company or its activities, the whole company will benefit (suffer) from it;

- Organised efforts to communicate a corporate agenda will result in a significant degree of correspondence between the attribute agenda of the company and the news media.

The last point is particularly important for media public relations. Media PR can indeed make a difference. Company news releases are estimated to influence as much as between 25% and 80% of news content. A substantial number (some say more than 50%) of the news stories in newspapers are substantially based on press releases. One study found that among the entire population of Fortune 500 companies, those with substantial press rooms on the web were ranked much higher on the Fortune list.[21] It is also worth noting that a news story in the general news section of a newspaper is often more friendly and positive than a similar story in the business section. News media have a fascination with celebrities and elites: 45% of a company's reputation can be attributed to the CEO. Consequently, PR activity aiming at news coverage devoted to the company should be separated from PR campaigns focussing upon the CEO.

Financial public relations

Meetings, newsletters and corporate advertising can also be directed towards financial publics. But even more important will be annual and financial reports giving bankers and potential investors the necessary information on the basis of which a sound financial reputation can be developed.

Media public relations

The purpose of media PR is to generate publicity and in that way reach other important audiences. Publicity results from the fact that the media cover events that have some news value, or write articles on issues that are company-related. Unless something special happens – normally unexpected and not so positive for the company – the media are not going to write or report positive news about the company. Usually, professional PR activity is necessary to draw the attention of the media.

The instruments of media PR are press kits and press releases, and their audiovisual counterparts Video News Releases (VNR) and Radio News Releases (RNR). A press kit is a set of documentation, containing photos, reports and a press release, which are sent to journalists or presented at a press conference. A press release is a document that contains the material that the company would like to see covered in the press. VNRs and RNRs are audiovisual news releases put on video or audio tape and sent to the TV or radio stations free of charge for unrestricted use.[22] They are composed in such a way that excerpts can be broadcast immediately, thereby assuring that the message reaches the audience undistorted. Many checklists have been proposed on how to write and present a good press release or a good newspaper article in general. The essentials are summarised in Table 10.4.

Table 10.4 Writing a news release

- Indicate the release date
- Answer the following questions in every news story: who, what, why, where and when
- Focus and clarity: know what you want to say
- The lead paragraph: structure your story – get the main news points in the first paragraph
- News story body: flesh out the details – use short paragraphs with only one point per paragraph
- Journalistic style: use short sentences and active verbs
- Imitation: follow the style and construction of existing articles
- Completeness: document all the facts and quote from reliable sources
- Editorialising: do not give your opinion
- Names: use proper style for spelling out names
- Include illustrative materials
- Closing: add a final paragraph
- Editing: review your copy twice, then review it again
- Accuracy and simplicity: strive for a perfect news release
- Contact details: give details of the person who can be contacted

Based on: Smith, J. (1995), *The New Publicity Kit*. New York: John Wiley & Sons; Pickton, D. and Broderick, A. (2001), *Integrated Marketing Communications*. Harlow: Financial Times Prentice Hall; Duncan, T. (2002), *IMC. Using Advertising and Promotion to Build Brands*. Boston: McGraw-Hill.

Table 10.5 Rules of good media relations

- Learn about what a medium considers newsworthy
- Make sure the story is accurate
- Only timely stories or those on the latest developments are news – old facts are of no use
- The facts or news of an event should be perceived as important by the readers of the medium
- Everything that deviates from the ordinary is potential news – everyday events are not news
- Facts endorsed by an authority (CEO or marketing manager) are perceived as more important than facts presented by a junior employee
- Human interest is important: to whom does it happen; who is involved; how important are they; is the story fun and/or emotionally engaging and does it strike a chord?
- Tension or drama created by conflicting points of view attract media attention
- Include the name and phone number of a contact person who can answer questions
- Do not expect a medium to copy your release as presented – it will be checked with other sources and modified

Based on: Burnett, J. and Moriarty, S. (1998), *Introduction to Marketing Communication.* Upper Saddle River, NJ: Prentice Hall; Duncan, T. (2002), *IMC. Using Advertising and Promotion to Build Brands.* Boston: McGraw-Hill.

By means of press conferences and interviews the company can comment on the issues that it considers important and try to present them as 'news'. However, in this over-informed society, not a lot of things are 'news'. Companies should avoid falling into the 'marketing myopia' trap as concerns the news value of 'important' company events. What is news to a certain medium depends on the characteristics of the message and the medium itself, and on the way the news is presented. In Table 10.5 some rules of good media relations are listed.

Marketing public relations

Product event sponsorship, i.e. sponsoring an activity in which the product plays a major role (for instance the Camel Trophy), is discussed in Chapter 11. Newsletters distributed to retailers, suppliers and other business contacts can be important instruments of public relations, complementing and reinforcing salespersons' efforts and sales promotion activity. Placing products in television shows or movies is an increasingly popular type of communication that is at the crossroads of PR and sponsorship.

Budgets

Public relations should be operating within the same discipline that applies to other business functions. This implies that a budget has to be fixed, and that measurable objectives should be defined. Different budgeting techniques can be applied (Table 10.6).[23]

Table 10.6 Public relations budgeting techniques

- Historical comparison
- Resources costing
- Action costing
- Competitive tendering
- Income proportion
- Industry comparison
- Capitation rating

Budgets may be based on historical comparison, i.e. on what has been spent in previous periods, possibly adjusted as a function of changed circumstances. New product launches may result in increased budgets; less competition may imply lower budgets. Overall, this method seldom leads to sound budgeting. Maybe the historical starting figure was inappropriate, or the company is doing so well that the PR budget can easily be reduced. Most importantly, there is a lack of strategic focus: by not taking into account the changing environment, great PR opportunities or dangerous threats calling for PR action may be overlooked. In the resources costing method management decides what resources are needed (an extra press officer, or an event co-ordinator) and calculates the costs implied. This method suffers from similar weaknesses to the previous one, although PR needs are to a certain extent taken into account.

In action costing a PR programme or activity is planned, and the cost to carry it out is calculated. This method has the virtue of starting from the task to be accomplished, but lacks long-term perspective. The competitive tendering method is very similar to the previous one. A PR programme is decided on and different PR agencies are requested to file a proposal and a budget. In the income proportion method a pre-specified proportion of margin or sales is devoted to PR. This method suffers from the same weakness as the historical comparison method. There is a lack of strategic focus, and the PR budget grows with sales – generally a situation in which less PR activity is needed. On the contrary, if there is a decline in sales, PR budgets decrease at a time during which they may be needed most. In industry comparison the industry average is used as a benchmark to decide the PR budget. Again, there is a lack of strategic focus, and no link with a pre-specified task.

In the capitation rating or achievement targeting method, audiences to be reached and objectives to be achieved are defined. For instance, a 30% awareness and a 70% favourable attitude with the general public and financial stakeholders by the end of the year may be the goals. Experience with other communications tools, such as advertising and direct mailing, may be used to calculate the budget required to achieve these objectives. This method is probably one of the most useful. However, as for all marketing communications activities, public relations is not an exact science, and the objectives to be achieved are often long-term oriented. Therefore it is difficult to set a PR budget. However, PR agencies increasingly face situations in which they are paid by results rather than on a mark-up basis.[24]

Measuring public relations results

Similar to most other communications instruments, the effectiveness of a public relations campaign can only be measured if clear objectives have been defined. These objectives have to be measurable and related to the PR activity. This implies that short-term or long-term awareness, opinion and/or attitude or goodwill changes will have to be measured with the targeted publics. Evolution of sales or market share is seldomly a good indicator, since they are not the main target objectives of PR activity. Furthermore, they are to a large extent influenced by other instruments of the marketing and communications mix. The result of public relations activity can be assessed by means of three categories of performance measures: input, output and achievement indicators:[25]

■ *Input indicators* measure PR efforts, such as the number of news stories disseminated, the number of interviews given, trade meetings organised, supermarkets visited or brochures sent. Input indicators measure efforts and not results. Therefore they are largely insufficient as measures of PR effectiveness. Nevertheless, they can be useful, since they can give a first indication of the activity undertaken.

■ *Output indicators* measure the result of the PR activity in terms of media coverage or publicity. Examples of such measures are the press space or television time devoted to the company, its events or brands, the length of the stories, the tone and news value of the headlines, readership/viewership levels, opportunity to see, tone of coverage, etc. Again, although output measures may be useful indicators of the result of PR activity, they do not give any information on how well the real objectives have been achieved.

■ *Achievement indicators* measure the extent to which a pre-specified objective has been met with a public of interest. They are very similar to some of the measures that are being used in the assessment of advertising effectiveness. Examples include: the share of the target audience that has been reached, changes in awareness and knowledge, changes in opinions and attitudes, evolution of the image and goodwill of the company, and the extent to which behaviour has changed.

Public relations and evaluation: does reality match the rhetoric?

It is good communications practice to set objectives and to measure the results, i.e. evaluate the effectiveness of the campaign. In a British study, 25 PR award-winning cases were studied. In total 102 different evaluations were made. In Chart 1 they are presented per type of measurement. Only a minority of the evaluations (12) used researched audience impact; almost half (44) of the evaluations are output measurements. Another third of the evaluations (29) is measured as a specific programme-linked result.

The 25 cases had a total of 73 identifiable objectives. In Chart 2 these objectives are listed, and compared with the reported evaluations. The campaigns that have single, clear objectives, involving no third party mediation (fundraising, lobbying, endorsement), are apparently easier to measure. On the other hand, awareness and sales objectives are not measured that frequently. There are more measurements of media and message placements, as there were objectives. This is probably due to the fact that awareness-building objectives are indirectly evaluated through the appearance of the product/company in the media.[26]

▶

Chart 1 Categories and occurrences of PR campaign evaluation

	Number of occurences
Researched impact	
Awareness	4
Attitude/opinion	3
Behaviour	5
Achieved specific programme effects	
Fundraising/sponsorship	6
Lobbying result	7
Government requesting input	3
Endorsement	4
Sales	8
Internal change	1
Output	
Media coverage	17
Use of message	11
Media reach	5
Media demand	11
Out-take	
Attendance/participation in PR events	5
Proactive demand from target publics	2
Website hits	1
Process	
Cost-effectiveness	3
Increased budget or expansion of programme	2
Awards	2
Crisis containment	2

Chart 2 Comparison of objectives and results measured

Objective	*Number of objectives*	*Number of objective-related and reported successes*
Corporate awareness	8	4
Product/service awareness	13	5
Market positioning	4	0
Sales promotion	8	8
Fundraising/sponsorship	5	6
Lobbying	6	7
Endorsement	5	4
Educational	3	3
Internal change	2	1
Media placement	9	17
Message placement	8	11
Crisis containment	2	2

Communications in times of crisis

A special type of circumstances in which public relations play an extremely important role is when the company faces an unforeseen crisis. By nature, a crisis is an event or a series of events that cannot be planned in advance. Crises can have multiple causes. A company's product may be found to contain toxic material, as in the Perrier case, a sinking ship like the *Exxon Valdez* may pollute the environment, a new car model like the Mercedes A may fail to pass the moose test, or a company executive may get involved in a personal or a financial scandal. Whether a crisis is a 'Cobra' (a sudden disaster) or a 'Python' (a slow-burning crisis or crisis creep),[27] good PR strategy should always take the possibility of a crisis into account and be prepared for it. A set of rules and procedures should be put in place well before any crisis emerges, as a result of which at least a scenario of crisis management is in place in the event of a suddenly emerging problem. Crises often turn into nightmares as a result of the lack of well-established procedures, which often have to do with the handling of the external and internal communication. Crises are expected to take place more frequently than before. All kinds of audiences, like consumer interest groups and the media, watch companies more closely, and modern communications technology results in a more rapid dissemination of the news on company incidents. Therefore, preparing for crisis management is an increasingly important task for PR professionals.

An important factor in crisis management is the way in which a company behaves and communicates *in tempore non suspecto*, i.e. in the pre-crisis period. The most important is to create a reservoir of goodwill. Some rules of conduct can be mentioned (Table 10.7).[28]

To know is to like. There is a strong correlation between knowing a company and liking it. Building awareness can be done most effectively by means of intensive communications with all important target groups. Target groups are not enemies or nuisances, but people the company may need the support of when things go wrong. Therefore, when these people have a problem or need assistance, a helping hand will not be forgotten when the company needs them. Telephone calls and letters should be responded to promptly so that audiences know that they are important to the company. Do not expect people with whom you have not communicated for a long period to remember you and offer help during a crisis.

The company should not pretend that problems do not exist. It has to show confidence and knowledge, but also humility. People with complaints may be disregarded,

Table 10.7 Pre-crisis communications rules

■ Communicate
■ Keep in touch and be responsive
■ Do not act as if problems do not exist
■ Build trust by communicating
■ Build brand equity
■ Build scenarios for the unexpected

Based on: Marconi, J. (1992), *Crisis Marketing. When Bad Things Happen to Good Companies*. Chicago, IL: Probus Publishing Company.

but the complaints will not go away and will rebound on the company in times of crisis. In many cases people have only limited contact with the company, often if they have a problem or a complaint. The way in which the company responds to their problem will largely determine the way they feel about the company. Trust has to be built by communicating, being honest and being a good corporate citizen. Image-building is a long-term and sometimes expensive process, the return on which becomes visible only when the reservoir of goodwill is needed to compensate for the negative image caused by a crisis. Building brand equity is important. A positive corporate image can often be established most effectively through well-known and highly valued brands.

Finally, a company has to learn to prepare and build scenarios for the unexpected. Although many crises cannot be predicted, the likelihood of some of them can be taken into account. If you operate oil tankers, one of them may sink, causing great damage to the environment; if you operate a steel mill, a serious accident may occur; if you manufacture drugs, people may die as a result of a human error in manufacturing, as in the B Braun incident in which two babies died as a result of a lethal confusion of ingredients and labels. In the pre-crisis or scanning phase, the company should make contingency plans. In a broader context, an 'issues audit' should be carried out. Issues are those potential areas that could have an important impact upon the operations of the company. The aim of an issues audit is to identify all that might be of consequence and help the company react to it and to plan ahead.[29] In general, a crisis can be prepared for by building contingency crisis management plans. In Table 10.8, a checklist for preparing for a crisis is presented.

In spite of all the preparations and the investment in goodwill, a crisis may occur and damage the company's image overnight as a result of mishandling the crisis. Often this counterproductive approach has to do with the way in which the communication is organised – or, more often, not organised – during the impact of the crisis.

Table 10.8 Preparing for and handling a crisis

- Prepare a list of issues, and their potential impact, to be circulated – which crises can occur?
- Identify areas of concern and of opportunity
- Monitor potential legislation that could affect markets
- Establish which publics should be taken into account
- Identify the executive responsible for leading on each issue
- Set up a crisis management team in advance
- Is the crisis management team well trained?
- Incident facilities are needed at all company locations
- Use simulations to test procedures – fine-tune all policies and procedures in 'peacetime'
- Establish a well-equipped crisis communications centre
- Develop and train your company spokespeople
- Develop policies that clarify how decisions will be made
- Provide each member of the crisis communications team with detailed background data on the company

Based on: Haywood, R. (1998), *Public Relations for Marketing Professionals*. London: Macmillan Business; Seymour, M. and Moore, S. (2000), *Effective Crisis Management: Worldwide Principles and Practices*. London and New York: Cassell; Anthonissen, P. (2002), *Murphy Was an Optimist*. Tielt: Lannoo.

During a crisis, the following rules have to be implemented:[30]

- *Designate a single spokesperson.* Often, the damage is done during the first hours and days of a crisis when all kinds of company executives give their – often contradictory – assessment of the facts. Every employee that comments speaks for the company.

- *Tell your story first and be honest.* It is much more difficult to neutralise rumours or to defend yourself against allegations, than to give a clear overview of the facts first. Furthermore, it is counterproductive to lie, since pressure groups or the media will find out sooner or later, with even more consequent harm to the company's image.

- *Never go 'off the record'.* There should only be one story which is the same for everybody. Act as if all questions and answers will be made public.

- *Keep your employees informed,* to avoid rumours that take on a life of their own and that are fed by the employees' speculations. Communicate internally and externally, in parallel.

- *Position your company* or products in a larger context, stressing the positive elements, to divert the attention from the element that caused the crisis.

- *Details*: give as much information about the incident as possible.

- *Compassion*: show understanding and regret, and make apologies.

- *Reassurance*: everything is under control, there is no further danger.

- *What are we doing about it*? Present in-depth research by an independent organisation.

Mitsubishi: using confrontational PR in support of legal battles

In April 1996 the US Equal Employment Opportunity Commission (EEOC) filed a lawsuit on behalf of 700 female employees at a plant of the Mitsubishi Motor Manufacturing Company (MMMC) in the city of Normal, Illinois. A further 29 women filed a private suit. Allegations were made about sexist remarks and molestation. The vice-president of MMMC set the tone in a first interview: 'We are surprised and horrified by the manner this is brought to the public's attention, and the public spectacle that has been made of these claims'. MMMC accused the Clinton administration of playing politics. The company also urged workers to call Washington and protest, and began to collect personal information on the 29 employees that had filed the private suit. In Normal, local businesses and politicians shunned the women, which to outsiders looked like support for MMMC through fear of losing trade and jobs. MMMC also organised a mass protest outside the offices of the EEOC in Chicago. Half of the employees were given a 'day off' and brought to Chicago, together with local dignitaries.

MMMC's efforts backfired. Its action was seen by the media as a staged attempt to intimidate the EEOC, television comedians made fun of the action and congresswomen condemned it. The National Organisation for Women started a boycott against Mitsubishi dealers, and started to influence other stakeholder groups, such as shareholders and investors. The media expanded the problem to corporate Japan, and started to report on abuses of female personnel in Japanese companies. Mitsubishi was forced to change its strategy. A number of top executives stepped down. The media reported that MMMC wanted to end its campaign again the EEOC, and that it wanted to settle the case as soon as possible. The company also invited representatives of the EEOC and members of congress to review its workplace policies. The Mitsubishi crisis is an example of a crisis that got out of control as a result of a lack of empathy, compassion and willingness to do something about the problem.[31]

After the crisis, the company enters the readjustment phase and has to rebuild a new reservoir of goodwill, based on the same principles discussed before.

Integrating public relations in IMC

Public relations is most frequently used to support the corporate image. However, marketing communications can also be reinforced by PR efforts, and PR efforts can build upon other marketing communications campaigns. Publicity can be generated following of sales efforts and successes: winning an important account, selling to well-known non-profit organisations or establishing links with famous organisations or events. Sponsorship efforts can be combined with public relations and advertising to build powerful events that generate a lot of publicity. Sponsored celebrities can be used for corporate hospitality, reinforcing sales efforts, corporate identity and image building, and in advertising. Public relations activities such as annual meetings, events and points of view can be announced through mass media advertising. Exhibitions and trade fairs can be used to hold press conferences, announcing new products, company news, etc., and to organise corporate hospitality events. Opening a new store or changing store appeal and image can be a starting point for organising events and generating publicity. In general, public relations can reinforce the awareness and the corporate reputation effect of many marketing and communication activities with a variety of stakeholders.

Summary

Public relations is the management of reputation. It is about building and maintaining long-term goodwill vis-à-vis a large variety of audiences and stakeholders. Depending on the nature of these stakeholders, different types of public relations can be distinguished. Marketing PR is directed towards marketing audiences and mainly supports marketing communications objectives. Corporate PR, such as public affairs, financial and media PR, supports corporate image and corporate reputation. A special type of PR activity is internal PR by means of which employees and shareholders are informed and/or motivated to co-operate in achieving the goals of the marketing and corporate communications plans. A broad variety of tools and media are being used in PR, ranging from personal and oral communications in internal PR, to press releases, corporate advertising, direct mailing and annual reports in corporate PR. A specific task of PR is communicating in times of crisis. Building goodwill by means of pre-crisis PR is essential to limit the fallout of a crisis situation, although PR activity during the crisis is equally important.

Review questions

1 What is the role of public relations in the communications mix, and what are its strengths and weaknesses?
2 What are the trends that influence public relations?
3 Who are the target groups of public relations?
4 What are the objectives of each type of PR activity?
5 What are the tools of internal communications?

6 What are the rules and techniques of good media public relations?

7 Compare the different PR budgeting techniques and their advantages and disadvantages.

8 How can the effectiveness of PR campaigns be assessed?

9 What are the basic rules of good crisis communications?

Further reading

Tench, R. and Yeomors, L. (2006), *Exploring Public Relations*, Harlow, Essex: Pearson Education.

Baines, P., Egan, J. and Jefkins, F. (2003), *Public Relations: Contemporary Issues and Techniques*. Butterworth-Heinemann.

Desanto, B. and Moss, D. (2001), *Public Relations: A Managerial Perspective*. Gower Publishing Co.

Haywood, R. (1998), *Public Relations for Marketing Professionals*. London: Macmillan Business.

Public Relations Review. www.jaipress.com

Ruff, P. and Stittle, J. (2003), *Managing Communications in a Crisis*. Gower Publishing Co.

Schenbler, I. and Herrling, T. (2003), *Guide to Media Relations*. Prentice Hall.

Seymour, M. and Moore, S. (2000), *Effective Crisis Management: Worldwide Principles and Practices*. London and New York: Cassell.

Case 10

SUEZ: Liquefied Natural Gas in New England

The Liquefied Natural Gas (LNG) industry was developed to link gas reserves in places like Indonesia, Algeria, Equatorial Guinea, Norway, Trinidad and Venezuela, with regions in need of natural gas. Japan and Korea, for example, import LNG to fulfill almost all their natural gas needs. Also, about half of Spain's natural gas needs are met by LNG import. Like many other countries, the US also satisfies part of its gas needs by using LNG. One of the top LNG importers to the US is SUEZ (by means of its subsidiary SUEZ LNG NA/Distrigas). This case focuses on SUEZ and the PR activities it engages in to enhance its ability to sell Liquefied Natural Gas in Massachusetts.

Company background

SUEZ is an international industrial and services group which is active in sustainable solutions in the management of electricity, gas, energy services, water and waste management. It is the 5th power producer and 6th gas operator in Europe, and the 10th power

producer worldwide. In energy services, SUEZ holds the first place across Europe. SUEZ employs approximately 160,000 people worldwide and earns about €41.5 billion in revenues.

SUEZ LNG NA is the business unit of SUEZ Energy North America which manages the company's LNG activities in North America. Its Everett Terminal in New England, the first LNG import terminal of the US, started to operate in 1971. The Everett Terminal currently provides about 20% of New England's natural gas needs, and LNG facilities as a whole are able to meet 35–40% of the region's natural gas demand on peak days. SUEZ' role in the power production of New England is also critical. The Everett Terminal has connections into two interstate pipeline systems and into a local distribution company's system. Through these connections, it serves nearly all of the gas utilities in the region and key power producers, including a power plant which can generate enough electricity for about 1.5 million homes each year in Greater Boston. Since New

England lacks underground natural gas storage, the terminal supplies LNG via truck to a network of local, customer-owned LNG storage tanks. SUEZ has about 40 customers who receive natural gas in vapor or liquid form, or a combination of the two.

What is Liquefied Natural Gas?

LNG is the same natural gas used by millions of people for heating and cooking, but in a different form. When natural gas is cooled to −260 degrees Fahrenheit, it liquefies and reduces to 1/600th of its original volume. This allows LNG to be transported and stored efficiently and economically. Moreover, LNG is neither explosive, corrosive, carcinogenic, nor toxic. It does not pollute land or water resources. LNG is not transported or stored under pressure, and natural gas vapours do not catch fire as easily as those of other fuels. All the foregoing makes LNG as safe, or even safer, to transport and store than most other fuels. To vaporise LNG, SUEZ and other LNG import terminal operators, in essence, run LNG through piping in hot water, and then use equipment to inject the natural gas into a connecting pipeline distribution system at the appropriate pressure.

SUEZ' vision on PR

PR has always been very important for SUEZ. In the beginning, when they entered the US market, they had to build trust in both the company and LNG. But even now, after more than 30 years of operations, PR is still considered business-critical. SUEZ cherishes 'local commitment and global vision'. Its business interests span much of the world, but SUEZ is eager not just to maintain but strengthen its presence everywhere it operates. To this end, SUEZ focuses largely on personal communication since it believes that much of its success is built on the strength of its relationships. Therefore, SUEZ considers it critical that its communication lines are open, active and personal. Its CEO, Senior Vice President of Operations, Vice President of Shipping, Director of Communications, etc. have to be familiar with, and interact with, the appropriate stakeholders. By engaging with these stakeholders, SUEZ hopes to ensure that its current business and prospects are strong in the months and years to come. The company tries to solidify its position as a credible and important player in the LNG market in North America, and hopes this reflects well on the subsidiary as well as the parent company. Having such solid relationships is indeed a necessity: if SUEZ is not considered as a credible partner in the eyes of its different stakeholders, this poses a substantial risk to their current and future business. Case Figure 10.1 gives an overview of the most important stakeholders SUEZ takes into account.

Government relations

SUEZ has built relationships with a variety of government officials at the federal, state and local level. Case Table 10.1 provides an overview of key governmental stakeholders.

SUEZ' major goal is to keep the policy-makers and elected officials informed about

1 the need for LNG in New England and the critical role of the Everett Terminal (20% of the natural gas demand)

Case Figure 10.1 Stakeholder groups of SUEZ

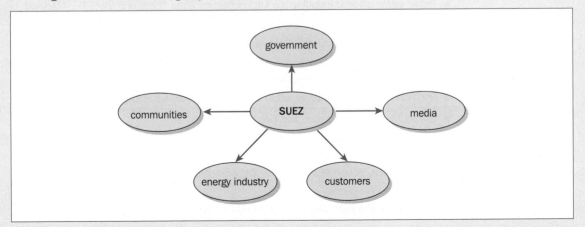

2 LNG's advantages as compared to other fuels (see above)

3 the safety and security records of SUEZ and the LNG industry.

Since the Everett Terminal is the only LNG import terminal that is located in an urban area in the US (although there are several LNG storage facilities in urban areas), the latter is extremely important. The company wants to make sure that everyone realises how LNG can be handled safely and, in particular how SUEZ has done so over the years. To this end, the company provides its own safety records and compares them to other alternatives. For example, there has never been a recorded incident of collision, grounding, fire, explosion, or hull failure that has caused a breach to a cargo tank of an LNG ship. In 1979 an LNG vessel ran aground near the Rock of Gibraltar, but no cargo was spilled. The *Exxon Valdez*, on the other hand, ran aground in 1989 and caused a natural disaster by spreading 11 million gallons of oil across 1,300 miles of coastline. In 2002 a nuclear submarine surfaced beneath an LNG vessel in the Mediterranean Sea. No damage occurred to the cargo tanks. In contrast, the oil tanker *Prestige* broke in two off the coast of Spain in 2002. Moreover, in 2003 there was a fuel oil spill in

Buzzards Bay and a gasoline barge fire and explosion on Staten Island. SUEZ hopes to prove with these records that LNG ships are among the best-built, most sophisticated and most robust in the world. Also, concerning LNG storage and trucking, the company can show excellent records. There has never been a report of either off-site injuries or property damage resulting from an incident at any LNG import terminal worldwide, or injuries or damage to land or water resources caused by a release of LNG from a truck.

With respect to security, all LNG ship officers, crew members and Everett Terminal workers are carefully trained and screened. Also, all LNG ships are boarded, inspected and escorted by the US Coast Guard through the Boston Harbour. Although SUEZ always has been very committed on safety and security, this became even more so after 9/11. To counter the fear of LNG ships becoming a target for terrorists, the company used a risk-based approach focused on consequence determination, potential threats (as provided by federal authorities) and their outcomes. Several initiatives were pro-actively taken to address credible threats and to ensure that deliveries would continue. SUEZ introduced a detailed security plan, hired more private security personnel, increased employee awareness, installed

Case Table 10.1 Key governmental stakeholders

Commonwealth of Massachusetts	■ Governor and key staffers within the Economic Affairs, Consumer Affairs, Telecommunications and Energy, and Public Safety offices ■ State Senators and Representatives of the district, and Senators and Representatives involved in Energy, Commerce and Public Safety ■ Massachusetts Port Authority ■ Public safety officers, including the Massachusetts State Police and State Fire Marshall
Federal	■ The US Coast Guard ■ The Federal Energy Regulatory Commission ■ The US Department of Energy ■ The US Department of Transportation ■ Senators and Representatives within the Massachusetts delegation
Local	■ Everett Mayor, Everett Police and Fire Departments ■ Everett Common Council ■ Everett Board of Aldermen ■ Boston Mayor, Boston Police and Fire Departments ■ Boston City Councillors ■ Chelsea City Manager, Chelsea Police and Fire Departments

onboard satellite tracking systems as well as cameras that monitor all areas of access, installed physical obstructions, etc. The security plan prescribes guidelines for decision making and responses to conditions or incidents that may occur during the transit within Boston Harbour. It was developed jointly with the many stakeholders of the port of Boston, including vessel agents, docking and harbour pilots, operational Coast Guards units, port authorities, citizen action groups, federal agencies and state and local emergency response organisations. The security plan was hailed by Homeland Defense Secretary Tom Ridge as one of the best in the country and became a model for the Coast Guard's Operation Safe Commerce Project, a national effort to improve transportation safety and security. Also, several countries including Australia, Algeria, Belgium, Qatar, Trinidad, Tobago, the UK and Japan have made requests for the plan.

SUEZ' lobbyists are in constant contact with both local and national officials. More specifically, they are in contact almost daily with local officials of one type or another in the city of Everett. With state officials and other local area entities the company has as much contact as is needed. This can vary from many times daily to weekly or bi-weekly. These contacts range from face-to-face discussions to provision of literature and reports.

Communities

SUEZ is led by the same objectives regarding community groups as with public officials: inform them on the need, the importance, the advantages and the safety and security of the product and the company. To this end, the company regularly tells the Chambers of Commerce that SUEZ is willing at any time to make a presentation to or answer questions from local groups such as neighbourhood associations and the Everett Common Council and Aldermen. In fact, about two to three times a year the latter call on the company to provide an update on its business. These Everett meetings are broadcast on local cable television increasing its reach enormously. Moreover, the company often presents for the Everett Public High School students. Since students often talk about this at home, SUEZ reaches both students and parents in this way. Furthermore, it has also often led to favourable local press coverage.

SUEZ also demonstrates its commitment to the local community by being an active member in the Everett Chamber of Commerce, The Everett Business-

Education Cooperative, the Everett Rotary Club, the Everett Kiwanis Club and the Chelsea Chamber of Commerce. Finally, the company is also a major benefactor to charities and civic efforts going from partial scholarships to students to sponsorship of the Little League baseball team. Moving beyond the City of Everett, SUEZ also supports the Citizens Energy/Distrigas Heat Assistance programme and the Courageous Sailing programme, which teaches inner-city kids to sail.

Energy industry

The company takes up an active role in several industry and trade groups. This ensures that it is well informed on significant issues (such as legislation) that could affect the industry. Moreover, doing so allows SUEZ to have a say in the messages that the energy industry spreads to the public. Furthermore, these industry and trade groups provide excellent networking opportunities. Case Table 10.2 presents some of the groups SUEZ is a member of.

Customers

To solidify its relationships with current and potential customers, SUEZ uses both direct and indirect means of communication. Direct communication consists of individual contacts between SUEZ' sales force and the (potential) customer. Indirect communication is obtained by

1 participating in key industry conferences where the company affirms its plans

2 press releases to, for example, the Northeast Gas Association, an association to which most of SUEZ' customers and prospects belong.

Media Relations

LNG is a hot, but also a very sensitive topic. SUEZ is well aware that reporters are eager to cultivate controversy on LNG. Therefore, it is important for the company to help frame the issue. To this end, the company has always responded in a very timely and helpful fashion to any requests for information, interviews, irrespective of the day (business day or weekend) and time (day or night). Besides these prompt responses, the company also behaves proactively by spreading press releases, articles and opinion pieces for various publications. For example, in February 2005 Frank Katulak, senior vice-president of operations for Distrigas of Massachusetts, wrote an opinion piece for a trade magazine for the chemical

Case Table 10.2 Industry memberships

ROLE OF SLNGNA	INDUSTRY OR TRADE GROUP
Founding Management Committee member	Center for LNG (includes BG, BP, Shell, ConocoPhilips, Chevron, and ExxonMobil), which is an active participant on Capitol Hill and provides information on LNG to the press
Member of the Board of Directors	Interstate Natural Gas Association of America (INGAA)
Founding member	University of Texas LNG consortium (includes BG, BP, Shell, ConocoPhilips, Chevron, and ExxonMobil AND the US Department of Energy), which was set up to develop public information from the basics to the safety of LNG
Member	Groupe International des Importateurs de Gaz Naturel Liquefié, an international association of LNG importers
Member	Northeast Gas Association
Member	Associated Industries of Massachusetts
Member	New England Council

engineering profession on the safety of LNG and its operations to counter the rumours of LNG ships being a natural target for terrorists. Also, in the autumn of 2005 an article was published in the Propeller Club Quarterly on the security plan of SUEZ.

To conclude, SUEZ considers it business-critical to communicate often and well with all stakeholders mentioned above. Remaining a credible company and partner in the eyes of all stakeholders is one of the main challenges the SUEZ team accepts every day. As the case clearly illustrates, PR activities are exceptionally important to SUEZ. To make a comparison, advertising equals only 5–10% of SUEZ' PR investments.

Questions

1 Which type of public relations has SUEZ engaged in?

2 Is SUEZ using direct or indirect PR?

3 What other types of PR could SUEZ have used? Which specific PR activities would you recommend?

4 Which of the PR target groups discerned by SUEZ do you think is most important? Why?

5 What do you think are the main objectives of the PR activities directed at the different target groups?

6 Do you think SUEZ handled the rumours of a credible threat of terrorism in a good way? What else could they have done?

7 How can SUEZ measure the results of its PR activities?

8 Is SUEZ right in attaching so much importance to PR? Would you complement its PR activities with other MC tools? If so, which ones would you choose?

Case based on information provided by: Rick Grant, CEO SUEZ Global LNG; Julie Vitek, Director External Affairs SUEZ LNG NA, Derrick Philippe Gosselin, Executive Vice President Strategy & Portfolio Management – Chief Strategy Officer, SUEZ Energy International and Katja Daman, SUEZ Energy International.
Katulak (2005), 'LNG – A Safe Alternative Fuel', CEP February 2005 (www.cepmagazine.org)
Joseph McKechine and Mark Skordinski (2005), 'LNG Case Study: Boston Public-Private Cooperation', *Propeller Club Quarterly*, Fall, 10–13.
Company website, www.suez.com

References

1 Sirgy, J.M. (1998), *Integrated Marketing Communication. A Systems Approach*. Upper Saddle River, NJ: Prentice Hall.

2 Haywood, R. (1998), *Public Relations for Marketing Professionals*. London: Macmillan Business.

3 *Public Relations Practice – Its Role and Parameters* (1984), London: The Institute of Public Relations.

4 Haywood, R. (1998), *Public Relations for Marketing Professionals*. London: Macmillan Business.

5 Brassington, S. and Pettitt, F. (2003), *Principles of Marketing*. London: Financial Times Management.

6 Haywood, R. (1998), *Public Relations for Marketing Professionals*. London: Macmillan Business.

7 http://groups.yahoo.com/group/brandhut/ May 2003.

8 De Pelsmacker, P. and Van den Bergh, J. (1998), 'Advertising Content and Irritation: A Study of 226 TV Commercials', *Journal of International Consumer Marketing*, 10(4), 5–27.

9 Bobo, C. (1997), 'Hitachi Faces Crisis with Textbook Response', *Public Relations Quarterly*, 42(2), 18–21.

10 Biurnett, J. and Moriarty, S. (1998), *Introduction to Marketing Communication*. Upper Saddle River, NJ: Prentice Hall.

11 Lages, C. (2001), *Dimensions of Public Relations Activity: An Exploratory Study*. PhD dissertation, University of Warwick: Warwick Business School.

12 Dibb, S., Simkin, L. and Vancini, A. (1996), 'Competition, Strategy, Technology and People: The Challenges Facing PR', *International Journal of Advertising*, 15, 116–27; Kitchen, P.J. and White, J. (1992), 'Public Relations – Developments', *Marketing Intelligence & Planning*, 10(2), 14–17; Lages, C. (2001), *Dimensions of Public Relations Activity: An Exploratory Study*. PhD dissertation, University of Warwick: Warwick Business School.

13 Thomsen, S.R. (1997), 'Public Relations in the New Millennium: Understanding the Forces that are Reshaping the Profession', *Public Relations Quarterly*, 42(1), 11–17.

14 Lages, C. and Simkin, L. (2003), 'The Dynamics of Public Relations: Key Constructs and the Drive for Professionalism at the Practitioner, Consultancy and Industry Levels', *European Journal of Marketing*, 37(1), 298–328.

15 KBC On-line, Effie Award. Belgium, 2003.

16 Dolphin, R. (2003), 'Approaches to Investor Relations: Implementation in the British Context', *Journal of Marketing Communications*, 9(1), 29–44.

17 *De Morgen*, 3 April 2002.

18 Haywood, R. (1991), *All About Public Relations*. London: McGraw-Hill.

19 Albrecht, K. (1990), *Service Within*. Homewood, IL: Dow Jones-Irwin.

20 Carroll, C. and McCombs, M. (2003), 'Agenda-setting Effects of Business News on the Public's Images and Opinions about Major Corporations', *Corporate Reputation Review*, 16(1), 6(1), 36–46.

21 Callison, C. (2003), 'Fortune 500 Company Websites and Media Relations: Corporate PR Practitioner's Use of the Internet to Assist Journalists in News Gathering', *Public Relations Review*, 29(1), 29–47.

22 McCleneghan, J.S. (1998), 'Are VNR's all they're Cracked Up to Be?', *Public Relations Quarterly*, 42(4), 35–8.

23 Haywood, R. (1998), *Public Relations for Marketing Professionals*. London: Macmillan Business.

24 Gofton, K. (1997), 'Rethinking the Rules', *Public Relations – Supplement*, 6–10.

25 Haywood, R. (1998), *Public Relations for Marketing Professionals*. London: Macmillan Business; See also Moss, D., Vercic, D. and Warnaby, G. (2003), *Perspectives on Public Relations Research*. London: Routledge.

26 Gregory, A. (2001), 'Public Relations and Evaluation: Does the Reality Match the Rhetoric?', *Journal of Marketing Communications*, 7(3), 171–190.

27 Seymour, M. and Moore, S. (2000), *Effective Crisis Management: Worldwide Principles and Practices*. London and New York: Cassell.

28 Marconi, J. (1992), *Crisis Marketing. When Bad Things Happen to Good Companies*. Chicago, IL: Probus Publishing Company.

29 Haywood, R. (1998), *Public Relations for Marketing Professionals*. London: Macmillan Business.

30 Lukaszewki, J.E. (1997), 'Establishing Individual and Corporate Crisis Communication Standards; The Principles and Protocols', *Public Relations Quarterly*, 42(3), 7–14.

31 Seymour, M. and Moore, S. (2000), *Effective Crisis Management: Worldwide Principles and Practices*. London and New York: Cassell.

Chapter 11

Sponsorship

Chapter outline

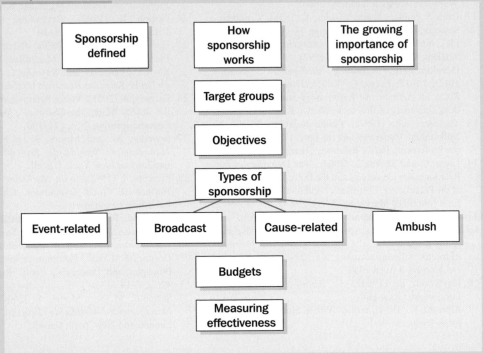

Sponsorship defined

How sponsorship works

The growing importance of sponsorship

Target groups

Objectives

Types of sponsorship

Event-related

Broadcast

Cause-related

Ambush

Budgets

Measuring effectiveness

Chapter objectives

This chapter will help you to:

- Understand the difference between sponsorship and other instruments of the communications mix
- Know how sponsorship works
- Understand why sponsorship is an increasingly important instrument of the communications mix
- Distinguish the target groups and objectives of sponsorship
- Learn about the different types of sponsorship, such as event-related sponsorship, broadcast sponsorship, cause-related sponsorship and ambush marketing, and their advantages and disadvantages
- Select sponsorship proposals on the basis of a set of relevant criteria
- Measure the effectiveness of a sponsorship campaign

Introduction

Although in most companies the share of sponsorship in the communications budget is still limited, worldwide it is an increasingly important instrument of the communications mix. Not only are sponsorship budgets increasing, sponsored events and causes are becoming more and more diverse. Although 'spouse-driven projects' still exist, the degree of professionalism in the selection and follow-up of sponsorship projects is becoming increasingly sophisticated and the communications effectiveness of sponsored projects has become a major concern. Contrary to advertising campaigns that are normally followed up by advertising or brand managers, sponsorship projects are often directly monitored by the corporate management, illustrating the importance that is attached to this type of activity – or the lack of maturity of this particular instrument. Sponsorship is different from other communications mix instruments. It is a flexible instrument that can serve a multitude of objectives, but it is more suited for some objectives than for others. As in advertising, a number of channels – types of sponsorship – may be used, each having their own advantages and strengths and disadvantages and weaknesses. The integration of this tool in the communications mix may be an even more important condition for success than that of the other communications instruments. In any case, in an increasing number of companies sponsorship has acquired the status of one of the cornerstones of the communications and marketing strategy.

Sponsorship: what it is and what it is not

Sponsorship can be defined as an investment in cash or kind in an activity, in return for access to the exploitable commercial potential associated with this activity.[1] The company promotes its interests and brands by tying them to a specific and meaningfully related event or cause.[2] It is a thematic communications instrument with which the sponsor assists the sponsee in realising his or her project. In return the sponsee co-operates in realising the communications objectives of the sponsoring company. If the latter is not the case, the investment of the 'sponsor' is nothing more than altruism, charity, patronage or benefaction. As such, 'sponsorship' has existed for centuries. The Roman Gaius Maecenas was a great sponsor of the arts, who gave his name to the concept of Maecenatism. The De Medici family of Florence became famous as sponsors of artists such as Michelangelo. The difference between this and contemporary professional sponsorship is that sponsorship is an integrated part of the communications effort, with explicit communications and commercial objectives. The benefits of charity, on the other hand, are mainly directed towards society and/or the beneficiaries.

Generally speaking, sponsorship shares two of the fundamental objectives of advertising, i.e. the generation of awareness about the product or company, and the promotion of positive messages about the product or company.[3] However, there are a number of important differences between the two, the most important one being that advertising allows greater control over the content and the environment of the message. Advertising messages are explicit and direct, and advertisers can decide when and where to place their ads. On the other hand, although sponsorship results in a less cluttered promotion of their products, companies also have less control over sponsorship, which makes their messages more indirect and implicit. As a result, in order to make sponsorship effective, accompanying communications efforts are called for.[4] Indeed, sponsorship can be described as a 'mute non-verbal medium', as opposed to advertising, in which messages are created using visuals, vocals and context.[5]

On the other hand, sponsorship is less cluttered and financially more attractive. It can be considered a cheap form of advertising. However, sponsorship may be less effective in gaining attention as a result of the distraction factor: spectators are primarily involved with the sponsored event (a soccer game or a work of art) and pay less attention to the environment of the event, such as the sponsor.[6] Indeed, exposure to a sponsor's name or logo is not the same as sponsorship effectiveness. Furthermore, in some cases the sponsor is closely associated with a popular sponsored event or cause, which may turn out to have a strong positive effect on corporate and brand image. Sponsorship is also easy for the consumer to understand: it essentially works on the basis of association between sponsor and sponsee. Advertising, on the other hand, often requires elaborate processing of the message.[7]

Sponsorship is different from event marketing, which, in turn, is a type of PR activity.[8] Certainly, sponsorship can be integrated into a PR campaign. During the world championship cycling in Valkenburg (1998), Rabobank was one of the structural sponsors. It invited about 5,000 guests, mainly employees and customers of Rabobank in the Netherlands and elsewhere. Invitations to cultural events, for instance to see David Bowie at the Seat Beach festival in Ostend and the musical *Oliver* in one of the 12 large theatres in the Netherlands, are examples of corporate hospitality, integrating sponsorship into a PR campaign by Nashuatec.[9] Event marketing can be defined as using a number of elements of the promotion mix to create an event for the purpose of reaching strategic marketing objectives. An example of event marketing is the Camel Trophy.

Finally, sponsorship should be distinguished from value marketing. Value marketing or societal marketing can be defined as a strategy in which a company links its activities to a philosophy of general societal interest. The company positions itself on the basis of a value system that is often not product-related. For instance, the international cosmetics company The Body Shop tries to combine fair business, social conscience and profitability. It produces environmentally-friendly products, based on natural ingredients, that are not tested on animals and which are sold in recycled or recyclable packaging. Raw materials are bought from Third World countries at fair prices. Sponsorship can be part of the value marketing strategy, but it is by no means its only instrument.[10]

Corporate social responsibility campaigns in The Netherlands

Companies set up corporate social responsibility (CSR) campaigns in which they sponsor cause-related projects that improve the quality of life in society, and by means of which they can improve their own reputation. The following examples are taken from the Dutch CSR network 'Samenleving & Bedrijf' (Society and Company).

Since October 2004 Microsoft Nederland has cooperated with the city of Amsterdam and local non-profit organisations to establish 'Community-Based Technology & Learning Centres (CTLCs)'. The project goes by the name of 'Computer neighbourhood' and tries to provide computer training to people with a lack of digital shills. The purpose of the project is to prevent people from getting isolated, and to empower less privileged inhabitants to enlarge their capabilities with respect to education, jobs, personal development and participation in society. The objective is to establish 16 CTCLs in which 1,100 people receive training. Eleven locations were set up where people from the neighbourhood could learn through short courses how to work with a computer, from chatting to e-mailing. More than 700 inhabitants have been trained

▶

so far. The project is part of the global Unlimited Potential initiative launched by Microsoft Community Affairs. Up to now, worldwide almost 30,000 CTLCs have been established in 95 countries. In these projects, Microsoft cooperates with 475 non-profit organisations.

The Shell Young Art Award project aims at stimulating young talent and entrepreneurship, besides acquainting youngsters with developments in modern art. In three Shell locations in Amsterdam, Rotterdam and The Hague artists present their work. A professional jury judges the work of the young artists and awards prizes. The initiative started in 2000 and so far dozens of young artists have been able to develop expertise in organising exhibitions of their works. The Shell Young Art Award is stimulating and leads to recognition and exposure. The prize-winning artists are allowed to show their work in museums. In this way the public can also get acquainted with their work. There is also an internal effect: many works of art have lead to intense discussions in the Shell offices.

Source: www.samen.nl accessed 6 March 2006.

How sponsorship works

A number of theoretical constructs can be used to understand the effects of sponsorship. Given the fact that sponsor messages are often simple and limited to company or brand names, one could argue that the effectiveness of sponsorship is based on the exposure effect (see Chapter 3), which implies that increased familiarity with the brand as a result of exposure to a sponsor's name in the long run generates a preference for the brand. As such, the main effect of sponsorship is that the brand ends up in the evoked set or the choice set of the consumer, without attitudinal-related effects. Additionally, it could be argued that both the episodic (event-based) and the semantic (as a result of longer-term exposure) memory of spectators and participants in a sponsored event is stimulated, which could lead to higher levels of brand awareness than those resulting from advertising exposure.[11]

Congruity theory could also explain the effectiveness of sponsorship. Basically, this theory states that people best remember information that is congruent with prior expectations. As a result, sponsorships that are consistent with the expectations of the target groups about the product could be better recalled.[12] Similarly, just as there seems to be a carry-over effect between the attitude towards the ad and the attitude towards the brand, it could be argued that there is the same effect between the prior attitudes towards the sponsored event or cause and the sponsoring brand. Furthermore, it can be expected that the more a person is involved with what is being sponsored, the stronger the carry-over effect between the sponsoring brand and the sponsored event will be.[13] Figure 11.1 illustrates this mechanism. The image of the sponsors of the 1996 Olympics appears to be mainly determined by the attitude towards Olympic sponsorship in general.[14]

Apart from these cognitively oriented theories, context effects can also partly explain how and why sponsorship works. The context of a message may be important in how a message is perceived. Since sponsorships tend to occur in positively evaluated environments, the resulting positive mood could enhance the positive image of the sponsoring brands.[15]

Finally, the behaviourist perspective may be relevant. The principles of operant conditioning posit that behaviour may be conditioned by the consequences that follow

Figure 11.1 Determining factors of the image of Olympic sponsors

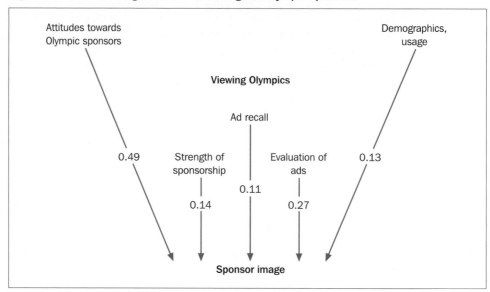

Source: Stipp, H. (1998), 'The Impact of Olympic Sponsorship on Corporate Image', *International Journal of Advertising*, 17(1), 75–88. Reproduced with permission of NTC Publications Limited.

it. On the basis of this principle it can be argued that sponsorship draws attention to a brand and in that way reinforces past favourable experience with the brand. The stimulus is being associated with a satisfactory experience and therefore reinforces it. When this point of view is accepted, it implies that sponsorship is only effective when it is directed towards consumers who are already using the brand. Another principle of operant conditioning is vicarious learning. By educating consumers on how a product can be used, vicarious learning increases the purchase probability. Applied to sponsorship, showing a famous and positively evaluated athlete using or endorsing a product may positively influence the target group.[16] This mechanism is very similar to the source effect in advertising: linking a relevant brand to a credible source (a bank to a classical concert, a beer to a famous entertainer) may improve its image.[17]

The growing importance of sponsorship

In 1984 the worldwide sponsorship market was estimated at US$2 billion. The estimate for 2001 is US$24.6 billion. Total sponsorship expenditures in Europe amounted to €7.4 billion in 2001, compared to €6.5 billion in 2000. Worldwide, the annual growth of sponsorship between 1990 and 1999 is estimated at between 10% and 15%. In the 1990s, the annual growth of advertising and sales promotion was only 6%. As a result, the relative importance of sponsorship in communications budgets has, on average, increased to 7%.[18] In some countries (Italy, South Africa and Australia), more than 13% of the advertising budget is spent on sponsorship.[19] Furthermore, part of the advertising budget is directly sponsorship-related in that it supports and leverages the sponsorship efforts (see below). It is fair to conclude that sponsorship is an increasingly important instrument of marketing communications (Table 11.1).

Table 11.1 Sponsorship as a percentage of advertising budgets in European countries

Country	Sponsorship as a % of advertising budget
Austria	6.0
Belgium	6.0
Denmark	6.1
Finland	7.1
France	6.0
Germany	7.2
Greece	8.0
Ireland	6.0
Italy	13.6
Netherlands, The	6.0
Portugal	8.0
Spain	8.0
Sweden	8.1
UK	4.8
Switzerland	6.0

Based on: Meenaghan, T. (1998), 'Current Developments and Future Directions in Sponsorship', *International Journal of Advertising*, 17(1), 3–28. Reproduced with permission of NTC Publications Limited.

UPS supports Olympic sponsorship with worldwide advertising campaign

UPS is the world's largest express carrier and largest delivery company. It entered the European market in 1988. It did not make a profit in Europe during the first 10 years. In 1996 UPS made the fundamental decision to revamp its European operations. It decided to become an official partner of the 2000 Olympics in Sydney. Research identified four weaknesses: low awareness of the Olympic sponsorship, low awareness of brand and service capabilities, an undifferentiated brand position, and the fact that potential customers were unaware of UPS as an enabler of global commerce. UPS launched a global campaign to redress this situation by leveraging its association with the Olympics in a relevant way. The Olympics provided a unique opportunity to associate UPS with the core Olympic values of trust, integrity, ambition and success. The creative execution of the campaign compared UPS with the Olympics: 'If UPS are good enough to deliver for the Olympics, they must be good enough for us'. The campaign showed UPS employees demonstrating their commitment to preparing to represent their country. The advertising campaign was implemented throughout Europe and worldwide, and stretched from the national trials to the games themselves, with special focus on key business periods March–May and the weeks before and during the summer Olympics in September 2000. Fifty-four campaigns ran in the US, Latin America, Asia and Europe, using global, pan-European and national media vehicles. Besides television, radio spots, magazine advertisements and outdoor advertising, sponsorship of key news programmes was also used. Research showed that UPS awareness increased by 5% to 10% in most countries, and so did most-often usage of UPS by 3% to 20%. Year-to-year revenue growth was 4% during the first quarter of 2001. The international export volume grew by 17%, led by Europe with a 25% increase. The UPS example shows that sponsorship programmes need to be accompanied by major investments in other communication campaigns to secure maximum impact.[20]

The (perceived) importance of sponsorship is not only reflected in the increasing budgets and the diversification in sponsored causes and events (see hereafter), but also in the level of (top) management involvement. Studies of managerial involvement in sports and arts sponsorship campaigns in the US and Australia show that in more than 50% of the cases senior management is involved in proposal assessment and agreement negotiations, and in about 25% of the cases in implementation and evaluation of sponsorship campaigns. Senior management is even involved in 75% of the renewal decisions.[21] This reflects the perceived importance of sponsorship, not only for marketing communications, but also for corporate communications and corporate image. The involvement of other departments mainly depends on the type of sponsorship. Sports sponsorship apparently implies the involvement of marketing or advertising departments, while art sponsorship is mostly seen as a PR matter. In Table 11.2 the results of a Canadian study are given and the involvement of different functional departments in sponsorship decisions are shown.[22]

There are a number of reasons why sponsorship is of increasing importance. First, there is a feeling that traditional mass media advertising is becoming increasingly expensive, increasingly irritating and, as a result of communication clutter, less effective. Sponsorship is believed to have the power to escape this clutter, to isolate the brand from the competition and to get the message across at lower cost, although some predict that sponsorship clutter may become equally widespread. Furthermore, sponsored events are increasingly broadcast, thereby leveraging the initial investment of sponsorship. Overall, media, especially television programme sponsorship (see below), is increasingly accepted, and substantially improves the levels of coverage of, and impact on, broad target groups.[23]

Due to increased leisure, sports and cultural activities, new sponsorship opportunities are emerging. Governments are less and less inclined to finance culture and other social activities, so forcing cultural and social organisations to look for financial support from private companies. Finally, legal constraints on tobacco and alcohol advertising are forcing the companies involved to look for other communications strategies to get their message across. Sponsorship is an obvious substitute to build awareness and image.

Apart from increasing expenditures, a number of other current developments in sponsorship can be discerned.[24]

- *A changing perception of sponsorship on the part of company executives.* An evolution towards more professionalism can be seen and management practice is becoming increasingly sophisticated.

Table 11.2 Key roles in the sports sponsorship decision (%)

Role	No influence	Some influence	Major influence
Marketing manager	26	20	54
Advertising manager	31	25	44
Sponsorship manager	49	11	40
Chief executive	25	40	35
PR manager	48	26	26
General manager	54	24	22
Board of directors	69	23	8
Outside consultants	52	43	5

Source: Thwaites, D., Anguilar-Manjarrez, R. and Kidd, C. (1998), 'Sports Sponsorship Development in Leading Canadian Companies: Issues and Trends', *International Journal of Advertising*, 17(1), 29–50. Reproduced with permission of NTC Publications Limited.

- *Changing expenditure patterns*. A greater part of the budget is spent on relatively new forms of sponsorship instead of on traditional sports and the arts. Broadcast or programme sponsorship, popular music and cause-related projects are becoming increasingly important.

- *The diffusion of sponsorship to an expanding range of industries*. In the early days sponsorship was mainly used by tobacco, alcohol and soft drinks companies and banks and car manufacturers. Nowadays retail groups and detergent manufacturers are joining the list.

- *The proliferation of sponsorship activity*. An increasing number of corporate sponsors, combined with a shortage of quality events, is leading to a greater exploitation of their properties by event owners.

- *Some sponsored events are evolving towards global projects*. The Olympic games, Formula One racing and worldwide sports sponsorship by Adidas are examples of this trend.

- *Sponsorship is becoming relationship-based* rather than transaction-based (structural versus punctual sponsorship), implying a longer-term co-operation between sponsors and sponsees.

- *Sponsorship is more and more broadcast-driven*. What is not on television is less attractive as a sponsorship project.

Sponsorship and the Olympics

The Olympic movement and the Olympic games could not be organised without the extensive support of strategic partners (sponsors) and television broadcast partnerships. Of the total 2001–2004 budget of the Olympic movement, 90% is generated through sponsorship and television broadcasting rights, and only 8% through ticketing and 2% through licensing. About

Chart 1 Olympic Games broadcast revenues

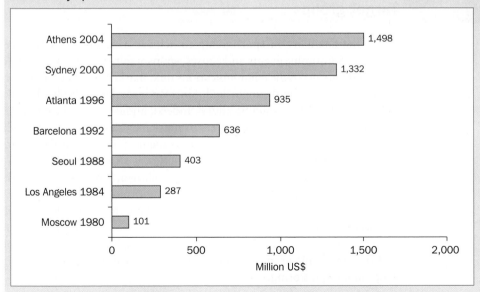

Chart 2 Olympic Winter Games broadcast revenues

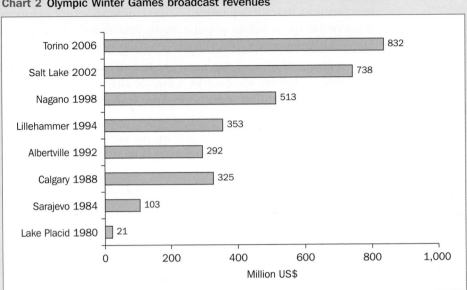

40% of all revenues are sponsorship contracts. Half of the budget is based on television broadcasting rights. Obviously it is the worldwide broadcasting of the Olympics that makes them extremely interesting for companies seeking global exposure and sales. In the following charts the broadcast revenues of the Olympic games and winter games from 1980 onwards are given. From this evolution it is clear that television broadcasts have become a major source of income for the Olympic movement, and that this source of revenue has increased exponentially over the years. Even for the 2008 Olympics, the television broadcast rights have already been negotiated. They amount to more than US$1.7 billion.[25]

Target groups

Given the flexibility of sponsorship to achieve a number of objectives and the wide range of sponsorable events and causes, sponsorship audiences are very diversified. Like other instruments of the communications mix, marketing and corporate communications target groups can be distinguished. Since sponsorship is explicitly linked to an event, an extra dimension should be added. Indeed, audiences can be contacted as active participants in the event (soccer players or musicians), as live spectators who attend events (fans or visitors of a museum), and/or as media followers of the event. In Figure 11.2 the particular sponsorship audience structure is shown. In Table 11.3 the results of a study on sports sponsorship in Canada are shown, illustrating the wide range of audiences that are targeted and their relative importance.[26] Obviously, depending on the objectives and the target groups of the global communications campaign, sponsorship projects will be selected that are best capable of reaching the desired target groups. For instance, products targeted at up-market demographic segments will sponsor tennis, golf and the arts, while brands targeting youngsters will focus on popular music festival or programme sponsoring.

Figure 11.2 Sponsorship audience structure

	(Potential) customers	Financial institutions	Community leaders	Employees	Channel members
Active participants					
Live spectators					
Media followers					

Table 11.3 Sports sponsorship target audiences in Canada

Audience	Mean importance (on 7-point scale)
Potential customers	5.79
Existing customers	5.62
Local community	5.60
General public	5.16
Business community	4.37
Workforce	4.33
Distributors	3.21
Shareholders	3.18
Suppliers	3.09
Ethnic groups	3.05
Government	2.74

Based on: Thwaites, D., Anguilar-Manjarrez, R. and Kidd, C. (1998), 'Sports Sponsorship Development in Leading Canadian Companies: Issues and Trends', *International Journal of Advertising*, 17(1), 29–50. Reproduced with permission of NTC Publications Limited.

World Cup sponsorship and brand perception

Does major investment in sports sponsorship actually benefit brand owners? This seems to be primarily the case amongst young consumers. The impact of sports sponsorship on other age groups is much more limited. In 2002, NOP World questioned 1,001 people from a representative sample of the UK population on behalf of the Superbrand organisation to test brand awareness and brand perception of the sponsors of World Cup soccer. Within the 15–24 year old range, 40% of people said that they would feel more confident about a brand if it sponsored high-profile sporting events such as the World Cup. Only 19% of the 25–34 year olds and 18% of the 35–44 year olds feel more confidence in a sponsoring brand. This percentage even lowers to 13% of the 45–54 year olds, and a mere 6% of the 55–64 year olds. For the over 65s, this percentage increases slightly to 11%. The impact of high-profile sporting events appears primarily to impress the younger age groups.[27]

Objectives

Sponsorship is a very flexible communications tool that can be used to achieve both marketing (product or brand) and corporate communications objectives. In Table 11.4 an overview is given of the two categories of objectives. In each of the categories a distinction can be made between the type of target group and/or the type of objective.[28]

Research indicates that, depending on the type of sponsorship and the type of company, different objectives are important. As far as **marketing communications objectives** are concerned, mainly awareness building, and to a certain extent image building, seem to be the objectives that sponsorship is most suited to achieve. These effects only become visible in the long run. Indeed, sponsorship effectiveness studies indicate that sponsors are not recognised better than their non-sponsoring competitors immediately after the sponsored event.[29] A direct increase in sales or market share is not the primary objective of sponsorship, although, for instance, a beverage supplier can obtain the sole rights for selling beverages at an event, and in this way boost sales. Linking a brand's name with a relevant event or cause is often used to improve the image with a specific target group of interest. Volvo sponsoring golf and tennis, and Adidas sponsoring, amongst others, soccer, are examples of this.

Table 11.4 Sponsorship objectives

Corporate communications objectives	General public	■ Increase general public awareness of company ■ Promote or enhance corporate image ■ Alter public perception of company ■ Involvement with the local community
	Channel members and trade relations	■ Build trade relations ■ Corporate hospitality ■ Demonstrate trade goodwill
	Employees	■ Enhance employee relations and motivations ■ Assist staff recruitment ■ Facilitate prospecting for the salesforce
	Opinion-formers and decision-makers	■ Increase media attention ■ Counter adverse publicity ■ Build goodwill ■ Reassure policy-holders and stockholders ■ Personal objective of senior managers
Marketing communications objectives	Awareness building	■ Increase awareness with actual customers ■ Increase awareness with potential customers ■ Confirm market leadership ■ Increase new product awareness
	Brand image	■ Alter perception of brand ■ Identify brand with particular market segment
	Sales/market share	■ Induce trial of new product ■ Increase sales/market share

Equally important are the corporate communications objectives of sponsoring. Most studies indicate that promoting corporate image and increasing goodwill with a variety of target groups are the most important corporate communications objectives of sponsorship.[30] But internal marketing objectives and motives can be equally or even more important. The Bank of Ireland sponsors Gaelic Football and the Bank of Ireland Proms. Besides corporate image objectives, employee-related goals are equally important. The bank tries to develop a corporate identity and a corporate image by transferring the values of the sponsored events to both external publics and their own staff. In the process staff pride is engendered. The bank is perceived as a desirable employer. Amongst the measurement of sponsorship effects the attitude of the company's own staff towards the sponsored event is of primary importance.[31] Given the fact that the struggle of the future will have to be concentrated as much on attracting high-quality staff as on finding customers, the employee-related effects of sponsorship are of increasing importance.

Another important category of objectives or motives of sponsorship is corporate hospitality, which can be aimed at own staff, salespersons, distributors or any other opinion leader or decision-maker. They can be invited to attend a soccer game, to follow a cycle race, to attend a concert or to obtain backstage passes at rock concerts. Creating goodwill and establishing stronger relations in an informal context are the primary objectives.

Corporate hospitality

Corporate hospitality is developing relationship marketing activities within the framework of a sponsorship programme. It involves, for instance, inviting employees, customers, suppliers, etc. to cultural or sports events, or the organisation of special events for these stakeholder groups at the occasion of sponsored activities. The selection of VIP events is a delicate exercise. The selection of groups requires an investigation into their interest in, and empathy towards, the sponsored event. If the managing director of one of the largest suppliers of the company is only interested in opera, and not in soccer, he or she should not be invited to a soccer game. Grouping the VIPs is another crucial decision. The result of the PR or relationship effort primarily depends upon the interaction between those invited. If they do not have anything to say to each other or are even hostile to one another, they should not be in the same group. Corporate hospitality can also lead to irritation, for instance if someone is invited to an event he or she does not like, or if other stakeholder groups feel discriminated against by not being invited. Therefore it is a good idea to conduct VIP treatment at a safe distance from the event itself, away from visitors who have paid to participate in the event. If the value of the VIP treatment is substantial, this can lead to ethical problems because the expectation is raised that the 'reward' for being invited should also be significant.

Corporate hospitality can also generate negative publicity in the media. An influential sports journalist from a Dutch television channel was interviewed in a newspaper, and was very critical about VIP events organised by sports sponsors: 'A cyclist championship for 15,000 VIPs in a concrete bunker on a car racing circuit – who was the fool who thought of that?' and 'During the final of the tennis tournament in Rotterdam, the VIP area was full of people in nice suits, talking about nothing important, while outside the world's numbers 1 and 2 were playing. No one I asked in the VIP area knew who they were'. Needless to say that this kind of negative media publicity can destroy much of the goodwill that was built up by the sponsorship programme, and should be avoided.[32]

One of the most important motives in sponsorship is the leveraging effect of the media coverage of the event. In some cases, as in tobacco or alcohol advertising, the ban on regular advertising leads to a situation in which sponsorship is the only way to obtain mass media exposure. But a lot of other sponsorship initiatives count on the 'bullhorn effect' of media coverage too. Sponsorship is indeed becoming more and more broadcast-driven, as illustrated in Table 11.5, in which the results of a British study are shown.

Although sponsorship is becoming increasingly professional, in many situations the decision to sponsor is motivated by personal interest, or 'management by hobby' of senior executives, or their husbands or wives. It goes without saying that many sports sponsorship budgets could have been spent more efficiently on other communications tools. There are many examples of sponsorships that end when the senior manager retires or gets another job. For instance, the Spanish soft drink brand KAS ended its sponsorship of a cycling team (with Sean Kelly as one of the top athletes) after its CEO retired. The sudden death in 1995 of Mr Furlan, CEO of the clothing company MG, was the cause of great concern amongst Italian professional cyclists, who feared that their successful team would cease to exist.

Table 11.5 Objectives of sponsorship

Objectives	% Agreement
Press coverage/exposure	84.6
TV coverage/exposure	78.5
Promote brand awareness	78.4
Promote corporate image	77.0
Radio coverage/exposure	72.3
Increase sales	63.1
Enhance community relations	55.4
Entertain clients	43.1
Benefit employees	36.9
Match competition	30.8
Fad/fashion	26.2

Source: Erdogan, Z.B. and Kitchen, P.J. (1998), 'The Interaction Between Advertising and Sponsorship: Uneasy Alliance or Strategic Symbiosis', in Kitchen, P.J. (ed.), The Changing World of Corporate and Marketing Communication: Towards the Next Millennia, Proceedings of the 3rd Annual Conference of the Global Institute for Corporate and Marketing Communication, Strathclyde Graduate Business School, 144–55. Reproduced with permission of Professor Philip Kitchen, The Queens University of Belfast.

Types of sponsorship

Sponsorship budgets can be directed towards different types of projects. In Figure 11.3 the main sponsorship types are shown. Four basic categories can be distinguished. Event-related sponsorship is the best-known category. Companies may sponsor a soccer competition, a team, an athlete, shirts or even a match ball, a golf tournament, skiing or a baseball game. They can lend their support, in cash or kind, to an exhibition, a series of concerts, a philharmonic orchestra or an artist. Or they can sponsor a rock concert, a beach festival or an annual traditional crafts exhibition. Broadcast or programme sponsorship is a more recent phenomenon, at least in Europe. A brand can

Figure 11.3 Types of sponsorship

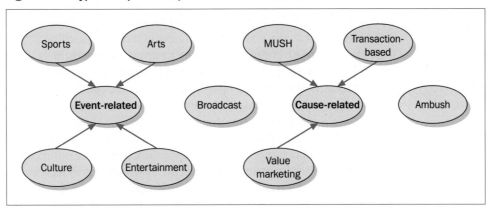

sponsor a sports programme, the weather forecast or a 'soap'. Cause-related sponsorship may be the oldest form of sponsorship, or rather charity. Rich people donating money to schools, the poor or other good causes is a phenomenon that has existed for centuries. The difference between those activities and cause-related sponsorship is that the latter is not just charity, but is integrated in the company's communications strategy. MUSH stands for Municipal, University, Social, Hospital sponsorship, and is a synonym for sponsorship of good causes. Transaction-based sponsorship (sometimes called cause-related marketing or point-of-purchase politics) is a type of sponsorship in which the company invests a pre-specified amount of money in a 'good cause' every time a consumer buys one of the company's products. Value marketing has been defined in the first section of this chapter. Sponsorship is only one aspect of value or societal marketing. Finally, ambush or parasitic marketing is a planned effort by a company to confuse the consumer regarding its affiliation status and to associate indirectly with an event in order to gain at least some of the recognition and benefits associated with being an official sponsor.[33] A company may be a minor sponsor of an event, but by spending considerable budgets on advertising support it creates the impression of being an important sponsor.

In Table 11.6 an overview is given of the budgets involved in each of these categories. Traditional event-related sponsorship still accounts for the bulk of the expenditures. On average, in Europe 75% of all sponsorship is devoted to sports, mainly soccer and Formula One,[34] and 16% to arts and culture. The majority of the rest is spent on broadcast sponsorship.

Table 11.6 Sponsorship expenditures (%) per category in some European countries

Sector	Germany	South Africa	Sweden	UK
Sports	62	80	65	61
Arts	22	7	15	11
Others	12	6	15	8
Broadcast	4	7	5	20

Based on: Meenaghan, T. (1998), 'Current Developments and Future Directions in Sponsorship', *International Journal of Advertising*, 17(1), 3–28. Reproduced with permission of NTC Publications Limited.

Event-related sponsorship

The opportunities and advantages of event-related sponsorship are multiple. Compared to advertising it is a cost-effective instrument in terms of reaching a particular audience. Given the variety of events in terms of targeted audiences, it is an excellent tool to reach broad as well as very specific market segments in terms of demographic and psychographic characteristics. Sponsorship of opera, exhibitions or rock concerts, and of cultural events in general, is usually very selective in terms of the market segment reached, while some sports sponsorship is capable of exposing broad target groups to the sponsor's message. Extensive media coverage of sports events leads to high levels of exposure of broad target groups to the sponsor's name. For instance, as far as cycling is concerned, 18.4% of managers and executives watch this sport regularly on television, as well as 18% of farmers, 16.5% of civil servants, 16.5% of blue-collar workers, 12% of pensioners and 9% of housewives.[35] Heineken sponsored the Rugby World Cup worldwide. It was estimated that in the UK, 83% of all men were exposed to the Heineken brand name, each of them at least 22 times.[36]

Event sponsorship is also flexible in achieving different kinds of objectives. It can increase awareness with actual and potential customers, improve the company's image and the image of the company's products. In Figure 11.4 public perception of some attributes of the corporate image of the Euro '96 sponsors is shown.

It is a tool in relationship building and corporate hospitality, it can be a platform for advertising campaigns, database building and sampling, and it is efficiently capable of avoiding advertising bans. For instance, as far as the latter is concerned, in a 1984 survey it was – sadly – found that the cigarette brands that were most widely recalled by children were those brands that were most commonly sponsoring televised sporting events.[37]

On the other hand, event sponsorship, and more particularly sports sponsorship, has a number of disadvantages and poses a number of threats. Spending large amounts

Figure 11.4 Attitudes towards Euro '96 sponsors

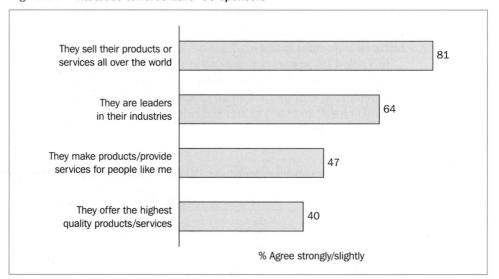

Source: Easton, S. and Mackie, P. (1998), 'When Football Came Home: A Case History of the Sponsorship Activity at Euro '96', *International Journal of Advertising*, 17(1), 99–114. Reproduced with permission of NTC Publications Limited.

Plate 1 InSites: the corporate housestyle of an online research and consulting agency

(Reproduced with permission of InSites Consulting)

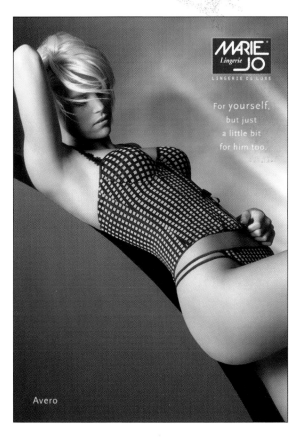

Plate 2 Marie Jo: when beauty meets luxury

(Reproduced with permission of Artex NV)

29 vacancies

for experienced professionals in sales & service

Multinational company is looking for dynamic and creative professionals to strengthen its sales & service organization. You thrive in a multi-lingual environment and are ready to add a new dimension to the word customer focus.

Sales positions:

1 senior sales engineer
1 sales engineer
1 sales support manager
1 sales desk manager
10 native or near-native sales assistants in the following languages: French, Spanish, German, Italian, English, French

Customer service positions:

9 customer service engineers, fluent in one of the following languages: English,Chinese, Italian, French
1 Customer service manager
1 Customer service administrator
1 customer service coordinator
1 spare parts manager
2 project managers

Barco adventure recruitment day

Apply now and receive your personal invitation for Barco's Recruitment Adventure Day on Saturday 15 October 2005. After a short company introduction, you will embark on an adventurous assessment day together with management and future colleagues. At the end of the day, you may well be part of the Barco family!

Your reaction

Send your resumé to the attention of Ms Els Depaepe, President Kennedypark 35, 8500 Kortrijk (els.depaepe@barco.com) or apply online via www.barco.com/jobs"

There's more to explore
You'll see

www.barco.com

BARCO

Visibly yours

Plate 3 Barco: Reinforcing the brand by means of a consistent housestyle

(Reproduced with permission of Barco)

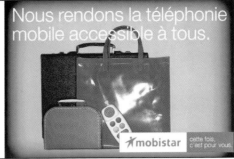

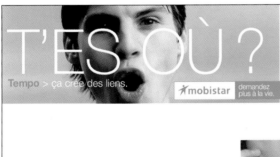

**Plate 4 Mobistar:
Celebrity endorsement
to affirm brand
credibility**

(Reproduced with permission of
Mobistar Belgium)

Plate 5 Electrolux: developing a brochune to help their new parents improve their knowledge of household applicances and care for their child

(Reproduced with permission of European Communication Strategies)

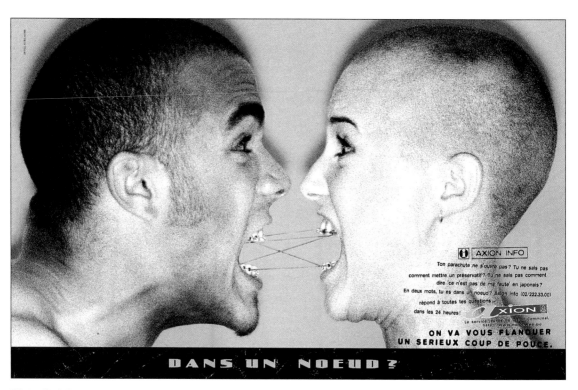

Plate 6 Axion: marketing bank products to youngsters

(Reproduced with permission of Gemeentekrediet, group Dexia)

Plate 7 Coral Black Velvet:
innovations call for communicating
category needs

(Reproduced with permission of Gesamtverband
Werbeagenturen GWA and J. Walter Thompson)

Plate 8 McDonald's: marketing to children requires a special approach

(Reproduced with permission of Leo Burnett)

Plate 9 Eastpak: the selling power of a creative idea

(Reproduced with permission of VF Corporation)

IT'S BIGGER

MVO:
It's bigger.

Tony assumes
"Superman" stance,
chest bulges.

MVO & SUPER:
It's stronger.

Tony's bicep flexes.

MVO & SUPER:
A whole new animal.

Tony's tail whips.
Frosties flakes move
towards camera
asteroid-like.

MVO & SUPER:
"50%" - "B1"
"NIACIN" - "B6"

Complete
Breakfast setting.

MVO:
...as part of a
nutritious breakfast.
Kellogg's Frosties
bring out the tiger...

Tony passes ball
towards camera.

MVO & SUPER:
In You!

We see a teenager
catching the ball,
he smiles.

Plate 10 Kellogg's Tony the Tiger: a 'character' becomes a celebrity

(Reproduced with permission of Leo Burnett)

Plate 11 The Marlboro Man: a personality symbol to support brand image

(Reproduced with permission of Leo Burnett)

Plate 12 Virgin: an aggressive price challenger using humour

Plate 13 Mastercard: influencing perceived behavioural control

(Reproduced with permission of Gesamtverband Werbeagenturen GWA and McCann-Erickson Europe)

'If a man is tired of London, he is tired of life.'

(Samuel Johnson 1709-1784)

Londen moe is levensmoe. Ook Victor Hugo
vond Londen 'een festijn voor fijnproevers'. En u?
Alles wat u altijd al graag had beleefd, vindt u
in Londen. In een sfeer die u nergens anders zo
opsnuift. U zal slechts één ding betreuren: dat u
niet lang genoeg kan blijven. See you there!

SEAFRANCE
SEALINK

BRITAIN
ZO VERSCHILLEND
ZO DICHTBIJ

Ja, stuur me gratis, in ruil voor deze bon - géén kopie, het A-Z
pocketboek over geestig Groot-Brittannië, incl. transport.

Naam: ....

Adres: ....

.... Tel.: ....

Aan B.T.A., Britse Toeristische Dienst, Louizalaan 306 - 1050 Brussel

---

Que disent les
policiers anglais
pour arrêter
un suspect?

STOP! OR I'LL SAY STOP AGAIN!

C'est un gars imposant de deux mètres avec un drôle
de casque. Toujours prêt à aider, il est stoïque, calme, ne
connaît pas la panique. C'est pourquoi il ne porte générale-
ment pas d'arme et donc ne dit jamais: 'Halte ou je tire!'.
C'est un symbole typique du flegme anglais.

P&O
European Ferries

BRITAIN
SI DIFFERENT
SI PROCHE

Oui, envoyez-moi contre ce bon votre guide gratuit et différent
'La Grande-Bretagne de A à Z' avec les moyens de transport.

Nom: ....

Adresse: ....

.... Tél.: ....

British Tourist Authority, Avenue Louise 306 - 1050 Bruxelles

---

Het Engels
is heel
makkelijk.

(Vooral als u Nederlands spreekt.)

Fax, voucher, Chunnel, minitrip, parking, hotel,
VIP, lunch, pudding, caddy, shopping, sweat-shirt,
compact disc, walkman.
Sandwich, ketchup, milk-shake, bowling, golf,
taxi, chewing-gum, hall, living,pressing, smoking,
brushing, cocktail, night-club, disco, rock.
Bloody mary, T-shirt, jogging, beefsteak, pop art,
modern style, video, hobby, change, bye bye, ticker,
stress, ferry, happy end. En goed week-end!

Stena Line

BRITAIN
ZO VERSCHILLEND
ZO DICHTBIJ

Ja, stuur me gratis, in ruil voor deze bon - géén kopie, het A-Z
pocketboek over geestig Groot-Brittannië, incl. transport.

Naam: ....

Adres: ....

.... Tel.: ....

Aan B.T.A., Britse Toeristische Dienst, Louizalaan 306 - 1050 Brussel

Plate 14 BTA: attracting tourists by means of cognitive humour

(Reproduced with permission of British Tourist Authority)

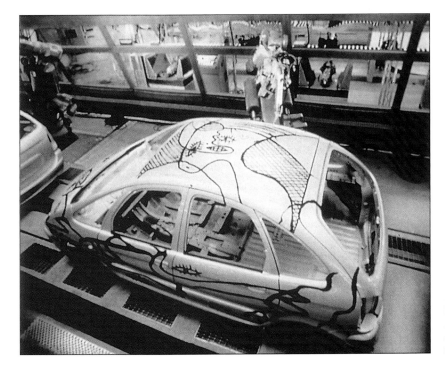

Plate 15 Citroën:
Picasso paints the Xsara

(Reproduced with permission of
Gesamtverband Werbeagenturen
GWA and Euro RSCG Works)

Plate 16 CKone: building a
brand image by eroticising it

(Reproduced with permission of
Advertising Archives)

Plate 17 Nicorette: giving up
smoking with a smile

(Reproduced with permission of
Gesamtverband Werbeagenturen GWA and
Abbott Mead Vickers BBDO)

Plate 18 L'Oréal: a tower in Berlin is a spectacular advertising medium

Plate 19 Whiskas: direct marketing loyalty programme to owners of cats and kittens in Germany

(Reproduced with permission of Federation of European Direct Marketing)

Plate 20 Smart: store image and
store design as positioning tool

(Reproduced with permission of Smart Center
Antwerpen)

Plate 21 Iglo: how to attract attention by means of in-store product presentation

(Reproduced with permission of Iglo-Ola, a Division of Unilever Belgium)

Plate 22 Red Bull: in-pub communication on Table Mountain (Cape Town)

Plate 23 Etap: unsinkable sailing pleasure exhibited

(Reproduced with permission of Etap Yachting n.v.)

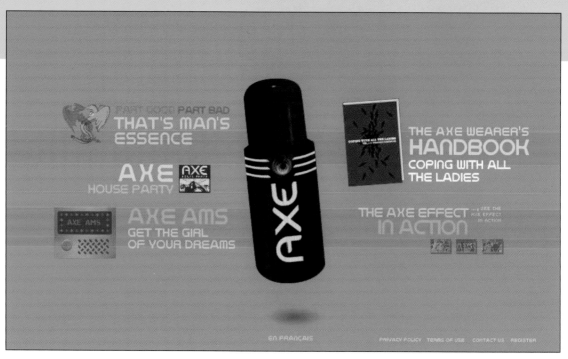

Plate 24 Axe: the Axe effect

(Reproduced with permission of Unilever, Inc.)

Plate 25 Umicore: supporting an industrial company repositioning by means of a new brand name and an integrated communications campaign

(Reproduced with permission of Umicore)

"I DON'T *work* WITH AMATEURS."

John Gainsford, Director of the Bellingham wine estate in Franschoek, South Africa is a very direct person.

"I say what I think. You have to have a PASSION about wine otherwise get out of the business. Wine is a product that lives – sheer poetry, romance, excitement. One bottle of wine is very, very important. One bottle can mean to us five years WORK, it can mean thirty, forty thousand cases."

So when John Gainsford distributes Bellingham wines around the world, he refuses to compromise.

"We're PROFESSIONALS and we want to work with professionals. I don't want wine that's due for New York ending up in London. I TRUST DHL, that when they undertake a job, they do it. I wouldn't work with them, if they hadn't the same passion that I have about my BUSINESS. The people at DHL haven't failed me yet, that's why I work with them. I don't work with amateurs."

We keep your promises

Plate 26 DHL: the French are not convinced by a South African wine grower

(Reproduced with permission of DHL Worldwide Network)

ABSOLUT VENICE.

Plate 27 Absolut Vodka: think global, act local

(Reproduced with permission of V&S Vin & Spirit AB. Absolut Country of Sweden Vodka & logo, Absolut, Absolut bottle design and Absolut calligraphy are trademarks owned by V&S Vin & Spirit AB. © 2006 V&S Vin & Spirit AB. Photo by Vincent Dixon)

Plate 28 McDonald's: selling arguments have to be adapted to local culture

Plate 29 Comfort Bultex: sits like it fits

of money on sponsorship can cause trouble with employees, especially if they are not properly informed about the relevance and economic justification of the sponsorship strategy. A company sponsoring a sportsman or woman or a team can alienate fans of the opponent.

Furthermore, unlike television sets and newspapers, sportsmen and women lead their own lives, and sometimes attract media attention that is not always favourable to the sponsor. The drugs scandal revealed in the Tour de France of 1998 was not particularly welcomed by the teams' sponsors, although Festina, the Spanish brand of timepieces and main sponsor of one of the offending teams, did not seem to suffer too much from the negative publicity. But even without such incidents, if the team or the sportsperson does badly, this can reflect negatively on the sponsor's image. Not surprisingly, a clean image is one of the main criteria on the basis of which sports or sports teams are selected for sponsorship.[38] Finally, although sports sponsorship can be used to transcend cultural, linguistic and geographic boundaries, some sports, like bull fighting, camel wrestling and dwarf throwing, are unfit for global brand sponsorship because they are culturally unacceptable in a number of countries.

Obviously, arts and cultural sponsorship is fundamentally different from sports sponsorship. First of all, arts audiences are different from sports audiences. The former are typically older and more affluent, and generally less numerous. The arts attract less media coverage and publicity, and are more suited to niche market segments than sports. However, some argue that the arts are increasingly attractive as sponsorship objects because of the increasing costs and saturation of sport sponsorship. Furthermore, a Toshiba study reveals that four times as many people visit museums and galleries as attended league football matches. Nevertheless, arts sponsors are believed to pursue corporate image and relationship and hospitality objectives rather than marketing goals. That makes arts sponsorship more of a PR tool than a marketing communications instrument.[39]

Coca-Cola: Integrating sponsorship into the marketing communications mix

For years Coca-Cola has been sponsoring big sports events all over the world. Obviously the World Cup in France could not be left out. Besides Coca-Cola's global approach to events like this, local adaptations were allowed. The Dutch agency localised Coca-Cola's sponsorship strategy as follows. Dutch teenagers could win a ticket to the World Cup for three bonus points and a good motivation, not as an international player, but as ball boy or girl, or as player in the games taking place just before the kick-off. Furthermore, Coca-Cola organised a fan day. For five bonus points Dutch fans could come to the Amsterdam Arena to wave their football heroes goodbye. For this successful localisation of a global sponsorship Coca-Cola received a nomination at the Esprix 1999, an award for exemplary Dutch Direct Marketing and Sales Promotion campaigns.[40]

Broadcast sponsorship

Broadcast or programme sponsorship is an increasingly important phenomenon. In the UK, broadcast sponsorship is estimated to be growing by approximately 15% per year.[41] In some countries, as in Belgium, government-owned television channels are not allowed to broadcast advertising messages, but are allowed to have their programmes sponsored, which makes broadcast sponsoring an extremely visible phenomenon. Broadcast sponsorship differs from plain advertising in a medium, in this case television, in that the sponsor has an influence on the content of the sponsored programme. Different types of broadcast sponsorship can be distinguished. Mentioning the name of a sponsor in a television programme is called billboarding: 'this programme was produced with the kind co-operation of company X'. Product placement involves the sponsor's product being used during the programme, and it is deliberately shown to the audience. Inscript sponsoring is a specific form of product placement. The sponsoring brand becomes part of the script of the programme. For instance if a programme is sponsored by a telecom company and the presenter asks the live audience to switch off their mobile phones, this establishes a connection between the sponsor and the programme. In prize sponsorship, the sponsoring company pays for awards or prizes, and is mentioned in the programme. In case of programme participation, product placement and billboarding are combined. The television channel produces a programme in close co-operation with a sponsor, for instance a tour operator that sponsors a travel programme, and pays for the prizes to be won in a contest during the programme.[42]

Product placement

In many cases, making movies would be impossible without product placement contracts between companies and movie producers. In the Bond movie *Die Another Day*, 20 brands are promoted by means of product placement. The total value of these contracts is estimated to be €45 million. James Bond (Pierce Brosnan) is civilised, appeals to both men and women, likes luxury and technology, and is popular around the world. Halle Berry, who features as the Bond girl Jinx, appeals to youngsters. Companies try to associate their image with the attractive features of the movie characters. Bond shaves with a Philishave Sensotec, drinks Finlandia vodka, wears an Omega Seamaster watch, and again drives an Aston Martin, after a couple of BMW-dominated Bond movies. Jinx drives a Ford Thunderbird in the same colour as her bikini (a special Thunderbird 007 series is also being made), uses the new Revlon lipsticks Mission Mauve and Hot Pursuit Pink, and wears a Swatch. Other product placers are Samsonite, Sony and British Airways.[43]

Product placement can be very effective, depending upon a number of moderating factors. A UK study of the impact of 10 cases of product placement in films resulted in the following conclusions:[44]

■ Product placement leads to an increase in brand salience;

■ Familiarity with a product category may have an inverse effect of product placement on brand salience;

■ Prior exposure to the film may have an inverse effect upon salience;

■ Liking of, and attention to, the film often increases brand salience;

■ People with a high degree of self-monitoring (wanting to behave as they perceive others expect) exhibit higher levels of brand salience than people with a low degree of self-monitoring after exposure to a product placed in a film.

Of all sponsorship types, broadcast sponsorship is closest to advertising and for that reason is capable of achieving similar objectives of awareness and image building. Furthermore, famous television actors featuring in the sponsored programmes can be used as celebrity endorsers in subsequent advertising campaigns, thus leveraging the sponsorship effort. Nevertheless, broadcast sponsorship is perceived more positively by the public. Sponsors are closely tied to the programme itself. In fact, they are physically part of it, to the extent that viewers even believe that sponsors actively participate in making the programme. Furthermore, sometimes the endorsing brand has a better image than the programme itself. Therefore, if the sponsor fits the programme well, this can lead to very positive carry-over effects between the two. Programme sponsorship also works in a different way. The long-term association between a likeable programme and a sponsor may lead to a very strong and positive brand image. Finally, broadcast sponsorship, as opposed to advertising, is perceived to benefit everyone. This has a major positive impact on viewer's acceptance of such sponsorships.[45] Belgian research reveals that these positive effects can only be expected if there is a long-term link between an exclusive sponsor and a programme. Short-term broadcast sponsorships are usually as ineffective as ordinary advertising or sports sponsorship campaigns.[46]

Desperate Housewives drive Ford

The Ford group owns eight car makes. To reach its customers the company increasingly relies upon product placement of its cars in movies and television shows instead of traditional advertising, the effectiveness of which is increasingly challenged. The Ford Explorer 4x4 already played a prominent role in *Jurassic Park*, and a Range Rover was prominently present in *Ocean's Twelve*, not to mention James Bond's Aston Martin. Fans of popular shows like *Desperate Housewives* now watch their favourite actresses drive car models of the Ford group: Susan drives a Volvo, and Lynette's husband goes to work in a Jaguar. Film- and programme-makers used to have to talk to each Ford brand separately, but now Ford has established 'Global Brand Entertainment', a company that supports the product placement of all Ford brands, from the Mazda Miata to the Aston Martin Vanquish.

Source: De Morgen, 4 May 2005.

Cause-related sponsorship

Cause-related sponsorship is a combination of public relations, sales promotions and corporate philanthropy, based on profit-motivated giving to good causes. MUSH sponsoring comes closest to traditional sponsoring in that money is given to good causes in return for exposure and image-building linkage with the good cause sponsored. Transaction-based sponsorship (sometimes called cause-related marketing) is different in that a company's contribution to a designated cause is linked to customers' engagement in revenue-producing exchanges with the firm.

Although the objectives of cause-related sponsorship are to a certain extent the same as those of other sponsorship activity, more emphasis is put on the impact on corporate or brand image as a result of the link between the company or the brand and the good cause sponsored. Research has shown that effective cause-related sponsorship programmes can enhance a company's reputation and brand image, and at the same time give customers a convenient way to contribute to non-profit organisations through their buying decisions. It is not only marketing professionals who believe that cause-related marketing can improve the image of their brands, consumers also seem to be interested. Studies indicate that as many as two-thirds of consumers are willing to take the company's contribution to good causes into account when taking a decision on which brands to purchase. A 2000 survey in 12 European countries indicated that two in five consumers bought a product because of its links to good causes. Cause-related marketing allows companies to attract and retain consumers, differentiate themselves from the competition and reach niche markets. Furthermore, cause-related sponsorship can motivate and engender loyalty in employees. In a 1999 study, 87% of employees in companies with cause-related programmes indicated a strong loyalty to their employer. Gradually, for many companies, cause-related sponsorship has evolved from a short-term, one-shot activity to a long-term strategic choice. Cause programmes are selected because they fit into company competences and long-term strategic objectives. Cause-related sponsorship places high demands on a company's strategy. A company wanting to engage in cause programmes successfully should be aware of the important principles of such activity: integrity, transparency, sincerity, mutual respect, partnership and mutual benefit. If not, the whole sponsorship programme will backfire, and the company will become known as insincere, opportunistic and lacking in credibility.[47]

Cause-related sponsorship programmes as a communications tool

In October 1999 ConAgra Foods, a company owning more than 80 household brands, launched Feeding Children Better, a cause programme to stop childhood hunger. By partnering with various anti-hunger organisations and using its extensive distribution, advertising and promotion resources, the company was able to bring more food into the charitable food distribution system and put child hunger on the agenda. Since the beginning of the programme, 50 Kids Cafes (places where kids can have a decent meal after school) have been funded, fresh food deliveries to relief organisations have increased dramatically and 29 trucks have been purchased for food banks with gifts from ConAgra. The programme received numerous sponsorship and non-profit awards.

Since 1995 Ford Motor Company has sponsored the Susan G. Komen's Breast Cancer Foundation. The support is not linked to Ford sales, but the company helps the organisation with donations, media support and in-kind gifts. The company also created the Ford Force, a united front of dealers, employees and the general public. More than 12,000 Ford employees and more than 3,000 dealers have participated in the activities of Ford Force. The results have been impressive, both for the Komen's foundation and for Ford. Website visits and toll-free telephone calls have increased dramatically, and there is a substantial increase in breast examinations. Ford has been able to create interest and sympathy among women, previously a lowly involved market segment.

Timberland, a lifestyle brand that sells footwear, apparel and accessories, and City Year, a national youth service organisation, have been partners for over 10 years. Timberland has donated more than US$ 10 million in grants and in-kind gifts since the beginning of the partnership. The partnership has helped to promote a service ethic among Timberland employees, who have contributed over 170,000 hours of community service. Timberland and City Year have co-ordinated numerous other service events and campaigns. Timberland also opened a City Year office in its headquarters. As a result, the company was voted by its peers as one of the '100 best companies to work for'.[48]

These examples illustrate that cause-related programmes can enhance corporate visibility and image, involve previously uninterested market segments and improve the commitment of the employees and future employees of the organisation.

A hybrid form of broadcast and cause-related sponsorship is the organised sponsorship of advocacy advertising on television. For instance, an insurance company could sponsor television spots in which parents are warned against situations that are potentially dangerous to children, such as water boiling on a stove, knives within reach, etc.

Ambush marketing

Ambush marketing occurs when an organisation deliberately seeks an association with a particular event without paying sponsorship fees, to persuade the audience that the ambusher is a legitimate or major sponsor. This can be done by sponsoring the media covering the event, by sponsoring subcategories within the event (one team or one player), or by overstating the organisation's involvement in the event by means of supporting advertising or sales promotion activity during the event.

Ambush marketers use several techniques, some of which are illegal, most of which are at least dubious, and some of which are legitimate. Ambush sponsors can use logos and brand names in non-authorised media: they can use sports logos and sports images without permission, exploit PR opportunities, sample non-official products or brochures, or run ambiguous advertising campaigns during the time of the event. They can co-operate with subsponsors of the event or with the media covering the event, or they can buy advertising spots or trailers that are embedded in an event that is, as such, sponsored by another company. They can publish 'congratulation ads' for athletes that have won a match or a medal or they can sponsor non-profit projects associated with the event.[49] Not surprisingly, official sponsors try to gain exclusive sponsorship and coverage of events in the media to prevent ambushers benefiting or the effectiveness of their own sponsorship efforts diminishing as a result of competitive action.

Ambush marketing in action

- Viewer recall and recognition scores for both sponsors and ambushers during the 1988 Winter Olympic Games revealed that the official sponsors were recalled more often than the ambushers in only four of seven product categories.[50]
- The spontaneous brand awareness of Sony rose by eight points to 61% during the 1991 Rugby World Cup. Sony was also mentioned as the main sponsor of this event. However, Sony was not the sponsor of the event itself, but of the ITV coverage.[51]
- When the Belgian top tennis player Kim Clijsters reached the final of Roland Garros in 2001, the insurance company Delta Lloyd, the official sponsor of the Belgian Tennis Federation, used her face in a newspaper advertisement the next day, referring to her performance. The federation had to intervene to prevent a lawsuit by the Clijsters management against the insurance company.
- To piggyback on soccer enthusiasm in the Netherlands, and in order not to allow Hyundai the advantage from being the official sponsor of the Euro 2000 European soccer tournament, Hyundai's competitor Daewoo launched an ambush campaign. Against a background of cheering soccer players, Daewoo advertised that car buyers would get a discount of €2,000 when buying a new Daewoo car. A judge ruled that this campaign was not a breach of the Euro 2000 'brand name'.[52]

Selection criteria

Selecting sponsorship proposals should be based on a careful comparison using appropriate selection criteria. In Figure 11.5 a five-step multi-attribute decision procedure of sponsorship selection is shown.

Multiple criteria can be used to assess and select sponsorship proposals. They can be divided into three categories, listed in Table 11.7.

Figure 11.5 Selecting sponsorship projects

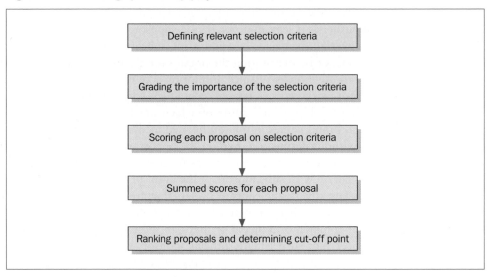

Table 11.7 Assessment criteria for sponsorship proposals

Sponsored event or cause	Potential promotional spin-off	Budget
■ Type of event or cause ■ Quality level or image of the event ■ Target groups ■ Compatibility between sponsored event and company's promotional strategy ■ Strategic fit between event or cause and company or brand name ■ Uniqueness of sponsorship or place of the company in the list of sponsors ■ Length of impact ■ Geographic scope ■ Company's role in decision-making ■ Protection against ambush marketing	■ Event's own communications plan ■ Estimated media coverage ■ Quantity and quality of exposure ■ Fit between company's and event's communications strategy ■ Interest with employees ■ Corporate hospitality potential ■ Sales promotion spin-off potential ■ PR spin-off potential ■ Advertising spin-off potential ■ Amount of supporting advertising or PR activity needed ■ Chance of negative or no media exposure ■ Measurability and evaluation of effectiveness	■ Costs in cash or kind ■ Alternative investment for budget and expected return ■ Budget for supporting marketing activity ■ Time implications for own staff

Depending on the type of company and the type of sponsorship projects, some criteria will be more important than others. But some of them should always be assessed as important. Sponsorship budgets and supporting marketing budgets, compatibility with the company's strategic objectives, the strategic fit between the event and the company's or brand's name, image and target groups will always be important. On the other hand, media exposure and other spin-off potential and competitive considerations may be more important in sports sponsorship, while corporate hospitality potential and the interest to employees might be more important in an arts sponsorship project. Some companies may be more concerned about their corporate image (e.g. service or business-to-business marketers), while fast-moving consumer goods companies may be more interested in the commercial spin-off potential, like sampling at the event, or organising a lottery-on-pack to attend an event.

The criteria listed should be used as a starting point. However, the selection of relevant criteria and the grading of their importance will largely depend on the type of company and its overall communications strategy. The eventual short list of potential candidates for sponsorship will ultimately depend on the relative weights of the criteria used and the available sponsorship budget.

Budgets

Obviously it is impossible to provide detailed guidelines as to the required budgets of a sponsorship campaign. Budgets should depend on the expected effectiveness or return in terms of exposure, communications effects and sales or market share impact (see below). As in communications campaigns in general, the objective-and-task method is called for. Sponsorship decision-makers should decide on the objectives they want to achieve, assess to what extent a sponsorship programme can contribute to these objectives and try to calculate how large an economically meaningful sponsorship budget should be. Needless to say, in most cases this is a cumbersome task. As an illustration, in Table 11.8 the budgets of major sponsors of professional cycling teams in 2002 are shown.

However, sponsorship-linked budgets are not limited to the expenditures directly related to the sponsored event or cause, but also encompass all communications efforts and budgets that are spent leveraging the investments in the activity or cause. Buying

Table 11.8 Budgets of major sponsors of professional cycling teams in 2002

UCI rank	Official UCI name (nationality)	Budget (€ million)	Activity	Sponsor since
1	Fassa Bortolo (Italy)	7.5	Building materials	2000
2	Deutsche Telekom (Germany)	12.0	Telecommunication	1991
3	Rabobank (Netherlands)	8.5	Bank	1996
4	Mapei*/Quick Step (Italy)	12.0	Glue/Laminates	1993
5	Lotto*/Adecco (Belgium)	4.5	Lottery/Interim bureau	1985
6	Banesto.com (Spain)	6.5	Bank	1989
7	Cofidis (France)	6.5	Credit organisation	1997
8	Once*/Eroski (Spain)	8.0	Lottery/Distributor	1989
9	US Postal Service (USA)	6.5	Postal services	1995
10	Domo*/Farm Frites (Belgium)	7.0	Carpets/Potato products	2002

* Sponsor from the year given in the 'Sponsor since' column.
Based on: Lagae, W. (2003), Marketingcommunicatie in de Sport. Pearson Education Benelux.

Table 11.9 Activities used to support sports sponsorship

Activity	Mean importance (7-point scale)
Signs and banners	5.83
Public relations	5.21
Advertising the sponsorship	5.14
Hospitality	4.85
Advertising the event	4.64
Point of sale promotion	4.24
Mainstream advertising	3.93
Competitions	3.31
Direct mail	2.78

Based on: Thwaites, D., Anguilar-Manjarrez, R. and Kidd, C. (1998), 'Sports Sponsorship Development in Leading Canadian Companies: Issues and Trends', *International Journal of Advertising*, 17(1), 29–50. Reproduced with permission of NTC Publications Limited.

the sponsorship rights is indeed 'just a licence to spend more money to leverage the initial investment'. For instance, Coca-Cola spent US$40 million to become an official sponsor of the 1996 Olympics, and an estimated $500 million to leverage this status.[53] A Canadian study revealed that only 37% of sports sponsors do not provide an additional support budget. But almost 20% allocate an additional budget of 50% of the sponsoring budget or more to communications support activities. In Table 11.9 the type of supporting activities and their relative importance is illustrated.

Indeed, there are different reasons why sponsorship should be supported by other media efforts. First, as has already been mentioned, sponsorship has its limitations. Very often brand awareness and brand image are supported, but other necessary communications and commercial objectives, like building knowledge about the brand and generating sales, will have to be achieved by means of additional communications support. But most importantly, the general principle of integrated communications also applies to sponsorship: the more it is supported by, and integrated in, the rest of the communications mix, the more effective it will be. For instance, among the sponsoring companies of the 1996 Olympics that also ran advertising on the events, 64% succeeded in creating the link. On the other hand, of the official sponsors that did not run advertising, only 4% created the link.[54]

Measuring sponsorship effectiveness

Similar to the measurement of the effectiveness of other communications tools, isolating the effect of sponsorship is complicated by a number of factors, such as the simultaneous use of instruments of the marketing and communications mix, the carry-over effect of earlier activities, creative management issues, the pursuit of multiple objectives and the discretionary nature of media coverage.

Sponsorship is to a certain extent similar to advertising in that one of its main objectives is to build brand awareness with specific target groups. Additionally, and equally important, brands try to improve their image by linking their name to the event sponsored. Furthermore, in a number of sponsorship projects, communications results are not only obtained during the sponsored event, but also as a result of their media coverage. Sponsorship research reflects these objectives and characteristics of this communications mix instrument.

Four types of sponsorship effectiveness can be distinguished (Figure 11.6). Two types of exposure can be distinguished: the number of people attending the event and the exposure resulting from the media coverage of the event. By counting the number of attendees at a sponsored event, and/or studying the composition of the audience present, the number of consumers reached and the frequency of their exposure to the brand name can be estimated. If the sponsored event is covered by the media, the number of lines, pages or times the brand name is mentioned, or the number of seconds it is shown on television or heard on the radio, can be calculated. On this basis, reach and frequency of exposure can also be estimated, as well as the monetary value of the exposure obtained. Evidently, frequency of exposure and reach only give an indication of the probability of having contacted parts of the target group, but nothing about the actual number of contacts, let alone of their quality or impact.

Figure 11.6 Types of sponsorship effectiveness measures

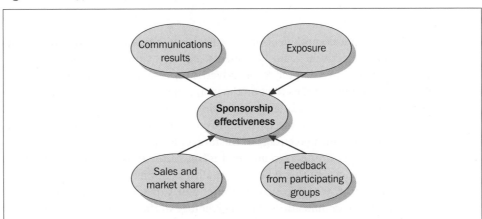

Worldwide Tour de France television exposure

The Tour de France is a major sporting event that attracts large corporate sponsors. One of the strengths of the Tour as an interesting event to sponsor is the three weeks of media coverage all around the world. In Chart 1 the number of hours of television coverage in 2002 in Europe and Asia is given. Chart 2 presents the average number of television viewers per day in 2000 for a number of European countries.

Chart 1 Number of hours of television coverage of the Tour de France in 2002

Europe	Number of hours	Asia-Pacific	Number of hours
Switzerland	203	Japan	90
Belgium	200	Australia	50
Denmark	152	China	35
France	122	New Zealand	33
Netherlands, The	100	Taiwan	20
Germany	72	Philippines	20
UK	64	India	12
Spain	63	Singapore	7
Italy	30	Hong Kong	2

Based on: ASO (2002), *Bilan-tv. Tour de France 2002*. Paris: ASO.

▶

Chart 2 Average number of viewers per day of Tour de France coverage 2000

Country	Number of viewers
Germany	4,000,000
Italy	2,870,000
US	2,080,000
Spain	1,670,000
Netherlands	820,000
UK	766,000
Belgium	680,000
Denmark	251,000
Switzerland	164,000
Portugal	144,000

Based on: ASO (2000), *Tv-exposure Tour de France 2000*. Paris: ASO.

Second, communications results can be measured. In this respect sponsorship campaign effectiveness measurements are very similar to the advertising campaign tests discussed in Chapter 9 on advertising research: brand awareness, correct sponsor attribution and the effect on the image of the sponsored event and the sponsoring brand can be measured. Besides increasing brand awareness, associating the brand with the sponsored event is the most important objective of a sponsorship campaign. As a result, measuring the percentage of the target group able to attribute correctly the name of the sponsoring brand(s) to an event is one of the most important measures of sponsorship effectiveness. In this type of test, a list of sponsored events is presented to a sample of consumers, who have to attribute (aided or unaided) the sponsors of the event. This results in an indication of the percentage of the target group that can correctly attribute sponsors to events, as well as measures of 'sponsor confusion'. Correct (aided and unaided) sponsorship attribution can be very low, while sponsorship confusion is in some cases stunningly high.

Virgin's Festivalbuddy

The airline company Virgin Express sponsors several music festivals. To counter the problem of festival visitors not knowing/remembering who actually sponsored the festival, Virgin decided to move from just being present during the festivals to involving festival visitors before and during the festival. To this end they launched the Festivalbuddy campaign. Festival lovers could *register by means of SMS or on the festivalbuddy website. Afterwards, Virgin sent them a* 'buddyword' by SMS. The challenge for the registered persons was to find another person with the same buddyword. Everyone who succeeded in this and presented themselves with their buddy at a Virgin stand on one of the festivals, won a free Virgin flight. The campaign created an enormous viral effect and was a real hype during several months in many communities. A Google-search on the word 'festivalbuddy' delivered about 80,000 results. Someone created a special 'festivalbuddy-matching' site and during the festivals several people wore a T-shirt on which their buddy word was printed in the hope to find their buddy. No doubt, Virgin succeeded in its objective of being linked to the sponsored festivals.

Based on: Cuckoo Awards 2006.

Additionally, the purpose of sponsorship is to associate the sponsoring brand or company with the sponsored event. Sponsorship research can therefore also focus on the link between the image of the brand and the event with members of the target group.

The effectiveness of sponsorship can also be conceptualised by means of the 'Persuasive Impact Equation'.[55] This equation integrates a number of important sponsorship impact factors at the communications level:

Persuasive impact = Strength of the link × duration of the link × (gratitude felt due to the link + perceptual change due to the link)

The more target group members are aware of the link between the sponsor and the sponsee, and the longer the duration of this perceived link, the more impact a sponsorship has had. The larger the gratitude felt as a result of the sponsorship, and the more positive the perceptual change of the image of the sponsor, the more impact the sponsorship has achieved.

Although increasing sales or market share is not the primary objective of sponsorship, its long-term effectiveness can also be assessed by estimating the sponsorship's commercial impact.

Finally, sponsorship effectiveness can also be measured on the basis of feedback from participating groups. Given the nature of some types of sponsorship, its effectiveness primarily lies in the reaction of participants to corporate hospitality sponsorship projects or the opinion of employees about sponsorship programmes. This will particularly – but not exclusively – be the case in cultural or cause-related sponsorship.

Integrating sponsorship in IMC

Sponsorship is probably one of the marketing communication tools that requires most support from other tools to be effective and at the same time offers ample opportunities for marketing communication spin-off activities. Sponsorship of events, teams and organisations can be referred to in television advertising during the event or in the advertisements of sponsored partners, by means of cross-reference to teams, celebrities, events . . . Television coverage of events can be used as an opportunity for programme sponsorship or product placement. Events can be an opportunity for couponing or sampling, but also for corporate hospitality. Cause-related sponsorship can be part of a public relations campaign aimed at building a good reputation for the company and its brands. It can enhance corporate identity building by means of the opportunities it offers to motivate and reward employees. During the sponsored event a microsite can be set up on which games, promotions and other customer contact opportunities are offered, which can subsequently be used for customer relationship marketing and direct communication. In-store merchandising can hook up to the sponsorship campaign by drawing the attention to the sponsored event and by offering special promotions connected with the sponsorship campaign.

Summary

Sponsorship is an increasingly important instrument of the marketing communications mix. This not only becomes clear from the increasing budgets spent on sponsoring, but also from the fact that the key roles in sponsorship decisions are often played by members of top management. Sponsors often try to escape the advertising clutter by linking their name to an event, and hope for beneficial carry-over effects from the event on company and brand awareness and image. Target groups for sponsorship are not only those that visit or participate in the event, but can also be any of the other marketing and corporate audiences of a company. Four basic types of sponsorship can be distinguished. Event-related (culture and sports) sponsorship is best known. Cause-related sponsorship, or sponsoring good causes, is the oldest form. Broadcast sponsorship is a more recent phenomenon, but is growing fast. The youngest type is ambush marketing, whereby a company tries to benefit from an event it does not sponsor. To integrate sponsorship effectively into the marketing communications mix, it is crucial to select the right sponsorship projects and to manage them at close range. Criteria that can be used to select projects can be event-related (type of event, quality level, target groups, uniqueness of sponsorship, fit with strategic objectives, etc.), spin-off related (indirect communications effects, media coverage, interest with employees, advertising and PR spin-off, etc.) and budget-related (cost in cash or in kind, time implications for staff, etc.). Sponsorship effectiveness can be measured on the basis of exposure, communications results, commercial results or on the basis of feedback from participating groups.

Review questions

1 What is the difference between sponsorship and advertising, public relations and value marketing?

2 How can the mere exposure effect, congruence theory and operant conditioning explain how sponsorship works?

3 What are the most important current developments in sponsorship?

4 How can sponsorship be used to reach a variety of objectives in different target groups?

5 What are the advantages and disadvantages of the various types of event-related sponsorship?

6 How can cause-related sponsorship contribute to a company's communications strategy?

7 What criteria can be used to select sponsorship proposals?

8 How can the effectiveness of a sponsorship campaign be measured?

Further reading

Adkins, S. (1999), *Cause-related Marketing: Who Cares wins*. Oxford: Butterworth-Heinemann.

Cornwell, T.B. and Maignan, I. (1998), 'An International Review of Sponsorship Research', *Journal of Advertising*, 27(1), 1–21.

Duffy, N. (2003), *Passion Branding: Successful Sports Sponsorship*. John Wiley & Sons.

Grey, A.M. and Shildum-Reid, K. (2003), *The Sponsorship Seeker's Toolkit*. McGraw-Hill.

International Journal of Advertising, 1998.

International Journal of Sports Marketing and Sponsorship.

Lagae, W. (2005), *Sports Sponsorship and Marketing Communications*, Harlow: Prentice Hall.

Case 11

Sponsoring championship football – France 98, Euro 2000 and the Nordic 2008 proposal

Football championships as strong brands

In recent years, the European and World football championships have been managed as high-profile events with sophisticated marketing communications campaigns, both from the point of view of the organising countries and the sponsors of the tournaments. Organising countries have positioned their championships as strong brands with unique core values, and have tried to attract sponsors that have the same core values. The sponsors of the championships have their own agenda and try to enhance the awareness and image of their brands among their target groups, piggybacking upon the worldwide interest for the football event. In a way, being a 'partner', or a structural sponsor, of a football championship is an exercise in co-branding. Sponsors start from the image and the core values that are being created by the organising countries, and try to position their brand images by developing sponsorship and other communications campaigns that are consistent with the brand values of the championship. In 1998 the World football championships were held in France ('France 98'); the European football championships in 2000 were held in Belgium and The Netherlands ('Euro 2000'). The Scandinavian countries were candidates for the organisation of the European championships in 2008 ('Nordic 2008'). First, the core values of these championships are discussed, and then the strategy and sponsorship campaigns of the strategic partners of France 98 and Euro 2000 are highlighted.

The core values of the football championships France 98, Euro 2000 and Nordic 2008

France 98

The slogan of France 98 was 'The beauty of a world at play'. Through this core theme the organisers wanted to communicate that the championships were more than a series of football games. It is remarkable that, compared with other championships, the word 'football' did not appear in this core theme. The slogan of the 1996 championships in the UK was 'Football comes home', and that of Euro 2000 was 'Football without frontiers'. Three emotional cues were attached to France 98: universality, excitement and sharing. Universality referred to the fact that football is the most popular sport worldwide; excitement had to do with the atmosphere during the matches; sharing referred to the shared emotions during the games. These three core values were used throughout all communications about the championships. In building this brand, events and the media played an important role. On 14 September 1995, the media were invited to officially start the campaign, with exactly 1,000 days to go to the championships. At the end of 1995 the pools and calendar of the preparatory tournament were officially composed during an event at the Louvre. The official mascot was presented in 1996, and a contest was organised to find a name for it (Footix). One year before the start of the campaign, the official poster of France 98 was presented (with Ronaldo, Platini and children from around the world). On 4 December 1997, the pools and calendar of the championship were composed at an event in a full stadium. The fact that France won the championship against super-favourite Brazil was, of course, a splendid apotheosis of four weeks of football. The organisation committee, the sponsors, FIFA (the international football organisation), the various cities in France where the matches were played and the media all worked together to consistently build the strong brand 'France 98'. The chaotic ticket sale was the only dark spot on the image of this football event.

Euro 2000

The European football championships in 2000 were jointly organised by Belgium and The Netherlands. The core theme of the tournament was 'Football without frontiers'. The co-operation between Belgium and The Netherlands stressed the international European character of the championships. Sharing exciting emotions was another core theme of the event. The public in the organising countries was critical about the decision to organise it in their countries, and they were particularly concerned about safety and traffic problems during the tournament. The communication campaign therefore used active media PR to stress the precautions taken to cope with these potential problems, and to convince the general public that everything was in place to organise an impeccable tournament. Numerous lifestyle events and tourist activities were organised to promote Euro 2000.

Nordic 2008
Value management was also a central issue in the proposal of the 2008 European championships campaign in the Scandinavian countries. Nordic 2008 is a co-operation between Denmark, Finland, Sweden and Norway. In their campaign, 'United Smile', the focus was on football players, the game and the spectators. The concept referred to the peaceful co-existence of top sport, emotions and positive behaviour of the football fans. In the practical implementation of this concept, the principle of the 'eHighway Express' was used. This principle refers to five 'e-values': easygoing, ecological, electronic, experiences and European. The organisers wanted to make the tournament accessible to everyone, and they wanted it to be organised as an ecological event in eight stadiums in all organising countries. The spectator is the MIP (Most Important Person). Above all, safety and fun is important. The stadiums complied with the very strict UEFA (the European football organisation) safety standards, public transport is widely available, the stadiums were all in beautiful cultural and historical cities at the waterfront, ticket sales were family-friendly, and 'smart tickets' should enhance the safety in the stadiums. Nordic 2008 wanted to unite the participating countries 'on the pitch', sharing positive emotions. The Scandinavian authorities and private companies all supported the United Smile theme.

The sponsors of France 98 and Euro 2000

In Case Table 11.1, the official partners and suppliers of France 98 and Euro 2000 are presented. The implementation of their sponsorship campaigns is discussed in the next sections.

France 98
For *Coca-Cola* it was very important to be associated with the championships. The main objective of its sponsorship was to appeal to its target groups and keep brand preference at a high level. Coca-Cola wanted to show that it shares and understands its consumers' passion for football. Refreshment, both physical and emotional, during and after the match, was the core message of its campaign. Coca-Cola focussed its communications during the tournament on 12–19 year olds. Fans from more than 60 countries were involved in promotional activities and events. The championships were promoted in three continents; the promotion trip was sponsored by Coca-Cola. In that way, it shared the enthusiasm of the fans in countries such as Nigeria, Saudi Arabia, South Korea, England, The Netherlands and France. A number of country-specific activities were also organised. For instance, the Cup was first kissed by Ronald Koeman on Dutch soil, after which it made a trip through the Netherlands to allow fans to share

Case Table 11.1 Partners and suppliers of France 98 and Euro 2000

France 98		Euro 2000	
Partners	*Suppliers*	*Partners*	*Suppliers*
EuroCard/MasterCard	Danone	Carlsberg	Adecco
Fuji Film	EDS	Coca-Cola	Adidas
Gillette	France Télécom	Fuji Film	Cisco
JVC	Hewlett-Packard	Hyundai	Connexxion
Philips	La Poste	JVC	KLM
Opel	Manpower	EuroCard/MasterCard	Lever Fabergé
McDonald's	Sybase	McDonald's	Nashuatec
Adidas		Philips	Nestlé
Snickers		Playstation	Total Fina
Coca-Cola		Pringles	Telfort
Canon		PSINet	
Budweiser		Sportal.com	

* Budweiser was replaced by Casio as a boarding sponsor in the stadiums because of a French law that forbids advertising for alcoholic beverages.

the passion by holding the Cup for a few moments. On 7 June 1998 a big 'fan day' was organised in Amsterdam. Fans could greet their football heroes and wish them success on their trip to France. By joining a contest, boys and girls could win tickets or a position as ball boy or girl in one of the matches. Also in Belgium a contest was organised: participants had to guess how long it would take the Belgian goalkeeper to run around a football pitch. The winner received the lifelong right to a ticket for a match in the first round of the European championships, together with his or her partner, all costs paid by Coca-Cola.

As a sponsor of France 98, *Adidas* wanted to communicate that it was more than just a manufacturer of football products. At France 98, Adidas was a sponsor, a supplier of balls, ball boys and girls, and 12,000 volunteers, and the only licenser of the official World Championship outfit. By clothing top players like Kluivert and Zidane, it wanted to communicate that top football players are very selective about the material they choose to wear. The core target group of 12–19 year olds was reached through music television channels. For instance, Kluivert appeared on *The Music Factory* in a specially designated programme to talk about football and many other things. Adidas visited all youth tournaments in Belgium and Holland with a test centre for Adidas products. Near the Eiffel Tower an Adidas football village was built to organise a youth tournament during the championships.

Opel sponsored France 98 to support brand awareness and to make the brand image more dynamic. The championships were used to create an emotional bond between the brand and the customers in its European markets. The 1998 championship was also considered the highlight and the logical continuation of the Opel sports sponsorship strategy of the previous years. Together with Visa, in France Opel made 700 cars available to accommodate guests invited to the Opel Club. The Opel subsidiaries in every country could decide in which way they wanted to benefit from the France 98 event. In all European countries the subsidiaries could support the Opel sponsorship by means of various promotional campaigns, such as advertisements, sales promotions, dealer incentives, etc. In Belgium and The Netherlands, a limited series of the Corsa Worldcup was manufactured.

For *Mcdonald's* France 98 was an opportunity to express its sympathy with top athletes and a unique sports event. Through in-store activities and the creation of a World Cup meal in 75 countries, McDonald's tried to carry over the fun and the excitement of the tournament to its customers. A Mc World Cup Special was offered with a spicy salsa sauce to make the association with Brazilian football. Furthermore, social programmes and local sports events were set up in various cities in France. Together with Fuji Film, the Young Photojournalist Contest was organised for children aged between 8 and 14 from The Netherlands, the UK, Italy and Argentina. The Mc Goal! Goal! Goal! campaign rewarded creative football with gifts to SOS Children's Village, the official social cause programme of FIFA.

A remarkable initiative was the sponsorship by *Snickers* of the Fair Play marathon between 4 December 1997 and 10 June 1998, which passed through 162 cities around the world. Every day two athletes ran half a marathon, totalling more than 7,000 kilometres. Around the marathon, 10,000 children were gathered through events and contests. Snickers also supported its sponsorship through extensive media advertising campaigns.

A new trend was the joint effort by the French Ministry of Youth and Sports and *Adidas, McDonald's* and *Danone* to organise a football tournament in 128 cities in France for boys born after 1984. The winning team in each city was combined with youth players from Brazil, Mexico and South Africa. The initiative aimed at stimulating integration, solidarity and sports. The campaign 'T'es jeune, t'es foot' was sponsored by *Coca-Cola* and *Crédit Agricole*. It tried to realise the dream of many boys and girls to participate in the championship as a volunteer or as a ball boy or girl.

Euro 2000

The sponsorship of Euro 2000 by *Hyundai* was part of an agreement to also sponsor the World Championships of 2002 in Japan and South Korea. For Hyundai, Euro 2000 offered an opportunity to improve its brand awareness and image in Europe because the brand name and logo of Hyundai were consistently exposed to the public, together with world-famous brands such as Coca-Cola, McDonald's and Playstation. During the tournament, Hyundai invested a lot in media campaigns to constantly draw attention to the brand in connection with Euro 2000. For instance, in May 2000 a television and poster campaign was rolled out to promote the Athos, Coupé and Accent models.

Coca-Cola was again an official sponsor of the European football championships in 2000. Together with the cities in which the tournament was organised,

Coca-Cola developed a campaign, the communications tools of which were city maps, fan villages and vending machines. In that way, Coca-Cola tried to establish good contacts with local administrations. The brand image was also supported by means of street soccer tournaments and 'refreshment zones'. The latter were locations within two to five kilometres of the stadiums or in the historical centres of the cities (parking lots, metro stations, newspaper kiosks, tourist venues, etc.), where the brand name was extensively presented and unique brand events could be experienced. For instance, in Amsterdam fans could find refreshment against an ice wall, and could drink a Coke in a uniquely constructed ice bar.

Nashautec, one of the official suppliers of the tournament, wanted to communicate that it is more than just a manufacturer of copiers, printers and fax machines, but that it also sells hardware and software and consultancy. Nashuatec Benelux installed 450 'remanufactured' (used) fax and copy machines and printers, and 70 technicians to control the data flows at Euro 2000. It wanted to show that the machines worked flawlessly in the capable hands of the Nashuatec people. The company also invited 2,500 business contacts, and rolled out several image advertising campaigns.

Questions

1 To what extent are the sponsorship and support campaigns of the France 98 and Euro 2000 sponsors consistent with, and building upon, the core values of France 98 and Euro 2000? Discuss the campaigns of every sponsor described in the case.

2 Could the sponsors have organised other types of activities? Which ones? Try to think of other types of sponsorships and other types of communications.

3 Are there any companies or brands in the list that seem less compatible with football championships, given their objectives and target groups? Why?

4 Try to think of sponsors that are compatible with the core values of the Nordic 2008 campaign. What activities could they undertake to support and build upon their Nordic 2008 sponsorship?

5 How would you measure the impact of the sponsorship campaigns?

Based on: Lagae, W. (2003), *Marketingcommunicatie in de Sport*, Pearson Education Benelux.

References

1 Meenaghan, T. (1991), 'The Role of Sponsorship in the Marketing Communication Mix', *International Journal of Advertising*, 10(1), 35–48.

2 Erdogan, Z.B. and Kitchen, P.J. (1998), 'The Interaction Between Advertising and Sponsorship: Uneasy Alliance or Strategic Symbiosis', in Kitchen, P.J. (ed.), *The Changing World of Corporate and Marketing Communication: Towards the Next Millennia, Proceedings of the 3rd Annual Conference of the Global Institute for Corporate and Marketing Communication*. Strathclyde Graduate Business School, 144–55.

3 Hastings, G.B. (1984), 'Sponsorship Works Differently from Advertising', *International Journal of Advertising*, 3(2), 171–8.

4 Erdogan, Z.B. and Kitchen, P.J. (1998), 'The Interaction Between Advertising and Sponsorship: Uneasy Alliance or Strategic Symbiosis', in Kitchen, P.J. (ed.), *The Changing World of Corporate and Marketing Communication: Towards the Next Millennia, Proceedings of the 3rd Annual Conference of the Global Institute for Corporate and Marketing Communication*. Strathclyde Graduate Business School, 144–55.

5 Meenaghan, T. (1983), 'Commercial Sponsorship', *European Journal of Marketing*, 7(7), 5–71.

6 Marshall, D.W. and Cook, G. (1992), 'The Corporate (Sports) Sponsor', *International Journal of Advertising*, 11(3), 307–24.

7 Bloxham, M. (1998), 'Brand Affinity and Television Programme Sponsorship', *International Journal of Advertising*, 17(1), 89–98.

8 Cornwell, T.B. and Maignan, I. (1998), 'An International Review of Sponsorship Research', *Journal of Advertising*, 27(1), 1–21.

9 Adfo Specialist Group (1999), *Rabobank Wielerplan* (*Rabobank Cyclism Plan*), Adfo Sponsoring Cases no. 2, Alphen aan den Rijn: Samson; Adfo Specialist Group (2000), *Nashuatec en Oliver*, Adfo Sponsoring Cases no. 5, Alphen aan den Rijn: Samson.

10 See also: Abshire, M. (2002), *Consumer Product Manufacturers: Maintain Giving in Uncertain Times*. Corporate Philanthropy Report 17 (March), 1–11; Polonsky, M. and Macdonald, E. (2000), 'Exploring the Link Between Cause-related Marketing and Brand Building', *International Journal of Nonprofit and Voluntary Sector Marketing*, 5 (February), 46–57.

11 Cornwell, T.B. and Maignan, I. (1998), 'An International Review of Sponsorship Research', *Journal of Advertising*, 27(1), 1–21.

12 Watson, J. and Watson, J. (2001), 'Sponsorship and Congruity Theory: A Theoretical Framework for Explaining Consumer Attitude and Recall of Event Sponsorship', *Advances in Consumer Research*, 28, 439–45.

13 Hansen, F. and Scotwin, L. (1995), 'An Experimental Enquiry into Sponsorship: What Effects Can Be Measured?', *Marketing and Research Today*, 23(3), 173–81.

14 Stipp, H. (1998), 'The Impact of Olympic Sponsorship on Corporate Image', *International Journal of Advertising*, 17(1), 75–88.

15 De Pelsmacker, P., Geuens, M. and Anckaert, P. (2002), 'Media Context and Advertising Effectiveness: The Role of Context Appreciation and Context–ad Similarity', *Journal of Advertising*, 31(2), 49–61.

16 Hoek, J., Gendall, P., Jeffcoat, M. and Orsman, D. (1997), 'Sponsorship and Advertising; A Comparison of Their Effects', *Journal of Marketing Communication*, 3(1), 21–32.

17 Hansen, F. and Scotwin, L. (1995), 'An Experimental Enquiry into Sponsorship: What Effects Can Be Measured?', *Marketing and Research Today*, 23(3), 173–81.

18 Irwin, R., Sutton, W. and McCarthy, L. (2002), *Sport Promotion and Sales Management*. Champaign: Human Kinetics.

29 Meenaghan, T. (1998), 'Current Developments and Future Directions in Sponsorship', *International Journal of Advertising*, 17(1), 3–28.

20 Euro Effie 2002.

21 Quester, P.G., Farrelly, F.J. and Burton, R. (1998), 'Sports Sponsorship Management: A Multinational Comparative Study', *Journal of Marketing Communication*, 4(2), 115–28; Farrelly, F.J. and Quester, P.G. (1997), 'Sports and Arts Sponsors: Investigating the Similarities and Differences in Management Practices', in Meenaghan, T. (ed.), *New and Evolving Paradigms: The Emerging Future of Marketing, American Marketing Association Special Conference Proceedings*. Dublin: University College, 874–86.

22 Thwaites, D., Anguilar-Manjarrez, R. and Kidd, C. (1998), 'Sports Sponsorship Development in Leading Canadian Companies: Issues and Trends', *International Journal of Advertising*, 17(1), 29–50.

23 Quester, P. (1997), 'Awareness as a Measure of Sponsorship Effectiveness: The Adelaide Formula One Grand Prix and Evidence of Incidental Ambush Effects', *Journal of Marketing Communications*, 3(1), 1–20.

24 Meenaghan, T. (1998), 'Current Developments and Future Directions in Sponsorship', *International Journal of Advertising*, 17(1), 3–28.

25 www.olympic.org/uk/organisation/facts/revenue, 23 May 2003.

26 Thwaites, D., Anguilar-Manjarrez, R. and Kidd, C. (1998), 'Sports Sponsorship Development in Leading Canadian Companies: Issues and Trends', *International Journal of Advertising*, 17(1), 29–50.

27 www.nop.co.uk/news, 23 May 2003.

28 Thwaites, D., Anguilar-Manjarrez, R. and Kidd, C. (1998), 'Sports Sponsorship Development in Leading Canadian Companies: Issues and Trends', *International Journal of Advertising*, 17(1), 29–50; Abratt, R., Clayton, B.C. and

Pitt, L.F. (1987), 'Corporate Objectives in Sports Sponsorship', *International Journal of Advertising*, 8(2), 299–311; Hansen, F. and Scotwin, L. (1995), 'An Experimental Enquiry into Sponsorship: What Effects Can Be Measured?', *Marketing and Research Today*, 23(3), 173–81.

29 Quester, P. (1997), 'Sponsoring Returns: Unexpected Results and the Value of Naming Rights' in Meenaghan, T. (ed.), *New and Evolving Paradigms: The Emerging Future of Marketing, American Marketing Association Special Conference Proceedings*. Dublin: University College, 692–4.

30 Cornwell, T.B. and Maignan, I. (1998), 'An International Review of Sponsorship Research', *Journal of Advertising*, 27(1), 1–21.

31 Grimes, E. and Meenaghan, T. (1998), 'Focusing Commercial Sponsorship on the Internal Corporate Audience', *International Journal of Advertising*, 17(1), 51–74.

32 Lagae, W. (2005), *Sports Sponsorship and Marketing Communications*, Harlow: Prentice Hall.

33 Irwin, R., Sutton, W. and McCarthy, L. (2002), *Sport Promotion and Sales Management*. Champaign: Human Kinetics.

34 www.communicatiecoach.com, 23 May 2003.

35 Lagae, W. (1997), 'Het Pokerspel van de Professionele Wielersponsoring' ('The Poker Game of Professional Cycling Sponsorship'), in Duyck, R. and Van Tilborgh, C. (eds), *Aan Marketing Denken en Doen. Marketing Jaarboek (Thinking of and Doing Marketing. Marketing Yearbook)*. Zellick: Roularta Books, 86–94.

36 Brassington, F. and Pettitt, S. (2003), *Principles of Marketing*. London: Pitman Publishing.

37 Cornwell, T.B. and Maignan, I. (1998), 'An International Review of Sponsorship Research', *Journal of Advertising*, 27(1), 1–21.

38 Thwaites, D., Anguilar-Manjarrez, R. and Kidd, C. (1998), 'Sports Sponsorship Development in Leading Canadian Companies: Issues and Trends', *International Journal of Advertising*, 17(1), 29–50.

39 Farrelly, F.J. and Quester, P.G. (1997), 'Sports and Arts Sponsors: Investigating the Similarities and Differences in Management Practices', in Meenaghan, T. (ed.), *New and Evolving Paradigms: The Emerging Future of Marketing, American Marketing Association Special Conference Proceedings*. Dublin: University College, 874–86.

40 *Esprix Jaarboek*, 1999, 86.

41 Brassington, F. and Pettitt, S. (2003), *Principles of Marketing*. London: Pitman Publishing.

42 Floor, J.M. and van Raaij, W.F. (2002), *Marketing-communicatiestrategie (Marketing Communication Strategy)*. Groningen: Wolters-Noordhoff.

43 *De Morgen*, 16 November 2002.

44 Johnstone, E. and Dodd, C. (2000), 'Placement as Mediators of Brand Salience within a UK Cinema Audience', *Journal of Marketing Communications*, 6(3), 141–58.

45 Bloxham, M. (1998), 'Brand Affinity and Television Programme Sponsorship', *International Journal of Advertising*, 17(1), 89–98.

46 De Pelsmacker, P., Van den Bergh, J. and Anckaert, P. (1998), *De Effectiviteit van Sponsoring (The Effective-*

ness of Sponsorship). Marketing Communication Research Centre, Research report no. 8. Ghent; De Vlerick School voor Management.

47 www.bsr.org, 23 May 2003.

48 www.bsr.org, 23 May 2003.

49 Lagae, W. (2005), *Sports Sponsorship and Marketing Communications*, Harlow: Prentice Hall.

50 Sandler, D.M. and Shani, D. (1989), 'Olympic Sponsorship vs "Ambush" Marketing: Who Gets the Gold?' *Journal of Advertising Research*, August/September, 9–14.

51 Smith, P.R. (1993), *Marketing Communication. An Integrated Approach*. London: Kogan Page.

52 Lagae, W. (2005), *Sports Sponsorship and Marketing Communications*, Harlow: Prentice Hall.

53 Sandler, D.M., Shani, D. and Lee, M.S. (1998), 'How Consumers Learn About Sponsors: The Impact of Information Sources on Sponsorship', in Meenaghan, T. (ed.), *New and Evolving Paradigms: The Emerging Future of Marketing, American Marketing Association Special Conference Proceedings*. Dublin: University College, 869–71.

54 Erdogan, Z.B. and Kitchen, P.J. (1998), 'The Interaction Between Advertising and Sponsorship: Uneasy Alliance or Strategic Symbiosis?', in Kitchen, P.J. (ed.), *The Changing World of Corporate and Marketing Communication: Towards the Next Millennia. Proceedings of the 3rd Annual Conference of the Global Institute for Corporate and Marketing Communication*, Strathclyde Graduate Business School, 144–55.

55 Crimmins, J. and Horn, M. (1996), 'Sponsorship: From Management Ego Trip to Marketing Success', *Journal of Advertising Research*, 36(4), 11–21.

Chapter 12

Sales promotions

Chapter outline

Importance of sales promotions	**Objectives and target groups**
Consumer promotions ■ monetary incentives ■ prizes ■ product promotions	**Trade promotions**

Are sales promotions effective?

Sales promotions research

Chapter objectives

This chapter will help you to:

- Understand why sales promotions are an increasingly important instrument in the communications mix
- Learn about the various types of promotions and their objectives and target groups
- Distinguish between the various consumer and trade promotion tools, and their advantages and disadvantages
- Understand to what extent sales promotions are effective
- Learn about the techniques to measure sales promotions effectiveness

Introduction

Unlike many other instruments in the communications mix, sales promotions are a category of techniques aimed at increasing sales in the short run, and therefore mostly used for a short period of time. Essentially, sales promotions are 'action communications' to generate extra sales, both from existing customers purchasing more products and by (temporarily) attracting new customers, on the basis of a temporary incentive or deal. The main characteristics of promotions are that they are limited in time and space, they offer better value for money and they attempt to provoke an immediate behavioural response. Although in sales promotions lead and lag effects can be distinguished, their effectiveness can be evaluated more directly than that of advertising and many other marketing communications instruments.

The effectiveness of promotions is often attributed to the operant conditioning mechanism: behaviour that is rewarded serves to reinforce future behaviour. Sales promotions are, as a result of this type of conditioning, quickly recognised by the consumer as a reinforcer, a reward, based on his past experience. For this mechanism to take place, the incentive has to be important enough for a consumer to notice a relevant difference from his or her anchorpoint, i.e. the 'normal' price quality expectation. In other words, the incentive has to exceed the 'just noticeable difference threshold'.[1] Promotions have to be substantial enough to trigger a behavioural response.

Although the main purpose of promotions is to trigger immediate sales, they can also be used more strategically, i.e. to generate, through trial purchases and subsequent learning effects, a change in the attitude towards the brand and, as a result, brand loyalty. In spite of this objective, sales promotions are often regarded as a threat to the long-term image and therefore profit potential of the brand because too frequent promotional actions give the brand a reputation of 'cheapness' and destroy the perception of its intrinsic qualities. Therefore – and also because the perception exists that in the long run promotional efforts are not always profitable – some manufacturers avoid the promotion instrument. The 'every day low pricing' (EDLP) strategy, permanent low prices for certain product categories, is sometimes used to replace *ad hoc* promotions.

The growing importance of sales promotions

Sales promotions are becoming an increasingly important instrument of the communications mix.[2] In 1980 American companies spent 44% of their advertising and promotions budget on advertising. Twenty years later in the US, still more money is spent on promotions than on advertising.[3] A similar situation exists in Europe. In the UK, for instance, estimates suggest that promotion budgets exceed advertising spends. Some sources claim that the advertising to sales promotion expenditure ratio has evolved from 60:40 in the mid-1980s to 30:70 in favour of sales promotions.[4] This evolution can be attributed to a number of factors (Figure 12.1).

In an increasing number of product categories, more and more brands and product lines are offered. For the consumers it is becoming increasingly difficult to distinguish

Figure 12.1 Factors affecting the increasing use of sales promotions

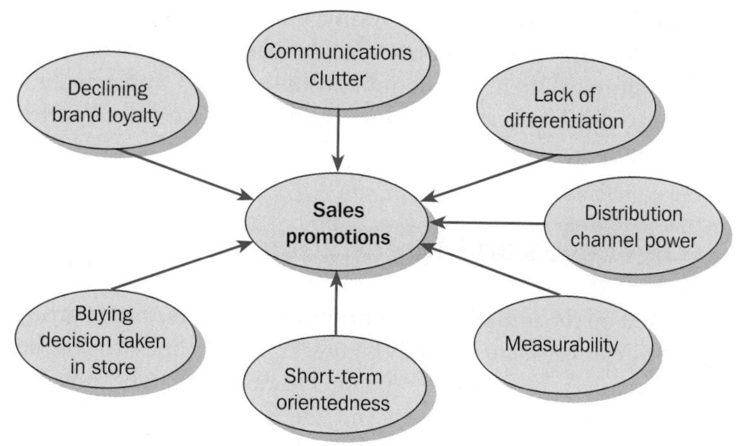

brands on the basis of their intrinsic qualities. Furthermore, functional differences between brands have become less important. Therefore, manufacturers find it increasingly difficult to differentiate their brands on the basis of advertising. Promotion is seen as a useful tool to attract the attention of target groups and to 'seduce' them into buying their brands. It is increasingly difficult to reach the consumer effectively by means of advertising. Individual ads get lost in communications clutter, and are hardly noticed by the majority of consumers. In a previous chapter the effects of communications clutter on brand confusion were illustrated. Furthermore, advertising avoidance behaviour by consumers is an increasingly important phenomenon, mainly as a result of the irritation caused by advertising (see Chapter 7). Therefore, marketers are looking for other tools to attract consumers' attention to their brands.

Consumers, at least for certain fast-moving consumer product categories, are less brand loyal, and are becoming increasingly price-conscious.[5] This results in an increased response to material incentives, such as promotions. The majority of buying decisions take place within the retail outlet. An increasing number of product or brand purchasing decisions are essentially impulse-buying decisions. Since communications efforts are most effective at the time and place when and where the consumer makes his or her decision, in-store communications elements and incentives become more attractive tools of persuasion.

Companies are becoming increasingly short-term oriented. However, the effects of traditional advertising campaigns only become visible in the long run. Product managers who want to see immediate results from their communications efforts will therefore be tempted to use promotion tools rather than long-term thematic advertising campaigns. The result of a promotion campaign can be more easily measured than that of an advertising campaign. Advertising is often aimed at obtaining intermediate effects, such as awareness and favourable attitudes, eventually leading to increased sales. Promotions are aimed at an immediate behavioural response, which can be readily measured. The immediate availability of results for most product managers is a very welcome characteristic of promotions. Finally, distribution channels are becoming increasingly powerful. Many brands are jostling for shelf space and, as a result, retailers are in a position to decide which brands will obtain shelf space under which conditions. Often, promotional tools are used to persuade the trade channel. Furthermore, the distribution channel is taking an increasing part in the promotional activity of manufacturers.

Objectives and target groups

Based on the initiator of the promotions and his target groups, several types of promotions can be distinguished (Figure 12.2). The initiator of the promotions can be either the manufacturer or the retailer. Promotions can be aimed at three types of audiences: distributors, the salesforce and the end consumer. Normally, retailers only promote to end consumers, whereas manufacturers can target their efforts at all three target groups. This results in four types of promotions:

- consumer promotions by manufacturers;
- consumer promotions by retailers;
- trade promotions by manufacturers, aimed at distributors;
- salesforce promotions by manufacturers.

The first two types are essentially similar in nature, since they are aimed at the end consumer. Specific tools of retail promotion are discussed in Chapter 14 on in-store communications.

Figure 12.2 Basic types of sales promotions

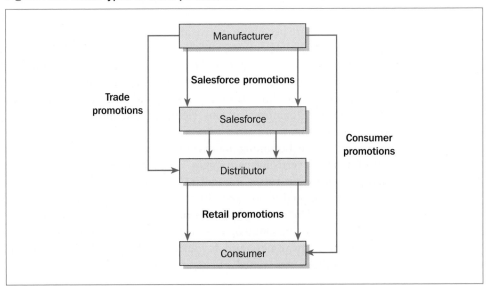

From trade to consumer promotions?

Recently there have been reports that, especially in food marketing, trade promotions are tending to gain in importance at the expense of consumer promotions. This evolution is attributed to the previously mentioned intensified battle for shelf space and the growing power of the distribution channels. However, a trade promotion survey of the food industry in the US showed that, on average, the allocation of funds between trade promotions and consumer promotions has not significantly changed between 1997 and 2002. The relative importance of trade promotions has only marginally decreased by two points to 49% of the total promotion and advertising expenses in 2002. The share of advertising has remained stable at 24%; consumer promotions have increased in importance to 27%. There are indications, however, that marketers are trying to monitor all their promotion efforts to ensure more impact. In trade promotion, this means that there is a shift in budgets from generic ads and displays to co-marketing partnerships with retailers (e.g. in-store events like demonstrations and recipe programmes), in which the latter also have to invest. Shifting the promotion focus from trade to consumer promotions does not necessarily work. For instance, Heinz suffered share and volume declines as a result of shifting its efforts to 'keep the consumers in the forefront'. It had to acknowledge that many of its products benefit more from trade efforts than from consumer-oriented campaigns.[6]

Consumer promotions can have several objectives and target groups[7] (Figure 12.3). Potential new customers can be attracted to try the product. Inducing trial by new customers is one of the most important objectives of a promotion campaign. This 'horizontal' effect results from brand-switching (i.e. consumers of competing brands purchase the promoted brand), or from attracting consumers who have never tried the product category before. The latter group is seldom inclined to try a product on the basis of consumer promotions alone. Trial promotions are particularly important when launching a new brand or a new item in a product line. When a retailer opens a new store, trial promotions (in this case by the retailer) can be an important tool to generate store traffic, in other words to make consumers enter the store.

Figure 12.3 Objectives and target groups of consumer promotions

Existing customers can be made loyal, and loyal customers can be rewarded for their loyalty. For a marketer it may be more important (and certainly less expensive) to retain a (loyal) customer than to convince a competitor's client to switch brands. Therefore, promotions are frequently aimed at inducing repeat purchase or rewarding loyal customers to stop them trying a competitor's product on promotion.

Promotions can be used to **increase market size**, as such, by stimulating the use of an entire product category. Promotions of this type are particularly suitable for market leaders who benefit most from a growing market or from a market without seasonal fluctuations. Examples are last-minute offerings, or selling ice cream during winter. Another way of inducing this 'vertical effect' of market growth is to increase sales with existing consumers. Consumer 'basket-filling' (e.g. by giving discounts when large volumes are purchased) not only increases sales, but also serves as a buffer against competitors' actions. As long as the consumer has sufficient stock of the product he or she may be less inclined to try a competitor's promotional efforts.

Finally, promotions can serve as **reinforcers of other communications tools**. An advertising campaign can have a greater impact if a promotion is included. The response to a direct mailing campaign may be much more effective if the mail is linked to a promotional offer. This symbiotic effect is often counted on in mail order catalogue selling.

The effect of marketing efforts are increasingly dependent on the co-operation of the distribution channel. To that end, trade promotions are used to persuade channel members to include the product in their mix, to give it appropriate shelf space, and to assist in promoting the product to the end consumer. One of the most important objectives of trade promotions is to gain the support of the distribution channel, both wholesaler and retailer, when **launching a new product**. In order for an end consumer to be able to buy the product, it has to be on the shelves in sufficient quantities and in a sufficiently large number of retail stores. Since the number of new brands is increasing steadily, the trade channel has to choose which ones to carry in their assortment and to promote. In that case trade promotions precede consumer promotions, and successful trade promotion is a prerequisite for an effective new product launch. In that respect, trade promotion is also 'trial' promotion in the sense that the distribution channel has to be persuaded to include the new product in its assortment. Furthermore, the success of a new product often depends on the number of retail outlets in which the product is on shelf. Therefore, trade promotions are often aimed at intensifying distribution in terms of the number of outlets in which the product is available.

For existing products, it is useful to **keep the trade channel motivated** to sell the brand. Trade promotions are aimed at maintaining shelf space or at inducing the retailer to promote the product by means of retailer promotions. One way to motivate the trade channel to push the product is by increasing its stock. Full warehouses induce the trade to pay more attention to selling the products in stock, i.e. to give them more shelf space and to promote the products actively themselves. On the other hand, trade promotions can be used to decrease the stock of a product in the trade channel rapidly, e.g. when a new product launch is being prepared.

In a more general sense, trade promotions are used to **keep the distribution channel loyal to a product (category)**. Much as in the case of 'rewarding' the consumer for loyalty to a brand by means of consumer promotions, the distribution channel may be rewarded for its loyalty in giving shelf space to a product by means of trade promotions.

The salesforce is an integral part of the distribution effort, since they are the first link in the distribution channel. As a result, offering them incentives to market the product well is a vital first step in any marketing strategy. Salesforce promotions are discussed in greater detail in Chapter 16 on personal selling. The most important objectives of salesforce promotions are to induce the salesforce to approach new customers, more specifically members of the trade channel, to try the product, or to increase the volume purchased by existing customers. In industrial marketing situations, new final customers can be the target.

The salesforce can also be encouraged to push new or existing brands as part of an integrated short-term sales promotions effort, or as a support to an advertising campaign. As in consumer promotions, a synergetic effect between salesforce promotions and other communications tools, such as advertising, can be established. Finally, the salesforce can be motivated to help the distribution channel to improve the exposure of the brand, by giving it more and better shelf space, keep the shelves filled, checking stocks, and pushing and improving the use of displays and other in-store communications material.

Depending on the objective of the promotions, a number of specific tools can be used. An overview of consumer and trade promotion techniques is given in the following sections.

IMC promotions

Promotions can be very creative, and can result in synergetic effects with other communications tools. Two examples of so-called offbeat promotions illustrate this.[8]

■ As a promotional stunt for **Dare**, a perfume brand, the Daring Adventure Programme was launched. Women were invited to write a story about their most intimate and adventurous dates. The winning stories were published in a booklet that was given as a premium to all buyers of Dare perfume. The campaign attracted a lot of media attention, trial purchase and consumer involvement.

■ **Odour Eaters** insoles organise a contest every year to award a prize, the Order of the Golden Sneaker, to the most stinking shoes. The name of the owner of the shoes is cited in the Hall of Fumes, and receives a cash prize. The shoes are exhibited in stores selling Odour Eaters. Again, the campaign results in a lot of publicity, consumer involvement and store traffic.

Consumer promotions

Depending on the type of incentive, three categories of consumer promotions can be distinguished, i.e. monetary incentives, product promotions and the chance to win a prize (Table 12.1).[9]

Monetary incentives

Different types of monetary incentives can be used, but they all lead to an improved price/quality perception by the consumer by lowering the price of the product.

Table 12.1 Consumer promotion tools

Monetary incentives	Chance to win a prize	Product promotions
■ Price cut on the shelf ■ Coupons ■ Cash refunds ■ Extra volume ■ Savings cards	■ Contests ■ Sweepstakes and lotteries	■ Sampling ■ Free in mail ■ Premiums ■ Self liquidators ■ Savings cards

The most direct monetary incentive is the price cut on the shelf in which the consumer gets an immediate discount when buying the product. This is the most immediate and simplest price promotion for the consumer, the manufacturer and the retailer. It can be used to generate trial, stimulate repeat purchase behaviour and for 'basket-filling' purposes. The advantage for the consumer is that the price cut is immediate and unconditional. The manufacturer can easily and quickly organise sales promotions of this type, and it does not lead to extra workload for the retailer. Furthermore, price cuts on the shelf almost invariably lead to additional turnover.

Price cuts are not always profitable

For a price cut to be profitable, certain – sometimes unrealistic – conditions have to be met. Suppose a six-pack of chocolate bars costs €2. The manufacturer's margin is €0.4. A price cut of 10% means that the chocolate bars are now sold at €1.8. If the price cut is fully absorbed by the manufacturer, this means that he is giving away half (€0.2/0.4) of his profit margin per chocolate bar pack. To enable him to earn as much total profit as before, twice as many chocolate bars will have to be sold, that is the sales volume will have to increase by 100%. Hence, a status quo in profitability implies a price elasticity of demand of 10, i.e. a price cut of 10% should lead to an increase in demand of 100%.

On the other hand, there are a number of disadvantages, the most important being the potential damage to the image of the product and the store. Although promotions always run the risk of damaging a brand's high-quality image, this is more specifically the case with immediate and directly visible price cuts. Consumers may doubt the quality of the product or the store in which too many price cuts are offered. When price cuts are used too frequently, the company runs the risk of selling discounts rather than products. Furthermore, too frequent price cuts influence the consumers' expectations of the normal price of a product: no price cuts may be perceived as price increases. Price cuts can be very expensive for both the manufacturer and the retailer. Large extra volumes may be required to compensate for the loss of margin per unit. Therefore, although the promotion campaign may be successful in terms of extra volume or extra trial, its profitability may be far from impressive.

Coupons are vouchers representing a monetary value with which the consumer can get a discount on a specific product. Coupons may be inserted in print ads, in direct mailings, or in newspapers and/or magazines. They can also be offered on-pack, in-pack or near-pack, or be distributed after a previous purchase. Normally, coupons have a limited lifetime. The percentage of coupons distributed that are used when buying a product is called the redemption rate. Coupons have been a promotional strategy for more than 100 years. By 1965 in the US more than 350 manufacturers were distributing 10 billion coupons annually. In 2001 it was estimated that 3,000 manufacturers distributed 310 billion coupons. Redemption rates are, on average, lower than 2%.[10] To increase the redemption rate and lower the cost of coupon distribution, more targeted procedures can be used, as illustrated below.

Database technology improves the effectiveness of sales promotions

Computer technology, barcode scanning and individualised store cards can be used to generate powerful databases, on the basis of which tailor-made couponing campaigns can be organised.[11]

■ In Dahl's Food Supermarket, customers can become a member of the **Vision Value Club**. The computer chip in the individual store card immediately registers the purchases at the checkout, and the consumer can, by means of a touch screen, immediately check which coupons are available, and print the ones he or she is interested in.

■ A similar system has been tested by Prisunic (Lille, France). By means of interactive touch-screens throughout the store and a personal store card the consumer can immediately print the coupons he is entitled to on the basis of his past purchasing pattern. Suggestions can even be made as to a combination of purchases of e.g. food items that give the opportunity to obtain extra coupons.

■ A number of manufacturers of fast-moving consumer goods organise mailings in Belgium under the name of **Sophie's Shopping Club**. Consumers are asked to fill in a questionnaire on their buying habits. The response rate was 12%, and 70% of the target group recall having received the mailing. Based on their answers €30 million of personalised coupons were distributed, the redemption rate of which was 9%, far better than in a traditional couponing campaign.[12]

As a promotional tool, coupons can serve a number of objectives, of which stimulating trial is a very important one. Couponing has the advantage that the consumer gets an immediate discount, provided that he or she has noticed and is prepared to use the coupon. The consumer does not have to do much to enjoy the promotion. Manufacturers can target a couponing campaign very well, in specific media and/or retail outlets, and for specific product categories and towards well-defined target groups. The retailer also benefits from couponing in the sense that it often generates extra sales. A problem with couponing is that it is often difficult to predict the redemption rate, and thus the couponing budget. Furthermore, instead of inducing trial, couponing may only have the effect of 'subsidising' already loyal customers. The latter is not necessarily a disadvantage, since 'basket-filling' by existing customers may be the primary objective of a couponing action. If the consumer is not price-sensitive, he or she will probably not notice the coupon or not use it, in which case the promotion action will be ineffective. Finally, the co-operation of the retailer is necessary since couponing means more work at the checkout.

The Procter & Gamble zero-couponing strategy

Procter & Gamble is one of the largest coupon distributors. In 1992 the company announced a new strategy. It decided to spend 50% less on couponing, and to adopt an EDLP (Every Day Low Prices) strategy, dropping retail prices by US$2 billion. In January 1996 the company launched an 18-month no-coupon test in a carefully chosen part of the state of New York, where 90% of the shoppers were known to use coupons. The vast majority of other manufacturers, retailers and wholesalers believed that this was a viable strategy, and some of them followed Procter & Gamble's lead. However, the no-coupon strategy was very unpopular among consumers. Many consumers considered coupons as 'an inalienable right'. Consumers in the test region started boycotts, public hearings and petition drives. Signs saying 'save our coupons' appeared in front gardens, and the local media were flooded with complaint letters to editors. The protests even made it into the national media. Public officials joined the protests, claiming that Procter & Gamble was the company of 'profit and greed' that hurt 'average Joe'. A resolution was voted to ask Procter & Gamble to abandon its strategy. Petitions with more than 20,000 signatures were sent to the company. After only 14 months, the company pulled the plug on its no-coupon test in April 1997. A settlement was agreed upon whereby US$4.2 billion worth of coupons was distributed that could be redeemed at any supermarket in the region by any consumer or for any food item. However, Procter & Gamble did not admit any wrongdoing. It still claimed that during the test period consumers received at least equally good value for money, without the cost and inconvenience of coupons. Nevertheless, the sales of Procter & Gamble were flat during the test period, while on average the use of coupons of competitors of Procter & Gamble and different product categories increased substantially. The company's experience has triggered new methods to distribute coupons. Instead of inserting them in media, more and more coupons are made available through shelf dispensers at the point of sale, in frequent buyer and loyalty programmes, in combination with free samples at the store, through direct mailings, the internet, or electronically at the checkout.[13]

Cash refunds are discounts offered to the consumer by means of refunding part of the purchase price after sending a proof of purchase. The refund is transferred to the customer's bank account. A cash refund is very similar to couponing in that it is mainly a trial-inducing promotion technique in which the consumer receives a price discount. Like couponing, the consumer has to do something, not by collecting coupons, but by sending back the proof of purchase.

Normally, cash refunds result in a more substantial discount than coupons. Therefore the resulting trial purchases tend to be higher. Furthermore, contrary to direct price cuts and couponing, the consumer has to pay the full price at the checkout. As a result, the consumer is less easily conditioned to expect lower prices and price expectations are less easily adjusted. As in the case of coupons, cash refund actions can be put in place very rapidly, and can be targeted to specific items of the product range. The main advantage for manufacturers is that the redemption of proofs of purchase enables them to build up a customer database. As compared to couponing, refunds do not result in extra work at the checkout. Therefore retailers prefer refunds to coupons.

Similar to couponing, it is difficult for the manufacturer to predict the success of a refund action, and hence the budget required. Again, there is the risk that existing customers will be subsidised instead of new customers being attracted. The main disadvantage for the consumer is that it takes more trouble to get the discount, especially if it means saving a number of proofs of purchase before part of the price is refunded. Sometimes the consumer has to wait a considerable time before the discount is refunded. Misunderstandings may occur if the consumer expects an immediate discount at the checkout or if it is not clear what part of the package the consumer has to send back to obtain the refund. The retailer may run the risk that the 'old' packages, of which no part of the price is refunded, are difficult to sell.

In product plus or extra volume promotions an extra quantity of the product is temporarily offered at the same price. In fact extra volume promotions are very similar to other types of price promotions since the price per unit of volume decreases. Promotions of this type are mainly used to induce 'basket-filling' by regular users. Consumers are not tempted to try a product for the first time if it is offered in larger volumes, quite the contrary. On the other hand, regular users may be attracted to the savings per unit proposition, and therefore buy more of the product.

Promotions of this type are very attractive for consumers since the advantage is immediate and unconditional. It does not result in extra workload or costs for the retailer, except the problem of fitting larger pack sizes onto the shelves. In terms of organisation, the product plus promotion is a very simple tool for the manufacturer. Follow-up campaigns are not necessary, and the promotion can easily be communicated on-pack or via an advertising campaign. The disadvantage is that extra volume promotions tend to be quite expensive. Special packages have to be designed, logistic problems may arise, and the extra volume sold does not always compensate for the implicit price cut. Retailers may experience logistic problems too, and may find it difficult to sell old stock without product plus promotion. Furthermore, as a result of the basket-filling, retailers may see a fall in sales after the promotion, since consumers have all the product they need for a while, and are not inclined to buy the same product immediately after the promotion. If this promotional tool is used too often or for too long, consumers' expectations as to the normal price/quantity rate may be conditioned in the wrong direction.

Award-winning promotions

The Esprix awards in the Netherlands make an award for the best promotion and direct marketing campaigns. Here are two examples of 2002 winners:[14]

- During a certain period of time, a special edition of the women's weekly magazine *Margriet* was given as a premium to every consumer who purchased a Nivea Vital product. This special edition entirely focussed upon the 1970s to offer the target group a nostalgic flashback to the time they were young and to create the right atmosphere to make the target group aware of the importance of the appropriate product for mature skin (Nivea Vital). The idea is based on the appreciation of a generation and its specific needs. The sales of Nivea Vital increased by more than 40%, and the promotion campaign resulted in market leadership for the brand.

- During the period before the release of a Harry Potter movie, Coca-Cola offered each family in the Netherlands a special six-pack of 1.5l bottles of Coke in a special and unique Harry Potter packaging format. The pack was cheaper than a normal pack of six bottles because of retailers' discounts. The box was used to creatively communicate the campaign in-store in most supermarkets. After a couple of months almost 200,000 Harry Potter Coca-Cola boxes were sold and became part of the decor of Dutch children's rooms. A unique packaging concept has successfully created a bond between the soft drink and its target group.

Monetary incentives may also be offered on the basis of repeat purchase of a brand or in a store. Savings cards, possibly combined with trading stamps, are promotion techniques on the basis of which customers receive a discount provided they have bought a number of units of the brand during a specific period of time, e.g. 'buy 10 items during one year, and you get a 20% discount when you buy the 11th item', or when trading stamps are handed in at the moment of purchase. This tool is often used by shops to stimulate store loyalty. The system is not very convenient for consumers, since they end up with dozens of saving cards in their wallet or purse if lots of brands or stores are using this type of promotion. If they forget the card, the item bought cannot be put on it. Furthermore, the discount is not immediate, it may take a long time before the consumer experiences the benefits of his loyalty. The advantage of the system is that the consumer is not conditioned to an immediate lower price. Moreover, promotions of this type (retention promotions) are very suitable for generating brand or store loyalty, since the benefit is dependent on repeat purchase. It is a very flexible promotion technique, since the number of trading stamps offered per purchase can be adapted to the objective at hand, e.g. to stimulate the sales of a specific item in a product range, double stamps can be offered. However, this promotional tool implies a long-term commitment by the manufacturer. If a large part of the budget is tied up in retention promotions, the short-term flexibility to react quickly to competitors' actions is lost. The system is widely used by shops of all kinds. The positive side-effect of using store cards is that the retailer can build up a consumer database and the purchasing history of each consumer can be tracked, and can be used to make future promotions more effective. Store cards, combined with scanning of barcodes of goods purchased, lead to powerful databases which are improving the ability of the retailer to understand consumer behaviour.

Contests, sweepstakes and lotteries

Contests differ from sweepstakes and lotteries in that in the former the participant can influence the outcome of the game. Creating a slogan or an advertising headline, recognising a voice or a piece of music, estimating how many people will send back a coupon, etc., are examples of contests. Lotteries and sweepstakes are based purely on chance. In a sweepstake, consumers receive a (set of) number(s), the winning ones of which are decided on in advance. This means that, if only 10% of the customers having received a set of numbers participate by buying a product, only 10% of the prizes have to be awarded. Sweepstakes are frequently used by mail order catalogue companies. In some countries some types of sweepstakes are forbidden by law.

Chance games are easy to organise, relatively cheap and appealing to consumers, depending on how gamble-prone they are, which is to a certain extent culturally determined. Consumers have much to win and nothing to lose. Therefore, contests and lotteries can be relatively effective promotion tools, provided the prizes are attractive enough. On the other hand, the benefit for the consumers is not unconditional or immediate. They have to participate actively to have a chance of winning. Chance games and lotteries are also plagued by 'professional players', a group of consumers obsessed by the possibility of winning something, and who therefore participate in all campaigns. There is only a very slim chance that this type of consumer will ever become loyal to the promoted brand. Furthermore, contests and lotteries are seldom capable of generating trial purchases. As a result, the potential of promotions of this type in attracting new customers or generating loyal ones is rather weak. Retailers are not particularly inclined to co-operate in promotions of this type since they do not generate long-term benefits for the store either. Finally, in most countries legal restrictions on contests and gambling exist, which result in either straightforward and thus not so creative contests, or near-illegal situations.

Contests as sales promotion tools

The Bavaria brewery realised that its slogan 'OK, now first a Bavaria' was no longer well known in the Netherlands. To counter this, Bavaria decided to launch a promotion campaign. The objective was not so much to increase sales, but to make the brand top of mind again. To this end a photo competition was organised. Although there is nothing special about organising a photo competition, it is unusual to organise a photo competition that convinced more than 10,000 consumers to respond without the possibility of earning big prizes. The promotion ran between May and September 1998. To make consumers aware of the contest, TV commercials, print advertisements, stickers, flyers, displays, beer mats and dispensers which were distributed in buses to holiday destinations were used. Consumers were encouraged to take holiday pictures on the theme of Bavaria and to come up with the funniest 'OK, now first a Bavaria' picture. Every week a winner was announced whose picture was used in an advertisement in the newspaper *De Telegraaf*. Every person who submitted a photo received a set of fridge magnets. Every winner received a photo book of the promotion and one winner received the winning prize of €2,450. Bavaria succeeded in mobilising a lot of tourists to take pictures on its theme. Bavaria regained its original brand experience and despite a price increase, its market share has increased in a stable to decreasing market. The promotion campaign won a Silver Esprix Award in 1999.[15]

L'Oréal rolled out a roadshow for its Maybelline brand. The 'Make-up on the Go Tour' travelled the UK from May until October 2002. A contest was organised for 16 to 24 year old girls, the prime target group of the brand. Girls winning the 'Face of Maybelline' contest in their region got an expenses-paid trip to New York.[16]

Product promotions

In product promotions the consumer is offered products free, either as an incentive to buy a product, or as a reward for having purchased it.

Sampling is a promotion technique that consists of distributing small samples of a product, sometimes in a specially designed package free of charge or at a very low cost. Sampling can be done in many different ways. The product can be distributed in every mailbox, or delivered at home. This technique is especially suitable for products with very broad target groups. If more specific targeting is called for, the sample can be mailed to the addresses of carefully selected target groups, or can be distributed at events where the target groups congregate, e.g. sports arenas or cultural performances. The sample can also be distributed in certain media, e.g. the scratch-and-sniff samples of perfume in magazines. The sample can be included in the package of a (complementary) product of the same product line. In the latter case only existing customers of the product line are being reached, to make them try an extension of the product line. Sampling can also be combined with demonstrations in or near stores. In fact, this is to a certain extent a combination of personal selling and consumer promotions. A salesperson at a demonstration stand tries to 'seduce' shoppers to try the product (usually food or drink), hoping that they will go on to buy it.

Sampling is the ideal promotion tool for generating trial, especially in those cases in which the product characteristics cannot be communicated very convincingly by means of advertising, and/or in those cases in which it is possible for a potential customer to get an idea of the product's benefits on the basis of trying it in small quantities. A possible disadvantage is that manufacturing and distributing small samples in large quantities, or demonstrations at supermarkets, may be quite expensive, and may lead to logistic problems for both the manufacturer and the retailer.

With free in-mail promotions, the customer receives a (nearly) free gift in return for a proof of purchase which has to be sent to the manufacturer. In that sense, promotions of this type are very similar to the cash refund, the only difference being that the consumer receives a gift instead of money. The main purpose of this type of promotion is not to generate trial, but to reward loyal customers, or to improve the link between the consumer and the brand. Moreover, such promotions can generate a lot of valuable information for the construction of a database on the interests and consuming habits of (potential) customers. This information can be used for future marketing action, and is one of the major advantages of this type of promotion. The disadvantages are that the consumer does not derive an immediate benefit, the logistics may be very expensive and time-consuming, and the benefit for the retailer is non-existent, since promotions of this type do not improve the link between the product and the store.

Premiums may be offered in-, on- or near-pack. They are small gifts that come with a product, e.g. a free glass when buying a bottle of cognac, or a pair of sunglasses when buying two bottles of sun lotion. Sometimes the package itself is a premium, like marmalade in a glass that can be used afterwards. Premiums tend to be successful, since for most consumers getting something for free is a powerful incentive. Such promotions can be used to generate impulse buying and trial, to reward existing customers and to stimulate repeat buying by offering a series of premiums that can be collected, like a set of glasses or stickers.

Consumers like this type of promotion because the benefits are immediately visible and easy to obtain. The budgetary implications for the manufacturer are clear in advance, and a premium can be easily combined with other types of promotions. Furthermore, there are no extra handling costs after the promotion campaign. The advantage for the retailer is that a premium campaign can generate extra store traffic and extra sales.

When are premium-based promotions effective?

To gain a better understanding of consumer reactions to premium-based promotions, an exploratory qualitative study among 12 consumers and a survey among 182 adult consumers were held in France. The results show that the consumer appreciation of this type of promotions is more positive when the premium is direct than when consumers can obtain it at a later point in time. Consumers also appreciate premiums more when the quantity of product to be purchased to obtain the premium is lower, when the value of the premium is mentioned, and when the interest in the premium is great. The more positive the consumer's brand attitude is, the more positive he or she is about the premium. Consumers that are characterised by deal-proneness and compulsive buying tendencies are also more likely to have a positive attitude towards premiums. Consumer's perception of the manipulation intent of the brand offering the premium is lower when the premium can be obtained directly, when the value of the premium is mentioned, and when the consumer is deal-prone and has an interest in the premium.[17]

If the consumer fails to respond to a premium, the whole campaign may fail. Furthermore, the wrong kind of premium may damage the long-term image of the brand. Finally, there is always the risk that only existing customers are subsidised, and that no extra trial or basket-filling results. The disadvantage for the manufacturer is that the production, handling and logistics costs may be quite substantial. The retailer may experience difficulties in displaying the product with the premium. Especially with near-pack premiums, shelf space has to be provided, and the retailer has to check for consumer fraud. As in other types of immediate purchasing incentives, the old stock of the product may be difficult to sell. If the premium is a product that is also being sold by the same retailer (a glass, sunglasses, etc.), sales of these items may fall.

Self-liquidators or self-liquidating premiums are presents that can be obtained in exchange for a number of proofs of purchase, and an extra amount of money. Sometimes self-liquidators can be obtained in the store, but more frequently they have to be ordered by mail. Similar to free in-mail promotions, self-liquidators are mainly used to stimulate repeat purchase and brand loyalty, rather than to generate trial. The advantage for the consumer is that he can obtain products of relatively high quality at a minimum cost. On the other hand, he has to go to some trouble to obtain a product, the quality of which is unknown. Indeed, it may be difficult to find a premium that is appealing to the target group. For the manufacturer, the follow-up of the campaign may be cumbersome, but valuable information about the consumer is obtained. If well communicated in-store, the campaign generates attention, to the benefit of both the manufacturer and the retailer.

Finally, savings cards and trading stamps may be used not only to offer consumers a discount some time in the future, but also to offer a gift. As such, the characteristics, advantages and disadvantages of these promotions are similar to savings cards with a cash incentive.

Premiums that make an impact

Every Dutch owner of a middle-of-the-range car of between three and six years old might have found a scratch ticket on their car during the months November and December 1998. Daewoo sampling teams visited car parks, shopping streets and office buildings in order to find possible candidates. The sampling team detected 650,000 cars and put a scratch ticket together with a Daewoo flyer on the window. The ticket contained the number of the registration plate. Up to €4,500 could be saved when the owner exchanged his old car for a new one. Furthermore, one lucky person could win a new Daewoo. The result of the promotion was that Daewoo sold 1,400 new cars in December, 70% above the objective. This is a remarkable result during a month in which sales traditionally are very poor, for within a few weeks the car is already a year old. Daewoo won a bronze Esprix award for its campaign.[18]

During the release of the Twentieth Century Fox film *X-Men* in 2002, Kellogg's ran an in-pack promotion that for the first time offered a metal premium in the cereals market. Children could collect a set of six X-Men metal ID tags. Research had shown that children were very keen on the idea of real metal ID tags because they saw them as trendy and aspirational.[19]

Different manufacturers may also co-operate to generate synergies between their promotional efforts (joint promotions). Similarly, a single manufacturer can offer a joint promotion for two different brands of his own. One item may be offered as a premium for the other, purchase proofs of different products may be requested to obtain a self-liquidator or a free in-mail present, and discounts may be made contingent on the purchase of different items at the same time. To increase the benefits for both the manufacturer and the retailer, they can co-operate in the organisation of promotion campaigns. Retailers can pay part of the manufacturer's promotion budget, perhaps in return for exclusiveness of the campaign in their stores, or they can provide the necessary in-store communication to draw attention to a promotion campaign. In Table 12.2 an overview is given of the different consumer promotions techniques, their main objectives, advantages and disadvantages.[20]

Table 12.2 Objectives, advantages and disadvantages of consumer promotions

Promotion objectives	A	B	C	D	E	F	G	H	I	J
Generate trial	+	++	++	--	--	--	++	--	++	--
Induce repeat purchase	+	+	++		++	--	--	++	++	++
Basket-filling	++	+	+	++	+		--		+	
(Dis)advantages										
Direct consumer benefit	++	++	--	++	--	--	+	--	++	--
Ease of obtaining benefit	++	+	--	++	--	-	++	--	++	--
Impact on brand image and brand loyalty	--	-			++	-		+		+
Manufacturer's workload and problems	++	+	-	-	+	--	-	--	-	--
Impact on consumer's price perception	--	-	+	-	--	+				+
Ease of targeting	--	++	++	--	++		+	++	-	--
Ease of budget planning	--	--	--	++	-	+	++	++	++	-
Database support	--	--	++	--	++	++	--	++	--	++
Immediate increase in sales	++	+		++	-				+	
Impact on store image and store loyalty	-				++	--			+	
Retailer's workload	++	-	+	-	-		-	--	-	

++ very positive   + positive   − negative   −− very negative

A price cut on shelf   F contests, sweepstakes and lotteries
B coupons   G sampling
C cash refunds   H free in mail
D product plus   I premiums
E savings cards   J self-liquidators

Trade promotions

Different promotion tools can be used to motivate the trade. They are summarised in Table 12.3.[21] Off-invoice allowances are direct price reductions to the trade, for instance during a limited period of time. They are the simplest form of trade promotions. The trade may receive a discount per unit purchased or a discount after he or she has sold a certain volume of the product. Discounts may also be given after a longer

Table 12.3 Trade promotion tools

- Off-invoice allowances
  - Individual case bonus
  - Volume allowance
  - Discount overriders
  - Count and recount
  - Free merchandise
- Slotting allowances
- Advertising/performance allowances
- Co-operative advertising allowances
- Buy-back allowances
- Dealer contests
- Dealer loaders

period of time, when a certain volume of sales has been reached (discount overriders). Also the count-recount method is retrospective in that the stock of the manufacturer's brand is counted at the beginning and at the end of a period, and a discount, for instance per case sold, is given. A slotting allowance is a one-time, up-front fee that is charged by retailers before they allow a new product on their shelves to cover the start-up costs of entering a new product into their system. Manufacturers often contest these allowances because they feel that they are subsidising the retailer's business. Advertising/performance allowances are monetary incentives aimed at encouraging the retailer to advertise the manufacturer's brand and are provided when proof of the ad is produced. In fact, the manufacturer pays part of the advertising campaign of the retailer. In some cases, a percentage of everything the retailer buys from a manufacturer is put into a co-operative advertising fund. The dealer adds an agreed-upon percentage to the fund, and uses it to advertise the brands of the manufacturer. To stimulate the retailer to put a new brand or a renewed version of the product on the shelves, the manufacturer sometimes offers to buy back the 'old' product, or commits to buying back the stock of the new product that is not sold during a specific period of time. This is called a buy-back allowance. To motivate retailers to sell more of the manufacturer's product, a contest among them may be organised in which, for instance, trips or other prizes can be won. In some cases, additional materials (dealer loaders) are offered during a promotional campaign, for instance, a refrigerator during a soft-drinks promotion. After the promotion, the retailer can keep the extra equipment.

Trade allowances result in a higher profit margin for the wholesaler or the retailer. This higher margin can (partly) be used to offer a discount to the end consumer by means of retail promotions, or to stimulate sales by means of more shelf space or other in-store communications tools. In those cases the trade promotions can eventually result in a favourable effect on end consumer purchases. If the (volume-based) trade allowance is used by the retailer only to increase inventory temporarily, the trade promotions will not result in an increase in sales to the end consumer. Although trade promotions have become increasingly important as a result of the growing power of the distribution channel, their effectiveness largely depends on the incentives given to the retailer to pass on the benefits to the end consumers and to stimulate short-term sales in-store.

Are sales promotions effective?

Various studies lead to the conclusion that, although promotions may be effective in the short run, they result in negative effects in the long run. Competitive campaigns neutralise the short-term effects, and the only result is an increase in promotions costs for the same amount of sales, and stable, long-term market shares. Furthermore, promotions have the reputation of undermining the effect of more strategic marketing instruments, such as advertising and sponsorship, which try to build brand image in the long run. Therefore, some manufacturers increasingly rely on the 'every day low pricing' (EDLP) strategy, aimed at maintaining a relatively low stable price for most of their products, as opposed to the 'high-low' (HILO) strategy in which frequent promotions are used. The following overview is a summary of the academic literature in which the effectiveness of promotions is studied. Most studies are based on monetary incentive consumer promotions, although in some studies product promotions are also covered. First, the effectiveness of promotions in the short, medium and long run is studied. In Figure 12.4 the potential effects of sales promotions are summarised. After that, attention is focused on moderating variables of promotions effectiveness. The results of the empirical studies discussed have to be interpreted with caution. They were carried out in different cultures and different time frames and, most importantly, the results were often obtained on the basis of experimental designs in which the potential synergetic effects with other instruments of the communications mix were ignored.

Figure 12.4 The potential effects of sales promotions

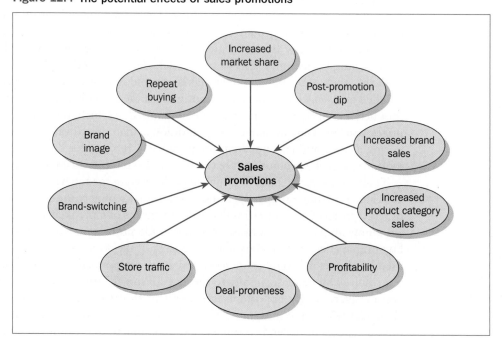

The effectiveness of sales promotions

In the short run most promotion campaigns lead to a substantial increase in sales and market share.[22] Promotional price elasticities of 10 in absolute value are no exception, and they largely exceed short-term advertising elasticities.[23] Product category sales and market shares of retailers are also positively affected. Although the effect of promotions on short-term profitability is unclear, some studies indicate that promotions lead to higher profits.[24] Furthermore, various studies indicate that 80% of the sales increase as a result of promotions is attributable to attracting buyers of competitive products.[25] However, the effects are asymmetric. Highly priced products are capable of attracting cutomers of lower-priced brands and distribution brands, while on the contrary the latter are far less capable of attracting customers of the former by means of sales promotions. If a promotions campaign only leads to a shift from one brand to another, product category sales will not be influenced, and no favourable effects for the retailer will result. On the other hand, sales promotions campaigns may attract new customers to the store, thus increasing the store's market share in its attraction area.[26] Furthermore, increased store traffic may lead to additional sales in other product categories.[27]

In the medium term (defined as 4–6 weeks after the promotion), the effect of the campaign on repeat purchase, and the lack of a 'post-promotion dip' become important indicators of effectiveness.

Promotions can have a negative effect on the medium-term image of the brand because consumers are influenced to choose the brand by the promotions rather than the intrinsic value of the product, and therefore could be less inclined to buy the product again when it is not on promotion. Hence, promotions may lead to less repeat buying.[28] According to the 'Mental Accounting Theory' and the 'Prospect Theory', consumers base their decisions on the difference between the actual stimulus and a stimulus of reference. Promotions can result in a decrease in 'reference price'; in other words, consumers get used to promotions and they adjust their price expectations as a result of frequent promotions, and will have to be offered more 'impressive' promotions to buy the product in the future.[29]

Promotions may also influence repeat buying decisions adversely because the long-term attitude towards the brand is being damaged. However, research has shown that promotions do not necessarily influence the long-term brand image. The more attractive (e.g. a large price cut), and the more immediate and unconditional the promotional offer is (e.g. a premium), the higher the potential damage to the long-term brand image. Furthermore, if the consumer is already a loyal customer before the campaign, and has already developed a clear attitude towards the brand, the effect of promotions on his or her long-term attitude towards the brand will not be affected. Similarly, in markets in which promotions campaigns are frequently used, and in markets in which most consumers are brand-switching anyway, the effect of promotions on brand attitude and thus repeat purchase will be limited.[30] It can also be argued that consumers are not involved deeply enough in purchasing fast-moving consumer goods, and therefore long-term attitudes are not affected by temporary promotion campaign.[31] Finally, consumers are getting used to a product as a result of trying it when it is on promotion, which increases the chance of repeat buying behaviour; in other words, promotions can put the brand in the choice set of the consumer. All in all, the overall effect of promotions on medium-term repeat buying behaviour seems to be limited.

When not only new customers are attracted by the promotions, but also existing customers buy more of the product during the promotion campaign, a 'post-promotion dip' in sales can result: as long as consumers do not consume the extra amounts of product they buy during the same period, they will buy less of the product in the period immediately after the promotion campaign. Therefore, to assess the effectiveness of a promotion campaign, both the sales during the campaign and after the campaign have to be measured. If the product is frequently on promotion, a pre-promotion dip may occur: consumers anticipate the campaign and postpone their purchase. The post-promotion dip has been studied extensively. When the campaign is mainly a 'basket-filling' exercise, its negative effects are well documented.[32]

Similar to medium-term effects, frequent promotions may lead to 'deal-proneness', with adverse effects on brand attitudes, market shares and sales in the long run. Research even indicates that frequent use of promotions leads to a 'prisoner's dilemma' as a result of which competitors retaliate in order not to lose market share, and long-term market shares are not affected. In a long-term market share analysis of 341 products it was shown that 60% of all market shares remained stable over a period of nine years. Only in 24% of the cases was a significant effect of promotions on market share evolution found.[33] Similarly, in a study of 400 products, 78% of market share appeared to be stable in the long run, which means that a maximum of 22% of the market share could have been affected by promotion campaigns (or by other marketing mix instruments, for that matter).[34]

Some researchers argue that the increasing intensity of promotional efforts are the result of increased variety-seeking behaviour and a diminishing brand loyalty (caused by the fact that in more and more markets undifferentiated products are offered), rather than the other way around.[35] Research also indicates that increased price-sensitivity, resulting in an increased 'deal-proneness', is affected by the frequency of promotion campaigns rather than the value of the promotions. All in all, the (negative and positive) effects of promotions in the long run seem to be limited.

Moderating factors of promotions effectiveness

General conclusions as to the negative or positive effects of promotions are contingent on a number of moderating factors, such as product and brand factors, consumer characteristics and the company's marketing strategy, which may influence promotions effectiveness.

Promotions will have a stronger effect on products of which the consumer can easily hold a stock, on products that are bought by large numbers of consumers and for which supporting communications campaigns, such as advertising and in-store communications, can easily be organised. Promotions will be less effective in very competitive markets. Research has shown that a promotions campaign is less effective when preceded by a competitor's promotion.[36] Furthermore, promotions seem to be more effective for brands with a small market share than for major market players. In the latter case, the effect of promotions is often limited.[37]

Also consumer characteristics may influence the effectiveness of a campaign. Variety-seeking consumers and consumer segments with high 'deal-proneness' are more influenced by promotions than others.[38] Indeed, in brand-switching segments promotions will be more effective than in loyal segments. In the latter case, consumers will, on average, be more involved in the product category, and as a result be more aware of promotions. The risk of 'deal-to-deal buying', i.e. postponing purchases until the next promotions campaign, is somewhat higher in those segments, and less frequent use of promotion campaigns is advised.[39]

Obviously, the effectiveness of a promotions campaign can be increased by integrating it in a marketing communications campaign, and thus supporting it by means of in-store communications, trade promotions, advertising campaigns and personal selling efforts towards the trade. Furthermore, the long-term effectiveness and profitability of promotion campaigns depend on a number of factors. In brand-loyal markets promotions of less value should be offered to retain customers. Brands with large market shares benefit from less frequent promotions, and distribution brands should avoid promotions altogether.[40]

Sales promotions research

Sales promotions can be pre- and post-tested. Sales promotions pre-testing is very similar to advertising pre-testing. Consumers may be exposed to sales promotions ideas, in a focus group setting or elsewhere, and may be invited to express their opinion about them. However, since the objective of most sales promotions campaigns is to provoke immediate buying behaviour, most promotions research will focus on behavioural response measures. Promotions are essentially aimed at stimulating trial purchase and at increasing sales with existing consumers. Therefore, effectiveness measures will focus on the evolution of sales compared with non-promotion periods, or on the comparison of different types of promotions as to their ability to generate extra sales.

When launching a new brand, or monitoring the sales evolution of an existing brand for which sales promotion campaigns are being used, the following analysis using consumer panel data can be carried out.[41] It is based on a decomposition of the market share of the brand as follows:

Market share = (attraction × conviction × domination × intensity)/shock absorption

Attraction = Number of buyers of our brand/total number of buyers of the product category.

Conviction = Number of loyal customers of our brand/number of buyers of our brand.

Domination = Average volume of our brand purchased per loyal customer of our brand/average volume of the product category purchased per loyal customer of our brand.

Intensity = Average volume of the product category purchased per loyal customer of our brand/average volume of the product category purchased per buyer of the product category. If the intensity rate = 1, the loyal customers of our brand are buying the same amounts of the product category as the average buyer of the product category.

Shock absorption = Total purchases in volume of our brand by loyal customers/total purchases in volume of our brand.

The definition of a 'loyal customer' is based on repeat purchase within a specified period of time. All indicators are measured per period (monthly, bi-monthly, etc.). All measures are volume-based. The attraction rate measures the penetration of the brand and is a measure of the effectiveness of trial promotions. The conviction rate gives an indication of loyalty promotions effectiveness, more specifically the success of repeat buying promotions campaigns. The domination rate indicates to what extent loyal customers are truly loyal. The higher the domination index the more exclusively loyal customers are loyal to a brand. It is an indication of the effectiveness of loyalty and basket-filling promotions. The intensity rate indicates the extent to which the brand is capable of attracting heavy users of the product category. If this indicator is larger than one, our brand is capable of attracting a more than proportional amount of heavy users. As such it is also an indication of the basket-filling capacity of promotional campaigns. The shock absorption index indicates to what extent our brand is vulnerable to competitive campaigns. The higher the shock absorption rate, the more our sales are based on loyal consumers, and the less vulnerable our brand is to switching behaviour caused by competitive actions. In Figure 12.5, an example is given of the launch of a new brand of detergent.

The effectiveness of promotions is often assessed by studying the evolution of sales over a period of time during which several types of promotions have been implemented. By studying the evolution of sales during the campaign, and comparing it to the sales

Figure 12.5 Monitoring the effectiveness of sales promotions campaigns: the launch of a new detergent

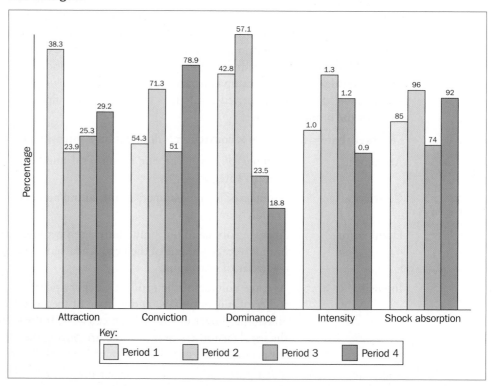

Based on: data from GfK Belgium.

level before and after the campaign, the extra sales volume generated by the campaign can be calculated. This type of analysis will also reveal potential 'sawtooth' effects, which follow the 'post-promotion dip' which is often the result of some types of promotions. Basket-filling promotions may induce consumers to buy large quantities of the product on promotion, after which they have enough stock for a number of weeks or months, and sales drop sharply in the post-promotion period. This phenomenon is illustrated in Figure 12.6. Obviously, if the only net result of promotions campaigns is that the post-promotion dip entirely compensates for the extra sales during the promotions period, the only thing that has happened is that the company has given up part of its profit margin. The success of a promotions campaign can be judged on the basis of the size of the positive difference between the extra sales during the promotions period and the drop in sales during the post-promotion dip.

In Figure 12.7 another example, based on retail panel data, is given of the baseline sales of a product, calculated on the basis of medium-term 'normal' sales, and the sales effect of promotions campaigns in subsequent months.

Obviously, the only relevant measure of promotions effectiveness is its long-term profitability. Sales volumes, sales prices and promotion costs will have to be combined into an economic analysis of the profitability of promotion campaigns.

Figure 12.6 The sawtooth effect of sales promotion campaigns

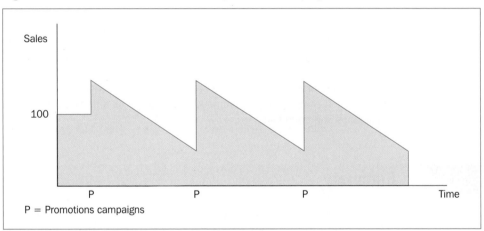

Integrating sales promotions in IMC

Like any other instrument of the marketing mix, sales promotion is most effective when it is integrated in the overall marketing communications efforts. First of all, the effectiveness of trade promotions can be enhanced by supplementing them with consumer promotions. Promotions can be announced via commercials in the mass media. Public relations can be combined with sales promotions to create events in which, for instance, samples and/or coupons can be distributed, or prizes can be won. Within the framework of sponsorship of events, teams or organisations sampling, couponing, demonstrations . . . can be used to get the public acquainted with the product and to stimulate trial. Coupons can also be inserted in direct mailings, or e-coupons can be distributed through the company's website or via interactive advertising on interactive digital television commercials. Product placement can be used

▶

Figure 12.7 Baseline sales and the sales effect of promotions campaigns

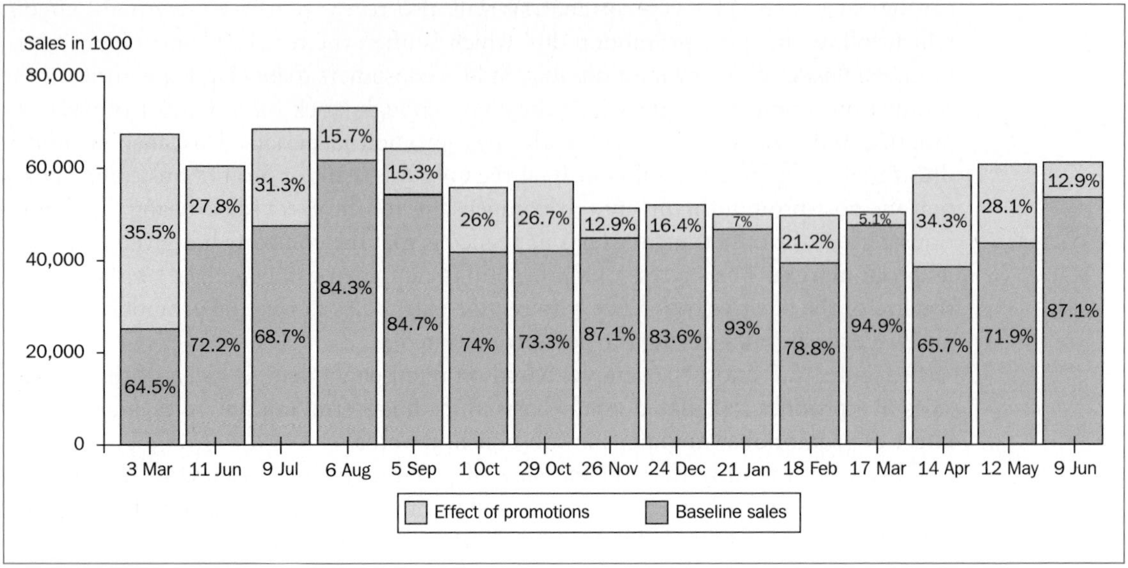

Based on: data from A.C. Nielsen Belgium.

to stir up the interest in a company's offerings via interactive promotional offers during product use in the television programme. Customer relationship efforts can be enhanced by linking them to various types of loyalty promotions: contests, saving cards, self-liquidators . . . In-store communications such as displays and merchandising modules can draw the attention to promotion campaigns, and promotions may serve as a traffic-building device for stands on exhibitions and trade fairs.

Summary

Although sales promotions are used to influence business results in the long run, a sales promotions campaign is a category of instrument that is primarily used to increase sales in the short run. Sales promotions have become increasingly important as a result of communications clutter, less brand loyalty, the lack of differentiation between brands and the short-term orientedness of many companies. Different types of sales promotions campaigns can be distinguished, mainly depending on whether they are targeted at retailers, the salesforce or end consumers. By means of sales promotions, various objectives can be pursued: attracting new customers, making existing ones loyal, increasing market size, reinforcing other communications tools, and rewarding loyal customers. Consumer promotions can take different forms. Three basic categories can be distinguished: monetary incentives (coupons, extra volume, savings cards) prizes (competitions, sweepstakes and lotteries) and product promotions (sampling, free in mail, premiums). The choice between these specific techniques depends on the objectives of the sales promotions campaign. Are sales promotions effective? In the short run, a number of potential positive and negative results can be discerned. Promotions can increase trial, loyalty and profitability, but can also lead to deal-proneness, brand-switching, a post-promotion dip and negative effects on profitability. In the medium and long run, the effects are unclear. The potential negative effect of sales promotions on brand image must be taken into account.

Review questions

1 Why are sales promotions becoming an increasingly important part of the marketing communications mix?

2 What are the objectives and target groups of sales promotions?

3 What are trade promotions used for?

4 What are the objectives of salesforce promotions?

5 Discuss the various tools of consumer promotions, their objectives and target groups, and the advantages and disadvantages for both the manufacturer and the retailer.

6 To what extent are sales promotions effective in the short and the long run?

7 Describe the 'launch analysis' of a new product and how it can be used to assess the effectiveness of a sales promotions campaign.

Further reading

Cummins, J. and Mullin, R. (2004), *Sales Promotion: How to Create, Implement and Integrate Campaigns that Really Work*. Kogan Page Ltd.

Horchover, D. (2002), *Sales Promotion*. Capstone Ltd.

Mela, C.F., Gupta, S. and Lehmann, D.R. (1997), 'The Long-Term Impact of Promotion and Advertising on Consumer Brand Choice', *Journal of Marketing Research*, 34 (May), 248–61.

Neslin, S.A. (2002), *Sales Promotion*. Marketing Science Institute.

Papatla, P. and Krisnamurthi, L. (1996), 'Measuring the Dynamic Effects of Promotions on Brand Choice', *Journal of Marketing Research*, 33 (February), 20–35.

Tellis, G.J. and Zufryden, F. (1995), 'Tackling the Retailer Decision Maze: Which Brands to Discount, How Much, When and Why?', *Marketing Science*, 14(3), 271–99.

Case 12

Febreze – safely eliminating odours

Febreze is one of Procter & Gamble's innovations in the fabric and home care market. After six years of research and testing, it was introduced in the US market in mid-1998, and proved to be very successful. Based on the US and UK test market results, P&G decided to enter the European market as well, launching Febreze in February 1999 in the UK, followed by France, Belgium and The Netherlands in March 1999. This case study mainly concentrates on the launch of Febreze in The Netherlands and Belgium, which took place in March 1999.

In line with P&G's mission of manufacturing and marketing products 'that improve the lives of consumers around the world', Febreze tries to fill the need of removing odours from fabrics without having to wash them. In contrast with hard surfaces, like floors and counters, soft surfaces composed of fabrics are much harder to clean and take care of. These fabrics are everywhere: from upholstery, to carpets, curtains and canvas shoes. In fact, generally in Europe about 75% of the household surfaces that need routinely cleaning are made of fabrics. Febreze, a completely new product in the market, is an environmentally friendly spray that eliminates odours on fabrics. After using the spray, a fresh scent similar to a laundry detergent is left, which lasts a few hours to one or two days. Febreze is not intended to replace cleaning, but to refresh household items and clothing that are not dirty, but do not smell clean. Examples are pet odour in the sofa, cigarette or cigar smoke in curtains or clothes, and cooking smells in kitchen fabrics. Several of these product uses have been discovered during consumer testing. The women who were asked to test Febreze found all kind of uses for it around their homes. And the more they used it, the more possibilities they discovered. This made it increasingly difficult to develop a product that tackles all kinds of odours on all kinds of fabrics effectively.

Pre-tests in The Netherlands and Belgium

Before launching the product in the Benelux market, pre-tests were carried out to get an idea of how convincing and engaging the product was and how easy to remember. The pre-test results showed that recall of the strategic information in the advertisement was quite high: 77% for The Netherlands and 62% for Belgium. The level of how convincing and how engaging it was, was average. When respondents were asked for comments, they responded with statements such as 'Too good to be true', 'If it's true . . . !', 'Is the product safe for my fabrics, my family?' The objectives of another study were to identify trial barriers and credible third parties to help overcome trial barriers. The conclusions of the pre-tests were that, in the trial phase, first, P&G needed to get the product into the hands of consumers ('seeing/using is believing'); second, consumers needed to be reassured on safety (especially in The Netherlands); and third, the versatility of Febreze had to be stressed.

Communications strategy

In response to the results of the pre-test study, P&G decided to implement a strong trial plan, to include the word 'safety' in the selling line to reassure consumers on the safety aspect ('Febreze *safely* eliminates odours from fabrics'), and to use TV commercials 'Discover the Uses' fully focusing on the versatility of Febreze. The communications plan is shown in Case Figure 12.1.

The objectives of the advertising campaign were to:

1 Create an awareness rate of 80% after four months of advertising.

Case Figure 12.1 The Febreze communications plan

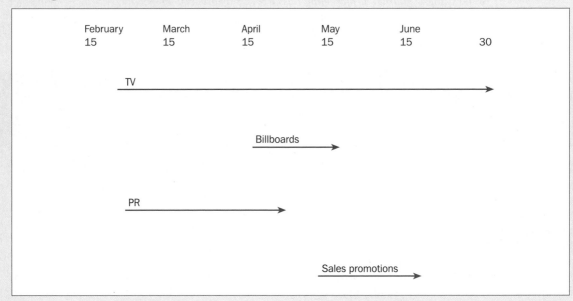

2 Generate trial by explaining the product/concept of Febreze, stressing its versatility, reassuring consumers on the safety aspect and telling them where they can find Febreze in the store (since it is a new product category).

3 Break through the media clutter by using 40-second TV ads in combination with a cut-down version of 10 seconds.

In different countries where Febreze had been launched, different selling propositions had been stressed. In the UK, one TV ad showed people in the living room spraying the product on the curtains which results in a cloud of freshness coming out of the curtains. Another ad shows the different possible product uses. In France billboards are used picturing clothes surrounded with a cloud of freshness. In the US one print ad illustrates how Febreze works its way into fabrics, leaving no trace. Another one shows a bottle of Febreze spraying all the possible product applications one after another: sofa, car, carpet, clothes and shoes.

Concerning the PR campaign, the problem of getting free media coverage was that even as a new product initially it was not very relevant to the press. Therefore, P&G had a research agency carry out an investigation on 'consequences of malodours in everyday life' with a special focus on newsworthy outcomes and differences in opinion between males and females, urban versus rural-dwelling people, and North versus South. Afterwards, a press conference was organised, both in the Netherlands and Belgium. First, the research agency presented the research results. Next, an external odour expert commented on the results and brought odours into a broader, more scientific context. Finally, the R&D and Marketing Department presented the Febreze concept. The research results confirmed that consumers think odours are important. About one in two consumers claim even to have left a room because of a bad odour. Futhermore, consumers realise that odours can have an influence on their social life (for example, bad odour as a reason for disliking someone). Odours are more important to Belgians than to Dutch people. Women as compared to men, and people under 50 as compared to older persons are more critical of odours, claim to perceive odours better and are more likely to think odours are important in their daily life.

Besides advertising and generating publicity, Febreze was also supported by a sales promotions campaign. The objective of the latter was to generate 30% household trial within the Benelux market. To this end samples of 100 ml bottles were distributed, among others, at the exit of supermarkets, with a leaflet stressing how to use Febreze correctly, how versatile and safe the product is, and that Febreze is available in 500 ml bottles to stimulate conversion. Three weeks after the sampling another sales promotions campaign was launched to prompt consumers to repurchase Febreze in a 500 ml bottle, consisting of a reduction of half a euro on every 500 ml bottle. By sustaining this price reduction, P&G could participate in the retailers' weekly brochures and the retailers could be more easily convinced to use POP material, such as displays. Furthermore, in-store product demonstrations were used. They demonstrated the product to consumers and mentioned that the product was on promotion. If the retailer did not carry a promotions programme, the consumers were given a coupon worth half a euro to persuade hesitant shoppers.

Results

One week after the start of the advertising campaign, the Benelux consumption was nine times higher than the week before. After two and a half months of advertising, awareness amounted to 60%. Only 3% mentioned safety as a barrier to trying Febreze. The PR campaign was quite successful as well: 60% of the Benelux shoppers aged between 20 and 49 were reached via free press and in-use shots (stills from the TV commercials) were frequently featured in the newspapers and magazines. According to P&G, the sales promotions campaign also proved to be effective. During the price reduction period, sales increased four-fold. The success rate of the product demonstrations ranged from good to excellent and mainly depended on the traffic of shoppers present in the store and the size of the supermarket.

Febreze has already been used by more than 25 million households around the world. The next challenge is to make this new product part of the daily cleaning routine of consumers.

Questions

1 What type of sales promotions did P&G use during the launch of Febreze?

2 Would you have chosen another type? If so, why?

3 Is it a good idea to launch a product like Febreze using price incentives?

4 Would you advise P&G to continue to use sales promotions after the introductory period? What are the advantages and disadvantages of repeated promotions?

5 How important do you think trade promotions versus consumer promotions were for introducing Febreze?

6 How would you advise P&G to test the effectiveness of its sales promotions?

Based on: Documents provided by Arnaud Demoulin, Customer Marketing Manager, Valérie Van Geel, Assistant Brand Manager, and Jochem De Boer, Assistant. Brand Manager, P&G Belgium–the Netherlands. A paper prepared by Ambrogio Foscarini, student of the Postgraduate Programme in Management, Free University of Brussels, Belgium. http://www.febreze.com/html/facts.html. Reproduced with permission of Procter & Gamble.

References

1 Antonides, G. and van Raaij, W.F. (1998), *Consumer Behaviour: A European Perspective*. Chichester: John Wiley & Sons.

2 See also Papatla, P. and Krisnamurthi, L. (1996), 'Measuring the Dynamic Effects of Promotion on Brand Choice', *Journal of Marketing Research*, 33 (February), 20–35; Mela, C.F., Gupta, S. and Lehmann, D.R. (1997), 'The Long-Term Impact of Promotion and Advertising on Consumer Brand Choice', *Journal of Marketing Research*, 34 (May), 248–61.

3 Duncan, T. (2002), *IMC. Using Advertising and Promotion to Build Brands*. Boston: McGraw-Hill/Irwin.

4 Pickton, D. and Broderick, A. (2001), *Integrated Marketing Communications*. Harlow: Financial Times Prentice Hall.

5 McDonald, C. (1992), 'Finding Out How – Unleashing the Power of Single-Source Data to Explain the Marketing Mix', *Admap*, (December), 21–5; Pickton, D. and Broderick, A. (2001), *Integrated Marketing Communications*. Harlow: Financial Times Prentice Hall.

6 *Advertising Age*, 24 March 2003.

7 See also www.incentivesatwork.com

8 Doyle, K. (1991), 'Offbeat Programmes', *Incentive*, (December), 21–4.

9 See also www.bcentral.com

10 Slater, J. (2001), 'Is Couponing an Effective Promotional Strategy? An Examination of the Procter & Gamble Zero-couponing Test', *Journal of Marketing Communications*, 7(1), 3–10.

11 De Pelsmacker, P. (1994), 'Een reis Langs de Nieuwste Vormen van Winkelpuntcommunicatie' ('A Journey to the Latest Forms of In-Store Communication'), in Van Camp, E. (ed.), *Marketing en Communicatie in de 21ste Eeuw: A Brave New World? (Marketing and Communication in the 21st Century; A Brave New World?)*. Roeselare: Roularta Books, 76–85.

12 *De Morgen*, 28 January 1999.

13 Slater, J. (2001), 'Is Couponing an Effective Promotional Strategy? An Examination of the Procter & Gamble Zero-couponing Test', *Journal of Marketing Communications*, 7(1), 3–10.

14 www.esprix.nl, 9 June 2003.

15 *Esprix Jaarboek* (1999), 60–1.

16 www.pandionline.com, 9 June 2003.

17 D'Astous, A. and Jacob, I. (2002), 'Understanding Consumer Reactions to Premium-based Promotion Offers', *European Journal of Marketing*, 36(11), 1270–86.

18 *Esprix Jaarboek* (1999), 60–1.

19 www.pandionline.com, 9 June 2003.

20 See also www.incentivesatwork.com

21 Duncan, T. (2002), *IMC. Using Advertising and Promotion to Build Brands*. Boston: McGraw-Hill/Irwin; Brassington, F. and Pettitt, S. (2003), *Principles of Marketing*. Harlow: Financial Times/Prentice Hall.

22 Allenby, G.M. and Lenk, P.J. (1995), 'Reassessing Brand Loyalty, Price Sensitivity and Merchandising Effects on Consumer Brand Choice', *Journal of Business and Economic Statistics*, 13(3), 281–9; Leone, R.P. and Srinivasan, S.S. (1996), 'Coupon Face Value: Its Impact on Coupon Redemptions, Brand Sales, and Brand Profitability', *Journal of Retailing*, 72(3), 273–89.

23 Sethuraman, R. and Tellis, G.J. (1991), 'An Analysis of the Trade off Between Advertising and Price Discounting', *Journal of Marketing Research*, 28 (May), 160–74.

24 For instance, Dhar and Hoch report profit increase between 113% and 235%: Dhar, S.K. and Hoch, S.J. (1996), 'Price Discrimination Using In-Store Merchandising', *Journal of Marketing*, 60 (January), 17–30.

25 Gupta, S. (1988), 'Impact of Sales Promotions on When, What and How Much to Buy', *Journal of Marketing Research*, 25 (November), 342–55; Blattberg, R.C. and Neslin, S.A. (1989), 'Sales Promotion: The Long and the Short of It', *Marketing Letters*, 81–97.

26 Grover, R. and Srinivasan, V. (1992), 'Evaluating the Multiple Effects of Retail Promotions on Brand Loyalty and Brand Switching Segments', *Journal of Marketing Research*, 29 (February), 76–89.

27 Mulhern, F.J. and Padgett, D.T. (1995), 'The Relationship Between Retail Price Promotions and Regular Price Purchases', *Journal of Marketing*, 59 (October), 83–90.

28 Rothschild, M.L. (1987), 'A Behavioral View of Promotion Effects on Brand Loyalty', *Advances in Consumer Research*, 14, 119–20.

29 Mayhew, G.E. and Winer, R. (1992), 'An Empirical Analysis of Internal and External Reference Prices Using Scanner Data', *Journal of Consumer Research*, 19 (June), 62–70.

30 Kahn, B.E. and Louie, T.A. (1990), 'Effects of Retraction of Price Promotions on Brand Choice Behavior for

Variety-Seeking and Last-Purchase-Loyal Consumers', *Journal of Marketing Research*, 27 (August), 279–89.

31 Davis, S., Inman, J.J. and McAlister, L. (1992), 'Promotion has a Negative Effect on Brand Evaluations – Or Does It? Additional Disconfirming Evidence', *Journal of Marketing Research*, 29 (February), 143–8.

32 Neslin, S.A., Henderson, C. and Quelch, J. (1985), 'Consumer Promotions and the Acceleration of Product Purchases', *Marketing Science*, 4(2), 125–45; Grover, R. and Srinivasan, V. (1992), 'Evaluating the Multiple Effects of Retail Promotions on Brand Loyalty and Brand Switching Segments', *Journal of Marketing Research*, 29 (February), 76–89.

33 Lal, R. and Padmanabhan, V. (1995), 'Competitive Response and Equilibria', *Marketing Science*, 14(3), 101–8.

34 Dekimpe, M.G. and Hanssens, D.M. (1995), 'Empirical Generalizations about Market Evolution and Stationarity', *Marketing Science*, 14(3), 109–21.

35 Farris, P.W. and Quelch, J.A. (1987), 'In Defence of Price Promotion', *Sloan Management Review*, 63–9.

36 Kumar, V. and Pereira, A. (1995), 'Explaining the Variation in Short-Term Sales Response to Retail Price Promotions', *Journal of the Academy of Marketing Science*, 23(3), 155–69.

37 Tellis, G.J. and Zufryden, F. (1995), 'Tackling the Retailer Decision Maze: Which Brands to Discount, How Much, When and Why?', *Marketing Science*, 14(3), 271–99.

38 D'Astous, A. and Jacob, I. (2002), 'Understanding Consumer Reactions to Premium-based Promotional Offers', *European Journal of Marketing*, 36(11), 1270–86.

39 Simester, D. (1997), 'Optimal Promotion Strategies: A Demand-Sided Characterization', *Management Science*, 43(2), 251–6.

40 Tellis, G.J. and Zufryden, F. (1995), 'Tackling the Retailer Decision Maze: Which Brands to Discount, How Much, When and Why?', *Marketing Science*, 14(3), 271–99.

41 GfK Belgium.

Chapter 13

Direct marketing

Chapter outline

- Direct marketing as a marketing communications technique

- Direct marketing objectives and target groups

- Direct marketing media and tools

- Relationship marketing

- Measuring direct marketing effectiveness

Chapter objectives

This chapter will help you to:

- Understand what direct marketing communications are, and why they are increasingly important in marketing communications
- Get an overview of the objectives and target groups of direct marketing communications
- Acquaint yourself with the direct marketing media, tools and techniques
- Understand why database marketing is so important, and how a database should be managed
- See how direct marketing communications can contribute to relationship marketing
- Measure the effectiveness of a direct marketing communications campaign

Introduction

The success of direct marketing, not only as a marketing philosophy, but also as a set of communications techniques, originates from the corner shopkeeper's philosophy of having close and personal contact with customers, knowing everyone's needs and wants, providing them with the best solutions to their problems and giving them excellent after-sales service. This makes them happy and loyal customers. The growing opportunities offered by technology, automation and database-supported marketing intelligence systems, and the reductions in computer hard- and software prices have encouraged marketers to execute their marketing activities with an emphasis on efficiency and quantifiable objectives. Advertising budgets are being cut and cost-effectiveness of communications media becomes crucial.[1] Direct marketing activities do not require huge production costs like, for instance, television commercials, and consequently are more accessible to all kinds and sizes of companies. They are also very flexible, highly selective (easy to target) media. Knowledge of customer habits and needs and other detailed market information are considered to be highly valuable tools for marketing strategy development. This is due to fundamental changes in the marketplace in the 1990s. The threat of high-quality/low-price private label brands have changed consumers' attitudes towards brands. As there is less and less difference between products, consumers are finding brand loyalty increasingly irrelevant. Manufacturers have to look for communications tools that motivate consumers to product trial and give them incentives to keep using their brands. These changes have led to the growing importance of one-to-one communications and relationship marketing, based on lifetime bonding of customers. Direct marketing has given added value to this kind of marketing activity in comparison to traditional mass marketing.

With the fast-growing internet penetration in the new millennium the number of e-mail addresses has been increasing at a fast pace, allowing direct marketers to develop e-mailing campaigns that are more flexible, and above all much cheaper than traditional direct marketing media. E-marketing and e-mailings will be discussed in Chapter 17, E-communication.

Direct marketing as a marketing communications technique

The definition of direct marketing has gone through various changes. In the beginning (the 1960s) it was considered as a type of distribution (direct selling through a different channel), as used by mail order companies. In the 1970s direct marketing became a marketing communications tool with emphasis on feedback and optimising response rates on mailings and other direct marketing tools. From the 1990s onwards long-term relationship building and increasing customer loyalty ('retention marketing') became the main issues in direct marketing.[2] These different views on direct marketing are reflected in the quite diverse definitions of direct marketing found in literature. Hughes defines direct marketing as 'any marketing activity in which you attempt to reach the consumers directly, or have them reach you'.[3] Kobs stresses the importance of a database as a basic tool for direct marketing activities (a communications tool according to him) in his definition: 'Direct marketing gets your ad message direct to the customer or prospect to produce some type of immediate action. It usually involves creating a database of respondents'.[4]

In general, direct marketing means contacting customers and prospects in a direct way with the intention of generating an immediate and measurable response or reaction. 'Direct' means using direct media such as mailings, catalogues, telephone or brochures, and not through intermediaries such as dealers, retailers or sales staff. An immediate response is possible via answering coupons, phone or a personal visit of the customer to the store or retailer. In order to make a direct contact with customers and prospects, a database is required. Databases can be considered as the heart of direct marketing. Some issues on database marketing are explored below.

There are a number of fundamental differences between direct marketing communications and media and traditional mass media communications. They are shown in Table 13.1. The basic philosophy of direct marketing is to consider each customer as an investment. Identification of each customer means you can target the most appropriate communication in an interactive way. Customers are personally addressed and are able to respond. Data involved with these transactions are stored in the database and may be used to establish long-term relationships by adapting a company's offer to the needs of the customer. Consequently the main goal of a direct marketer is to increase customer share (i.e. the quantity and frequency of purchases of each individual customer) rather than market share.

The importance of direct marketing in European countries has consistently been increasing during the last decennium. Even during the past economic recession years direct marketing expenditures kept rising. Within Europe, Germany is the largest direct marketing market, although second placed UK is gaining share. The importance of direct marketing varies considerably in different European countries. In the Netherlands, direct marketing expenditures exceed those of traditional advertising (117.7%) whereas in Greece direct marketing expenditures are only 9% of traditional advertising spends. In Denmark this percentage is 78.4% while in Sweden it is 48.7. The breakdown of total direct marketing expenditure per European country is shown in Figure 13.1.[5]

During the last decade direct marketing has moved from a typical and traditional mail order company activity to an important communications tool of banks, insurance companies, not-for-profit organisations, supermarkets, car manufacturers, etc.

Table 13.1 **The difference between mass and direct media**

Mass media	Direct media
■ Segmenting	■ Individualising
■ Recall, recognition and image measurement	■ Response measurement (per client)
■ Mass one-way communications	■ Targeted two-way communications
■ Market share	■ Customer share

Figure 13.1 **Total direct marketing expenditure in Europe, 2001**

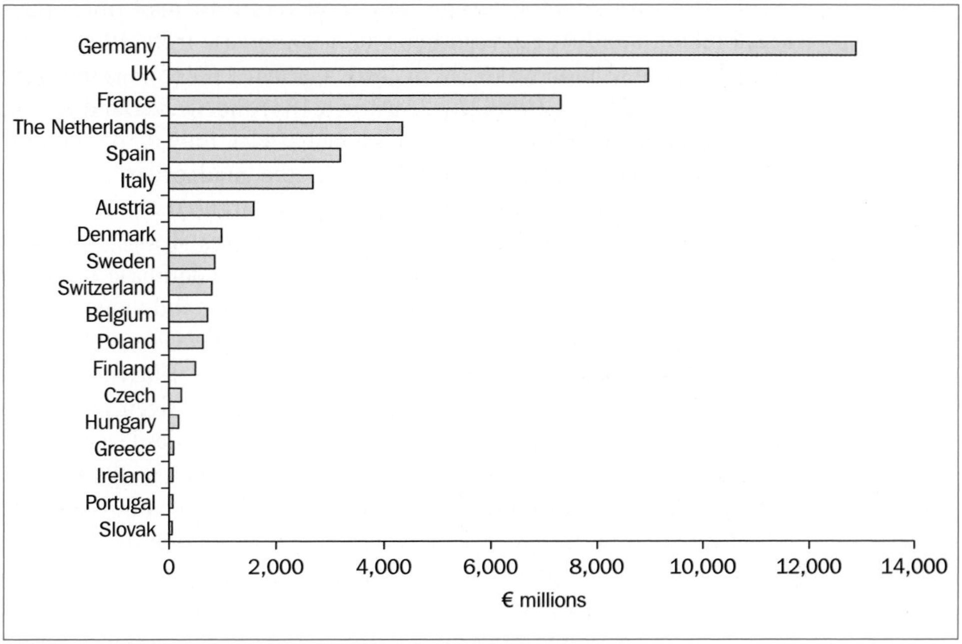

Country	€ millions

Chart showing total direct marketing expenditure by country (€ millions), x-axis from 0 to 14,000:
Germany (~13,000); UK (~9,000); France (~7,300); The Netherlands (~4,300); Spain (~3,200); Italy (~2,700); Austria (~1,600); Denmark (~900); Sweden (~800); Switzerland (~700); Belgium (~600); Poland (~550); Finland (~450); Czech; Hungary; Greece; Ireland; Portugal; Slovak

Based on: FEDMA (2002), *Survey on Direct and Interactive Marketing Activities in Europe*. Reproduced with permission of the Federation of European Direct Marketing, www.fedma.org.

Objectives and target groups

Direct marketing may be the appropriate communications tool for different purposes. They are presented in Figure 13.2.

Direct sales

Direct marketing communications may be used as a direct sales channel or distribution technique: selling products and services without face-to-face contact with intermediaries (salespersons, dealers or retailers). The best example is the mail order business. Catalogues

Figure 13.2 **Objectives and target groups of direct marketing communications**

are mailed to prospects and orders are taken by phone or by mail. The success of mail order sales varies across Europe. The total return of mail order operators exceeded €52.4 billion in 2001, representing a 17.1% increase from 1996. Turnover per capita in the European Union was €132 in 2001. Germany (€265) has the highest turnover per capita, followed by the UK (€221), Austria (€183) and Switzerland (€143). The lowest per capita turnover figures in 2001 were Hungary (€7), Italy (€14) and the Slovakia (€15).

As the roots of direct marketing lie in the mail order industry, many authors, including Alan Tapp, a direct marketing guru, argue that the real strength of direct marketing, as illustrated by mail order and success stories, still relates to what he calls 'transactional direct marketing' or selling. The database compiled by companies allows them to segment their target groups by needs and values and to maximise the probability of response. It also allows marketers to develop profiles of the most profitable customers, and hence target new prospects more efficiently. According to Tapp, this efficiency at transaction marketing is what has driven marketing's growth and many marketers leave direct marketing at that 'direct sales level'.[6]

New financial services organisations and brands such as the European online bank Egg (www.egg.co.uk) have been developed to function as direct sales businesses. Egg initially started in the UK in 1998 where it is now serving over two million customers and has been operating in France since 2002. Egg offers a range of direct banking services including credit cards, savings, loans and mortgages. It also provides its customers with top-of-the-range online banking facilities and even TV banking. With the Egg Money Manager, clients can see all their online accounts in one place, whether they are held with Egg or not. Having an Egg account also offers other benefits: customers can even e-mail money to their friends – all they need is the friend's e-mail address. Egg's products and services are specifically tailored to fit the direct marketing medium and they are simplified so that customers require less advice as part of the decision-making process. This considerably improves response and conversion rates through building consumer confidence. On the other hand, the new brand had to be independent and therefore could not leverage the heritage or awareness of its parent company. It had to build its own customer base and generate awareness and trust on its own terms.[7]

Sales or distribution support

Direct marketing can also be used to support the activities of the sales team, dealers or retailers. Although the actual selling is done by intermediaries, direct marketing tries to prepare, stimulate and facilitate sales. It can also be used to follow up sales. For instance, the Dutch airline KLM uses direct marketing to motivate independent travel agents to buy KLM tickets for long-distance flights. Direct marketing is also often used to support personal sales. Sales visits are rather expensive, but a high frequency of contacts has to be maintained or even increased because of the highly competitive market environment. In this case direct marketing has a funnel function (see Figure 13.3). Reducing a high number of potentials to a limited number of qualified prospects (to be visited by the sales representative) is the main objective. Direct marketing will take over some of the sales team's tasks to reduce costs.[8]

Hewlett-Packard tried to increase its market share in the Dutch PC notebook market by developing a direct marketing campaign that, unlike most campaigns, did not focus on primary product features but stressed Hewlett-Packard's facilitating

Figure 13.3 Direct marketing as a sales supporting tool

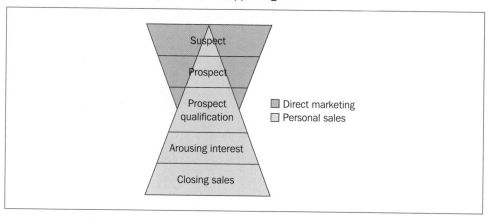

role in home-working. The campaign, which consisted of a mailing and the minisite www.hphomework.nl with lots of practical content for home- and teleworkers, aimed to help people find the right 'work–life balance' and in the process build brand preference among notebook buyers. As a result of the campaign, Hewlett-Packard's market share in the Netherlands for notebook PCs rose from 4.2% at the beginning of the direct marketing campaign to 6.1%, all in one year. The HP Homework campaign created by Publicis received a Silver Esprix award for best direct marketing campaign in 2002.[9]

Customer retention and loyalty

Direct marketing is also the appropriate tool to improve relations with customers and increase their satisfaction and loyalty. Customer loyalty is important for different reasons. One study involving 27 brands showed that the most loyal customers (12%) are responsible for 69% of the sales figure of a brand.[10] Others claim that lack of loyalty slows company performance by 25%–50%. Customer switching is costing British companies an estimated sales loss of £100 billion each year and another £100 billion to win back lost customers. Relationship marketing has two positive effects: customer retention, in combination with gaining new customers, leads to a higher number of customers. Second, the longer they stay, the more profitable they become. The return per customer will increase, operational costs will decrease, positive word-of-mouth will lead to new customers and loyal customers are less price-sensitive. Figure 13.4 shows how profits increase year on year thanks to the different effects of customer loyalty.[11]

Corporate expenditures on loyalty programmes are booming. The top 16 retailers in Europe, for instance, spent more than €1 billion on loyalty initiatives. Nevertheless, the role of direct and database marketing in achieving higher levels of customer loyalty is not undisputed. A fair amount of academic research seriously doubts that loyalty schemes, magazines or other tactical initiatives make much difference. Emotional loyalty is said to be only a reality when personal interactions take place.[12] Moreover, large-scale and longitudinal studies have found that the relationship between loyalty and profitability is much weaker than proponents of customer relationship marketing (CRM) and loyalty programmes claim. One study discovered little or no evidence to

Figure 13.4 Profit per client as a function of customer retention

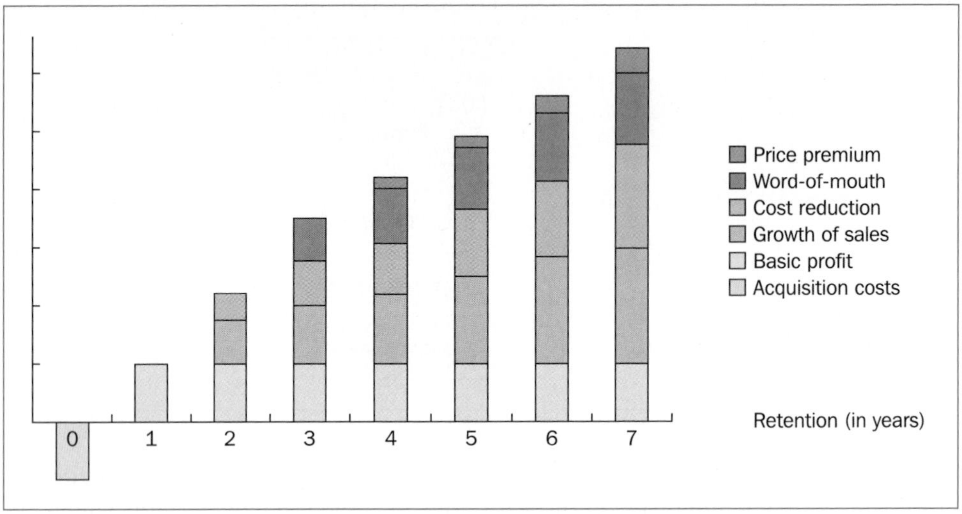

Based on: Reichheld, F.F. (2001), *The Loyalty Effect. The Hidden Force Behind Growth, Profits and Lasting Value*. Boston: Harvard Business School Press. Reproduced with permission of Harvard Business School Publishing.

support Reichheld's hypothesis that customers who purchase steadily from a company over time are cheaper to serve, less price sensitive or effective at bringing in new business by positive word-of-mouth advertising. Instead of focussing on loyalty alone, a trend among many marketers, companies will have to measure the relationship between loyalty and profitability in order to identify the really interesting consumers. To track the performance of its loyalty programme one US high-tech corporate service provider set up a costing scheme to measure all costs for each customer during five years. The results took them by surprise. Half of the customers who had regularly been buying for at least two years (the company thought these could be called 'loyal' customers) barely generated profit while about half of the most profitable customers were buying high-margin products in a short time, before completely disappearing.[13]

Whiskas is leading the premium segment of the cat food market. To sustain this position it was essential to lead a direct dialogue with the consumer to strengthen brand loyalty and increase the lifetime value of the brand users. Using direct response television advertising, addresses of owners of kittens in Germany were collected at the earliest possible age of the cat (see Plate 19). The dialogue programme consisted of a welcome package providing relevant information to make life with the cat more comfortable and convenient in the first year of the cat's life, together with distributing product samples. After this welcome package, addresses were transferred to the Whiskas loyalty programme, ensuring four contact moments per year. The cat owners receive a quarterly full-colour, 22-page magazine with content that is closely linked to the core brand values: best possible care and nutrition for the cat and responsible cat ownership because 'nobody knows cats better than Whiskas'. The programme led to a significant increase in brand preference and buying intention, and above-average response rates.[14]

Direct marketing media and tools

To meet the communications objectives different direct marketing media and tools can be used. Two types may be discerned: addressable and non-addressable media. They are presented in Figure 13.5.

Figure 13.5 Direct marketing media and tools

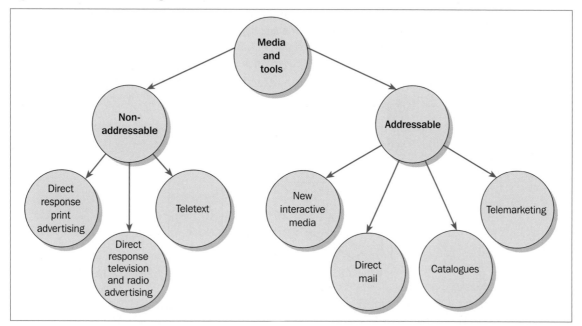

Although it may seem a paradox, direct marketing communications can also make use of mass media or non-addressable media, but the difference with mass communications is that they are used to generate a direct response among receivers of the message. Direct response advertising (direct response print ads, television and radio advertising) makes up an important part of the advertising activity. For instance, in the US approximately two-thirds of all advertising is response-generating.

Direct response print advertising

Direct response print advertising or coupon advertising means placing an advertisement in a newspaper or a magazine with the following characteristics:

- direct feedback from the reader (respondent) to the advertiser by returning a coupon or calling a phone number;
- a clear link between the response (feedback) and the message advertised;
- identification of the respondent.

Direct response print advertising is not addressable and not individually targeted at one single consumer. The advertisement is placed in a mass medium (newspaper or magazine). The primary goal of direct response ads is to select interested consumers or companies (in a business-to-business context use) out of a large audience. Direct response advertising is also a good way to provide interested consumers and prospects with more information than can be 'packed' in a traditional ad. By responding with an answering coupon, the interested potential customer can obtain more detailed information. Ads with a coupon seem to be quite effective in that they are able to produce up to 20% better attention scores than other ads.

Thanks to the directness and feedback of direct response ads some interesting research on effectiveness can be carried out. In the first figure the impact of print ad format (full-page or part-page) on response success is shown.[15] The results lead to the conclusion that doubling the ad format will not lead to a 100% growth in response.

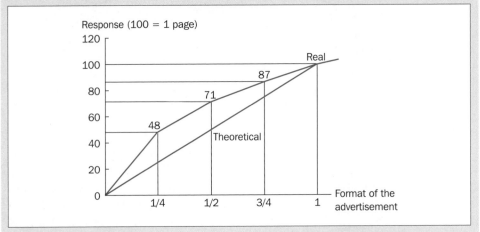

Reproduced with permission of Kogan Page.

Increasing the frequency of a direct response ad will rarely lead to a rise in response figures. A second ad published shortly after the first one will most of the time have a lower response rate. The first exposure will reach the majority of the interested audience. This is shown in the next figure.

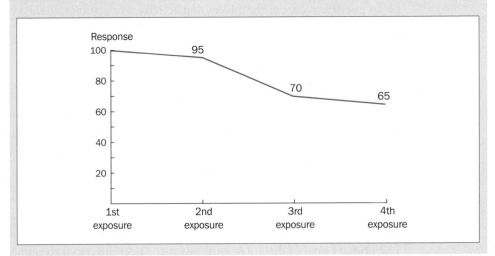

To incite readers to react to a direct response print ad, usually three different techniques are combined:

■ *Motivational information*: information that gives the readers a reason to react. The visual and headline used in the ad are important because they draw the attention of the readers and have 15 or 20 times more chance to be seen than the rest of the ad. Visuals and headlines should get the attention and give motivation to read the rest of the ads. Motivational information is information appealing to the needs of the readers.

■ *Activating information*: this informational content of an ad stresses what the reader should do to react and how he or she can react. Active language (words like 'now' and 'quick') and clear response instructions ('come', 'call', 'cut') are crucial.

■ *Facilitating instruments*: these will help the reader to react and will break down potential problems and barriers. Examples are: a dotted line around a coupon, the picture of scissors, a phone number that is easy to remember etc.

Direct response television advertising

Direct response television (DRTV) uses television as a medium to generate reactions. It is thus, with regards to principles and key success factors, quite comparable to print response advertising in newspapers and magazines. In the US half of all TV commercials include a response phone number. DRTV commercials are principally used for direct selling or information enquiry purposes (both 40%), for competitions (21%) and for sampling, gifts and shop visit invitations (each 10% use).[16] Quite often, different direct response propositions are combined in one commercial or DRTV is integrated in a multi-step strategy to generate extra sales. The power of DRTV as a sales tool is proved by the success of teleshopping programmes (for instance, Home Order Television on the German cable station DF1) or even teleshopping channels (like QVC, Home Shopping Europe or Polonia 1, the first Polish channel, operated by the Polish media holding Fincast, that is focusing on teleshopping in Poland).

Direct response television commercials are different from traditional television advertising or direct response ads in a number of ways. The first is the choice of a response method. Providing the possibility to react by phone will create more response than a simple mail-answering method. The phone number will have to stay long enough on screen (11 seconds) to allow viewers to memorise the number. Visual and auditory support and repeating the phone number will also increase response. Another difference with traditional television ads is that direct television advertising is more efficient during the cheaper broadcasting hours. Traditional TV advertising has as its main objective to be seen by as many viewers as possible. DRTV commercials want to generate the highest and most profitable response. Broadcasting DRTV spots in the morning and afternoon is the most efficient way to do so because they will lead to the largest percentage of viewer response. The reason for this is that viewers do not want to be disturbed during prime time while they are watching their favourite programmes and shows. Calls for action at those broadcasting hours will be less successful.

DirecTel, a German mobile phone operator, used DRTV adverts to promote an aggressive price offer for a mobile phone and XtraCard to be sold through a telephone ordering service. The campaign was targeted at beginners in the world of mobile telephony who want to use a mobile phone without being tied down to a contract and financial commitments. The DRTV adverts were broadcast between June and September on the channels ProSieben, RTL2 and DSF, among others. During this period, 15,000 calls were registered, a 40% higher response than for previous marketing actions.[17]

Direct response radio advertising

Similar to direct response TV advertising, direct response radio advertising is an interactive form of radio advertising, aimed at generating direct behavioural responses from the listening audience using the phone, post or internet. Although direct response radio advertising can be used both for mass and niche markets in a consumer or business-to-business environment, content analysis of broadcast commercials has shown that services like banking and insurances and the tourism industry in particular use this kind of advertising. Compared to other advertising media, radio suffers from characteristics such as external pacing, volatility and lack of attention. However, it also has some advantages. It is relatively cheap both in renting and production costs as the average costs of a radio-GRP tend to be five to ten times lower than the average costs of a TV-GRP. Radio advertising is also a selective medium, allowing advertisers to limit reach to certain geographic areas or demographic and lifestyle groups, as the specialised music and news programming of radio stations usually attracts specific audiences. Radio is also a very flexible medium to advertisers as commercials can be delivered shortly before the first broadcast. The last advantage is its availability to a broad public in any place, at any time. Although radio advertising has been lacking attention as a direct response medium for a long time, more recently there is a growing awareness of the powerful role radio can play in direct marketing. The growing penetration and use of mobile telephones is facilitating response to advertising in cars and other places where a fixed phone line is not available. However, research has shown that it is less effective and efficient to broadcast direct response radio commercials between 7 a.m. and 9 a.m., and between 4 p.m. and 6 p.m.; those broadcast between 2 p.m. and 4 p.m. were most effective. Spots broadcast on Monday, Tuesday and Wednesday were also significantly more effective than those broadcast on other days of the week. Position in the commercial break and total length of the commercial break had no implications for the effectiveness.[18]

Teletext

Advertisers may rent one or more teletext pages to spread their message and generate response. The popularity of this medium is different from one country to another and depends on the tradition of commercial teletext broadcasting. In the UK, for instance, teletext is widely used by advertisers since ITV teletext is heavily used by the British public.

Addressable media are media by means of which it is possible to communicate individually with each customer or prospect. The most important addressable media are direct mail, telemarketing and catalogues.

Direct mail

Direct mail are written commercial messages, personally addressed and sent by mail. A direct mailing usually consists of an envelope, a sales letter accompanying a brochure and an answering card. Pros of direct mail are the selectivity, the opportunity to personalise messages, flexibility in the use of very creative ideas, and the ability to communicate fast, target specific groups and customise messages and offers. The con is that the response to mailings is usually rather low. This is due to the 'clutter' and the resulting 'junk mail' image of direct mail. Direct mailing is still the most frequently used direct medium and the high number of mailings per capita (Figure 13.6[19]) stimulates receivers to be very selective in what mailings they open and wish to read.

Figure 13.6 Addressed direct mail per capita in Europe, 2001

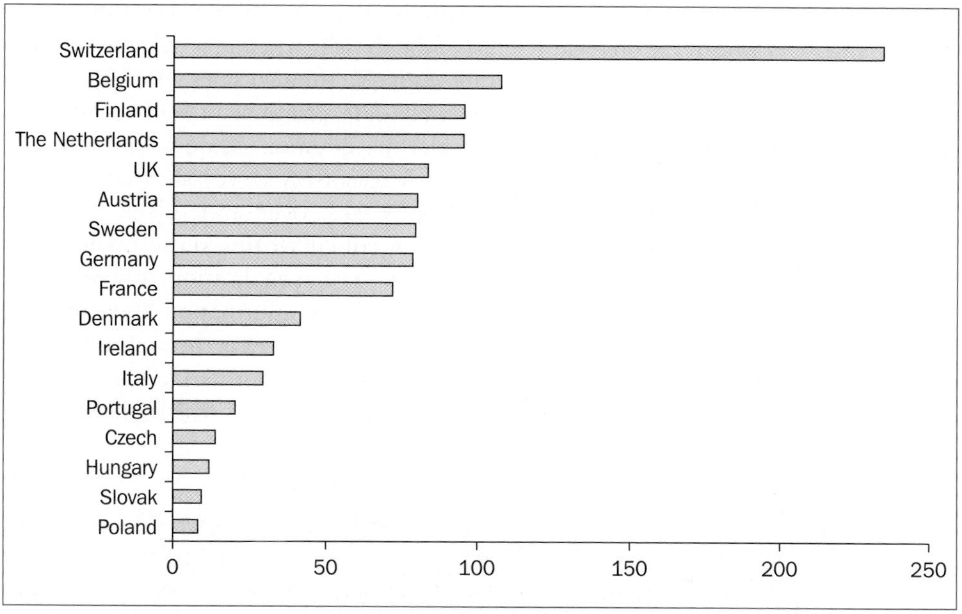

Based on: FEDMA (2002), *Survey on Direct and Interactive Marketing Activities in Europe*. Reproduced with permission of the Federation of European Direct Marketing, www.fedma.org.

Belgian Post eradicates junk mail

Despite increasingly sophisticated database marketing techniques and lip service for targeted marketing communication efforts, the average consumer is still swamped with junk mail from companies that send their direct mails undifferentiated to all more or less potential consumers. The Belgian Direct Marketing Organisation has opened a website on which people can sub-scribe to the so-called 'Robinson list', indicating that they do not want to receive unsolicited direct mails. It is a kind of 'opt-out' mechanism for paper mailings that is similar to the opt-in legislation for electronic communication as a result of which companies are not allowed to send e-mails to people without their prior and written consent. The Belgian Post has taken the initiative to hold a survey amongst the whole Belgian population to find out for which products each person still wants to receive mail and for which products he/she definitely does not want to be 'stalked'. As such, the initiative is a combination of the opt-in and opt-out principle. It is aimed to be a win–win situation for both advertisers and consumers: the consumer only receives the commercial communication they are interested in, while companies avoid the cost of sending their communication to large groups of consumers who are not interested in receiving it. For those consumers who do not complete the questionnaire, the Post sticks to its current principle: nobody ends up on a list, and those who do not reply keep on receiving the same (junk) mail as before.

Source: *De Morgen*, 26 November 2005.

Switzerland is the most frequently mailed European country with an average of 234.5 addressed mailings per capita. Belgium, the Netherlands and Finland are also mail-intensive countries. Poland, Slovakia, Hungary and the Czech Republic are the least direct mailed countries with less than 14 addressed mailings per capita in 2001.[20]

One of the important goals of database marketing is to increase the level of customer intimacy, not only to generate response but also sales. With the fully customised text and graphics that today's variable data printing, in both print and electronic communications, has made available, the question is, does the use of a high degree of personalisation help these goals. A recent US survey showed that name-only personalisation increased response rates by 44% over static black-and-white mailings (that averaged 0.46% response). Adding colour to this static mailing increased response by 45% and together with name-only personalisation, response rates increased by 135%. Adding dynamic database-resident information even increased the rates by over 500%. Responses followed a similar pattern through all product categories in consumer and business-to-business markets. Another German study reported that the success rate for fully customised direct mailings is nearly three times higher than for standard mailings.[21]

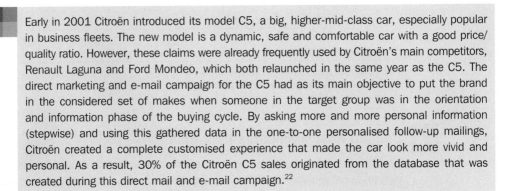

Early in 2001 Citroën introduced its model C5, a big, higher-mid-class car, especially popular in business fleets. The new model is a dynamic, safe and comfortable car with a good price/quality ratio. However, these claims were already frequently used by Citroën's main competitors, Renault Laguna and Ford Mondeo, which both relaunched in the same year as the C5. The direct marketing and e-mail campaign for the C5 had as its main objective to put the brand in the considered set of makes when someone in the target group was in the orientation and information phase of the buying cycle. By asking more and more personal information (stepwise) and using this gathered data in the one-to-one personalised follow-up mailings, Citroën created a complete customised experience that made the car look more vivid and personal. As a result, 30% of the Citroën C5 sales originated from the database that was created during this direct mail and e-mail campaign.[22]

Every direct marketing or mailing campaign will require a different success measure according to the initial marketing or communications goals.[23] A classic illustration of this is a company selling a Caribbean island through a direct mailing campaign. A brochure with an accompanying letter was sent to 500 key prospects each having enough money, being eager for privacy and being sun worshippers. Only one response was received but it led to the sale of the island, making the direct mailing campaign 100% effective.

RSGB Mailmonitor is providing a measure of effectiveness in the UK based on a panel of 1,350 households selected on a nationally representative basis. The table shows that even if response is not immediate, a mailing could be effective at a later stage.

Reactions to mailings in the UK (Based on the RSGB Mailmonitor)

	Number of items (m)	% of direct mail
Total direct mailings	1,411.44	100.00%
Kept for future reference	292.73	20.74%
Read, threw away	198.73	14.08%
Read carefully, threw away	91.18	6.46%
Placed an order	68.88	4.88%
Passed to someone else	34.72	2.46%
Entered competition	20.32	1.44%
Made appointment/visit	6.49	0.46%
Telephoned for quote	1.97	0.48%
Any action	**714.99**	**51.00%**

Reproduced with permission of Centaur Communications Ltd.

According to this monitor, half of the mailings resulted in one reaction or another. But response rates seem to vary considerably from one industry to another. In 1994 the market with the best response rates to its mailings was the food and beverages industry with 23.6% response. There are three main reasons why this industry had an astonishingly high response rate compared to the other markets. First, until now direct mailings had not often been used in this industry and would therefore account for a higher attention and reaction rate. Second, food and beverage items have a small cost per item which makes the barriers for trial lower. Third, most mailings in this market have a relatively simple message. Across the different consumer product markets an average response rate of 5.7% was calculated. In terms of individual mailings, analysis suggested that the smaller the mailings and the more targeted the direct mailing campaign, the higher the response rate is likely to be.[24]

Telemarketing

Telemarketing may be defined as any measurable activity using the telephone to help find, get, keep and develop customers.[25] The use of telemarketing as a direct marketing medium has increased enormously. Total European telemarketing expenditures were €12.3 million in 2001, an amount that has steadily grown over the last decade. Developing markets are Greece and Slovakia, with growth rates of +275% and +400% respectively in 2001. However, these markets are still very small compared to the biggest telemarketing spenders, the UK (€4.7 million) and Germany (€3 million).[26]

Telemarketing may be considered as a number of different activities that can be defined on the basis of two dimensions, i.e. the party taking the initiative (inbound versus outbound telemarketing), and the extent to which it is used as a sales-generating versus a sales-supporting direct marketing tool (Table 13.2).[27]

Outbound telemarketing means that the marketer is taking the initiative to call clients or prospects; inbound implies that interested customers or prospects are using the phone to contact the company and ask for product information, order a product, ask for help with a problem or file a complaint. Outbound telemarketing means outgoing telephone calls (from the marketer's point of view) and inbound incoming calls. Using telemarketing to take orders is especially common in mail order companies or for direct response advertisers. Telesales involve actively calling consumers or companies with the

Table 13.2 **The different functions of telemarketing**

	Sales-generating	Sales-supporting
Inbound telemarketing	■ Taking orders	■ Product and company information ■ Customer service, helpdesk ■ Complaints service
Outbound telemarketing	■ Tele-sales	■ Organising meetings/dates for the salesmen ■ Tele-prospecting ■ Updating commercial databases ■ Supporting other marketing communications ■ Generating traffic ■ Tele-factoring

Based on: Walrave, M. (1995), Telemarketing: Storing op de Lijn? (Telemarketing: Badly Connected?). Leuven/Amersfoort: Acco.

purpose of selling products or services. Tele-prospecting is searching for prospects by phone. Two other uses are controlling and actualising databases and settling dates for the sales team. Telemarketing might also be a good way of creating synergetic media effects when it is used together with other marketing communications activities. For instance, the response to a direct mailing might be increased by calling to announce the arrival of the mailing. Telemarketing can be used to generate more traffic at the point-of-sales or to collect debts (tele-factoring). A survey of France Télécom revealed that 35% of French companies use the phone for active sales (telesales) purposes; 44% used the phone to take orders; 53% to set dates and meetings.

The phone is the most direct of all direct media tools and has some advantages. It is a flexible, interactive and quick medium. A telemarketing campaign may be launched at any moment and its effectiveness is very easy to track immediately. On the other hand, it is quite a hard-selling and intrusive medium and with its costs being 10–20 times higher than a mailing it is a rather expensive tool. However, costs should be gauged against response figures to make a correct evaluation.

Catalogues

A catalogue is a list of products or services presented in a visual and/or verbal way. It may be printed or electronically stored on a disk, a CD-ROM or a database. Germany is the worldwide number one catalogue country with an average DM425 spent per capita per year. Catalogues are, of course, mostly used by mail order companies. In 1992, 40% of the Dutch people bought from a mail order company, in France 57% did, in Belgium 38% and in Germany 45%. Although customers are not able to feel, try, smell, taste, etc. the product in a catalogue, it does give them the freedom to go through the catalogue, choose among a wide range of products and save time.

There are different types of catalogues.[28] Reference catalogues are an extensive overview of all products with their characteristics, references and prices. This kind of catalogue is typically nothing more than a purely technical description of the products or services range. They are more used in industrial markets and are appropriate if a relationship with a customer has already been developed. The hard-selling catalogue is a sales-generating tool that should be able to sell without further involvement of a salesperson, a dealer or distributor. These catalogues are used by clothing, soft- and hardware, books and CD mail order companies. Just like the reference catalogues they have a functional sales goal. Other types of catalogues are more supporting sales and used as guidelines or helping tools during a sales conversation or during a shop visit. For instance, the Ikea catalogue is used as a guide during a stroll in Ikea shops. A second goal of these catalogues is to invite and stimulate people to visit the store (traffic-generating objective).

New interactive media

New media are often a combination of existing media such as telephone, cable, television and computers into new applications. That is why they are also called multimedia. Interactive media are characterised by the fact that they deliver tailor-made information to the users at the moment that the user wants to have this kind of information. In other words, the user is directing the information process. Media such as CD-I, CD-ROM, internet, interactive teletext, websites and e-mail are the most important new interactive media. In Chapter 17 these techniques will be explored in more depth.

Database marketing

A database is a collection of interrelated data of customers and prospects which can be used for different applications such as analysis, individual selection, segmentation and customer retention, loyalty and service supports.[29] The minimum requirements of a good marketing database are personal customer data, transaction (purchase history) data and communications (received mailings, incentives, marketing actions and market reactions) data. The database could also file which products, company departments and salespersons are involved with a certain marketing action. In fact, a database stores three kinds of data: market information, relationship data and company data (Figure 13.7). They are mostly stored in a relational database, such as Access and Oracle, that use SQL (structural query language) to make links between individual data.

There are two possible sources of data:[30] internal and external. Most companies already have the basic information needed to start a database:[31] order and invoice information, such as customer names, addresses, account numbers, purchase data, method of payment, etc. These customer files are internal data which may be the first basis to start up a database. External data are all types of lists compiled outside the company which can be bought or hired for direct marketing purposes. Examples are subscriber lists of newspapers and magazines, or databases segmented on lifestyle and consumption habits.

The success of any direct marketing campaign depends heavily on the quality and structure of the database used. The effectiveness of direct marketing campaigns will increase with improved targeting. The latter means that individuals may be reached with a relevant message improving response and reducing irritation levels. Repeat business and new business are the key factors to company growth. The former will need communications with the current loyal customers. Those heavy users are often small in

Figure 13.7 The marketing database

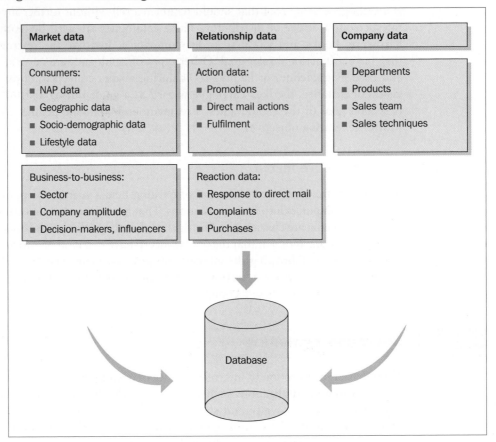

number and thus only accessible through direct marketing targeting. Strategic use of the database and accurate segmentation based on the registered consumer profiles will be crucial to these goals. For new business success depends on the ability to identify potential customers with the correct profile to be hot prospects for the kind of products or services the company has to offer. Learning from the current customers and keeping all kinds of useful information about these customers in a database will make it easier to make a good list of prospects. For example, Seagram (a liquor company) knows that two-thirds of all American adults will never drink liquor. It would be a waste of money to invest in mass marketing and advertising. Creating a database to identify potential new customers would be a better investment.

As the marketing database is a crucial instrument of direct marketing communications, it is important that it is correctly managed. Most of the data will quickly expire and frequent updates are required to prevent the database from losing its value. There are five potential pitfalls for a marketing database:

■ *Incompleteness*: some data are not collected for all records in the database. This may be due to a bad data collection procedure or to a compilation based on different sources.

- *Data expiration*: some data expire quickly, for instance, function (job title) and home address may rapidly change, but the name of the customer usually stays the same during his or her entire adult lifetime.

- *Unreliability*: some data might be false because the source is not trustworthy. For instance, data collected through the internet sometimes contain many fictitious names and addresses.

- *Inconsistency*: some data are not automatically changed, although they are linked to others, for instance a phone number is not adapted to a newly entered home address.

- *Duplications*: two or more identical records may be stored due to different spellings resulting in two or more of the same mailings to customers and prospects, which might irritate them and is costing money to the direct marketer.

At least one person in the organisation should be appointed to manage the database in order to avoid these mistakes.

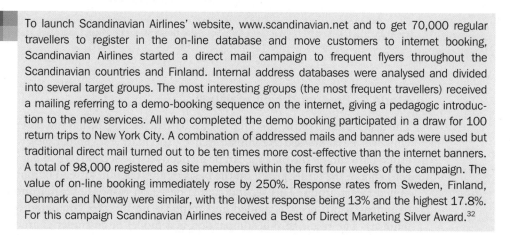

To launch Scandinavian Airlines' website, www.scandinavian.net and to get 70,000 regular travellers to register in the on-line database and move customers to internet booking, Scandinavian Airlines started a direct mail campaign to frequent flyers throughout the Scandinavian countries and Finland. Internal address databases were analysed and divided into several target groups. The most interesting groups (the most frequent travellers) received a mailing referring to a demo-booking sequence on the internet, giving a pedagogic introduction to the new services. All who completed the demo booking participated in a draw for 100 return trips to New York City. A combination of addressed mails and banner ads were used but traditional direct mail turned out to be ten times more cost-effective than the internet banners. A total of 98,000 registered as site members within the first four weeks of the campaign. The value of on-line booking immediately rose by 250%. Response rates from Sweden, Finland, Denmark and Norway were similar, with the lowest response being 13% and the highest 17.8%. For this campaign Scandinavian Airlines received a Best of Direct Marketing Silver Award.[32]

The growing importance of one-to-one marketing[33] has made it clear that generating and managing customer information has moved from a strategic opportunity to a strategic necessity. Companies that are the first to detect and answer customer needs with the right product or service at the right moment, offered through the right channel have a substantial competitive advantage. A file with address data is not enough to support marketing decisions and drive customer loyalty programmes. More sophisticated database techniques have to be used. In Figure 13.8 five stages in the use of database marketing are shown:[34] from the use of the database as a file with addresses (untargeted approach) to the use of database marketing to get the right product through the right channel at the right moment to the customers (event-driven database marketing).

Stage 1: Untargeted marketing

Often, the starting point of database marketing in a company is the phase in which a company uses a database of prospects. They are selected on certain criteria to fit with the target group of the product or service the direct marketer will promote in the mailing sent to this broad group of potential customers.

Figure 13.8 Five stages in the use of database marketing

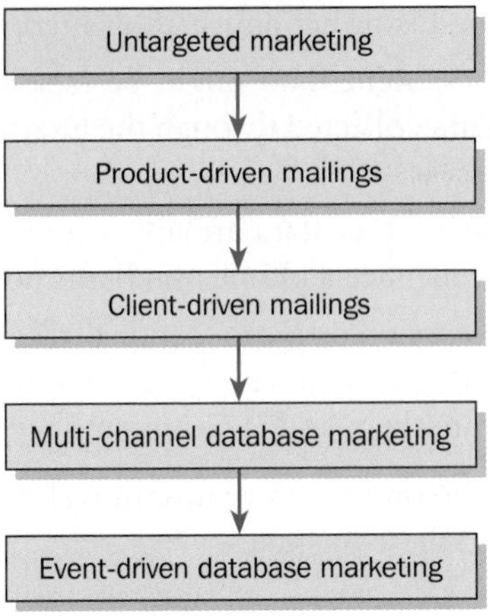

Based on: Bügel, M.S. (1997), 'Van Direct Mail naar Event-Driven Marketing' (From Direct Mail to Event-Driven Marketing), *Tijdschrift voor Strategische Bedrijfscommunicatie*, 3(2), 98–106.

Stage 2: Product-driven mailings

The disadvantage of the first step in database marketing is that the criteria to determine who will be addressed are constituted by the marketer. Sometimes when the wrong criteria are chosen the mailing can be ineffective. The second step in database marketing is to choose the target group on the basis of a test action instead of mailing a predetermined target group. This second step is based on response scoring models. A sample of potential prospects is mailed and response profiles are compared to non-response patterns. The result of this comparison is a model of customer characteristics with a predictive value for response. This model is then used to give a score (the likelihood of response or, in other words, the need of every customer for the product or service offered in the mailing) to every potential prospect. Those prospects for whom the estimated returns (based on response chance) would be higher than the mailing cost are then selected for mailing. Product-driven database marketing uses customer information to select the right customers for a certain product or service. This is a more targeted form of direct marketing offering more relevant propositions to consumers and lowering mailing costs for the direct marketer.

On the other hand, there are two cons: too much focus on action-driven mailings could lead to cannibalisation of the sales of other products or services, i.e. stealing sales from some of the other products of the company. Furthermore, incentives and loyalty systems used in these product-driven mailings could subsidise consumers who would have bought the products without these incentives. This has a negative influence on profits.

Stage 3: Client-driven mailings

To take the negative aspects of product-driven database marketing into account, a measure for individual client relationship value can be developed. The decision to contact certain customers will depend on the change in this relationship value rather than the profits on individual actions. Only customers who increase their relationship after a certain action are targeted. This introduces the concept of lifetime value[35] or the expected return a certain customer will deliver during the years he or she has a relationship with the company. This implies an estimation of the lifetime of a client as well as the profitability of every individual customer (share of wallet).[36] In this stage the direct marketer tries to target the right customers with the right products.

Stage 4: Multi-channel database marketing

This database marketing technique integrates the knowledge on channel sensitivity into marketing activities. Some prospects are more open to direct mail than others. In this approach actions to sell the same kind of products or services are sent through different sales channels (direct sales, personal selling, etc.). Which combination of sales channels will be used depends on the sensitivity of every individual customer and the costs of each channel. Both types of data are stored in the marketing database. Multi-channel marketing uses the database to offer the right product to the right client through the best channel.

Stage 5: Event-driven database marketing

In stage 4 products and services are promoted and proposed during the action period. But consumers' needs are not always felt during this action period. The chance of a mailing arriving just in time, i.e. when the consumer actually considers a certain purchase, is slim. By the time he is planning the purchase there is only a slight chance that he will remember the mailing and the action of competitors could get more attention. To avoid this, it is necessary to adjust the timing of mailings and other marketing actions to the moment when customers' needs become prevalent. Needs often arise as a consequence of certain events in the life of a customer (marriage, buying a house, birth of a child, moving, etc.), or they are related to the relation between the client and the company (e.g. an information request two weeks ago, for a bank: €2,500 on a customer's account, etc.). In event-driven database marketing customers are actively followed to detect changes in needs and to offer them the right products at the right moment (through the right channel). Smart chip cards, internet and call centres may be used to keep track of these changes. Instead of traditional promotion planning done by a marketer, all actions take place at the most effective moment for each individual client.

Privacy concerns

With the rising use of databases linked to the growing desire to get to know individual customers, consumers are concerned about what companies know about them and how those companies obtain and use personal information. The primary source of consumer privacy concerns revolves around personal or individual-specific data such as names, addresses, demographic characteristics, lifestyle interests, shopping preferences and purchase histories. Growing numbers of marketers are assimilating and using information from (and about) individual consumers and renting or exchanging data or lists describing habits and characteristics of individual consumers. The privacy literature suggests that most of the individual-specific consumer information used for marketing purposes falls into five broad categories: demographic characteristics, lifestyle characteristics (including media habits), shopping or purchase habits, financial data and personal identifiers such as names, addresses, social security numbers. A survey has found that consumers are most willing to provide marketers with demographic and lifestyle information and least willing to provide financial information (such as annual household income, the kind of credit cards they possess and the two most recent credit card purchases) and personal identifiers. On the other hand, the majority of respondents were always willing to share their two favourite hobbies, age, marital status, occupation or type of job and education. Although most consumers understand the need for financial information when purchasing on credit, a request for income information, particularly from a non-financial or non-insurance service marketer, has a profound negative effect on purchase intentions. Most consumers desire more control over information collection and use. They want to control what companies do with their information as well as control the number of catalogues and the amount of advertising material they receive. Only 33% of companies inform consumers of the uses of the information they collect. As communicating the uses of information can be seen as an essential first step in allowing customers to opt out of databases and information use, it can be assumed that the number of companies providing customers with the option to control the dissemination of their information is far below the 33%. The Direct Marketing Association strongly recommends an opt-out format (allowing consumers to remove their names from a list by checking a box on a form). Apart from the control of information disclosure, privacy also has to do with control over unwanted intrusions such as telemarketing, unwanted direct mail or unsolicited commercial e-mail (spam). The internet channel in particular has fostered a new set of privacy concerns resulting from the ease with which data in this channel can be collected, stored and exchanged. Additional consumer concern results from the volume of spam due to the low absolute cost and waste inherent in sending commercial e-mails. Nevertheless research has shown that consumers are more likely to request name removal from telephone lists than e-mail lists. But on the other hand, removal from e-mail lists was more desired than postal mail lists.[37]

Relationship marketing[38]

Marketers still tend to spend more and exert more effort on gaining new customers than on keeping the current customers satisfied and loyal. An estimation revealed that the part of marketing budgets assigned to promotional activities aimed at attracting new customers is five times greater than the budget spent on current customers.[39] But the efforts involved in attracting new customers are much higher than those required to keep the current customers loyal. In fact, some claim that companies can realise profit increases of 35%–85% just by decreasing customer loss by 5%. Moreover, as mentioned before the profit per customer can also be assumed to increase the longer a customer stays with the company. This is the result of diminishing acquisition costs, lower operational and service costs per client per year, combined with a rise in the average yearly purchases per loyal client, declining price sensitivity and, last but not least, positive word-of-mouth (more referrals) attracting new customers cost-effectively.[40]

In relationship marketing a marketer's challenge is to bring quality, customer service and marketing into close alignment, leading to long-term and mutually beneficial customer relationships.[41] In other words, the direct marketer tries to create and maintain relationships of value. For example, Harley-Davidson created the Harley Owners Club which has about 200,000 members worldwide. Besides motorbikes, Harley-Davidson also offers an insurance programme, a travel agency, an emergency roadside service, two magazines, member competitions and 750 local chapters. Nestlé regularly sends information to young mothers. It employs qualified dieticians to operate its customer service lines and runs a chain of baby cafés to cater for families away from home.

The fundamental importance of relationship marketing is related to the principle that customer satisfaction, loyalty and profitability are correlated. Lifetime value, or the net present value of the profits a company will generate from its customers over a period of time (usually 4–5 years), is an important concept for the direct marketer involved with relationship or retention marketing. By computing the average lifetime value of its customers, the company will be able to determine how much it can invest in attracting and making loyal potential new customers. Not all customers should be made loyal.[42] It makes no sense building up a loyal but unprofitable relationship. With the Pareto principle in mind, 80% of time and promotional efforts should be allocated to 20% of the customers. To identify these customers the information assembled about the customer's past behaviour will help the direct marketer select the right customers for further loyalty development. Apart from traditional socio-demographic and psychographic segmentations, customer portfolio segments can be measured in terms of number of customers, number of purchases (frequency of purchase), recency of purchases and contribution to sales and profits (monetary value).[43]

During a relationship, customers can progress from being a prospect to being a customer, client, supporter and, at the top of the loyalty ladder, an advocate (see Figure 13.9).[44] The latter are so involved with the organisation that they are very loyal

Figure 13.9 The loyalty ladder

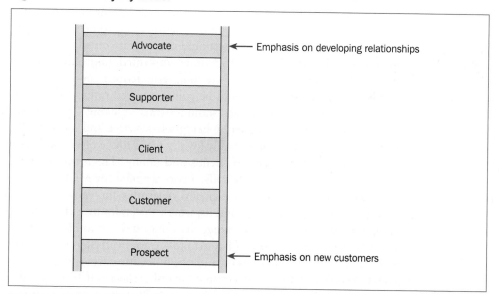

Based on: Jenkinson, A. (1995), *Valuing Your Customers: From Quality Information to Quality Relationships Through Database Marketing*. London: McGraw-Hill.

and influence others by positive word-of-mouth. The relationship direct marketer wants to encourage its customers as far up the loyalty ladder as possible.

Customer loyalty will be won by being better than competitors (offering superior products and services) or by loyalty strategies. There are two strategies to stimulate customer loyalty: a rewarding strategy and a relationship strategy. The former implies rewarding loyal behaviour by giving 'hard' advantages to reinforce and maintain customer loyalty. Examples are frequent flier programmes, gifts, prizes or money. Rewarding strategies are targeted to rational calculating customers. But, as these rewards are easy to copy or exceed by competitors, they are rarely the best strategy when they are not used in combination with a relationship strategy. The latter consists of creating tight relations with customers by gathering information about each individual customer and using it intelligently by providing soft, personalised and customised advantages. Examples are sending targeted and relevant messages, special events for customers, etc. These relationship strategies are targeted at affective-oriented customers. For instance, someone calls a local florist and orders a bouquet for his mother's birthday; the next year he gets a postcard from the florist three weeks before his mother's birthday which reflects the number and type of flowers he ordered last year and with the message that it only takes one phone call to send her flowers again. Which of the strategies should a direct marketer choose? Rewarding programmes are effective to use as a first step in the process of building a close relationship. They will bring in customers in the programme. However, this will not be enough to keep customers loyal.

A marketer introducing a loyalty programme should consider the following strategic points involved with sharing value with customers.[45] To profit from loyal customers, marketers should offer the best value to the best customers: the clients creating most profit should benefit from this situation, which will make them even more loyal and profitable. For instance, a company could consider offering lower prices to its loyal customers. Unfortunately, most companies forget this and deliver products or services of the same quality to all customers. The value created by a customer loyalty programme should lead to higher returns than costs. A reward programme may never be a cost and should not attract price- or promotion-sensitive customers of competitors instead of rewarding loyal clients. Rewards should concentrate on stimulating desired behaviour (loyalty, word-of-mouth) and discourage unwanted, unprofitable behaviour (customer defection). Loyalty programmes are long-term actions and not short-term promotions and long-term advantages should be communicated rather than promoting switching behaviour. Loyalty programmes should attract valuable customer segments and discourage less valuable segments by being self-selective and individually correcting. For example, MCI's Friends and Family loyalty programme offered 20%–50% discount on calls to a specified network of friends and family. The proposition is most attractive to heavy users of long-distance calls, a core segment for MCI.

In the customer's mind, five elements determine the value of a loyalty programme: cash value, the number of options, aspiring value, relevance and convenience. The value should be calculated as a percentage discount on the amount a consumer has to spend to be able to get the reward. A free trip to a Caribbean island or a new car has a higher aspiring value than a discount on a phone bill. Customers should also be able to choose from different benefits. A programme is only relevant if the aspired benefit is within reach; if it takes years to collect the necessary air miles to make a free trip it will not be of any relevance to a customer. If it takes a lot of administration, whether for the customer or the retailer, a loyalty programme has a small chance of success. This is what is meant by 'convenience'.

Measuring direct marketing effectiveness

Direct marketing and interactive marketing are behaviour-oriented in nature, and therefore research into the effectiveness of direct and interactive marketing campaigns will invariably be tests of 'counting' behavioural response. The number of people responding to a free telephone number in a direct response television commercial, the number of people returning a coupon included in a print ad or the number of people placing an order as a result of a direct marketing campaign, are examples of effectiveness tests.

Evidently, all communications effectiveness tests are aimed at subsequently improving the communications effort. In direct marketing, which is essentially database-driven, the optimisation of a direct mailing campaign can be based on response scoring models, i.e. a procedure in which a number of indicators of behavioural response in the past are combined. A well-known response scoring model is the RFM-model. For all customers in a database, three behavioural response parameters are measured:

- *Recency*: the time elapsed since the last purchase;
- *Frequency*: the frequency with which a customer places an order;
- *Monetary value*: the average amount of money a customer spends per purchase.

Obviously, the shorter the time elapsed since a customer placed an order, the more frequently he or she buys something, and the higher the average amount of money spent, the more positive the expected response is following the next mailing campaign.[46] For each of the three variables a number of categories can be defined, and each category can be given a 'value' or score, representing the importance of each category for future response. This is illustrated in Table 13.3.

Table 13.3 The RFM model

Recency	Score	Frequency	Score	Monetary value	Score
Last 6 months	100	Once a year	0	Less than €100	0
7–12 months	80	Between 2 and 4 times a year	30	More than €100	20
13–24 months	60	More than 4 times a year	70		
25–36 months	30				
37 months or more	0				

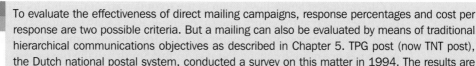

To evaluate the effectiveness of direct mailing campaigns, response percentages and cost per response are two possible criteria. But a mailing can also be evaluated by means of traditional hierarchical communications objectives as described in Chapter 5. TPG post (now TNT post), the Dutch national postal system, conducted a survey on this matter in 1994. The results are described in the table below.

		Private (%)	Business (%)
Recall	■ spontaneous	29	16
	■ aided	44	44
	■ not recalled	27	40
Reading	■ entirely	12	9
	■ browsed	29	28
	■ not yet	24	16
	■ not read	8	7
Attitude	■ very interesting	13	11
	■ a bit interesting	11	10
	■ not interesting	15	14
	■ don't know	2	2
Response	■ planned to react	8	6
	■ no intent to respond	10	9
	■ don't know yet	6	6

Business-to-business mailings on average have lower scores than mailings to private addresses. Companies tend to receive more mailings and company executives have less time to open and read them. Only 9% read them in full but still one in three take the time to have a quick glance.

Evidently, the values attached to each category are to a certain extent arbitrary, but can also be derived from the analysis of past response behaviour. The RFM-values can now be used selectively to mail those members of the target group that have the highest score on one or two of the three factors, or on a combination of all three. It can, for instance, be decided to mail only those customers that have a score of at least 80 on the recency value, as well as a score of 30 on the frequency factor, or only to mail those database entries that have a combined score of at least 100. Response scoring models can improve the effectiveness of mailing campaigns. It remains advisable, however, to pre-test a campaign before sending it out to a sample of target group members.

Some publications have criticised the RFM score model as a poor way to measure loyalty. One problem is that patterns of buying behaviour for frequently purchased goods are different than those for infrequently bought goods. RFM ignores the average time between purchases as a key variable, while the probability that someone who is within historic range of buying frequency will buy again in the future is higher than for someone who is way past the average time between two purchases. RFM analysis would determine that someone who buys more frequently and has bought recently to be the more loyal and therefore direct marketing activities and investments would be targeted at the wrong profile of customers. Take, for instance, two customers, Mr Smith and Ms Jones, who both start to buy goods from a company in month 1. During the first year they purchase at different rates: Smith buys again in the second, sixth and eighth month, whereas Jones purchases again in the eighth month. A simple RFM analysis suggests that Smith is more loyal and thus more interesting for direct marketing investments than Jones because his purchases are more frequent and recent. But Smith usually buys every 2.3 months and yet by month 12 he hasn't bought anything for four months. Jones, too, hasn't bought anything since month 8, but she normally doesn't purchase anything for seven months. On this basis, the chance that she will buy again in the future is higher than for Smith.

This is a case of 'event-history modelling'. In its simplest form, the formula to calculate the probability that a customer will keep on buying is t^n, with n the number of purchases the customer made during a period (in this case a year), and t the fraction of the period represented by the time between his first and last purchase. Unlike RFM, this model is particularly good at predicting how soon a customer's buying activity will drop off and might prevent heavy overinvestment in profitable but disloyal customers.

The second main disadvantage of a scoring model such as RFM is that the monetary value is mostly based on revenue rather than profitability. The cost of servicing customers who buy only small quantities of low-margin products often exceeds the revenue they bring in. Therefore revenue, the average profit earned on each customer, must be brought into the analysis. By multiplying the probability figure for each period (e.g. a quarter) by the historical average profit number, the sum will be the estimated profit for each customer over the next year.

After analysing your customers' profitability and the projected duration of the customer relationship, all customers can be placed into one of the four categories in the matrix shown in Figure 13.10 (overleaf).

Integrating direct marketing communication in IMC

Direct marketing communication should be well integrated into the IMC mix. First of all, different forms of direct marketing can be combined. For instance, a telemarketing campaign can serve as input for a better targeted direct mail shot. Direct marketing communication and customer relationship management can support personal selling by generating leads, collecting information and identifying prospects, thus making sales calls more effective. Sales call results can be ploughed back into the CRM system and they can be used for follow up. Database enrichment as a result of direct mailing or telemarketing can also be used for handling requests and complaints, cross-selling, generating traffic to exhibitions and trade fairs, and provide important information about customer characteristics, attitudes, preferences and buying behaviour. Results of sales promotion and advertising campaigns can be integrated into the customer database and can be used to find out which advertising appeals worked and which promotion campaigns were effective. These impact analyses can be used to generate more impact with future direct marketing, promotion and advertising efforts. Direct marketing communications can also be used to direct (potential) customers to a website, to register and react to in-bound calls resulting from a direct-response advertising campaign, or to contacts generated through the company website.

Summary

Direct marketing communications are an increasingly important instrument of the communications mix, and have the unique characteristics of being able to reach the consumer personally and directly, and immediately measure the effects. Direct marketing can serve a number of objectives, such as direct sales, sales and distribution support, and customer retention and loyalty enhancement. Direct marketing uses a multitude of tools and media. Some of them are non-addressable mass media instruments, such as direct response print and television ads and teletext. Others are addressable or personalised, such as direct mail, telemarketing and catalogues. A prerequisite for successful direct marketing communications is building, maintaining and managing a marketing database which enables the company to collect individualised information on all its customers and prospects, and use it in one-to-one marketing communications campaigns. Depending

Figure 13.10 Reinartz and Kumar's matrix for categorising customers and relationships

	Short-term customers	Long-term customers
High profitability	**Butterflies** High profit potential Actions: ■ Aim for transactional satisfaction and milk accounts ■ Cease investments soon enough	**True friends** Highest profit potential Actions: ■ Communicate consistently ■ Build attitudinal and behavioural loyalty by delighting them
Low profitability	**Strangers** Lowest profit potential Actions: ■ Make no investments in these relationships ■ Make profit on each transaction	**Barnacles** Low profit potential Actions: ■ If share of wallet is low, focus on up- and cross-selling ■ If size of wallet is small, impose cost controls

Source: Reinartz, W. and Kumar, V. (2002), 'The Mismanagement of Customer Loyalty', *Harvard Business Review*, (July), 86–94.

on the sophistication of data collection and data use, five types of databases and direct marketing techniques can be distinguished. Given the fact that keeping existing customers loyal is far less expensive than gaining new customers, relationship marketing, using databases and direct marketing techniques, becomes increasingly important. Based on database information on customer response to previous campaigns, several techniques, such as the RFM model, have been developed to assess the effectiveness of direct marketing communications campaigns.

Review questions

1 Why is direct marketing becoming increasingly important?

2 What are the typical characteristics of direct marketing communications, and to what extent do they differ from mass marketing communications?

3 What are the objectives and tasks of direct marketing communications?

4 How can mass media advertising be used in a direct marketing communications campaign?

5 Compare the various media and tools of addressable direct marketing communications. What are the advantages and disadvantages of each tool?

6 How can telemarketing be used as a direct marketing communications tool?

7 How important is a database for direct marketing communications and how can it be managed?

8 What are the stages in the evolution of database marketing use?

9 What is the importance of relationship marketing and how can direct marketing communications techniques contribute to customer loyalty?

10 How can the RFM model be used to measure the effectiveness of a direct marketing campaign?

Further reading

Bird, D. (2000), *Common Sense Direct Marketing*. London: Kogan Page.

Bush, R., Smith, R. and Cresswell, P. (2003), *The B2B Handbook: A Guide to Achieving Success in Business-to-Business Direct Marketing*. London: Base One.

Curry, J. and Curry, A. (2000), *The Customer Marketing Method. How to Implement and Profit from Customer Relationship Management*. Riverside, NJ: Simon & Schuster Inc.

Drozdenko, K. and Drake, P. (2002), *Optimal Database Marketing: Strategy, Development and Data-Mining*. Thousand Oaks, CA: Sage Publications.

Gentle, M. (2003), *The CRM Project Management Handbook. Building Realistic Expectations and Managing Risk*. London: Kogan Page.

Hughes, A. (2000), *Strategic Database Marketing: The Masterplan for Starting and Managing a Profitable Customer-based Marketing Program*. Hightstown: McGraw-Hill Education.

Molineux, P. (2002), *Exploiting CRM: Connecting With Customers. (The Management Consultancies Association Series)*. London: Hodder & Stoughton Educational.

Mullin, R. (2003), *Direct Marketing: A Step-by-Step Guide to Effective Planning and Targeting. (Marketing in Action Series)*. London: Kogan Page.

Peppers, D. and Rogers, M. (1996), *The One-to-One Future: Building Relationships One Customer at a Time*. New York: Piatkus Books.

Sargeant, A. and West, D. (2001), *Direct and Interactive Marketing*. Oxford: Oxford University Press.

Stone, B. and Jacobs, R. (2001), *Successful Direct Marketing Methods*. Hightstown: McGraw-Hill Education.

Stone, M., Band, A. and Blake, E. (2003), *The Definitive Guide to Direct and Interactive Marketing: How to Select, Reach and Retain the Right Customers*. London: Financial Times Prentice Hall.

Tapp, A. (2001), *Principles of Direct and Database Marketing*. London: Financial Times Prentice Hall.

Thomas, B. and Housden, M. (2002), *Direct Marketing in Practice*. Oxford: Butterworth-Heinemann.

Warwick, M. (2003), *Testing, Testing, 1, 2, 3: Raise More Money with Direct Mail Tests*. Hoboken, NJ: Jossey Bass Wiley.

Case 13

Direct marketing at Tesco – 'Join the Club . . .'

Tesco is a fast-growing UK-based international retailing group, operating almost 2,000 stores in 10 markets (including Eastern Europe and South-East Asia). Its core business is food retailing, of which it holds a 16.7% market share in the UK. With a national turnover of €33.67 billion, Tesco is not only market leader, but also one of the most profitable retailers in its home market. With an international turnover amounting to €41.15 billion, Tesco is ranked seventh among the world's biggest food retailers. According to Tesco's Chairman, Terry Leahy, the company's 'organic growth is stronger than that of any other international retailer'.

The leading British grocer operates four different types of store: hypermarkets (Tesco Extra), supermarkets (Tesco Metro), convenience stores and petrol station stores (Tesco Express). The food retailer also operates a successful on-line shop (Tesco.com), which was introduced in 1996 on a small-scale basis, and slowly expanded to cover almost the entire UK by

2000. Tesco's virtual store managed to achieve its breakeven point in 2001, making a profit of €17.74 million in 2002. Expansion of the on-line business to other countries (including the US through a joint venture with Safeway) is on its way.

Tesco ClubCard

With the mission 'to create value for its customers, to earn their lifetime loyalty' (see Case Table 13.1), Tesco launched its ClubCard in February 1995. The innovative magnetic-strip card allowed customers to collect points and save money. For every pound spent, they would receive one point, worth one penny. Rapidly, around 14 million customers signed up to the programme and Tesco overtook J. Sainsbury's as the UK's leading grocery retailer.

However, Tesco's loyalty programme turned out to be much more than a mere points reward scheme. Indeed, Tesco's ClubCard has caused a considerable stir in the marketing world. Tesco recognised that the most valuable asset provided by the card is consumer insight. In an interview for the *McKinsey Quarterly*, David Reid, Tesco's Deputy Chairman, acknowledges the strategic importance of the loyalty cards, stating that without them 'it would be like flying blind'.

Indeed, the cards collect all sorts of information on Tesco's customers, from shopping frequency to shopper basket contents. This valuable information sheds more light on its shoppers' driving forces which permits Tesco to develop more appropriate strategies to meet the needs of individual customer groups. For instance, this caused Tesco to adapt the product ranges stocked in different stores to the particular types of customers patronising them. Sophisticated insight, gained from analysing ClubCard data also allows Tesco to target specific awards more accurately. Thus, Tesco can direct high-rate saving schemes at families, discounts on holidays at elderly people and free 'Me Time' pampering sessions at women. Such a targeted

approach saves the company over £300 million a year. Direct marketers have always known that good targeting is the key to efficiency and effectiveness.

Tesco's *ClubCard Magazine*

Tesco introduced its *ClubCard Magazine* with the following aims:

- To create a fun, information-packed magazine that communicates core Tesco brand values and services;
- To engender lasting brand loyalty and contribute significantly to customer awareness of new areas;
- To increase take-up of other Tesco ventures, especially non-food.

At Forward Publishing, they realised very quickly that you can't talk to someone in their twenties in the same way that you would to a person in their sixties. A single magazine just wouldn't do. And what better way to make use of the vast amount of customer information that Tesco has accumulated than to craft perfectly targeted magazines for people at different life stages?

From the ClubCard data, five life stages could be identified and different copies of the *ClubCard Magazine* were developed for each of them. In the magazine the latest products, ranges and services are introduced and practical features, hints and tips are offered – all adapted to the target audience. The *ClubCard Magazines* are mailed in spring, summer and autumn to the 7.5 million customers who earn over 250 ClubCard points on their purchases over a 12-week period. Every Christmas a newsstand size bumper issue is distributed to stores. Soon Tesco's *ClubCard Magazine* reached the highest circulation of any magazine in Europe. Incredibly, the circulation is 95% higher than the highest-selling women's newsstand titles.

The magazines also offer great targeted advertising opportunities to a wide supplier base. Brand-tracking after each mailing provides a clear picture of sales growth. Receiving increasing advertising support as a result of their success, the targeted *ClubCard Magazines* proved to be an important communication tool for Tesco.

Taking it one step further with Tesco Lifestyles

The marketing services consultancy agency 'Dunnhumby', which handled the initial trial, launch and continuing development of Tesco's loyalty programme, introduced 'Tesco Lifestyles' in 2001, a major new lifestyle customer segmentation based on the extensive ClubCard data. Shopper basket

Case Table 13.1 Tesco vision and values

Vision	To create value for customers to earn their lifetime loyalty
Values	No one tries harder for customers Treat people how we like to be treated
Brand promise	Every little bit helps

Source: Tesco Annual Report, 2002.

analysis and lifestyle information (e.g. family orienta-tion, calorie consciousness, environmental concern, etc.) allowed them to give Tesco's ClubCard holders a Lifestyle code, enabling highly detailed targeting of quarterly ClubCard statement mailings. This way, key customer groups, such as the 50,000 vegetarians shopping at Tesco, could be targeted even more effectively and given special attention. Not only life 'stage' but also life 'style'-based magazines were developed (such as *Tesco Recipe Magazine* and *Tesco Vegetarian Magazine*) – see Case Figure 13.1 and Case Tables 13.2 and 13.3.

The data-mining skills of marketing consultancy agency 'Dunnhumby' were valued so highly at Tesco that it decided to acquire a majority shareholding in the company in 2001. From that moment on, Tesco could start sharing consumer profiles from its ClubCard database with its suppliers. The success of Tesco ClubCard had awakened interest in direct marketing among fast-moving consumer goods manufacturers, who could also use this valuable information to profile the buyers of their product categories. This would also allow more accurate targeting of their offers and promotions. These pro-motions could be targeted via Tesco-owned media channels, such as the quarterly statement mailings or

mailing campaigns to selected 'clubs' within ClubCard (such as wine lovers, pregnant women, mothers with newborns or toddlers, etc.). According to a state-ment provided by 'Dunnhumby' (November, 2002), the latest ClubCard quarterly statements now con-tain more than four million coupon variations and produce a sales uplift in the region of £30 million.

Case Table 13.2 Tesco lifestyle segmentation

Upmarket (24%)	Customers who are very health-oriented in terms of food, and real gourmets, enjoying finer foods.
Mid-market (54%)	Mainly families, contemporary mainstream or with kids, and time-conscious people that lead a busy lifestyle and therefore need quick and easy food. These customers are slightly traditional and health-oriented.
Less affluent (23%)	Price-sensitive customers, slightly traditional. They look for value and buy working-class brands.

Source: Tesco/Dunnhumby

Case Figure 13.1 Tesco's lifestyle-based customer segmentation

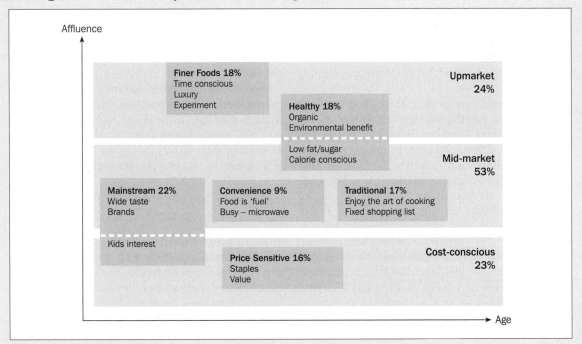

Source: Tesco/Dunnhumby.

Case Table 13.3 Tesco lifestyle segmentation – lifestyle groups

Price Sensitive (16%)	This group are the most likely to buy 'value' lines either due to necessity or because they provide good value for money and are the least affluent. They purchase a narrow range of products which tend to be processed and canned rather than fresh.
Mainstream (22%)	This segment represents the middle ground in terms of grocery shopping and is more likely to contain families with children at home. They have a trust for brands despite not being particularly affluent, which may be partly driven by pester power and, as such, tend not to be adventurous.
Traditional (17%)	This segment contains customers with a traditional outlook, who are predominantly older, however their affluence levels have some variation. They prefer traditional meals based around meat and vegetables and enjoy cooking and baking.
Convenience (9%)	These customers like convenience in food preparation and for them the microwave is an important feature in the kitchen. They tend not to be adventurous; however, there are differences in household composition and affluence reflected in the variety of food they consume. They can be families with older children who buy convenience in order to cater for different meals being consumed at different times or younger adults for whom cooking is a chore.
Healthy (18%)	This group is driven by different elements of health and dieting but with varying points of focus. There are traditional attitudes to healthy living which include plenty of roughage, households who buy diet foods or customers driven by organic foods.
Finer Foods (18%)	This segment is the most affluent and upmarket but displays different levels of adventurousness and has different requirements in terms of convenience. Some of these customers are fairly traditional, high spenders whilst others enjoy cooking but don't always have the time.

Source: Tesco/Dunnhumby.

It also claims that sales effectiveness of new stores has been increased by 50% since 'Tesco Lifestyles' was introduced because of the ability to optimise the product range to better match potential shoppers' lifestyles and because of better customer targeting of marketing activity.

Nestlé Purina, one of the UK's biggest pet food manufacturers, was the first to take this opportunity to join forces with Tesco and in April 2003 launched a co-branded direct marketing campaign aimed at building customer loyalty, both to the Felix cat food range and to the Tesco supermarket chain. The mailing, targeted at thousands of consumers profiled from Tesco's ClubCard data, was sent in a Tesco-branded envelope and included a booklet entitled 'Keeping your cat purrfect . . . with a helping hand from Tesco and Felix', offering tips on keeping cats healthy and comfortable. The direct marketing campaign also featured a series of discounts on Felix-branded products as well as promotional material on Tesco Personal Finance pet insurance products and Purina PetCare services.

Customised communications: Coupons@Till
Another innovative media channel introduced by Tesco in 2002 is the till receipts delivered to customers at the cash register. Through 'Coupons@Till' shoppers can receive customised coupons printed on their till receipt. These highly personal coupons are based on the customers' actual purchase history as recorded through the ClubCard scheme. Although this system may help reduce mailing costs, according to *Precision Marketing* (May 2002) its biggest benefit is that it will enable Tesco to provide even more targeted offers.

Building relationships at store level
As 30% of a retailer's customers appear to be responsible for 75% of its sales (*Financial Times*, 9 November 1996), it may be worthwhile for store managers to communicate with their highest-spending customers in a more personal way. The information provided by ClubCard data at store level could be used to identify these large spenders. Tesco encourages, for example, parents-to-be to sign up to its Baby Club at a point in time when they are likely to increase their

spending in this area considerably. In an attempt to build a profitable long-term relationship with this group, Tesco provides them with a targeted magazine and special customised offers. At the individual store level, this relationship can be even further developed as it pays to market to this valuable group on a more individual basis (e.g. by sending birthday cards, organising special events, etc.). Based on store-level ClubCard information, store managers can also personally telephone defecting or dissatisfied customers.

Facing the loyalty wars . . .

According to Tim Mason, Marketing Director of Tesco Stores, one of the greatest management insights derived from the ClubCard data is the 'Fallacy of Averages' as a basis for understanding customers and marketing to them. As a result of its ClubCard programme, the Tesco supermarket chain has managed to be at the forefront of customer knowledge for several years now and it has been using this information very successfully. Therefore Tesco has been elected as the company which makes the best and most innovative use of direct marketing techniques in a Top Client Companies survey conducted by *Precision Marketing*, the UK's weekly business magazine devoted to targeted, accountable and responsive marketing

(*Precision Marketing*, June 2003). However, as the other supermarket chains follow Tesco's successful example and adopt their own customer cards and loyalty programmes, the company will be faced with a new challenge: to stay ahead in the loyalty wars . . .

Questions

1 What are Tesco's objectives with its ClubCard?

2 How does Tesco differentiate between its customers? (Consider the ClubCard magazines, the quarterly ClubCard statements, Coupons@Till, etc.)

3 Evaluate the information stored in the ClubCard database. What different types of data are kept? In what way is Tesco able to use its ClubCard database, considering the five stages in database marketing development?

4 How does Tesco's ClubCard data enhance Tesco's efficiency and effectiveness in communicating with its customers?

5 What methods are available to measure the effectiveness of the Nestlé Purina and Tesco co-branded direct marketing campaign?

6 Do you think Tesco's customer card is a good means for creating loyalty?

7 What is the challenge Tesco is currently facing and what can it do to stay ahead?

Case prepared by Malaika Brengman, Free University of Brussels. *Based on:* Cuthbertson, R. (2003), 'Every Little Helps: Interview with Crawford Davidson, Director of ClubCard at Tesco, UK', *European Retail Digest*, (March), 37, 26; Child, P. (2002), 'Taking Tesco Global', *McKinsey Quarterly*, 3, 2002, http://www.mckinseyquarterly.com/article_page.asp?ar=1221&L2=21; Dunnhumby, (2002), 'Tesco ClubCard Case Study', November; Kleinman, M. (2001), 'Tesco to Offer Profiles of ClubCard Customers', *Marketing*, 2 August 2002; Knox, S. (2002), 'Building Customer Relations in the Value Chain', Cranfield University School of Management; http://www.marketing.unsw.edu.au/PDFFiles/Simon_Knox_presentation.pdf; 'Tesco Plays its ClubCard Right', *Marketing Week*, 3 November 1995; 'The Loyalty Wars', *Brand Strategy*, 24 December 2002; 'Tesco ClubCard Shake-up to Pave Way for Mail Cutbacks', *Precision Marketing*, 3 May 2002; Mauri, C. (2001), 'Card Loyalty. A New Emerging Issue in Grocery Retailing', Working Paper n° 42, Bocconi University School of Management, http://www.sdabocconi.it/dr/file/wp42.pdf; Peck, H. (2002), 'Tesco ClubCard Forever?', Cranfield School of Management, August; M+M Eurodata; LZ NET; M+M Planet Retail; Forward Publishing website; documents provided by Nigel Lawrence (Dunnhumby).

References

1 Bell, F. and Francis, N. (1995), 'Consumer Direct Mail – Just How Effective Is It?', *Seminar on Advertising, Sponsorship and Promotions: Understanding and Measuring the Effectiveness of Commercial Communication.* Madrid: ESOMAR publications.

2 Hoekstra, J.C. (2002), *Direct Marketing: Van Respons tot Relatie (Direct Marketing: From Response to Relationship).* Groningen: Wolters-Noordhoff.

3 Hughes, A.M. (1995), *Second Generation Strategies and Techniques for Tapping the Power of your Customer Database.* Berkshire: McGraw-Hill Trade.

4 Kobs, J. (2001), *Profitable Direct Marketing. A Strategic Guide to Starting, Improving and Expanding any Direct Marketing Operation.* Chicago: McGraw-Hill/Contemporary Books.

5 Federation of European Direct Marketing, (2002), *Survey on Direct and Interactive Marketing Activities in Europe.* www.fedma.org.

6 Tapp, A. (2001), 'The Strategic Value of Direct Marketing: What Are We Good At? Part 1', *Journal of Database Marketing*, 9(1), 9–15.

7 Shannon, R. (2002), 'Grasping the Direct Marketing Advantage', *Journal of Financial Services Marketing*, 7(1), 75–9.

8 Goldberg, B.A. and Emerick, T. (1999), *Business-to-Business Direct Marketing.* Direct Marketing Publishers.

9 www.esprix.nl

10 Baldinger, A.L. and Rubinson, J. (1996), 'Brand Loyalty: The Link Between Attitude and Behavior', *Journal of Advertising Research*, 36(6).

11 Reicheld, F.F. (2001), *The Loyalty Effect: The Hidden Force Behind Growth, Profits and Lasting Value*. Boston: Harvard Business School Press.

12 Tapp, A. (2001), 'The Strategic Value of Direct Marketing: What Are We Good At? Part 1', *Journal of Database Marketing*, 9(1), 9–15.

13 Reinartz, W. and Kumar, V. (2002), 'The Mismanagement of Customer Loyalty', *Harvard Business Review*, (July), 86–94.

14 Federation of European Direct Marketing, *Best of Europe Cases 2000/2001*.

15 Bird, D. (2000), *Common Sense Direct Marketing*. London: Kogan Page.

16 Vergult, C., De Wulf, K. and Van Vooren, E. (1997), *DRTV, Technische Kenmerken en Beleving. Op Zoek naar Succesfactoren (DRTV, Technical Characteristics and Responses. In Search of Success Factors)*. Research report, Direct Marketing Research Centre, Ghent: Vlerick Leuven Gent Management School.

17 Federation of European Direct Marketing, *Best of Europe Cases 2000/2001*.

18 Verhoef, P., Hoekstra, J. and Aalst, M. (2000), 'The Effectiveness of Direct Response Radio Commercials. Results of a Field Experiment in the Netherlands', *European Journal of Marketing*, 34(1/2), 143–55.

19 De Rijcke, J. (2000), *Handboek Marketing*. Garant: Leuven, Apeldoorn.

20 Federation of European Direct Marketing, (2002), *Survey on Direct and Interactive Marketing Activities in Europe*. www.fedma.org.

21 Morris-Lee, J. (2002), 'Custom Communication: Does it Pay?', *Journal of Database Marketing*, 133–38.

22 www.esprix.nl

23 Bell, F. and Francis, N. (1995), 'Consumer Direct Mail – Just How Effective Is It?', *Seminar on Advertising, Sponsorship and Promotions: Understanding and Measuring the Effectiveness of Commercial Communication*. Madrid: ESOMAR publications.

24 Croft, M. (1994), 'Food for Thought', *Precision Marketing*, 5 December, 14–15.

25 Liederman, R. (1990), *The Telephone Book. How to Find, Get, Keep and Develop Customers*. London: McGraw-Hill.

26 Federation of European Direct Marketing, (2002), *Survey on Direct and Interactive Marketing Activities in Europe*. www.fedma.org.

27 Walrave, M. (1995), *Telemarketing: Storing op de Lijn? (Telemarketing: Badly Connected?)*. Leuven/Amersfoort: Acco.

28 Van Vooren, E. (1994), *Direct Marketing Actieboek: Bondige Tips voor Business-to-Business Marketers (Direct Marketing Action Book: Shorthand Tips for Business-to-Business Marketers)*, Zellik: Roularta Books.

29 Tapp, A. (2001), *Principles of Direct and Database Marketing*. London: Financial Times Prentice Hall.

30 Tapp, A. (2001), *Principles of Direct and Database Marketing*. London: Financial Times Prentice Hall.

31 Katzenstein, H. and Sachs, W.S. (1992), *Direct Marketing*. New York: Macmillan.

32 Federation of European Direct Marketing, *Best of Direct Marketing 2000/2001*.

33 Peppers, D. and Rogers, M. (1996), *The One-to-One Future: Building Relationships One Customer at a Time*. London: Piatkus Books.

34 Bügel, M.S. (1997), 'Van Direct Mail naar Event-Driven Marketing' ('From Direct Mail to Event-Driven Marketing'), *Tijdschrift voor Strategische Bedrijfscommunicatie*, 3(2), 98–106.

35 Hughes, A. (2000), *Strategic Database Marketing: The Masterplan for Starting and Managing a Profitable Customer-based Marketing Program*. Hightstown: McGraw-Hill.

36 Peppers, D. and Rogers, M. (1996), *The One-to-One Future: Building Relationships One Customer at a Time*. London: Piatkus Books.

37 Phelps, J., Nowak, G. and Ferrell, E. (2000), 'Privacy Concerns and Consumer Willingness to Provide Personal Information', *Journal of Public Policy & Marketing*, 19(1), 27–41; Milne, G. and Rohm, A. (2000), 'Consumer Privacy and Name Removal across Direct Marketing Channels: Exploring Opt-in and Opt-out Alternatives', *Journal of Public Policy & Marketing*, 19(2), 238–49.

38 De Wulf, K. (1998), 'Relationship Marketing', in Van Looy, B., Van Dierdonck, R. and Gemmel, P. (1998), *Services Management: An Integrated Approach*. London: Financial Times Pitman Publishing.

39 Bunk, R. (1992), 'Fluktuation Minimieren. Was Kunden Bindet' ('Minimise Fluctuations. It Keeps Customers Loyal'), *Absatzwirtschaft*, 4, 36–47.

40 Riechheld, F.F. and Sasser, W.E. (1990), 'Zero Defections: Quality Comes to Services', *Harvard Business Review*, (September/October), 105–11.

41 Christopher, M., Payne, A. and Ballantine, D. (1994), *Relationship Marketing: Bringing Quality, Customer Service and Marketing Together*. Oxford: Butterworth-Heinemann.

42 Reichheld, F.F. (2001), *The Loyalty Effect. The Hidden Force Behind Growth, Profits and Lasting Value*. Boston: Harvard Business School Press.

43 Curry, A. and Curry, J. (2000), *The Customer Marketing Method. How to Implement and Profit From Customer Relationship Management*. Riverside, NJ: Simon & Schuster Inc.

44 Jenkinson, A. (1995), *Valuing Your Customers: From Quality Information to Quality Relationships Through Database Marketing*. London: McGraw-Hill.

45 O'Brien, L. and Jones, C. (1995), 'Do Rewards Really Create Loyalty?', *Harvard Business Review*, 73(3), 75–82.

46 David Sheppard Association, (1999), *The New Direct Marketing. How to Implement a Profit-Driven Database Marketing Strategy*. Berkshire: McGraw-Hill Education.

Chapter 14

Point-of-purchase communications

Chapter outline

```
        ┌─────────────────────────────────┐
        │  Objectives and tools of point-of- │
        │  purchase communications           │
        └─────────────────────────────────┘

        ┌─────────────────────────────────┐
        │  Effectiveness of point-of-purchase │
        │  communications                    │
        └─────────────────────────────────┘

┌──────────┐ ┌──────────────┐ ┌──────────────┐ ┌──────────────┐ ┌───────────┐
│  Store   │ │  Store       │ │  Product     │ │  Store       │ │ Packaging │
│  image   │ │  organisation│ │  presentation│ │  atmosphere  │ │           │
└──────────┘ └──────────────┘ └──────────────┘ └──────────────┘ └───────────┘
```

Chapter objectives

This chapter will help you to:

- Understand why point-of-purchase communications are important
- Learn about the tools and objectives of point-of-purchase communications
- Learn how effective the various tools of point-of-purchase communications can be
- Get an overview of different aspects of point-of-purchase communications, such as store image, store organisation, product presentation, store atmospherics and packaging

Introduction

Point-of-purchase (POP) communications are a very powerful tool as they reach consumers at the point when they are making the decision which product or brand to buy. As indicated in Chapter 5, purchase intentions often do not result in an actual purchase because of situational factors such as out-of-stocks, competitive brands that are on promotion and attention-grabbing displays. Besides altering purchase intentions, the store environment also significantly influences consumer behaviour in the sense that about one-third of unplanned purchases can be attributed to the fact that the point-of-sales environment makes consumers recognise new needs while they are shopping.[1] Indeed, many consumers seem to make choices at the point of purchase and do not know in advance what brand they are going to buy. Furthermore, consumers spent more and more time on the road and out-of-home, which makes it harder for traditional media to reach them.[2] No wonder that point-of-purchase communications are receiving more and more attention.[3] Mexico witnessed a steady growth in POP spendings of 12% to 15% for a couple of years resulting in a total spending of more than $160 million. Brazil's POP spendings saw a 100% growth annually for 10 years until the 2001 crises came around. Also in the US, POP spendings have been increasing for years, except immediately after the disaster of 11 September 2001, spendings declined by 11% to $15.5 billionwith. German POP spendings in 2000 were estimated at €1.5 billion with growth figures forecasted for the years to come. A similar trend can be expected for the rest of Europe. Reebok learnt the advantage of POP a couple of years ago. In 1996 the company reduced its advertising budget in favour of a better retail presence to fight its competitor, Nike, more effectively. Reebok's total advertising and marketing budget was increased by $74 million, of which $30 million was destined for the Atlanta Olympic Games and the remainder ($44 million) to improve in-store and retail communications.[4]

According to marketers, retailers have also become more favourable and flexible towards this type of communication.[5] Point-of-purchase communications are most effective when they form part of an integrated communications plan, which means that, for instance, they reflect what consumers have seen on TV or billboard ads, and correspond with PR efforts or sponsorships.[6] Indeed, it has been shown that, for instance, when advertising and POP communications are combined, as compared to using advertising only, sales increase by more than 100%.[7] Also the combination of POP and a price cut appears to have enormous advantages over and above the use of POP or price cuts only.[8]

After having discussed why point-of-purchase communications are important, the objectives and tools will be highlighted, and attention will be devoted to the effectiveness of point-of-purchase communications tools. Finally, other aspects of point-of-purchase communications such as store image, store atmospherics, store organisation, product presentation and packaging will be discussed.

The importance of point-of-purchase communications

The Point-of-Purchase Advertising Institute (POPAI) conducted a consumer buying habits study in several European countries.[9] To this end, the POPAI institute used entry–exit interviews, meaning that the consumers were interviewed twice, once before entering the store (to measure the planned budget and the planned purchases), and again after leaving the store (to measure the budget spent, the actual purchases and the perception of POP material).

Purchases can be classified into four categories. In the case of specifically planned purchases the consumer has bought the specific product and brand she intended to buy before entering the store. Generally planned purchases assume that the purchase of the product, but not a specific brand, was planned before entering the store. Substitute product or brand purchases occur when the consumer intended to buy a specific product or brand, but actually purchased another product or brand. Unplanned purchases are defined as the purchases that the consumer did not plan in advance. In Europe an average of 67.2% of brand purchase decisions are made in the store, which is comparable to the in-store decision rate of 72% for American consumers (Figure 14.1 and Table 14.1).[10] The number of in-store decisions are highest for younger and higher-income consumers, larger households and consumers accompanied by children.

Figure 14.1 In-store decision rates

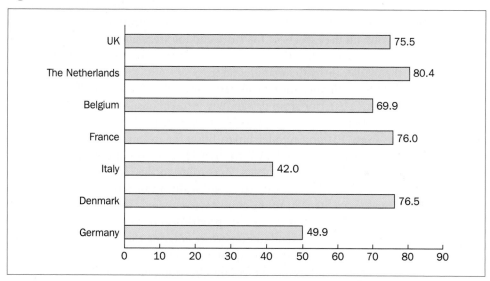

Source: POPAI Europe (1998), *The POPAI Europe Consumer Buying Habits Study*. Co-ordination by Retail Marketing In-store Services Limited, Watford, Herts: POPAI Europe. Reproduced with permission of POPAI Europe.

Table 14.1 Purchase classification

	UK	France	Italy	The Netherlands	Denmark	Belgium
Specifically planned	24.5%	24.0%	58.0%	20%	23.5%	31%
Generally planned	8.0%	12.0%	19.0%	24%	16.0%	9%
Substitute product or brand	3.7%	6.0%	6.0%	4%	7.7%	4%
Unplanned	63.8%	58.0%	17.0%	52%	52.8%	56%

Source: POPAI Europe (1998), *The POPAI Europe Consumer Buying Habits Study*. Co-ordination by Retail Marketing In-store Services Limited, Watford, Herts: POPAI Europe. Reproduced with permission of POPAI Europe.

The numbers of unplanned purchases should not be exaggerated. All the purchases that one really needs, but did not think of in advance, are also considered as 'unplanned'. For example, some consumers do not write a shopping list in advance, but walk down all the aisles to spot what they need. Furthermore, large differences can be observed between different countries.

Objectives and tools of point-of-purchase communications

Point-of-purchase or POP advertising, also called in-store, point-of-sales or POS advertising, can be defined as any promotional material placed at the point of purchase, such as interior displays, printed material at shop counters or window displays. (See Plate 22)[11] However, it also includes in-store broadcasts, video screen demonstrations, shopping-trolley advertising, shelf talkers, coupon dispensers, wastepaper baskets and interactive kiosks (devices by means of which the consumer can interactively retrieve information about the shop and the products in the shop). POP communications are not only concerned with POP advertising. The store image, store design, the scent and the music in the store, the way the products are placed on the shelves and the packaging of the products form an integral part of POP communications. In short, POP communications involve all the aspects of the store and the store environment that can signal something to customers about the quality, price or product assortment, whether it is initiated by the retailer or by the manufacturer.

POP communications can serve several objectives or functions (Figure 14.2). An attractive exterior store design may attract consumer's attention and may differentiate the store from its competitors, so increasing the likelihood that the consumer will enter the store. Fashion retailer Hugo Boss, for example, installed a 106-inch screen in its Regent Street store in the UK to show Hugo Boss's latest collections as well as fragments of sponsored sporting events. According to the retail manager the screen can be seen from the other side of the street and really attracts people to the shop because it brings a sense of excitement to the store environment.[12] In supermarkets eye-catching displays may attract attention to specific products and may induce the consumers to buy a product they did not intend to buy before entering the store. Effective POP material should remind consumers of ongoing or previous advertising, PR, sales promotion or other campaigns, reinforcing the communications message. Because of the high amount of advertising clutter today, consumers have difficulty remembering the different messages

Figure 14.2 Point-of-purchase communications objectives

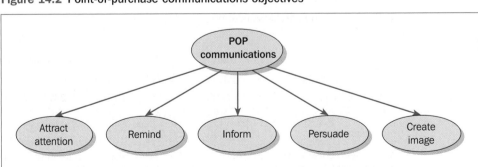

and often confuse brands. POP material is a good tool to aid consumers in this. Apple, for example, used pictures of Gandhi, Amelia Earhart, Jim Henson and Einstein on branded banners to help brand their new vendor shops in compUSA locations (shop in the shop system). These celebrities perfectly illustrate Apple's unique selling proposition and remind people of the baseline used in all advertising, 'think differently'.[13]

Besides reminding, POP material can also inform consumers. Detailed information on a VCR or a computer can be shown on large displays, the store's design may signal the intended target groups, or an interactive display may help consumers decide on what kind of wine is best served with certain meals. Procter & Gamble, for example, used an interactive kiosk called the Oil of Ulay/Tesco Consultant to launch its Oil of Ulay Colour Collection range. By means of touch screen technology consumers are asked to enter details on eye, hair, skin colour and skin type. The Oil of Ulay/Tesco Consultant then suggests products from its Ulay range, such as lipsticks, foundation, eye shadow and mascara. According to P&G, Oil of Ulay Colour Collection reached market leadership in the UK cosmetics market within a month.[14]

Design Wizard Does it All

The British DIY chain Do it All installed in several of its stores the Design Wizard, a custom-build computerised in-store design system. The customer can make a selection from 12 room settings (kitchen, bedroom, etc.), 428 different wallpapers, 311 borders, 36 paints and several carpets. In total 18.5 million different combinations are possible. By simply clicking on their choices, the Design Wizard shows a photo-realistic image of what the room would look like. Furthermore, the Design Wizard calculates the amount of wallpaper and paint needed, and tells the consumer immediately how many of the items the store has in stock. Afterwards the system suggests several decorating accessories that can help the consumer in his decorating task. Other Design Wizard POP material such as wobblers, posters, leaflets, floor and hanging signage have been designed in-house to lead the consumer to the decorating department. Do It All invested $100,000 in the project.[15]

Another objective of POP communications is to persuade consumers, to influence their decision-making at the point of sale and to trigger impulse purchases. Finally, POP communications serve to help with building an image, both of the retailer and the products sold.

No hot Nikes at Foot Locker any more

Nike was founded in 1972 and Foot Locker in 1975. Foot Locker started with a new concept: a store devoted to athletic shoes only. This aroused Nike's interest and Nike wanted very badly to get in there. Selling its shoes in an athletic shoe store would rub off on its own image. In the beginning, Foot Locker was hesitant since it did not want to sell 'unbranded footwear' and Nike was still unknown at that time. Over the years the two companies grew together and were able to benefit from each other's strengths. Nike's ad campaigns triggered demand for its shoes and Foot Locker's extensive network of stores made the shoes available everywhere for the consumers. Nike got prominent displays in Foot Locker stores and Foot Locker got Nike's newest models. This allowed Foot Locker to grow five times as fast as its competitors. To drive sales, Foot Locker began to aggressively discount its products over the last few years. Nike, on the

▶

other hand, wanted to preserve its image of cutting-edge fashion king. This led to a dispute between the two companies that began in the beginning of 2002. When Nike posed rigid terms on the selection and price of shoes it would sell to Foot Locker, Foot Locker announced a cut in its Nike order by 15% to 25% in the hope that Nike would reconsider its terms. Nike responded in the opposite way: it slashed its planned shipments to Foot Locker by 40%, withholding its most popular and newest sneakers. Consumers can no longer find Nike's hottest shoes at Foot Locker, shoes that Nike is selling to Foot Locker's competitors now. Moreover, Nike's campaigns are no longer driving consumers to Foot Locker's stores. All this induced a serious drop in sales, a negative impact on its image and an enormous marketing challenge for Foot Locker.[16]

In order to be able to communicate the store, the products and the brands offered effectively, market segmentation and a clear understanding of the characteristics of target groups are essential components of a marketing communications strategy. For example, with fashion clothing the most important attributes seem to be price, quality, product selection and service offered by the personnel.[17] However, different target groups will prefer different levels of these characteristics. Knowing the exact preferences of your target groups is essential to fine-tune the interior and exterior design of the store, the POP material present in the store, the product assortment and the overall image of the store. For example, the fashion retailer catering to wealthy women must design his store in a way that looks exclusive and expensive. On the other hand, if you want to communicate that you have low prices and that consumers can get bargains, it may not be a good strategy to have the products neatly arranged by size or colour. A chaotic mélange and large price displays attracting bargain hunters like a magnet seems to be a better strategy to communicate the bargain possibilities.[18]

House of Fraser turns into House of Segments

The objective of the House of Fraser was to become the best upper-mass-market department store chain in the UK, ranking between Harvey Nichols and Debenhams. The chain wanted to get rid of its problems of former years, among which were low sales densities, and an unclear definition of its customer base. The embodiment of this new approach was a £12 million, 81,000 sq. ft outlet in Nottingham, opened in October 1997. House of Fraser and the design company Kinnersley Kent Design worked together to identify the target customer groups. The main target group remained the quality classic market consisting of people who like details and wear brands like Jaegar. But the strategy also sought to target fashion lovers, smart careerists, label lovers and smart dressers. For each segment, profiles were drawn, including the first and second choice brands. Smart careerists, for example, are more likely to purchase Planet or Mondi, while fashion lovers are expected to be in favour of DKNY, Oasis or French Connection. The design company tried to reflect the personality of each consumer segment in the physical environment. To this end, large boards were made picturing the images of the targeted segment, as well as colour pallets, and materials (limestone, maple, glass, etc.) that would reflect the segment's personality. Those boards were used to ensure consistency and to give concession operators (such as Tommy Hilfiger, Bobbi Brown, CK, Versace, etc.) an idea of the offering. Translating this into the global store environment, while retaining the House of Fraser identity, was done by blurring the edges of the different departments especially designed for the targeted segments. Instead of circulating through the racks, consumers have to follow walkways and can have a glance at what the department has to offer through display units containing cut-out circles filled with glass.[19]

The effectiveness of point-of-purchase communications tools

In-store communications have an enormous potential impact on the consumer. Several studies show that displays and shelf talkers are able to trigger purchase responses, sometimes even when the price reduction is negligible.[20] Therefore, POP material is receiving growing interest and is used more and more often. Special product presentations on existing shelves, displays, billboards and pallets are most often used (see Plate 24). According to POPAI, these are also the POP materials that are remembered by most consumers (see Figure 14.3). In another study, about 1,000 US shoppers were asked to indicate the POP elements to which they pay particular attention when grocery shopping and the POP elements that have motivated them in the past to buy a product or brand they had not planned to purchase beforehand.[21] Figure 14.4 summarises the results. According to the consumers, in-store samples seem to be particularly effective. More than two in three respondents claim that these attract attention and have in the past persuaded them to buy the product or brand. Moreover, 68.3% say they try in-store samples almost every time they are available, while 26.3% say they do this occasionally. Of course, trying a sample is not the same as buying a product. Some 13% admit to buying the product or brand almost every time they try a sample, while about 73% claim to buy the tried product occasionally. Besides in-store samples, coupons, on-pack promotions and displays are also deemed very effective. It is interesting to know that according to this study, 50% of the grocery shoppers who use shelf coupon dispensers most frequently use the coupon for brands they have not tried before, while

Figure 14.3 POP awareness in supermarkets

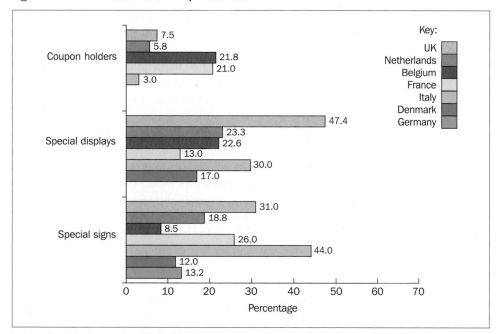

Source: POPAI Europe (1998), *The POPAI Europe Consumer Buying Habits Study*. Co-ordination by Retail Marketing In-store Services Limited, Watford, Herts: POPAI Europe. Reproduced with permission of POPAI Europe.

Figure 14.4 Attention and purchase motivation of different POP elements

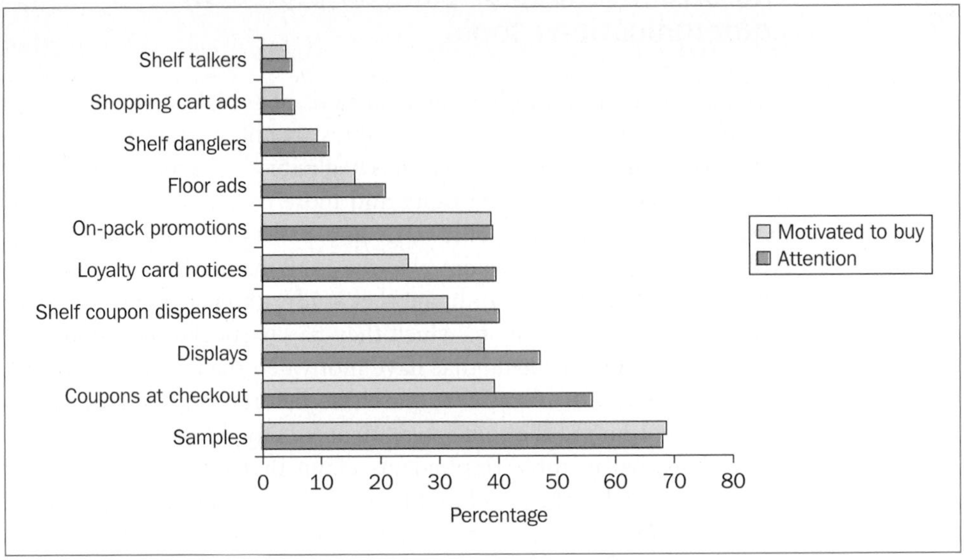

Source: *Grocery Incentive Study 2002* (http://www.pmalink.org/research/CDPgrocery_F.asp). © Copyright 2003 by the Promotion Marketing Associaton, Inc., 257 Park Ave. South, New York, NY 10010. All rights reserved, including the right to disseminate in any format or media. Reproduction or other use of this work in any form is forbidden without written permission of the publisher.

a quarter use the coupon only if it is for the brand they intended to buy.[22] Other studies have also demonstrated the effectiveness of shelf coupon dispensers. It has been found, for example, that consumers tend to respond even more easily to shelf coupons than to price reductions of the same amount.[23] Floor ads or floor graphics and shopping cart ads also appear to work, sometimes even better than assumed by the respondents of the foregoing US study. Nestlé, for example, tested its floor graphics in Germany. To this end, floor graphics were placed in aisles of six test stores and compared to six similar control stores without floor graphics. According to 3M, the developer of Nestlé's floor graphics, sales were 23% higher in the test as compared to the control stores. Furthermore, brand recall of products advertised by means of floor graphics amounted to 47%, as compared to 19% for wall posters and 10% for shelf stickers.[24] Walls promoted its Solero ice cream by means of shopping cart ads in 100 Asda supermarkets. The most memorable image from a recent television ad was used as the basis for the poster. It featured a man with an iceberg capping his head eating a Solero ice cream. The baseline read 'the mind cooler'. One in four trollies were decorated with a poster on the outside, as well as on the inside, so that both the trolley pusher and other shoppers could see the message. The cost of the campaign was estimated at 63 pence per 1,000 exposures. Sales of Solero were monitored in 32 Asda stores, half of which ran the trolley advertising campaign. The results showed a sales increase of over 20% in the test as compared to the control stores.[25]

The spot where POP material is installed also exerts an influence on purchase behaviour. In a US study, in-aisle displays resulted in 58% unplanned purchases, as compared to 61% for displays at the end of aisles and 64% for displays placed at the checkout.[26]

POP material should not only work for the consumer, it should also work for the retailer. Indeed, retailer support is indispensable for a good POP campaign. Therefore it is useful to know which POP elements retailers are in favour of and what they think of current practice. The American POPAI Institute discovered that 70% of retailers prefer POP displays with a mobile element rather than static displays. The reason is that movement is more likely to attract the attention of shoppers. According to retailers, moving displays as compared to no POP support result in a sales increase of 83%. Also interactive kiosks look very promising. However, about 90% of the interactive projects over the last decade failed. More attention should be devoted to setting clear objectives and to developing the appropriate content. The kiosk should be placed in a quiet corner rather than in a crowded, noisy aisle. Moreover, it should be clear to the customer what the kiosk is for, how it can help the customer and how the customer can make use of it.[27]

Retailers recognise the importance of POP communications, but unfortunately they experience many shortcomings in current practice. As the greatest weaknesses they mention that the displays often are inappropriate for the channel of trade, are of the wrong size, are poorly built and are unattractive.[28] Retailers' advice on how to improve POP communications is summarised in Table 14.2.[29] Marketers, on the other hand, have complaints about retailers. The most important ones are summarised in Table 14.3.[30] Clearly, a good relationship and open communication between retailers and manufacturers

Table 14.2 Suggestions to improve POP

1 Strive to be classy and not gaudy.
2 Gather more information from sales staff.
3 Avoid cheap-looking solid white bases.
4 Get your POP designers out into the field more often.
5 Keep in mind that you have to clean around these displays.
6 Use materials that will not look shop-worn after a week.
7 Better seasonal timing of POP.
8 Have a dummy display first to trouble-shoot it for design errors.
9 Produce smaller sizes with an option to utilise multiples (fit together) if the space is available.
10 Discuss the programme with our visual merchandising personnel as well as the product merchants.

Based on: 'P-O-P Times/POP Design Trends Survey 1998', in P-O-P Times, The News Publication of Point-of-Purchase Advertising, Display and Packaging (December 1997), 4. Reproduced with permission of Hoyt Publishing Company.

Table 14.3 Complaints about retailers

1 They are lazy, stupid and don't want to merchandise properly.
2 Every retailer has different rules.
3 Their willingness to accept POP initially is not matched by a willingness to implement it at the store level.
4 They are slow decision-makers – they make unreasonable delivery schedule demands.
5 They will knock out our POP for any vendor with a higher profit margin.
6 You cannot depend on them to place it in the proper location.
7 They are more worried about slotting fees than sales.
8 When only half empty, a display is thrown away.
9 The last one in the door wins the space.
10 No concern for the abuse of displays by competitors.

Based on: 'P-O-P Times/POP Design Trends Survey 1998', in P-O-P Times, The News Publication of Point-of-Purchase Advertising, Display and Packaging (December 1997), 4. Reproduced with permission of Hoyt Publishing Company.

can solve many problems. Manufacturers should not only focus on their own needs and profits but also on those of the retailers. Collaborating with retailers to increase category sales instead of just the manufacturer's own sales, differentiating the POP programme for different stores to give the retailer a unique programme, communicating and working with retailers to find out what works for them and what does not can raise goodwill enormously and lead to real partnership.[31]

Besides the use of specific tools, there are a number of other angles and aspects of POP communications. They are summarised in Figure 14.5, and discussed in the next sections.

Figure 14.5 Other point-of-purchase aspects

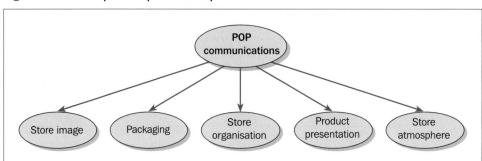

Seducing consumers on the shop floor

Increasingly, consumers decide which product or brand to buy while shopping. Since it is important to communicate with the consumer at the time and the place where they take a purchase decision, in-store communication techniques are increasingly important, and are becoming increasingly sophisticated.

The Cyber Solution laboratory of the Japanese telecom company NTT has developed a system they call 'information rain'. Cameras observe the customers and, based upon the information that is generated in this way (for instance, the amount of time the customer looks at a certain shelf), advertising messages are generated and projected on the body of that customer.

Music is an important in-store marketing tool. According to the Canadian marketing expert Jean-Charles Chebat, the best music is original songs, not 'easy listening' versions of songs. Nor is it a good idea to turn on a radio channel, or to buy a couple of CDs and play the same songs all the time. The latter irritates the staff who, in turn, project their irritation on the customers. The choice of the type of music can be adapted to specific target groups that shop at different times of the day: older consumers shop during the day (play their hits), at noon, mostly hurried and/or stressed people pop in (calm music is called for), after four o'clock teenagers take over (a bit louder and modern), and during weekends it is mostly families who do their shopping. They want to shop efficiently and need fast music to create the illusion of a 'blitz visit'. At the check-out they need slow music to create the perception of shorter queuing times. The customers do not need to know the music. They just need to recognise it, giving them the feeling that the shop atmosphere fits in with their lifestyle. Combining smell and music is even more effective. Fast music calls for citrus odours; slow music connects with lavender. Supermarkets creating the right atmosphere using music and smell have seen their turnover increase by as much as 40%.

▶

The luxury brand Delvaux decided to play more jazz and pop-electro music in its shops, instead of classical music, because they want to attract younger people. The British clothing retailer Donaldson plays sixties hits, because their public mainly consists of baby boomers. The Swiss Chocolate chain Galler discovered the positive impact of the smell of vanilla on its clients, and artificially creates it in all its shops. People with a sweet tooth cannot resist the smell of burned nuts or cacao beans. In shops were Galler operates cacao burners, turnover increased by 20%.

Source: De Morgen, 15 October 2004, 25 July 2005.

Store image

Store image can be defined as 'an individual's cognitions and emotions that are inferred from perceptions or memory inputs that are attached to a particular store and which represent what that store signifies to an individual'. It consists of both affective and cognitive factors.[32] The way the store is organised, the way the personnel dress and behave, the quality of the merchandise, the POP advertisements, the service, the location, price levels and the store's reputation all combine to form the image of the store and its products (see Plate 20).[33] However, the attributes of store image and the importance of specific attributes are industry- and situation-specific. Cleanliness may be an essential aspect of store image for food retailers, while it may be less crucial for fashion shopping. The situation, such as the purpose of a store visit, may also alter the importance of store attributes. Store location may be less of a determining factor in recreational than in urgent shopping trips.[34]

It is important for retailers that their store has the intended positive image in the eyes of their target groups since store image seems to be one of the fundamental determinants of store loyalty.[35] Therefore, the retailer should carefully think over what he wants consumers to see and feel as this is the basis on which they form an image of the store. In general, store image is created by external and internal impressions of the store. External characteristics are very important since they determine the first impression a consumer gets from the store. If this first impression is unfavourable, the consumer may not even enter the store. Therefore, the retailer should pay attention to the store front, the entrance, the placement of signs, the display window, etc. and make them attractive to the target consumers and conform to the store image the retailer wants to convey. Internally, the layout of departments and traffic aisles, the arrangement of displays, the price level, the quality, the depth of the assortment, the service level, the personnel, the store atmospherics, the type of customers, etc. create a store's image.[36]

Related to store image is the concept of store personality. While store image refers to a mental representation of all dimensions that are associated with a store, store personality is limited to dimensions that reflect human traits.[37] As for brand personality, a scale for store personality has also been developed. The scale consists of the following five factors:[38]

1 Enthusiasm (welcoming, enthusiastic, lively, dynamic).

2 Sophistication (chic, high class, elegant, stylish).

3 Unpleasantness (annoying, irritating, loud, superficial).

4 Genuineness (honest, sincere, reliable, true).

5 Solidity (hardy, solid, reputable, thriving).

Different consumer segments will appreciate a different store personality and a different store image. Indeed, a store cannot appeal to, or be an ideal store for, all people. Tailoring a store's characteristics to the psychological and physical needs of a selected target group is the key to making their store impressions and shopping experiences as satisfactory as possible, and in trying to convert casual entrants into loyal customers.[39]

Although store image is indeed very important, research shows that store location is the major determinant of store performance in terms of sales. Increasing the attractiveness of the store by a superior assortment, opening hours, service or more varied offerings (such as a pharmacy, video rental, florists stall, banking services, etc.) cannot make up for a poor location. Given a certain location, store sales can be improved by making the store more attractive. However, increasing attractiveness not only goes hand in hand with increasing sales, but also with a lower sales productivity since these additional offerings are usually quite expensive.[40]

Store organisation

How a store's total space is divided into areas or departments can have an enormous impact on its profitability. First, a retailer should try to maximise the space devoted to selling activities and minimise the non-selling space (customer services, inventory, repair counter, etc.) in order to get a high space productivity. The ratio between selling and non-selling space is usually 4 to 1. Second, the allocation of space determines to a large extent the store atmosphere, which can have an influence on the willingness of consumers to shop in the store. After dividing the total space into selling and non-selling areas, product categories have to be assembled in natural groupings. A logical grouping facilitates the location and comparison of products, making the shopping experience more enjoyable for the consumer. Furthermore, consumers apparently allocate a certain time to shopping. If they find what they need quickly, they appear to spend the rest of the time browsing around which increases the likelihood of additional purchases.[41] Next, a retailer has to decide where to place the different merchandise groupings in the store. Two important criteria for merchandise location are consumer buying behaviour and merchandise compatibility. With regard to the former, low involvement products, for which consumers are not willing to spend time looking, will be placed in high exposure areas, such as major aisles, checkouts, etc. High involvement, or speciality items on the other hand, can be placed in less accessible areas since the consumer is willing to devote more effort to finding them. Furthermore, frequently purchased items can be located in such a way that consumers are led past as many other products as possible.[42] Merchandise compatibility concerns the location of related products in the same area. White wine can be located near the fish department, spaghetti sauces near the pasta, ties near shirts, etc.[43]

Scanning data reveal interesting insights for store organisation

Customer and loyalty cards and scanning applications are gaining ground all over the world. Albert Heijn, a Dutch chain of supermarkets, has launched a customer card that provides personal offers. In the UK, supermarkets experiment with cards that give the customer advantages even outside the store. Delhaize in Belgium is considering publishing a magazine with different offers depending upon customers' family situation. Store cards combined with scanning data are important sources of information. Supermarkets know whether you drink beer or wine, whether or not you use condoms, whether or not you are a vegetarian, whether or not you have pets, whether you buy vegetables or fruit in their store, etc. They even know whether or not you have been shopping elsewhere. If you buy pet food on a regular basis and then do not do so for a few weeks, supermarkets know that you have been buying it elsewhere. Scanning data offers a lot of strategic information on target groups and individual consumers. Besides that, it can also be used for store organisation. The Belgian supermarket GB, for example, has reorganised its home collection department on the basis of scanning data. The data showed that consumers usually buy a bath robe, bath towels and a bath carpet at the same store visit. In order to service the customer better, these products are now arranged in each others' vicinity.[44] Another example can be found in the American night shops. By means of scanning data, it was found that consumers who buy babies' nappies often buy beer at the same time. An explanation for this odd finding was found through a survey. Women often realise in the evening that only one nappy is left for their lovely baby. Fortunately, their husbands are still at work, so they can ask them to stop at the night shop. The fathers make the purchase, but are a bit embarrassed to do so or think they deserve a little treat. Therefore they decide to treat themselves to beer. American night shops have reorganised their shops and have put the beer next to the babies' nappies.[45]

Studies show that particular store layouts are very attractive to consumers. Consumers seem to walk through the store, for example, in a counter-clockwise direction. They try to avoid turns and like to continue to walk in the direction they are going.[46] Furthermore, customers usually look to and buy products situated on their right-hand side. Broad aisles and aisles on the walls are most preferred and, as a consequence, are visited by the majority of the shoppers.[47]

The way a store is organised can have impressive implications for marketers. If consumers fail to locate desired products, this may produce feelings of frustration and anger. This probably induces very low satisfaction levels, and may even lead to a premature interruption of the search process. The shopper may opt for a substitute product and/or for another store in the future, which results in lost revenues.[48]

Product presentation

After store organisation has been taken care of, attention should be devoted to the way products and brands are presented to the consumer and how the shelves are filled (see Plate 21). Shelf management is not easy. The most important aspects that have to be considered are the product assortment, the space allocated to each product and the shelf position. The retail assortment (product lines, brands, styles, services, etc.) has to match consumer needs.

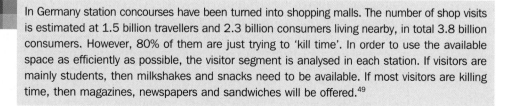

In Germany station concourses have been turned into shopping malls. The number of shop visits is estimated at 1.5 billion travellers and 2.3 billion consumers living nearby, in total 3.8 billion consumers. However, 80% of them are just trying to 'kill time'. In order to use the available space as efficiently as possible, the visitor segment is analysed in each station. If visitors are mainly students, then milkshakes and snacks need to be available. If most visitors are killing time, then magazines, newspapers and sandwiches will be offered.[49]

A common practice in shelf management is that shelf space is allocated according to market share or retail margin. However, space allocation based on market share is an example of circular reasoning, since shelf space depends on market share, which in itself partly depends on shelf space.[50] Indeed, a study compared sales in three situations. The first showed the product in its regular location; the second showed the product in its regular location but with more shelf space; the third condition displayed the product in two locations. Depending on the product, increased shelf space induced a sales increase ranging from 19% to 39%. A second location proves to be even better, leading to between 77% and 243% sales increase.[51] Recent shelf space allocation models also include product profitability for each item, demand interdependencies (a fixed amount of shelf space requires that an increase in the space of item X may raise the sales of X, but the decreased shelf space of item Y may at the same time cause a fall in the sales of Y), inventory levels and product stock-outs.[52] Stock-outs can be a serious problem. A study indicated that about 41% of the consumers confronted with a stock-out purchase a different size of the same brand; one-third bought a competitive brand; 14% went to another store to find the stocked-out brand; 13% delayed the purchase.[53] However, across studies the percentage of consumers visiting another store in case of stock-out ranges from 6% to 83%, partly depending on the product category. Those percentages increase when the item is missing on a second purchase occasion.[54] With promotional advertising, stock-outs of advertised items are a recurrent problem. Such stock-outs may generate negative feelings in the consumer, especially in those people who have made a special trip to the store to buy a bargain.[55]

Concerning shelf position, there seems to be general agreement that products positioned at eye level generate the best results. The second best position is probably immediately to the right of the brand leader or the visually most dominant brand on the shelf. The reason for this is that consumers watch the shelf in the way they read; as a consequence their eye is most likely to move from the most visually dominant brand to the right and downward.[56] Most complete product lines with regard to sizes and colours are usually placed at eye level, while assortments with missing elements appear in lower racks.[57] Another rule is to put high-margin products on the most visible shelves, while cheap products are placed on the floor rack. Other criteria to take into account are the weight of the products (put heavy products on the floor) and the turnover of the products. Products that sell very well need to be frequently replenished. Such products need to be positioned at an easily accessible place.[58]

Store atmospherics

Atmospherics can be defined as the effort to design buying environments to produce specific emotional effects in the buyers that enhance their purchase probability,[59] since atmosphere is apprehended through the senses. The dimensions of store atmosphere are shown in Figure 14.6. Taste is not considered a meaningful dimension of the store atmosphere since one cannot taste an atmosphere. However, in-store 'degustations', a sales promotion instrument, may be regarded as an atmospheric dimension for food retailers.

The atmosphere adds a valuable characteristic to the product and mainly serves three functions.[60] First, the atmosphere can generate attention by using specific colours, music, etc., which make a store stand out. Second, the atmosphere creates a message by

Figure 14.6 Dimensions of store atmosphere

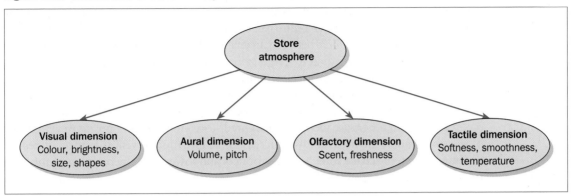

using the atmospheric characteristics in such a way that they express, for example, the intended store audience. Third, the atmosphere creates affect by arousing people, which may tip the scale in favour of buying certain products or brands (Figure 14.7).[61]

Although empirical research in this field has been scarce, the few studies to date seem to support the idea that physical attributes in the store induce emotional states, which in turn affect consumer behaviour.[62] An experiment in a British supermarket revealed the following.[63] Four French and four German wines were put on the super-market's wine shelves. On days that French accordion or Gallic favourites such as the 'Marseillaise' or can-can music was played, Beaujolais and Côtes du Rhône sold extremely well (40 French versus 8 German bottles), while on the days that German, side-splitting Keller music was played, the German wine sales rose (12 French versus 22 German bottles). Interviews revealed that consumers were certain that the kind of music did not influence their purchase. Also in a restaurant setting it has been shown that when visitors' preferred music is playing they stay significantly longer in the restaurant and spend significantly more on both drinks and food.[64] Another study investigated an ambient effect, consisting of specific combinations of music and light-ing, and a social effect consisting of the number and the friendliness of the personnel. Background classical music with soft lighting as compared to foreground top 40 music with bright lighting induced a significantly more pleasurable feeling, except when the less attractive ambient environment was offset by very friendly personnel. Feelings of pleasure and arousal were found to increase the customers' willingness to buy.[65] In a store setting in which the visual dimension or store design factor (colour, layout and displays), the store social factor (number of employees, the outfit of the employees) and the store ambient factor or aural dimension (music) was manipulated, it was found that all three factors had a significant direct impact on store perceptions (such as

Figure 14.7 Relation between store environment and consumer behaviour

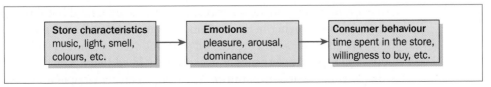

Based on: Mehrabian, A. and Russell, J.A. (1974), *An Approach to Environmental Psychology.* Cambridge, MA: MIT Press.

merchandise quality perceptions, price perceptions, etc.) and an indirect impact on store patronage intentions via the evoked perceptions. The impact of the design factor appeared to be much stronger than that of the social and ambient factors, though.[66] With regard to aroma, the link between aroma advertising and increased sales still has to be proved. However, according to The Aroma Company's Simon Harrop's experience, a pleasant aroma induces a better response than no aroma, or worse, an unpleasant smell.[67] One study[68] showed that products in a scented shop were perceived to be better than identical goods in an unscented shop, while another study found that a scented versus an otherwise identical unscented store induced more positive evaluations of the store and of the merchandise, increased the intention to visit the store, increased the intention to purchase some of the products and lowered the perception of the time that consumers had spent in the store.[69]

The impact of colour on consumers' approach-avoidance behaviour

In a recent experimental study involving almost 800 respondents, the Mehrabian and Russell framework shown in Figure 14.7 was applied to store environmental colour. In total, 32 different colours were tested for a hypothetical design store: eight different hues or pigments (green-yellow, red, blue-green, purple-blue, green, yellow-red, yellow and blue), each in two different brightness levels (a bright and dark version of the colour) and in two different saturation levels (saturated version containing a large proportion of the pigment versus an unsaturated version containing a large proportion of grey). The results revealed that for two of the eight hues a significant difference on evoked feelings could be found. Blue elicited significantly more pleasure and less tension in consumers than green-yellow. Moreover, brighter colours induce significantly more pleasurable feelings and less tension than darker colours, while more saturated coloured stores were judged by the respondents as significantly less tense. These results show that the first part of the model in Figure 14.7 is confirmed: store colour has a significant impact on consumers' feelings. Furthermore, evidence was also found for the second part of the model in Figure 14.7: the pleasure evoked by the store colour was positively related to respondents' approach behaviour towards the store (i.e. willingness to spend time in the store, to spend money in the store, etc.), while colour-evoked tension had a negative impact on approach behaviour. The conclusion of this study seems to be that store keepers had better avoid painting the store walls in green-yellow and rather choose a (bright version of) blue instead. If blue does not fit the rest of the interior, yellow-red or yellow are also good alternatives.[70]

Besides affecting the time that consumers spend in the store or their willingness to buy, high pleasure feelings seem to be related to high customer satisfaction levels.[71] This is important since customer satisfaction seems to be the driving force of customer loyalty.[72] In Table 14.4 two German Ikea stores possessing different characteristics concerning store layout, store atmospherics and product presentation are compared.[73] Consumers' mood improved with shopping in the pleasant store, while it deteriorated in the less pleasant store. Customer satisfaction – influenced both by store environment and mood – was higher in the pleasant as compared to the less pleasant store. Furthermore, the good mood in the pleasant store induced consumers spontaneously to spend more money on articles, simply because they liked them. The drawback of this study is that it is impossible to know which store elements were mainly responsible for the observed effects. Was it the bright colours, the well-structured route or the unexpected presentation of the products? Or was it the combination of these characteristics? Another

Table 14.4 Differences between two Ikea stores

	Store 1: Pleasant store	Store 2: Less pleasant store
Store atmospherics	■ Renovated one year ago ■ Bright colours	■ Many signs of deterioration ■ Dim colours
Store layout	■ Well-structured route with no crossings and possible shortcuts ■ Many striking signs in different colours	■ Many crossings and possible shortcuts ■ Few, not very striking signs, some only handwritten
Product presentation	■ Presentation out of the ordinary, unexpected ■ Integration of furnishings to complete rooms ■ New supplies highlighted	■ Expected, ordinary presentation ■ Functional grouping of furnishings ■ New supplies presented amidst others

Based on: Spies, K., Hesse, F. and Loesch, K. (1997), 'Store Atmosphere, Mood and Purchasing Behavior', *International Journal of Research in Marketing*, 14, 1–6. Reproduced with permission of Elsevier Science BV.

study investigated the effect of several store characteristics on in-store induced emotions and store attitude.[74] Characteristics included product assortment, value, salesperson's service, after-sales service, facilities, location and atmosphere. The conclusion of the study was that characteristics of the store environment have a pronounced influence on consumers' emotions in the shopping environment, which in turn have an influence on how a consumer thinks and feels about the store (store attitude).

In conclusion, the majority of the atmospherics research seems to support the relationship between store atmospherics, emotions and consumer behaviour. Some practitioners even say that 'fifty % of consumers' decisions are made because of the environment they are in'.[75] Therefore, a good understanding of store atmospherics and store dynamics is very important, both for the manufacturer and the retailer.

Packaging

Besides protecting the product and making distribution easier, packaging fulfils several communications functions, such as attracting brand attention, identifying the brand and the product, facilitating brand and product recognition, and informing consumers of price, ingredients and product use.[76]

As for advertising in general, the packaging should try to attract and keep the consumer's attention to be effective. In order to do so, the package should possess an attention-grabbing colour, an unusual size or form, or be novel or complex. Recent multimedia techniques are a useful tool to design and test new packages. However, paying attention to the packaging is one type of consumer response; a positive pack-aging evaluation is another. Research shows that packages that deviate considerably from what is standard for the product category indeed attract a lot of attention, but they also lead to negative package evaluations. Moderate package deviation seems to be the best trade-off in serving the purpose of drawing attention and generating favourable evaluations.[77] It is important to realise that shoppers on average spend only five to seven seconds glancing at a package. Therefore, although some complexity might be favourable to attract attention, the package or label should not be too complex. The point of difference of the brand should be made clear at a glance and should not require shoppers to read the full label or to read the back label. Putting too many messages on the label might increase the likelihood of shoppers missing every benefit statement.[78] Furthermore, although the new multimedia techniques can be very helpful in modernising packaging, marketers should try to avoid the 'seven packaging sins' and pay attention to the following:[79]

- Define the objectives you want to reach with the new packaging: on what criteria should it score more positively than the current packaging?
- Define the priorities for the different characteristics (conspicuousness, recognition, product expectations, etc.) of the package.
- In testing, both the old and the new packaging should be tested to find out which aspects have improved or detoriated.
- In testing, both the own and the competitive packaging should be tested to learn own strengths and weaknesses.
- Test the product concept and brand image in order to discover what the package signals to the consumer.
- Test before the package development has begun.
- Test alternative packages in order not to have to start all over again when the test appears to be negative.

According to one study,[80] brand choice can be predicted from observations of the visual attention to the packages of competing brands. Brands that are fixated longer (meaning that the eyes pause longer on the brand), that receive more intra-brand saccades (meaning quick jumps of the eyes from the brand to another brand) and more inter-brand saccades (meaning quick jumps from one attribute of the brand to another attribute), are more likely to be purchased. This conclusion holds, irrespective of the time pressure or shopping motive of the respondents, although the research also shows that time-pressured shoppers skip more textual but not pictorial information, while this is the other way round for highly motivated shoppers. This study shows that measuring eye movement can be a valuable pre-test method for new packages.

In a study by P.I. Design International, results indicate that children's favourite colours are: purple, red, yellow, blue and green. Children disliked light, dark, smudgy and sophisticated colours. The use of over-large colour blocks was perceived as boring. Using foil and blister packaging seemed to be attractive to kids. The same study advised not breaking through standard flavour colour codes such as pink or red for strawberries, brown for chocolate, etc. It helps children to understand and recognise what they prefer. Multi-packs may also lead to confusion and should be transparent, permitting children to see exactly what is inside. Children like bubble typographs and find straight refined fonts cold and unfriendly. Colourful and exciting funny illustrations are preferred to realistic photographs. Children find the latter typical for adults and, as a result, dull.[81]

An important conclusion from recent research is that packaging can influence consumer behaviour long after the actual purchase has been made. It appears that larger pack sizes encourage greater usage volume per usage occasion, although there is, of course, a limit on how much detergent or pasta a consumer wants to consume at one time.[82] One reason for this greater usage volume seems to be the lower perceived unit cost of larger packages. Another explanation is that, because of the large package, consumers are less worried about running out of the product.[83] Besides an encouragement to use more, larger packs sometimes also induce people to consume the product more frequently, simply because of the presence of the product in the household inventory.[84]

Integrating point-of-purchase communications in IMC

The purpose of many marketing communications efforts is to ultimately generate traffic to the point of sale (POS). Since the store is the place 'where the rubber meets the road', the communication tools at the point of sale should be well integrated into the communication mix and should convince the consumer actually to buy the product that has been promoted through other communication campaigns. If well-integrated with other communication efforts such as advertising, public relations and sponsorship, POS-communication itself can build traffic to the store and to product (categories) in the store. In-store communication can enhance the effectiveness of sales promotions by appealingly promoting the campaign on the shop floor and/or by referring to advertising in which merchandising campaigns or promotions were announced. In a broader perspective, store image, organisation and atmospherics, and product in-store presentation can build and reinforce the image of the company and its brands, as built up in advertising and sponsorship.

Summary

Point-of-purchase communications are a powerful marketing tool, since they reach consumers at the moment when, and the place where, they are taking decisions. Since the vast majority of consumers make buying decisions at the point of purchase, in-store communications are of crucial importance. Point-of-purchase communications have to be particularly well integrated with sales promotions and distribution strategies. The objectives of in-store communications are to attract the consumer's attention, to remind him or her of ongoing or previous advertising, to inform, to persuade and to build an image of the brands on shelves. Several instruments of in-store communications can be used, such as shelf displays, floor graphics, trolley advertising, moving displays and interactive kiosks. Besides these specific communications instruments, store image, store organisation, store atmospherics and product presentation are also important. They all add to the impression a consumer has when making buying decisions in store. Finally, packaging is an important tool of in-store advertising.

Review questions

1 Why are point-of-purchase communications so important, given consumer buying behaviour?

2 What are the tools and objectives of point-of-purchase communications?

3 How effective are the various point-of-purchase tools?

4 How can store image influence sales?

5 What is the importance of store organisation and product presentation?

6 How do store atmospherics help to achieve communications objectives?

7 In what way can packaging influence buying behaviour?

Further reading

International Journal of Retail and Distribution Management

In-Store Marketing

Journal of Retailing

Liljenwall, R. and Maskulka, J. (2002), *Marketing's Powerful Weapon: Point-Of-Purchase Advertising*. Washington, DC: Point-Of-Purchase Advertising International.

P-O-P Times

The Promotion Marketing Association, (http://www.pmalink.org/research/).

Case 14

POP in the c-store – the case of Red Bull

No longer are convenience or c-stores just great pit stops for filling up gas tanks; they have become an easy alternative to grocery stores. A study shows that only 12.4% of customers stop at a c-store because they need gas, while about one in three stop because they are hungry or thirsty. A couple of years ago, the convenience stores redefined themselves by adding several products. Nowadays many c-stores offer quick-serve meals, dry cleaning services, express mail counters, pharmacies and internet access, besides the food, snacks and drinks they used to offer. About 75% of the c-stores have a petrol distributorship, while more than 40% run a branded food service programme. Due to the high number of different items that are for sale, c-stores have become overcrowded with signage and POP-material.

Customer segments

C-stores try to offer convenience by being a little of everything to everybody. They target males and females, teens and grown-ups. This makes in-store marketing a really difficult task. The segments differ, the time of shopping differs (see Case Figure 14.1), but the reason remains the same: convenient shopping. Of all purchases at c-stores 30% are planned and 20% are made on impulse. The key is to have POP material that stimulates the different consumers, while not making the relatively small shops 'overcluttered'.

Different needs

Supermarkets differ substantially from c-stores (Case Table 14.1). Although c-stores have recently grown from an average of 2,400 square feet to an

Case Figure 14.1 When do shopper visit c-stores?

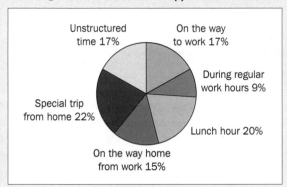

Reproduced with permission of Hoyt Publishing Company.

Case Table 14.1 Most important differences between c-stores and supermarkets

Aspects	Differences
Space	Space is much more crucial for c-stores than for supermarkets
Time	Customers are more in a hurry in c-stores than in supermarkets
Flexibility	Because of the quick replacement and reorganising of POP material in c-stores, they need to be more flexible
Variety	A lot of POP in such a small space in c-stores requires more variety to be noticed
Functionality	C-stores are looking for functional rather than aesthetic POP material

average of 3,800–4,400 square feet, the proportion of square feet to the number of available products (different stock-keeping units, SKUs) is rather small. Therefore, although recently more space has become available for in-store material, most of the manufacturers' POP displays are too big. So, displays that are accepted in grocery stores and supermarkets will not even be considered in c-stores. The reason for this is that the square footage needed for the display can generate far more sales from other products. Furthermore, since c-stores' *raison d'être* (impulse buying), is different from that of supermarkets, c-stores do not need smaller versions of supermarket POPs, but specially designed POP material which they currently often make themselves. Besides space, time is another challenging aspect of c-stores. Visitors do not have the time to browse through the store or interact with displays. This speed flows over to the retailers who change their window signs and internal POP material every week. Therefore, they ask for flexible POP items, as well as a lot of variety which makes it stand out and be noticed by the customers.

Main characteristics that c-store retailers value in POP are convenience and ease of placement. Case Table 14.2, based on *P-O-P Times' Trend Report* (1999) shows c-stores' least and most preferred POP material. POPAI's 2002 study indicates that advertising at the cash register and on the outside window enjoys a particularly high recall.

The Miller Brewing Company is one of the first manufacturers to come up with hundreds of POP items developed especially for c-stores. The items began to appear in c-stores in spring 1999. Items include metal branded pricing signs, curb stickers, metal curb signs, cooler signs, beer bottle cooler door handles and a 'faux display'. The latter is 'a vacuum-formed plastic cube, which, when seen from the road, looks like a mass stacking of 12-packs of Miller cans'. Another way of attracting attention seems to be the use of gas pump talkers, which formed part of a very successful campaign launched by Red Bull.

Red Bull

One of the key market segments that Red Bull targets is motorists, hence c-stores seemed an especially attractive distribution channel for the product. However, at the beginning of 1998 Red Bull was a new and unknown product. Since oil companies are not obliged to stock the product, Red Bull distributor's (Ubevco) first worry was to get Red Bull into the already over-crowded c-store. To this end, it announced a major c-store campaign in the UK in the hope that this might persuade the c-market. The campaign mainly consisted of having covered fuel nozzles, also called sqawkers or gas pump talkers. Pump talkers are attached to gas hoses by means of durable, self-locking hose clamps. In fact, they function as a kind of mini-billboard while customers are filling their car up. The advantage of gas pump talkers is that they have a completely captive audience for the three minutes it takes for the average 25-litre fill. Red bull's gas pump talkers read as follows. 'Tired? Red Bull [a picture of the can] revitalises mind and body. Improves concentration, improves reaction times, improves endurance. Caution: Do not drink when you want to sleep.' The campaign ran in Elf, Total, Q8, Murco, Repsol and Maxol stores. For the first campaign, 182 Fina sites agreed to collect data. Of these 182 sites only three had stocked Red Bull before the one-month campaign started. Compared to the month prior to the campaign, sales jumped enormously (see Case Table 14.3). The 179 other Fina sites did not stock Red Bull prior to the campaign. However, 152 of them put Red Bull on their shelves before the end of the campaign, which increased Ubevco's distribution by 85%.

Red Bull's communications campaign not only consisted of gas pump talkers, but also used sampling,

Case Table 14.2 Most and least preferred POP material

Most preferred POP	Least preferred POP
Translites for menuboards	Coupon dispensers
Case stackers	Electric signage
Shelf organisers	Sidekicks
	Pallet displays

Case Table 14.3 Sales increase in Fina sites that stocked the product before the campaign

Fina convenience stores	Sales increase
Site 1	167%
Site 2	180%
Site 3	530%

Case Table 14.4 Awareness rates of Red Bull for different types of POP techniques

Medium	Awareness rate
Average for other outdoor media	26%
Average for gas pump talkers	80%–90%
Lowest for gas pump talkers	50.8%

sponsoring of the Sauber Petronas Formula One team, and an in-store campaign consisting of a free Formula One poster for every can of Red Bull bought. The whole campaign had a significantly positive impact on awareness (Case Table 14.4), and both distribution and sales. However, Red Bull is most pleased with the gas pump talkers. Compared to the cost of other forms of outdoor media, gas pump talkers are relatively cheap, costing £50 to cover all the fuel hoses on one forecourt during one month. According to the company supplying the gas pump talkers, the talkers are also more effective than other outdoor media tools.

Red Bull is really sold on the medium. It immediately invested in subsequent campaigns in the UK and started planning a huge pan-European programme, starting with a big entry in the German market.

Meanwhile, several manufacturers, such as Nestlé and Dr Pepper, have followed Red Bull. Gas pump talkers are becoming a popular technique worldwide.

Questions

1 Do POP communications serve the same functions in a c-store as in a grocery store or supermarket?

2 Why do you think c-stores change their POP material more frequently than supermarkets?

3 More and more people pay at the pump. What is the major advantage and disadvantage of this trend for c-stores? How does this influence their need for POP material?

4 Would you advise a c-store to use atmospheric elements, or do you think this is less important for c-stores than for supermarkets or other retailers?

5 How could the Red Bull campaign have been made even more effective?

Based on: Cosgrove, J. (2002), 'Convenient POP. POPAI's latest advertising study details what works and what doesn't in convenience stores', *Beverage Industry*, May, 38–40; 'Convenience Store, You've come a long way, baby', 1999. *P-O-P Times, The News Publication of Point-of-Purchase Advertising, Display and Packaging*, 12, 4, 46–55; Special report, 'Ambient Media is Providing Retailers and Suppliers with Yet Another Way of Advertising Their Products Instore and Influencing Consumers' Buying Decisions', 1998. *In-Store-Marketing* (January), 32; 'Marketing at the Gas Pump', 1997, *P-O-P Times. The News Publication of Point-of-Purchase Advertising, Display and Packaging*, 10, 12, 34; Case prepared by Malaika Brengman, Limburgs Universitair Centrum.

References

1 Park, C.W., Iyer, E. and Smith, D.C. (1989), 'The Effects of Situational Factors on In-Store Grocery Shopping Behavior: The Role of Store Environment and Time Available for Shopping', *Journal of Consumer Research*, 15, 422–32.

2 Liljenwall, R. and Maskulka, J. (2002), *Marketing's Powerful Weapon: Point-Of-Purchase Advertising*, Washington, DC: Point-Of-Purchase Advertising International.

3 *PROMO Magazine Annual Report on the Promotion Marketing Industry*, http://www.pmalink.org/annual_studies.asp, (2003); Parmar, A. (2002), 'POP Goes the World', *Marketing News*, 11 November, 13.

4 'Winning The Retail Race' (1997), *In-store Marketing* (April), 22–3.

5 Flack, J.A. (2002), 'Putting Up with POP', *Marketing Week*, 11 April, 33–4; 'Special Report, Food Service POP' (1998), *P-O-P Times, The News Publication of Point-of-Purchase Advertising, Display and Packaging* (April), 32–44.

6 Chadwick, P. (2003), 'POP Dos and Don'ts', *Promotions & Incentives*, April, 45–7.

7 Leeds, D. (1994), 'Accountability is In-Store for Marketeers in '94', *Brandweek* (14 March), 17.

8 Tellis, G.J. (1998), *Advertising and Sales Promotion Strategy*, Reading, Mass.: Addison-Wesley.

9 POPAI Europe (1998), *The POPAI Europe Consumer Buying Habits Study*, Co-ordination by Retail Marketing In-store Services Limited, Watford, Herts: POPAI Europe; POPAI (1995), *Measuring the In-Store Decision Making of Supermarket and Mass Merchandise Store Shoppers*, Englewood Cliffs, NJ; POPAI.

10 POPAI Europe (1998), *The POPAI Europe Consumer Buying Habits Study*, Co-ordination by Retail Marketing In-store Services Limited, Watford, Herts: POPAI Europe; POPAI (1995), *Measuring the In-Store Decision Making of Supermarket and Mass Merchandise Store Shoppers*, Englewood Cliffs, NJ: POPAI.

11 Rosenberg, J.M. (1995), *Dictionary of Retailing and Merchandising*. New York: John Wiley & Sons.

12 'Boss Switches to Interactive CD System' (1998), *In-Store Marketing* (January), 6.

13 '"Think Different" Boutiques Boost Sales' (1998), *Point of Purchase Magazine*, 4(3), 56.

14 'Procter & Gamble Backs Health and Beauty Product Launch with Twin Interactive Kiosk Strategy' (1997), *In-Store Marketing* (October), 7.

15 'Digital DIY' (1998), *In-Store Marketing* (February), 24–5.

16 Tkacik, M. (2003), 'Rubber Match: In a Clash of Sneaker Titans, Nike Gets Leg Up on Foot Locker', *Wall Street Journal*, 13 May.

17 Birtwistle, G., Clarke, I. and Freathy, P. (1998), 'Customer Decision Making in Fashion Retailing: A Segmentation Analysis', *International Journal of Retail & Distribution Management*, 26(4) (http://www.europe.emerald-library.com/brev/08926db1.htm).

18 Kotler, P. (1973), 'Atmospherics as a Marketing Tool', *Journal of Retailing*, 49(4), 48–64.

19 'House of Change' (1997), *In-Store Marketing* (October), 22–3.

20 Inman, J.J. and McAlister, L. (1993), 'A Retailer Promotion Policy Model Considering Promotion Signal Sensitivity', *Marketing Science*, 12, 339–56; Inman, J.J. and Winer, R.S. (1998), *Where the Rubber Meets the Road: A Model of In-Store Consumer Decision Making*, Working Paper, Report no. 98–122, Cambridge, MA: Marketing Science Institute.

21 *Grocery Incentive Study 2002*, The Promotion Marketing Association, (http://www.pmalink.org/research/CDPgrocery_F.asp).

22 *Grocery Incentive Study 2002*, The Promotion Marketing Association, (http://www.pmalink.org/research/CDPgrocery_F.asp).

23 Dhar, S.K. and Hoch, S.J. (1996), 'Price Discrimination Using In-Store Merchandising', *Journal of Marketing*, 60, 17–30.

24 'Building the Nesquik Brand' (1998), *In-Store Marketing* (March), 28.

25 'Special Report: Ambient Media is Providing Retailers and Suppliers with Yet Another Way of Advertising Their Products in Store and Influencing Consumers' Buying Decisions' (1998), *In-Store Marketing* (January), 32–3.

26 Inman, J.J. and Winer, R.S. (1998), *Where the Rubber Meets the Road: A Model of In-store Consumer Decision Making*, Working Paper, Report no. 98–122, Cambridge, MA: Marketing Science Institute.

27 'Special Report: Touchscreen Kiosks, Trolley Displays and Talking Shelves – Interactive Multimedia is Coming to a Shop Near You. But is it Working?' (1997), *In-Store Marketing* (September), 25–31.

28 'Does P-O-P Measure up?' (1997), *P-O-P Times, The News Publication of Point-of-Purchase Advertising, Display and Packaging* (December), 36–52.

29 'Backroom Brawling' (1997), *P-O-P Times, The News Publication of Point-of-Purchase Advertising, Display and Packaging* (December), 4.

30 'Backroom Brawling' (1997), *P-O-P Times, The News Publication of Point-of-Purchase Advertising, Display and Packaging* (December), 4.

31 Botsford, D. (2002), 'Getting the Retail Support You Want', *Brandweek*, 43(22), 19.

32 Brengman, M., Geuens, M. and Faseur, T. (2002), 'Capturing the Image of Second-hand Stores: Investigating the underlying image dimensions', *Asia Pacific Advances in Consumer Research*, 5, 387–93.

33 Zimmer, R. and Golden, L.L. (1988), 'Impressions of Retail Stores: A Content Analysis of Consumer Images', *Journal of Retailing*, 64(3), 265–91.

34 Birtwistle, G., Clarke, I. and Freathy, P. (1999), 'Store Image in the UK Fashion Sector: Consumer versus Retailer Perceptions', *International Review of Retail, Distribution and Consumer Research*, 9(1), 1–16.

35 Osman, M.Z. (1993), 'A Conceptual Model of Retail Image Influences on Loyalty Patronage Behaviour', *International Review of Retail, Distribution and Consumer Research*, 3(2), 133–48.

36 Lewison, D.M. (1997), *Retailing*, sixth edition, Englewood Cliffs, NJ: Prentice Hall; Kunkel, J.H. and Berry, L.L. (1968), 'A Behavioral Conception of Retail Image', *Journal of Marketing*, 32 (October), 21–7.

37 D'Astous, A. and Lévesque, M. (2003), 'A Scale for Measuring Store Personality', *Psychology & Marketing*, 20(5), 455–69.

38 D'Astous, A. and Lévesque, M. (2003), 'A Scale for Measuring Store Personality', *Psychology & Marketing*, 20(5), 455–69.

39 Lewison, D.M. (1997), *Retailing*, sixth edition, Englewood Cliffs, NJ: Prentice Hall.

40 Reinartz, W.J. and Kumar, V. (1999), 'Store-, Market-, and Consumer-Characteristics: The Drivers of Store Performance', *Marketing Letters*, 10(1), 5–22.

41 Miller, R. (2002), 'In-Store Impact on Impulse Shoppers', *Marketing*, November 21, 27–8.

42 Inman, J.J. and Winer, R.S. (1998), *Where the Rubber Meets the Road: A Model of In-Store Consumer Decision Making*, Working Paper, Report no. 98–122, Cambridge, MA: Marketing Science Institute.

43 Lewison, D.M. (1997), *Retailing*, sixth edition, Englewood Cliffs, NJ: Prentice Hall.

44 'De Supermarkt Weet Wanneer Je Vreemd Gaat' (The Supermarket Knows When You Are Doing It Somewhere Else) (1998), *De Morgen*, 14 March, 70.

45 'Het is Bewezen: Wie's Avonds Luiers Koopt, Drinkt Blond Bier' (It Has Been Proven: Persons Who Buy Diapers in the Evening, Drink Blond Beer), (1998), *Intermediair*, 24 (9 June), 19.

46 Spies, K., Hesse, F. and Loesch, K. (1997), 'Store Atmosphere, Mood and Purchasing Behavior', *International Journal of Research in Marketing*, 14(1), 1–17.

47 Van der Ster, W. and van Wissen, P. (1987), *Marketing & Detailhandel*, fourth edition. Groningen: Wolterns-Noordhoff.

48 Titus, P.A. and Everett, P.B. (1996), 'Consumer Way Finding Tasks, Strategies, and Errors: An Exploratory Field Study', *Psychology and Marketing*, 13(3), 265–90.

49 'Stationshoppen' (Shopping in the Station) (1999), *Media Mix Digest*, 34(5), 7.

50 Mulhern, F.J. (1997), 'Retail Marketing: From Distribution to Integration', *International Journal of Research in Marketing*, 14(2), 103–24.

51 Wilkinson, J.B., Mason, J.B. and Paksoy, C.H. (1982), 'Assessing the Impact of Short-Term Supermarket Strategy Variables', *Journal of Marketing Research*, 19 (February), 72–86.

52 Mulhern, F.J. (1997), 'Retail Marketing: From Distribution to Integration', *International Journal of Research in Marketing*, 14(2), 103–24; Urban, T.L. (1998), 'An Inventory-Theoretic Approach to Product Assortment and Shelf-Space Allocation', *Journal of Retailing*, 74(1), 15–35.

53 Emmelhainz, M.A., Stock, J.R. and Emmelhainz, L.W. (1991), 'Guest Commentary: Consumer Response to Stockouts', *Journal of Retailing*, 67, 138–44.

54 Borin, N. and Farris, P. (1995), 'A Sensitivity Analysis of Retailer Shelf Management Models', *Journal of Retailing*, 71(2), 153–71.

55 Mulhern, F.J. (1997), 'Retail Marketing: From Distribution to Integration', *International Journal of Research in Marketing*, 14(2), 103–24.

56 Young, S. (2002), 'Winning at Retail', *GCI*, August, 61–4.

57 Lewison, D.M. (1997), *Retailing*, sixth edition, Englewood Cliffs, NJ: Prentice Hall.

58 Van der Ster, W. and van Wissen, P. (1987), *Marketing & Detailhandel*, fourth edition, Groningen: Wolterns-Noordhoff.

59 Kotler, P. (1973), 'Atmospherics as a Marketing Tool', *Journal of Retailing*, 49(4), 48–64.

60 Kotler, P. (1973), 'Atmospherics as a Marketing Tool', *Journal of Retailing*, 49(4), 48–64.

61 Mehrabian, A. and Russell, J.A. (1974), *An Approach to Environmental Psychology*. Cambridge, MA: MIT Press.

62 For example, Donovan, R.J. and Rossiter, J.R. (1982), 'Store Atmosphere: An Environmental Psychology Approach', *Journal of Retailing*, 58 (Spring), 34–57.

63 North, A.C., Hargreaves, D.J. and McKendrick, J. (1999), 'The Influence of In-Store Music on Wine Selections', *Journal of Applied Psychology*, 84(2), 271–6.

64 Caldwell, C. and Hibbert, S.A. (2002), 'The Influence of Music Tempo and Musical Preferences on Restaurant Patrons' Behavior', *Psychology & Marketing*, 19(11), 895–918.

65 Baker, J. and Levy, M. (1993), 'An Experimental Approach to Making Retail Store Environmental Decisions', *Journal of Retailing*, 68(4), 445–60.

66 Baker, J., Parasuraman, A., Grewal, D. and Voss, G.B. (2002), 'The Influence of Multiple Store Environment Cues on Perceived Merchandise Value and Patronage Intentions', *Journal of Marketing*, 66, 120–41.

67 'Special Report: Ambient Media is Providing Retailers and Suppliers with yet Another Way of Advertising their Products in Store and Influencing Consumers' Buying Decisions' (1998), *In-store Marketing* (January), 29–33.

68 Ethridge, M. (1996), 'We Follow Our Noses to Stores', *Akron Beacon Journal* (20 January), B1.

69 Spangenberg, E.R., Crowley, A.E. and Henderson, P.W. (1996), 'Improving the Store Environment: Do Olfactory Cues Affect Evaluations and Behaviors?', *Journal of Marketing*, 60 (April), 67–80.

70 Brengman, M. (2002), *The Impact of Colour in the Store Environment. An Environmental Psychology Approach*, Doctoral Dissertation, Ghent University, Belgium.

71 Dawson, S., Bloch, P.H. and Ridgway, N.M. (1990), 'Shopping Motives, Emotional States, and Retail Outcomes', *Journal of Retailing*, 66 (Winter), 408–27.

72 Bloemer, J. and de Ruyter, K. (1998), 'On the Relationship Between Store Image, Store Satisfaction and Store Loyalty', *European Journal of Marketing*, 32(5/6) (http://www.europe.emerald-library.com/brev/00732ef1.htm).

73 Spies, K., Hesse, F. and Loesch, K. (1997), 'Store Atmosphere, Mood and Purchasing Behavior', *International Journal of Research in Marketing*, 14(1), 1–17.

74 Yoo, C., Park, J. and MacInnis, D.J. (1998), 'Effects of Store Characteristics and In-Store Emotional Experiences on Store Attitude', *Journal of Business Research*, 42(3), 253–63.

75 Miller, R. (2002), 'How to Exploit POP Around the Globe', *Marketing*, August, 27.

76 Schoormans, J.P.L. and Robben, H.S.J. (1997), 'The Effect of New Package Design on Product Attention, Categorization and Evaluation', *Journal of Economic Psychology*, 18(2), 271–87.

77 Schoormans, J.P.L. and Robben, H.S.J. (1997), 'The Effect of New Package Design on Product Attention, Categorization and Evaluation', *Journal of Economic Psychology*, 18(2), 271–87.

78 Young, S. (2002), 'Winning at Retail', *GCI*, August, 61–4.

79 'De Zeven Verpakkingszonden' (The Seven Packaging Sins) (1999), *Marketing Mix Digest*, 34(3), 5.

80 Pieters, R. and Warlop, L. (1999), 'Visual Attention During Brand Choice: The Impact of Time Pressure and Task Motivation', *International Journal of Research in Marketing*, 16(1), 1–16.

81 Clark, S.H.L. (1997), 'How Packaging Works with Children', in Smith, G. (ed.), *Children's Food Marketing and Innovation*. London: Chapman & Hall, 119–25.

82 Wansink, B. (1996), 'Can Package Size Accelerate Usage Volume?', *Journal of Marketing*, 60(3), 1–14.

83 Folkes, V., Martin, I. and Gupta, K. (1993), 'When to Say When: Effects of Supply on Usage', *Journal of Consumer Research*, 20 (December), 467–77.

84 Wansink, B. (1994), 'Antecedents and Mediators of Eating Bouts', *Family and Consumer Sciences Research Journal*, 23 (December), 166–82.

Chapter 15

Exhibitions and trade fairs

Chapter outline

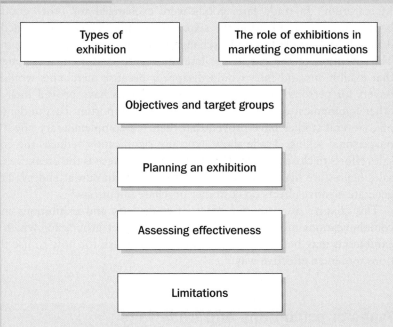

Types of exhibition

The role of exhibitions in marketing communications

Objectives and target groups

Planning an exhibition

Assessing effectiveness

Limitations

Chapter objectives

This chapter will help you to:

- Understand the role of exhibitions and trade fairs in marketing communications
- Learn about the objectives and target groups of trade fairs and exhibitions
- Plan an exhibition
- Assess the effectiveness of exhibition participation
- Understand the limitations and drawbacks of exhibitions as a marketing communications tool

Introduction

An exhibition or trade fair is a place where manufacturers and retailers of a certain product category or sector meet each other to talk about trade, to present and demonstrate their products and services, to exchange ideas and network and actually to buy and sell products.

Exhibitions and trade fairs are one of the oldest communications tools. They originate from the Roman period. Merchants traded at fixed places called 'Collegia Mercatorum'. In trade fairs goods were exchanged for other goods until coinage became more widespread in the sixteenth century. Value was defined by supply and demand. Most trade fair and exchange buildings were built during the Middle Ages. The invention of the car in the late nineteenth century made some people predict that exhibitions and fairs would disappear because merchants would travel to meet buyers for personal selling. However, exhibitions have proved their added value to other communications mix elements and are an important part of the communications mix. Several studies have proved that there's a complementary effect of trade shows on personal selling. Trade show exposure significantly reduces the cost of follow-up sales efforts to close the sale. This cost reduction exceeds the breakeven, and return-on-sales figures are higher among show attendees than non-attendees. Trade shows also generate positive effects on customer purchase intentions.[1]

This chapter discusses the place of trade fairs and exhibitions in the marketing communications mix and the objectives and target groups for which trade fairs and exhibitions may be used, and provides a framework for how to use this communications tool in an effective way.

Types of exhibitions and trade fairs

Exhibitions can be broadly divided into public fairs and trade fairs (Table 15.1).

Public or general fairs are open to the general public. There are two kinds of public fairs: general interest fairs and special interest fairs. The former target a broad audience and often exhibit a wide and diverse range of products and services. They are strongly promoted and aim to attract as many visitors as possible, especially buying visitors. For instance, the Vive La France Exhibition in January 2002 attracted more than 38,000 visitors over three days. More than 350 exhibitors were selling goods and services

Table 15.1 **Types of exhibition**

Public fairs	Trade fairs
■ General interest	■ Horizontal
■ Special interest	■ Vertical
	■ Conference-bound
	■ Trade mart

linked to France: for instance, Chateau de Cassaigne selling wines and Armagnac, Bonne Maman, producers of jam preserves, and Poilane the Bakeriers, which sells only 3% of its bread in Paris and exports to Japan and the US. Michelin Travel publications was showing an extensive range of maps, guides and digital travel assistance products and services.[2] Special interest fairs are fairs targeted at certain segments of the general public. They often put emphasis on informing visitors rather than making them buy. For instance, Adventure Affair is a fair for exciting and active leisure activities such as bungee jumping, mountain climbing, survival trips, etc.

Trade fairs are open to people working in a certain field of activity or industry. There are four kinds of trade fairs. In horizontal trade fairs exhibitors from one single industry exhibit their products and services to professional target groups, such as sales agents or distributors, from different industries. Companies selling chemical components may participate in that type of exhibition to market their products to buyers from different industries (food, detergents, etc.). In vertical trade fairs different industries present their goods and services to target groups belonging to one single field of activity. Various marketers of building materials, wooden doors, plumbing equipment, etc. may participate in trade fairs aimed at construction companies.

Conference-bound exhibitions[3] are small exhibitions linked to a conference. They have a low reach, but may be highly effective as a result of their high selectivity on the target group. This kind of exhibition in combination with a conference or symposium has become very popular both because it is financially attractive to conference organisers and because they offer an effective way to reach target groups that are hard to reach through other communications media. The fair conference formula is very popular in the United States, as opposed to exhibitions which are more explicitly aimed at buying and selling. Unlike their European counterparts, American companies do not enjoy buying and selling in the open. In Europe the concept of a 'market', where sellers and buyers of competing products stand next to each other and try to out-shout each other has always existed.

A trade mart is a hybrid kind of exhibition, i.e. half exhibition, half display, with a high frequency. Participants rent a permanent stand and aim to sell. Participants in trade marts have samples permanently on display.

In Table 15.2 an alternative classification of exhibitions is presented, based on types of visitors and exhibitors.[4] Other classifications include: public versus private fairs, indoor versus outdoor exhibitions and static versus mobile exhibitions.

Table 15.2 Types of exhibition based on the type of visitors and exhibitors

		Visitors	
		Vertical	*Horizontal*
Exhibitors	*Vertical*	**Focussed shows** Reserved for companies and clients from a specific sector	**Multi-industry visitors** Companies from a specific industry exhibit to a diverse public
	Horizontal	**Multi-industry exhibitors** Different companies exhibit to a specific public	**Diversified trade shows** Different companies exhibit to a diverse public

Based on: Shoham, A. (1992), 'Selecting and Evaluating Trade Shows', *Industrial Marketing Management*, 21, 335–41. Reproduced with permission from Elsevier.

In 2001 there were 1,858 exhibitions in the UK, attracting a total of 17.3 million visitors in 458 different venues. On average, exhibiting companies attended eight of these exhibitions in 2001, a similar number to previous years. Table 15.3 shows the top five public and trade exhibitions in the UK in 2001. An on-line listing of exhibitions can be found at www.exhibitions.co.uk.

Table 15.3 Top public and trade exhibitions in the UK

	Exhibition organiser	Venue	Attendance
Top 5 UK public exhibitions			
1 Daily Mail Ideal Home Show	DMG World Media	Earls Court, London	426,528
2 International Motorcycle & Scooter Show	MCI Exhibitions	NEC, Birmingham	206,434
3 BBC Clothes Show Live	Haymarket Exhibitions	NEC, Birmingham	170,702
4 London Boat Show	National Boat Shows	Earls Court, London	158,515
5 BBC Gardener's World Live	Haymarket Exhibitions	NEC, Birmingham	145,466
Top 5 UK trade exhibitions			
1 Spring Fair Birmingham	Trade Promotion Services	NEC, Birmingham	79,961
2 World Travel Market	Reed Exhibitions	Earls Court, London	38,871
3 The Furniture Show	CMP Information	NEC, Birmingham	36,685
4 Autumn Fair Birmingham	Trade Promotion Services	NEC, Birmingham	32,851
5 IFSEC/Security Solutions	CMP Information	NEC, Birmingham	27,991

Source: Association of Exhibition Organisers & ABC, August 2002.

The role of exhibitions in marketing communications

Like direct marketing and personal selling, exhibitions and trade fairs are considered to be a more personal and thus a 'below-the-line' communications tool. Demonstrations, one-to-one contacts with customers and prospects, direct selling and public relations are combined in this medium. Exhibitions have the advantage that all the senses (listening, watching, feeling, tasting and smelling) can be stimulated. Through new media such as Event TV, i.e. a television station broadcasting live from exhibitions, above-the-line effects can also be generated.

Table 15.4 shows the result of a study among 311 Belgian companies that were asked to rank their most important promotional tools.[5] A comparison was made between rarely exhibiting companies and frequently participating companies.

Personal selling and direct marketing are most frequently cited as important communications tools. For exhibitors trade fairs take third place, but non-exhibitors think that advertising, own events and PR are far more important. The same study concluded that for investment goods, personal selling was significantly more important than for consumer goods and services. Trade fairs and exhibitions proved to be of little importance for services. On average only 8% of the communications budgets in these industries was spent on trade fairs, compared to 15% in investment and consumer goods.

In business-to-business markets, trade shows represent the third largest marketing expenditure after advertising and sales promotions. They consume an average of 17% to

Table 15.4 **The place of exhibitions in the communications mix**

Exhibiting companies		Non-exhibitors	
Tool	Score/5	Tool	Score/5
1 Personal selling	4.09	1 Personal selling	3.51
2 Direct marketing	3.48	2 Direct marketing	3.13
3 Own events	3.36	3 Ads in professional magazines	2.99
4 Exhibitions	3.35	4 Own events	2.83
5 PR	3.34	5 PR	2.82
6 Ads in professional magazines	3.19	6 Exhibitions	2.23
7 Sponsorship	2.33	7 Sponsoring	2.03

Source: De Pelsmacker, P., Van den Bergh, J. and De Schepper, W. (1997), *Febelux Research on the Image of Exhibitions and Trade Fairs Among Companies and Communication Agencies*. Ghent, Belgium: De Vlerick School voor Management.

20% of a typical business-to-business marketing budget.[6] For instance, Lansing Linde is the UK's leading forklift truck manufacturer and service provider. For Lansing exhibitions are an important part of its marketing mix, the only part that lets it demonstrate its lift trucks to potential customers. Lansing Linde also uses exhibitions as platforms to generate press coverage in major trade magazines.[7]

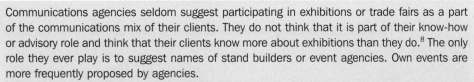

Communications agencies seldom suggest participating in exhibitions or trade fairs as a part of the communications mix of their clients. They do not think that it is part of their know-how or advisory role and think that their clients know more about exhibitions than they do.[8] The only role they ever play is to suggest names of stand builders or event agencies. Own events are more frequently proposed by agencies.

Positive characteristics of trade fairs, according to communications agencies are interactivity (more personal contacts), the possibility of generating sales leads, and demonstrating products or services. They tend to see the more negative aspects of exhibitions, such as too many people (of which there is a large proportion of uninterested visitors) and the fact that sales leads are concentrated, which could raise problems in reaction time. The biggest problem is the poor targeting and positioning of most exhibitions and trade fairs which leads to a substantial waste in contacts, making exhibitions a rather expensive medium per useful contact. Communications agencies think that organisers of exhibitions want to fill their capacity with as many participants as possible rather than select the right participants for the right target groups. Another problem is that there are too many exhibitions, often run simultaneously. This makes it difficult for agencies to select the right and effective exhibitions for their clients. A last barrier is the fact that it is a labour-intensive activity for participants and is thus viewed as an expensive medium. This corresponds with the view of companies.

One of the most important problems inhibiting agencies from selecting exhibitions from the mix and making proposals to their clients is the perceived cost. Trade fairs will take up a substantial part of the communications budget, from which the agency itself will probably not earn anything (compared to the 15% commission fee on above-the-line media). Besides that, agencies are not aware of the different exhibitions due to a lack of information such as audience descriptions, profiles of exhibitions, and of ten think that exhibitions are aimed at target groups that are too diverse.

Objectives and target groups

A company should first focus on the objectives it wants to achieve by participating in an exhibition or trade fair. Exhibition goals vis-à-vis the overall communications and marketing objectives should be formulated, often integrating specific goals of sales and marketing departments. In Figure 15.1 a number of objectives are listed which may positively influence the decision to participate in exhibitions and trade fairs.[9]

Selling products is especially important for companies in markets in which an important proportion of the annual sales is done in trade fairs. Examples are cars, clothing and chinaware. Trade fairs and exhibitions are important to make the first contacts with prospects and to generate leads that could eventually lead to sales. On the other hand, they are also meeting places where clients are met and contacts are reinforced. Moreover, the public of exhibitions is highly selective since they would not come to the fair if they were not interested in the exhibited products or services. A study indicates[10] that 82% of a potential market of companies would never have been contacted if it weren't for the personal contacts and exchanges at exhibitions and trade fairs. A research report from the Center for Exhibition Industry Research (CEIR) says it costs 56% less to close a lead generated at an exhibition than a lead generated in-field ($625 versus $1,117). Booths at exhibitions lead to hundreds or thousands of face-to-face interactions with highly targeted individuals.[11] Launching and/or testing a new product can be another important objective of trade fair participation. Visitors and other participants of exhibitions learn about new products. A company can use trade

Figure 15.1 **Marketing communications objectives and trade fair participation**

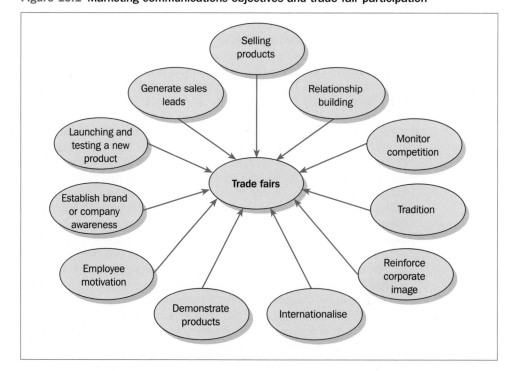

fairs as a 'test market' for new products by observing visitor interests, reactions and intentions to buy certain innovations.[12] Possible improvements and new applications may be discovered in that way. For instance, Nivea for Men used an exhibition to launch its range of grooming products under the 'for men who dare to care' theme. Pre-show mailings, tube posters and show sponsorship drove people to the stand where sampling, interactivity and a competition took over. Nivea supported its product launch with media coverage as a result of the exhibition and gave out thousands of free samples to its target group. Another example is Procter & Gamble launching Sunny Delight, a range of fruit drinks, at a top retailing trade show. In this case, the objectives were push marketing to get the new drinks noticed among the distribution as well as to earn shelf space. P&G attracted 35% to 40% of the entire exhibition audience to its colourful stand with free prize draws and product sampling, generating thousands of leads for sales call follow-up. Sunny Delight is now the UK's biggest selling drink.[13]

New companies can have a quick take-off in a market by immediately marketing their products and services to the target market in a direct way. Trade fairs may help to increase brand and company awareness rapidly within the target market, and to make deals with customers they would not have met as quickly using other communications tools. One of the major strengths of trade fairs is that products and services can be demonstrated and potential buyers may experience the value of products by trying them out, looking at them, touching them, etc. Potential customers can have all the technical details they want and the products' features and unique selling points can be demonstrated.

In an era when food retailers are seeking to differentiate themselves, the SIAL show in Paris, an international food, beverage, wine and spirits exhibition, provides a show-case of innovative products in three ways. The exhibition floor offers a range of products divided into product areas, then subdivided by country of origin. A trend showcase provides a specific array of products that are among the most outstanding of the new products. The show's own SIAL d'Or Awards spotlight items that are distinguished as fresh, inventive and trendy by a panel of judges. For instance Makrill, an Estonian company, provides surimi (minced fish) to Wal-Mart. At SIAL, the company introduced a line of surimi-filled ravioli products that were the first in the export marketplace. Another company showing at the SIAL trade fair, Lily O'Brien, a chocolate producer based in County Kildare, Ireland, had developed a product line for retailer Costco that is innovative in packaging. The company produced a packaged set of two boxed product assortments. One offers flavours related to popular desserts such as key lime pie, while the other plays on the popularity of coffee. Among its innovative approaches to the market are single-serve chocolates and a chocolate multipack designed in the likeness of an ice cream to capitalise on the popularity of frozen desserts. The biannual SIAL exhibition in Paris attracts more than 130,000 delegates and is one of the biggest events in the world for the food industry. It offers foreign and small companies the opportunity to demonstrate their innovative products to the world's biggest retailers.[14]

Exhibitions are a part of a company's relationship marketing programme with its customers and are also a public relations tool to support the corporate image of the company and the quality and fame of its brands. Companies not participating in certain exhibitions or trade fairs may send out negative signals to the market. Customers and prospects will have questions about the absence of a company at a trade fair, and competitors will try to profit from its absence. Multinational companies may increase their international brand awareness and sales through participating in foreign trade fairs.

This could lead to new contacts and sales contracts in new foreign markets. For instance, Russian and Asian trade fairs may help European companies develop markets outside Europe. Often they will be able to enjoy financial and organisational support from governmental export departments. Overseas trade shows are the least costly and most efficient way to check out international opportunities for franchisors with expansion plans who want to determine interest in their concept before making further investments. National Franchise exhibitions in Birmingham, Valencia, Brazil, Hong Kong, Singapore and Milan have all averaged between 15,000 and 30,000 attendees.[15]

There is no quicker way to learn about the new products and policies of competitors than by participating in exhibitions and trade fairs. Competitor analysis and comparing own products and prices with those of competitors could also be an objective for participating in an exhibition. Trade fairs often offer the opportunity of building relationships with customers. Clients feel important if they are treated as a VIP (champagne, food, personal demonstrations of novelties, etc.) at fairs and exhibitions. Companies often have special guest suites and activities reserved for their best customers. Sometimes exhibitions and VIP arrangements for sales people in luxury hotels, etc. are used as an incentive to enhance personnel morale and to motivate employees. Besides that, new sales people may be recruited at exhibitions and trade fairs. Finally, some companies stick to their tradition of participating in certain exhibitions and do not consider other communications objectives because 'we do it every year, it is a tradition'.

In Table 15.5 the results of a study of exhibition objectives among 124 UK companies[16] are compared with a study among 311 Belgian firms.[17] As Table 15.5 shows, the six most frequently formulated goals are similar for both countries: interaction with new and existing customers, promoting existing and new products, learning about

Table 15.5 Objectives of trade fair participation in the UK and Belgium

Objective	UK (N = 104)		Belgium (N = 311)	
	Mean (10 points)	Rank	Mean (5 points)	Rank
Meeting new customers	8.87	1	4.25	1
Launching new products	8.68	2	3.86	4
Taking sales orders	7.69	3	2.82	23
Enhancing company image	7.52	6	3.89	3
Interacting with existing customers	7.67	4	3.73	7
Promoting existing products	7.53	5	3.82	5
Getting information about competitors	4.84	10	3.66	8
Getting an edge on non-exhibitors	4.57	12	–	–
Keeping up with competitors	4.86	9	–	–
Enhancing staff morale	3.90	13	1.72	26
Interacting with distributors	4.80	11	–	–
Doing market research	5.77	7	–	–
Meeting new distributors	5.01	8	–	–
Increasing company awareness	–		3.93	2
Reaching as many people as possible	–		3.76	6
Increasing brand awareness	–		3.63	9
Reaching people in an effective way	–		3.60	10

Based on: Blythe, J. (2002), 'Using Trade Fairs in Key Account Management', *Industrial Marketing Management*, 31, 627–35; De Pelsmacker, P., Van den Bergh, J. and De Schepper, W. (1997), *Febelux Research in the Image of Exhibitions and Trade Fairs among Companies and Communication Agencies*. Ghent, Belgium: De Vlerick Leuven Gent Management School.

competitors' new products and enhancing the corporate image are the most important reasons why companies choose to participate in exhibitions or trade fairs. Taking sales orders seems more important in the UK, whereas brand and company awareness are more frequently formulated goals in Belgium.

Overall, an exhibition or trade fair combines a number of the following functions: sales generation, promotion, contact generation, demonstration, research, promotion of the company and its image, and public relations.

For a stand to be successful both sales teams and marketing must work in tandem. An exhibition should be as much about customer relationships as about sales. Quantel, a manufacturer of high-end creative software for the film and TV industry, regularly exhibits at the National Association of Broadcasters show in Las Vegas and at the International Broadcasting Convention in Amsterdam. Its goal is to generate more sales leads but not at the risk of diluting the brand equity. At the same convention, Microsoft TV wanted to make visitors aware of its name in the broadcasting marketplace while ensuring that the salesforce could engage visitors with the product in a suitable environment. At the stand, physical barriers were discarded and the stand was divided into zones by changes in colour, furniture, textures and materials. Large screens and chill-out areas enabled visitors to see the message.[18]

What is the perception of marketing managers as to the suitability of exhibitions to reach these objectives, compared with other communications mix instruments? This is illustrated in Table 15.6. It shows that exhibitions only score higher than competing media on competitor intelligence goals (observing the competition). To support company awareness and image, trade fairs also get high scores, nevertheless half of the surveyed companies stated that advertising in specialist magazines is equally valuable in reaching that specific objective. The results of this study suggest that exhibitions tend to be weaker in attaining the formulated goals, even in those that were regarded as particular strengths of exhibitions.

Exhibitions and trade fairs can be directed at a number of quite different target groups, each having their own expectations and information needs. This will have an influence on designing the stand and choosing what kind of information is presented in what way. Target groups include customers, prospects, competitors, suppliers, own personnel and journalists (media). All this depends on the type of exhibition.

Table 15.6 Trade fairs as instruments to reach specific marketing communications objectives

For objective X	Competing medium Y is	Worse	Equal	Better
Meeting new customers	Direct marketing	12.7%	32.9%	54.4%
Enhancing company image	Magazines	6.8%	52.7%	40.6%
Interacting with customers	Personal selling	2.9%	20.2%	76.9%
Promoting existing products	Personal selling	15.5%	24.1%	60.3%
Launching new products	Own events	3.7%	14.3%	82.5%
Getting competitor intelligence	Magazines	29.9%	46.4%	23.7%
Discovering market trends	Magazines	19.7%	37.6%	42.7%
Increasing company awareness	Magazines	7.4%	58.8%	33.7%
Reaching as many people as possible	Magazines	17.9%	32.8%	49.3%
Increasing brand awareness	Magazines	5.3%	44.2%	50.4%
Reaching people in an effective way	Personal selling	15.5%	24.1%	60.3%

Based on: Shipley, D. and Wong, K.S. (1993), 'Exhibiting Strategy and Implementation', *International Journal of Advertising*, 12, 117–30.

Visitors may have a number of reasons for attending an exhibition. They may want to increase their knowledge about products, services and companies, discover novelties and evolutions, contact other people working in the same area, and prepare specific purchases.

As a result, areas of interest and typical questions of exhibition visitors are:[19]

- comparing different suppliers and having an overview of supply;
- technical novelties and trends;
- scientific information;
- product and system information;
- technical information;
- user conditions;
- prices and sales conditions;
- competitor analysis;
- who the preferred supplier is;
- who may be potential partners;
- training.

The more heterogeneous the target groups of the exhibition, the more simple a stand concept will have to be.

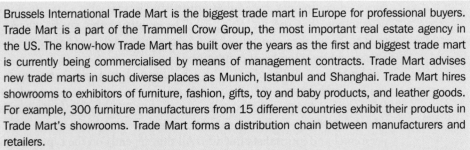

Brussels International Trade Mart is the biggest trade mart in Europe for professional buyers. Trade Mart is a part of the Trammell Crow Group, the most important real estate agency in the US. The know-how Trade Mart has built over the years as the first and biggest trade mart is currently being commercialised by means of management contracts. Trade Mart advises new trade marts in such diverse places as Munich, Istanbul and Shanghai. Trade Mart hires showrooms to exhibitors of furniture, fashion, gifts, toy and baby products, and leather goods. For example, 300 furniture manufacturers from 15 different countries exhibit their products in Trade Mart's showrooms. Trade Mart forms a distribution chain between manufacturers and retailers.

The advantages for the tenants (manufacturers) are that they can receive own as well as competitors' customers in a permanent showroom. By taking part in the permanent exhibition the tenants can avoid having to visit different retailers' showrooms on the road. Furthermore, the tenant can offer the retailer a total image of the whole sector in an adapted infrastructure which is easily accessible.

The advantages for the retailers are that they can visit their suppliers in a very short time period, they can take a look at all the different products and can make comparisons before buying. Furthermore, retailers can reduce stock since they have the possibility of a continuous supply. By visiting Trade Mart retailers can discover novelties in their sector and be a step ahead of competitors by introducing these novelties in their stores.

Trade Mart hires showrooms to about 1,500 manufacturers. However, due to the rise of category killers, discounters, factory outlets and electronic retailing, the classic retail market at which Trade Mart is oriented is declining. In order to retain its market share in this declining market, Trade Mart asked itself three questions. How to segment the market, how to position the store formula and what marketing mix to use? Regarding segmentation, Trade Mart decided to stick to the five business sectors in which it has built up experience, but to try to attract non-visitors in these sectors and to increase the number of revisits and purchases. To this end non-visiting retailers were personally invited by means of a personalised letter and a tele-marketing action. They were welcomed with breakfast, a gift and had the opportunity to win a holiday. To increase revisits, a savings card was given which entitled the holder to a convenient trolley bag after four visits. Concerning the positioning of Trade Mart, research results show that many retailers experienced a *déjà vu* effect. Trade Mart was associated with being big, having a lot of light and air, but the value of a visit was not so clear to the retailers. Therefore, Trade Mart started working on a clear positioning. It wanted to become *the* shopping centre 'for professionals only' in which retailers discover new products during every visit, receive useful information concerning particular themes and trends and where they are frequently treated with activities, events and presents.

As far as the marketing mix is concerned, Trade Mart wants to protect itself from ending in a vicious circle of lowering prices and degrading quality. Concerning product and service every-thing had to be directed at customer convenience and efficiency. New products, for example, are now grouped together in one showroom. Retailers can visit this showroom first and then look for additional products at the individual tenants' showrooms. Furthermore, Trade Mart started co-operating with a Dutch Trendwatcher to be able to offer information sessions for retailers regarding fashion and shoe trends. During the organised 'purchase days' the retailers are welcomed with a gift, free bus service, free coffee and croissants, a guaranteed parking space for early birds, and a 'caddy' boy who brings the purchased products to the car. Above all, a visit to Trade Mart has to be fun, and the stress is on a good atmosphere, humour and emotion, not on commotion. Trade Mart has adopted the vision that a store can only survive in the long run if it serves its customers more quickly, nicely, easily, cheaply and better than other shops. To convey its positioning, products and services, Trade Mart has changed to a new, dynamic communication starting with a new Trade Mart logo. The positioning remains 'for professionals only'. To make this positioning explicit Trade Mart engages in three operations: inform, signal and show. Trade Mart's sales representatives frequently visit the tenants to inform them when novelties are coming. Trade Mart signals these novelties by providing them with 'new' signs to highlight them in the showroom, and the tenants have to display the novelties temporarily in their showroom. Trade Mart employs ten sales people who are continuously look-ing for professional manufacturers to take part in Trade Mart. An interactive website has been created to improve contacts with customers. All invitations and brochures are characterised by an emotional appeal to stress the fun aspect. Focus is about 50% on people, not only on products. Testimonials from both tenants and retailers are used to attract new clients.[20]

Planning an exhibition

The success of participating in an exhibition is highly determined by the preparation. As planning and implementing exhibitions is a labour-intensive and long-term process, a checklist should be used throughout the entire procedure. Most projects start one year in advance of the actual exhibition. The logical steps one should follow when planning an exhibition are shown in Figure 15.2.[21]

In the first stage of this process exhibitions are considered as a medium or commun-ications tool and compared to other media to reach the communications goals as stated in the communications plan of the marketing strategy. A company should also choose

Figure 15.2 The exhibition planning process

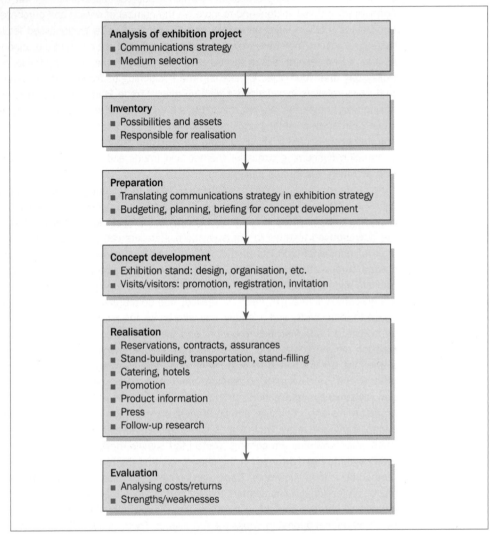

Based on: Van Den Tempel, W. (1985), 'Beursdeelneming en Return on Investment' (Trade Fair Participation and Return on Investment), in *Beurzen en Tentoonstellingen: praktijkhandboek voor communicatief exposeren* (*Trade Fairs and Exhibitions: A Practical Guide to Expose and Communicate*). Deventer: Kluwer. Reproduced with permission of Kluwer Bedrijfswetenschappen.

an exhibition that is most representative for the communications objectives it has planned. A number of selection criteria will help marketers to make the right choice:

- *Reach of the exhibition or trade fairs*: both quantitatively (number of visitors) and qualitatively (profile of visitors);
- *Costs and estimated return* of fair participation;
- *Programme of the exhibition*: the subject of the exhibition should correspond with the characteristics of the products or services a company is selling;
- *Presence of competitors*: not participating could send negative signals to the market of buyers, and competitors may use your absence as a strategic tool in negotiations with your (ex-)clients;

- *Reputation and fame* of an exhibition and its organiser;
- *Number of participants*;
- *Media attention* for former editions;
- *Own experiences* with former editions of the exhibition;
- *Supporting activities*, such as workshops, readings, conferences;
- *Timing of a trade fair*: fairs should be scheduled into the planning of a company and sales leads generated at a fair need sales capacity immediately after the fair.

Types of visitors and the type of products or services presented at trade fairs were the most important selection criteria among UK companies.[22] Other important criteria include estimated numbers of leads, numbers of visitors, costs and publicity. Date and duration of the event and reputation of the organiser were the least important criteria. For instance for financial advisors, fairs for senior citizens can draw big crowds of retirees looking for financial information, but there's a good chance that every broker and insurance agent will be present at the fair as well. The same can be said for specific financial expos. Therefore financial advisors should be more creative in their choice of public fairs. For instance, expositions for expectant parents might be interesting to reach parents and grandparents. Health fairs can also be interesting. Even boat shows or construction equipment trade shows could be important fairs for the financial advisor. The former attracts people with enough money for boats, who will certainly also have funds to invest. The attendees of the latter are owners of, or upper management in, companies that could need retirement plans and other financial advice.[23]

In the next phase, budgets, time and capacity are checked and one person is made responsible for the planning and implementation of the trade fair. Next a strategy and exhibition goals are defined, together with the budget, back-timing and briefing for the development of stands, animation, etc. This is developed further in the next steps. Later, the participation is evaluated through the tools discussed in the next paragraph.

The promotion stage is one of the more important exhibition supporting activities of the planning process. A direct mailing to invite clients and prospects (with free entrance tickets) is often employed. Advertising on radio and television may be used to bring the exhibition and stand to the attention of the public. Advertisements in the exhibition catalogue will help visitors find your stand and have an important after-fair promotion effect. A study revealed that free entrance tickets (51% of all exhibiting companies), direct mails (42%) and ads in the catalogue (42%) are the most frequently used pre-promotion tools. Press releases and ads in above-the-line media are less frequently used.

Companies who successfully develop integrated marketing communications programmes emphasising trade shows do so because these trade fairs create sales for them. These companies create a competitive advantage through their use of shows in two ways: they are twice as likely to close sales from their trade show exposure and they are able to gain these sales more efficiently, at a lower cost per sale. They also obtain up to three times more exposure because they can exhibit in more shows at the same cost. These companies have additional expertise, enabling them to make better use of trade shows. In addition, responsibility and authority for the show operations and success lie with someone who has and can develop expertise. A study clearly indicates that success is not based on preference for shows but rather on the performance of activities that lead to success. Less successful companies can increase success by identifying someone in the organisation to take the exhibit marketing responsibility.[24]

Assessing effectiveness

After participating in an exhibition, a company should evaluate the effectiveness of its efforts. There are four major reasons for measuring the results of every exhibition:[25]

- To justify investments (by calculating return on investments, just like for any other item in the marketing budget);
- To help choose the right exhibitions;
- To improve trade show activities (before, during and after the show);
- To encourage goal-driven activities.

This means that results should be compared with the objectives. Sales figures from current clients as well as new customers, and market and competitive information gathered at the fair are criteria to evaluate whether the exhibition brought value for money.[26] Sometimes exhibiting companies evaluate a fair by asking their sales reps about the contacts they have had during the fair. Often this leads to stories about jealous competitors or first contacts with important new customers 'in the near future'. This is not the most objective nor appropriate tool for analysing exhibition success. Others look at increases in sales returns after a fair, but this would only be a good evaluation if direct selling was the main goal of participating. Future sales returns cannot be predicted as many contracts have not yet been signed.

The coverage or reach of exhibitions and trade fairs differs from that of traditional print or other media. Gross reach has to do with the number of exhibition visitors, net reach could be the number of stand visitors. But effectiveness does not depend on the number of visitors only, but also on the quality of visits. Since 2000 the Audit Bureau of Circulations (ABC) has provided an independent 'currency' by which the success of exhibitions and trade shows can be compared. The two types of certificates issued are 'standard', which amounts to a number count only, and 'profile', which has audited demographics of the visitors. International Confex, for example, a trade fair targeting the travel industry and held every spring, has a profile certificate.[27]

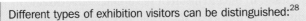

Different types of exhibition visitors can be distinguished:[28]

- *The brochure hunter*: his only goal is to get a brochure, a sticker or something else. He disappears very quickly from a stand.
- *The explorer*: wants to know everything about novelties. He has an endless flow of questions and is a time-consuming and difficult stand visitor.
- *The tourist*: he is not really interested, and often just visits the exhibition to accompany someone else.
- *The information hunter*: wants as much information as possible. Could sometimes be working for a competitor. Giving her a lot of information is important, it will help to create a good image of your company and eventually she might choose you because you gave her the best information.
- *The returner*: a supplier disguised as a visitor trying to get you as a new client.
- *The (future) client*: the ideal visitor of course, might ask for serious trade fair discounts.

Needless to say, not all types of visitors are equally useful and relevant.

In order to be able to assess the effectiveness of trade fair participation, a number of research methods can be applied.[29] During the course of the fair, the following research can be carried out:

- *Counting the distributed information material* (brochures, etc.): this is a way to estimate the interest in the company and its products and services, and is also a technique to evaluate image-building objectives.

- *Counting the number of passers-by and stand visitors*: may be used for different objectives. Possible counting mistakes may occur when certain people visit the stand more than once to ask for additional information or after comparing other stands.

- *Counting the number of personal contacts*: especially appropriate when objectives include sales leads and supporting new and current trade relations. The number of contacts and the quality of those contacts (hot/medium/cold prospects) should be distinguished.

- *Analysis of visitor flows on the stand*: through time-lapse video registration it is possible to observe and analyse behaviour and walk patterns of visitors during an entire exhibition day.

- *Observing visitor behaviour*: by observing stand visitors (where do they stop, what are they looking at? etc.) it is possible to detect what visitors find important and what is catching their attention. Eye-camera tests and tachistoscope tests (described in Chapter 9 on advertising research) are tools that are used for this kind of observational research.

- *Questionnaires for stand visitors*: this offers all possible ways of measuring effectiveness for different objectives such as evaluating pre-exhibition communications impact, stand concept and response to informational and other needs, company image testing, etc. However, on-stand face-to-face interviewing could be quite annoying for visitors (taking up their time).

Other analytical tools can be used to measure the effectiveness of an exhibition after the fair:

- *Questionnaires with stand visitors*: this implies that visitors' personal data have been stored. Strengths and weaknesses, awareness and recall can be tested, and suggestions for further exhibitions may result from this kind of research.

- *Surveying stand personnel*: as mentioned above, it could be hard to delete the subjective opinions and views, etc.

- *Response analysis on sent invitations*: how many of the invited persons have visited the stand? What were the reasons why invited people did not come to the stand?

- *Sales returns*: what are the sales results of the fair? Is the increase in return large enough, compared to the objectives?

- *Ratio-analysis*: some ratios help to measure effectiveness of exhibitions:[30]
  - Exhibition coefficient I = value of transactions generated at the fair / total fair costs
  - Exhibition coefficient II = yearly sales of the company / yearly fair costs
  - Visitor price = (Trade fair costs / number of fair visitors) × 1,000
  - Stand contact price = Trade fair costs / number of stand contacts
  - Costs per stand worker[31] = Trade fair costs / number of stand personnel
  - Costs per m² = Trade fair costs / amount of m²

When an exhibitor wants to make comparisons with other marketing and communications instruments throughout time, the next ratio[32] may be helpful:

$$\text{Sales efficiency quotient} = \frac{\text{order administration costs on the trade fair}}{\text{order administration cost through other sales channels or media}}$$

The first condition to be able to measure effectiveness is the presence of quantitatively defined concrete objectives. A study of 311 Belgian companies revealed that 27% of the exhibition participants always set objectives before participating in exhibitions and trade fairs; 29% hardly ever sets objectives; 57% of all surveyed companies claim that they track the effectiveness of the exhibitions in which they participate.[33]

To conclude, trade show performance has traditionally been evaluated by outcome-based measures such as different sales-related activities (for instance, on-site sales and sales immediately after the trade show). But on the other hand, behaviour-based control systems can also be used to evaluate participation in a trade fair. In a behaviour-based control system, the process rather than simply the outcome is addressed. In this system the booth personnel are directed to perform behaviours that are part of the marketing strategy. Four behaviour-based dimensions can be identified:[34]

■ *Information-gathering activities* including all activities related to the collection of information about competitors, customers, industry trends and new products at the trade show;
■ *Image-building activities* related to building corporate image and reputation at the trade show;
■ *Motivation activities* directed at the motivation of company employees and customers;
■ *Relationship-building activities* with established customers as well as new customers.

Limitations of fairs and exhibitions

There are a number of reasons why companies could have a negative attitude to participating in trade fairs and exhibitions. Visitors are overwhelmed with lots of information during a short period of time, and it is likely that communicating a message in this clutter will be ineffective. Competitors are easy to contact and comparisons are possible. It is likely that a client will find a better offer for his or her preferences at the fair; on the other hand, it is also possible to gain new customers (ex-clients of your competitor). Trade fairs are often hectic and exhibitions with a high visitor number will only lead to very superficial contacts. Exhibitions are exhausting. Weary visitors are difficult to contact and will not be very willing to buy. Half of visitors spend a maximum of 3–4 hours on an exhibition.

In Table 15.7 the most frequently mentioned reasons why trade fairs are not chosen as a communications tool are shown.[35] The most important barrier to exhibiting is the high cost. Low sales responses and satisfaction about the current communications mix are also high scoring reasons.

Table 15.7 Reasons for not integrating trade fairs in the communications mix

Reasons for not exhibiting	Mean (on 7-point scale with 1 = not a reason and 7 = a very strong reason), N = 24
1 Costs too much	6.08
2 Does not generate enough sales	4.92
3 Present promotion mix is satisfactory	4.83
4 Too few of my customers attend the exhibition	4.83
5 There are no suitable trade fairs to attend	3.33
6 Exhibitions are not traditional in my industry	3.27
7 Too many competitors attend the fair	2.25
8 I've never considered exhibiting	1.33

Based on: Shipley, D. and Wong, K.S. (1993), 'Exhibiting Strategy and Implementation', *International Journal of Advertising*, 12, 117–30. Reproduced with permission of NTC Publications Limited.

On-line trade shows

Although traditional trade shows still have advantages for companies that want to showcase their products, on-line shows have emerged as an attractive option for those with audiences that are too focussed to justify the expenses of a real-world show. Recession, tight corporate travel and marketing budgets, and terrorism have taken their toll on traditional exhibitions. In 2002 attendance at trade shows fell by 2% and sales of exhibition space declined by 5%. Meanwhile the popularity of on-line shows is growing. Although in 2002 only 5% of exhibitors' budgets was spent on-line, an increase to 10% is expected for the coming years. Most of those budgets will be spent on more specialised exhibits, smaller shows with targeted audiences and refined messages. *EE Times* magazine is targeted at such an audience of electronic engineers. In November 2002 the magazine moved its IP/System on Chip conference to cyberspace for the first time. Using software from Israeli firm Unisfair, *EE Times* created a website depicting a conference centre, complete with virtual visitors walking paths to the conference hall and an exhibition space. A click on the conference hall took the real visitors, paying nothing for the two-day event, into a virtual auditorium where presenters' slides filled the screen while their speeches were broadcasted via streaming audio. In the exhibition hall attendees could view exhibitors' displays and chat with sales reps. Exhibitors such as IBM, Intel and Motorola could get details on who viewed products and contact visitors in real time. The on-line trade show drew about 600 live attendees, with another 1,100 viewing an archive of the event. Due to its success, the show was immediately rescheduled.

Trillium software, maker of software for organising data, regularly pays to have a booth at on-line trade shows run by dataWarehouse.com, a website for data-warehousing managers. This site has had quarterly on-line trade shows since July 2000. For exhibitors, running a booth is far cheaper on-line than at traditional shows. A booth at *EE Times'* System on Chip show costs from $3,000 to $20,000, depending on prominent placement, colours and options for linking to products or press releases. For attendees at on-line shows there are no costs. Another advantage of on-line shows is their global reach. Nearly 40% of dataWarehouse.com's visitors are from outside the US, with India, the UK and Benelux countries represented most. At *EE Times'* Chip show, 13% of visitors were from Asia and 11% from Europe.

However, virtual shows have one big disadvantage when compared with their real-world counterparts: the lack of personal face-to-face contact. Virtual exhibition halls and on-line chat might be successful but can't beat the ability to see, touch and play with a product or shake hands with a potential business partner. As traditional shows involve more effort from, and higher costs for, attendees, leads generated are more likely to turn into actual sales as less serious shoppers are weeded out. Some virtual trade shows are trying to make their events more realistic by using technologies that allow individuals to be represented by lifelike avatars who can move and interact in a simulated world on-line. Another standard feature of traditional exhibitions, the goodie bag of promotional items given out by exhibitors and organisers, is also very important. DataWarehouse.com sends out gifts to a random sample of about two-thirds of visitors halfway through each show.[36]

Integrating exhibitions and trade fairs in IMC

Obviously, exhibitions and trade fairs can be announced in advertising campaigns, on websites, or awareness and interest can be created through press conferences, but in the first place exhibition and trade fair activities should be well integrated into the direct marketing and personal selling efforts. Direct marketing can be used to announce the fair to customers and stakeholders. Information collected at the fair can be ploughed into the customer database and be used for more effective mailing campaigns or for better advertising and promotion. At the trade fair, prospects can be identified and deals can be closed. It is an opportunity to invite loyal customers and to build a stronger relationship with them. Exhibitions and fairs are also opportunities to hold press conferences and organise corporate hospitality events. Prospects, identified through sales efforts and direct marketing campaigns can be invited to the fair for a more personal approach. In general, fairs and exhibitions can make direct marketing and sales efforts more effective, and the latter can turn fairs and exhibitions into powerful tools by adequately preparing for them.

Summary

Exhibitions and trade fairs are mainly, but not exclusively, used in business-to-business marketing as places for merchants of a certain product category or industry to meet and talk. Different types of exhibitions can be distinguished, such as public fairs, horizontal and vertical trade fairs, conference-bound exhibitions and trade marts. The place of exhibitions, especially in business marketing communications, is considered to be almost as important as direct marketing and personal selling. The objectives of exhibitions can be very diverse: to launch and test new products, establish brand or company awareness, demonstrate products, reinforce corporate image, monitor the competition, build relationships, generate sales leads and sell products. Exhibitions and trade fairs have to be planned carefully. After an analysis of the exhibition project, and making an inventory of what is needed, the actual exhibition has to be prepared, a concept for a stand has to be developed and the exhibition has to be realised (reservations, stand building, catering, press, etc.). After the exhibition, the results have to be evaluated. This can be done by counting the distributed information and the numbers of passers-by and personal contacts, by analysing the flow of visitors and observing visitors' behaviour, or by surveying them. Sales returns can be measured.

Review questions

1 What is the importance of trade fairs and exhibitions in the marketing communications mix?

2 What are the main objectives of trade fair participation, and for which objectives are exhibitions and trade fairs most suited?

3 What are the basic steps and considerations in the development of an exhibition participation plan?

4 How can the effectiveness of exhibitions and trade fairs be assessed?

5 What are the limitations of trade fair participation?

Further reading

Arnold, M. (2002), *Build a Better Trade Show Image: Establishing Brand by Designing a Dynamic Exhibit Experience*. Kansas City: Tiffany Harbor Productions.

Levinson, J., Smith, M. and Ray-Wilson, O. (1997), *Guerrilla Trade Show Selling: New, Unconventional Weapons and Tactics to Meet More People, Get More Leads, and Close More Sales*. Hoboken, NJ: John Wiley & Sons.

Miller, S. (2000), *How to Get the Most out of Trade Shows*. New York: McGraw-Hill.

Rice, G. and Almossawi, M. (2002), 'A Study of Exhibitor Firms at an Arabian Gulf Trade Show: Goals, Selection Criteria and Perceived Problems', *Journal of Global Marketing*, 15(3/4), 149–72.

Robbe, D. (1999), *Expositions and Trade Shows*. Hoboken, NJ: John Wiley & Sons.

Siskind, B. (1997), *The Power of Exhibit Marketing*. Bellingham, WA: Self Counsel Press.

Case 15

Etap – unsinkable sailing pleasure

The Belgian company Etap Yachting was established in 1970. Since the beginning, Etap has stressed the safety factor and, more specifically, the unsinkability of its yachts. Etap's first product was launched in 1972. Because of their unique construction (the 'sandwich construction') the yachts are unsinkable. Thanks to Etap's use of this construction from the very beginning, today Etap benefits from the fact that its name is synonymous with unsinkable yachts. Furthermore, its products are characterised by a contemporary, original style, consisting of several unique design features as well as novel materials. Functionality,

maintenance-friendliness and durability have always been taken to heart. At the end of the 1970s, Etap started distributing in the Netherlands, France and Germany, after which the rest of Europe, the US and Japan followed. In 2005, Etap's home market takes only 5% to 10% of total turnover, which clearly illustrates Etap's international character.

In 2005 Etap realised a turnover of about 11 million Euro, 20% of which was in The Netherlands and in France, 15% in Germany, and 10% in the UK. The USA, Japan and Australia together accounted for another 10% of turnover. For a number of years,

Etap sold 200–220 boats per year. However, in recent years the number of boats sold is down to about 150, due to the on average larger scale of the boats sold (less, but larger boats).

Market

The yacht market is mainly situated in the industrialised world (Europe, Japan, the US and Canada) and forms part of the larger market of pleasure boats dominated by motor boats (65% market share). In Europe the largest markets are France and Germany, followed by the Netherlands, the UK and the rest. In France each year about 1,800 new sailing yachts are registered. In Germany, it is 1,100. Currently, sailing yachts are typically built out of polyester, giving the yachts a very long life. For this reason the market soon became saturated, leading to a structural decrease in the demand for new yachts. Today, in Europe, for every new yacht built five secondhand yachts are sold. A recent tendency in the market is the increasing importance of charter activities: the rental of ships, skipper included or otherwise. Therefore, more and more ships are being built especially for the charter market.

The competitive landscape of sailing yachts is divided among:

■ a few very large worldwide suppliers such as the Beneteau-Jeanneau group, Bavaria, Dufour, Catalina and Hunter;

■ a few shipyards that can be described as larger small and medium-sized enterprises, among which are Hallberg Rassy, X-yachts, Etap Yachting, Amel and Alu-bat;

■ a large number of very small suppliers whose annual production consists of only a few ships.

The first group offers product lines in all different categories such as cruising, racing, catamarans and charters, while most shipyards in the second category are targeting a niche market to remain competitive with the former group. For example, unsinkability combined with style and maintenance-friendliness is the unique positioning of Etap. Furthermore, Etap builds yachts ranging from 21–48 feet. The latest introduction, Etap 46DS in 2003, extended the range from 39 to 48 feet. This range makes Etap one of the few international shipyards that still build ships under 30 feet. The reason why Etap follows this strategy is that it wants to build customer relations in an early stage of watersports practice. This is very important to Etap since niche products are often characterised by a higher brand loyalty.

The distribution of yachts usually takes place by means of a network of very small companies (about five employees), depending to a large extent on the shipyards as far as product presentation and communications activities are concerned. Some shipyards partly or fully utilise direct selling to the end customers. After-sales service is usually provided by small, independent companies. Etap distributes its products by means of a network of distributors in the larger European markets. For instance, in Germany and the UK five, and in France seven, distributors work with Etap. The distributors have a regional responsibility and usually follow up on the contacts that are generated as a result of Etap's marketing efforts. Importers make their own marketing plan for the country in which they import. Etap gives them financial and logistical support. Smaller or more distant markets are supplied by means of an importer, while in the home market direct selling takes place.

Communications strategy

Etap makes use of three major communications tools: a website (www.etapyachting.com), exhibitions and advertising in magazines specialising in watersports. The extranet section of the website is used for information transfer between distributors. Up to 65% of the total marketing budget (website excluded) is allocated to international trade shows. At these shows two types of brochure are distributed: one providing a general view of what Etap has to offer for consumers with a general interest in the product category, and one with detailed, technological information of each sailing yacht in Etap's product portfolio for consumers with specific interests. The rest of the budget is mainly spent on magazine advertising. Concerning the latter, Etap advertises in specialised water sports magazines in countries in which it has a distribution structure. Usually advertisements are placed in both the largest and the most specialised magazine in each country. Countries in which Etap advertised in 2005 were Belgium, Germany, The Netherlands, France, Italy, the UK, Austria, Switzerland, Australia, Japan and the USA. In countries in which an importer is present, the organisation and cost of advertising is the importer's responsibility; in other countries Etap organises and pays for the advertising campaigns. Materials for advertising and POS materials and brochures for distributors are produced and paid for by Etap. The company seldom advertises in media directed at the general public, unless it wants to announce a special event, such as wharf open-door days. Furthermore, a limited amount of sponsorship is allocated to watersports activities and for organising local or global events such as Etap contests and Etap club meetings. Besides these 'paying communications tools', it goes without saying that PR activities are very important for Etap. Product tests and product reviews published in international media have an important influence on potential buyers.

In all marketing communications tools, an advertising agency makes sure that the typical corporate style of Etap is retained. Special attention is devoted to graphic and pictorial elements and to the repetition of Etap's USP 'unsinkable sailing pleasure'. (See Plate 23.)

Exhibition strategy

The communications objectives Etap wants to reach by participating in exhibitions are fourfold. First, Etap wants to raise awareness of Etap and its USP, the unsinkability of its sailing yachts, in all people interested in water sports. Second, Etap wants to encourage visitors to ask agents for further information in order to start a sales process. A third objective is to maintain relationships with existing customers, while a fourth is to announce new products. Etap's primary target group is families. Experience has taught that the initiator of the buying process is usually aged 45+, and enjoys a high income. Sailing families are often self-employed or belong to middle or senior management. They are very likely to be interested in technology and take safety to heart, despite the fact that they enjoy an adventurous sport. However, more broadly there are five different groups of people with whom Etap would like to communicate during an exhibition: interested consumers, existing customers, competitors, the media and suppliers.

Interested consumers are subdivided into three groups:

1 Prior contacts for whom the exhibition may trigger a purchase.
2 Consumers who did not know about Etap in advance, but who are sufficiently interested to address with follow-up activities.
3 Consumers who did not know about Etap in advance, and who have concrete plans to buy a yacht at the exhibition.

Etap concentrates its efforts mainly on the first two groups. Developing a sales strategy for the third is assumed to be too concentrated on short-term rather than long-term results. The classification of potential customers according to the level of interest and the probability of a successful closure is based on an evaluation on three criteria:

1 To what extent is the customer convinced of the superior price/quality relation of an Etap yacht?
2 To what extent is the customer's budget realistic (taking into account a possible trade in of an existing yacht)?
3 To what extent is the customer's timing realistic?

The success of an exhibition is evaluated on the basis of this categorisation, as well as on sales generated. The classification is also used to estimate future sales from the leads generated at the exhibition. A sales person is assumed to know after five minutes to whom he is talking and whether or not the visitor is showing sufficient interest. Interested visitors are asked to fill out a form with personal data, to which the sales person adds comments after the visit. These forms are used as sales leads for follow-up activities.

Concerning existing customers, Etap does not follow the strategy of looking at them as possible repurchasers, but rather wants to build a long-term relationship with them. Solving problems, sharing experiences and trying to make them feel part of Etap are the main objectives. The presence of competitors is useful in order to collect information on new products and prices. Meeting the press has the advantage of maintaining relationships and setting dates for the presentation of new products or for test sailing. Suppliers' participation is very useful since it enables Etap and its competitors to visit several suppliers in a very short time period.

Preparation of exhibitions

The preparation of exhibitions implies a number of activities:

- Depending on the budget, determine at which exhibitions Etap will be present with which types of boats, based on a yearly meeting with Etap sales managers and distributors
- Communicate exhibition calendar to distributors
- Reservation of exhibition surfers, based on a study of preferential locations

- Technical file: arranging electricity in the stand, reserving equipment to install vessels, stage-setting of the stand, ordering entry cards, parking permits, technical control of stand construction, choosing necessary stand materials, organising transportation for exhibited yachts and stand materials . . .

- Press contacts: preparing and sending press kits, informing the press about exhibited models . . .

- Adapting website and enabling visitors to make a personal appointment

- Timely advertisements in professional magazines

- Organisation and schedule of Etap staff present at the exhibition, travel, accommodation for staff

- Informing distributors about types of vessels exhibited and promotion campaigns

- Direct mailing to customers and prospects about novelties presented

- Training of sales staff and exhibitors about prices, promotions, new products . . . by employees of the shipyard or by external trainers (the latter for instance for training in price negotiation, personal organisation, direct mail . . .)

- Preparation meetings with Etap staff and distributors at the exhibition stand

- Logistical organisation for building and removing the stand

- Final control of the stand by Etap sales managers.

Furthermore, follow-up on the leads generated by the exhibition takes about six weeks.

As indicated before before an exhibition takes place many things have to be taken care of. Therefore, every year a meeting is held with all agents and sales personnel to determine the exhibition calender for the next year. For example, Etap typically takes part in the exhibitions detailed in Case Table 15.1.

The delivery date for yachts and communications activities need to be co-ordinated with this calender. Media space needs to bought in advance in order for Etap to advertise its participation in exhibitions in the relevant magazines. Preparations need to be made with regard to direct mail activities. Participants of the exhibition often need additional training to inform them on prices or new products. Depending on the objectives of the training, the training sessions may be given by employees of the shipyard or by external trainers. Sessions on price negotiation, personal organisation or direct mail, for example, are typically in the hands of external advisers. During the exhibition, shipyard employees and agents work very closely. Furthermore, work is not over when the exhibition ends. Follow-up of the leads generated at the exhibition takes about six weeks.

Etap does not define specific objectives for each fair, and consequently does not measure all performance indicators and results exactly. However, the level of success of exhibitions is qualitatively and quantitatively assessed on the basis of multiple criteria:

- Number of vessels sold at the exhibition. The distinction is made between 'lucky shots' and successfully closing a sales process

- Number of vessels sold up to 8 weeks after the end of the exhibition, with sales directly linked to the exhibition

- Subjective impression of sales persons about the number of visitors and the level of interest for the Etap stand

Case Table 15.1 **Etap's programme of exhibitions, 2005**

Time	Place	Nature of exhibition
January	Düsseldorf	Dry
February	Ghent	Dry
March	Tulln	Dry
July	Sydney	Water
September	Ijmuiden	Water
September	La Rochelle	Water
September	Southampton	Water
September	Friedrichshafen	Dry
October	Barcelona	Water
October	Hamburg	Dry
December	Paris	Dry

- Total number of visitors at the exhibition
- Documentation material distributed
- Number of addresses collected at the information desk
- Number of appointments made to visit a yacht
- Extent to which appointments made in advance actually take place
- Visitors' comments, especially with regard to new vessels.

In general, Etap considers exhibitions as the most important source of 'customer intelligence'. By observing, listening and talking to (potential) customers, the sales and research staff get an idea of possible improvements to existing products and what to take into account when developing new ones.

Questions

1 Which type of exhibition does Etap Yachting make use of?

2 Why do you think Etap spends almost two-thirds of its marketing budget on exhibitions?

3 In view of Etap's communications objectives, do you think exhibitions are the most efficient communications tool to reach these objectives? Which other alternatives are there?

4 Would you advise Etap to make more use of other communications tools, such as advertising or sales promotions?

5 Is it Etap's main intention to generate sales during exhibitions? Explain.

Thanks to Jan Verhaege, Marketing Director, Etap Yachting n.v. for providing documentation and preparing this case study. Reproduced courtesy of Etap. www.etapyachting.com

References

1 Smith, T., Gopalakrishna, S. and Smith, P. (1999), *Trade Show Synergy: Enhancing Sales Force Efficiency*. ISBM report 24-1999. Institute for the Study of Business Markets, Pennsylvania State University.

2 Posner, M. (2002), 'Vive La France Exhibition', *Journal of the Institute of Credit Management*, March, 24.

3 Groenendijk, J.N.A., Hazekamp, G.A.Th. and Mastenbroek, J. (1992), *Public Relations & Voorlichting: Beleid, Organisatie en Uitvoering* (*Public Relations and Press Relations: Management, Organisation and Implementation*). Zaventem: Samson bedrijfsinformatie.

4 Shoham, A. (1992), 'Selecting and Evaluating Trade Shows', *Industrial Marketing Management*, 21, 335–41.

5 De Pelsmacker, P., Van den Bergh, J. and De Schepper, W. (1997), *Febelux Research on the Image of Exhibitions and Trade Fairs among Companies and Communication Agencies*. Ghent: De Vlerick School voor Management.

6 Pinar, M. Rogers, J. and Baack, D. (2002), 'An Examination of Trade Show Participation in a Developing Country: An Exploratory Study in Turkey', *Journal of European Marketing*, 11(3), 33–52.

7 *Exhibition Work: The Case for a Powerful, Cost-effective Marketing Medium*. The Association of Exhibition Organisers (AEO), (2002), www.exhibitionswork.co.uk.

8 De Pelsmacker, P., Van den Bergh, J. and De Schepper, W. (1997), *Febelux Research on the Image of Exhibitions and Trade Fairs among Companies and Communication Agencies*. Ghent: De Vlerick School voor Management.

9 Anderson, A.H. and Kleiner, D. (1995), *Effective Marketing Communication: A Skills and Activity-Based Approach*. Oxford: Blackwell Business.

10 Ingram, T.N. and Laforge, R.W. (1989), *Sales Management: Analysis and Decision Making*. Chicago: The Dryden Press.

11 Chapman, B. (2001), 'The Trade Show Must Go On', *Sales and Marketing Management*, 153(6), 22.

12 Kotler, P. (1984), *Marketing Management: Analysis, Planning and Control*. London: Prentice Hall.

13 *How to Exhibit. Maximising the Power of Exhibitions*. The Association of Exhibition Organisers (AEO), (2002), www.exhibitionswork.co.uk.

14 Duff, M. (2002), 'European Food Expo Beckons U.S. with Trends not Found at Home', *DNS Retailing Today*, 41(21), 8–48.

15 Fishman, B. (2003), 'International Trade Shows: The Smartest Ticket for Overseas Research', *Franchising World*, 35(3), 25–8.

16 Shipley, D. and Wong, K.S. (1993), 'Exhibiting Strategy and Implementation', *International Journal of Advertising*, 12, 117–30.

17 De Pelsmacker, P., Van den Bergh, J. and De Schepper, W. (1997), *Febelux Research on the Image of Exhibitions and Trade Fairs among Companies and Communication Agencies*. Ghent: De Vlerick School voor Management.

18 Greaves, S. (2002), 'Unifying Sales and Branding at Events', *Marketing*, (November), 25.

19 Wenz-Gahler, I. (1995), *Messenstand-Design* (*Trade Fair Stand Design*). Leinfelden-Echterding: Alexander Koch.

20 Freddy Vander Mijnsbrugge, Director Brussels International Trade Mart.

21 Van Den Tempel, W. (1985), 'Beursdeelneming en Return on Investment' (Trade Fair Participation and

Return on Investment), in *Beurzen en Tentoonstellingen: praktijkhandboek voor communicatief exposeren* (*Trade Fairs and Exhibitions: A Practical Guide to Expose and Communicate*). Deventer: Kluwer.

22 Shipley, D. and Wong, K.S. (1993), 'Exhibiting Strategy and Implementation', *International Journal of Advertising*, 12, 117–30.

23 Klein, L. (2003), 'How to Make Trade Shows Work for You', *National Underwriter*, 107(1), 11.

24 Tanner, J. (2002), 'Leveling of the Playing Field: Factors Influencing Trade Show Success for Small Companies', *Industrial Marketing Managemment*, 31, 229–39.

25 *How to Measure Exhibition Success: A Workbook for Marketers*. The Association of Exhibition Organisers (AEO), (2002), www.exhibitionswork.co.uk.

26 Anderson, A.H. and Kleiner, D. (1995), *Effective Marketing Communication: A Skills and Activity-Based Approach*. Oxford: Blackwell Business.

27 Greaves, S. (2003), 'Events Answer Industry Needs', *Marketing*, (February), 27; Benady, D. (2003), 'Show You Count', *Marketing Week*, (February), 41–4.

28 De Vries, L. (1985), 'Profiel en Typologie van de Bezoeker' (Profile and Typology of the Visitor), in *Beurzen en Tentoonstellingen: Praktijkboek voor Communicatief Exposeren* (*Trade Fairs and Exhibitions: A Practical Guide to Expose and Communicate*). Deventer: Kluwer.

29 Meffert, H. and Ueding, R. (1996), *Ziele und Nutzen von Messebeteiligungen: Zusammenfassung einer Empirisch Gestützten Untersuchung auf der Grundlage einer Befragung Deutscher Aussteller* (*Objectives and Use-fulness of Trade Fair Participation: Summary of an Empirical Study Amongst Trade Fair Participants*). Cologne: Institüt für Marketing-Universität, Ausstellungs- und Messe-Ausschus der Deutschen Wirtschaft (AUMA).

30 Postma, P. (1986), *Marketing voor Iedereen* (*Marketing for Everyone*). Amsterdam: Omega Books.

31 Deelen, M. and Muys, W. (1991), *Verkoopactief Deelnemene aan Beurzen* (*Sales-Active Trade Fair Participation*). Deventer: Kluwer Bedrijfswetenschappen.

32 Meffert, H. and Ueding, R. (1996), *Ziele und Nutzen von Messebeteiligungen: Zusammenfassung einer Empirisch Gestützten Untersuchung auf der Grundlage einer Befragung Deutscher Aussteller* (*Objectives and Useful-ness of Trade Fair Participation: Summary of an Empirical Study Amongst Trade Fair Participants*). Cologne: Institüt für Marketing-Universität, Ausstellungs- und Messe-Ausschus der Deutschen Wirtschaft (AUMA).

33 De Pelsmacker, P., Van den Bergh, J. and De Schepper, W. (1997), *Febelux Research on the Image of Exhibitions and Trade Fairs among Companies and Communication Agencies*. Ghent: De Vlerick School voor Management.

34 Hansen, K. (1999), 'Trade Show Performance: A Conceptual Framework and Its Implications for Future Research', *Academy of Marketing Science Review*, 1999(8), 135–50.

35 Shipley, D. and Wong, K.S. (1993), 'Exhibiting Strategy and Implementation', *International Journal of Advertising*, 12, 117–30.

36 Saranow, J. (2003), 'The Show Goes On: Online Trade Shows Offer a Low-cost, Flexible Alternative for Organizers – Especially in These Days of Tight Travel Budgets', *Wall Street Journal*, 28 April, R.4.

Chapter 16
Personal selling

Chapter outline

Personal selling as a marketing communications tool		Personal selling activities

The personal selling process

Salesforce management

| Organisation and planning | Recruitment and selection | Training motivation compensation | Evaluation |

Chapter objectives

This chapter will help you to:

- Assess the place of personal selling in the marketing communications mix
- Understand the advantages and disadvantages of personal selling as a marketing communications tool
- Understand the various stages in the personal selling process
- Understand the components of salesforce management
- Know how a salesforce should be organised and planned
- Learn how a salesforce can be trained, motivated and compensated
- Assess the effectiveness of the salesforce

Introduction

Like marketing practice in general, personal selling has come a long way. The aggressive selling orientation, which gave rise to personal selling's bad reputation of trying to sell products to consumers who did not need them, has been replaced with a customer orientation with a focus on building long-term relationships instead of immediately closing a sale. In other words, personal selling is moving from transaction-based methods to relationship-based methods. The latter focusses on solving customers' problems, providing opportunities and adding value to customers' business over an extended period of time.[1]

A lot of marketing practitioners started their career as a sales rep. The reason why many companies start new recruits in a personal selling function is that it is an ideal position to get to know the customers and the market, which is essential for marketing communicators, as well as for all other marketing functions.

In this chapter personal selling is defined, and its objectives and target groups discussed. Moreover, attention is devoted to the pros and cons of using a salesforce. Finally, sales management, consisting of planning and organisation, recruitment and selection, training, motivation and compensation, and evaluation of the salesforce is dealt with.

Personal selling as a marketing communications instrument

Personal selling can be defined as two-way, face-to-face communications used to inform, give demonstrations to, maintain or establish a long-term relationship with, or persuade specific members of a particular audience.

Contrary to some of the other marketing communications tools, personal selling always implies interaction with the customer. It is a two-way, interpersonal communications tool which is said to involve face-to-face contact. The latter should not be interpreted too strictly since telephone selling, which does not really imply a face-to-face activity, also forms part of personal selling. Personal selling is an important element of the marketing communications mix, especially for business-to-business communications. In addition, manufacturers of consumer goods, such as PCs, insurance or loan companies, and not-for-profit organisations, such as collecting funds for charity or third world relief, find personal selling indispensable.

Depending on the target groups, different types of personal selling can be distinguished. Table 16.1 gives an overview of the major selling types with the corresponding target groups.

Trade selling is concerned with selling products to supermarkets, groceries, pharmacies, etc. Companies like Unilever, Procter & Gamble and Coca-Cola, for example, have a strong negotiating position towards the trade because no store can afford not to have these brands on their shelves. The salespersons of less familiar brands may have a much tougher job convincing the trade to allocate shelf space to its products.

Missionary selling means informing and trying to convince not your direct customers, but the customers of your direct customers. An excellent example of missionary selling

Table 16.1 **Types of personal selling**

Type of selling	Target group
■ Trade selling	■ Supermarkets, groceries, pharmacies, etc.
■ Missionary selling	■ Target group of customers of your direct customers
■ Retail selling	■ Consumers
■ Business-to-business selling	■ Businesses
■ Professional selling	■ Influencers of your target group
■ Direct selling	■ Consumers

Based on: Marks, R.B. (1988), *Personal Selling: An Interactive Approach*. Boston: Allyn and Bacon; Govoni, N., Eng, R. and Galper, M. (1986), *Promotional Management*. Englewood Cliffs, NJ: Prentice Hall.

can be found in the pharmaceutical industry. Pharmaceutical sales reps, for instance, try to persuade pharmacists to buy their products and local practitioners to prescribe the company's drugs to patients. The direct customers of the pharmaceutical company are, however, wholesalers and not the pharmacists or the doctors.

Retail selling involves direct contact with the end consumer. Retail selling is responsive in nature since the customer usually approaches the salesperson for help. Although the required knowledge and skills of the salesperson depend upon the type of product being sold (e.g. a hair dryer versus a computer), the level of experience and training needed is on average much lower than for salespersons dealing with business-to-business selling.

Business-to-business selling, or industrial selling, is concerned with selling components, semi-finished products or finished products or services to other businesses. The salesforce need to know their company's products and the client's needs thoroughly in order to present the company's products as an attractive alternative for the client.

Professional selling deals with approaching influencers or prescribers. For example, a company specialised in indoor lighting or home decoration can try to influence architects, engineering firms or interior decorators to incorporate their products in their future assignments.

Direct selling refers to selling products or services directly to consumers in a face-to-face manner. This usually takes place in consumers' homes or in the homes of friends, but not in permanent retail locations. Well-known examples of direct selling companies are Tupperware, Avon, Amway, Mylène, etc. Amway, for example, sells its 450 products by means of 3.6 million independent sales agents in more than 80 countries.[2]

Personal selling is an integral part of the integrated marketing communications effort. As a result it should reinforce the effects of advertising, PR, sales promotions, exhibition, direct marketing, etc. Considering the hierarchy of effects model, discussed in Chapter 3, one can state that advertising and PR are well suited for building awareness and appreciation, while the objective of personal selling is rather to assist consumers in learning about the product and to try to advance them to the conative or behavioural phase. In other words, personal selling's goal is to find potentially interested people, to inform them, to illustrate by means of demonstrations how the product works, to build close relationships, to guide customers to a purchase and to offer after-sales service. Selling is no longer the central issue; customer satisfaction is.

The boost of direct selling

Over the past 10 years, the number of direct sellers in Europe has increased from 1,379,194 to 3,120,245, realising a sales figures increase from €5,484 to €8,082.1 million. However, enormous differences between the European countries illustrate that direct selling has more appeal in some countries than in others, as shown in the following table.

Sales figures in million € in 2001	Countries	Range of number of direct sellers across countries
<50	Denmark, Estonia, Ireland, Luxembourg, Portugal, Slovakia, Turkey	62–164,000
50–99	Belgium, Croatia, Czech Republic, Finland, Greece, Hungary, The Netherlands, Norway, Sweden	15,077–140,667
100–499	Austria, Poland, Russia, Switzerland	6,278–400,000
500–999	Italy, Spain	109,000–152,626
≥1,000	France, Germany, UK	182,000–411,000
8,082.1	**Total in Europe**	**3,120,245**

Based on: www.fedsa.be (Federation of European Direct Selling Associations).

Moreover, it has to be mentioned that, notwithstanding the increasing popularity of direct selling, several direct selling companies now look for additional sales channels. Avon, for example, sells beauty products in over 100 countries. These products can be bought through an Avon representative invited to your home, but also directly from Avon on the Web by means of eRepresentatives or in an Avon Salon.[3]

A salesperson has become a manager of customer value. Getting to know customers' current needs, anticipating their future needs, providing customer-oriented solutions and communicating honestly can create trust and satisfaction. Particularly during the build-up and maturity stage of a relationship, sales reps seem ideal for fulfilling these objectives.[4]

Another objective of personal selling is representing the company. A salesperson is an important factor in corporate image-building (see also Chapter 1). Especially in a business-to-business context, customers often only have contact with the salesperson. In these situations, the salesperson is the company, and the way he or she acts, the way he or she dresses, and the car he or she drives form the company image. Equally important is representing the customers by collecting information and feedback from them and passing it to the organisation.

Personal selling has some unique advantages. However, as with all communications tools, some disadvantages can be noted. Table 16.2 gives an overview of both.

In view of the fact that zapping and zipping of advertisements occurs more and more often, that people put a sign on their mailbox refusing advertising leaflets, that they can install a device in their radio to avoid commercials, that direct mail messages may never be opened, but end up in the wastepaper basket, the major advantage of personal selling is the impact it has. A salesperson is much more likely to break through (eventually), attract people's attention and be remembered afterwards. A salesperson can adapt his or her message to the type of customer he or she is dealing with, or in other words bring a targeted message. Depending on the buyer readiness stage the

Table 16.2 Advantages and disadvantages of personal selling

Advantages	Disadvantages
■ Impact	■ Cost
■ Targeted message	■ Reach and frequency
– Information	■ Control
– Demonstration	■ Inconsistency
– Negotiation	
■ Interactivity	
– Amount of information	
– Complexity of information	
– Feedback	
■ Relationship	
■ Coverage	

consumer is at, the salesperson can make the customer aware of the product, give detailed information to increase knowledge, raise interest, preference or conviction by demonstrating the product or letting people use the product, or by negotiating on the price, after-sales service, etc. the customer can be persuaded to buy the product. Furthermore, product lines that are not relevant to the customer can be ignored in favour of other product lines. Another advantage of personal selling is interactivity, or two-way, personal communication. Interactivity has several advantages: the likelihood of miscommunication is reduced, which implies that the message can be longer and more complex. Moreover, the salesperson gets immediate feedback, and can act as the customers' advocate by informing the company of the current and future needs of customers, and about which aspects of a selling proposition are most valued. In this way, the salesforce becomes a resource for the company management to guide policy and marketing strategy formulation.[5] The personal nature of a sales call makes it easier to build a relationship with the customer. Good salespersons first screen potential customers and direct their effort and attention to qualified prospects. This means that, unlike with advertising, waste coverage is reduced to a minimum.

What are the disadvantages of personal selling? First of all, it is quite expensive. Therefore, administrative tasks should be assigned to in-house employees as much as possible so that the distinctive knowledge and capabilities of the salesperson can be fully employed in dealing with customers. As a consequence of this high cost, a company cannot afford to send its salespersons to all customers too often. Therefore, reach and frequency will remain limited. Because of the high cost and the availability of advanced communications technology, many salesforces are being reduced in size. For example, Pearl Assurance, which has one of the last door-to-door insurance salesforces in the UK, is about to cut its entire 1,000-strong salesforce.[6] Another disadvantage is that the company does not have full control over its salesforce, as it has over other communications tools. In the case of a commercial, the company knows exactly which image and message are going to be conveyed. However, this is not the case with a company's salesforce. Different salespersons may represent the company in a different way. Since the salespersons sometimes form the only contact a customer has with the company, inconsistent behaviour or messages may lead to an inconsistent company image and can create confusion as to what the company really stands for.

The personal selling process

Although every sales call will be different, depending on the type of business, the type of customer and the specific customer needs, the personal selling process in general consists of the stages, shown in Figure 16.1.

Locating and qualifying prospects

The first stage in the personal selling process, locating and qualifying prospects, is often also referred to as prospecting, and consists of three steps:[7]

- *Building the prospect profile.* Since a product will never appeal to every customer, the salesperson will first have to think of characteristics that make a good prospect. For example, if you are selling a computer program like 'route planning', which describes the shortest route, the travel time and distance between two locations, good prospects are customers or companies employing staff who are on the road a lot. Bus companies, companies owning a salesforce, taxi organisations, etc. fulfil the identified characteristic.

- *Building a prospect list.* With the prospect profile in mind, a prospect list should be developed. In the example of the route planning program, co-ordinates of bus companies, large industrial organisations, etc. could be selected from Yellow Pages or other directories. Furthermore, the prospect list should be completed with direct enquiries. These enquiries may come from reactions to direct mail actions, advertising, PR activities or visitors of trade shows.

- *Qualifying prospects.* On the basis of the prospect list, prospects have to be identified or qualified. A qualified prospect is someone who needs the product, who has the authority to buy the product and who is able to pay for the product. Qualifying prospects often occurs by making telephone calls after which the prospects can be categorised as a hot, warm or cold lead. Qualifying prospects is important in order not to waste too much time chasing prospects who are neither interested nor able to buy the product.

Figure 16.1 Steps in the personal selling process

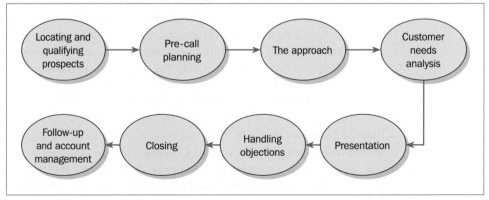

Source: Dalrymple, D.J. and Cron, W.L. (1992), *Sales Management.* New York: John Wiley & Sons. © 1992 Wiley. This material is used by permission of John Wiley & Sons, Inc.

Pre-call planning

Before contacting the qualified prospects, the salesperson has to look for information on the prospect in order to have an idea of the offering the prospect may be interested in. Questions the salesperson should be able to answer are listed in Table 16.3.

Furthermore, the salesperson has to make up his or her mind on what he or she is going to say, and what he or she wants to accomplish (for example, agreement to a trial period, agreement to a meeting, etc.). Another aspect is thinking about how to deal with sales resistance and identify different selling strategies depending on the type of sales resistance faced.[8]

The approach

The approach stage consists of two steps: gaining access and establishing rapport.[9]

- Different approaches can be used to gain access or make an appointment with qualified prospects. Phoning in advance or writing a letter with some additional information attached to it are probably the most successful methods. 'Cold calling', which refers to making a visit without an appointment, is less likely to be successful since most of the time the prospect will not have the time to receive the salesperson.

- Establishing a rapport starts after the salesperson gains entry to a prospect's office. Since the first impression is very important, this step should be approached with care. Adhering to the dress code, offering a business card, showing respect and mentioning the fact that you know that the prospect's time is valuable are good starting points. Furthermore, body language cannot be ignored: words make up only 7% of communication, tone, rate of speech and inflection make up 38%, while 55% takes place with non-verbal action such as facial expression, eye contact and gestures.[10] Finally, salespersons often consider it a good idea to engage in non-business conversation with the prospect to get acquainted. However, research shows that effective, as compared to non-effective, salespersons engage in much less non-business communication and more in providing solutions to the customer's problems.[11]

Table 16.3 Checklist of information needed from prospects

- What is the company's core business?
- What products does it sell?
- Who are the target customers?
- What are the company's long-term objectives?
- Who are the members of the decision-making unit?
- Who is the company's competition? Are these companies customers of ours?
- How well is the company satisfied with its present supplier?
- Can this company give us enough business to make this call worthwhile?
- Is the company's staff technically well trained? Can we help them develop their skills?
- Do we (or can we) use their products in our company?
- Does any one of our managers have personal contact with one of their managers?

Puma had been facing a decrease in its turnover for several years. To halt this trend, to reinforce its position against the other international sports brands and to facilitate the salespersons' job, Puma decided to come up with an original approach. Dutch theatre students were hired to bring about the 'Return of the Puma'. Hysterically yelling, wearing torn and bloodstained clothes as if attacked by a puma, the actors ran into sports shops, threw a torn up envelope on the counter with the accompanying message: 'The beast is loose'. One thing is certain, shop workers remembered the visit and were fully aware of the 'Return of the Puma' campaign. This facilitated the visit of salespersons afterwards since they had something to talk about. About 80% of the prospects took the time to take a look at Puma's new collection. Shop-in-shop and displays have been placed in 22 stores and more than 50 new Puma outlets have been installed. Puma has proved that with a good idea and little money, a lot can be achieved. The campaign was rewarded with a bronze Esprix award.[12]

Customer needs analysis

In this stage the salesperson has to find out what the real needs of the prospect are, what benefits and what value the prospect is looking for. Asking questions in a non-irritating way and careful listening are key aspects here. For example, when General Motors told a Goodyear salesperson all about the characteristics GM wanted the tyres for its Corvette sports car to possess, Goodyear was able to include this information in the design of its tyres and to come up with a tyre that perfectly fulfilled GM's needs.[13]

Presentation

During the sales presentation, the salesperson stresses the product's features and points to benefits for the prospect (cost- or time-saving, user-friendliness, etc.), keeping the prospect's needs in mind. Three general types of presentations exist:[14]

1 *Tailored sales proposals* are customised and take the prospect's needs as a starting point. Obviously this is the most highly recommended type of presentation. However, it is also the most difficult one in which only experienced salespersons succeed.

2 *Organised presentations* suggest that salespersons follow a company-prepared outline or checklist, although they remain free in the wording they use. For new and inexperienced salespersons this is useful because it makes sure that the main points will be covered.

3 *Canned presentations* are strictly structured and prepared in advance by the company. A canned presentation can take the form of showing a slide show accompanied by some remarks, as can be done for example at trade shows, reading from brochures or giving a memorised presentation. The latter can be employed in door-to-door selling, for instance.

Handling objections

Objections are likely to be raised during every sales presentation. Therefore, a salesperson has to think over in advance which objections might be raised and how they can be handled. Table 16.4 describes some techniques that can be used to handle objections.

Table 16.4 Techniques for handling objections

Technique	Explanation
1 Repeat the objection	If the prospect makes a vague objection, ask to be explicit in order to find out whether the objection is real or just an excuse. For example, if the prospect mentions that a competitor offers better service, ask which services the competitor offers and in what way they are better.
2 Agree and counter	This is the 'yes, but' technique. Agree with the objection, but handle an argument that compensates the objection. For example, when a prospect mentions that recharging the battery for the Nokia is annoying, a salesperson can counter by saying that it is not so bad, since the recharge can take place before the battery is totally down (so you can make a mobile phone call at the same time), and that the recharge battery is much cheaper.
3 Boomerang	This technique agrees with the prospect and turns the objection into a reason to buy. If a prospect objects that a certain computer program is almost outdated and that he would rather buy the latest software program, the salesperson can reply by mentioning the fact that since the program has been on the market for a while, all the bugs have been detected, while bugs might be a serious problem with new software.
4 Feel, felt, found	If the prospect turns to emotional objections in the sense that the purchase does not make him or her feel right, this can be handled by mentioning that others felt the same way, but afterwards found it to be the right decision.
5 Denial	In contrast with the other techniques, denial involves contradicting the prospect. This is a risky technique and care must be taken not to offend the prospect. Furthermore, it is only justified if proof can be provided that the prospect is wrong.

Based on: Brassington, F. and Pettitt, S. (2003), *Principles of Marketing* (3rd edition). Harlow: Pearson Education.

Closing

Although closing is assumed to follow naturally from carefully carrying out all the previous steps, a lot of salespersons seem to find closing the sale difficult. In order to recognise the 'closing moment', salespersons should be attentive to signals given by the prospect. These can be gestures (nodding), asking questions (warranties, discounts) or making comments (we need delivery in two weeks). Different closing techniques can be used. They are presented in Figure 16.2.[15]

On the basis of the prospect's earlier agreement to aspects of the sales presentation, the deal is assumed close, in other words the salesperson assumes that the prospect has made the purchase decision and carries on with handling the details of the sale. The salesperson stresses the fact of earlier agreement by stating, for instance, 'You've agreed that our machine can help you save in production time, so let us order it immediately'. As a special case of the assumed close, the either-or close also assumes that the purchase decision is made, but asks the customer for a decision on some details of the close. The social validation closing technique is based on recognition of the influence reference groups can have. Indications of 'Firm X has been using this product for over a year now, and they are very satisfied' can be used to persuade the prospect.

Since it can be assumed that a prospect is more willing to purchase a product from a company if this purchase can be seen as reciprocation for a favour that the selling company has done for the prospect in the past, the norm of reciprocity tries to appeal to this social norm by making the prospect feel obliged to buy. The if–then closing technique

Figure 16.2 Closing a deal

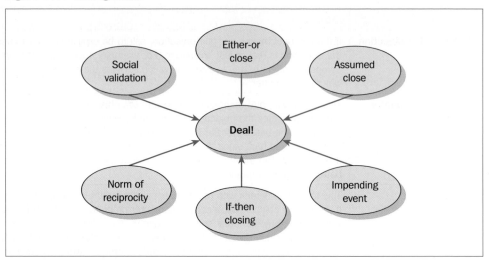

Based on: Hawes, J.M., Strong, J.T. and Winick, B.S. (1996), 'Do Closing Techniques Diminish Prospect Trust?', *Industrial Marketing Management*, 25(5) 349–60.

is derived from the norm of reciprocity and tries to commit the prospect to a sale by offering additional service, a favour or concessions, such as 'If I arrange special credit terms, then you will buy'. By using the impending event technique, a salesperson encourages a prospect to buy before some future event takes place which will render the purchase less favourable for the prospect. The impending event close is based on the scarcity principle of persuasion, which assumes that the more scarce a product is, the more valuable it becomes, inducing a penalty for purchase deferment. Two explanations can be offered for the value increase of scarce products. The first explanation is based on the law of supply and demand, making a scarce commodity a valuable commodity. The second stems from the theory of psychological reactance. According to this theory, consumers react to products becoming scarce because it reduces their freedom to possess it. Therefore, people are more motivated to possess the product that is becoming scarce, making it more valuable.[16]

An Austrian study[17] investigating the influence of the above-mentioned closing techniques on the trust that the prospect has in the salesperson found that trust seems to be highest when no closing technique is used (4.67 on a 7-point scale) and lowest when an assumed or either-or close is used (4.04 and 3.98 respectively). Although this does not mean that it is not beneficial or effective to use a closing technique, salespersons should be aware of the fact that a hard-sell approach using certain closing techniques reduces the prospect's trust in them.

Follow-up and account management

Closing is not the final step. The salesperson needs to take care of the customers after the sale as well. This after-sale service implies that the salesperson has to check whether the customer is satisfied, and this concerns everything related to the product sold: delivery times, the quality of the product, the installation, the training, the billing and the maintanance. He or she has to represent the customer in the company, as well as the company to the customer. Furthermore, the salesperson should cultivate the contacts that he or she has in the company and try to build long-term relationships since the latter are the key factor to future sales. Follow-up does not only consist of delivering after-sale service, but also of call-backs to prospects who did not buy. The salesperson should make notes of the objectives of the prospects, the persons in charge, the prospects' needs and the reasons why the sale was not closed, in order to learn as much as possible of the prospect so that certain mistakes can be avoided in the future.[18]

Sales management, i.e. managing salesforce activities, consists of different activities. They are summarised in Figure 16.3.

Figure 16.3 **Salesforce management**

Planning and organising the salesforce

The first task of salesforce management consists of setting objectives: how many sales does the company want to reach in total and for different geographic areas, different products, etc.? Next, the company has to decide on the type, the size and the structure of the salesforce.

Concerning the type of the salesforce, a company can employ either a direct salesforce (full-time employed in the company) or a contractual salesforce, consisting of independent representatives or agents that sell contractually, on a commission basis. A direct salesforce can be employed internally, as well as externally. The internal salesforce can help customers by phone, by answering frequently asked questions or doing a part of the prospecting job, which reduces the work of the usually more expensive external salesforce who visits the customer. Concerning the choice between a direct and a contractual salesforce, it would be – from an economic point of view – beneficial to hire a contractual salesforce or sales representatives as long as the variable sales commission paid to the contractual salesforce is smaller than the costs associated with a direct salesforce (overhead costs, salary and or commission).[19] In Figure 16.4 this is the case until sales reach point SE, where the cost of the commissions paid to the reps equals the overhead and salary and/or commission costs paid to the company's own salesforce. Because of this, some companies switch between manufacturers' representatives and a direct sales-force several times during the company's main product's life cycle. Sales representatives would be used in the introduction and growth phase, a direct salesforce during the maturity and decline phase, and telephone selling in the later decline phase.[20]

However, the economic aspect is not the only important factor in deciding, for example, whether or not to convert sales representatives to a direct salesforce. The mar-keting environment, product sophistication, sales range and reach, relationships with customers, control, competence, costs of hiring and training good salespersons, and channel access, must be considered as well.[21] The importance of all these factors has to be assessed in order to be able to make a sound decision on the type of salesforce.

Figure 16.4 Salesforce cost

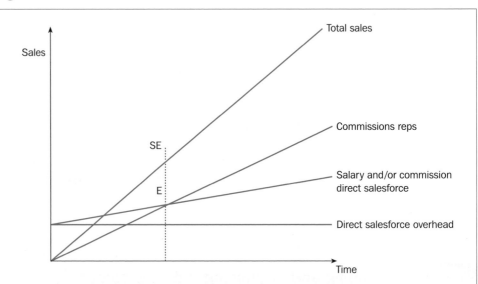

Source: Dishman, P. (1996), 'Exploring Strategies for Companies that Use Manufacturers' Representatives as Their Sales Force', *Industrial Marketing Management*, 25(5), 455. Reproduced with permission of Elsevier.

The optimal size of a salesforce is often computed by means of the workload approach.[22] The different steps in this approach are as follows:

1 Estimate the *call frequency* for different types of customers. Very attractive customers and customers with a decision-making unit consisting of several people will need more visits.

2 Estimate the *duration of a call* for the different types of customers. Customers that purchase very frequently can be serviced with a shorter call.

3 Estimate the *workload to serve all the accounts*.

4 Estimate the *workload one salesperson can handle*.

5 Calculate the *number of salespersons required* by dividing the total workload by the work-load one salesperson can handle.

Suppose a computer company made the following estimates:

1 Call frequency (a year) required for:
- Institutions   3
- Small and medium-sized companies   6
- Large, multinational companies   8

2 Duration of a call:
- Institutions   45 minutes
- Small and medium-sized companies   60 minutes
- Large, multinational companies   90 minutes

3 Estimate the workload to serve all the accounts:
- Institutions $3 \times 45 \times 400 = 54,000$
- Small and medium-sized companies $6 \times 60 \times 500 = 180,000$
- Large, multinational companies $8 \times 90 \times 200 = 144,000$

                                                  378,000 minutes = 6,300 hours

4 Estimate the workload one salesperson can handle:
During an 8-hour workday, a salesperson can devote only a certain percentage of his or her time to sales calls. Travel time, preparation of sales calls, prospecting, etc. also have to be taken into account. Assume a salesperson spends 5 hours a day making sales calls. Available workload a year: 5 (hours a day) × 5 (days a week) × (46 weeks) = 1,150 hours

5 Calculate the number of salespersons required:
6,300 hours/1,150 hours = 5.5, so 6, or 5 + a part-time salesperson need to be employed.

In general, a company has four broad alternatives to structure its salesforce, although a combination or hybrid form also occurs:[23]

1 *Geographically-based.* In this case a salesperson is assigned to a geographic area in which he or she sells all the products of the company.

2 *Product-based.* Due to large differences between the different products, salespersons are assigned to a product or product line in which they can specialise.

3 *Marker or customer-based.* The salesperson sells the entire product line to a specific type of customer, for example banks, schools, steel companies, etc.

4 *Function-based.* The sales job is broken down into different functions in which different people specialise. The customer is then served by a team of specialists: one taking care of the initial contact, another responsible for the installation, another for servicing, etc.

Advantages and disadvantages of the different structures are summarised in Table 16.5.

Colomer, selling Spanish leather

The Spanish company, Colomer Group, manufactures high-quality leather products for clothing, footwear and gloves. Worldwide, Colomer's 15-strong salesforce serves 800 customers (mainly designers), of which 600 are based in Europe. The salesforce is organised on product and geographic lines. In the European leather market, the company employs three sales representatives for clothing, one for footwear and one for gloves. Moreover, an independent sales agent is hired for every country. Most of the small designers require only one to two sales calls a year, while more attention has to be paid to top designers in the Italian market. About 20 days a year are devoted to sales training.[24]

Table 16.5 Advantages and disadvantages of alternative salesforce structures

	Advantages	*Disadvantages*
Geographic	■ Lower travel time leading to lower costs ■ Clarity in who is responsible for whom: one salesperson for one customer ■ No geographic or customer duplication	■ Salesperson has to sell the whole product line ■ Difficult for dissimilar, complex products: no specialisation ■ Perhaps too much attention to easy-to-sell products
Product	■ Experts in the products and the necessary selling processes ■ Better control of selling effort	■ High travelling costs ■ Geographic and customer duplication
Market	■ Better understanding of customer's needs ■ Better control of selling effort to different markets	■ Higher costs ■ Salesperson has to sell the whole product line, but needs of different customers are more similar
Function	■ Customer-oriented ■ Specialists	■ Duplication of calls ■ Need for co-ordination

Based on: Ingram, T.N., LaForge, R.W., Avila, R.A., Schwepker, C.H. and Williams, M.R. (2001), *Sales Management. Analysis and Decision Making* (4th edition). Orlando, FL: Harcourt College Publishers.

Procter & Gamble revamps salesforce

Although many companies have moved from a product- to a customer-centred approach, Procter & Gamble recently reverted from a customer- to a more product-oriented selling force, structuring its sales department exactly as it was 10 years ago. P&G hopes to reverse its two-decade sales erosion by bringing in expert sales persons. As a consequence, a P&G sales rep will no longer be responsible for all paper products, from paper tissues to diapers, but will focus on a limited category within paper products, such as female hygiene products. Most of P&G's competitors hold on to a salesforce structured around accounts or outlets.[25]

Recruiting and selecting the salesforce

Motivation, selling skills and personality variables are important determinants of later sales performance. To assess selling skills, a special scale has been developed consisting of the following components:[26]

1 Interpersonal skills (ability to express oneself non-verbally, speaking skills, etc.).

2 Salesmanship skills (ability to present the sales message, ability to close the sale, etc.).

3 Technical knowledge (knowledge of the market, of own and competitor products, etc.).

Although a lot of research has been conducted on finding the personality traits that will predict good and bad performance, no general conclusions can be drawn. In one of the studies more than 200 purchasing agents were asked what characteristics they did and did not appreciate in salespersons. Table 16.6 summarises the results.

Other research shows that salespersons' effectiveness is higher the more they enjoy interpersonal competition and feel confident in their ability to perform well.[27]

Table 16.6 Appreciation of salespersons' characteristics

Good	Bad	Ugly
■ Honesty	■ Poor listening skills	■ Pushy
■ Patience	■ Wastes my time	■ Smokes in my office
■ Dependability	■ Begins by talking about sports	■ Complains
■ Adaptability	■ Puts down competitors' products	■ Gets personal
■ Admits mistakes	■ Too many phone calls	■ Calls me 'dear' or 'darling'
■ Loses a sale graciously	■ Walks in without an appointment	■ Plays one company against another
■ Problem-solving capabilities	■ Poor presentation	■ Wines and dines me
■ Knows my business	■ Fails to ask about needs	■ Know-it-all attitude
■ Well prepared	■ Lacks product knowledge	■ Bullshitters

Adapted from: Dalrymple, D.J. and Cron, W.L. (1992), *Sales Management*. New York: John Wiley & Sons. © 1992 Wiley. This material is used by permission of John Wiley & Sons, Inc.

However, since the tasks of different salespersons can be totally different, the first thing to do is to write an accurate job description including what activities the salesperson will have to perform and how important each of them is. Next, one has to define the profile of the salesperson most suited to fulfil the job. Communication and negotiation skills may be much more important in one selling job, while technical and problem-solving skills may be crucial in another.

Training, motivating and compensating the salesforce

Before a new salesperson starts dealing with the customers, he or she usually has to participate in a sales training programme. However, also more experienced salespersons can regularly be assigned to a training programme. Training can be formal, organised by an external company or the employing company itself, or informal, on-the-job training. The training can deal with several main topics, such as the history, objectives, strategies, etc. of the company itself, the characteristics of the products that the company sells compared to those of the competitors, the general market situation, the type of customers the salesperson has to deal with, and/or selling techniques.

Although everybody recognises the importance of training and research indicates that training increases sales performance,[28] a lot of companies still have difficulties in designing effective training programmes.[29] In view of the importance of adequate sales training and the fact that sales training usually demands a huge investment, companies should give careful attention to assessing training needs, setting training objectives, co-ordinating training practices and evaluating training programmes in order to get the most out of their investment. Factors that should be taken into account when setting the training budget and deciding on specific training are the expected difference in job performance between trained and untrained sales persons, the length of time the impact of the training is likely to last and the retention rate of trained employees (i.e. how long trained employees remain in the organisation).[30] A good method to increase the effectiveness and efficiency of training programmes is to conduct a sales training evaluation[31] or audit[32] on a regular basis.

Whirlpool's sales training: Live with the brand

Sales training does not always have to consist of classroom courses. On the contrary, on-the-job training or real-life experience with the product can foster sales rep confidence and product knowledge even more. To achieve the latter, Whirlpool rented an eight-bedroomed farmhouse equipped with Whirlpool washers, dryers, dishwashers, microwaves and refrigerators. Sales training consisted of living in the house and taking care of the household, including cooking, doing the laundry and carrying out other household chores.[33]

Although some salespersons may be self-motivated to do a good job, management must recognise that most people need to be motivated, and even more important need to be kept motivated over time. This can be done in negative and positive ways. An example of a negative way is the threat of a pay cut or dismissal. However, in general it is better to concentrate on positive motivators. Offering interesting training programmes as a reward is one way. Another technique is to give salespersons more autonomy. Research indicates that when salespersons feel they have autonomy, job satisfaction is positively reinforced.[34] Furthermore, the behaviour of the sales manager plays a crucial role.[35] Instead of simply telling the salesforce what to do, the sales manager should show what and how things need to be done by providing an appropriate behaviour model that is consistent with both the manager's personal values and the organisational objectives. Empirical research shows that by being such a role model, the sales manager can increase the trust the salesforce has in him or her, which results in a positive impact on job satisfaction and overall performance.[36]

Other motivating factors are meetings at regular intervals, setting sales quota, clearly defining what is expected (no role ambiguity) and avoiding role conflict. Empirical research[37] points out that minimising role conflict and role ambiguity reduces emotional exhaustion. Emotional exhaustion can be defined as a feeling that the emotional 'tank' is empty and as a lack of energy,[38] and is supposed to be the first stage of burnout. Furthermore, a reduced level of emotional exhaustion seems to increase a salesperson's job satisfaction and commitment to the organisation, reducing the intention to quit. Since the salesperson actually has a quite lonely job, the organisational climate has an important influence on motivation. Organising social activities, making the salesperson feel part of the company, and organising sales contests can increase the motivation level. Moreover, research points out that disengaging salespersons who need a boost can be remotivated by being assigned a mentoring job.[39] Mentoring newcomers involves 'exposing' the protégé to internal and external contacts and providing selling skills training. The exposure task may provide recognition for the mentor which may enhance motivation and job satisfaction. Furthermore, it may require the mentor to re-establish a network of internal and external contacts, improving social relations and making the mentor reconnect to the organisation. The selling skills training requires the mentor to update his or her own skills. This may lead not only to increased motivation and satisfaction, but also to improved performance.

Finally, money serves a motivating function. In order not to lose good salespersons to the competition, fair and competitive compensation plans should be defined. Compensation plans perform three functions:[40] they remunerate the employee for his or her work (compensation); they guide efforts towards activities that are consistent with the organisation's objectives and priorities (management and control); they induce the salesforce to dedicate themselves fully to the task (motivation).

Three basic compensation methods exist: straight salary, straight commission and a combination plan.[41] Straight salary plans offer salespersons a fixed amount each pay period. This method is recommended in situations in which it is difficult to estimate the performance of the salespersons, where the job consists of many non-selling tasks or to motivate salespersons to develop relationships instead of aggressively trying to close sales. Straight commission plans provide the salespersons with a percentage of the sales or gross profits that they generate. It may be used to induce salespersons to sell products quickly. Combination plans are most often used and consist of a fixed base salary combined with a commission or bonus. This is an ideal method when a company wants to keep reasonable control of the costs, while at the same time providing an incentive to generate additional sales.

Performance evaluation

The objective of the evaluation or control of salesforce performance is to direct a salesperson's performance in such a way that both the short-term and long-term objectives of the company are reached.[42] In order to evaluate sales performance, salespersons have to fill in call reports indicating how many calls are made a day, which customers were called on, who was visited, what was discussed, which problems were encountered, how the sale is going, etc., as well as a workplan of intended activities and calls. Other sources of information are customer feedback and personal observation.

Performance can be measured in qualitative or quantitative terms. Qualitative performance methods involve subjective evaluations of the salesperson's attitude (satisfaction and commitment), product knowledge, customer knowledge, appearance, absenteeism, communication and presentation skills. A quantitative evaluation method can range from a purely behaviour-based to a purely outcome-based control strategy. Behaviour-based control strategies control the input (how many calls were made), while outcome-based control strategies measure the output (how many sales were generated). Table 16.7 summarises the characteristics of these two strategies.

Table 16.7 Behaviour-versus outcome-based control strategy

Behaviour-based	Outcome-based
■ Monitoring of intermediate states (e.g. sales activities)	■ Monitoring of final output (sales and profits)
■ Close supervision required	■ Minimal supervision required
■ Low span of control	■ High span of control
■ Interference with salesperson's activities required	■ Limited contact with salespersons
■ More complex and subjective evaluation	■ Simple performance plans
■ Fixed remuneration	■ Simple compensation plans (e.g. commissions)
■ Risk for the company	■ Variable remuneration (commissions)
	■ Risk for the salesperson

Based on: Anderson, E. and Oliver, R. (1987), 'Perspectives on Behavior-Based versus Outcome-Based Salesforce Control Systems', *Journal of Marketing*, 51 (October), 76–88; Oliver, R. and Anderson, E. (1995), 'Behaviour- and Outcome-Based Sales Control Systems: Evidence and Consequences of Pure Form and Hybrid Governance', *Journal of Personal Selling and Sales Management*, 25 (Fall), 1–15.

Research indicates that behaviour-based control strategies seem to have a higher motivational impact on salespersons, compared to outcome-based control strategies.[43] Moreover, a high formal and informal control as compared to a low formal and informal control proved to lead to a higher salesperson's effectiveness.[44] Notwithstanding, it has been repeatedly observed that salespersons are not fond of formal controls and that they do not hesitate to behave opportunistically when confronted with behaviour- or outcome-based control strategies. For behaviour-based control measures, salespersons may provide incorrect competitive data, inflated activity reports, etc.; for outcome-based control measures, salespersons may go for less difficult goals such as pay visits to clients or areas that increase short-term but not long-term company results.[45] In reality, a combination of qualitative and quantitative techniques, and a comparison with previous performances and the performances of other salespersons, may give the most accurate picture of how a salesperson is performing and whether or not corrective action is needed. More and more, companies also include customer satisfaction in their control measures.[46]

Integrating personal selling in IMC

In every stage of the personal selling process, sales activities can be supported by other tools of the communication mix. In the prospecting phase, advertising and direct marketing communication can help to build brand awareness and interest. Websites, trade fairs and direct mailings can assist in identifying prospects, and prepare for a more effective sales pitch and sales process. Sponsorship and events, by offering opportunities for corporate hospitality and for bringing the customer into contact with the company and its products, can also reinforce the sales efforts. Furthermore, sales input can enhance the effectiveness of other communication tools. Important first-hand information about complaints, remarks, observations, attitudes, preferences and buying behaviour can be obtained through direct contact with the customer, and can be used to enhance databases and to improve other marketing communication campaigns.

Summary

Personal selling is two-way, face-to-face communication with customers and prospects, the main purpose of which is to assist consumers in learning about the product and to close the sale. It is often used in business-to-business marketing situations and in high involvement consumer product categories. Although it is an expensive communications tool, it has a great impact on customers and it is an excellent instrument for building long-term relationships because of its interactive and personal nature. Different hierarchical steps in the personal selling process can be identified: locating and qualifying prospects, pre-call planning, approach, customer needs analysis, presentation, handling objections, closing the deal, and follow-up and account management. A salesforce also has to be managed. Recruitment and selection of the salesforce, planning and organisation of salesforce activities, training, motivation and compensation, and performance evaluation are important aspects of salesforce management.

Review questions

1 How can personal selling be integrated in the marketing communications strategy?

2 What are the advantages of personal selling?

3 Apply the different stages in the personal selling process to selling a specific product of your choice. What is the interaction of personal selling with other instruments of the marketing communications mix in each stage?

4 By means of which techniques can a sale be closed?

5 On what factors does the organisation of a salesforce depend?

6 How can a salesforce be motivated?

7 How can the effectiveness of a salesforce be assessed?

Further reading

Anderson, R. and Dubinsky, A. (2004), *Personal Selling. Achieving Customer Satisfaction and Loyalty*. New York City: Houghton Mifflin.

Dalrymple, D.J., Cron, W.L. and DeCarlo, T.E. (2003), *Sales Management: Concepts and Cases (8th edition)*. New York: John Wiley & Sons.

Ingram, T.N., LaForge, R.W., Avila, R.A., Schwepker, C.H. and Williams, M.R. (2001), *Sales Management. Analysis and Decision Making (4th edition)*. Orlando, FL: Harcourt College Publishers.

Jobber, D. and Lancaster, L. (2003), *Selling and Sales Management (6th edition)*. London: Financial Times/Prentice Hall.

Journal of Personal Selling and Sales Management.

Case 16

Tele Atlas – the reference in digital mapping

Tele Atlas was founded in the Netherlands in 1984. By 2003 Tele Atlas has become a worldwide leading provider of digital maps of both Europe and North America, covering 388 million inhabitants in 18 European countries and 313 million inhabitants in North America. The company has offices in 21 countries and database partners in Singapore, Australia and Hong Kong. Tele Atlas offers several types of applications which can be categorised in three broad product groups:

1 Navigation products consisting of car navigation systems (global positioning system – GPS – in the car) and navigation software installed in personal digital assistants (PDAs such as in Palm, HP iPaq, etc.).

2 Geographic databases used in geo-marketing (such as for determining where to build a new McDonald's restaurant, where to have additional telephone pylons for GSM providers, where to build additional bus stops, etc.).

3 Location-based services (LBS) (to determine where the nearest ATM is, to find a friend, etc.).

Revenues in 2002 amounted to €78.3 million, an increase of 10% from 2001. Of these revenues, 71.5% can be attributed to the navigation products. Tele Atlas' main competitor on the global digital mapping market is the American company Navtech, which has a turnover of €113 million.

Tele Atlas' sales and marketing teams

Tele Atlas changed its organisation structure in 2003, moving from a territory-oriented to a function-oriented company. This means that from now onwards, the company completely focusses on being a global company in all aspects. Therefore, marketing and sales decisions are no longer taken on a country-level, but are taken on a global level under the supervision of the Sales and Marketing Director Worldwide. Notwithstanding, different sales and marketing teams exist for different countries such as Austria, the Benelux, France, the UK, Germany, Iberia, Italy, Switzerland, Scandinavia and Japan. The size and structure of the sales teams depends on the size of the market. For example, in the Benelux and Scandinavia, the structure of the Sales and Marketing team is as shown in Case Figures 16.1 and 16.2.

Due to a very high tax system (180%), penetration of navigation products in Scandinavia is very low. As a consequence, the Scandinavia Sales and Marketing team is smaller than in other countries. The team consists of a Sales and Marketing Director, an Account Manager who is mainly responsible for the Swedish market and a Sales and Marketing Co-ordinator addressing the full Scandinavian market. So, no division is made according to the navigation and Geo-LBS market.

In larger regions, special account managers take care of the Geo and LBS products. These products are exclusively situated in the business-to-business sector

Case Figure 16.2 Structure of the Scandinavia Sales and Marketing team

and represent a serious investment for the end customers (which are companies and not consumers). Therefore, the account managers will treat every customer on a personal basis and follow a customised approach for each of them. In the Benelux, Tele Atlas has approximately 75 Geo and LBS customers; in Scandinavia it has about 25. For developing the Geo and LBS products, Tele Atlas licenses its digital map databases to software companies or platform owners such as Ad Hoc Solutions and TomTom (formerly known as PalmTop Software).

The Sales Manager Navigation Products deals with car navigation system manufacturers such as Blaupunkt, Clarion, Kenwood, Siemens-VDO, VDO Dayton (formerly known as Carin) and Becker. Car navigation manufacturers provide the hard- and

Case Figure 16.1 Structure of the Benelux Sales and Marketing team

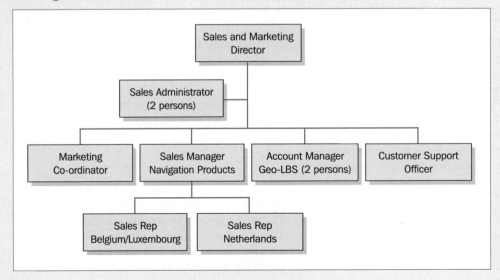

software and work with one or two data providers only. Therefore it is very important for Tele Atlas to convince the leading suppliers of car navigation systems to co-operate. For example, Harman International Industries (known under the brand name Becker) used to work with Navtech, but in October 2002 Tele Atlas succeeded in making a worldwide agreement with the company. By closing this deal, Tele Atlas now co-operates with all leading car navigation system manufacturers. In view of the importance of these co-operations, it goes without saying that building good relationships is a crucial task of the sales manager here.

Besides car navigation system manufacturers, the Sales Manager Navigation Products also pays a lot of attention to car importers and car manufacturers like VW Audi, Mercedes-Benz and Peugeot. The sales reps focus more on the channels, such as car accessory and car electronic dealers (see Case Figure 16.3 and Case Table 16.1). The number of key accounts in the Benelux amounts to 280 while the total number of customers is almost 1,000. A similar ratio of key accounts to total customers can be found in other regions.

In the past it was impossible for Tele Atlas to approach Opel, Ford, Toyota, Citroën, VW Audi and other dealers directly. The company could only have contact with the car importer. However, direct contact is becoming more and more a necessity. For

Case Table 16.1 Distribution of navigation products

Car importer	Main importer for specific car brands in a country
Car dealer	Outlet or chain selling cars and accessories
Car accessory dealer	Dealer selling everything which can be added to, or replaced on, a car
Car entertainment dealer	Dealer selling car radios, mobile phones to be installed in cars, navigation systems, etc. (e.g. ARC, Musical Car, Essec, Quality Center, Helo, Auto Electro, etc.)
Consumer electronic dealer	Dealer selling white, brown and IT products (e.g. Mediamarkt, Dixons, Expert)
Infotainment dealer	Dealer selling books, CDs (e.g. FNAC)
Specialist	E.g. petrol stations

Mercedes, Peugeot and Ford dealers, Tele Atlas has already established this direct approach which offers the company more opportunities for providing direct information. Motivating dealers to pay sufficient attention to navigation CDs and updates is not an easy task. Indeed, at least three disadvantages of car navigation CDs can be noted:

Case Figure 16.3 Tele Atlas' trade channel model for navigation products

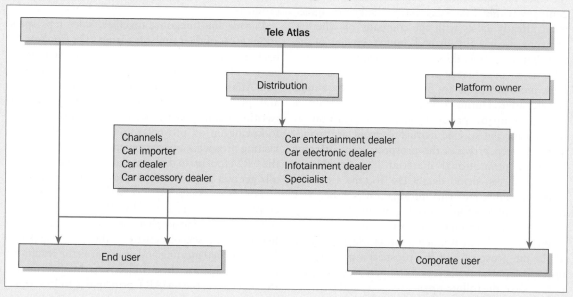

1 The revenues for the dealer are negligible in comparison to the profits obtained on for example cars.

2 The penetration rate of car navigation systems is still fairly low (only 7% of European cars, or 3.5 million of the 50 million cars, are equipped with a navigation system).

3 Customers do not 'pull' the product (the product is not mature yet and customers are unaware of the different digital map providers, they only know the hardware suppliers such as Siemens-VDO, Blaupunkt, etc.).

However, car navigation systems are gradually becoming standard accessories in the business segment, especially in leased vehicles, which means that the market volume is growing. Moreover, more and more car manufacturers are launching special offers as they used to do with airbags, air conditioning, etc. This may induce not only higher sales of first-time CDs, but also an increase in updates and specialty CD-ROMs. Nevertheless, because of, amongst others, the problems of motivating dealers to push the company's products, Tele Atlas has started to approach the customer directly.

The personal selling process for important prospects

The sales rep usually looks for information about important prospects before making contact. Information can be found on the internet and other public sources. If the prospect is an international company, the sales rep will search for information about the company within Tele Atlas to see whether an agreement already exists with the company or whether someone else has already had contact. In view of the fact that Tele Atlas does not have many sales reps, who as a consequence are responsible for a large area, most prospects are first approached by e-mail or telephone. During a first face-to-face contact, a general company presentation and a presentation tailored for the specific market segment are made. The sales rep provides the prospect with different kinds of promotional material like brochures, product sheets, demo data CDs (for the Geo/LBS prospects only), etc. This information is either sent to the prospect before a meeting or supplied during the meeting. The main objective during the first meeting is to obtain as much information as possible about the prospect and the prospect's products in order to supply a realistic and competitive price proposal. Next, the follow-up on prospects and partners is extremely important. Therefore it's necessary to keep track of the prospect and to closely follow up on the proposal made. Tele Atlas Scandinavia, for example, succeeded in gaining Ericsson as a customer by being proactive and having an excellent follow-up of its contacts. Tele Atlas does not prescribe a special follow-up procedure, but normal communication tools such as e-mails, phone calls and visits are used, or in other words, whatever tool is necessary to build a good relationship with the prospect and partner. Larger partners have one main contact person within Tele Atlas and are normally managed by one sales rep only, but another sales rep (from Tele Atlas Europe) is always informed about agreements, special issues, etc. in order to give good and ongoing support to the partner in the best possible way. The account manager regularly has physical contact with key accounts. For example, every month he or she pays a visit to TomTom (Palmtop Software), an important customer in the PDA market, while non-physical contacts take place weekly. In order to create and maintain brand awareness and build a good relationship with prospects and partners, Tele Atlas sends newsletters (paper or electronic) on a regular basis with information about new product releases and other topics. In case customers experience problems, they can get assistance not only from their account manager or sales rep, but also from the Customer Support Officer for platform owners, by means of the extranet in case of Geo and LBS products, or by means of the e-commerce site, Navshop (www.navshop.com) in case of navigation products.

Putting the foregoing together, sales reps spend about 30% of their time preparing sales (looking for background information, preparing presentations, etc.), 25% to 30% discussing and meeting with the Tele Atlas team, 20% on communications (e-mailing and phone calls), 10% on relationship building (writing thank you letters, taking clients to lunch, following up on prospects and customers), 5% on visiting prospects and customers and 5% on keeping the CRM tool up to date (for the latter, sales reps usually get assistance from the sales administrator).

For every sales rep, as well as for all other employees, a Management by Objectives principle is followed. This means that the employee and his or her supervisor sets objectives for the following period in an informal meeting and afterwards the results are evaluated against these objectives. In determining the objectives, the SMART principle is followed, i.e.

objectives should be Specific, Measurable, Acceptable, Realistic and Timeable. Let's take an account manager as an example. In this case, objectives are set concerning sales in existing accounts (e.g. realise sales of €1,480,000 before end of the year), key account management (e.g. visit an important account at least five times a year, increase exposure on the market, forecast future sales, determine opportunities for maintenance contracts, upgrades, etc.) and development of new business and market targets (e.g. make a contract with at least one new internet service provider to use Tele Atlas data, work out a concrete action plan to approach potential customers/partners). Everyone in the sales and marketing team has a mixed salary consisting of a certain percentage fixed salary and a certain percentage commission. Depending on the function within the team, up to 40% of the salary can be commission. For example, if the account manager's objectives are fully met, he or she receives a commission of 40% of the salary on top of the fixed salary, resulting in a salary of 140%. If less than 80% of the objectives are met, the account manager receives zero commission. If 80% of the objectives are met, he or she receives 50% of the commission, resulting in a total salary of 120%. If the objectives are exceeded, for example 125% is achieved, then the commission is doubled, giving the account manager a salary of 180%. Moreover, if a country manages to sell more than its objectives, the country is awarded a bonus. This bonus is shared between the sales reps and the other employees, but half of it goes to the sales reps.

Besides the sales objectives, the sales team is also evaluated on the extent to which training objectives are met (e.g. was a seminar concerning 'How to collaborate successfully with indirect sales channel partners' attended, was a foreign language course successfully completed, etc.) and on skills and competencies. For example, the sales rep will be evaluated to see how he or she scores on:

- effective communication (how he or she makes opinions, feelings and information known to others by speech, writing, bodily movements, etc.);
- being efficient (completing tasks in an orderly and planned way, meeting deadlines, etc.);
- being flexible (dealing effectively with changes in tasks or work conditions);
- commitment (the way of feeling/thinking about the company, colleagues, etc.);

- product knowledge;
- customer-orientation (anticipating and providing solutions to internal and external customers, etc.);
- achievement drive (wanting to get sales results, etc.);
- etc.

On the basis of these evaluations, areas for improvement are specified (e.g. develop a proactive attitude).

Moving towards a customer-oriented approach

Only since the beginning of 2003 did Tele Atlas start to develop a customer-orientation. From now onwards the company focusses its marketing communications on both its business partners and the end-consumer. Its main communications objective is 'to increase the consistency, frequency and quality of communication both internally and to the outside world while making sure that the messages given are unambiguous and worldwide identical'. The main message the company wants to deliver is that 'If there's a way, Tele Atlas will find it'. Even more, it wants customers to know that Tele Atlas offers the most accurate, most up-to-date digital maps available, and as a consequence is 'the reference in digital mapping'. Moreover, it wants to make people aware of the necessity of updates since 20% of the road network changes every year. Therefore the old CDs are pretty soon outdated: new roundabouts are missing, street directions have changed, etc.

A first direct communication tool to the end consumer consists of the e-commerce site, Navshop, which was launched in February 2003. The system collects e-mail addresses and keeps track of all visitors in the sense that a customer is immediately recognised when he or she revisits the site. Before the launch of Navshop, the company only possessed names and addresses of approximately 130,000 of the 3.6 million European navigation system users. As soon as more addresses are available, Tele Atlas can start with direct mailings which can be personalised towards certain segments of the market. Since the marketing budget per country does not exceed €1 million, above-the-line communications are not really an option for the company.

By combining a push (towards the dealers) and pull (towards the end consumer) strategy, Tele Atlas hopes to build more awareness in end consumers, to enhance its image both in the business-to-business and the business-to-consumer market, and to become 'the reference in digital mapping' in the minds of all its target groups.

Questions

1 How do the specific characteristics of the digital mapping market influence the organisation and activities of the sales representatives?

2 Is the fact that more and more car dealers can be approached directly, instead of indirectly through importers, an advantage or a disadvantage for Tele Atlas? In what way will this influence the activities of the sales representatives?

3 How do you evaluate Tele Atlas' move to the end consumer (launch of the Navshop, etc.)? Should it engage in more business-to-consumer communications? Would this consumer approach harm its relationships with its distributors?

4 On the basis of which criteria is the salesforce organised? Would you advise the use of other criteria?

5 How do you evaluate the motivation and compensation system? Can you think of alternative (and better) ways of motivating and compensating the salesforce?

6 How is the performance of the sales reps evaluated? Can you think of alternative evaluation systems? Which would you recommend?

Sources: Tele Atlas Annual Report 2002; www.teleatlas.com; Interviews with Laurent De Hauwere (Marketing Director Europe), Pia Steen Hansen (Sales and Marketing Co-ordinator Scandinavia), Vincent Maenhaut (Sales and Marketing Director Benelux) and Sandra Deblander (Marketing Co-ordinator Benelux).

References

1 Ingram, T.N., LaForge, R.W., Avila, R.A., Schwepker, C.H. and Williams, M.R. (2001), *Sales Management. Analysis and Decision Making* (4th edition). Orlando, FL: Harcourt College Publishers.

2 www.amway.com

3 www.avoncompany.com

4 Jap, S.D. (2001), 'The Strategic Role of the Salesforce in Developing Customer Satisfaction Across the Relationship Lifecycle', *Journal of Personal Selling & Sales Management*, 21(2), 95–108.

5 Cross, J., Hartley, S.W., Rudelius, W. and Vassey, M.J. (2001), 'Sales Force Activities and Marketing Strategies in Industrial Firms: Relationships and Implications', *Journal of Personal Selling & Sales Management*, 21(3), 199–206; Wotruba, T. (1996), 'The Transformation of Industrial Selling: Causes and Consequences', *Industrial Marketing Management*, 25(5), 327–38.

6 Denny, C. (2002), 'Pearl's Entire Sales Force To Go', *The Guardian*, 2 December.

7 Dalrymple, D.J., Cron, W.L. and DeCarlo, T.E. (2001), *Sales Management* (7th edition). New York: John Wiley & Sons.

8 Hunt, K.A. and Bashaw, R.E. (1999), 'New Classification of Sales Resistance', *Industrial Marketing Management*, 28(1), 109–18.

9 Ingram, T.N., LaForge, R.W., Avila, R.A., Schwepker, C.H. and Williams, M.R. (2001), *Sales Management. Analysis and Decision Making* (4th edition). Orlando, FL: Harcourt College Publishers.

10 Dalrymple, D.J. and Cron, W.L. (1992), *Sales Management*. New York: John Wiley & Sons.

11 Gellerman, S. (1990), 'The Test of a Good Salesperson', *Harvard Business Review* (May–June), 64–72.

12 *Esprix jaarboek*, 1999, 62–3.

13 *The Wall Street Journal*, 15 March 1984, 33.

14 Ingram, T.N., LaForge, R.W., Avila, R.A., Schwepker, C.H. and Williams, M.R. (2001), *Sales Management. Analysis and Decision Making* (4th edition). Orlando, FL: Harcourt College Publishers.

15 Hawes, J.M., Strong, J.T. and Winick, B.S. (1996), 'Do Closing Techniques Dimnish Prospect Trust?', *Industrial Marketing Management*, 25(5), 349–60.

16 Brehm, S.S. and Brehm, J.W. (1981), *Psychological Reactance: A Theory of Freedom and Control*. New York: Academic Press.

17 Hawes, J.M., Strong, J.T. and Winick, B.S. (1996), 'Do Closing Techniques Diminish Prospect Trust?', *Industrial Marketing Management*, 25(5), 349–60.

18 Dalrymple, D.J., Cron, W.L. and DeCarlo, T.E. (2001), *Sales Management* (7th edition). New York: John Wiley & Sons.

19 Dishman, P. (1996), 'Exploring Strategies for Companies that Use Manufacturers' Representatives as their Sales Force', *Industrial Marketing Management*, 25(5), 453–61.

20 Dishman, P. (1996), 'Exploring Strategies for Companies that Use Manufacturers' Representatives as their Sales Force', *Industrial Marketing Management*, 25(5), 453–61.

21 Dishman, P. (1996), 'Exploring Strategies for Companies that Use Manufacturers' Representatives as their Sales Force', *Industrial Marketing Management*, 25(5), 453–61.

22 Cravens, D.W. and LaForge, R.W. (1983), 'Salesforce Deployment Analysis', *Industrial Marketing Management* (July), 179–92.

23 Ingram, T.N., LaForge, R.W., Avila, R.A., Schwepker, C.H. and Williams, M.R. (2001), *Sales Management. Analysis and Decision Making* (4th edition). Orlando, FL: Harcourt College Publishers.

24 Brassington, F. and Pettitt, S. (2003), *Principles of Marketing* (3rd edition). Harlow, Essex: Pearson Education.

25 Bittar, C. (2001), 'P&G Eyes Sales Force Revamp Amid Slump', *Brandweek*, 42(36), 32.

26 Rentz, J.O., Shepherd, C.D., Tashchian, A., Dabholkar, P.A. and Ladd, R.T. (2002), 'A Measure of Selling Skill: Scale Development and Validation', *Journal of Personal Selling & Sales Management*, 22(1), 13–21.

27 Krishnan, B.C., Netemeyer, R.G. and Boles, J.S. (2002), 'Self-Efficacy, Competitiveness, and Effort as Antecedents of Salesperson Performance', *Journal of Personal Selling & Sales Management*, 22(4), 285–95.

28 Roman, S., Ruiz, S. and Munuera, J.L. (2002), 'The Effects of Sales Training on Sales Force Activity', *European Journal of Marketing*, 36(11/12), 1344–66.

29 Honeycutt, E.D. (1996), 'Conducting a Sales Training Audit', *Industrial Marketing Management*, 25(2), 105–13.

30 Honeycutt, E.D., Karande, K., Attia, A. and Maurer, S.D. (2001), 'A Utility Based Framework for Evaluating the Financial Impact of Sales Force Training Programs', *Journal of Personal Selling & Sales Management*, 21(3), 229–38.

31 Lupton, R.A., Weiss, J.E. and Peterson, R.T. (1999), 'Sales Training Evaluation Model (STEM)', *Industrial Marketing Management*, 28(1), 73–86.

32 Honeycutt, E.D. (1996), 'Conducting a Sales Training Audit', *Industrial Marketing Management*, 25(2), 105–13.

33 Anonymous (2001), 'Welcome to the Real Whirled: How Whirlpool Training Forced Salespeople to Live with the Brand', *Sales & Marketing Management*, February, 87–8.

34 DeCarlo, T.E. and Agarwal, S. (1999), 'Influence of Managerial Behaviors and Job Autonomy on Job Satisfaction of Industrial Salespersons, a Cross-cultural Study', *Industrial Marketing Management*, 28(1), 51–62.

35 Deeter-Schmelz, D., Norman-Kennedy, K. and Goebel, D.J. (2002), 'Understanding Sales Manager Effectiveness. Linking Attributes to Sales Force Values', *Industrial Marketing Management*, 31, 617–26.

36 Rich, G.A. (1997), 'The Sales Manager as a Role Model: Effects on Trust, Job Satisfaction, and Performance of Salespeople', *Journal of the Academy of Marketing Science*, 25(4), 319–28.

37 Babakus, E., Cravens, D.W., Johnston, M. and Moncrief, W.C. (1999), 'The Role of Emotional Exhaustion in Sales Force Attitude and Behavior Relationships', *Journal of the Academy of Marketing Science*, 27(1), 58–70.

38 Babakus, E., Cravens, D.W., Johnston, M. and Moncrief, W.C. (1999), 'The Role of Emotional Exhaustion in Sales Force Attitude and Behavior Relationships', *Journal of the Academy of Marketing Science*, 27(1), 58–70.

39 Bolman-Pullins, E. and Fine, L.M. (2002), 'How the Performance of Mentoring Activities Affects the Mentor's Job Outcomes', *Journal of Personal Selling & Sales Management*, 22(4), 259–71.

40 Barkena, M.G. and Gomez-Méjia, L.R. (1998), 'Managerial Compensation and Firm Performance: A General Research Framework', *The Academy of Management Journal*, 41(2), 135–45.

41 Ingram, T.N., LaForge, R.W., Avila, R.A., Schwepker, C.H. and Williams, M.R. (2001), *Sales Management. Analysis and Decision Making* (4th edition). Orlando, FL: Harcourt College Publishers.

42 Borghgraef, S. (1996), 'The Effects of Sales Force Control Systems on Salespersons' Job Performance and Sales Organization Effectiveness: An Empirical Test', in Beracs, J., Bauer, A. and Simon, J. (eds), *Marketing for an Expanding Europe, Proceedings of the 25th EMAC Conference*. Budapest, 89–97.

43 Baldauf, A. and Cravens, D.W. (1999), 'Improving the Effectiveness of Field Sales Organisations, A European Perspective', *Industrial Marketing Management*, 28(1), 63–72; Piercy, N.F., Cravens, D.W. and Morgan, N.A. (1997), 'Sources of Effectiveness in the Business-to-Business Sales Organization', *Journal of Marketing Practice: Applied Marketing Science*, 3, 43–69.

44 Borghgraef, S. (1996), 'The Effects of Sales Force Control Systems on Salespersons' Job Performance and Sales Organization Effectiveness: An Empirical Test', in Beracs, J., Bauer, A. and Simon, J. (eds), *Marketing for an Expanding Europe, Proceedings of the 25th EMAC Conference*. Budapest, 89–97.

45 Ramaswami, S.N. (2002), 'Influence of Control Systems on Opportunistic Behaviors of Salespeople: A Test of Gender Differences', *Journal of Personal Selling & Sales Management*, 22(3), 173–88; Ramaswami, S.N. (1996), 'Marketing Controls and Dysfuncitonal Employee Behaviors: A Test of Traditional and Contingency Theory Postulates', *Journal of Marketing*, 60 (April), 105–20.

46 Jap, S.D. (2001), 'The Strategic Role of the Salesforce in Developing Customer Satisfaction Across the Relationship Lifecycle', *Journal of Personal Selling & Sales Management*, 21(2), 95–108.

CHAPTER 17

E-communication

Chapter outline

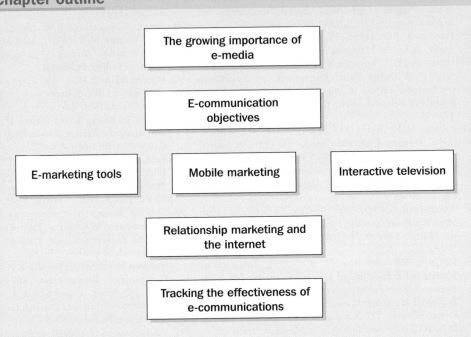

The growing importance of e-media

E-communication objectives

E-marketing tools

Mobile marketing

Interactive television

Relationship marketing and the internet

Tracking the effectiveness of e-communications

Chapter objectives

This chapter will help you to:

- Assess the importance of the internet and other new media as interactive communications tools
- Distinguish the different types of e-marketing tools related to different communications objectives
- Understand the internet as an advertising medium, its success factors, and the different types of internet advertising
- Learn about new evolutions such as mobile marketing, interactive digital television, blogging and podcasts
- Understand how the internet contributes to relationship marketing
- Learn how the effectiveness of e-communications can be measured

Introduction

Mass marketing communications techniques have dominated communications strategies for decades. Gradually, direct marketing principles have been adopted that allow access to each member of the target group on an individual basis. The next stage in this evolution is the trend towards real interactivity, i.e. not only is the marketer capable of communicating with his or her target group on a one-to-one basis, but also individual members of the target group are capable of responding to, and interacting with, the sender of the message. Although some direct marketing communications techniques also allow a certain degree of interactivity, the increasing penetration of internet and mobile phones and the rise of new interactive media such as interactive television are bound to change the nature of marketing communications interactivity. Moreover, people's media attention is fragmenting. Mobile phone penetration in Europe now exceeds 85%. So, marketers have to follow them into the new media they are consuming. The internet is fundamentally different from traditional, and even direct, marketing communications tools: consumers can go all the way from awareness to interest to desire to action, all within the same medium and within the same session.[1] Its unique characteristics and current evolutions are further explored in the first section of this chapter. The next sections focus on the different interactive media a marketer can use for different communications objectives, with specific sections dedicated to new evolutions such as interactive television and mobile marketing. Related topics such as relationship marketing and loyalty marketing using the internet are also considered. Specific ways to measure the effectiveness of internet presence is discussed in the last section. Although the internet has the capability to support all aspects of company processes (including logistics, e-commerce, e-procurement, etc.), this chapter will specifically focus on the use of new media for marketing communications purposes.

The growing importance of e-media

The internet refers to the computer network infrastructure enabling the exchange of digital data on a global scale. Worldwide 395 million hosts[2] are interconnected through cable and telephone networks. Through historical developments (the internet was first a military tool developed to make communication possible in case of nuclear wars and was later adapted by academics to share and exchange information) and intentional efforts, nowadays the internet is a unique, independent medium that is not owned or operated by a commercial or government body. Although the internet is also the network serving e-mail applications, news servers (newsgroups), ftp (file transfer), gopher (pure text-based information exchange) etc., it is often used as a synonym for the World Wide Web (WWW), the interactive and graphical communication medium invented by Tim Berners-Lee, physicist at the European Centre for Nuclear Research (Cern).[3] The Web is characterised by the use of hypertext mark-up language (HTML) that allows documents consisting of text, icons, sounds or images to be shared by different users, regardless of the computer operating system they use. The hyperlinks (text- or image-based) make it possible to navigate quickly through documents and pages by simple mouse-clicking. The growth of the WWW can be attributed to the user-friendly, consumer-operated pages utilising this hypertext capability.[4]

In April 2006 there were, on a global scale, 68.4 million domain names[5] (an indication of the number of websites). Worldwide, 1 billion people (291 million of whom are in Europe) are connected to the internet. The penetration of the internet, i.e. the number and percentage of people that have access to the net, in European countries is discussed by Danny Meadows-Klue below. Scandinavian countries have the highest share of their inhabitants on-line in Europe, with penetration rates of more than 60%. When looking at absolute figures, Germany (48.7 million online), the UK (37.8 million), Italy (28.8 million) and France (26.2 million) are the largest European players.

Europe: online advertising crosses tipping point

By Danny Meadows-Klue, Danny@DigitalStrategyConsulting.com[6]

As online advertising becomes mainstream marketing, Danny Meadows-Klue reflects on the diversity of today's digital landscape across Europe, and how the biggest changes are yet to come.

Markets cascade

The big switch to bringing online advertising into the mainstream media mix continues across Europe. Online advertising has already crossed into the mainstream of media in eight European markets, and a clear cascade effect is underway. Key opinion formers in each European country are embracing online and causing their markets to leap. Our latest market tracking study – which collates online adspend from 14 countries – confirms the total online advertising comfortably broke €4.5bn in 2005 confirming the consistently steep growth. The world of marketing is changing; and the web is at the very forefront of how marketing is evolving.

Market share: the key metric to watch

The UK continues to lead the European markets, both in terms of total online spend and the share the web takes of all media spend within the country. Share is the key metric in determining how sophisticated the market is and in the UK this has reached 8.4% following twelve consecutive record-setting quarters of recorded spend. Belgium, Denmark, Finland, France, Germany, The Netherlands and Poland have also crossed the 2% threshold for the share the web takes in their national market, with Germany, France and the UK accounting for more than 80% of the overall European market.

However, with audiences across the continent spending 20% of their 'media time' online, it's no surprise marketers are turning their attention to the web, now that key hurdles including the standardization of advertising formats, the arrival of video and the reach of web marketing, have all now been crossed.

Drivers of growth

Several markets have had ten or more successive quarters that have each seen new records set for the amount invested in online marketing. Regardless of what happens in the wider marketing community, online is on the rise; rapidly. We have isolated more than twenty drivers of the industry's growth. The relative mix of drivers varies with each country, and although the size of the potential market is set by the online population and its engagement with the channel, the scope varies greatly.

The explosive growth of search engine listings is a common theme across Western Europe and Scandinavia, but alongside this, dozens of other online advertising formats also drive growth.

▶

Online's share of total media spend across Europe

The market share of online vs other media is the most revealing way of seeing how the use of digital has advanced. Across Europe share is rising, and the rate varies from around 1% to 7.8% in the most mature markets.

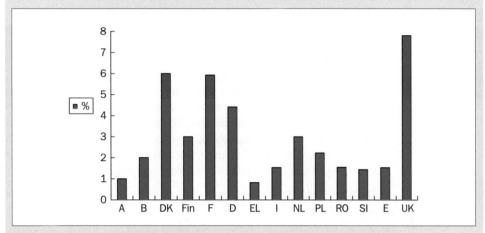

Source: IAB Europe / Digital Strategy Consulting 2006

There's a new generation of web banners that are using sophisticated 'behavioural targeting' techniques to learn about the viewer's interest and provide tailored messaging,. Television-like commercials can now be easily produced, allowing TV assets to be rebroadcast online and the campaign stretched further. The creative power of the engaging 'rich media' formats that take commercial messages across the whole web page has given creative directors a new freedom in design. And the standardization of advertising formats and some of the workflow processes, has removed a barrier that long held agencies back from recommending the web.

But that doesn't mean every advertiser has discovered what online can do. Like any marketing innovation, there are some firms who lead, and some who follow. Online may be enjoying a high – and rapidly growing – share of advertising spend in Western and Northern Europe, but this hides a more interesting insight: most European firms are yet to start advertising online at all. Our figures represent a simple average of an entire country. Dig deeper and you'll find companies who have become experienced in online advertising putting 20% or more of their budgets into the web, while others in the same business sector may be yet to even start.

Building brands; generating response

Ironically, one key challenge that help the industry back was its diversity; it can support every aspect of the marketing mix. Smart online marketers realize it's about more than having a successful website. They have discovered how online marketing can support every aspect of a customer's journey – from the early stages of raising awareness of a brand, through the sale itself, and into the after sales service. That's why the proportion of investment into online continued to grow as more and more firms discover the power of web advertising as both a branding and direct marketing medium.

Nigel Morris, President Worldwide of the communications agency Isobar, is clear the growth is unstoppable: 'The world of media is changing and agencies across Europe need to be braver in crafting a new mix of media that really explores the rich variety of digital tools available and the vast European audiences you can reach with them'.

Advertisers: time to look again

If the last time you thought about online was six months ago, then it's time to take a fresh look. This is a medium that does anything but stand still and the reason it remains the fastest growing marketing channel is the power of its results. Whether for brand building or direct response, more and more marketers are turning to online, upweighting its role and using the expanding range of tools to create the right digital media mix for them.

With the majority of consumers connected in most European countries, and the amount of time they spend online constantly growing, the internet has already become the third most used media channel. Across much of Europe it averages 20% of the total time we spend with all media, a staggering leap in the focus we give to it.

Among many demographics, it has leapt even further, becoming a staple part of their lifestyle, in everything from entertainment and shopping, to keeping up with the news and talking with their friends. Media consumption patterns have suddenly shifted, and marketers are catching up. Against a background of media fragmentation, and falling advertising effectiveness in television, it is no surprise that this ceaseless growth of online proves attractive. However, dig deeper and there are even more compelling reasons:

- Daytime is primetime – audiences that could never be reached before are now available and attentive
- A medium of a thousand niches – combines exceptional lifestyle targeting with a mass reach
- Accountability and making budgets stretch further – a strategic advantage of digital channels

'It's no longer a question of whether to invest; it's now a matter of how much', says Michael de Kare-Silver, Managing Director of the AKQA agencies across Europe. 'Marketers have realised there is no escaping the enormous impact that Digital is having. The key now is to work out how to fit this new opportunity into the rest of the marketing mix.'

Factfile: top 3 markets

France

44% of population online (21.6m users) and 75% of connections are on broadband. 59% of users claim they shop online and €1.1bn was spent in online advertising in 2005. The annual increase was 74% and 5.9% of all advertising media spend now goes online. 'Among IAB France's great achievements in 2005, the NetImpact 3 study has showed the direct impact of online advertising when it comes to sell goods in retail stores and supermarket', explains Bruce Hhoang of IAB France. 'This brand new measure paves the way to new commercial media potentiality and confirms the power of online advertising. We're also proud to announce a great 2005 first semester report in online ad spend, with a 70% growth compared to the same period in 2004.'

Germany

58% of population online and 60% of connections are of the faster broadband type. 58% of users claim they shop online and at least 14% of all media time is spent online. Total advertising spend was €885m in 2005, rising 60% year on year to account for 4.4% of all advertising media spend.

United Kingdom

62% of the population is online (29.3m users), and 71% of their home connections are broadband. 18m people shopped online and more than £1.3bn was spent online, making the UK the largest market in Europe. The market is growing 62% year on year and accounting for 7.8% of total advertising spend. 56% of the investment goes into search engines.

Search engines: a revolution in customer acquisition

Search accounts for more than 40% of all online advertising spend in many countries including the UK and USA. It's changing the nature of customer acquisition marketing and the simplicity of search – any manager can try it out with a credit card – means you can experiment, test and refine easily. In the UK search is now bigger than the total national radio industry, and we believe will top consumer magazines when spend for 2006 is announced. 'We expect in 2006 to see search becoming much more integrated with other advertising media, not only across the online platform, but also with offline campaigns. Clients are beginning to see the benefits of incorporating search into campaign planning instead of treating it as a stand-alone medium', says The Search Works – Nick Hynes, CEO.

Search has revolutionised direct marketing. It is the purest marketplace; buyers meet sellers and do so at the very moment the buyer is actively looking. The efficiency this creates has not been lost on either the advertiser or the web user and is one of the keys to its sudden appearance as a mainstream business tool. Search delivers the most qualified of prospects; a self-selecting audience that is ready to act. The commercial propositions this taps into have become much more sophisticated than an immediate sale. They could be to encourage an appointment (such as making a request to test drive a car), make deeper product information available (downloading a brochure), building a customer database (by inviting users to subscribe to a newsletter), or making the purchase itself. These customers have sought out those brands. They're actively seeking information, and hence 'ready to act'.

Media substitution: clear evidence from the UK

As online's share of the market has grown, spend is being drawn from other channels. Although some of this spend is migrating from the print editions of publications – particularly consumer magazines and directories – much is moving to the internet pure play firms, in whose hands the market remains highly concentrated.

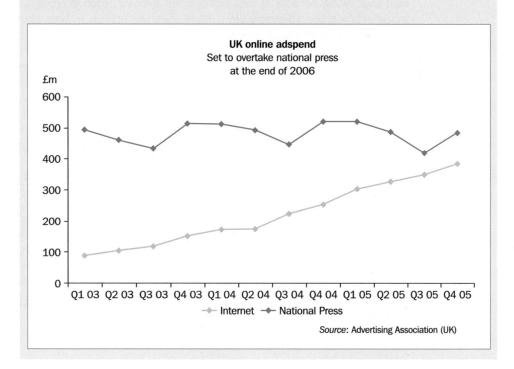

UK online adspend
Set to overtake national press
at the end of 2006

Source: Advertising Association (UK)

Direct mail is suffering severely as customer acquisition budgets move to search, and retention budgets move to e-mail marketing (the spend on which is not currently tracked). Classified advertising in newspapers and magazines is finally migrating to the web, with recruitment the largest single advertising sector online in several markets, and much of the advertising spend evaporating in favour of free to air models such as CraigsList.org, or disintermediation as consumers access company websites directly.

Which industry sectors have invested the most in online advertising?

Financial services and recruitment are the largest two client categories in many countries. Their products are a natural fit with the early web environments and as the firms refocused their marketing to include the web, audiences found the services useful and a virtuous circle developed.

This picture has changed a great deal. Initially the sectors that explored online advertising were IT and telecoms. In the mid nineties their products were a perfect fit for the first wave of web users whose interests and employment were heavily skewed in favour of the same sectors. Next it was the turn of the sectors whose products can be reviewed, inspected, compared and even sold, without the need to touch them. The early explosion of book and CD retailing relied upon customers knowing the title of what they wanted to buy and then following links to online bookstores. Travel and financial service products were natural early migrants as well, and although every sector has its own early adopters, the migration in spend only happens when enough firms realise the potential of the new marketing channel.

Although some industry sectors embraced online early on, others were much slower. There were structural barriers in the industry that had to be conquered before some sectors would begin to move en masse. For example, the lavish advertising creative of the motoring industry rendered poorly in the early online advertising formats, but the rapid take-up of video and 'rich media' creative formats since 2002 has tackled this. Fast moving consumer goods (FMCG) held back initially because of concerns over the audience reach of online, and because the model of how online advertising drove offline sales was unclear. In both cases these barriers have now been lifted enough to give the brands the confidence to invest.

Small and local firms found the internet particularly difficult to engage with and most held back for a long time. Smaller firms found it difficult to engage with the internet because there was no roadmap and many of the routes they tried proved to be a combination of time consuming, expensive, or slow to deliver results. Initially not enough customers were using it in enough ways. However all this has now changed. Any firm can enjoy a basic site for almost nothing, and they need little in the way of technical skills to achieve this. That's why managers in smaller and 'local' firms are increasingly focusing on the web, and in particular search engine advertising, as a way to attract customers.

Where next?

With the market share in the UK topping 8% in 2005, it seems reasonable to assume that online will cross the 10% threshold by the end of 2006. The last ten years has shown how the UK can behave like a laboratory for the rest of Europe. In 2006 online will overtake national press; now the question is: could the growth even match the scale of television. Few marketers in the UK would bet against that today. The revolution in media consumption has happened, and now online marketing is crossing its tipping points in each European market.

Danny Meadows-Klue is a founding partner of Digital Strategy Consulting, a boutique practice that helps media owners get the right strategy for their online businesses. Danny@DigitalStrategyConsulting.com

E-communications objectives

While we are witnessing more enthusiasm for the integration of internet marketing tactics in today's marketing plans, few brand managers have a clear idea of which of these tactics are most appropriate for accomplishing which marketing objective. In many cases, a trial and error process is undertaken, often heavily influenced and stimulated by whichever tactic the internet or advertising agency is trying to sell to the brand manager. As this calls for a need to develop an overall framework that allows marketers to categorise the different digital marketing tactics, InSites Consulting has developed such a framework, on which the following is based.[7]

Basically the e-marketer can focus on four specific marketing goals when turning to digital tools:

■ *Generating brand awareness*: putting or reinforcing the brand in the evoked set (i.e. the set of brands that is considered when the need or desire for the product or service arises) of consumers. In line with most research and cases found on this subject, stimulating brand awareness is ideally achieved via on-line advertising, content sponsorship, advergames and viral marketing.

■ *Shaping brand image and brand attitudes*: defining, reinforcing or changing the set of associations that differentiate the brand from competing products and improve consumers' knowledge and judgement about a brand. According to literature on the subject, shaping brand attitude is best achieved by brand sites, on-line advertising, anchor deals, e-mail marketing, mobile marketing, on-line contests and peer-to-peer games.

■ *Generating trial*: attracting new buyers to the brand by attracting brand switchers (i.e. consumers of competing brands) or consumers who have never tried the product category before. Trial stimulation implies an increase in the brand penetration rate in a certain market. Mobile marketing, e-mail marketing, on-line contests, e-couponing and e-sampling are the best on-line marketing instruments to atain this objective.

■ *Creating loyalty*: influencing consumers' buying behaviour in the sense of increasing the number of satisfied and committed buyers. Striving for customer loyalty is also a cost-saving strategy as research indicates that the cost of attracting new customers can be as much as six times greater than the cost of retaining customers. E-mail marketing, brand websites, virtual communities and certain e-rewarding games and on-line loyalty promotions contribute to the objective of generating and sustaining brand loyalty.

Generating traffic to a website is often stressed in publications but is not actually a marketing communications end goal, except for e-commerce sites for which traffic is essential. Of course it is important to engage customers by the e-marketing actions that a company undertakes, but in the end site traffic will have to lead to one of the four objectives defined above. This is also the case for increasing market and consumer knowledge through employing e-direct marketing and database programs.

In the next section each type of e-marketing tactic is described and illustrated with examples.

E-marketing tools

Marketers have a large number of different e-marketing communications tools at their disposal. In this section we describe each instrument of the e-communications mix. The multimedia capabilities of the net allow advertisers to use content, graphics, movement, audio and video. Almost every traditional communications tool has an on-line twin, take for instance e-coupons or on-line contests and seminars. Since almost every internet user has his or her own e-mail address, marketers can build a direct communication line with customers and prospects at lower costs than traditional direct marketing. The huge success of mobile telecommunications in Europe opened new opportunities for companies to use wireless advertising to reach their target groups. Digital interactive television is for most European countries still in a test phase, but the UK is the leading nation for this new medium and other countries will surely follow soon.

Brand websites

Brand websites are sites with specific brand-related information and/or services. A brand site can be used to communicate with the target groups and also as a platform that enables interaction with, or between, customers or the collection of individual customer data, for instance by letting them subscribe to receive e-newsletters. Coca-Cola encourages site visitors to register and leave their personal data in exchange for 'goodies' like games, downloads (screensavers, . . .) etc., (Plate 24). On the one hand, evidence has been found for the brand attitude forming capabilities of a brand website that delivers information and applications that enforce the brand positioning of the brand.

Hilton Hotels created an emotional website (hiltonjourneys.com) to support the hotel chain's corporate brand image. The three main parts of the website are, in an interactive and animated way, constructed around the idea that travel should pamper, empower and entertain.

In the 'entertain' section the site focuses on Hilton's sponsorships such as the Grammy Awards or Extreme Makeover Home Edition. In the 'pamper' section more information on the Hilton beds can be found as well as more details on Hilton's resorts and spa vacations as well as weddings at Hilton. The 'empower' section describes Hilton's services for business travellers such as the Wi/Fi high-speed internet access, Starbucks coffee, in-room fit kits, the Hilton eat right menu and business centre. Alongside the visitor interaction into each section testimonial video interviews of celebrities are integrated into each part of the site. Site visitors can also leave their personal information to receive weekly offers from the hotel chain or immediately book a stay at one of Hilton's hotels.

On the other hand, brand websites are also essential to sustain or increase effectively the loyalty of user groups. A brand website is necessary for 'maintenance communication' all year round, 24 hours a day, with loyal customers and brand lovers. If heavy users of a brand feel bonded with the brand and the company, they will also expect to find more product information on the internet and might even want to contact the people behind their favourite product. However, merely having a website is in most cases a waste of budget since only the leading brands supposedly benefit from spontaneous traffic towards their brand sites. Brands with a moderate or low unaided brand aware-ness are likely to be disillusioned by the reach of their website. Hence, websites need continuous traffic-generating efforts. Successful traffic generators are on-line advertis-ing, search engine optimisation and including the URL on corporate media (stationery such as business cards, letter headings and brochures), on packaging and in off-line advertising. The way a site is marketed has a substantial impact on the types of customers it attracts. Loyal customers are attracted by referrals, whereas 'butterflies' are attracted by promotional discounts and general untargeted banner advertising.[8]

A brand site does not have to be continuously hosted but can be used for a short period during a product launch. These temporary sites are also called micro-sites. The growing complexity of corporate sites and the limitations of banner advertising have induced advertisers to develop this new way of providing richer on-line experiences with more complex messages (than traditional media). A micro-site is a small website that exists for a specific purpose, and often doesn't contain more than fives or six pages. Companies often buy a specific URL related to the launch or promotion of a new product or ser-vice and then use the micro-site to enhance brand experience. Retailers frequently use micro-sites to highlight certain goods out of their massive assortment. Because of the many possibilities of adding content, audio, video and interaction, micro-sites have many advantages over banners and other standardised ad formats. But just like a stand-ard brand or company site, micro-sites need promotion to get found and noticed by the target group. Micro-site-based campaigns have a limited shelf life that is comparable to any other advertising campaign. For companies selling low-interest or impulse-buy products, such as insurance companies or fast-moving consumer packaged goods such as soft drinks and candy bars, micro-sites are an interesting alternative to large and expensive websites that often demand enormous efforts to generate traffic to them.

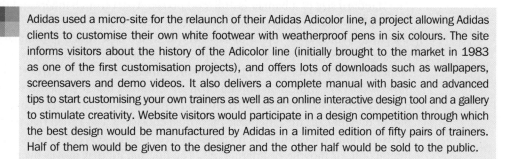

Adidas used a micro-site for the relaunch of their Adidas Adicolor line, a project allowing Adidas clients to customise their own white footwear with weatherproof pens in six colours. The site informs visitors about the history of the Adicolor line (initially brought to the market in 1983 as one of the first customisation projects), and offers lots of downloads such as wallpapers, screensavers and demo videos. It also delivers a complete manual with basic and advanced tips to start customising your own trainers as well as an online interactive design tool and a gallery to stimulate creativity. Website visitors would participate in a design competition through which the best design would be manufactured by Adidas in a limited edition of fifty pairs of trainers. Half of them would be given to the designer and the other half would be sold to the public.

Search engine optimisation

The biggest issue with having a brand or company website is to attract visitors to the site. Unlike traditional advertising with its interruptive nature, on-line marketing com-munications often require an action from the consumer as the internet is a pull medium. To find this traffic marketers use a combination of off-line and on-line marketing com-munications techniques. One specific on-line technique is to improve the listing in search engines. As 47% of web users tend to use search engines to find on-line informa-tion and the top 10 search query results get 78% more traffic than the others, this so-called 'search engine optimisation' is important to many companies, not least to on-line stores and e-commerce sites. Some web agencies are specialists in registering sites in top and niche search engines and in improving their rankings at the engine. For this purpose they use specific metatags, page titles, reciprocal linking, hidden keywords and multiple domain names as these are the factors that influence search engine robots' behaviour.

BMW Germany was penalised by Google after a search engine software engineer found out that the car manufacturer had been trying to influence search results and improve the ranking of its site when Google users searched for 'used car'. BMW admitted using so-called doorway pages that attract spiders (software agents searching the net for content that are used by search engines to make an index of new web pages). Although BMW immediately removed the pages after the news came out, it was banned from top search results and degraded to a low page ranking position.

Source: BBC News, BMW given Google 'death penalty', 6 February 2006.

Another way of increasing search engine share-of-voice is keyword buying, one of the on-line advertising techniques explained below.[9]

Online advertising

Online advertising can be defined as commercial messages in standard formats on specific rented spaces on websites of other companies. Different formats can be discerned, among which the banner is the best known. Banners are graphic images (animated gifs or Java-applets) used as advertisements. Several standard formats (defined by number of pixels) exist: some are known as buttons (very small rectangles or squares), rectangles and skyscrapers (a thin and small format, typically along the right side of a web page). The standard size of a banner is 468×60 pixels. Apart from banners and their variants, other forms such as pop-ups and interstitials exist. Pop-ups are banners that appear in a separate window on top of or beneath (in which case called pop-unders) the visited website. Interstitials are ads that appear temporarily when loading a new web page. Sometimes they cover part of the browser; sometimes they take over the entire screen. Superstitials are additional pop-up browser windows that are opened when a new web page is opened; they are very intrusive and irritating. Interstitials can be static (an image file) or dynamic. In the latter case they often consist of a so-called rich media ad, i.e. an ad using animated content such as audio/video, Flash, Java, etc. to create special effects, interaction, or moving or floating ads. The floating ad that moves over the browser in an animated way and is usually very effective in getting the attention of the website visitor is also called 'shoskele' or overt.

A specific type of targeted on-line advertising is keyword buying. This is advertising on large search engines such as Google that is triggered by specific keywords and search terms and which appears alongside the search results. These 'smart ads' ensure higher impact and low waste for advertisers looking to target genuine potential customers. This type of advertising uses the unique benefits of the Web as a pull medium.[10] Unlike the other types of online advertising that are CPM-based (cost per thousand) ad formats, keyword buying uses a PPC model (pay per click). This means that advertisers using keyword buying on Google adwords, Yahoo! search or MSN search only pay for each click – through on their sponsored link. The prices per click vary and are set by bidding on keyword combinations. The more popular the keyword, the more expensive. Search engine marketing (SEM) is one of the fastest growing online advertising businesses. Another smart way of linking is affiliate marketing or affiliate networking. This is often used by on-line retailers. Amazon.com, the on-line book and CD shop, employs this technique most successfully, with more than 1 million who offer small banner advertisements on their sites that direct the visitors to their sites to the Amazon site. Each partner earns 4–8.5% referral rates depending on the number of items shipped every time a customer clicks on the banner and buys at Amazon. To Amazon this affiliate network accounts for a quarter of its revenues.[11]

The cost of on-line advertising differs substantially between the different formats, with pop-unders, banners and skyscrapers the cheapest and rich media ads, interstitials and keyword buying the most expensive. Of course this strongly correlates to the effectiveness and impact of each ad format. Table 17.1 shows the performance of each ad format according to a study by Romeo and Nyhan.[12]

Several research findings confirm the summary in Table 17.1. Although standard creative rectangle banners still dominate the on-line advertising industry, they have poor click rates in relation to other creative sizes such as the pop-up and skyscraper.[13] The larger the ad format, the more visible and more effective the ad will be.[14] Size also accommodates more interactivity and technological flexibility. Skyscrapers and large rectangles were shown to be three to six times more effective than standard banners in increasing brand awareness and message association.[15] Rich media ads showed considerably more stopping power compared to non-animated ads, were more memorable and were twice as good for lifting brand awareness, message association and brand preference.[16] If the ad is active, engaging and moves viewers from passive viewing to active processing, the memorisation capability is generally high.[17] According to a study by Pfizer and Dynamic Logic, the time people spend with their mouse navigating and interacting through the ad (interaction time) is an exact indicator of brand favour. Interaction depth, defined as how deep a person delves into an ad, shown by, for example, how many tabs have they clicked on, is an indicator of purchase intent.[18] Rich media ads are best when selling the product requires a 'show and tell' element (just like TV advertising).

It is remarkable that the level of effectiveness in general strongly correlates with the perceived annoyance of an ad format by site visitors, as shown in Table 17.1. Only

Table 17.1 Performance of, and viewers' annoyance at, online advertising formats

Ad format	Performance*	Irritation*
Banner	*	*
Rectangle	**	***
Skyscraper	**	**
Pop-up	***	*****
Pop-under	**	****
Rich media ad	****	****
Interstitial	****	****
Keyword buying	*****	*

* The number of stars in the columns represents the general performance and annoyance caused for each ad format.

Based on: Elkin, T. (2003), 'Size matters; so does prize', Advertising Age, January, 13; Dynamic Logic (2001), 'Branding 101: an overview of branding and brand measurement for online marketers', (March), www.dynamiclogic.com

keyword buying proves to be very effective without being irritating. Irritation by ad formats cannot be ignored because of its possible negative effect on brand attitude. Although larger ads are noticed more and communicate better, they are also often too disruptive for consumers, for instance due to their slow download. Consumers might take away a negative perception of the ad and, in consequence, of the advertised brand.[19]

Lancaster, a global cosmetic brand, launched its first on-line promotion campaign for its new pure skin care product line in Spain. The Lancaster website is very basic and, in fact, not much more than an on-line store and the brand did not have local websites to promote its global brand. The on-line campaign was preceded by a traditional media campaign in typically glossy magazines. Although the main goal was to increase the number of sales, it also had other objectives: launching the new skin care product, creating a client database and driving users to selected retail outlets. Lancaster placed banners on major websites for women to target Spanish women aged between 17 and 35. The click-through rate of this campaign was 2.4%, a good result thanks to the right targeting. The campaign was supported by a micro-site offering a product presentation, an automated on-line test and free advice from the dermatology department. Thousands of on-line consultations with the dermatologist through e-mail created a highly reliable database of potential customers, since users obtained feedback on their personal skin problems.

Less standard advertising formats are advertorials, content sponsorship and anchor deals. These three formats are not supported by media sellers and so result from direct negotiations with each specific website owner. Advertorials are informative ads with an editorial approach but also a clearly identified advertiser. They can be used to communicate product and services news or attributes, third party endorsements, research or trends and can include visuals and links to the site of the advertising company. The content of the advertorial should be informative and engaging to reinforce messages in traditional media. They can also be linked to promotional activities where consumers are encouraged to read content to win prizes. Advertorials improve the opinion about the sponsoring company and increase awareness, influence image and encourage interest.

Content sponsorship consists of placing an advertiser's message in an area on a website that stands out from other advertisements, for instance a fixed and exclusive presence in a chosen section that is relevant to the advertiser's brand. Area and topic sponsorships are the two most common types. Homepage restyling, an adaptation of the look and feel of a web page using the colours, corporate style and images of the advertisers is another popular form. Many consumer product companies are moving towards this kind of on-line alliance strategy after being confronted with the long development timeframes and the high costs involved with building and maintaining an own-brand site, not to mention the high cost of driving and retaining web traffic.

Procter & Gamble has a long tradition of associating products with content and content syndication dating back to radio days and early 1950s television (the first 'soaps' were initially sponsored by P&G which explains their name). For its Bounty brand, P&G used a modernisation of the same concept via on-line content sponsorship of 'Real Families, Real Fun' which featured a real-life view of family activities. The programme gathered input from a nationwide panel of young families by offering home projects, recipes, trips and entertainment ideas. The programme was launched on several portals and category sites and ran for six months. All programming carried the message 'this editorial programme is made possible by Bounty' and the content was syndicated, resulting in higher exposure across the Web. The programme was linked to Bounty's new website, launched simultaneously with 'Real Families, Real Fun'. By clicking on the Bounty logo, families could learn what the brand had to offer them.

Anchor deals represent the presence of a brand on certain content sites and portals as a supplier of brand-related content continuously for a long period. In exchange for co-branding on all Pepsi bottles, in-store displays and so on, Yahoo! handled all the technical assistance for the Pepsistuff.com website. The site became the centrepiece of the most successful campaign Pepsi ever ran. Consumers logged on to the site by entering a code found under the caps of Pepsi bottles. Each code was worth 100 points and could be redeemed for prizes such as DVDs and digital rewards (music downloads, credits at Yahoo! auctions, etc.) More than 50% of redeemed prizes were digital, saving Pepsi lots of money. Pepsi also saved $10 million by not having to print prize catalogues and the anchor deal with Yahoo! resulted in 2.9 million people providing their name, e-mail address, zip code and date of birth, a valuable database for organising polls, launching new products such as the Pepsi Blue (the new Pepsi-with-berries fusion launched in Spring 2003) and promoting the music celebrity endorsement with Britney Spears and Shakira.

Targeting on-line advertising

It has been proved that on-line advertising is most effective when it is well-targeted. Marketers can target broadly using content targeting or specifically using several criteria:

- *Context/content targeting*: using web page content and context to target on-line ads. For example, Unilever targeting people interested in cooking and lifestyle (predominantly women aged between 20 and 49) for its brands Hertog, Knorr, Magi and Blue Band by using advertorials and content sponsoring on the website of *Life & Cooking*, a television cookery programme in the Netherlands.[20]

- *Web server/browser*: a web server or ad server can deliver ads based on the profile of the user connected to the site, including IP (Internet Protocol) address, browser, operating system, and the date and time of the server request. A marketer can display targeted ads based on these simple characteristics, for instance IP addresses reveal the geographic location of the user.

- *Registration/customer data*: a website or ad network can show targeted ads based on user registration data (obtained from memberships, participating in contests, purchases, etc.).

- *Clickstream/behavioural data*: as visitors click through a site or different sites, ad networks and sites can show ads that are related to the kind of content the internet user is viewing.

- *Collaborative filtering*: on-line ads can be shown to a particular user based on matching his or her profile with other users that share common interests.[21]

Global beer brand Budweiser sponsored the Happy Hour on CBS Marketwatch. Interestingly enough there is no direct link between the message and the content of the site itself: Bud on a site dedicated to preparing and filing taxes or on stock portfolio site sections. This seems to ignore the consensus view of the definition of contextual relevancy. However, Bud chose to sponsor the right timeframe (quitting time on Friday, the right moment for most business people as they will soon be leaving for the weekend and will probably stop first at a pub or a grocery store).

On-line events and seminars

Even face-to-face communications tactics such as exhibitions, trade shows and events have been translated to an on-line environment. Victoria Secret, the American undergarment brand, introduced one of the first commercial on-line events in 1999 when it held its web-based fashion show. It was announced in advertisements in the *New York Times*, TV commercials during the Super Bowl football game and other traditional advertising media. The on-line event drew 1.2 million visitors, an 82% increase in web traffic. In subsequent years the on-line fashion shows were continued. On-line seminars, with experts that first give an exposition and afterwards participate in chat sessions, are also becoming more common in business-to-business markets and professional segments. Chapter 15 on exhibitions and trade fairs has a section on on-line trade fairs. As broadband penetration increases, bandwidth problems will disappear and on-line events, workshops, seminars and narrowcasts will gain popularity as they save time and money both for the organisers and the participants and allow a much wider and more international reach.[22]

Advergames and on-line games

On-line games are a rich media type of brand-related on-line entertainment used as a tool for brand interaction and experience. In other words, advergames use interactive game technology to deliver embedded messages to consumers. The advertising message can then become an integral part of playing the game. Advergames are often used in combination with e-mail and viral marketing campaigns as their entertainment value increases the value perception of the mail receivers and tends to evoke consumer responses beyond their own personal interaction, such as forwarding the message to friends and relatives. In this way advergames can reach up to four times the initial number of gamers through referrals. Games can drive traffic to websites, for instance candy producer Nabisco's website dedicated to games, Candystand.com, is attracting 3.5 million visits per month, with each visit lasting on average half an hour. Games can also be used to expand the company's marketing database while engaging consumers in a bit of fun, like Guinness did on its brand site when launching the Extra Cold sub-brand.[23] Subscription-based on-line games, are an effective way of capturing data and constructing an opt-in database of names and e-mail addresses.[24]

Developing an on-line game or advergame carries a price tag that can range from a few thousand euros (to re-skin already developed game engines with simple graphics and game play) to several thousand euros to build a proprietary game with sophisticated

3D graphics and complex artificial intelligence. Adapting a successful existing game for the marketer's purpose is less expensive and less risky but also limits the degree of impact and brand immersion. On top of the production cost, marketers should also consider a placement and maintenance cost that can vary from nothing for a self-hosted turn-key game to thousands of euros a month for full-service hosting on another site.[25]

Although the costs of creating an advergame clearly exceed those of rich-media banners, interaction time and brand immersion should be considered as well. On-line games and advergames are tools that permit the on-line marketer to build brand awareness and brand image through a more interactive user experience.[26] For example, players of the Jurassic Park III game played for an average of 19 minutes, which is obviously a guarantee of a bigger mind-share among the target groups. The retention value of advergames is said to be 10 times higher than the retention value of traditional broadcast commercials. They allow voluntary self-induced exposure to brand communications and are a non-intrusive and non-interruptive way of internet advertising. Depending on the approach, a high percentage of players don't even see the game as 'advertising'.[27] Advergames are also used to teach consumers the prime benefits of a product and increase their brand knowledge by making a brand's core values and attributes central in the on-line game.

It is important to note that over-billboarding of a game should be avoided, particularly if teens and twenty-somethings are the main target groups. A game should be built around a brand's values and not carry its logo throughout the entire game. The game idea should be melded with the characteristics of the brand and make sense for the products as well as for the gamer.[28]

Vicks, your diary defender

Procter & Gamble used an advergame on the internet for Vicks in the UK to support the launch of its Vicks First Defence nasal spray (sold in pharmacies). The microgel nasal spray fights colds at the early signs by spraying a substance with low pH on viruses at the back of the nose. The advergame is an adaptation of a classic destroyer game to fit with the Vicks' characteristics: the gamer flies over a daily planner and has to destroy the viruses as well as protect very important days in the agenda, such as, Valentine's Day. An original way of promoting a pharmaceutical product.

Viral marketing

Quite often the success of advergames and on-line games strongly depends on the strength of on-line word-of-mouth advertising, also called 'word-of-mouse' advertising. Viral marketing is the set of techniques that is used to spur brand users and lovers, game participants or advocate consumers among the target group to promote their favourite brand to friends and relatives. They are put to work to spread the word about the brand or product by using e-mail, SMS, 'tell or send to a friend' buttons or other referral tools on websites. Viral marketing attempts to harness the strongest of all consumer triggers: personal recommendation. Viral marketing uses the snowball principle and the typical network nature of the internet strongly supports the quick exponential growth in the message's exposure and its influence in a rather effortless way. Just like viruses, viral marketing strategies take advantage of rapid multiplication to explode the message to thousands or millions of 'victims'. One of the first and probably most successful viral campaigns was set up by Hotmail. By simply using the free web-based e-mail package, consumers hawked the message as every message they sent contained a Hotmail ad ('Get your own private free e-mail at http://www.hotmail.com'). Hotmail grew to 12 million accounts in its first year, 1996. Compared to the results of its print campaigns (100,000 new subscribers) this result was impressive.[29]

Member-get-member action can also be considered as a viral technique when its goal is to enlarge an e-mail database in a very short time. An example of this kind of viral action was the Dove Moments campaign for the Unilever brand in The Netherlands. Using the website dovemoments.nl, visitors could request a 'Dove moment' (a package of Dove samples) for a friend (referral) by composing a personalised e-letter. A hundred thousand sample packages were delivered in the first month of the campaign, resulting in a new database of the same size in only one month.[30] Viral marketing helped on-line auction site eBay to cut its acquisition costs as half of eBay's customers come from viral marketing. It also helped to cut retention costs as research showed that those customers acquired through friend and relative referrals cause lower costs than those acquired by traditional advertising efforts. Other typical viral examples are screensavers (remember the Bud Frogs and Dancing Hamsters/Babies), e-cards and rich media e-cards, and funny commercials, pictures or cartoons. Viral sweepstakes, often linked to games, are also popular. In these, contestants' chances of winning increase if they get their friends to sign up for the game as well. Lastminute.com had great success with these kinds of on-line marketing tactics. The Easter Groovy Movie campaign consisted of a micro-site that allowed users to create a short animated movie that could then be sent to five friends via e-mail once the sender's details had been entered. All entrants were then registered for a weekly newsletter. In an earlier seasonal promotion around Valentine's Day, the Office Flirt Test promotion, 150,000 visitors to the site resulted in a total of 1 million web pages viewed (so-called page impressions).[31]

Viral marketing campaigns work best between groups with strong common interests. This implies that they allow marketers to spread selective messages to selective groups. By using viral marketing tactics carefully, marketers may avoid negative reactions and gain an excellent return on investment by increasing the reach of a marketing message to a targeted group that is much larger than the audience originally covered. Viral marketing is increasingly popular for three reasons. First, entire social networks are on-line today as a large number of everybody's friends and family members have started to use the Web or will soon. Second, contacting individuals on-line is virtually cost-free and it is possible for each individual to contact hundreds more without much effort or cost.[32] According to a survey, 81% of those who receive viral messages pass them on to at least one other person, and almost half of those receivers are likely to pass the message along to two or three other people.[33] Finally, for 68% of surfers, word-of-mouth is the top source for learning about new websites, which puts referrals and viral marketing in second place after search engines (74%) and above links on other sites (65%), ads (46%) and on-line advertising (45%).[34]

HP uses 'fishy' tactics

Hewlett-Packard developed an engaging interactive application that encouraged the use of the multiple original print (MOP) function on HP printers as opposed to printing a single copy and taking photocopies. The MOPy Fish is a lifelike virtual pet goldfish swimming around the user's desktop in its own aquarium. To survive, just like a Tamagotchi, the fish needs regular feeding and attention. Each day MOPy Fish owners are rewarded points and each time they use the multiple print option on their PC they gain 20 points. The points can then be exchanged on the HP website for aquarium accessories which in turn enhance the environment of the fish. MOPy Fish is an example of strategic viral marketing that successfully increased awareness and use of the multiple original print function, drew users to the HP website and created a digital one-to-one relationship between HP and its customers. Only a few months after the launch the pet fish was downloaded more than 16 million times and it is in the *Guinness Book of Records*.

Just as with off-line word-of-mouth advertising, word-of-mouse is not driven by marketers and it is hard to keep control over the messages. This could imply negative associations with the brand and a dilution of brand assets as the same strengths could work against a company if dissatisfied customers share their anger with their contacts. Therefore marketers should consider pre-testing viral marketing campaigns on a small scale. If viral messages contain audio or video components, some internet users might consider them as bandwidth and mailbox space-consuming 'spam' (unwanted and unsolicited e-mail).

On-line contests and sweepstakes

Related to on-line games are the internet versions of contests and sweepstakes. They are particularly effective for generating enthusiasm, building name recognition and rewarding long-time customers. On-line contests often have an off-line component, for instance in TV or radio ads to get attention or on packaging, leaflets, etc. to communicate the contest. Sometimes codes such as access codes or lottery numbers are distributed either in or on packaging but relate to the brand's (promotional contest) website. A contest should arouse a customer's interest and demand interaction. E-contests can just draw winners at random (sweepstake) or ask for a certain skill or creative involvement (contest). For example, Heineken held a beer-mat contest asking participants to create and design their own beer mat. Just like advergames, on-line contests seem to be growing in popularity.[35] Keys to success are an appropriate play value of the contest and appropriate incentives to participate. The latter is determined by the business a company is involved in and the goal of the contest. For instance, if the objective of the contest is to create a customer database, a company should offer one of its products as the prize. This relevancy will attract the right entrants, since providing an incentive to people who can and will buy your products and services should be the goal. A contest or sweepstake with a high number of participants might look successful at first sight but if it attracts the wrong people, those who enter any contest just to win something, the campaign won't be effective and customer acquisition costs will rise. Prizes should also create a sense of value, uniqueness and emotional appeal to winners. If the prize is large enough or attractive enough, people will take the time to enter and fulfil requirements such as registration and they will even tell their friends and colleagues about the contest. Of course, contests and sweepstakes will only work if people know about them, and if you want people to come back regularly, it will be necessary to award prizes on a daily or weekly basis.[36]

Frozen dessert retailer Häagen-Dazs created interest around its new dessert, the Dazzler, with an on-line contest and promotion. With every purchase in a Häagen-Dazs outlet, consumers received a game card during a two-month period. On the card was a code that when entered on the Häagen-Dazs website took customers to a game page where they could play an on-line match-and-win game. Site visitors had to select three of the nine 'Dazzlers' on the page, which revealed a prize. If the three prizes revealed were the same, the visitor won that prize. Häagen-Dazs was giving away $11 million worth of prizes, including a three-year Jaguar XK8 lease, $5,000 shopping sprees, free ice cream for a year and gift certificates for the Banana Split Dazzler. Contest participants were asked to register with information such as age, zip code, and e-mail address to enter the contest.[37]

E-sampling and e-couponing

Companies (especially those in the consumer packaged goods business) can use the internet as a means of promoting their products by sampling or couponing, for instance banner advertising leads consumers to a data-capture page where they leave their details to receive samples or coupons. Traditionally, brands had a few options for reaching consumers with a sample: sampling at events, on street corners, in the mailbox, with newspapers or magazines, on door hangers, and in-store sampling. Now the internet adds a new way of sampling (combined with mail addresses) at a lower cost per converted person because of the opt-in request. E-sampling gives marketers the option to carry out extremely accurate one-to-one demographic, geographic and psychographic targeting, whereas traditional sampling is often based on convenience targeting (street corners, shop) or neighbourhood clusters (mailbox sampling). There is also less waste or duplication as 'one sample item per household' can be controlled and consumers make a conscious choice to request a sample themselves. As targeted users can be part of a marketing database that tracks their behaviour and engages them over time, e-sampling is less of a one-shot and more part of a CRM campaign. Companies can also get real-time, instant consumer feedback on usage and likeability of the sample without high costs or much effort.[38] For some businesses e-sampling can be completely handled on-line, for instance software companies providing free downloads or demo versions of their software, often with an expiration time of 30 to 60 days. On-line music and book stores like Amazon allow their customers to sample 30-second clips of music or fragments of books before ordering.[39]

E-coupons are the on-line equivalent of print coupons and can be redeemed on-line (on e-commerce sites) or printed. They can be delivered via e-mails or via a website. Just as with e-sampling, they offer the ability to monitor the user's online shopping behaviour (if redeemed on-line) and can reach an audience that would not bother to cut out print coupons in newspaper or magazine advertisements. Apart from these advantages, on-line couponing can also save money compared to the off-line printing costs and advertising costs. E-couponing also makes it possible for the advertiser to experiment with split/run tests (choosing which offer/design combination has the best response results and then quickly adapting the coupon's value or message) and to make immediate and automatic responses by tailoring the coupons to the demographic profile of the consumer. Research found that about 30% of the web population uses on-line coupons.[40]

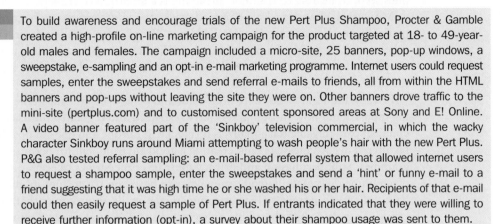

To build awareness and encourage trials of the new Pert Plus Shampoo, Procter & Gamble created a high-profile on-line marketing campaign for the product targeted at 18- to 49-year-old males and females. The campaign included a micro-site, 25 banners, pop-up windows, a sweepstake, e-sampling and an opt-in e-mail marketing programme. Internet users could request samples, enter the sweepstakes and send referral e-mails to friends, all from within the HTML banners and pop-ups without leaving the site they were on. Other banners drove traffic to the mini-site (pertplus.com) and to customised content sponsored areas at Sony and E! Online. A video banner featured part of the 'Sinkboy' television commercial, in which the wacky character Sinkboy runs around Miami attempting to wash people's hair with the new Pert Plus. P&G also tested referral sampling: an e-mail-based referral system that allowed internet users to request a shampoo sample, enter the sweepstakes and send a 'hint' or funny e-mail to a friend suggesting that it was high time he or she washed his or her hair. Recipients of that e-mail could then easily request a sample of Pert Plus. If entrants indicated that they were willing to receive further information (opt-in), a survey about their shampoo usage was sent to them.

E-mail marketing

The one 'killer' application that is most used by internet users is e-mail. Just as in traditional direct marketing, e-mail marketing can be used inbound and outbound.[41] In fact, e-mail marketing is basically not much more than using the internet and e-mail for direct marketing practices. The net provides speed, flexibility and low costs compared with traditional direct marketing media and customisation and full individualisation are much easier and cheaper. With these features, e-mail marketing usage has grown significantly during the last five years. One of the clear reasons for this surge in volume and spending is that e-mail marketing is more effective in terms of response than traditional direct mail or other web campaigns such as banners or interstitials. Click-through rates of commercial e-mails range between 2% and 10%, and response figures of 32% are achieved for highly targeted personalised messages and up to 18% for e-mail newsletters. Banner click-through rates are still far below 1% and a traditional average direct marketing response rate is 2%.[42] Moreover, it is estimated that an e-mail marketing campaign costs between 60% and 65% less than a traditional postal direct marketing campaign by eliminating postage, paper and printing expenses. This also implies that e-mail made it possible to start using direct marketing for lower-cost items and that communicating with less frequent buyers now is profitable.[43] E-mails reach their destination within a few seconds of sending, and responses will also typically arrive within 48 hours of a communication. Compared to the usual six weeks response time for a traditional direct mail campaign, this speed of delivery and response is clearly another advantage of e-mail marketing.[44]

Marketers also appreciate the easy and inexpensive way of tailoring messages to groups of customers or even individuals. Content of e-mails and newsletters can be customised to specific customer interests and needs and running tests on small samples to refine messages before finally mailing them to the entire target market is cheap. Research has shown that personalisation has profound effects on results. The average click-through rates can be expected to double when messages are fully personalised.

Personalisation effects grow over time: where impersonal e-zines (electronic magazines sent by e-mail or e-newsletters) are still able to reach curious people, only the personalised ones seem to be able to continue attracting the attention of readers.[45]

Measurement and tracking of e-mail marketing effectiveness can be carried out automatically and if necessary at a detailed level. There's also a link with viral marketing as it is easy for receivers of a promotional e-mail message to pass it along to other readers simply by forwarding it to friends or relatives who they think might be interested in the offer.

Privacy and legal issues were once a hot and controversial issue in the e-mail marketing industry but now most markets have restricted and regulated the use of commercial e-mails, spam (unsolicited e-mails) is forbidden in Europe and opt-out possibilities should be offered in each message sent, creating a good environment for permission-based programmes. Still, permission and privacy must be cornerstones of every e-mail marketing programme. Successful e-mail campaigns are based on trust. 'Opt-in' means that users have voluntarily agreed to receive commercial e-mails about topics that they find interesting. They do so by subscribing on websites and checking a box. 'Opt-out' means that users have to uncheck the box on a web page to prevent being put on an e-mail list. 'Opt-in' is better than 'opt-out' as the quality of the database or list will be better.[46] Companies should always stress the purpose of collecting addresses and guarantee that the information will not be disclosed to third parties or misused. However, the real threat for e-mail marketing is overuse due to its low cost and reputation for outperforming other on-line actions and traditional direct marketing. Some analysts predict that response rates will seriously be driven down due to each consumer's inbox being flooded by thousands of commercial messages and massive opting-out. Another limitation of the new direct marketing medium is the lack of good opt-in e-mail databases. Supply is limited which results in companies renting the same lists, with bombarded and tired consumers as a consequence. Often the first and most difficult challenge for marketers who want to launch an e-mail campaign is to create a good target database of prospects and customers.[47] The second challenge is then to deliver the right content as low relevance of content and high mailing frequency both incite consumers to unsubscribe from a mailing list. A survey among 1,000 e-mail users concluded that the preference in e-mail content differs between males and females. Men are more interested in thematic content such as compelling news and information while for women promotional content like discount offers and samples are welcome.[48]

Aberlour, a Scottish brand of single malt whisky, used an e-mail marketing campaign to build awareness among the target group and generate pre-Christmas sales of its 10-year-old single malt whisky. Apart from this it wanted to test a previously untried market: women buying whisky as a gift for their husbands or friends. The last campaign objective was to build a database of whisky enthusiasts who gave their permission for further activities and communications. Aberlour bought two e-mail lists, both of which matched the profile of the typical whisky drinker. A sequential e-mail campaign rolled out over a two-week period consisted of three stages: an initial invitation to enter a prize draw and win a case of whisky, a reminder e-mail to everyone who didn't respond to the first e-mail and a final e-mail to all prize draw losers with a follow-up drive-to-retail offer. As a result, over 10% of the cold list were permissioned to Aberlour's database, the drive-to-retail offer achieved a 1% conversion rate and over 95% of the entries volunteered further profiling information.

Mobile marketing

Mobile marketing or wireless advertising consists of all the activities undertaken to communicate with customers through the use of mobile devices to promote products and services by providing information or offers. It typically consists of commercial or sales promotional messages sent to mobile phones by using permission-based SMS or MMS (multimedia messages such as digital pictures, audio tunes and video), advertising or WAP/i-Mode advertising (internet advertising viewed by the internet connection of the mobile device). Mobile marketing will be more productive and useful to marketers in the near future when time- and location-based information services as well as real MMS will become widely available and popular (supported by GPRS and 3G technology). Location-aware advertising messages (for instance, you receive a wireless coupon on your mobile phone or PDA that is related to a shop or restaurant in your immediate neighbourhood) are expected to create five to ten times higher click-through rates compared to internet advertising messages. Wireless advertising can be broken into two categories: push and pull. Push advertising is categorised as messages that are proactively sent out to wireless users and devices like alerts, SMS messages or even voice calls. It should be reserved for companies that have established a relationship and obtained permission to push communications to wireless users. Due to privacy issues and user backlash, pushed mobile advertising will seldom be used for new customer acquisition. Pull advertisements are messages shown to users as they are navigating WAP or wireless sites and properties. Both push and pull advertising should be carefully targeted and of relevance to the viewer to improve customer response and acceptance. Users should never feel that viewing the advertiser's message is costing them airtime.[49] A mobile phone is primarily used for two-way communication. Companies should therefore incorporate a two-way aspect into any mobile marketing campaign. Every single message sent out must be of real value to each recipient as the mobile phone is a very personal device and every useless message sent will have an intrusive connotation.[50] A study revealed that the degree of acceptance of SMS marketing is significantly influenced by the level of exposure and the knowledge that marketing messages are controlled by a known and trusted service provider. In this respect, SMS advertising is considered as acceptable as TV and radio advertising.[51]

Mobile marketing examples

- France Loisirs, a French member club with 3.8 million members in France (1 in 5 French families) is offering books, music, DVDs, etc. using six catalogues every year, websites and 200 shops. To stimulate the 35–55-year-olds in France in reading books, France Loisirs held a communication campaign which involved three media: postcards, e-mail and SMS messages. The latter had the best opening and reading rates (90%) which proves that mobile marketing is not only an effective medium for youngsters but also for an older audience.

- El Corte Ingles, a Spanish department store asked customers to send an SMS in order to receive promotional discounts in different departments of the store. The mobile marketing action succeeded in obtaining a high redemption rate of 77%, with 5% of customers even presenting more than one coupon.

- To launch its new S40 model Volvo sent SMS to its European clients in order to let them download a short documentary of the new model. 49% of the Volvo drivers who received the SMS responded: 36% actually downloaded the movie clip to their mobile phone and 13% used the internet to watch the movie. The documentary was called 'the mystery of Dalarö', a small island near Stockholm, Sweden, where 32 inhabitants had bought the S40 model on the first day of the campaign, all from the same dealership, which claims that they normally never even sell 32 cars in an entire year. The documentary was shot by direc-tor Spike Jonze and left the viewer seriously wondering whether the story was fact or fiction.

■ ABN Amro, a Dutch financial institution, used mobile marketing to promote personal loans to their clients. Clients who received the SMS simply had to return an SMS with the text 'LOAN' to a shortcode number to get a loan. In total ABN Amro received 11,000 SMS in 12 weeks, a 50% higher result than the previous e-mail campaign.

Source: Wellens M., La communication toutes-boîtes face aux nouvelles technologies media, Mémoire de Fin de Cycle d'Executive Master in Marketing, December 2005.

SMS has many advantages as a marketing tool. It is still considered a novelty and a more personal and engaging form of communication than e-mail. Just like e-mail, SMS is instantaneous, but it has an even faster and wider reach than e-mail as the mobile device usually accompanies the user and SMS can be received anywhere, at any time. It also allows for more precise targeting as every mobile phone is tied to one single person, whereas computers are often shared. Recipients are also able to call back imme-diately for further information when prompted by an SMS message. Production costs and lead times of SMS messages are negligible. The average response rate to commer-cial SMS messages is 10% to 15% while an average campaign cost is only €24,000.[52] As SMS actions are quite intrusive, they should always be launched on an opt-in basis, which implies that they should be regarded as a complement for other marketing com-munications. In most cases it needs a traditional medium (above-the-line, packaging, etc.) to broadcast the invitation to participate. An SMS message is most appreciated when the content is appealing (an offer, a game, an incentive, a contest) and attractive. The most effective wireless campaigns are sweepstakes. An instant-win contest is a good way to acquire a database of consumers.

SMS text messaging is an excellent advertising medium for reaching young adults. In the UK, 24% of all cellphone users would be willing to receive text-based advertising on their cellphone;[53] among 14–17 year olds this rises to over 50%. A survey in the UK has concluded that SMS marketing is most suitable for brand awareness generation, improving brand attitudes and generated direct responses. Mobile advertising worked best for advertising low-ticket items. It also generated a viral marketing effect, with 17% of receivers forwarding the SMS message to third parties. Concerning the brand-ing power of mobile marketing, 66% of people spontaneously remember the average SMS campaign and 12% spontaneously recall the brand being advertised (44% aided recall), with the best campaign obtaining more than 50% unaided brand awareness and 80% prompted awareness. SMS is said to be 50% more successful at building brand awareness than TV and 130% more successful than radio. An average 36% of SMS campaign recipients say they are more likely to buy the product advertised as a result of the campaign, rising to 71% for the best campaigns. In a large-scale research project, Enpocket interviewed 5,200 consumers after they had seen some of the 200 tested SMS campaigns during the period October 2001 to January 2003. On 94% of occasions the messages were read by the recipient and 23% of people forwarded the marketing message to a friend. The average campaign had a 15% response rate (the best marketing campaign 46%), 8% replied, 6% visited the website, 4% visited a store and 4% bought the advertised product.[54] Until now we can conclude that the power of SMS marketing is outperforming that of direct mail and e-mail, but on the other hand this is easily explained by the use of voluntary opt-in databases and the fact that SMS campaigns are not yet a very common marketing technique, giving it a unique aspect with not much advertising clutter negatively influencing the effects. It can be predicted that the effectiveness of SMS campaigns will decline as the number of campaigns increases.

When using mobile marketing techniques, a lot of legal and moral implications have to be taken into account. The Mobile Marketing Association (MMA) is the key institute regulating the mobile industry. The key guidelines of the MMA code of conduct can be summarised as follows:

1 Consumers must have given explicit consent to receive messages prior to any communication being sent.

2 Every communication must clearly indicate who the message is from.

3 Every communication must have clear opt-out options.

Other legal instruments (e.g. the Data Protection Act) require companies to treat consumer data fairly. It should clearly be indicated to consumers how often they will receive messages and what types of messages will be sent.[55]

Interactive television

Interactive (digital) television, or i(D)TV, is television content that gives viewers the ability to interact with programmes and to use a number of interactive services such as t-government, t-banking, t-commerce, t-learning (for instance, language lessons on the TVL channel of the Italian station Stream or CBeebies in the UK aimed at toddlers), information, games, video-on-demand and communication (t-mail), all supported by a set-top-box.[56] The new medium offers some new possibilities for marketers as they are now able to move buyers through the complete buying process. Interactive advertising, for example, allows viewers to ask for extra information about products and services, receive coupons or samples and even buy a product, all with one push of a button. iDTV will also enhance the possibilities of understanding the viewing behaviour of the target group as well as developing personal relationships with viewers and making tailored interactive advertising content adapted to the needs of the viewers.[57] Apart from interactive commercials, the iDTV medium provides advertisers with other possibilities:

- *Programmercials or programme sponsoring*: for instance a tour operator sponsors a travel programme on iDTV that gives viewers the opportunity to receive more information about a destination, order a catalogue or book a holiday;
- *Advertising messages or logo's on the electronic programme guide*, visited on average five to ten times by the iDTV viewer;
- *Linking with certain t-services*, for instance the *Financial Times* sponsoring the t-banking application on iDTV;
- *Bannering during programmes*;

- *Walled gardens*, a kind of website created specifically for iDTV, and linked with an interactive commercial or an iDTV programme, for instance through product placement.[58]

A campaign on interactive digital television to promote the launch of Microsoft's Xbox 360 games console was one of the most successful to have ever run in the UK. Not less than 1.9 million viewers were driven to an iDTV ad on Sky Active entertainment channel showcasing the features and available games of the Xbox 360. The results were more than four times the conversion rate of an average red-button campaign. Microsoft used a mix of online and press advertising to drive consumers to the iDTV commercial that contained a secret code allowing viewers to go to an additional level of secret video content. The first seven players to crack all the codes were able to insert their names onto a leader board.

Source: *New Media Age*, 2 February 2006.

New advertising formats on interactive digital television

The development of digital television brings along the possibility of developing new interactive advertising formats.[59] Interactive advertising implies a control shift from the advertiser to the consumer,[60] who can decide to gather information of any kind and to process this information. TV advertising shifts from a push to a pull philosophy. The consumer's motivation to interact with commercials becomes a key issue. From this control shift arises the advertiser's opportunity to build a dialogue with his consumers, reducing the irritating effect of TV advertisements.[61] Several new formats have been developed (see Table). One of them is the *Dedicated Advertising Location* (DAL, mini-DAL). This format consists of a 30-second TV ad embedded with clickable content 'micro sites' featuring an individual still screen which provides additional information.[62] The viewer can navigate through the extra information, thereby increasing the actively involved time, enlarging the cognitive processing of the advertising message, and, as a result, extending the advertising effectiveness. A study by Bellman (2004)[63] demonstrated that the effects of three exposures to a traditional analogue commercial is equivalent to one exposure to a DAL, assuming the consumer interacts with this DAL. In the *impulse response format*, the extra information is placed on top of the screen like an internet banner.[64] It is mostly used to give the viewer the possibility of ordering coupons, samples or brochures. An important difference between the impulse response format and the DAL is that, in the former, the viewer stays in the linear broadcast stream. With the DAL, on the other hand, if the viewer presses the red button that appears onscreen, he enters a second (broadband) stream, where the extra information appears, similar to an internet site. As a result, he will miss part of the programme. With this problem in mind, Lekakos *et al.* (2001)[65] introduced the *micro site*. A picture-in-picture or split screen divides the television screen in two parts, and allows the user to navigate through the advertising content without missing part of the linear broadcasting stream. Yet, because the attention of the viewer is divided in two simultaneous streams, this format may lead to less effective advertising. Another new format, not resulting in content overlap, is the '*contact me*' function that appears during the commercial. With a press on the red button, the user can choose to be contacted by the advertiser. Because all the identification information is saved in the set-top-box, little user effort is required.[66] Besides using the new formats, advertisers also have to cope with higher skipping rates of commercials through the introduction of the PVR (Personal Video Recorder) and VOD (Video on Demand). Advertising messages that are skip-proof, in other words embedded in the television content, e.g. *product placement*, sponsorship, virtual advertising, on-screen banner advertisement during programmes, and advertainment (a programme totally made by an advertiser),[67] will gain importance.[68] New variants of product placement, like interactive product placement, where the user clicks on a button appearing in the programme, bringing him to the DAL of the advertiser, are likely to emerge. Virtual advertising or sponsorship uses image manipulation, made possible by the digitalisation of television, e.g. virtual billboards at live sports events or in news items. This format enables advertisers to promote global products locally.[69] The use of logos and banners, adopted from the internet, will also become visible on television. Alongside the broadcasting stream, IDTV allows advertisers to reach their target audiences through *banners and logos on the Electronic Programme Guide* (EPG), permitting the viewer to choose his favourite programme from a schedule overview. Besides this, the broadcaster's portal can also be used to put on advertising messages. In the '*walled garden*', a limited broadband space, comparable with the internet, advertisers can become visible through sites, games, gambling, chatting, etc. Consumers owning the IDTV technology can receive emails on their television. This opens up new options for direct marketing. *Video On Demand* allows the user to choose a movie, soap or other content, and is a possible way to let commercials be pulled by the user; a challenge for advertising professionals to make their commercials as attractive as possible.

IDTV advertising formats

In broadcast stream	Besides broadcast stream
<u>In Ad</u>	<u>Walled garden</u>
■ Dal (mini-dal)	■ Logos/banners
■ Microsite	■ Website
■ Impulse response	■ Games
■ Contact me	<u>EPG/IPG</u>
<u>In content</u>	■ Logos/banners
■ Product placement	<u>VOD</u>
■ Sponsoring	■ Advertisement
■ Advertainment	■ Long commercial
■ Interact.PP	<u>Direct mailing (email)</u>
■ Virtual advertising	
■ On screen banners	

The impact of digital television for marketers is considered important because the market penetration of televisions is so much higher than that of personal computers. As technology develops further, the distinction between the PC, TV and telephone will completely blur. This is called media convergence.[70]

WEB 2.0: a new direction for the internet

With technology-fuelled changes in recent years, marketing is increasingly about two-way mass conversations between internet users. 'Web 2.0' is a concept used to describe this architecture of participation. A Google search for 'definition of Web 2.0' brings up 29,400 different results, but it can be seen as a collection of emerging technologies enabling social networking by offering internet users the ability to add, edit and tag content of different kinds (text, sound, video, images) and to collaborate and share information online. This so-called 'consumer-generated content' includes weblogs (blogs), video blogs (vlogs), podcasts, wikis and RSS feeds. It is said to differ from earlier web developments, retroactively referred to as 'Web 1.0', in that it is a move away from static websites through which internet users navigate using the structure imposed by the site and merely read the content fed to them without playing an active role to a more dynamic and interactive World Wide Web in which users participate and connect to each other using services as opposed to sites. One of the earliest Web 2.0 applications was Napster, a peer-to-peer file swapping tool that leveraged personal music catalogues across its user base and facilitated music sharing. More recent examples of Web 2.0 platforms are:

- Google Maps: a satellite based 3D map of the world allowing users and advertisers to pinpoint and comment on certain locations, buildings or shops.

- Flickr (owned by Yahoo!): an application facilitating uploading and sharing of photos while tagging each picture with keywords.

- Wikipedia: a Britannica-rivalling popular online encyclopedia completely constructed and continuously updated by a community of volunteering contributors. 'Wikis' are collaborative websites comprising the continually updated work of many people.

- Del.icio.us (also owned by Yahoo!): an online collection of favourites (bookmarks listed by a community of web users) tagged with certain topics.

- Upcoming.org (again acquired by Yahoo!): a search engine looking for events on certain topics (generated by users).

- Social networks such as Myspace and Orkut (with more than 25 million visitors): sites where you can create a personal profile and contact soulmates.[71]

All examples of Web 2.0 applications have some common characteristics: they use new communication channels such as Really Simple Syndication (better known as **RSS**). RSS involves the syndication of content using standardised protocols permitting end-users to make use of this content in another context ranging from another website, an RSS reader, another desktop application (such as Apple's iTunes). RSS allows users to subscribe to any content that supports the format. The RSS broadcasted content that can be integrated in another context is also called '(RSS) feed'.

A **podcast**, also one of the new Web 2.0 buzzwords, is nothing more than a sound file with an RSS feed that can be listened to by any MP3 or audio player (not only iPods as the name would suggest). This technology makes it easy for people to create their own audio recordings and post them on the Web. According to a Bridge Ratings study about 5 million radio listeners have downloaded at least one podcast in 2005.[72] Some advertisers are already experimenting with developing their own podcasts or integrating their advertising or brand into existing podcast initiatives. Volvo paid $60,000 for a six-month sponsorship of the monthly podcast of Weblog's Autoblog. Over that period the show was downloaded 150,000 times.[73] BMW launched bmwaudiobooks.com, a site with free to download 45-minute audio books by leading authors featuring BMW product placements. The books are intended to be the length of the average car journey and new tales are put available every two weeks.[74] Since the new MP3 players also allow video downloading and playing the next development in Web 2.0 will be the 'vodcast' (video podcasts). Stanford University is offering educational material (lectures, speeches, sport reports, news, interviews and videos) to their students via iTunes. Maybelline, a cosmetics brand, has launched a series of beauty podcasts in France, featuring tips to get a perfect make-up with weekly videos and a traditional audio podcast section sharing make-up suggestions. Online retailer Amazon has started Amazonwire, a podcast featuring exclusive interviews with authors, musicians, movie directors and other people behind the range of products they sell. In Germany Coke Light launched its own podcast as part of the 'Live Life Light' campaign. The podcast, lasting 15 minutes, featured inspirational content to help people discover the beautiful side of life and 'think positive'.[75]

Weblogs, or contracted '**blogs**', are frequently updated personal web journals that allow owners to publish ideas and information. Blog readers can read and evaluate material and add new content, thus creating a conversation that spans time zones and continents. Some blogs are just expressions of individual opinions and analysis, while others aggregate information or serve mainly to direct readers to other blogs, websites or other sources. Some are company-internal and only accessible to employees or departments within a company. Others are posted on public websites and available for anyone to see and react. The earliest blogs were started in the late 1990s but real interest has skyrocketed over the past years. Technorati, the leading search engine for weblogs, estimated that there were more than 38.4 million weblogs in May 2006 and the so-called blogosphere is said to double every 6 months with a creation of 75,000 new weblogs every day. Daily posting volume tracked by Technorati was over 1.2 million posts per day in April 2006, which equals about 50,000 posts per hour.[76] Blogs take the pulse of consumer trends and can build customer relationships as well as exposing shoddy products. One of Kryptonite's popular U-shaped bike locks had to be recalled and exchanged after a blog posting on bikerforum.net said it could be picked with a bic pen. The story raced through the blogosphere and was picked up by the *New York Times* and other big media. The product exchange implied a cost of $10 million dollars for Kryptonite. Blogs derive power from several sources: inexpensive and easy-to-use software allows everyone to start publishing. They are unedited and unfiltered and may include links to other blogs or sites, news articles, photos, video or audio providing readers with fast access to additional information. Companies like IBM, Microsoft, Boeing, Sun Microsystems, Hewlett-Packard and General Motors have started several public blogs to provide further visibility and credibility. GM vice-chairman Robert Lutz has even achieved a celebrity status with his blog (fastlane.gmblogs.com) that focuses on new designs and GM cars.[77] A blog can be an effective and low cost way to:

- influence a public conversation about your brand or company: by giving the latest accurate information, which is often picked up by journalists since studies have shown that half of them regularly read corporate blogs to detect news items.
- improve brand visibility and credibility: by giving the company a more human voice but also by obtaining higher rankings in search engines.
- improve customer relations and receive quick feedback, suggestions and complaints.[78]

A corporate blog allows a company to keep an ear to the ground to hear what's being said and if necessary react with corrective information. A South African winery, Stormhoek, made use of blogs to enter the UK market. The founder sent sample bottles to 150 bloggers in the UK without the obligation to say anything about the wine but a lot of them ended up writing about it. By interfacing with the blogosphere, Stormhoek changed the way it looked at its primary customers (supermarket chains) and the end-users (the supermarket's customers). Simply telling the blog story to supermarket buyers and importers made the sales process easier and as a result the wine got a 19% share of its category in the UK market and sales doubled from 50,000 cases in 2004 to 100,000 in 2005.[79]

Relationship marketing and the internet

The basis of loyalty programmes consists of collecting data that are related to the customer's behaviour. What kind of customer is he or she? What does he ask for? What does she buy? What interests do they have and how can we tailor our e-communication to his or her wants? Customer profiles drive what the website looks like, which e-mails he or she receives, what kind of offers he or she receives, etc. The Web is not about fragmenting audiences but about creating one-to-one relationships for marketers and increasing the bond between consumers and producers. Database applications, like collaborative filtering used by Amazon.com, focus on customer retention rather than acquisition. The internet is well suited for the evolution towards an individualised, tailored value proposition. It offers addressability, two-way continuous interactivity, customisation capabilities, on-demand availability and seamless transactions. Marketers can leverage interactive media to identify self-selected users, enhance loyalty by providing value-added services, use what they learn about their customers to customise existing products or create new products and services, and start an ongoing on-line communication with customers. E-mail communication with customers is more personal and intimate than the traditional letter with glossy brochure. When a customer sends an e-mail to a company, the person who replies to the e-mail suddenly becomes the representative for the whole company.[80]

An increasing proportion of contact with customers is conducted via the Web rather than the phone. E-CRM focuses on the electronic relationship with customers and allows marketers to deliver cheaper and faster CRM (customer relationship marketing). Although the initial software investments can be high, the automation and personalisation of the marketing dialogue with the customer imply significant savings and faster response. E-CRM is a web approach to synchronising customer relationships across communications channels, business functions and audiences. It empowers customers to access tailored information and services that are tied to products in ways that are less expensive and more convenient than traditional ways. E-CRM represents a shift from employees taking care of customers directly to allowing customers to use self-service tools that make them an active part of the buying and servicing process.

The internet is a good instrument for this e-CRM as it enables companies to find out more about each customer and thus to empower customers to control the process. E-CRM-initiated websites, intranets and extranets let customers obtain the tailored information they need before making a purchase or help them solve problems in an after-sales-service site without help from more costly sales and support staff or call centres. The core issue in CRM and e-CRM is to collect the right data and turn that data into useful information to leverage customer service, marketing and sales. The salesforce can benefit from the fact that the internet qualifies sales leads and shortens the sales cycle. Marketers learn what promotions work best and how their target group reacts to advertising, and better understand the needs, desires and consumer behaviour of their customers. Customer service is supported by customer-care sections on the website or extranet that are available 24 hours a day without extra costs.

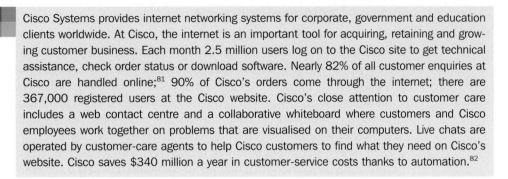

Cisco Systems provides internet networking systems for corporate, government and education clients worldwide. At Cisco, the internet is an important tool for acquiring, retaining and growing customer business. Each month 2.5 million users log on to the Cisco site to get technical assistance, check order status or download software. Nearly 82% of all customer enquiries at Cisco are handled online;[81] 90% of Cisco's orders come through the internet; there are 367,000 registered users at the Cisco website. Cisco's close attention to customer care includes a web contact centre and a collaborative whiteboard where customers and Cisco employees work together on problems that are visualised on their computers. Live chats are operated by customer-care agents to help Cisco customers to find what they need on Cisco's website. Cisco saves $340 million a year in customer-service costs thanks to automation.[82]

The essence of CRM is to have a single comprehensive database with a complete history of the prospect or customer that can be accessed from any of the customer touch points (sales, call centre, personalised website and customer service).[83] Dell provides a Premier Pages service for its corporate clients. Premier Pages are sites dedicated to a particular customer and only accessible to that customer. Each dedicated site holds a record of all previous interactions between the customer and Dell and can be used to communicate with the customer and inform him or her about exclusive offers. The collaborative software that Amazon.com, the online book and CD retailer, uses allows communication of personalised advice on products that the software predicts to be interesting for a certain customer.[84] LivePerson software (www.liveperson.com) offers website integration with live customer-service representatives in real time.[85]

Tracking the effectiveness of e-communications

The company website is a way to reach customers directly and deliver information to them, take their orders and build relationships. The net is also a medium used to place advertising and to create a direct communication line with customers and prospects. For these reasons it is important for marketers to know how their website and on-line marketing campaigns are performing and how they can improve the effectiveness and efficiency of their site and digital strategy. As the internet is an interactive and computer-supported medium, all information about site traffic is stored on the net server in server log files. Analysing these files is one way of tracking website performance. About half of the Belgian and Dutch marketers are of the opinion that the results of on-line marketing actions are more measurable than those of most other traditional marketing actions. The only other technique of which the effectiveness is even easier to measure, in their view, is direct marketing.[86]

Assessing the effectiveness of e-marketing involves finding answers to questions like:

- Are the corporate and marketing objectives identified in the e-marketing strategy being met?
- Are the marketing communications objectives identified in the e-marketing plan achieved?
- How effective are the different promotional tactics used?[87]

Measuring website effectiveness

The most basic method of using feedback to measure site effectiveness is by asking for feedback on the website. This can be done by asking visitors to leave a contact e-mail address or by inserting a feedback form on one of the web pages. Both methods will only elicit the most extreme (negative and positive) reactions, and are not representative of the site audience. Moreover, little feedback may be expected. Including a feedback form may provide more detailed feedback and more direction as specific questions and categories of information can be included in the feedback form.

Each time a user clicks on a link or interacts with a site, the server of that site will automatically add data into a number of computer files called server logfiles. There are four commonly used logfiles generated by most web servers:

- access_log;
- agent_log;
- referrer_log;
- error_log.

The access_log file records the name of the file transmitted, a timestamp and the IP address of the client that requested the page. The agent_log files contain the name of the browser used each time the website is accessed. The referrer_log file lists the web page that each user accessed prior to accessing any web page on our site (i.e. the site from where a visitor came before entering our site) and the error_log file is just a record of occurring errors.[88] These logfiles provide traffic information (hits, visits, times, bytes), domains (internet service providers, proxies, firewalls), referrers (browsers, dependent action) and browsers (types and platforms). As the logfiles are nothing more than large text files, some tools have been developed to analyse these files. Software such as WebTrends and services such as Nedstat and Hitwatchers keep track of the numbers. Logfiles cannot be used to identify specific users (as they only record host names) or client sessions. Therefore cookies are often used for these two purposes, in combination with logfile analysis. Metrics that logfile analysis can deliver are:

- the number of hits: a request for a file on a web server – this not very useful and not reliable as every text or graphic file that is included in a web page is considered as one hit;
- the number of page views: a request for a total page;
- entry and exit pages;
- the number of unique visitor sessions: visits during a period of, for example, 20 minutes;
- the number of unique visitors (if combined with cookies);[89]
- visitor frequency report (repeat visitors);
- session duration: the length of time a visitor spends on a site;
- country of origin;[90]
- browser and operating system used;
- referring URL and domain (where the visitor came from).

Logfile analyses have limitations and a number of weaknesses, such as under- and overcounting.[91]

To really find out who visits a website and what his or her evaluation of the site, the brand and the sales effects are, visitor surveys (on-line or off-line) are necessary. Surveys may give socio-demographic, psychographic and webographic (with regard to the use of the internet) profiles of visitors. They can also measure attitudes, satisfaction and intentions, and are a good way of tracking the effectiveness and success of a website. InSites Consulting (www.insites-consulting.com), a leading European internet research agency, developed a model to evaluate the performance of a website using scientifically tested questionnaires and constructs, adaptable to specific research questions and needs (see Figure 17.1). In pre-testing, usability testing and post-testing of websites, qualitative market research techniques such as focus groups and in-depth interviewing can be used in conjunction with quantitative internet panel surveys to add research insights to the website visitor surveys. Website users' input should be integrated with the design process to ensure targeted and effective website building.

The InSites Consulting model[92] to measure website effectiveness consists of different parts that permit an in-depth assessment of the site based on an on-line questionnaire filled out during the site visit:

User profile of the website

The user profile is described in terms of (firm) demographics and webographics (such as internet experience and usage, type of connection, etc.) as well as a personal/professional or socio-demographic profile (such as customer, function, role in the decision-making unit, dealer, employee, etc.). This information is crucial in order to detect the extent to which the site attracts the right visitors: does the 'anticipated target group' correspond to the 'actual target group'?

Traffic analysis and generation

In-depth information can be gathered concerning the way users of the site arrive at the site (traffic analysis). What is the performance of the different traditional media used to

Figure 17.1 Assessing website marketing performance: the InSites Consulting model

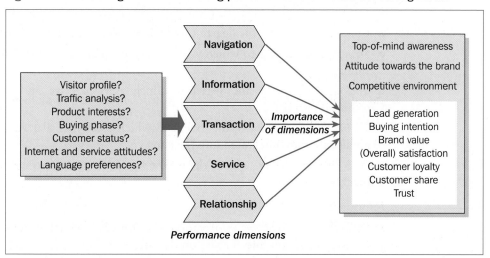

Source: developed by InSites, www.insites-consulting.com.

attract visitors to the site? How many and which visitors are redirected from other (sub)sites (dot-com – local sites)? In addition, this section will also provide insights into the motives for the site visits.

Product interest, knowledge and buying phase

Visitors to the site will be asked to provide insights into their area(s) of interest. More specifically, with which product categories and information are they concerned? From the (on-line) marketing and sales viewpoint, it is also important to ascertain which stage of the buying cycle visitors have reached. Have visitors to the pages recognised a product need, are they processing information about the products, are they currently comparing supplier and product information, do they wish to order products or are they just seeking after-sales service and feedback?

Current customer status

Similarly, it is important to know about current product ownership (such as number of products, looking for new products or replacement of an existing product), customer status, relation towards the company or brand (for example, loyalty).

Content needs and attitudes for value-added services

The customers' interest in several concepts for on-line applications (such as on-line demos, product configuration, accessory information, etc.) can be tested. Furthermore, different attitudes towards on-line marketing and service through the internet (such as e-mail offers, community application/references, attitude towards brand banners and others, call-me-back buttons, etc.) are measured.

Performance of the site

In order to analyse the functionality and effectiveness of websites, InSites Consulting will apply its comprehensive web performance model. The model is multidimensional and contains a variety of metrics that have been tested scientifically.

1   Navigation

- *Design* and *layout*: the extent to which users perceive the site as visually attractive;
- *Content readability*: the degree to which users consider the texts easy to read;
- *Structure*: the extent to which visitors perceive that navigation through the site is simple;
- *Technical reliability*: the degree to which users perceive the site to be free of technical problems;
- *Technical advancedness*: the extent to which users find that advanced technical applications are integrated into the site;
- *Web page processing speed*: the extent to which users perceive that pages load quickly.

2   Information

- *Availability of relevant information*: the degree to which visitors find that there is enough relevant information on the site;
- *Information credibility*: the extent to which users judge the information to be credible;

- *Information recency*: the extent to which users consider the information to be up to date.

3 Transaction

- *Information search usability*: the extent to which users consider that the product/ service they want to buy can be easily reached on the site;
- *Transaction process information*: the extent to which users perceive that the site offers clear and sufficient information on the rest of the buying cycle;
- *Product/service assortment*: the degree to which visitors perceive that the site offers a broad range of products/services;
- *Product/service quality*: the extent to which users perceive that the quality of the product/service corresponds to what they expect.

4 Service

- *Contact possibility*: the extent to which users consider that the company can easily be reached for voicing questions, feedback and complaint;
- *Responsiveness*: the extent to which users feel that the company (will) respond(s) swiftly to questions, feedback and complaints.

5 Relationship

- *Website personalisation*: the extent to which users perceive that the site takes their personal wants and needs into account.

Competitors and brand awareness

Do visitors to our site also visit the competitors' sites? What is their overall assessment of these sites in comparison to the site information on our site? These questions allow the company to find out to what extent visitors are loyal to the site. Simultaneously, the company will ascertain which on-line position it holds in relation to its main competitors. In addition, the top-of-mind awareness and branding perception within the industry will be assessed among visitors.

Marketing effectiveness and customer behaviour

This monitor can provide insights into the degree to which visitors are becoming interesting leads (for example, intention to contact dealer or sales representative/company), whether they intend to buy a certain product, how they value the brand, how satisfied they are with the website, etc.

By relating the web performance metric scores to these marketing effectiveness variables, InSites Consulting provides an understanding of the commercial importance of the different site features. For example, based on correlation and regression analyses, the importance of site design for satisfying users or the weight of information credibility for spurring customer loyalty will become clear. By comparing the performance on several web dimensions with their importance, a web performance quadrant will enable the company to focus on the major problem areas of the website.

Measuring the effectiveness of on-line advertising

The effectiveness of banner advertising depends on different aspects: the location of the banner, and the message content and execution. How relevant is the website on which the banner is posted to the target audience? A banner ad for a CD company will probably be more effective when placed in a music-related website. This is very similar to the case of traditional advertising that is likely to be more effective when placed in media that target the relevant customers group well. Again, much like in traditional advertising, the quality of the banner for attracting attention and its placement on a web page will have a great impact on its effectiveness.

Although, as a consequence of the interactive nature of the medium, web advertising effectiveness measurement will be based on the behaviour of web users, a certain hierarchy of effects can be defined: internet users may be exposed to a message, they may engage in looking for more information 'behind' the banner and they may even click through to the web page of the advertiser. Based on this distinction, different types of ad effectiveness measures can be defined:[93]

- Graphical ad impression is the delivery of a graphical advertisement to a browser.
- Cached/textual ad impression is the delivery of an advertisement to a browser that has cached the advertisement, has graphics turned off or does not support graphics.

Both of the above measures, often added to obtain total ad impressions, are in fact exposure measures. Furthermore, since in the internet environment it is unlikely that an ad is seen by different people at the same time, it is also a measure of the number of contacts made by an ad.

- Click-through is a click by a user on an advertisement. As such, it can be compared with the response to a direct response ad in traditional media.
- Ad transfer is the successful arrival of a user at the advertiser's website. Evidently, most click-throughs will result in ad transfer. This measure can be considered an indication of the number of people who are really motivated to visit an advertiser's web page.

In web ad tracking, the above-mentioned indicators are often summarised into the following rates:

- Graphical click-through rate: total number of click-throughs divided by total number of ad impressions for graphical advertisements;
- Total click-through rate: total number of click-throughs divided by total number of ad impressions;
- Ad transfer/total impressions: total number of ad transfers divided by total number of impressions;
- Ad transfer/click-throughs: total number of ad transfers divided by total number of click-throughs.

Impression, click-through and ad transfer can be measured for different banners used by the same advertiser, and on a daily basis, to track web ad effectiveness.

For e-couponing, e-sampling and mobile marketing, conversion and response rates are the most important metrics. To measure the effectiveness of an e-mail marketing campaign, the following metrics can be used:

- Sent mails:
  - number attempted
  - number successfully sent;

- Click-through rates:
  - percentage of recipients who clicked on a link
  - overall e-mail CTR and CTR for specific links
  - of different formats/offers, etc.;
- Unsubscribe rates;
- Open rates:
  - percentage of recipients who opened the e-mail
  - only possible for HTML mails;
- Conversion rates (tracking to e-commerce landing page or internet survey);
- Click-stream analyses;
- E-mail pass along rates to measure viral marketing;
- Coupon codes redeemed if coupons are inserted.

Apart from these measures, the most important issue for marketers is what happens after users click-through an on-line advertisment or visit a website. Does the on-line marketing strategy lead to conversion? What is the effect of the e-marketing campaign on brand equity and purchase intention? For e-commerce sites, purchase behaviour is easy to link to e-marketing tactics, but for most companies and businesses the effects on sales are difficult to trace as they often take place in the off-line distribution system. Using post-campaign research that consists of an initial tracking of brand awareness, brand image and intention to buy before the campaign and a post-campaign survey tracking the same metrics can deliver this kind of information. InSites Consulting also offers an e-ROI methodology that tracks behaviour of customers and prospects after they have visited a company's website by using a re-contact survey. In this way InSites is able to calculate the return on investment of a website and on-line advertising campaign.

Integrating e-communications in IMC

Many e-communication tools are essentially electronic equivalents of traditional marketing communications. Therefore, they can be used either as supplements or as substitutes to traditional tools. Microsites can be set up to accompany and reinforce new product launches, sales promotions or sponsorship campaigns. Generating traffic to websites is one of the most important first steps. This can be done via web-advertising, but also by means of off-line advertising, promotion, sponsorship, PR . . . campaigns or in-store communication. Websites and e-mail campaigns can also be used to build up and maintain databases for direct marketing, personal selling and relationship building. Traditional media such as television, radio and print advertising and telemarketing can be used to generate traffic and contacts on the site. The electronic component of these efforts should be consistent and well-integrated with traditional instruments to obtain a truly multichannel customer approach. Interactive digital television can generate detailed information on the viewing and clicking behaviour of viewers, and various types of interactive advertising and promotion can be tested and the information generated can be integrated into databases and traditional advertising and direct marketing campaigns. A special aspect of electronic communication is its integration into the IT environment of the company. Online applications should enable marketers to efficiently interact with their target groups, and marketers should only develop campaigns that can be technically handled by the IT-department.

Summary

In large parts of Europe the internet reaches more than half of the population. Mobile phone penetration is even higher and interactive digital television is expected to penetrate even further within a few years. As a consequence, consumers' media attention is fragmenting and marketers will have to follow them into the new digital media. They therefore employ a number of e-marketing tactics that all contribute to the communications objectives: creating brand awareness, shaping brand attitudes, generating trial and sustaining loyalty. Brand websites are essential for most brands to support brand image and communicate with customers. Merely having a website is not enough and other off-line and on-line advertising tools such as search engine optimisation will be required to drive traffic to the site. Because of the time and budget involved, more and more companies tend to create temporary mini-sites called micro-sites to draw users and bring a new product or service to their attention. On-line advertising is on the rise in Europe and new ad formats regularly see the light. Although rich media ads, pop-ups and skyscrapers perform better than traditional banners, these new formats affect budgets and often cause irritation. Keyword buying and content sponsorship are formats that are known to work on their strengths: relevance to the target group. New ad types that are very popular due to their customer engagement and impact are advergames or on-line games. Although the cost of this kind of interactive advertising tends to be much higher than for other ad formats, the interaction time leads to a higher brand immersion. Related to these games are viral marketing actions, which make good use of the network characteristics of the net community, on-line contests, and e-sampling and e-couponing, which have a number of advantages over their off-line counterparts. The same is true for e-mail marketing, the digital form of direct marketing communication, which has recently been joined by action-driven mobile marketing communications to the cellphones of consumers. A new era for marketers lies in development when looking at the commercial developments in interactive digital television in Europe. Finally, the internet, as an intrinsically interactive medium, can also be used to develop and sustain customer relationships, for instance via customer service pages on the net or virtual communities. The effectiveness of e-communications can be assessed by the use of logfile analysis, customer feedback forms and visitor surveys.

Review questions

1 How is the internet and on-line advertising market in Europe evolving?

2 How can a brand or company website contribute to a marketing plan?

3 Discuss the different kinds of on-line advertising and compare them in terms of performance, cost and irritation?

4 What other e-marketing tools are available? For which communication objective would you choose them?

5 What is meant by 'viral marketing'?

6 What are the dos and don'ts of e-mail marketing?

7 Explain the added value of mobile marketing to an e-marketing plan?

8 How can marketers benefit from a new evolution such as interactive digital television?

9 How can the internet help to develop relationships between a company and its customers?

10 What use are virtual communities to a company or brand?

11 How can the effectiveness of e-marketing tactics be tracked?

Further reading

Chaffey, D. and Smith, P.R. (2005), *E-marketing Excellence*. London: Butterworth-Heinemann (Elsevier).

Damani, R., Damani, C., Dana, F. and Linton, J. (2005), *Online Marketing: Online Media Planning, Pay Per Click, Search Marketing, Organic Search Engine Optimization, Email Marketing, Affiliate Marketing, Rich Media and Banner Advertising, Viral Marketing, Social Networks and Analytics*. New York: Imano.

Meadows-Klue, D. (2005), *A Marketer's Guide to Online Advertising*. London: Butterworth-Heinemann (Elsevier).

Scobble, R. and Israel, S. (2006), *Naked Conversations. How Blogs are Changing the Way Businesses Talk with Customers*. New Jersey: John Wiley & Sons.

Case 17

NOKIA CONCEPT LOUNGE: creating online buzz around the brand

Background

The roots of the company Nokia go back to the year 1865 when a forest industry enterprise was established in Finland by mining engineer Fredrik Idestam. In 1898 the Finnish Rubber Works Ltd was founded and in 1912 the Finnish Cable Works began operations. Gradually Nokia and the two other companies became owned by the same few owners and eventually, in 1967, the three companies were merged to form the 'Nokia Corporation'. In the 1980s Nokia strengthened its position in the telecommunications and consumer electronics markets through a number of acquisitions such as Mobira, Salora, Televa and Luxor of Sweden, as well as the consumer electronics operations and part of the component business of the German Standard Elektrik Lorenz, the French company Oceanic (also consumer electronics) and the Swiss cable machinery company Maillefer. In the late 1980s Nokia became the largest Scandinavian information technology company by acquiring Ericsson's data systems division, and expanded its cable industry through the acquisition of the Dutch cable company NKF. Since the beginning of the 1990s Nokia has concentrated on its core business: telecommunications. Today Nokia is a world leader in mobile communications with net sales of €34.1 billion and an operating profit of €4.6 billion in 2005 and more than one in three mobile phones sold globally is a Nokia phone. The company obtains these results by 'connecting people' (Nokia's corporate slogan) to each other and the information that is relevant to them with products like mobile phones, devices and solutions for imaging, games, media consumption and business. Nokia also provides equipment, solutions and services for network operators and corporations.

Now, as the features and functionality of mobile devices extends from voice to imaging, games, entertainment and business applications, Nokia has entered a new growth period.

Market situation and challenges for Nokia

In 2005, Nokia's sales and marketing expenditure was €3.0 billion, representing 8.7% of net sales. According to a survey published in July 2005 by Interbrand, the Nokia brand was recognised as the sixth most valued brand in the world.

In order to reach Nokia's objective of 40% of the global market share and maintain high profitability, Nokia needs to be able to understand consumer and market trends and be effective in supplying the right products to satisfy them, and to spot trends and opportunities in the converging digital industry and the continuous development of technology. Nokia needs to maintain its brand equity, manage price erosion and mobile device commoditisation. Design and ease of use have always been key attributes of Nokia phones, therefore it is crucial for Nokia to stay competitive in these areas.

Club Nokia

In order to cope with this challenging future, Nokia wants to support and improve the brand image of Nokia as a leader in design and product development, while at the same time strengthening its relationship with the community of current Nokia users. To support the relationship with its customers in consumer markets Nokia has created a customer loyalty programme called 'Club Nokia'. Six advantages for club members are given:

- the monthly e-magazine (e-mail newsletter) with tips and tricks to get more out of the Nokia phone and contests with which CDs, DVDs, free tickets, etc. can be won.
- Exclusive promotions on Nokia devices, accessories and software for mobile phones.
- Mobile phone testing: only Club Nokia members are selected to test and keep new Nokia handsets and give their user feedback and opinion on new Nokia products and solutions
- The opportunity to pre-order new phone models to get them among the first consumers.
- Exclusive new product demonstrations for members.
- Free tickets and VIP packages to concerts, shows, parties, sports events
- Special occasion events (New Year, Valentine's Day . . .)

- Tailor-made VIP support: preferential treatment such as faster service for repair and maintenance during the warranty period and exclusive access to the Club Nokia Careline and to information, user guides, manuals and software.

In Europe Club Nokia currently has a total of 21 million members.

Nokia Concept Lounge

In the second half of 2005 Nokia created the Nokia Concept Lounge website as a platform for discovering and exchanging ideas for future mobile communications. On the website three different future concepts of Nokia designers were showcased to start a discussion and share ideas about the future of mobile communications on the one hand and inspire design students to send in their own concepts and innovative ideas on the other:

- the Zond: a phone with integrated rotating video-camera as well as a projector allowing mobile communications with full sound and motion. The concept designer was inspired by R2D2 (a robot with integrated projector in the Star Wars movies)
- Sky: a mobile device with a double seamless touch-screen allowing access to all personal information (video, TV, voice, e-mail, SMS, text). This design was inspired by a butterfly.
- Strap-up: a wearable (around the wrist) device that is operated by user-defined movements. Each hand movement automatically generates a logo message or pre-defined SMS text that can be sent to other mobile phones or e-mail. This allows users to communicate without talking. The designer was inspired by Indians using smoke messages.

Together with this site Nokia launched the Nokia Benelux Design Awards, a contest in Belgium, Luxemburg and The Netherlands to gather creative new ideas of industrial and product design students around the world. The latter were encouraged to send in their designs and ideas for future mobile communications. The winner of the design contest would earn a cash grant of €5,000, a premium category Nokia phone and a trip to Helsinki where he or she could meet the Nokia designers team.

The three main elements of the website reflected the objective of creating a total community experience from the site and the Nokia Concept Lounge campaign:

1 Presenting Nokia's concepts

2 A forum and community to submit and discuss ideas in which participation was rewarded by the chance to win Nokia phones and digital pens

3 The design contest for students.

Objectives of the Nokia Concept Lounge campaign

In terms of objectives the Nokia Concept Lounge was designed as one of a number of EMEA Club Nokia benefits in the second half of 2004 and first half of 2005 in order to meet Club Nokia's targets of influencing consumer behaviour and increasing Nokia's brand loyalty. Key goals of the Concept Lounge campaign were:

■ to provide a Nokia and Club Nokia brand enhancing consumer experience related to design and product development content

■ to increase the 'brand mystique' of Nokia phones among Club Nokia members

■ to involve members in product design and increase personal brand involvement

■ to give members the feeling that Nokia is listening to their needs, wants and desires

■ to raise the awareness, uniqueness and excitement of Nokia's design and product development and reinforce Nokia's position of being at the fore-front of design and technology.

Promotion of the Nokia Concept Lounge site and the Nokia Benelux Design Awards

To promote the Nokia Concept Lounge website and the design contest a number of tools were used:

■ the e-mail newsletter to Club Nokia members: 37% of the Club Nokia e-mail recipients opened the newsletter and 40% of the viewers clicked-through to go to the website

■ community marketing: seeding the competition in local web communities. This resulted in an inter-community 'Pimp my phone' competition with members posting their idea links in forum and chat messages. The effect of this was over 12,000 visits to the Nokia Concept Lounge site mostly in the first 2 months of the campaign

■ built-in viral actions: an e-mail with a link direct to the submitted idea and encouraging people to visit the idea on the Nokia Concept Lounge website and vote for it. 80,000 directly referred bookmarks came from this viral campaign

■ promotion via Nokia websites (nokia.com, nokia.be, nokia.nl, nokia.fr and nokia.pl)

■ PR announcing the Nokia Benelux Design Awards, resulting in more than 27 press articles in every major Benelux publication for 3 months

■ online campaign (only in The Netherlands): a mix of targeted advertorials, bannering and search engine marketing (SEM) resulted in 40,546 clicks to the website. Case Table 17.1 shows the details of the online ad and advertorial placements on the Dutch fashion website fashion.nl, on good2B.com (Dutch lifestyle site with daily news on art, fashion, parties and design), Partyscene (a Dutch party portal targeted at young people with an active interest in going out and the dance scene) and Trendystyle (a portal for women with fashion, beauty and makeup trends). Case Table 17.2 shows

Case Table 17.1 The online ad and advertorial placements on fashion.

Website	Bought Views	Delivered Views	Clicks	Delivered Views	Cost (€)
Fashion.nl 336x280	56,260	53,394	148	95%	1,800
Good2B 336x280	fixed	281,527	590	nvt	765
Good2B advertorial	fixed	0	112	nvt	1,912
Netdirect	18,888	0	28,953	153%	6,800
Partyscene 120x600	130,000	123,175	191	95%	3,900
Trendystyle 336x280	60,000	60,152	254	100%	2,400
Total	**265,148**	**518,248**	**30,248**	**195%**	**17,577**

Case Table 17.2 **The results of SEM on Google and Overture**

TOTAL GOOGLE + OVERTURE				
Period	*Impressions*	*Clicks*		*Costs €*
01.09.05–30.09.05	325,843	1,594		757.42
Entire campaign (30.06–30.09)	2,928,553	10,298		5,097.04

the results of SEM on Google and Overture (now called Yahoo! Search).

Results of the campaign

The total number of visits to the Nokia Concept Lounge website amounted to 485,422 (by the end of February 2006) with an average monthly number of 45,000. During the campaign period (April 2005–February 2006) peak moments could be noted during campaign communication highlights: the campaign launch (April 2005: 71,511 visitors), the online marketing campaign in The Netherlands (July 2005: 59,073 visitors) and the announcement of the winners (October 2005: 97,842 visitors). On average one Nokia Concept Lounge visitor saw 8.65 pages; 46% of all the site visitors viewed the 3 Nokia concepts; and 19% were interested in the Nokia Benelux Design Awards. 53,500 visitors clicked to learn more about sharing ideas. Only 190 visitors wanted to learn more about the prizes of the design contest which suggests that more altruistic motives were behind submitting ideas to Nokia. In total about 4,000 visitors have uploaded design ideas, 780 with multimedia files. The top 15 of the ideas submitted received 46,593 visitors. The page with the award winners received 126,112 visitors. In total the Concept Lounge website was picked up by 4,597 different blogs on the internet, while over 16,000 blogs covered the Design Awards (peaking at the beginning of October 2005 when the winners were announced).

The winner of the Nokia Benelux Design Awards was Tamer Nakisçi from Turkey for his conceptual device 'Nokia 888', a mobile device that changes its shape depending on what is happening, like when receiving a phone call. The bracelet-like 888 is envisioned to use a liquid battery, feature speech recognition, a flexible touch screen, and a touch sensitive body cover. A video showing off the device's potential features shows off close to a dozen functions, including an alarm clock, PDA, GPS, phone, push e-mail receiver, digital wallet and jewellery. Publishing the design contest winners resulted in wide international news coverage in the press and especially on the Web. The buzz around the winning design in blogs exceeded the buzz around the Nokia N90, Nokia N71 and Nokia 8800 as can be seen in graphs 17.1 and 17.2. Together with the launch of new products, the Nokia Benelux Design Awards helped to increase the sustainability of buzz around Nokia design.

The Nokia Concept Lounge campaign won three international awards: Web Awards (New York) Standard of Excellence, Bronze for best interactive campaign in the Epica (Europe) Awards and 'Best branded community project' at the Future Marketing Awards (Europe).

Case questions

1 What do you think of the Club Nokia idea, the benefits offered and the Club Nokia website? What other benefits could Nokia offer to club members in order to increase brand loyalty?

2 For Nokia the online marketing campaigns are key communication strategies. When considering the target group, market situation, the Benelux market and communication objectives, can you underwrite this strategy?

3 Which online campaign in The Netherlands obtained the best campaign results. Use case Tables 17.1 and 17.2 to calculate return on investment of the different placements. Suggest different reasons for this placement being the most successful in terms of ROI?

4 Considering the objectives of the campaign, did Nokia use the best e-marketing tactics? What other creative tactics could be used by Nokia to achieve the same objectives?

5 Do you think mobile marketing and interactive digital television should be considered as a part of the e-marketing plan by Nokia's marketers? What kind of marketing actions would you propose in these new media?

6 How was the effectiveness of the Nokia Concept Lounge campaign measured in this case? What other metrics could be useful when paying attention to the communication objectives of the Nokia Concept Lounge campaign? What would be the best way to obtain these kinds of metrics?

Source: Nokia.

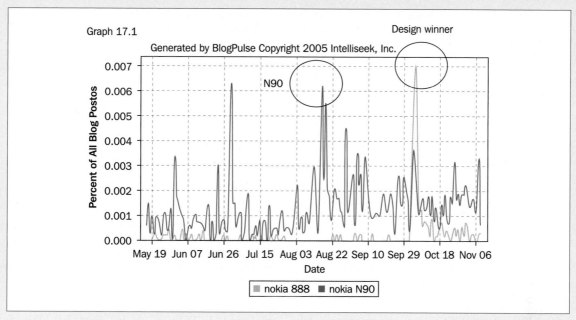

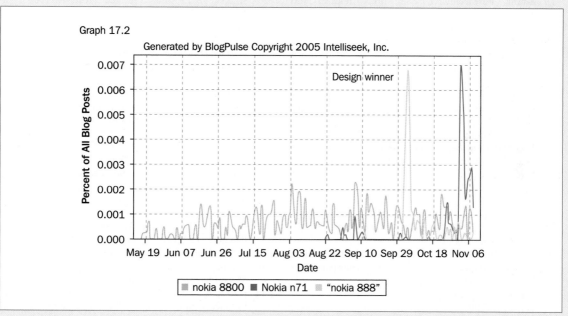

References

1 Butterfield, L. (2003), *AdValue. Twenty Ways Advertising Works for Business*. Oxford: Butterworth-Heinemann.

2 Based on Network Wizards Internet Domain Survey, (January 2006), http://www.isc.org/ds/

3 Samiee, S. (1998), 'The Internet and International Marketing: Is there a Fit?', *Journal of Interactive Marketing*, 12(4), 5–21.

4 Peters, L. (1998), 'The New Interactive Media: One-to-one, but Who to Whom?', *Marketing Intelligence & Planning*, 16(1), 22–30.

5 Based on Domain Tools.

6 Meadows-Klue, D. (2006), 'Europe: online advertising crosses topping point', contributed for this book on behalf of the IAB Europe.

7   De Wulf, K., Van den Bergh, J., Vergult, C. and De Boek, F. (2003), 'Using Internet Marketing Tactics to Support FMCG Brands: an overview of lessons learned', *White Paper published by InSites Consulting*. http://www.insites-consulting.com.

8   Reicheld, F. and Schefter, P. (2000), 'E-loyalty, Your Secret Weapon on the Web', *Harvard Business Review*, July/August, 105–13.

9   Strauss, J., El-Ansary, A. and Frost, R. (2003), *E-Marketing. 3rd edition*. New Jersey: Prentice Hall.

10 Adams, R. (2003), *www.advertising. Advertising and Marketing on the World Wide Web*. Cambridge: The Ilex Press Limited.

11 Strauss, J., El-Ansary, A. and Frost, R. (2003), *E-Marketing. 3rd edition*. New Jersey: Prentice Hall.

12 Elkin, T. (2003), 'Size Matters; So Does Prize', *Advertising Age*, January, 13.

13 Adlink Research/Engage, OAR, Summer 2001.

14 Briggs, R. (2001), *Measuring Success: An Advertising-Effectiveness Series from the IAB*, 1(3), 1–5.

15 Interactive Advertising Bureau/Dynamic Logic, *Ad Unit Effectiveness Study*, March–June 2001, www.dynamiclogic.com.

16 Adlink Research/CNET.com press release, July 2001.

17 Adlink Research/Millward Brown, 2000.

18 Webchutney (2002), *Juxtaposition Compiler*.

19 Dynamic Logic (2001), 'Branding 101: An Overview of Branding and Brand Measurement for Online Marketers', (March), www.dynamiclogic.com.

20 Weima, K.W. (2002), *Webvertising. Tools voor een Effectieve Campagne (Tools for an Effective Campaign)*, Alphen aan den Rijn: Kluwer.

21 Allen, C., Kania, D. and Yaeckel, B. (2001), *One-to-One Web Marketing. Build a Relationship Marketing Strategy One Customer at a Time*. New York: Wiley Computer Publications.

22 Strauss, J., El-Ansary, A. and Frost, R. (2003), *E-Marketing. 3rd edition*. New Jersey: Prentice Hall.

23 *Interactive News*, August 2002.

24 Prensky, M. (2002), 'The Motivation of Gameplay', *On the Horizon*, (August).

25 Chen, J. and Ringel, M. (2002), 'Can Advergaming be the Future of Interactive Advertising?', White paper published by Fast Forward (www.kpe.com).

26 Abcnews.com, November 2002.

27 Pintak, L. (2001), 'It's Not Only a Game. Advergaming Set to Become a Million Dollar Industry', 23 May, www.turboads.com/richmedia_news/2001rmn/rmn20010523.shtml.

28 Rogers, A. (2002), 'Game Theory', www.fastcompany.com/build/build_feature/yoya.html.

29 Neuborne, E. (2001), 'Viral Marketing Alert!', *Business Week*, (March).

30 Adformatie Online (2001), 'Veel Respons op Dove Moment' ('Much Response to Dove Moment Campaign'). http://www.adformatie.nl/nieuws/Nieuws20001-06-26.html#item11027.

31 Smith, P.R. and Chaffey, D. (2002), *eMarketing Excellence: The Heart of eBusiness*, Oxford: Butterworth-Heinemann.

32 Krishnamurthy, S. (2000), 'Is Viral Marketing All It's Cracked Up to Be?', Clickz.com. www.clickz.com/mkt/onl_mkt_comm/article.php/823941.

33 Jupiter MMX, 2002.

34 DBT Database & Internet Solutions (2001), 'Viral Marketing', December, www.dbt.co.uk.

35 Strauss, J., El-Ansary, A. and Frost, R. (2003), *E-Marketing. 3rd edition*. New Jersey: Prentice Hall.

36 'Supermarket sweep', *Advertising Age, Direct & Database Supplement*, October, 16, 2000 and various online sources: www.kcustom.com/articles/winemover.htm, www.kresch.com/articles/art012.htm, www.the-marketing-agency.com/sweepstk.html (2003).

37 Saunders, C. (2001), 'Häagen-Dazs Launches Web Promotion for New Dessert', *Internet News*, June, www.internetnews.com/IAR/article.php/788831.

38 *Internet Sampling: Reaching Consumers* (2001), Congress presentation, 10th Annual Conference on Global Electronic Marketing (GEM), 8/22/01, San Diego, USA, www.gmabrands.com/events2001/gemcon/weiss.pdf.

39 Strauss, J., El-Ansary, A. and Frost, R. (2003), *E-Marketing. 3rd edition*. New Jersey: Prentice Hall.

40 ACP (Association of Coupon Professionals) (2001), *A Guide to Internet Coupons*, www.couponpros.org.

41 Chaffey, D., Mayer, R., Johnston, K. and Ellis-Chadwick, F. (2003), *Internet Marketing. Strategy, Implementation and Practice*. Essex: Financial Times/Prentice Hall.

42 Waring, T. and Martinez, A. (2002), 'Ethical Customer Relationships: A Comparative Analysis of US and French Organizations using Permission-based E-mail Marketing', *Journal of Database Marketing*, 10(1), 53–69.

43 Rapp, S. and Martin, C. (2001), *Max-e-marketing in the Net Future. The Seven Imperatives for Outsmarting the Competition in the Net Economy*. New York: McGraw-Hill.

44 Furger, R. (2000), 'E-mail's Second Shot', *Upside*, 12(4), 160–8.

45 Postma, O. and Brokke, M. (2002), 'Personalisation in Practice: The Proven Effects of Personalisation', *Journal of Database Marketing*, 9(2), 137–42.

46 Strauss, J., El-Ansary, A. and Frost, R. (2003), *E-Marketing. 3rd edition*. New Jersey: Prentice Hall.

47 Khera, R. (2002), 'E-mail Marketing Primer: 12 Tips for Successful Campaigns', *The Magazine for Magazine Management*, 30(9), 53.

48 EMarketer (2002), 'Does Permission E-mail Marketing Push Consumers to Purchase?', *eMarketer e-zine*, October, 28.

49 Cameron, D. (2001), 'SMS Text Messaging for Easy, Targeted and Responsive Online Marketing', www.imagesofone/articles.

50 Haig, M. (2002), *Mobile Marketing: The Message Evolution*. London: Kogan Page.

51 Enpocket Insight (2002), 'Consumer Preferences for SMS Marketing in the UK', www.enpocket.com, August.

52 FEDMA and Forrester (2001), *The Marketer's Guide to SMS*, December.

53 Barwise, P. and Strong, C. (2002), 'Permission-Based Mobile Advertising', *Journal of Interactive Marketing*, 16(1), 14–24.

54 Enpocket InSight (2003), 'The Response Performance of SMS Advertising', www.enpocket.com, February.

55 De Kerckhove, A. (2002), 'Building Brand Dialogue with Mobile Marketing', *Advertising and Marketing to Children*, July–September, 37–42.

56 Wise, T. and Hall, D. (2002), *Pause or Play? The Future of Interactive Services for Television*. Accenture.

57 Lekakos, G. (2002), *An Integrated Approach to Interactive and Personalized TV Advertising*, Athens University of Economics and Business.

58 Bernoff, J. (2002), *Smarter Television. The Forrester Report*, (July).

59 For a more comprehensive overview, see: Cauberghe, V. and De Pelsmacker, P. (2006), 'Belgian Advertisers' Perceptions of Interactive Digital TV As a Marketing Communication Tool', Proceedings of the ITV 2006 Conference, Athens.

60 Stewart, D.W. (2004), 'The new face of interactive advertising: It's time to rethink traditional ad research strategy', *Marketing Research*, 16(1), 10–15.

61 Godin, S. (1999), *Permission Marketing: Turning Strangers into Friends, and Friends into Customers*. London: Simon & Schuster.

62 + 63 Bellman, S. (2004), 'The impact of adding additional information to television advertising on elaboration, recall, persuasion'. Paper presented at the ANZMAC Conference, Wellington.

64 Body, W. (2004), *New Media and Popular Imagination*. Oxford: Oxford University Press.

65 + 66 Lekakos, G., Papakiriakopoulos, D. and Chorianopoulos, K. (2001), 'An integrated approach to interactive and personalized TV advertising', in M. Bauer, P.J. Gmytrasiewicz and J. Vassileva (eds), *User Modeling 2001: 8th International Conference*. Berlin/Heidelberg: Springer-Verlag.

67 Body, W. (2004), *New Media and Popular Imagination*. Oxford: Oxford University Press.

68 Saatchi and Saatchi Quatro. (2005), 'What's new? IDTV for advertiser'. Retrieved at October 2005 at http://whatsnewsaatchi.blogspot.com/.

69 Body, W. (2004), *New Media and Popular Imagination*. Oxford: Oxford University Press.

70 Pickton, D. and Broderick, A. (2001), *Integrated Marketing Communications*, Essex: Prentice Hall/Financial Times.

71 Otten, R. (2005), 'De online toekomst heet Web 2.0 (The future of on line is called Web 2.0)', *NRC Handelsblad*, December, 12. www.nrc.nl.

72 www.emarketer.com (13 January 2006).

73 Green, H. (2005), 'Searching for the pod of gold', *Business Week Online*, 14 November. www.businessweek.com.

74 Andrew, A. (2006), 'BMW drives into audio book podcasts', *The Times*, February 04.

75 Several postings on adverblog.com (2006).

76 Sifry, D. (2006), 'State of the Blogosphere', April 2006 Part 1: On Blogosphere growth. Posted on 1 May 2006 on Technorati's weblog: www.technorati.com/weblog/.

77 Dearstyne, B.W. (2005), 'Blogs. The new information revolution?', *Information Management Journal*, September/October, 38–44.

78 Heires, K. (2005), 'The blogosphere beckons: should your company jump in?', *Harvard Management Communication Letter*, 2(4), November.

79 'Invisible marketing: What every organization needs to know in the era of blogs, social networks and Web 2.0', whitepaper, www.marqui.com.

80 Smith P.R. and Chaffey, D. (2002), *eMarketing Excellence: The Heart of eBusiness*, Oxford: Butterworth-Heinemann.

81 Chaffey, D., Mayer, R., Johnston, K. and Ellis-Chadwick, F. (2003), *Internet Marketing. Strategy, Implementation and Practice*. Essex: Financial Times/Prentice Hall.

82 Strauss, J., El-Ansary, A. and Frost, R. (2003), *E-Marketing. 3rd edition*. New Jersey: Prentice Hall.

83 Allen, C., Kania, D. and Yaeckel, B. (2001), *One-to-One Web Marketing. Build a Relationship Marketing Strategy One Customer at a Time*. New York: Wiley Computer Publications.

84 Jobber, D. and Fahy, J. (2003), *Foundations of Marketing*. Berkshire: McGraw-Hill.

85 Strauss, J., El-Ansary, A. and Frost, R. (2003), *E-Marketing. 3rd edition*. New Jersey: Prentice Hall.

86 Van den Bergh, J. (2002), '45% of Belgian Marketers Actively Set Up Internet Actions', Press release of the *eBenchmark Survey* of InSites Consulting, December, 9. www.insites-consulting.com.

87 Chaffey, D., Mayer, R., Johnston, K. and Ellis-Chadwick, F. (2003), *Internet Marketing. Strategy, Implementation and Practice*. Essex: Financial Times/Prentice Hall.

88 Sen, S. (1998), 'The Identification and Satisfaction of Consumer Analysis-Driven Information Needs of Marketers on the WWW', *European Journal of Marketing*, 32(7/8), 688–702.

89 Weima, K.W. (2002), *Webvertising. Tools voor een Effectieve Campagne (Tools for an Effective Campaign)*. Alphen aan den Rijn: Kluwer.

90 Chaffey, D., Mayer, R., Johnston, K. and Ellis-Chadwick, F. (2003), *Internet Marketing. Strategy, Implementation and Practice*. Essex: Financial Times/Prentice Hall.

91 Chaffey, D., Mayer, R., Johnston, K. and Ellis-Chadwick, F. (2003), *Internet Marketing. Strategy, Implementation and Practice*. Essex: Financial Times/Prentice Hall.

92 www.insites-consulting.com (2003).

93 Bhat, S., Bevans, M. and Segupta, S. (2002), 'Measuring Users' Web Activity to Evaluate and Enhance Advertising Effectiveness', *Journal of Advertising*, 31(3), 97–106.

Chapter 18

Business-to-business communications

Chapter outline

Business-to-business marketing, target groups and products

Differences between business and consumer marketing

Business buying behaviour and marketing communications

Marketing communications in a business-to-business environment

Chapter objectives

This chapter will help you to:

- Understand the specific nature of business-to-business marketing, its target groups and products, and the important differences between business and consumer marketing
- Learn about business-to-business buying behaviour, and how it affects marketing communications
- Understand the typical characteristics of business-to-business marketing communications, and how they work
- See how specific the business-to-business communications mix is

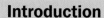

Introduction

Although large parts of this book focus on business-to-consumer marketing communications, in fact the majority of marketing activity takes place between companies. Therefore, business-to-business communications are an important marketing communications topic. Evidently, in a business-to-business environment, largely the same principles of sound communications hold. However, there are a number of important differences between communications in a consumer environment and in a business environment. First, products, customers and markets are different. Buyer decision-making behaviour is generally more complex, and other factors influence the buying decision and the way in which customers seek information. As a result, marketing communications will have to be adapted to these different circumstances, not only in terms of the communications techniques, but also regarding the instruments that are used, or at least the relative emphasis that is put on some instruments at the expense of others.

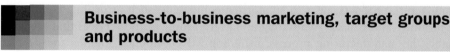

Business-to-business marketing, target groups and products

Business-to-business marketing can be defined as all activities that are related to marketing products to organisations (commercial, government and distributors) in order for them to resell the products or to use them in the production of consumer or industrial products, or to facilitate the activities of the company. Business-to-business marketing has a larger scope than industrial marketing. The latter refers to the marketing of often complex goods or services to companies that manufacture consumer and industrial products. The former also includes marketing consumer products to resellers or marketing not to individuals but to organisations.[1]

The customer groups of business-to-business marketing consist of three categories (Table 18.1) which are not mutually exclusive, i.e. a company can buy goods or services to use them, while at the same time it can be an OEM. Resellers or distributors buy products to market them to the next intermediary in the distribution chain or to the final consumer. Supermarkets buy food products from manufacturers like Nestlé and Coca-Cola, and sell them to end consumers. The Apple Education Centres sell the Apple hard- and software to schools and universities. Original equipment manufacturers buy industrial goods and incorporate them in their own products. Monroe sells shock absorbers to car manufacturers who build them into their cars. Users are industrial companies that buy industrial products or services to support or enable the production

Table 18.1 Business-to-business marketing target groups

- Commercial organisations
  - Resellers
  - Users
  - Original equipment manufacturers (OEMs)
- Government organisations
- Private not-for-profit organisations

process or the activities of the company in general (machinery, copiers, computers, paper, cleaning products, etc.).

Government organisations buy products, such as paper, fax machines and computers, and services, such as opinion polls or laboratory tests, to use them, or products such as bricks and machines to build into other equipment, such as in road construction or power plants. Government buying procedures are characterised by complex decision-making and legal constraints. Private not-for-profit organisations constitute a variety of organisations, such as schools, hospitals, religious organisations, pressure groups, cultural organisations, etc. Usually they buy products as users.

Business-to-business goods and services can be classified into categories in a number of ways.[2] Four basic types of products can be distinguished (Table 18.2). Entering goods are goods that are part of a final product. They can be raw materials, such as copper ore or vegetable oil, semi-finished products such as steel cords or chemical substances, or parts, such as hard disks and gearboxes. Foundation goods or capital goods are pieces of equipment that are necessary to manufacture other products. Two categories can be distinguished. Installations, such as buildings and plants, are the basic equipment needed to manufacture products, next to supporting equipment, such as drilling equipment, office furniture and trucks. Facilitating goods are products and services that facilitate or enable the manufacturing process, including MRO supplies (maintenance, repair and operating), such as paint and cleansing material, and services, such as advertising agencies or maintenance contracts. Reseller goods are usually consumer products that are purchased to market them to the next stage in the distribution process or to the final consumer. Car dealers buy cars from manufacturers to sell them to the public. Supermarkets purchase pet food to market it to final customers.

Table 18.2 Business-to-business products

- Entering goods
- Foundation goods
- Facilitating goods
- Reseller goods

Differences between business and consumer marketing

Business marketing differs from consumer marketing in a number of ways, some related to the market and the marketing environment, others to the appropriate marketing mix. They are summarised in Table 18.3. Business market structures tend to be more oligopolistic (fewer sellers) and oligopsonistic (fewer buyers). This implies that business marketers know their customers better and can approach them in a more individualised way. Consumer markets are often monopolistically competitive in that there are a number of sellers trying to differentiate their products, and many buyers. Business marketers often face derived instead of direct demand. Demand for many business products only exists because, at the end of the line, there is a direct demand from end customers. As a result, business marketers can seldom influence end demand directly. Furthermore, there is no direct relationship between end demand and derived demand. A company

Table 18.3 Differences between business and consumer markets

Market structure	Product/service mix
■ Competition	■ Product life cycle
■ Demand and demand levels	■ Product specification
■ Reverse elasticity	■ Branding
■ Buying behaviour	■ Services
Marketing philosophy	■ Equipment compatibility
■ Market perspective	■ Consistency of quality
■ Market segmentation	**Price**
■ Innovation	■ Competitive bidding
■ Buyer/seller interaction	■ Price negotiation
Distribution	■ Leasing
■ Channel length	■ Product life-cycle costs and benefits
■ Product knowledge	■ Discount structures
■ Channel complexity	**Marketing communications**
■ Delivery reliability	

Based on: Gross, A.C., Banting, P.M., Meredith, L.N. and Ford, I.D. (1993), *Business Marketing*. Boston: Houghton Mifflin.

may need a piece of equipment to manufacture 100,000 bars of chocolate, but as long as demand is not well over 100,000 it is not going to buy a second machine. This leads to a situation of heavily fluctuating demand for business products, and thus a greater sensitivity of sales to business cycle fluctuations. In most consumer markets, price elasticity of demand is negative: if prices fall, demand increases, and vice versa. In business markets the phenomenon of reverse elasticity is quite common: if prices decrease, companies might postpone buying in the expectation of further price cuts.

Although consumer markets tend to become increasingly global over time, a lot of consumer products are still adapted to local tastes and habits. This is far less the case in business markets that are more homogeneous on a global scale. Market segmentation does not take place on the basis of demographic or psychographic characteristics, but on the basis of the type of industry, the end markets served, the level of technology and the characteristics of the decision-making unit, such as the number of members of that unit, centralised versus decentralised decision-making, the types of people in the unit, institutional characteristics, etc. In consumer markets innovation is often consumer-based and therefore aimed at style and incremental changes. In a business marketing environment innovation tends to be much more technology-driven and research and development-based.

Although consumer marketers are becoming, or trying to become, more consumer-focussed, in general business markets are traditionally much more customer-oriented. Indeed, business marketers often have to deal with relatively few customers directly, often through face-to-face contacts. This implies that they know the needs and wants of their customers very well, and the marketing process is highly individualised and interactive. Furthermore, often companies buy and sell on the basis of reciprocity: car manufacturers need computers, but computer companies also need cars, and therefore they might agree to buy and use each other's products. In general, relationship marketing, i.e. building long-term, high-service relations with customers, is far more frequently practised in a business-to-business environment. Finally, most business marketers have to take the phenomenon of key accounts into consideration. Key accounts are the limited number of customers that are of crucial importance in that loosing them would cause huge problems.

Dupont: corporate brand building in a business-to-business environment

Dupont de Nemours was founded in 1802 in the US to manufacture gunpowder. The first overseas office was opened in London in 1905. Much of Dupont's success can be attributed to its expertise in polymer chemistry. The company has continuously been at the forefront in developing new materials, such as cellophane packaging, nylon, Teflon and Kevlar. By 1990 50% of its sales came from outside the US. The company is ranked in the top 10 on the Fortune 500 list of industrial companies, and employs some 90,000 people in 80 countries. More than 2,000 employees and US$1.8 billion are devoted to research and development. But communication also contributed to Dupont's success. The corporate message, associated with the well-known oval Dupont logo, started as 'Better things for better living through chemistry'. In 1980 the words 'through chemistry' were dropped to stress the broader scope of the company's product range. The new slogan 'The miracles of science' was launched through a global communications campaign with TV, print and poster advertising and promotional and public relations activities. The company was one of the first industrial companies to understand the importance of corporate branding in a business-to-business environment by means of consistent communications.[3]

In business marketing, industrial products are often marketed. They generally have a shorter product life cycle than consumer products due to the speed of technological changes. Furthermore, industrial products are often much more customised, i.e. tailored to the needs of individual customers, than consumer products. Many industrial products do not have a brand name, or at least brand names are less intensively used as marketing instruments. That does not mean that brands cannot be important in an industrial context. Given the nature of the products concerned, very often the corporate branding strategy is used: the company name and reputation is used as an endorsement for the products. Business customers demand and receive many more services than most private consumers. Pre- and post-transaction services and installation services in particular are important instruments of the marketing mix. Equipment compatibility is an important factor in product specification and buying decisions. Original equipment manufacturers attach a lot of importance to the extent to which product and components can be integrated into their products without problems. Consistent quality is an attribute of the product environment which is more crucial to business customers than to individual consumers.

Due to the complexity of the products sold, business distribution channels are generally short and direct. Often, the company sells directly to the customers by means of its own salesforce, or sales agents are used as the only intermediaries. Therefore it is extremely important that the distribution channel and/or the salesforce has a thorough knowledge of the often complex technical characteristics of the products sold. On the other hand, business marketers often have to deal with a variety of different and often complex channels. Selling to a government organisation requires a different approach from marketing to different types of OEMs. Finally, in business markets delivery reliability is much more crucial than in most consumer markets.

Bruhn: improving the corporate image through personalised communication

The Danish company Bruhn distributes Canon office machinery in Denmark. From its sales-force Bruhn learned that several companies did not want to deal with Bruhn. Bruhn decided to settle this matter and began a dialogue with 435 of the largest companies in Denmark. The objective was to find out the prejudices companies held against Bruhn and to clear these out in order to eliminate possible barriers for future sales. The campaign was called 'I can handle the truth – not the uncertainty'. As a first step, a direct mail questionnaire was sent to the selected companies. In an accompanying letter Bruhn's CEO urged the chief buyers to fill in the questionnaire and, above all, to tell the truth. After two other mailings, a fourth mailing was sent in which Bruhn's CEO stated his new vision for Bruhn. Each buyer received a personal letter based on the answers in their questionnaire. This is an example of a real one-to-one dialogue which proved to work very well. Bruhn succeeded in turning 20.5% of the responding chief buyers into customers. The campaign was rewarded with a gold Best of Europe Award.[4]

As far as price is concerned, although many industries and companies use 'official' list prices, they are only indicative. Price negotiations and discount structures are common practice in a business marketing environment. Companies often make use of competitive bidding systems, ranging from the solicitation of quotations to very formal sealed bid procedures. Although the purchasing price is an important criterion, very often considerations of product life-cycle benefits and costs will play an equally import-ant role, i.e. the extent to which a product has an influence on the total cost and benefit structure of the company over its whole life cycle.

All these differences have an impact on the way the company communicates. In the next section the impact of the specific characteristics of business buying behaviour on marketing communications is discussed. The influence of the differences in market situation on marketing communications strategies and tools is then highlighted.

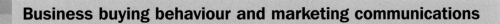

Business buying behaviour and marketing communications

Business buying behaviour depends on a number of factors that are substantially different from the consumer marketing environment. The number of customers and prospects (potential future customers) is considerably lower than in consumer markets, implying a closer relationship between buyers and sellers. Orders tend to be relatively large, which increases the importance of gaining or losing one of them. Purchase motives in business buying processes tend to be more rational, economic, objective and profit- or efficiency-oriented. Purchase risks are very high. Buyers are often technically qualified and highly involved specialists. This is seldom the case in consumer markets. Since the market situation is often both oligopolistic and oligopsonistic, individual business buyers tend to be more powerful than in consumer market situations. On the other hand, a company often faces substantial switching costs as a result of changing suppliers. This results in greater buyer loyalty.

Differences in business ad characteristics between the UK and the US

Similar to consumer advertising, business-to-business ads may differ between cultures. In a comparative study of US and UK business ads, the following differences were found:[5]

- In the US emotional appeals are used more frequently (21.4%) than in the UK (11.7%).

- A greater part of the ad is used to portray the product in the US (on average 40.1% of the page) as compared to the UK (30.5% of the page).

- US advertisers use the quality proposition more often, while the UK ads more frequently use the high sales potential appeal.

- 89% of the headlines of UK ads could be classified as informational. This is only the case for 58% of the US ads. US ads use emotional appeals in 40% of the cases. This is in contrast with the general perception that the US is more 'hard sell'-oriented.

The authors of the study note that the cross-cultural differences in business ads are much less pronounced than is usually found in consumer marketing communications. Business advertising tends to be more global and homogeneous than consumer advertising campaigns.

Possibly the most important difference between consumer and business buying behaviour is the size of the buying unit. When individual consumers buy a product, they may be influenced by reference groups, but generally buy products on their own or with other members of the household. In business buying situations a buying centre or decision-making unit (DMU) is often comprised of several members who play different roles in the buying process. The DMU can be large or small, depending on the size of the company, the newness of the buying situation and the degree of formal structure of the company. In large, highly structured companies the DMU can be large and complex. As to the newness of the product, often a distinction is made between a new task, a modified rebuy and a straight rebuy. Furthermore, different functional responsibilities can be represented in the DMU, such as top management, purchasing, maintenance, transportation, R&D and manufacturing management. Depending on the type of buying situation, these functional areas will influence the decision to a different extent. In Table 18.4 an overview is given of the relationship between the stage in the product life cycle, the newness of the task and the size and composition of DMUs. Members of the DMU can also play various roles, such as information gatherer, key influencer, decision-maker, purchaser and user. Often a number of these roles are combined in one person, or a person can have a part in more than one role.

Table 18.4 Type of buying situation and nature of DMU in business marketing

Stage of product life cycle	Type of purchase situation	Size of DMU	Key functions in DMU
Introduction Growth Maturity	New task Modified rebuy Straight rebuy	Large Medium Small	Engineering and R&D Production and top managers Purchasing

Based on: Howkins, D.I., Best, R.J. and Coney, K.A. (1992), *Consumer Behaviour. Implications for Marketing Strategy.* Homewood, IL: Irwin.

The organisational decision-making process consists of a number of stages, i.e. problem or need recognition, product specification, information search leading to a short list of suppliers, obtaining proposals and evaluating them, supplier selection and purchase decision, product usage and, finally, evaluation. In different stages of this buying process, different functional roles and hierarchical levels tend to have an impact on the decision. Lab technicians, operators and heads of department are mostly involved in the first stages of the decision-making process. Purchasing managers or buyers, and to a lesser extent finance managers and accountants, are important in supplier selection and obtaining proposals. The evaluation of proposals is mainly monitored by top management and heads of departments. The involvement of the board of directors is highest in the supplier selection stage. Overall, the role of top management and heads of department is important in all stages of the process.[6]

Although marketing communications can be important in the other stages of the decision process, it is particularly in the information search stage that their role is crucial. Therefore, it is important to consider the relative importance of the sources of information considered in the various stages and circumstances of an industrial buying situation.

In Table 18.5 an overview is given of the information sources that a business-to-business buyer can use during the buying process. The taxonomy is based on two criteria, i.e. whether the source is personal (face-to-face) or not, and whether it is commercial (paid for by the seller) or non-commercial.

Traditionally, the role of personal commercial sources of information is emphasised. More particularly the role of the salesperson is stressed. However, studies show that other sources of information tend to be important. In an American study, two samples of 400 and 232 organisational buyers and purchasing managers were interviewed on the sources of information they use when making a buying decision. In Table 18.6. their perceived usefulness of various sources of information is shown. In the first sample,

Table 18.5 Sources of information during the buying process

	Personal	*Impersonal*
Commercial	Salespeople Telemarketing Trade shows Interactive websites E-mail	Advertising Direct mailing Sales literature (catalogues, brochures, etc.) Sales promotions Informational website Mass e-mail (spam)
Non-commercial	Top management Using department Terminal users Outside consultant Colleagues Purchasing department E-mail Chat rooms	News publications Trade associations Rating services List services Bulletin boards

Adapted from: Moriarty, R.T. and Spekman, R.E. (1984), 'An Empirical Investigation of the Information Sources Used during the Industrial Buying Process', *Journal of Marketing Research*, 21 (May), 137–47; Deeter-Schmelz, D.R. and Kennedy, K.N. (2002), 'An Exploratory Study of the Internet as an Industrial Communication Tool. Examining Buyer's Perceptions', *Industrial Marketing Management*, 31, 145–54.

Table 18.6 Usefulness of information sources

Source of information	Usefulness sample 1 (% of respondents)	Usefulness sample 2 (score on 5-point scale, 5 = very important)
Third-party location information	50.1	4.44
The internet, websites	21.1	3.21
Advertising in trade journals/magazines	20.4	2.80
Colleagues' experience/word-of-mouth	16.7	4.10
Personal experience/travel to meetings	14.4	4.47
Direct-mail brochures	13.6	3.87
Personal sales calls	3.4	2.95
Trade associations	3.1	–
Direct-mail promotional items	3.1	2.73
Attendance at trade shows	2.9	3.36
Articles in trade journals/magazines	2.9	3.20
Newsletter from meeting facilities	–	2.66

Adapted from: Deeter-Schmelz, D.R. and Kennedy, K.N. (2002), 'An Exploratory Study of the Internet as an Industrial Communication Tool. Examining Buyers' Perceptions', *Industrial Marketing Management*, 31, 145–54.

respondents had to list their useful sources of information (unaided recall); in the second sample, a list of sources was presented and the respondents had to score their usefulness on a five-point scale. Third-party location information (e.g. conventions and visitor bureau resources), the internet, personal experience, colleagues' experiences and word-of-mouth, and direct-mail brochures are perceived to be the most important sources of information in both samples. In sample 2, the internet is only ranked 6 in order of importance in the usefulness of information tools. In Table 18.7 the actual use of the internet for various purposes is measured in the same sample of purchasing managers. Again, importance ratings are given. Apparently, besides e-mail exchange, the internet is mainly used in the information gathering and exchange stage of the buying process. It is used far less as a truly interactive tool of supplier selection, placing and following up orders.[7]

In a study on a complex investment decision, five information sources were identified:

1 Promotion agency-controlled information (personal or impersonal commercial).
2 Non-commercial impersonal sources (news articles, etc.).
3 Personal independent or non-commercial sources (consultants, etc.).
4 Internal information sources.
5 Outside consultants.

Internal sources appeared to be by far the most important ones, while both non-commercial and commercial impersonal sources were the least important.[8]

Research shows that as the procurement decision progresses, the role of personal non-commercial sources of information becomes more important. The impersonal sources of information appear to be greatest in the early stages of the decision process. This implies that after the initial stage of information search, during which mainly impersonal commercial or non-commercial sources of information are used, the opinion of 'significant

Table 18.7 Use of the internet as an information gathering tool

Purpose of internet use	Average score (1 = never, 5 = always)
E-mail	3.96
Gathering product information	3.28
Searching for new suppliers	3.24
Gathering information regarding current suppliers	2.94
Providing information to suppliers	2.61
Gathering competitive information for your company	2.56
On-line ordering	2.47
On-line order status checks	2.45
Accessing supplier documents	2.37
Gathering external customer information for company	2.32
On-line customer support	2.29
Electronic data interchange	2.21
Discussion groups with other customers	1.55
Just-in-time inventory planning	1.51
On-line payments	1.41
Conducting reverse auctions	1.18

Based on: Deeter-Schmelz, D.R. and Kennedy, K.N. (2002), 'An Exploratory Study of the Internet as an Industrial Communication Tool. Examining Buyers' Perceptions', *Industrial Marketing Management*, 31, 145–54.

others' or reference persons, such as consultants and competitors, is more important.[9] Public relations can be an important tool with which to build goodwill with these reference groups, which can result in positive effects on the decision-making process of potential customers. Another component of personal non-commercial sources of information are the members of the DMU. Again, approaching all members of the DMU is imperative for the business marketer. For the buyer, organising efficient internal communications between the members of the DMU is crucial in taking a purchase decision. As the decision process proceeds towards supplier selection, internal reports and internal communications become more important. Obviously influencing reference groups also implies integrated PR efforts towards all relevant audiences. The build-up of goodwill may result in favourable media exposure.

Evidently, many factors influence the use of information sources by the various members of the DMU. For instance, younger, innovative and better educated decision-makers are inclined to rely on a wider variety of sources of information, especially external ones. Large companies tend to formalise their information search more than smaller ones. In addition, the higher the decision risk or the decision turbulence, the more external sources of information will be sought, especially during the early stages. Also, different members of the DMU in different types of companies often have different motives and therefore need different types of information. Initiators, influencers, deciders, buyers and gatekeepers of intermediaries (wholesalers, suppliers, resellers) are often interested in pricing, after-sales service, inventory management and technical information. End users often focus on timely delivery, technical information, volume discounts and product support.[10]

Regional differences and buying behaviour in China

China is an enormous country, and it would be a mistake to assume that all Chinese companies, regions and managers are similar. More particularly, various regions have had a distinctly different history and have been exposed to the Western style of doing business in a totally different way. For instance, the northern region has few foreign investors and foreign partners, and is rather traditional. The south pioneered the economic reforms in China, and companies and customers in the south have been extensively exposed to overseas investors and products. The work pace is faster and markets change rapidly. The Shanghai region (eastern coast) was the economic and financial heart of Asia before 1949, and has been influenced by Western culture for decades. Numerous multinational companies have operations in China, and therefore the business style in Shanghai is very westernised. In the table, the three regions are compared on the basis of a number of criteria that relate to business (buying) behaviour.[11]

Comparison of industrial customers' characteristics in three Chinese regions

Characteristics	Northern region	Southern region	East coastal region
Exposed to Western technology	Less	More	More
Adoption of new ideas	Least	Most	Moderate
Initiation of contact	Difficult	Moderate	Moderate
Friendship maintenance	Easy	Moderate	Moderate
Guanxi orientation (personal friendship/connection)	Strong	Less strong	Weak
Long-term relationship orientation	Strong	Less strong	Moderate
Keeping promises	Poor	Moderate	Strong
Negotiation time	More	Moderate	Less
Approval time	More	Moderate	Less
Calculative decisions	Less	Moderate	More
Credit	Poor	Moderate	Good

Based on: Lee, D.Y. (2003), 'Segmentation and Promotional Strategies for Selling CARB Bearings in China', *Journal of Business and Industrial Marketing*, 18(3), 258–69.

As the buying decision process proceeds, and as companies work with the same suppliers more often, the nature of the relationship between the company and its suppliers will alter. In Table 18.8 the communication tasks, tactics and types in different stages of the relation-building process is given. In the pre-relationship phase, awareness-building takes place by means of one-way mass media communication tools and tactics. In the negotiation stage, interactive communication starts to take place, aimed at persuading the

Table 18.8 Communication tasks, tactics and types in different stages of the relation-building process

Relation-building phase	Pre-relationship	Negotiation	Relationship development
Communication task	Awareness	Persuasion	Commitment
Communication type	Supplier → Buyer	Supplier ↔ Buyer	Supplier ↔ Buyer
Communication tactics	Mass media Reputation management Referrals	Influence tactics	Part-time marketing Episodal communication EDI Customer visits

Adapted from: Andersen, P.H. (2001), 'Relationship Development and Marketing Communication: An Integrative Model', *Journal of Business and Industrial Marketing*, 16(3), 167–82.

potential buyer by means of personal selling efforts, implying multiple contacts between the seller and the DMU of the buyer. In the relation-building phase, commitment is built through interactive communication. In this stage, the communication does not have to be continuous any more (part-time marketing). Episodal communication means that interaction information is automatically recorded and stored in a database, and the company acts upon it through semi-automised internet (e-mail) contacts and electronic data interchange (EDI). Websites can be used as permanent relation-building tools. They can be integrated with and supplement personal contacts between sellers and buyers.[12]

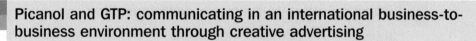

Marketing communications in a business-to-business environment

The two major consumer marketing communications instruments, i.e. advertising and sales promotion, are relatively unimportant tools in business communications. Personal selling is by far the most important tool, together with the technical documentation the salesperson brings along. Trade shows, although only marginally important, nevertheless play a much greater role in business communications than in consumer marketing. The role of direct mailing, database marketing and certainly the internet has increased in recent years (see also Tables 18.6 and 18.7).

Picanol and GTP: communicating in an international business-to-business environment through creative advertising

Picanol is a Belgium-based company that manufactures different types of weaving machines. More than 2,600 weaving mills all over the world use Picanol equipment. The machines are renowned for their high productivity, reliability and flexibility. Picanol provides many special features on its machines for enhanced added value and to increase their productivity. GTP is an independent subsidiary of Picanol that offers worldwide services to Picanol customers and other textile manufacturers. While Picanol sells and installs weaving machines, GTP provides services, technical and electronic maintenance, parts, accessories and upgrades on a continuous basis. It also sells 'GTP approved' second-hand machines. GTP positions itself as a full-service company of services and accessories for the textile industry that helps its customers concentrate upon their core business by leaving all maintenance and service activities in the hands of GTP. In 2002 the company decided to reinforce its image worldwide by launching an integrated communication campaign, using corporate brochures, mailings, an internet site, a CD/give-away, exhibitions and trade fairs, road shows and press conferences and, last but not least, advertising. The same creative concept was used throughout all communications tools. To communicate that the manufacturer is able to concentrate on his work, and that GTP takes care of all the rest, a musical metaphor was used: 'As a musician you can concentrate upon your music, we take care of all the other problems: concert halls, scores, instruments maintenance . . .). In the visual execution of the campaign, musical instruments (piano, harp, violin, etc.) are shown in which textile threads replace the strings, and other recognisable textile utensils are built into the instruments. Also country-specific instruments are used. This creative metaphor is universal and can be used in various cultural settings. It can be applied to all the communications tools. At the same time it is modern, stylish and emotional, and suggests quality and top class.[13] Although advertising is not as intensively used in industrial marketing situations as it is in business-to-consumer contexts, creative advertising can be a relevant tool in the communications mix of industrial marketers.

In Figure 18.1 the most important distinctive characteristics of business communications are summarised. As already indicated in the previous section, personal communications tools, and primarily the salesforce who call and/or visit customers and prospects, play a very important role in business marketing. In fact, to a large extent even trade shows can be considered to be a relatively 'personalised' means of conversation. Business communications are not only personal, they are to a large extent also personalised or individualised. Direct mailing, but also trade shows and certainly personal selling, provide the opportunity of communicating directly with individual customers and prospects. Third, business communications are interactive. Interactivity is to a certain extent a common characteristic of direct mailing, personal selling and trade shows. Customers can be approached individually, but they can also respond to the communications. Furthermore, communications in a business environment are usually much more tailor-made than in consumer markets. Customers often have specific needs and effective communications require tailor-made solutions being offered and communicated. Finally, business products are often technically complex, and lead to high involvement decision-making processes, the consequence of which is that marketing communications will be more rational and more objective attribute-oriented. Brand images and emotions play a less important role in business communications. Business advertising and direct mail often pave the way, laying the groundwork for the salesforce by creating awareness and interest in the company and its products, and as such often have a supportive role in the communications process.

Compaq: direct-to-customer communication

Hardware suppliers are turning more and more to direct marketing. Although this communications tool is too expensive to address individual consumers, it often produces good results in a business-to-business environment. However, the trade is very sceptical about direct contact between supplier and customers. Even Dell Computers, pioneer in direct trade, works for certain products in the B-to-B segment with trade partners. The same goes for Compaq. Compaq is increasingly trying to avoid trade partners and is undertaking efforts to get to know its customers better. Currently, Compaq is building a database. Compaq plans to launch the project 'Compaq Dialog', the objective of which is to build long-term communications with its business-to-business customers. At the end of 1998 Compaq launched a direct mail campaign in which it addressed 96,000 existing or potential customers. By completing four questions, the respondent received a present. However, anyone who turned down the first present offered could gain a more valuable present at a later stage. Further, by means of mail, fax and call centres, Compaq tried to enter into a dialogue with its customers through its website. Sixty per cent of existing and potential customers replied by using the electronic highway. Compaq also plans the launch of an electronic customer magazine.[14]

Do communications work differently in a business environment from in a consumer environment? Figure 18.2 shows a model of how communications (and, more particularly, advertising) work in a business-to-business marketing environment. It is an adaptation of the ELM, discussed in Chapter 3, to a business marketing situation. The central new concept, as compared with the traditional ELM, is the buy task involvement (BTI). It is a feeling of personal relevance that members of the DMU experience when facing a specific buying situation. The model acknowledges the fact that the personal values of the members of a DMU and the personal consequences of the purchase decision play a

Figure 18.1 The distinctive characteristics of business communications

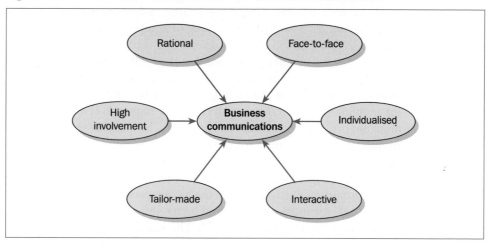

Figure 18.2 A model of business-to-business communications effects

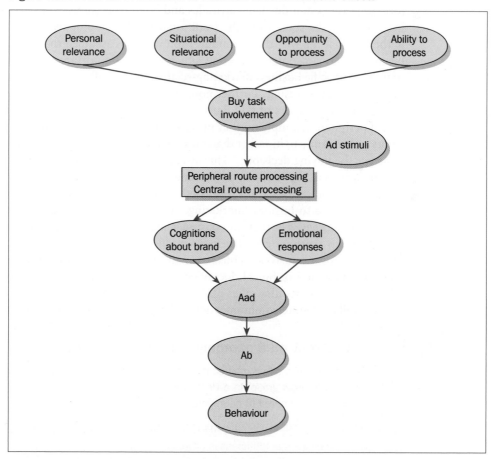

Adapted from: Gilliland, D.I. and Johnston, W.J. (1997), 'Toward a Model of Business-to-Business Marketing Communication Effects', *Industrial Marketing Management*, 26, 15–29.

role in how communicative stimuli will be processed, because they influence BTI. If a DMU member attaches a lot of importance to doing a good job, his BTI will be higher. If the buying decision involves a piece of equipment with which he has to work on a daily basis, his BTI will also be higher. Next, situational sources of relevance influence BTI, such as the role of the individual in the DMU, and the importance of the purchase to the individual and the company. If the individual plays an important role in the DMU, and mistakes in the buying decision have important negative consequences for the individual or the company, BTI will be higher. BTI will also increase if there are more opportunities to process information. The greater the amount of communications stimuli the DMU member is exposed to and the more frequent the repetition of messages, the higher BTI will be. Ability also plays a role in the development of BTI. The more a person knows about the problem and the product, the easier it becomes to process information. Furthermore, as the buying process enters its final stage, the members of the DMU are more informed and better able to process the information.

All four categories influence BTI. The higher the BTI, the more likely it becomes that a member of the DMU will process the information in the ad centrally. If BTI is low, depending on its antecedents and determining factors, the more likely it is that the information is processed peripherally, and the more important the communications format becomes in influencing attitudes and buying decisions. The latter line of reasoning is exactly the same as in the traditional ELM. The importance of this model lies in the fact that the way the communication works is assumed to be exactly the same in business as in consumer marketing situations, the important difference being that a number of specific business marketing-related factors influence the likelihood of central or peripheral processing. Furthermore, it acknowledges the fact that, depending on the determining factors of BTI, business-to-business communications can also be processed peripherally, implying that in some circumstances the format of the ad, and the emotional response to it, rather than the content of the ad and the cognitive reaction, may influence the buying decision.[15] This insight is increasingly put into practice in business communications, especially in advertising (see below).

The communications tools discussed in previous chapters of this book can all be used in business-to-business marketing. Some of these tools, such as promotions, will be used less intensively than in consumer marketing, although it is a frequently used instrument in marketing to resellers (trade promotion). Other tools are used more often, or almost exclusively in business marketing, such as trade shows and exhibitions, and catalogues and technical documentation. A large part of the personal selling and telemarketing activity also takes place in the business-to-business environment, and PR activity and corporate communications, and direct mailing play a significant role.

How can direct mail campaigns be made effective?

The effectiveness of a direct mail campaign depends on the opening, reading and response behaviour of the target group. In a Belgian study the following characteristics of business-to-business mailings appeared to be important for effectiveness:[16]

■ Standard A4 envelopes increase opening behaviour.

■ The presence of a stamp increases envelope opening.

■ The use of normal paper envelopes increases the chance of the envelope being opened.

▶

- Opening behaviour is not affected by the number of mailings respondents received on a given day.
- Generally speaking, no reader or situational characteristics are related to opening behaviour.
- No letter or reply instrument characteristics have a significant impact on reader behaviour.
- Situational factors (such as the number of mails received) do not influence reading behaviour.
- Personal factors, such as the manager's attitude towards direct mail, are important influencing factors of reading behaviour.
- Reading behaviour has a significant impact on response behaviour. If a mailing is read more thoroughly, the chances of response increase.
- Marketing managers seem to respond more frequently to mailings than other managers.
- Mailings related to building, maintenance and industrial equipment show high response rates.
- A positive attitude on the part of managers to direct mail enhance response chances.

In Table 18.9 the most frequently used business marketing communications tools or materials are presented and divided into media-specific and non media-specific instruments. Advertising has traditionally played a minor role in business communications, and the instrument was and is mainly used in trade journals targeted at a specific specialised audience. In recent years, however, there has been a major shift in the advertising budget from the specialised media to the more general ones, and an increasing use of communications techniques that are also used in consumer marketing. In the US consumer magazines and television represent 73% of the business-to-business advertising budget.[17]

Table 18.9 Business marketing communications instruments

Media-specific	Broadcast	■ Radio spots ■ Television spots ■ Infomercials
	Print	■ Trade magazine ads ■ Consumer magazine ads ■ Newspaper ads
Non media-specific	Selling materials	■ Corporate and product brochures ■ Technical specification sheets ■ Direct mail ■ Telemarketing ■ Trade show participation ■ Corporate and product videos
	Publicity	■ Press releases ■ Product photography ■ Press conferences and events ■ Ghost-written articles ■ Technical articles

Based on: Gilliland, D.I. and Johnston, W.J. (1997), 'Toward a Model of Business-to-Business Marketing Communication Effects', *Industrial Marketing Management*, 26, 15–29.

Traditionally, business-to-business advertising has been described as 'heavy, ponderous, deadly serious and boring'.[18] This qualification can be attributed to the specific characteristics of the business environment, i.e. the importance of technical aspects of products and services, the importance of the products for the economic performance of the buyer, and the complex decision-making units. Business ads, for that reason, tend to be more factual and rational, and tend to emphasise the company name rather than its products, because customers are also buying reliability, after-sales service and technical support, in other words, a relationship with a trustworthy partner.

Advertising business-to-business consultancy services: PWC

In recent years, the consultancy industry has witnessed important mergers and acquisitions, accompanied by renaming and re-branding of the companies involved. Re-branding and repositioning tasks are always accompanied by major communication campaigns in which a variety of tools can be used. This is illustrated by the story of PWC.

In 1999 a number of companies merged into PricewaterhouseCoopers (PWC). The merger was accompanied by a creative advertising campaign intended to build brand awareness and brand image among its high-profile business customers worldwide. The 2001 'PWC Corporate Finance and Recovery' campaign in the European business press was shortlisted as Best Business Press Campaign for the prestigious European Media and Marketing Awards. The company supplements its advertising efforts by sponsoring various initiatives, such as the Fast Track 100 and Profit Track league tables, which identify the fastest growing and most profitable UK companies. PWC also produces reports and survey results that are of interest to the boardrooms of its clients, and is strongly involved in the World Economic Forum at Davos and the European Business Forum. PWC's website is used to promote stakeholder dialogue and supports the company's extensive community programme, such as the sponsorship of the web-based Maths Enhancement Programme with the University of Exeter. PWC also places a lot of importance on internal marketing to inform and motivate its 20,000 employees.[19]

On the other hand, there are a number of reasons why business advertising should not be so different from consumer advertising. After all, the human element is present in both situations, and some of the functions of advertising are common to both markets. As to the second factor, in business-to-business communications, advertising is used to create awareness and interest, and to build preference or reinforce the attitude after the customer has purchased the product. As far as the first factor is concerned, people are not all that different on and off the job, and are always subject to emotions, values and even biases. Some studies even suggest that once basic performance criteria are met, business decisions are largely based on psychological factors, such as earlier experience with a vendor, vendor credibility, experience, flexibility and reliability to serve customers in the future, and vendor commitment to a particular technology. A study of the portrayal of women in business ads even suggests that a substantial number of female members of business DMUs finds business ads sexist, and would, therefore – all 'objective' characteristics of competing offerings being equal – buy from a company that advertises in a less offensive way.[20] Given the increasing role of women in business, that is an observation worth taking into account. It is clear that business ads can also be effective when they focus on these 'intangibles', rather than stressing objective product characteristics.[21]

All in all, studies show that the content and format of business ads are significantly different from consumer ads in a number of ways. The most striking differences seem to be that fewer people are depicted in business ads, the proportion of advertising space devoted to copy tends to be greater in business advertising, product characteristics are more frequently mentioned, and psychological – as opposed to functional – appeals are seldomly used in business advertising.[22]

Just because advertisers and advertising agencies are doing something, it does not always mean that they are doing the right thing. What are the dimensions of an effective business-to-business ad? Research shows that a successful business ad should score on four dimensions: characteristics of the ad, the reader's feelings about his or her relationship with the ad, the selling proposition and the company's orientation or visibility. To score positively on each of the dimensions, business ads should clearly use a rational approach. The ad should explain the product and the benefits of the product, its quality and performance. The information should be presented in a logical order. On the other hand, the size of the text should be closely monitored. Too much text and too much information decrease ad effectiveness. On the other hand, the use of illustrations and pictures, as long as they are relevant to the target group, enhances ad effectiveness. Including too many people in the ad reduces its impact, and when people are shown, the target group should be able to identify with them. All in all, business ads differ and should differ from consumer ads, but there is no reason to assume that business ads should be dull, and packed with text and information overload.[23]

Summary

Business-to-business marketing is different from consumer marketing in that the former is aimed at different (industrial or other organisational) target groups, different types of products and market situations are involved, competitive structures are often different, and it is generally much more truly global. Traditionally, due to the oligopolistic and oligopsonistic nature of many business markets, customer satisfaction concern is much more predominant in business marketing situations. One of the most important characteristics of a business-to-business environment is the complexity of decision-making units. For marketing communications this implies that for each customer a number of members of the decision-making unit will have to be approached with different yet consistent messages. Furthermore, depending on the complexity of the buying task and the stage in the decision-making process, different members of the DMU will be targets for marketing communications. Business communications tend to be more personal, individualised and interactive. They are more tailor-made and often include high involvement decision processes. As a result, they tend to be quite rational and objective (some say dull), and the marketing communications mix tends to be radically different. However, people are people, and engage in private consumption situations as well as in business buying situations. The same basic factors affecting information processing, such as the elaboration likelihood, affect buying behaviour. And although industrial advertising is still substantially different from consumer ads, there is no reason to believe that most of the persuasion mechanisms found in consumer communications would not hold in a business situation too.

Review questions

1 What are the specific characteristics of business-to-business marketing and how does it differ from consumer marketing?

2 What are the consequences of complex decision-making units for business marketing communications?

3 How can business marketing communications be adapted to the various stages in the decision-making process?

4 In what way are business marketing communications different from consumer marketing communications?

5 How can the elaboration likelihood model be applied and adapted to a business marketing communications situation?

6 Generally speaking, in what way does a business marketing communications mix differ from a consumer communications mix?

7 How different is business advertising from consumer advertising?

Further reading

Coe, J.M. (2003), *The Fundamentals of Business-to-Business Sales and Marketing*. New York: McGraw-Hill Trade.

De Bonis, J.N. and Peterson, R.S. (1997), *AMA Handbook for Managing Business-to-Business Marketing Communications*. McGraw-Hill/Contemporary Books.

Industrial Marketing Management, www.sciencedirect.com/science/journals/

Journal of Business and Industrial Marketing, www.mcb.co.uk/cgi-bin/journal1/jbim

Journal of Business-to-Business Marketing, www.haworthpress.com

Wright, R. (2004), *Business-to-Business Marketing*. Harlow: Addison-Wesley Publishing.

Case 18

From Union Minière to Umicore: rebranding and repositioning an industrial company

Umicore defines itself as a materials technology group. Its activities are centred on four business areas: advanced materials, precious metals products and catalysts, precious metals services and zinc specialties. The company focuses on application areas where it can capitalise on its expertise in materials science, chemistry and metallurgy, both in everyday products and in new technological developments. Umicore defines for itself and its products over 250 applications in 26 activity areas and in 45 industries (see Case Figure 18.1. for the company structure).

Applications range from rechargeable batteries to automotive pollution control, mining tools, solar cells and water repellent lens coatings. The company has achieved a substantial growth over recent years. In 2000, the company had subsidiaries in 25 countries, employed 8,000 people, and had a turnover of €3.8 billion. In 2006, Umicore has industrial operations on all continents and serves a global customer base with its 70 sites in 35 countries and its 14,000 employees. In 2005 the turnover was €6.6 billion. Umicore focuses on sustainable innovation-led

Case Figure 18.1 Company structure

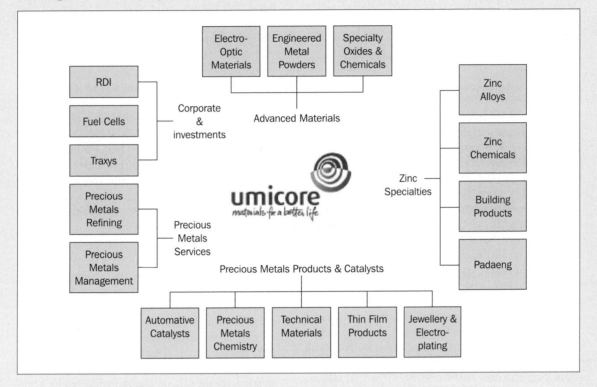

growth, fuelled by high value-added products. Therefore, the company has extensive R&D capabilities. More than 500 employees worldwide are involved in research and development activities, in six countries: a central facility in Belgium, and dedicated units in Germany, Japan, Canada, France and Liechtenstein. R&D spending is over 5% of revenues.

Union Minière: a graveyard brand

For many years and until 2001, the company was known under the name 'Union Minière'. This name referred to its former core business of copper mining and dated back to Belgium's colonial past in the Congo. By the end of the previous century, the company was beginning to feel the burden of a – what appeared to be – inappropriate and even counterproductive name. Union Minière had an excellent reputation amongst its customers and in the industry, but for nearly all other stakeholder groups, the name was a liability. The fact that it was a French name in bilingual Belgium was also considered by some to be a drawback. The company's activities were not correctly perceived by the general public, reducing its attractiveness as an employer; for

attracting new potential customers, especially in the field of advanced materials, the name appeared to be a real obstacle, and also potential investors and the financial markets put Union Minière in the wrong category, and often dismissed it for the wrong reasons. A Research International Survey (November 2000) concluded that Union Minière was a 'graveyard brand', i.e. a brand with a high aided awareness (82%), but very little spontaneous awareness. More than three-quarters of those interviewed did not know or misunderstood the activities of the company. A lot of respondents – not surprisingly, given the name – associated the company with mining. Although industry experts recognised that Union Minière was a modern company operating internationally, its image among the broader public was that of a competent, but old-fashioned, group: 'a big introvert company in the dated, heavy industry with a colonial history that lacks vitality and appeal'. Time and again, investors and analysts urged the company to change its name. The name was also perceived as a handicap by the senior management of the company, because it evoked inappropriate category associations, acted as a mental block for the financial partners, triggered negative impressions of the past, and – important for a global company – was difficult to pronounce abroad.

Integrated communication, brand adaptation or rebranding?

Various strategies could have been adopted to close the gap between the corporate identity and the corporate image, or between the attitudes triggered by the brand name and the real, present-day position of the company. The company could try to close the gap between its identity and its image by keeping the name, but changing the brand values amongst stakeholders. This could be done by means of an integrated communication campaign. The second option was to keep on capitalising on the well-known brand name, but adjust it to signal a change. The third option was to show a radically different corporate identity by changing the brand name and house style. Each option had advantages and disadvantages. Keeping the brand name and changing the image by means of a communication campaign seemed to be a suboptimal and uncertain solution. The power of communication to overcome the negatives evoked by the name should not be overestimated. It was hard to tell how long and how many resources it would take to really change the corporate image by means of communication. Adapting the brand or rebranding, as an obvious sign of change, would facilitate this communication job. The basic choice seemed to be either to gradually change the image of Union Minière by means of communication, or to organise a short-term, big bang by (partly) changing the brand name.

The advantages of a name change are that it is an obvious sign of change, it raises the attention for the company, ensures consistency with the activities of the company, gets rid of the negative brand equity elements of the past, lowers the barriers in the financial community, and facilitates communication. The disadvantages are that it takes a budget to develop and implement a new identity, the existing name recognition is lost, and there is a risk of destabilising the customers. In changing the name, various alternatives were explored:

- *Restrict the name to UM.* This would avoid some of the negative connotations of the full name; carry limited risks (everyone already knew the company as UM); get rid of the problem of pronouncing the name for non-French speakers; allow easy labelling of activities; and lead to less urgency to adapt all brand carriers. On the other hand, this option could have limited impact (*fait divers*), no significant influence on the image, was not an eye-opener for communication, and there was a risk that 'Union Minière' would still be used for a long time.

- *Use UM, but change the full name of the company behind it (e.g. UM Materials).* The advantages are that it would be an internal sign of change, and at the same time signal a gradual evolution externally. On the other hand, the change in itself would have little impact, the risk of negative associations of the past remains, the required budget would be similar to the creation of a completely new identity, and the question would be: which new definition of UM to choose?

- *Go for a completely new umbrella brand name.* This option is undoubtedly the most expensive and most time-consuming one. There is a risk of confusion and destabilisation, although in a business-to-business context this is controllable because the customers are known. It would take a lot of time to fully establish the new identity. And last, but not least, the company would need to redefine its position in a credible and realistic way, to reinforce the idea of 'change' triggered by a new brand identity. The advantages of this 'big bang' option were that it could be a carrier of the idea of 'change' that the company wanted to signal, it would be an eye-opener to raise attention, and facilitate communication. At the same time it could invigorate the internal stakeholders to make the external promise come through. The advantages of an umbrella brand (brand name used for all UM activities and products) that is positioned at an abstract, visionary level (as opposed to a functional benefit positioning) is that it is cost efficient, makes integrated communication more easy, facilitates diversification, allows cross-fertilisation, and offers considerable stretch potential. On the other hand, with umbrella branding, negative associations or adverse publicity are transferred on all activities of the company, existing brand values may not be relevant to new activities, and there is a risk of it becoming banal if the coherence between products and activities is not obvious.

The executive Committee of Union Minière decided to go for a new umbrella brand name that should preferably retain a reference to UM, but be different enough to underline the change that the company underwent, in other words, to adjust the image to overcome the past.

Rebranding and repositioning

The executive committee of Union Minière developed a briefing to create a new brand name that fitted the company's mission and values. This brand name was to be linked to UM, but different enough to signal a change. It was to be a non-descriptive name that should be distinctive, easy to memorise, able to cross linguistic borders, and timeless, that could serve as an umbrella-brand name for all activities, and that should be protectable (trademark, company name, dotcom). The brand characteristics of UM in the past, and the desirable brand connotations for the future as defined by the management, are given in Case Table 18.1. The summary of the core values of UM were described as in Case Table 18.2.

The new brand identity (name, logo, base line) was ready and approved by the board of directors on 13 June 2001 (see Plate 25) and ready to be rolled out and communicated.

Communicating the new identity and position

A company like UM has many important stakeholder groups: internal stakeholders (employees), shareholders, financial opinion makers, media, customers and end-users, governments, pressure groups, recruits . . . The challenge was to communicate the corporate identity change by means of an integrated communication campaign. 'D-day', the announcement of the new name and identity to the general assembly, was scheduled for 3 September 2001. A communication campaign was designed around the event that consisted of the following stages:

1 Pre-communication
   ■ March–June: initial announcement of plans, both internally, by means of internal communication

Case Table 18.1 Past and future connotations of the UM brand

Past	Future
■ Mining and refining, commodities	■ Refining, production and recycling, value-added
■ 'Congo Belge', copper, established and establishment	■ Global, diversified, re-invented, transparent
■ Engineers, operating excellence, push: production-oriented	■ Innovators, EFQM, pull: customer-oriented
■ Factual leadership	■ Recognized leadership and growth
■ Financial disappointment, environmental/social issues	■ Financial, environmental and social equity, credibility
■ Classic, stratified	■ Entrepreneurial, communication
■ Blurred naming, diffuse image	■ One brand, one vision, one image

Case Table 18.2 Brand values of UM

Starting point: Materials for a better life			
Central values (ideals)	Discovery	Sustainability	Success
Expressive values (feelings)	Contemporary (ingenious)	Responsible (citizenship)	Self-confident (underpromising, overperforming)
Instrumental values (thoughts)	Prosperity Material comfort	Durability	Reliable
Objective characteristics	Engineered materials	Recycling	Leading and global (big and stable)
Brand essence: technology for people and the world			

tools, such as a teasing card stating 'have a nice holiday and the new beginning will be surprising', an invitation for a launch event on 9 September, and an information newsletter in various languages

- August: preparing the ground, teasing internal stakeholders to raise attention for D-day, and externally, by announcing the general assembly of 3 September
- Development of new corporate identity manual
- Preparation of brochures, presentations . . .
- Replace 'old' brand vehicle materials: stationary, flags, gifts, website, brochures, newsletters, computer-generated documents, signage, corporate video . . .

2 D-day: 3 September 2001

- 11 a.m.: Announcement of new identity to shareholders and general assembly approval
- Press release and press conference, to communicate the new identity and the rationale for change
- 12 p.m.: Unveiling of new plates and major sign boards at headquarters and sites (see Plate 25)
- Information sessions for all communicators on site, supported by a self-explanatory communication toolbox
- Personalised mailing to all affected by the name change: employees, commercial relations, financial community, local communities . . .

3 Launch week: boost awareness and announce the rebirth of the company to the financial community and the general public

- VIP event for opinion leaders and the media in the Brussels Stock Exchange

- Event for personnel and their families, with some 5,000 people attending
- Advertising in primary media with 'news value': full page newspaper advertisements and radio spots
- Advertisements in financial magazines.

4 September–October: image campaign

- To the international financial community: selection of international press: newspapers and magazines in the USA, UK, France, Germany, The Netherlands and pan-European
- To the customers: selection of professional press worldwide (such as Metal Bulletin)
- New in-house company magazine in six languages: Umicore.link
- Merchandising: Umicore diary, coffee cups, mouse pads, bags
- Presence at exhibitions.

The objectives of the campaign were to create maximum brand name and logo awareness in all countries within one year, to establish legitimacy ('who we are and what we stand for'), and to achieve a significant shift on key image elements such as: dynamic, future-oriented, transparent . . . The budget of the campaign in 2001 was set at €8 million. In Case Table 18.3 the major budget items are shown. It was estimated that, for 2002 and 2003 an advertising budget of about €4 million per year should be foreseen.

Results

The company did not measure the results of the campaign formally with all stakeholders, but infers the success of the operation on the basis of the following:

Case Table 18.3 Budget breakdown for the development, communication and implementation of the new corporate identity

Budget item	Cost (Euro)
Corporate identity development and registration	950,000
Campaign (production and media investments)	4,550,000
Events (VIP and employees)	300,000
Direct mail (customers and employees)	200,000
Implementation (stationary, signs . . .)	1,200,000
Coordination and contingencies	800,000
Total budget	**8,000,000**

- Development and implementation of brochures, video, website, stationary . . . went well. However, after three months, signage and computer-generated documents were not yet fully adapted to the new identity
- Unanimous positive reports in the media
- Personnel event of 9 September 2001 was a success
- 60% of the company's employees reacted positively to the new name, and 30% were neutral
- The company's stock market valuation increased significantly over the ensuing years – although the same change was obviously only one element in the ongoing strategic repositioning of the group. Unaided awareness of company name was 13% as opposed to 2% before the name change
- A Belgian study revealed that 78% of the respondents had seen and understood the Umicore image campaign in the newspapers (as compared with 45% on average for all newspaper campaigns). 83% called the company 'international', 70% 'a leader', 63% 'successful', and 58% 'innovative'. The advertising campaign was called striking (78%), original (68%) and credible (65%)
- Website traffic was six-fold the pre-D day volume
- Spontaneous job applications tripled

- The campaign received an ABAF (Association Belge des Analystes Financiers) award for excellence in financial communication.

Questions

1 Do you agree with the analyses that has led to Umicore's corporate re-branding campaign? What are the advantages and disadvantages of the other options, such as changing the company's image by means of a communication campaign, or adapting the brand instead of re-branding completely?

2 Do you believe the new brand architecture is credible and consistent with the company's activities?

3 Assess the communication campaign that was used to launch the new corporate identity. How could it have been improved? Which other instruments, tools and channels could have been used?

4 The company gives a number of indications of success of the campaign. Do you think they are credible, justified and impressive? How could they have measured the results of the campaign in a more formal way?

Sources: www.umicore.com Interbrand and VVL/BBDO: 'Union Minière. Towards a new image', 2001; VVL/BBDO: 'Union Minière. Exploration of the DNA-structure', 2001; VVL/BBDO: 'Le cas d'Union Minière/Umicore: d'une industrie lourde à une enterprise moderne', 2001; E. Cornelis: 'Umicore name change: threat or opportunity?', 2002; Fons Van Dyck, Strategic planning director, VVL/BBDO; Thomas Leysen, CEO Umicore; Eddy Cornelis, communication manager Umicore.

References

1 Coe, J.M. (2003), *The Fundamentals of Business-to-Business Sales and Marketing*. McGraw-Hill Trade.

2 An extensive categorisation can be found in Gross, A.C., Banting, P.M., Meredith, L.N. and Ford, I.D. (1993), *Business Marketing*. Boston: Houghton Mifflin; Coe, J.M. (2003), *The Fundamentals of Business-to-Business Sales and Marketing*. McGraw-Hill Trade.

3 www.superbrands.org and www.dupont.com, 9 June 2003.

4 Best of Europe, 1998.

5 Cutler, B.D. and Javalgi, R.G. (1994), 'Comparison of Business-to-Business Advertising', *Industrial Marketing Management*, 23, 117–24.

6 Abratt, R. (1986), 'Industrial Buying in Hi-Tech Markets', *Industrial Marketing Management*, 15, 295.

7 Deeter-Schmelz, D.R. and Kennedy, K.N. (2002), 'An Exploratory Study of the Internet as an Industrial Communication Tool. Examining Buyers' Perceptions', *Industrial Marketing Management*, 31, 145–54.

8 Brossard, H.L. (1998), 'Information Sources Used by an Organization During a Complex Decision Process. An Exploratory Study', *Industrial Marketing Management*, 27, 41–50.

9 Belizzi, J.A., Minas, L. and Norvell, W. (1994), 'Tangible versus Intangible Copy in Industrial Print Advertising', *Industrial Marketing Management*, 23, 155–63.

10 Albert, T. (2003), 'Need-based Segmentation and Customized Communication Strategies in a Complex Commodity Industry: A Supply Chain Study', *Industrial Marketing Management*, 32, 281–90.

11 Lee, D.Y. (2003), 'Segmentation and Promotional Strategies for Selling CARB Bearings in China', *Journal of Business and Industrial Marketing*, 18(3), 258–69.

12 Andersen, P.H. (2001), 'Relationship Development and Marketing Communication: An Integrative Model', *Journal of Business and Industrial Marketing*, 16(3), 167–82.

13 www.picanol.be; Saatchi and Saatchi Business Communications, Belgium.

14 *Marketing Mix Digest*, (1999), 34(5), 8.

15 Adapted from Gilliland, D.I. and Johnston, W.J. (1997), 'Toward a Model of Business-to-Business Marketing Communication Effects', *Industrial Marketing Management*, 26, 15–29.

16 De Wulf, K., Hoekstra, J. and Commandeur, H. (1999), 'The Opening and Reading Behaviour of Business-to-Business Direct Mail', *Industrial Marketing Management*, 29, 133–45.

17 Gilliland, D.I. and Johnston, W.J. (1997), 'Toward a Model of Business-to-Business Marketing Communication Effects', *Industrial Marketing Management*, 26, 15–29.

18 Lambert, D.R., Morris, M.H. and Pitt, L.F. (1995), 'Has Industrial Advertising Become Consumerized? A Longitudinal Perspective from the USA', *International Journal of Advertising*, 14, 349–64.

19 www.pwcglobal.com and www.superbrands.org, 9 June 2003.

20 La Tour, M.S., Henthorne, T.L. and Williams, A.J. (1998), 'Is Industrial Advertising Still Sexist?', *Industrial Marketing Management*, 27, 247–55.

21 Bellizzi, J.A., Minns, L. and Norvell, W. (1994), 'Tangible versus Intangible Copy in Industrial Print Advertising', *Industrial Marketing Management*, 23, 155–63.

22 Lambert, D.R., Morris, M.H. and Pitt, L.F. (1995), 'Has Industrial Advertising Become Consumerized? A Longitudinal Perspective from the USA', *International Journal of Advertising*, 14, 349–64.

23 Lohtia, R., Johnston, W.J. and Aab, L. (1995), 'Business-to-Business Advertising. What are the Dimensions of an Effective Print Ad?', *Industrial Marketing Management*, 24, 369–78.

Chapter 19

International communications

Chapter outline

Chapter objectives

This chapter will help you to:

- See why companies go international
- Learn why the international communications process is different from communicating in the home market
- Understand the importance of differences between the components and the dimensions of culture for international marketing communications
- Learn about the importance of legal and regulatory differences for international marketing communications
- See how media use differs between countries
- Understand the factors that influence the standardisation and adaptation of the international marketing communications mix

Introduction

More and more companies are operating internationally. In 2005 the value of world exports amounted to more than 9 trillion euros and world imports even exceeded 9.5 trillion euros.[1] Following this trend, international communications have also grown enormously. However, communicating internationally is not without its problems. International marketing communications management differs from domestic communications management in that one has to operate in a different environment with different demographic, economic, geographic, technological, political and legal conditions. Cultural and legal differences between a company and its foreign marketplace can cause many problems and difficulties. The translation from the message strategy 'what to say' into a creative strategy 'how to say it' (see also Chapter 7) is even more problematic in international marketing communications than it is in domestic communications. The different cultural components can have a major impact on international communications campaigns. The different regulations regarding communications instruments are important. Furthermore, marketing communications have to consider differences in media availability and the popularity of different media. Due to differences in the international marketing environment, a company has to consider the major question: to what extent should it localise (adapt) or globalise (standardise) its marketing communications across different cultures?

Why go international?

International marketing is a complex and difficult activity in which many companies fail. Even a well-established international company like McDonald's does not seem to be able to get a foothold in the South African market due to fierce local competition. Nevertheless, more and more companies are going international.

Table 19.1 gives an overview of several advantages and disadvantages of engaging in international marketing.[2] The basic reason and the (long-term) objective for going international are always to increase sales and profits.

The international communications process

Communications are always a difficult process. Even when the message comes through, misunderstanding can arise when, for example, different people attach different meanings to the same word. Other problems are the distortions a message may undergo during the communications process due to the low quality of the media channel, the distraction of the consumer when he or she is exposed to the message, prejudices of the consumer which leads him or her to interpret the message in a distorted way, low involvement of the consumer which leads to limited attention paid to the communication, etc. In an international context, the communications process is even more complex and more difficult. Figure 19.1 shows the different elements in the process. Because the sender and the receiver have a completely different background, different values, different norms, different expectations, a different view of the world, etc. it is difficult

Table 19.1 Potential advantages and disadvantages of international marketing

Potential advantages of international marketing	Potential disadvantages of international marketing
1 Possibility of creating economies of scale	1 Costs of marketing mix adaptations
2 Growth potential even when there is no or limited growth in the home country	2 Risks of unstable governments
3 Possibility of avoiding fierce competition in the home country	3 Risks of unstable currencies
4 Keeping up with competitors who are going international	4 High entry requirements, different standards, different laws and rules
5 Creation of an international brand image or offering an international service to multinational clients	5 Difficulty of understanding local culture, habits, values, norms, etc.
6 Possibility of disposing of large inventories which the company wants to get rid of	6 Difficulty of getting a foothold in the local distribution channel (e.g. Japan)
7 Possibility of profitably using excess capacity	
8 Possibility of extending the product life cycle if the product is in another life-cycle stage than in the home country	
9 Benefiting from lower labour costs, freer regulations, etc.	
10 Geographic diversification which lowers country-specific risks	

Figure 19.1 The international marketing communications process

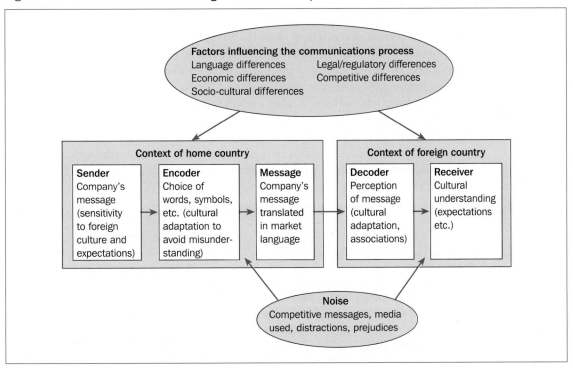

Based on: Bradley, F. (2002), *International Marketing Strategy.* London: Pearson Education; Hollensen, S. (2004), *Global Marketing, A Market-Responsive Approach.* London: Pearson Education.

to send a message that the receiver interprets as it is intended by the sender. In order to accomplish this, a company needs to understand the elements of the foreign market environment thoroughly and try to understand fully the local customers and business partners. What are they interested in, what do they value most, should brand attributes or brand image be stressed, do they want a lot of information, is price or quality more important, what words, images, colours and symbols should be avoided etc.? Because environmental aspects are extremely important in international marketing and international communications, these factors will be discussed in more depth. More specifically, the impact of cultural, legal and media use differences will be highlighted.

Cultural differences and marketing communications

Hofstede[3] describes culture as the 'collective programming of the mind which distinguishes the members of one group or category of people from those of another'. In order to succeed in international communications, marketing communications managers have to understand these cultural differences. The reason for this is that, since consumers grow up in a certain culture and are used to that culture's values and beliefs, they will respond differently to marketing communications.[4] Often, marketers and marketing communications executives fall victim to the self-reference criterion.

The self-reference criterion (SRC) refers to our unconscious tendency to refer everything to our own cultural values.[5] People often expect that foreigners have the same values, same interests, etc. as they do themselves, and if this is not the case, they consider their own habits, values, etc. to be superior. In order to be able to understand other cultures, the marketer has to try to avoid the self-reference mistake, and not take for granted everything he or she is used to. Numerous marketing blunders have been made due to the self-reference criterion. For instance, Fomabo, a Dutch construction company, tried to penetrate the Malaysian market. In The Netherlands, Fomabo was a low-cost company. It made use of a special technique that made it possible to keep labour costs low, but required higher material costs. However, in Malaysia labour costs are very cheap and the Fomabo technique resulted in building houses that were 10%–15% more expensive than competitors. The self-refence criterion led the company to think that building houses in the Netherlands is the same as building houses in Malaysia, without taking local cost factors into account.[6]

Maybe today's youth is not so global after all

Coca-Cola tested more than 30 commercials using a panel of Singaporean teens. Assuming that contemporary youth is global and Asian youngsters can be mirrored to American ones, ads showing things that are typical of American youth, such as body-pierced, grungy kids in a car listening to rock music and head-banging, shirtless youngsters crowd-surfing at a concert and youngsters going down a store aisle on a grocery cart were shown to Singaporean youngsters. However, the ads were not really appreciated by the Singaporean teens. They considered the ads far too rebellious and unruly. The head-banging car scene was particularly disliked. One 18 year old made the comment 'They look like they're on drugs constantly. And if they're on drugs, then how can they be performing at school?' Coke concluded that ads have to be 'within bounds of societal approval' in order to be liked by young Singaporeans. According to the managing director

▶

of Viacom's MTV India, Asian teens are far more conservative than American or European youngsters. Rebellion, anger or the need to question authority, which are all elements of global youth culture, do not appeal in Asia. Asian youngsters may wear earrings, belly-button rings and ponytails, but they are still very conformist, a value deeply seated in Asian culture.[7]

Bajaj Auto, India's largest scooter and motorcycle producer, faired better. Its commercial pictured an Indian boy and his Caucasian girlfriend cruising around on a Bajaj motorbike. Since in India most marriages are still arranged and strict caste codes still operate, this scene is pretty provocative. However, this provocation is set off by the next scene: the youngsters arrive at a temple and the boy covers his girlfriend's head with a shawl. The commercial shows rebellion, but it does not push it too far. According to the creator of the ad, the message of the commercial is 'we are changing, testing boundaries, but we have pride in our core values'. Indian youth loved the ad and Bajaj motorcycles achieved a sales increase of 25% during the seven months following the launch.

Another example of the self-reference criterion would be advertising a laundry detergent in Arab countries, showing from left to right the different stages the laundry goes through: at the left a very dirty shirt, in the middle the laundry detergent brand, and at the right an extremely clean shirt. But Arab people read from right to left. It would not make an effective ad to show a laundry powder making an extremely clean shirt very dirty.

The SRC also cropped up in the promotion of the toothpaste brand Pepsodent. Claiming how white the brand makes your teeth in Asian countries in which yellow teeth are a status symbol is not an example of smart advertising.

Many other examples of the self-reference criterion are frequently mentioned. For instance, to be successful in sales negotiations, do not shake hands or touch Japanese negotiators, do not address German or French people by their first name, do not try to make a business deal over the phone with English business people, remember the style consciousness of Italians with respect to dressing and prepare for their bureaucracies, and practise your singing skills when having a formal appointment with Indonesians since you will probably be asked to take your turn in singing.[8] In Figure 19.2 some important components of culture are given.

Verbal language

Language is an important communications element. Subtle differences or different pronunciations may convey totally different meanings. In Asian countries such as Japan and Thailand, language differs according to who is speaking. The suffixes Thai women use are different from those Thai men use. In Japan the level of formality of the language depends on the gender and the status of the speaker.[9] For marketing communications this means that the seller always has to place him or herself in an inferior position. Furthermore, translation of words may lead to more space requirements which can alter the overall layout of the ad. For instance, 25% more space is needed when translating from English into a Roman language and 30% from English into German. Furthermore, the meaning of words may alter as a result of translation. For example, Germans associate 'ruhig' with a forest, sleep, church, a cemetery and a bed, while 'tranquille' makes the French think of the countryside, a forest, a house, a library.[10]

In general, people like to be addressed in their own language. However, this is not always the case. French people should be addressed in French, while many Asian ads

Figure 19.2 The major components of culture

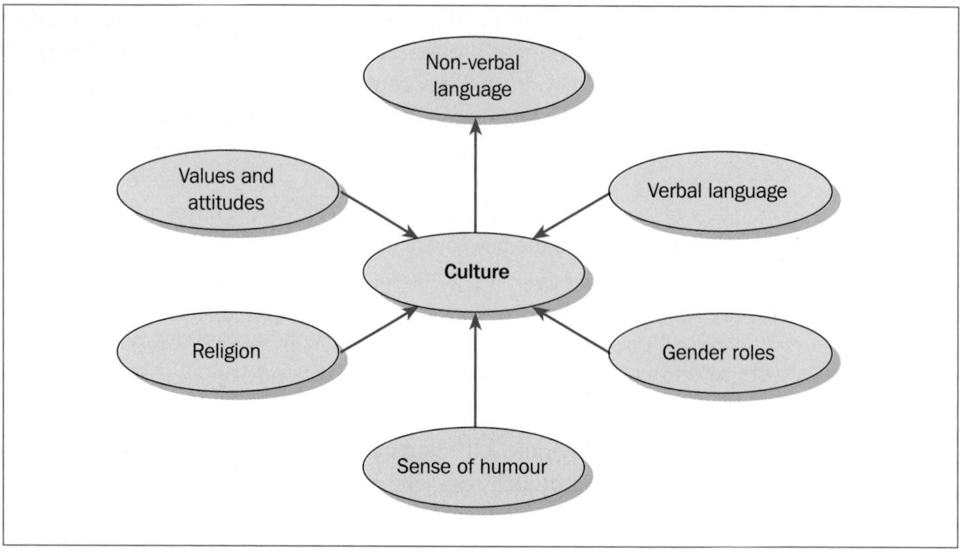

contain English words to achieve positive country-of-origin effects.[11] Marketing communications executives should know which language is most effective for their different international target groups. In general, it is recommended that the company, and especially sales reps, master some foreign languages. Many Japanese companies demand that all its employees speak English.[12] Foreign language skills in several European countries such as Denmark, Finland, The Netherlands, Belgium and Poland are pretty good, with UK companies lagging a bit behind. The latter are more likely to assume that all customers understand English.[13]

Despite the fact that translators usually know the foreign language quite well, translation errors frequently occur. One way to avoid such errors is to translate and back translate, which should result in the same words or sentence(s) as the original one(s). Some examples of translation errors are:[14]

■ The Pepsi slogan 'Come alive, you're in the Pepsi generation' was translated into German in 1960. The result became 'Come alive out of the grave'.

■ GM's brand Chevy Nova translates in Spanish as 'doesn't go', while Nescafé was understood as 'no es café'.

■ A Copenhagen airline office promises to 'take your bags and send them in all directions'.

■ A Hong Kong dentist claims to extract teeth 'by the latest Methodists'.

■ A Japanese hotel left the following notice to hotel guests: 'You are invited to take advantage of the chambermaid'.

■ 'Let Hertz put you in the driving seat' became 'Let Hertz make you a chauffeur'.

■ The truck brand Fiera from Ford became 'ugly old woman' when translated into Spanish.

■ Mitsubishi renamed its Pajero model in Spanish-speaking countries because Pajero is related to masturbation.

Non-verbal language

Non-verbal language is very important for salespersons and in sales negotiations. Aspects of non-verbal language include:[15]

- *Timing*: How important is it to be on time, what is the time concept? If you have a meeting at 3 pm with the Chinese, you can expect them to be there at 2.30 pm, while a meeting with Arab people might result in a delay of about 30 minutes. Furthermore, is time money or do people consider it to be indefinitely available? A time-is-money person (such as in Europe and the US) might have difficulties working with people who do not adhere to this time concept. The same goes for the difference between monochronic (M time) versus polychromic (P time) use of time. M time people (such as Europeans and Americans) do one thing at a time and stick to preset schedules. When a meeting takes longer than planned, they will leave the meeting and go to the next one. P time people (such as the Japanese), on the other hand, are more committed to persons, ongoing discussions, meetings, etc. than to schedules. They take things as they come. In negotiations, sales promotions schedules, point-of-purchase agreements, etc. the difference in M and P time orientation can lead to serious problems. Finally, a distinction can be made between a time orientation towards the past, present or future. Many European countries have an orientation towards the past, using the past to explain where we are now. Americans are more future-oriented, while Muslim countries are rather fatalistic and adhere to a present-time orientation.

- *Space*: Asian and Arab people tend to stand very close to one another, Western and American people leave more space and find it rather threatening when people stand close to them. According to Hall's 'proxemics', Western countries are characterised by three primary zones of space: the intimate zone (0–45 cm), the personal zone (45 cm–1 m) and the social zone (1–2 m). However, within Europe differences concerning optimal space also appear: the further south you go, the smaller the distance gets.

- *Touch*: Northern Europeans, the English and Americans are said to have a low-touch culture, demonstrating low contact in public, while southern Europeans, Arabs and eastern Europeans are said to have a high-touch culture. However, although a country may belong to a high-touch culture, one should keep in mind subtleties in touching rules in advertising and in sales negotiations. Touching a woman is usually a more sensitive area, and especially in Arab countries this may cause problems.[16] Moreover, who touches who also depends on the culture. In Europe it is usual to see people of the opposite sex (a couple) walking hand in hand on the street. This is not the case for many Asian and Arab countries. Here you would rather see people of the same sex (not a couple, but just acquaintances) holding hands.

- *Colours*: Colours have different meanings in different cultures. Not knowing these cultural meanings may lead to international failures, often merely due to the wrong package colour. An example is the Dutch company Daf, which tried to introduce its trucks in Saudi Arabia. Trucks were used most often in the building sector. In this sector all machines (e.g. bulldozers and cranes) belonged to Caterpillar. Since Caterpillar's products are strong and reliable, and since Caterpillar's products are yellow, yellow became associated with strong and reliable material in the building sector in Saudi Arabia. Daf trucks were orange. Only after Daf painted its trucks yellow did sales begin to rise.[17] In the US and Europe, green is often associated with freshness and good health, but in countries with dense green jungles it is associated with disease instead. Red suggests good fortune in China but means death in Turkey. White stands for purity and cleanliness in many European countries, but suggests death in many Asian countries. Black has negative connotations in Japan, India and Europe, but is perceived positively in the Middle East.[18]

- *Gestures*: Cultures differ in the way they greet each other: shaking hands, bowing, kissing, etc. Furthermore, moving the head back and forth is an affirmative sign in most Western countries, but means 'no' in Greece and Bulgaria. Patting a child on the head is a sign of affection in Western cultures, but an insult in Islamic countries. Raising three fingers when ordering a drink means you want three drinks in Western countries, but in Japan you would be ordering two drinks since they count the number of fingers that are down instead of up.

- *Eye contact*: Looking someone straight in the eye is regarded positively by Europeans and Americans because it is perceived as a sign of honesty. However, in Japan you show respect by lowering your eyes.

Values and attitudes

Values and attitudes are our guide in determining what is right and what is wrong, what is important and desirable. To a great extent, consumer behaviour is determined by values and attitudes. Therefore, it is extremely important to understand different cultural values and beliefs. Some researchers claim that cultural values form the core of advertising messages and that advertising reinforces cultural values.[19] Since different cultures cherish different values, different cultures, not surprisingly, emphasise different communication appeals. Even in the US and the UK, two countries in which the marketing environment is very similar (economic development, language, legal restrictions, marketing institutions, technology, etc.), differences in culture lead to different types of advertising appeals. A study investigating beer ads in the two countries found that American ads predominantly depict American values such as achievement, individualism/independence and modernity/newness, while British ads show British values such as tradition/history and eccentricity (acting strangely or whimsically, often to humorous ends). Furthermore, in British ads the beer is more often shown being drunk on regular occasions, while in American ads product use is depicted during special occasions or the usage is not shown at all.[20] Empirical studies show that it is also advisable to follow a culture-congruent communications strategy since consumers seem to respond more positively to culture-congruent appeals (see Plate 26).[21] In Table 19.2 the results of two studies on cultural standards in a number of countries are summarised.

In Asian cultures, such as China, Vietnam, Japan, etc., a well-known norm is saving one's face, a norm many Europeans have difficulty understanding.[22] This has important consequences for interactions with Asian people in the sense that Asians will try to avoid or retreat from potentially embarrassing social situations. Another consequence is that only after a positive personal relationship is built, will business contacts be successful for Asian people, while most Europeans are more task-oriented.

Religion[23]

Religion influences international marketing in a profound way. First of all, it influences what is allowed to be said or shown in a marketing message. For example, Seiko got

Table 19.2 Cultural values in the US, Germany, France and Vietnam

Cultural values in the US	Cultural values in Germany	Cultural values in France	Cultural values in Vietnam
Individualism	Formalism	Individualism	Interest for studies
Egalitarian orientation	Power orientation	Democracy	Hierarchy
Action orientation	Performance of one's duty	Rationalism	Patience, persistence
Achievement/competence orientation	Family orientation	Creativity and inventiveness	Charity, benificence
Interpersonal distance regulation	Interpersonal distance regulation		Honesty, truthfulness
Social acceptance	Physical distance regulation	Valuing culture	Gratefulness
Calmness/'easy going'	Frankness/ outspokenness		Face saving
Patriotism	Personal property		Sense of the family
Relation between sexes	Traditional role expectations		Loyalty
Future orientation			Tenacity

Adapted from: Holzmüller, H.H. and Stöttinger, B. (1998), 'A Pragmatic Concept for Developing the Cultural Sensitivity of Marketing Managers', in P. Andersson (ed.), *Proceedings of the 27th Emac Conference, Marketing Research and Practice, Track 2: International Marketing*. Stockholm, 213–36; Chan, N. and Prime, N. (1998), 'Vietnamese and French Value Systems: Empirical Study and Managerial Implications', in P. Andersson (ed.), *Proceedings of the 27th Emac Conference, Marketing Research and Practice, Track 2: International Marketing*. Stockholm, 333–47.

into trouble when it ran its worldwide advertising campaign in Malaysia saying 'Man invented time, Seiko perfected it'. According to Islam, God and not man invented time, so the message had to be changed to 'Man invented timekeeping, Seiko perfected it'. In France Volkswagen had to withdraw its billboards for the new Golf since it was said to mock the Last Supper. A modern version of the Last Supper is shown, the last meal Jesus had with his disciples. Instead of 'Drink, this is my blood', Jesus says 'Let's rejoice since the new Golf is born'.

Second, religion influences the value people attach to material goods. According to Islam and Buddhism, material wealth is immoral, while in the Western world wealth is a symbol of achievement. Therefore, status appeals can be expected to be more successful in Western countries than in Islamic or Buddhist countries. Third, religion has an influence on what products can and cannot be consumed. An ad for a refrigerator should not show beef or pork inside the refrigerator if the ad is meant to run in countries with a Hindu or Islamic culture. (See Plate 28.)

Sense of humour

Some countries make more use of humour than others. Ads in the UK, for instance, are more likely to contain humour than in the US or France, while a higher percentage of ads in the latter countries are humorous than in Germany. Furthermore, different cultures seem to appreciate different types of humour. Incongruent humour is more often used in German (92%) and Thailand (82%) than in the US (69%) and Korea

(57%). The English like black humour, the Germans slapstick and demeaning humour, while the Japanese seem to prefer black humour and dramatisations.[24]

Gender roles

Since communications have to be made in a way that consumers can identify with, a lot can be learned about a nation's perception of gender roles by analysing how men and women are depicted in advertising. A review of content analyses in different countries leads to the conclusion that gender roles in advertising differ to a great extent from one country to another. In Malaysia, women are usually depicted in the home taking care of the children. In Singapore, women are concerned with looking beautiful and are often shown in white-collar and service occupations. German and Japanese advertising stick much more to traditional gender roles than ads in Denmark, France, New Zealand and the US. Australian and Swedish ads have a more balanced and non-traditional way of presenting men and women in advertising.[25] The former differences of a culture's view on gender roles is not only important for creating advertising, but also for salespersons. Using traditional gender roles, such as talking about the 'lady's kitchen', the 'lady's vacuum cleaner', etc. when trying to sell a house to a young European couple will not be appreciated by these women since more and more men and women share household chores while in Muslim countries, such as Malaysia, it would be unwise to infer that men could have a role in the housekeeping.

High- and low-context cultures

Hall introduced the concept of the communication context. According to him,

> 'a high-context communication or message is one in which most of the information is either in the physical context or internalized in the person, while very little is in the coded, explicit, transmitted part of the message. A low-context communication is just the opposite; i.e. the mass of the information is vested in the explicit code.'[26]

In other words, in low-context cultures, a lot of emphasis is placed on words. One is as accurate, explicit and unambiguous as possible so that the receiver can easily decode the message and understand what is meant. In high-context cultures words are one part of the message, the other part is formed by body language and the context, i.e. the social setting, the importance and knowledge of the person. In the latter case, the message is more ambiguous and implicit. The Japanese, for example, have 16 ways to avoid saying 'no'.[27] Needless to say, the greater the context difference between the domestic and the target country, the more difficult to communicate and the better salespersons should be trained in how to make their message clear. Advertising appeals also differ to a great extent in different context cultures. For example, Japanese ads have been shown to contain fewer information cues, less emphasis on the product's benefits, fewer comparisons and to consist of more emotional appeals than American ads.[28] In other words, in Japan a soft-sell approach is preferred, while in the US a hard-sell approach is more frequently encountered.

Cultural dimensions[29]

According to Hofstede five cultural dimensions can be distinguished which can explain the differences in cultural components across countries (Figure 19.3).

Figure 19.3 Hofstede's five cultural dimensions

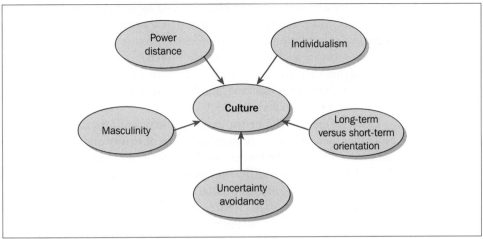

Several researchers consider the value attached to individualism versus collectivism to be one of the most basic dimensions of a culture.[30] The characteristic of individualism is that there are loose ties between people and that they look after themselves and their immediate family only. In collectivistic cultures people belong to strong, cohesive in-groups (often extended families) who look after and protect each other in exchange for unquestioning loyalty. Central to individualism is giving priority to personal goals over the goals of the group, as well as an emphasis on differentiation and achievement, while collectivism stands for the reverse: harmony, conformism, group goals, participation and team work above all. This leads to differences in advertising appreciation. An empirical study shows that Americans respond more favourably to an individualistic appeal, while Chinese people react more positively to a collectivistic appeal. It should be added, though, that a culturally incongruent appeal is less harmful when the appeal matches the product use condition. For example, a Chinese individualistic appeal for a toothbrush is less harmful than a Chinese individualistic appeal for a camera.[31]

The degree of power distance refers to the extent to which authority plays an important role, and to what extent less powerful members of the society accept and expect that power is distributed unequally. In high-power distance cultures (e.g. Malaysia), a few people have all the power and make all the decisions. The other people carry out orders. In low-power distance cultures (e.g. Denmark, Austria) power is not concentrated in the hands of a few and interactions between people occur on a more equal basis. In the latter case people are used to evaluating information and making decisions themselves. For communications this might mean that expert endorsers are more appropriate in high-power distance cultures in which people are used to being and expect to be told what to do, while information-dense ads might be more appropriate in low-power distance cultures in which people appreciate making decisions on the basis of information offered.[32]

In masculine cultures, assertiveness, competitiveness and status are valued highly while in feminine cultures caring for others and quality of life are central values. In feminine cultures men's and women's values and roles coincide, while there is a larger gap in their roles in masculine cultures.

Uncertainty avoidance refers to the extent to which people feel uncomfortable with uncertainty and ambiguity and have a need for structure and formal rules in their lives. Communications for uncertainty avoidance cultures can focus on expert appeals and providing information and guarantees to reassure consumers.

Long-term versus short-term orientation deals with values such as pragmatic future-oriented thinking, virtue, thrift, perseverance and a sense of shame versus conventional, history or short-term thinking, fulfilling social obligations, respect for tradition and a sense of security and stability.

Based on these five dimensions, 10 synthetic cultures can be derived (see Table 19.3). Note that these cultures are simplifications of reality and that such extreme cultures do not exist. However, the tendencies demonstrated in each of them do exist in real world. Table 19.4 shows how different countries score on Hofstede's dimensions and on the communications context dimension.

Depending on our own culture, we can easily misinterpret the behaviour or a communications message of people of another culture. For example, an individual belonging to a low-power distance-oriented culture can perceive foreigners as bossy, rigid, servile or cowardly, while feminine-oriented individuals may see others as aggressive or macho and think that they show off and have a 'baby doll' attitude towards women. Long-term-oriented people often think others behave irresponsibly and throw away money, while collectivistic individuals often perceive foreigners as insulting, heartless and rude.[33]

How do people belonging to different cultures react?[34]

Imagine the following situation:

A sales representative is going to a formal business meeting in a foreign country. The meeting is with a marketing manager he has never met before. When he arrives at the airport, a warmly smiling woman dressed casually in jeans and sandals welcomes him. What would he think:

Reaction	Culture	Explanation
She must be a secretary	Masculine	In masculine countries gender roles are unevenly divided, with men holding more of the higher positions than women
She must be the person with whom I am going to have the meeting	Feminine or uncertainty tolerant	In the first case: he is not surprised that it is a woman In the latter: he does not mind that she is casually dressed
It is wonderful to be welcomed so warmly	Collectivistic	Makes him feel that he is accepted in the inner group
How dare someone meet me in such an informal outfit	High-power distance	He is disappointed because no impressive delegation is there to show appropriate respect
There must be an error	Uncertainty avoidance	He is confused because he expected a formally dressed person since people show their position through their clothing

Table 19.3 Summary of Hofstede's synthetic cultures

Culture	Obsession	Communication	Words with positive connotation	Non-verbal behaviour	Stereotypes
Individualistic	Individual freedom	Explicit, noisy	Pleasure, I, me, self-actualisation, individual, etc.	Eye contact, far space	Hurried, loners
Collectivistic	Group harmony	Implicit, tone and pauses, quiet	We, face, harmony, sacrifice, tradition, honour, etc.	Close space with in-group	Never alone, devious
High power	Respect for status	Very verbal, but polite and quiet	Respect, master, wisdom, protect, obey, orders, etc.	Restrained, formal, far space	Hierarchical and seek to please
Low power	Equality	Talk freely in any context, noisy	Rights, complain, negotiate, fairness, criticise, question, etc.	Informal, unceremonious, close space	Unruly, impolite and jealous
Masculine	Winning, material success	Verbal and noisy, like to criticise and argue	Career, competition, success, excel, big, fast, tough, power, action	Eye contact, physical contact, close space, hand gestures	Macho, competitive, like winners
Feminine	Caring, solidarity	Small talk, agreement, quiet	Quality, caring, solidarity, modesty, tender, touch, small, soft, etc.	Warm, friendly, close space	Sexless, complaining, pamper losers
Uncertainty avoidance	Certainty	Very verbal, structured and somewhat noisy	Structure, duty, order, certain, clear, secure, safe, predictable, tight, etc.	Hand gestures, but no physical contact, far space, hurried (time is money)	Rigid, arguing, obsessed with rules
Uncertainty tolerance	Exploration	Imprecise, quiet, use open-ended questions	Spontaneous, loose, creative, flexible, tolerant, relativity, etc.	Informal, unhurried, close space	Unprincipled, talk nonsense
Long-term orientation	Long-term virtue	Direct and focused, quiet	Work, save, invest, afford, economy, duty, virtue, effort, etc.	Restrained, unceremonious, far space	Dull, workaholics
Short-term orientation	Face saving, keep up with the Joneses	Talk a lot, like talking about the past	Quick, spend, today, gift, relation, tradition, show, image, receive, etc.	Warm, formal, ceremonious, attentive, close space	Big spenders, irresponsible

Based on: Hofstede, G.J., Pedersen, P.B. and Hofstede, G. (2002), *Exploring Culture. Exercises, Stories and Synthetic Cultures.* Yarmouth, Maine: Intercultural Press.

Table 19.4 Positioning of countries on cultural dimensions

	Countries scoring high on left dimension attributes	Countries scoring average	Countries scoring high on right dimension attributes	
Collectivism	East and West Africa, Latin America, Portugal	Arab countries, Greece, Japan, Spain, Turkey	Australia, Switzerland, Scandinavia, France, UK, US, Germany, The Netherlands, Belgium	Individualism
Low power	Scandinavia, Austria, Switzerland, Germany, Ireland, US, UK, The Netherlands	Spain, Taiwan, Greece, Japan, Italy, Portugal	Malaysia, Guatemala, Arab countries, West African countries, Philippines	High power
Feminine	Scandinavia, Portugal, The Netherlands, Turkey	Belgium, France, Greece, Spain, Arab countries	Austria, Canada, UK, Ireland, Italy, Japan, Switzerland, US	Masculine
Uncertainty tolerant	Scandinavia, UK, US, Ireland, Canada, India	Arab countries, Austria, Switzerland, Germany	Belgium, France, Greece, Japan, Portugal, Spain	Uncertainty avoidance
Short-term orientation	Pakistan, Nigeria, Canada, UK, US, Australia, Germany, Poland, Sweden	India, Thailand, Hungary, Singapore, The Netherlands	China, Hong Kong, Taiwan, Japan, South Korea	Long-term orientation
High context	Japan, China, Arab countries, Latin America	Italy, Spain, France, UK	North America, Scandinavia, Germany, Switzerland	Low context

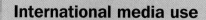

International media use

Different countries have different media preferences. Therefore, besides adjustments due to foreign regulations, the domestic media mix needs adaptation to local habits, local preferences, as well as to the target groups the particular media reach in foreign countries. Table 19.5 presents an overview of media expenditures for different countries and in Figure 19.4 TV viewing time in selected countries is illustrated. It is apparent that the relative importance of the different media varies to a great extent from one country to another. TV is the most important advertising medium in countries like Hungary, Portugal, Poland and Slovenia, while it is much less frequently used in more print-oriented countries such as Austria, Finland, Ireland, Luxembourg and Switzerland. Figure 19.4 shows that the time consumers spend on watching TV differs substantially between countries and, as a consequence, so does the likelihood that people can be reached by the specific medium. Moreover, 'prime time' also differs between countries. In contrast to Eastern Europeans, Northern Europeans watch very little TV in the morning. Italians have a first peak during lunchtime, Spanish people at 'siesta' time (3.15 p.m.). In northern Europe a peak is reached only in the evening, around 9.15 p.m. This is considerably earlier than the evening peak in Spain and Greece which starts at 10.30 p.m.[35]

The foregoing clearly illustrates that the international communications manager has to look for information concerning media importance, media usage, media coverage and media preferences before planning the international media mix.

Table 19.5 Media percentages of advertising expenditures in selected countries

	TV	Radio	Daily press	Magazines	Other press	Cinema	Outdoor	Internet
Austria	24.3	7.7	28.8	17.5	13.4	0.6	7.2	0.5
Belgium	44.2	10.7	22.1	12.6		1.2	9.3	
Denmark	35.3	1	36.5	7	13.9	0.9	5.4	
Finland	19.2	4.4	49.6	16.5	5.7	0.2	2.9	1.6
France	32.8	16.3	13.1	19	4.6	0.7	13.4	
Germany	42.7	5.3	23.6	21.6	2.4		3.1	1.5
Greece	33.8	4.6	14.2	32.1			15.2	
Iceland	28.9		59.4	7.5	1.5		2.6	
Ireland	16.9	7.5	63.1	3		0.8	8.8	
Italy	35.7	9.7	24	25.2	1.4	1.4	2.7	
Luxembourg	10.6	20	43.7	20.9		1.2	3.5	
Netherlands, The	47.4	8.7	16.9	9.6	13	0.3	4.2	
Norway	30.5	4.4	43.7	7.1	3.9	0.9	3.6	5.9
Portugal	63.2	6.5		22.4		0.4	7.6	
Spain	55.4	8.8	22.7	6.1	2	0.5	3.9	0.6
Sweden	41.6	2.2	38.6	11.9		0.4	5.4	
Switzerland	18.8	3.9	39.8	18.3	5.5	1.1	11.5	0.5
UK	43.7	7	18	12.6	6.8	1.8	8.2	1.9
Poland	58.3	8.1	13.5	14.2		0.9	5	
Hungary	65.4	4.3	11.9	11.8		0.4	5.7	0.5
Slovenia	58.3	6.2	14	15		0.4	5	1
Czech Republic	48.3	6.1	20.1	20.2		0.3	5	

Based on: IP Peaktime (2005), *Television 2005. European Key Factors*. Neuilly-sur-Seine, Cedex, Brussels: IP.

Figure 19.4 TV viewing time per individual per week, 2005

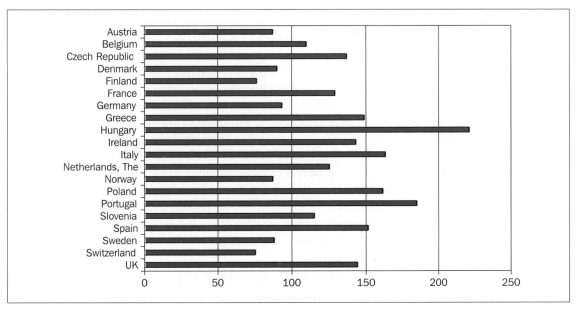

Based on: IP Peaktime (2005), *Television 2005. European Key Factors*. Neuilly-sur-Seine, Cedex, Brussels: IP.

International regulations

In order to retain trust and credibility, advertising needs to meet high ethical standards. The advertising industry in many countries has recognised this fact and has started to regulate its industry by establishing codes of practice or sets of guiding principles, a process called self-regulation. Although the features and operation of the self-regulatory systems may be quite different in different countries, they all share the same goal: 'ensuring legal, decent, honest and truthful advertising, prepared with a sense of social responsibility to the consumer and society and with proper respect for the rules of fair competition'. Self-regulation has existed for over 60 years. The International Chamber of Commerce was the first to publish its International Code of Advertising Practice (ICC Code) in 1937. All the codes in use today, all around the world, are based on this code. Self-regulatory organisations (SROs), which are funded by the advertising industry, ensure that the rules are applied. If an advertiser is not willing to comply voluntarily with the decision of the SRO, media may be refused for future advertising, negative publicity may be used, or the case can be referred to the appropriate statutory authority. Due to its flexibility, speed and low cost, self-regulation makes an ideal complement to the law.[36]

ICC codes

The ICC has issued several codes, including an International Code of Advertising Practice (1997), Sales Promotion (2002), Direct Marketing (2001), Sponsorship (2003), Children and Young People (2003), electronic media (2004) etc.[37] According to these codes, marketing communications should not contain statements or visuals which offend, denigrate, mislead or abuse the trust of consumers or another party. Consumers should be able to recognise the communication as a marketing tool. No testimonials should be used 'unless they are genuine, verifiable, relevant and based on personal experience or knowledge'. All marketing communications tools should avoid imitation of competitive and non-competitive actions in case this imitation might mislead or confuse consumers. For sales promotions, it should be clear to consumers how they can obtain the promotional offer (i.e. what are the exact conditions), the value and nature of the promotion should not be misrepresented and any geographic, age, quantity or other restrictions should be clearly indicated. Concerning children and young people, marketing communications may not be framed in a way that takes advantage of their youth or lack of experience or that strains their loyalty towards their parents or guardians. In case of direct marketing or sales promotions, no products should be delivered for which consumers have to pay unless consumers have requested the supply of these products. Also, no offers that could be perceived as bills or invoices for unordered products should be made. Moreover, data can be collected 'for specified, explicit and legitimate purposes only' and consumers should be provided with the opportunity to 'opt out' from marketing lists or to require that their data cannot be handed over to third parties. This has a serious impact on the possibilities of creating or buying databases with the intent to use them for direct marketing purposes.

European Advertising Standards Alliance (EASA)

The EASA[38], created in 1992, is Europe's single voice for the advertising industry and acts as a co-ordination point for the self-regulatory bodies of the respective European countries. The latter should not imply that Europe will come to one general system for all its member states, but rather that all main principles will be adopted. As the director general of EASA puts it: 'We must be careful of a one size fits all approach and allow markets the freedom to develop a system which responds to the EASA's Common Principles as well as the needs of that particular country, its advertising concerns and consumers'.[39] The EASA principles exist in addition to other European (and national) laws such as the prohibition of having more than 12 minutes of commercial messages an hour, the prohibition on tobacco advertising and the prohibition of associating alcohol consumption in advertising with driving, physical performance, social or sexual success or therapeutic qualities.

The Alliance has three major goals: to promote self-regulation; to support existing self-regulatory systems; to ensure that cross-border complaints are resolved speedily and effectively. For example, the Italian self-regulatory office ran an advertising campaign on television, radio, press and poster sites with the tag line 'We love advertising so much that sometimes we have to restrict it'. The ads featured a heart covered by a seatbelt and had the purpose of informing Italian consumers of the role of the Istituto Auto-disciplina Pubblicitaria. In Belgium a website was launched inviting consumers to fill in an on-line complaint form. Consumers should include a description of the ad, where, when and in which media the ad appeared and the reason why they are complaining.[40] In 2004 EASA received 196 cross-border complaints. Of these, 93% were filed because consumers thought the communication contained misleading information. Only 6% of the complaints pertained to offensive advertisements. Distinguishing between media, 95% of the cross-border complaints pertained to direct mail, 1% to press, 2% to internet, 1% to TV advertising and 1% to unsolicited faxes sent to companies.[41] Besides the foregoing activities, the self-regulatory bodies in several European countries (but not in Austria, Switzerland, Germany, Greece, The Netherlands and Spain) can be called upon to give advice on advertisement copy before campaigns are launched.

Advertising to children: the call for regulation

Many countries have strict rules and legislation about advertising to children.[42] The negative social consequences of advertising to children underpin the rationale for advertising restrictions, and the debate has mainly focused on food products.[43] Notwithstanding this extensive regulation, there is not a strong agreement that advertising directed at children should be banned.[44] In the context of the obesity debate, Berman (2005)[45] states that there is no reason to believe that a complete ban on advertising would have any impact on childhood obesity rates, and Eagle, Bulmer and Hawkins (2003) and Eagle et al. (2004b)[46] also conclude that there is a growing body of evidence that banning food ads targeted at children would be both inequitable and ineffective. Nevertheless, many parents seem to be in favour of stricter legislation on and control of (food) advertising directed at children. Burr and Burr (1976)[47] in their study of 400 US parents, had already noticed a call for greater federal legislation. And Chan and McNeal (2003)[48] also concluded that parents feel strongly that advertising should be banned on children's programming. On the other hand, Spungin (2004)[49] wonders whether, without food advertising, parents would buy better food. In this study 40% of parents thought they did not have enough information about providing their children with a healthy diet, and they did not particularly like advertising bans. In any case, Nathanson et al. (2002)[50] concluded that a high perceived threat and concern about television content leads to more support for censorship.

▶

Besides these 'hard' regulations, there are also 'soft' measures. The most widely known are self-regulatory initiatives by the advertising industry. Gray (2005),[51] an advertising man, states that advertising self-regulation is the best way to control advertising, and refers to the 'International Code of Advertising Practices' of the International Chamber of Commerce (ICC). The CARU (Children's Advertising Review Unit), a self-regulatory body in the US, claims to ensure that advertising directed at children is truthful, accurate and appropriate.[52] However, in the 1970s, it had already been found that there is a great deal of sarcasm about self-regulation, and as long as there are concerned parents who question the efficacy of industry self-regulation efforts, children's advertising is likely to remain a controversial issue.[53] Soft measures do not only refer to self-regulation by the industry, but also to initiatives such as the formation of parent monitor groups, independent organisations or multi-party bodies (consisting of parents, educators, broadcasters . . .).[54]

As far as the support for hard or soft measures is concerned, Walsh, Laczniak and Carlson (1998)[55] concluded that many options on regulations and control had been offered, but that mothers were inconsistent in their views and preferences.

Communications rules in European countries

As mentioned above, although all codes and most national laws are based on the ICC code, regulations may differ greatly from one country to another, even within the EU. As a consequence, an ad or a communications practice such as direct marketing or sales promotions may be acceptable in one country, but may be prohibited elsewhere. Therefore, it is advisable for a company to be well briefed on local regulations.

Differences in regulations exist, among others, concerning the products that can be advertised, the creative appeal, the media and advertising material that can be used.

Products

Several countries impose specific restrictions on the advertising of alcoholic drinks. France, Belgium and a number of other countries demand that ads for alcoholic beverages include the phrase 'consume in moderation'. In China there is a ban on tobacco and liquor advertising, except in hotels and other establishments frequented by foreigners. In The Netherlands and Belgium, confectionery advertising has to show a toothbrush, making it clear to children that they have to brush their teeth after consuming the product. In the UK, TV advertising for sensitive products such as female sanitary protection products and condoms was prohibited until 1986. Now it is permitted, but it may not be shown during family viewing times, and it may not contain explicit information that may embarrass women. Promoting toys is not allowed in Greece from 7.00 to 22.00 hours.

Creative appeals

Some creative appeals may be used in certain countries, but not in others. Only recently did the European Commission approve a law permitting comparative advertising. In

Japan comparative advertising is allowed, but is rarely used since explicitly offending a competitor is considered taboo in Japanese culture. Another appeal that may cause problems is erotic advertising. Europe is less stringent on that matter than, for instance, America. One also has to be cautious with the use of children. In Austria and France, for example, children are not allowed to promote a product, but may be shown consuming. In Portugal children can be used actively on the condition that the product is directly related to them.[56] Furthermore, in Belgium advertising is not allowed five minutes before and after a programme targeted at children,[57] while the Polish parliament recently decided to prohibit advertising aimed at children altogether. However, the latter regulation received a lot of criticism: how can you define an ad targeted at children? Is a chocolate bar meant to be for adults or for children?[58]

Media availability

Legislation on media availability differs from one country to another. TV advertising has been allowed in Denmark only since 1987, in Sweden since 1992 and in Saudi Arabia since 1993. In Italy no billboards can be placed near motorways, no outdoor messages are allowed near panoramic routes, inside parks or near bus shelters. In France, no commercials for wine and spirits can be shown in cinemas. Billboards promoting these products are prohibited in the cities, in airports and in railway stations. In Belgium, only public welfare messages are permitted near motorways. In Norway, coupons, sweepstakes and promotional gifts are prohibited.[59]

Durex TV and print campaign

Durex ran a TV campaign on MTV across Europe a few years ago. One of the ads featured an enormous sperm-like crowd following a man walking down the street to meet his girlfriend. When the couple meet, the sperm crowd gets blocked by a huge latex wall. The sperm get trapped in a huge condom, after which the base line 'Durex: For a Hundred Million Reasons' appears. Since most US television channels do not permit condom advertising, Durex ran a radio campaign in the US instead. The ads were made up of playful interviews with couples who talked about their sexual experiences. For example, in one ad a girl giggled 'We were on vacation and I lifted my skirt', at which her boyfriend responds 'Yeah, I think she was in her exhibitionist phase then'. Due to media availability, ad theme and ad execution were completely different for Europe and the US.[60]

Advertising material

Several countries pose restrictions on whether or not, or to the extent to which, foreign material may be used. Some countries demand, for example, that local presenters, local voices, local music and/or local technical people be used. A study among 46 countries shows that 22% of countries prohibit foreign-produced ads and 38% impose partial restrictions.[61] Malaysia, for example, imposes full restrictions, while Peru, Australia and the UK have partial restrictions.

Standardisation or adaptation

Once a company decides to go international, one of the most important strategic decisions to be made is to what extent a global marketing strategy in the foreign market(s) must be followed. A standardised campaign can be defined as a campaign that is run in different countries, using the same concept, setting, theme, appeal and message, with the possible exception of translations. A local approach implies that elements of the communications strategy are adapted to local circumstances.

Obviously, the standardisation or globalisation of the marketing mix has a number of advantages, the most important one being economies of scope. But often the international marketer will have to adapt or localise his marketing mix to a different foreign environment.

In order to create a global brand, not all marketing mix elements can or have to be standardised. In general, strategy, objectives and image are more likely to be globalised, while pricing, distribution and marketing communications are more easily localised.[62]

The globalisation/localisation debate goes back more than 40 years and continues today.[63] Some claim that the needs and desires of consumers are becoming more and more homogeneous around the world, justifying the use of a global communications programme.[64] Others point to the different cultural backgrounds, different lifestyles, different norms, different values, different experiences, etc. that exist around the world and do not believe in the merits of global communications.[65] Obviously, both approaches have advantages and disadvantages.

Pros of globalisation

A major advantage of globalisation is the cost savings that can be realised. Standardisation across the world induces enormous economies of scales and might lead to huge savings in manufacturing costs, personnel costs and communications costs. Not only can the price of the communications programme be reduced, but also the quality can be enhanced. Really good creative ideas are scarce. Global campaigns offer the advantage of globally exploiting a great creative idea. Other advantages are that global campaigns make things simpler for the company in the sense that co-ordination and control of the communications programme in the different countries become easier. Moreover, a global image can be created across different parts of the world. Brands that have communicated globally include: Nivea, Martini, L'Oréal, Xerox, Parker pens, etc.

Comfort Bultex® brings a standardised message

Comfort Bultex® is a foam filling for seating applications (such as sofas, chairs, etc.). It has a unique cell structure, is very durable and promises its customers reliability, responsibility and above all, a comfortable life and inner harmony. Within its market it is a leading brand in Belgium, Holland, France, Germany and Sweden, whereas southern and eastern parts of Europe are developing markets. To reinforce Comfort Bultex® as a pan-European branding concept an integrated marketing communications campaign was developed. Contrary to competitors' messages, the campaign did not use functionality and technical information as central arguments, but combined aesthetic/emotional values with functional values. An ▶

advantage was that this concept works throughout the value chain, from furniture manu-facturers and designers to furniture retailers and consumers. For the trade press, for example, different ads were developed, all showing a different type of fruit (a peach, an apple, a pear or cherries), stressing its specific shape. The base line always ran as follows: 'Comfort Bultex®, sits like it fits'. The copy mentioned things like 'Comfort Bultex® follows the contours of your body perfectly and supports them by just the right amount. Without sagging, without losing its shape. A guaranteed, unequalled seating comfort.' Some ads gave more technical details. Besides trade press advertising, the IMC mix consisted of brochures, technical leaflets, trade shows, sales support, point of sales materials and the website. Every tool stressed the same message and the same values. The campaign was a true global campaign and won a business-to-business communication award (see Plate 29).[66]

Pros of localisation

People living in different cultures differ in their beliefs, previous experiences, attitudes, values, etc. According to de Mooij, values are rooted strongly in history and seem pretty resistant to change. Different values might lead to different needs and a different consump-tion behaviour (see Plate 28). Research indicates that when countries converge with respect to national wealth, cultural dimensions (such as the ones identified by Hofstede) increas-ingly explain differences in country-level consumer behaviour. For example, people in uncertainty avoidance cultures (such as France, Germany, Italy and Belgium) consume more mineral water and buy more insurance products than those in uncertainty tolerant cultures (such as the UK and Scandinavia). More consumers in individualistic countries possess a private garden, a separate house (instead of an apartment), a personal radio, a computer and have an internet connection than consumers in collectivistic countries, and in masculine cultures more expensive watches and jewellery are bought than in feminine countries.[67] Even in cases where consumers' needs are homogeneous, this does not automatically mean that people want to satisfy these needs in a similar way. Nescafé, for example, offers more than 100 varieties since consumers in different countries prefer different blends and flavours. Furthermore, different cultures have different attitudes towards instant coffee. A couple of years ago, instant coffee's share of the total coffee market was more than 90% in the UK, 85% in Japan, 50% in Canada, 35% in France, 32% in the US and 10% in Germany,[68] making global advertising less obvious. Philishave modifies its ads because of the different shaving habits in different countries.[69] Nokia adapted its 6,100 series mobile phones and, for example, raised the ring volume for the noisy crowds in Asia.[70] Komatsu enlarged the door handles of its mechanical shovels for the Finnish market because Finnish workers often wear gloves against the cold.[71]

Another consequence of a different culture and different experiences is that it may be hard, if not impossible, to create advertising that is understood in a similar fashion by people living in different countries. The more distant the cultures are, the more prob-lematic this will be. Remember the difference between high-context and low-context cultures. A Japanese ad which is meant to be primarily understood by the context and not by the words used may be completely incomprehensible to Europeans, even if it is appropriately translated. Different cultures often have different education levels. This may lead to advertisements that are too difficult or too complex for some nationalities. The question is not only whether ads, symbols and pictures are understood, but rather how they are understood. Rain in countries with a very dry climate has a totally different meaning to that in rainy countries such as the UK, The Netherlands and Belgium. Gerber baby food experienced a problem with putting a picture on its package. It used the same packaging in Africa as in the US, showing a cute baby on the label. However, in Africa it is customary to put a picture on the label of what is inside the packet because most people are not able to read. Needless to say, African consumers were rather upset.[72] Sometimes regulations or media availability make it impossible to run a global marketing communications programme. As mentioned before, in Europe, until recently, comparative advertising was prohibited.

Another argument in favour of a local approach is that local managers are more motivated if they can add to the creativity of the communications programme rather than just run a programme set up by the headquarters. Furthermore, when competitors adapt their communications mix, it may be difficult to use a global approach. In the latter case competitors have the advantage of tailoring the messages and appeal to the real interests and values of the consumers. Finally, products are often at different stages of the product life cycle in different countries. This makes it impossible to use a global approach, since the information needed will differ depending on which stage of the life cycle the product is in.

The Chinese image of global brands

Since the majority of Chinese consumers are not familiar with the Roman alphabet, the first thing to do when international companies enter the Chinese market is to choose a proper Chinese name. This is not an easy task and a company has several possibilities. First of all, the brand name can be directly translated. In this case, the Chinese name sounds like the original name, but has no specific meaning in Chinese. This strategy is followed by Nike, for example. Secondly, the company can opt for free translation. In this case, the name is translated according to its meaning, but has no phonetic link with the original brand name. Schindler, for example, sounds like 'Xunda' in Chinese and means 'quick arrive'. Finally, the company can go for a mixed translation. This is the most popular alternative and results in a name that both sounds like the original brand name and has a meaning in Chinese. For example, Gucci's Chinese name sounds like 'Guzi' and means 'Classic looks', while Nivea sounds like 'Niweiya' and means 'Girl keep elegance'.

Besides deciding on the translation method, a company also has to decide on the sound of the new name. Every Chinese syllable can be pronounced with four different intonations. So, a two-syllable name can have sixteen different tone combinations, making an impact not only on the ease of pronunciation but also the connotations. Next, different combinations of characters have to be selected. Although different combinations can have the same pronunciation, they have completely different meanings. For example, Ford sounds like 'Fute' in Chinese and can have two different meanings: 'happiness' and 'bending over'. Since neither really fits Ford, Ford opted for a direct translation without a meaning. Ford's competitors fared better and have strong meanings. BMW is renamed as a 'horse' which in Chinese legend is connected with speed. Citroën is a 'dragon', referring to power, and Rover is a 'tiger' which is linked with prestige. So, it is important to realise that by giving the brand a Chinese name, not only a local name is given, but also a local image and a local identity, which can be very different from the original one. Only 7% of Chinese names have an almost identical meaning to the original one. A good example here is Volkswagen, for which the Chinese name means 'the

▶

masses' or 'the people'. More than 50% of Chinese names have a positive connotation that is absent in the original name. For example, Polaroid does not have a real meaning in Roman language but its Chinese name 'Shoot get instant photos' accurately describes Polaroid's benefits. About 12% have a different connotation. Examples here are Yahoo! which in Chinese means 'elegant tiger' and Lux soap which is called 'strong man'. It is interesting to note that Lux is pronounced with exactly the same sound and tone in Taiwan but has a different meaning. In Taiwan, Lux refers to 'beauty', a meaning that fits the brand better. However, when Lux entered the Chinese market in the 1980s, 'beauty' was not an acceptable name since it referred to 'decadent bourgeois aesthetics' under the orthodox communist doctrine. Another example of different meanings in Chinese and Taiwanese is Johnson & Johnson. It is called 'strong life' in China and 'tender/delicate life' in Taiwan. The company opted for 'strong life' in China because in view of the 'one child' policy, parents would rather have strong than delicate babies.

The foregoing illustrates that obtaining a global image is not always easy. For 2 million Chinese consumers, BMW is not 'the ultimate driving machine' but 'a treasure horse'. If the same image is not possible, try to go for a meaningful name since it enhances image and association formation. Moreover, if possible, emphasise a Western image rather than a local image in the new name since the Chinese regard Western products very favourably.[73]

Think global, act local

Probably the best way to approach international markets is not to adhere to one of the extreme strategies of globalisation or localisation, but to opt for a 'global commitment to a local vision',[74] or in other words to 'think global, but act local'. If the brand positioning is a good one, it should be rolled out in most countries. Also, an excellent creative idea can work nearly everywhere. However, advertisers should always look at the creative idea through the eyes of the locals. Even the best ideas might need some adaptation in execution to get into the mind-set of local people or to respect their cultural values.[75] An example would be to work out a global creative idea, but to adapt the advertising so that local presenters, experts or celebrities are employed, or that reference is made to local history or national symbols (Big Ben in London, the Eiffel Tower in Paris, the Atomium in Brussels, the gondolas in Venice (see Plate 28), etc.). Coca-Cola records radio spots in about 40 languages and uses 140 different music backgrounds.[76] Goodyear and Kraft develop a pool of ads from which each country selects the most appropriate one.[77] Miele runs campaigns with a different pay-off line. In Germany, Spain and Switzerland Miele is 'a decision for life', in Austria Miele is 'reliability for many years', and in the Netherlands, Belgium, the US and Canada 'there is no better one'.[78]

Globalising and standardising at Unilever and Procter & Gamble

For decades, Unilever adapted both its 'brand hardware' and 'software' to local markets. Due to cost considerations, local Unilever companies are no longer allowed to adapt the brand hardware, consisting of product formula, packaging and product range. However, a brand's software, such as the brand name, advertising, PR and event marketing, is still localised. For example, although standardised products are used, Unilever decided to retain different brand

▶

names for its fabric softener in each country (Lenor in the UK, Kuschelweich in Germany, Coccolino in Italy, Mimosin in Spain, Snuggle in the US and Robijn in Belgium). Also, the Coccolino teddy used in the Italian market and the figures Darren and Lisa used for the UK market are retained because the cloth puppets and teddy have been used for years and they connect well with local people. Dumping them would be throwing away valuable brand equity. Moreover, cost savings that can be achieved by standardising brand hardware are much higher than can be achieved by globalising an advertisement campaign.

Similar reasoning is followed by Unilever's competitor, Procter & Gamble. It learnt the hard way that globalisation is not always the way to go. Changing the name of the Mexican soap brand Escuda into Safeguard led to a serious sales decrease. After the name was changed back to Escuda again, sales went back up. Since then, P&G is thinking of the hard points it wants to keep consistent across regions. For example, the machine used to make Bounty has to be standardised, but the brand name, the colours, etc. can be adapted to meet local needs, as can the advertising. For Pampers, for example, widely varied copy is used for the Middle Eastern, Latin American and South African campaigns.[79]

The Designated Driver in Europe

The Bob campaign finds its origin in Belgium, in December 1995. The objective of the campaign is to raise awareness of the dangers of driving while intoxicated and focuses on the designated driver (DD) approach. BOB is the person designated at the start of the evening to be the one who does not drink. He is the one who drives and brings everyone home safely. BOB is established as a sympathetic figure, someone to look up to: 'Because of BOB, we do not have to worry and we can have a great party.' Right from the start, the campaign was a big success both in terms of mentality and behavioural change. Owing to this success, to date the concept has been picked up by 16 other European countries and has been supported by the EU Commission since 2001. The EU's objective is to reduce the number of road victims by 50% by 2010. Every country adheres to the concept mentioned above (the designated driver does not drink and brings the others home safely). Other common features are that both men and women can be the designated driver, that a rotation among the group is promoted, and that a driver should be designated before the group goes out. For the rest, every country adapted the campaign to reflect local mentality and culture. The campaigns in the different countries have a totally different look and feel: partly focusing on different target groups; employing different running periods; and making use of different communication tools.

Some countries followed the Belgian approach of a figure embodying the designated driver, although the name of this person can differ. For example, in Belgium, Greece and The Netherlands the DD is called BOB, in Poland Krzys, in the UK Des and in Denmark the Team Player. Not only the names, but also the slogans differ for each country. For example, in Belgium it is about 'chose a Bob and it's a party', or 'no party without Bob' ('Kies een Bob en 't is feest', 'pas de fête sans Bob'), while in The Netherlands the slogan runs as 'do you Bob or do I Bob?' and 'Bob, you can come home with him'('Bob jij of Bob ik?', 'Bob, daar kun je mee thuis komen'). In the UK they talk about 'Des will save you from the night bus', and 'No thanks, it's my turn to drive'. In other countries, the campaign focuses on behaviour. For example, in France 'the one who drives is the one who does not drink' ('celui qui conduit est celui qui ne boit pas') is used as a slogan, in Ireland they have 'drive straight and designated', and in Portugal '100% cool'.

▶

In terms of target groups, countries who have recently adopted the campaign focus principally on young males. Countries in which the campaign has already been running for several years (Belgium, The Netherlands, the UK . . .), have enlarged the target group to include other age groups as well.

With regard to the running period of mass media campaigns, in Belgium the campaign typically runs in December and January, in France in October and November, in Greece in January and February and during the summer months, in The Netherlands from December to February and during the summer months, in Spain from September to November, and in the UK from October to January.

A wide variety of communication tools are used in the different European countries, for example in Belgium, The Netherlands, Poland and the UK billboards are very popular. In addition, in The Netherlands the Dutch Korfball Association also promotes Bob. In Malta, among other things, bus shelters are used. In Denmark, hardly any mass media campaigns are used, but they do use, for example, outdoor events with a driving simulator. In Portugal, besides posters, night brigades are installed who reward '0% alcohol DD' with petrol vouchers, cinema tickets, etc. In Ireland, a trade competition has been organised to reward the most original ideas on the DD concept in bars and pubs. In France contests are organised to come up with original ideas on how to select the DD. Moreover, several countries created a special DD-website.

The European DD campaign clearly illustrates the 'think global, act local' idea, reflecting one common concept and one common objective, but with many differences on all other aspects.

Based on: BOB final report 2003–04, and slideshow on the main elements of the Pan-European designated driver campaigns 2005 (http://www.efrd.org/main.html).

When to use global communications

Whether or not a global approach is successful depends to a great extent on how similar the foreign culture is to the domestic one on the one hand, and on the nature of the product on the other. Obviously, an ad broadcast in The Netherlands and Germany needs less adaptation than an ad broadcast in England and Saudi Arabia. Furthermore, some product categories seem to lend themselves better to a global approach than others (Figure 19.5).[80]

Some products can be sold to similar target groups across countries. This boils down to global segmentation or finding groups of consumers that share similar opinions, values, interests, etc. across borders instead of looking for different target groups in different countries. Young people or people with a higher education, for example, are very similar, whether they are French, Italian, German, Belgian or American. The reason for this is that these groups, in general, are more open-minded, less culturally bound, more receptive to international media, make more use of international media, have more international contacts and/or go abroad more often. This factor explains the success of MTV, Calvin Klein and Dell computers.

Products that can be sold on the basis of image appeals are also more suited for global communications. Images, visual messages and international music lend themselves more to standardisation than a spoken or written message. Examples of successful campaigns in this category are Marlboro, Levi's, Coca-Cola, Martini, Smirnoff vodka, perfume ads and airline campaigns.

Figure 19.5 Product suitability for global approach

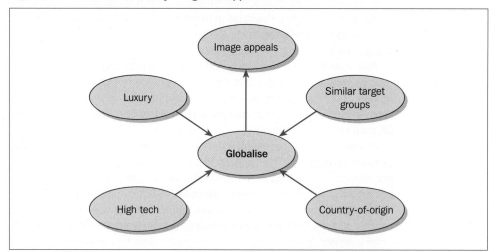

Based on: Fannin, R. (1984), 'What Agencies Really Think of Global Theory', *Marketing and Media Decision* (December), 74–82.

Luxury products are targeted at upper-class people who buy the product for the status it brings. Because only the status and no product information needs to be communicated, these appeals are easier to standardise.

Although innovative, high-tech products, such as the latest computers, the latest software, etc. need an informational appeal, these products seem to be used everywhere in the same way, which can justify a global appeal.

Products with a country-of-origin appeal can be more easily globalised. Belgium is famous for its chocolates, France for its wine, Japan for its technology, Germany for its durability, Switzerland for its watches. Products that use a country-of-origin positioning may well be advertised by means of a global approach.

Summary

The world has become a global village. Companies are increasingly faced with the challenge of marketing their products internationally. In that case, they are often faced with different cultures and habits. Marketing communications, as one of the most visual aspects of the marketing activity, have to avoid falling into the 'self-reference criterion' trap, i.e. believing that the foreign environment is similar to the environment in the home market. Cultural differences and factors have to be taken into account. Culture is the collective programming of the mind that distinguishes one group of people from another, and involves people's opinions, attitudes, preferences and perceptions. The marketing communicator has to take account of different cultural components, such as verbal and non-verbal languages, values and attitudes, religion, sense of humour and gender roles. Also, the cultural dimensions specified by Hofstede should not be neglected. Needless to say, all these components will reflect how marketing communications are perceived and can persuade people. For efficiency reasons, companies would like to standardise their marketing effort across countries and cultures, but given the differences in the marketing environment, marketing and marketing communications strategies will often need to be adapted. Companies have to find ways to combine global strategies with local adaptations of strategy to comply with differences in culture, media use and legislation between their foreign markets.

Review questions

1 What are the major advantages and disadvantages of international marketing?

2 Why is the international marketing communications process different from home market communications?

3 What is the self-reference criterion and how can it affect international marketing communications?

4 What are the components of culture and how can they influence international marketing communications?

5 According to Hofstede, on the basis of which dimensions can culture be distinguished, and what is their impact on international marketing communications?

6 How can international regulations influence the communications mix?

7 How can differences in media usage and media preferences influence international advertising?

8 What are the advantages and disadvantages of standardising the communications mix?

9 Which types of product can be easily globalised and why?

Further reading

Advertising Self-Regulation in Europe, The Blue Book, 2005. Brussels: European Advertising Standards Alliance.

De Mooij, M. (2005), *Global Marketing and Advertising: Understanding Cultural Paradoxes,* 2nd edn. Thousands Oaks, CA: Sage Publications.

Hofstede, G. (2003), *Culture's Consequences: Comparing Values, Behaviors, Institutions and Organizations Across Nations.* Thousand Oaks, California: Sage Publications.

Hofstede, G.J., Pedersen, P.B. and Hofstede, G. (2002), *Exploring Culture. Exercises, Stories and Synthetic Cultures.* Yarmouth, Maine: Intercultural Press.

Mueller, B. (2004), *Dynamics of International Advertising.* Peter Lang Publishing.

Usunier, J.C. and Lee, J.A. (2005) *Marketing Across Cultures.* Harlow: Pearson Education.

Case 19

L'Oréal's Biotherm and Biotherm Homme: a global brand of skin care products

The L'Oréal Group

The L'Oréal group, with headquarters in Clichy, France, was founded in 1907, and is the world's number one company in cosmetics. The group is very focused on this activity: 98% of turnover is sales of 135 different cosmetic products. The group has 52,000 employees of 100 different nationalities, 15,000 of whom work in 42 production facilities around the world. Another 3,000 employees work in 30 different disciplines of R&D. The group is present in 130 countries with almost 300 subsidiaries. In 2004 group turnover was 14.5 billion euros, 1.6 billion of which was profit. The world market for hygiene and beauty in 2002 was about 100.16 billion euros, 13.9% of which was made up of L'Oréal products. The competition is heavy and global, with companies such as Procter & Gamble, Unilever, Beiersdorf, Wella, Estée Lauder and LVMH. Western Europe, North America and Asia Pacific each account for 26–29% of sales. Skin care accounted for 27% of sales, hair care 26%, hygiene 19%, make-up 17% and fragrances 12%.

L'Oréal's vision is that cosmetics are part of the universal quest for beauty and well-being. As a form of self-expression, they are personal, part of social life, and they serve a daily need for self-confidence and contact with others. L'Oréal claims to put all their expertise and research resources to work for the well-being of men and women, in all their diversity, around the world. Consequently, the company's focus centres around three important principles:

- unfailing attention to consumers and understanding and anticipating their individual needs and aspirations
- respect for personal diversity; the company strives to match personal diversity with the diversity of their products and brands (age, type of skin, over time, culture . . .)
- the effectiveness of the products is built upon in-depth research and a dedication to invest in innovation, product safety and the highest standards of reliability and product quality.

With respect to R&D, about 3,000 employees worldwide are working in 30 different research disciplines. In 2004, more than €500 million was invested in R&D. In 14 research centres around the world, 120 molecules have been developed over the last 40 years, each year 4,000 formulas are developed, and the company has 30,000 active patents.

The attention to consumer needs and personal diversity is reflected in the branding and product range strategy of the group. The company markets 17 global brands, 16 of which are responsible for 95% of cosmetics sales. They can be divided into four categories (Case Table 19.1). Each brand has its own well-designed brand proposition, and brand equity is continuously built and supported by means of advertising and other forms of marketing communications. L'Oréal also recognises that there is no single model of beauty. Each culture has unique personal care segments, unique styles of dress and self-expression, unique traditions in cosmetics and, above all, its own unique vision. The company tries to serve these diverse needs by designing a diverse product range with products attuned to each culture and its needs. For examples:

- Softsheen.Carson: The world leader in haircare products for people of African descent
- Lancôme and L'Oréal Paris: European taste and traditions
- Shu Uemura: Standard bearer for Japanese style
- Maybelline NY & Redken: Trendsetters in the US
- Armani: Italian style

The L'Oréal products are available in supermarkets, hair salons, pharmacies, cosmetic boutiques and other specialist outlets, and also online and through mail order distribution. Brands are available in different outlets, depending on the category they belong to (see Case Table 19.1).

Biotherm

Biotherm is one of L'Oréal's luxury brands. It was founded in 1950 and covers a comprehensive range of face care (53% of sales), body care (20%), sun

Case Table 19.1 L'Oréal product and brand structure

Type of product	Consumer product	Professional product	Luxury products	Active cosmetics
Definition	Are priced competitively and distributed through mass-market retailing channels	Meet the requirements of hair salons and provide customers with a wide range of innovative products	Offer customers products and premium service in department stores and specialty stores	Dermo-cosmetic products sold in pharmacies and specialist retailers
Brands	■ L'Oréal Paris ■ Garnier ■ Maybelline NY ■ Softsheen.Cars on ■ CCB Paris	■ L'Oréal professional ■ Kérastase ■ Redken ■ Matrix ■ Mizani	■ Lancôme ■ Biotherm ■ Helena Rubinstein ■ Kiehl's ■ Shu Uemura ■ Giorgio Armani ■ Ralph Lauren ■ Cacharel ■ Viktor & Rolf	■ Vichy ■ La Roche – Posay ■ Innéov ■ SkinCeuticals

care (4%), make-up (6%), and skin care for men (16%). The brand originated with the discovery of an active ingredient found in thermal springs in the French mountains, which was called 'Pure extract of thermal plankton'. This basic component contains essential trace elements, minerals salts, proteins and vitamins, and is mixed with natural ingredients. Due to its biological affinity with the skin, Biotherm has a soothing, regenerating and stimulating effect. Its three basic functions are: cleansing, toning and treating. It is claimed to lead to a clearer healthier, softer, silky, vital and energised skin and a flawless complexion.

Biotherm is positioned on the basis of the following verbatims: young, well-being, positive attitude (de-dramatised, wink), simple, fresh, pure, minimalistic, direct, assertive, and complicity. The product range is organised by skin type (dry, normal . . .), and also on the basis of special needs and lifestyle elements. For instance, the following specialised products belong to the Biotherm programme: Age Fitness (anti-ageing), Densit Lift (anti-wrinkle) and Acnopur (to treat skin imperfections). Lifestyle products are Hydra-Detox (to eliminate toxins generated by urban pollution), D-stress (against stress-induced skin fatigue) and Aqua Sport (to keep the body toned and fit). Biotherm is distributed in almost 14,000 stores worldwide, 12,000 of which are in Europe. Sales in 2003 totalled about €350 million, and were

estimated to show double-figure growth in the years thereafter. In Case Figure 19.1 a positioning map is shown, based on two dimensions: 'serious–sensation' and 'new luxury–classic luxury'. Biotherm is positioned in the 'serious–new luxury' corner of the map. Its largest most direct competition is Clinique (16.4% market share). In Case Table 19.2, the market position of Biotherm and its main competitors in a number of European countries and for a number of product categories is given.

The Biotherm brand image in different countries
In February 2003 focus group studies were conducted with 80 women in various countries. The objective of this qualitative research project was to explore the brand image of Biotherm, and to assess the strengths and weaknesses of the brand and the brand communications. The focus groups were composed of both users of Biotherm and competitive products. In Case Tables 19.3–19.6 the composition of the focus groups in Germany, France and Spain are given along with the results of the survey. Although the composition of the groups was similar in the three countries, the results differ in some respects. For instance, while in Germany, the brand is accused of being featureless, in Spain consumers complain about the origin of the brand and the water, and in France the perception is that there is a lack of seduction, femininity and sensuality. In terms

Case Figure 19.1 Biotherm's positioning versus the competition

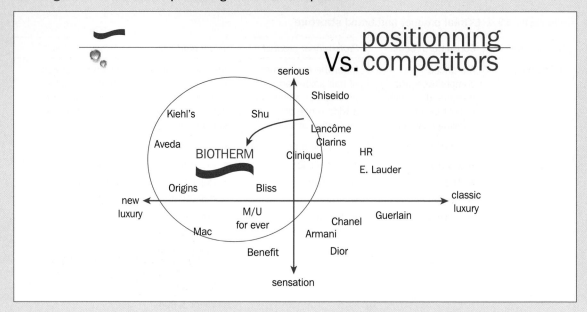

Case Table 19.2 Biotherm and the top three other brands in selected European countries and markets (2002) (percentages are market shares)

Country product category	France		Germany		Italy		Spain	
Care	Clarins	20.5	Shiseido	12.8	Shiseido	11.9	Lancôme	13.7
	Lancôme	12.0	Biotherm	12.1	Lancôme	9.9	Clarins	10.3
	Sisley	9.5	Lancôme	11.4	Lauder	9.9	Clinique	9.9
	Biotherm	7.6	Clarins	8.3	Biotherm	5.9	Biotherm	9.4
Face care	Clarins	16.4	Shiseido	15.0	Shiseido	12.6	Lancôme	14.6
	Lancôme	12.7	Lancôme	10.7	Lauder	11.5	Lauder	11.3
	Sisley	10.2	Lauder	8.9	Lancôme	10.4	Clinique	11.0
	Biotherm	6.1	Biotherm	8.7	Biotherm	4.8	Biotherm	8.4
Body care	Clarins	45.3	Biotherm	35.5	Clarins	29.2	Clarins	30.3
	Biotherm	14.5	Clarins	14.8	Biotherm	13.1	Biotherm	20.4
	Dior	8.6	Lancôme	14.1	Dior	7.9	Lancôme	9.6
	Lancôme	6.0	Dior	5.8	Lancôme	7.4	Dior	6.0

Case Table 19.3 Composition of focus groups on the Biotherm brand image in Germany, Spain and France

France Paris 3 groups	SPAIN Madrid 3 groups	GERMANY Düsseldorf 4 groups

■ 7 BIO. users
   25–35 yrs old
	■ 7 BIO. users
	   25–35 yrs old
		■ 7 BIO. users
		   20–30 yrs old

	■ 7 BIO users
	   30–40 yrs old
		■ 7 BIO. users
		   35–45 yrs old

■ 6 CLINIQUE
   25–35 yrs old
	■ 6 CLINIQUE
	   25–35 yrs old
		■ 6 CLINIQUE
		   25–35 yrs old

■ 6 ORIGINS AVEDA
   users 25–35 yrs old
		■ 6 SHISEIDO
		   25–35 yrs old

Case Table 19.4 Brand image of Biotherm in Germany

	☺ *Strengths*	☹ *Weaknesses*
Image/value	■ Rich and stable mental picture ■ French endorsement ■ Real consistency between fundamental values (naturalness, purification, softness, sobriety) and their expression through products (colors, smells, feel: lightness . . .)	■ Risk of being too insipid, featureless
Product offer	■ Clear, readable instructive offering, complete, accessible ■ Legitimacy for face and body ■ Powerful HYDRATION benefits, 'Intelligent' Freshness SKINCARE, Respect, Softness, Safety, Calming	■ Lack of distinct benefits ■ Problem of product descriptions, not in German
Ads		■ Lack of LIFE, of MOVEMENT, of DYNAMISM, of EMOTION
Target	■ Woman aged 30–40, sweet, natural, young-minded, rather sporty, healthy, easy-going	■ Club BIOTHERM not personalized enough

Case Table 19.5 Brand image of Biotherm in Spain

	☺ *Strengths*	☹ *Weaknesses*

Image/value	■ Eau Naturelle Bienfaisante (more sea-water) at the heart of life → Freshness, Cleanliness, Health Physical and psychological effects
	■ Research: confidence, scientific
		■ What about origins
		  – of the water
		  – of the brand

Product offering	■ Simple and serious offering ■ Enhancement of Makeup offer ■ 'Mission' for hydration + refreshing, regenerating and relaxing actions ■ Good value for money	■ Lack of substance (Well-being, health)
Ads	■ Attractive color (Celluli-choc, Hair Resource) ■ Central role of regenerating water	■ Agua! Too much water, pale, lack of consistency
Target	■ Woman aged 30–40, natural, spontaneous, sporty Bohemian (20–30) and non conformist (ut.CLINIQUE)	■ Women are too smooth, disincarnate, not convivial enough, lacks seduction Lack of assertion

of product offering, German consumers believe that there is a lack of distinct benefits, and they complain that the product description is not in German. French women feel that there is a lack of status for younger consumers, and the product has too 'pharmaceutical' a feel. On the other hand, consumers in all three countries agree that the advertisements for Biotherm lack life, emotion, dynamism, dream and sensoriality.

Men and body care

In a 2003 study, Publicis investigated which taboos had disappeared from the masculine mind the years

Case Table 19.6 Brand image of Biotherm in France

	☺ *Strengths*	☹ *Weakness*
Image/value	■ Natural, Simplicity, Freshness, dynamisme Heathy	■ Lack of seduction, feminity sensuality
Production offer	■ Strong water, tonifying Hydrating, freshness Relaxing ■ Natural ingredients	■ Lack of status for younger ■ Too Pharmaceutical
Ads	■ More selective; more modern	■ Lack of dream ■ Lack of sensoriality
Target	More young people: 25–35	■ Not fashion

before, and what significant new behavioural patterns appeared to have emerged, in other words which were the new ways in which men could be addressed. Four key points of communication were identified. They are summarised in Case Figure 19.2. Almost half of the men today like the idea of having a masculine and feminine side, especially young men. The result is a 'blurring' of behaviour: muscles, health, but also youth, perfection and facial beauty are important. There is a growing trend among men to care for their appearance and to care about themselves. Skin care is considered to be at the crossroads of physical hygiene and the desire to seduce. Being authentic, good-looking, seducing and pure, is increasingly important. A large proportion of men want to have more free time to take care of themselves. And sport, along with the gay phenomenon, is one of the structural themes of the New Man. But the 'eternal man' remains eternal. Values such as being in control, strong, ambitious, forceful, and full of authority are still positively valued, contrary to a man who is passive, hesitating and lost in dreams.

Case Figure 19.2 New ways to address men and the link with cosmetics

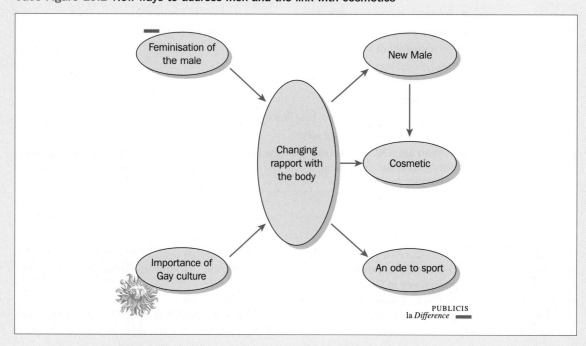

Biotherm Homme

The skin and skin treatment of men and women are fundamentally different in a number of ways. Men have between 6,000 and 25,000 hairs in their beard; this is much more than most women. Typically, men spend 3,000 hours of their lives shaving (that is 140 days). A man's skin is more oily and is more susceptible to acne. The male skin is 16–20% thicker than a woman's skin, and therefore less fragile. On the other hand, the male skin tends to age more rapidly, and wrinkles appear more quickly. Therefore, there is a need for a skin care product especially designed for men. Additionally, the aforementioned evolutions in men's attitude towards body care signals a market potential for a specific male body care product. Biotherm Homme, a skin care programme for men launched in 1985, is experiencing a strong growth in recent years. This complete line of skin care products for the face and the body is the world's market leader in men's care (2004, value shares). The men's skin care market has been growing steadily for the past 10 years (even twice as fast if you add in the guys who borrow products from their girlfriends or wives).

The positioning of Biotherm Homme can be summarised as follows: 'There is more to skin care than aftershave. You have no qualms about your individuality. You are comfortable looking after your body, skin and general well-being. You want to keep things simple, quick and effective. You want immediate results that make you feel good about yourself.' The brand statement is: 'Biotherm Homme, men's skin care coach' because only a coach can provide men with a custom-made programme that respects and soothes their skin. This coach is 'the creator of men's skin care treatment'. It has created personalised programmes specifically for men: high precision shaving formulas, face care treatments with extremely targeted ingredients, technical body care products. Each individual should be able to find the product that is best suited to his personal skin care needs.

In March 2003 a qualitative brand study in four focus groups of men aged 20–45 was carried out in Germany. In this study, the brand statement was tested as well as a number of advertising campaigns for both Biotherm and some of its competitors, merchandising programmes and product offers. The conclusion was that the idea of a 'coach' was too business-like and authoritative, did not fit into the need for autonomy of men, and lacked pleasure,

character, sensuality and emotionality. However, the notion of personalisation, and the description of ingredients and scientific research were noted as strong points. In terms of advertising effects, the conclusions were that they were identifiable, attractive, aesthetic, masculine, informative and simple. However, the non-German name of the product, the 'coach' idea and the non-selective packaging were negative points, leading to low spontaneous recognition. The conclusion was that the brand statement needed to be redefined, using elements such as: skin care specialist, scientific knowledge, innovation, highlighting skin care benefits and sensations. The communication elements to stress were the specific characteristics of the product, and the sensuality of the product and the models, and the key colour codes on each product. It was further concluded that, in order to build brand loyalty, the identification of men with the product needed to be enhanced by means of clear claims, visible skin results, identification of skin types, needs and benefits, and identification of products offer.

Questions

1 Is the vision and branding strategy mainly global (standardised) or local (adapted to local cultures? Explain and give examples.

2 Looking at the different types of needs that people can experience (for instance, Maslow), to which needs do L'Oréal in general, and Biotherm and Biotherm Homme in particular, appeal? Do you believe these needs are universal?

3 Clinique is mentioned as one of the closest competitors of Biotherm. Why? In what ways is the positioning of Biotherm and Clinique similar or different (use communication materials, websites . . . to illustrate)?

4 Summarise the main similarities and differences of the results of the focus group discussions in the three countries studied. Can you find a relationship between the cultural characteristics of the countries and the attitudes and perceptions of the group members from these countries?

5 Is Biotherm Homme positioned differently in different countries? (consult communication materials, websites . . .). Why or why not?

6 Are the conclusions and the marketing communication implications of the German Biotherm Homme study correct? Would you adapt the communication strategy in a different way?

Source: www.loreal.com; www.biotherm.com; Materials provided by Teresa di Campello and Joëlle Van Rijckevorsel, L'Oréal.

References

1 *International Trade Statistics 2005* (www.wto.org).

2 Brassington, F. and Pettitt, S. 2006, *Principles of Marketing (4th edition)*. London: Pearson Education.

3 Hofstede, G. (1991), *Cultures and Organizations: Software of the Mind*. London: McGraw-Hill.

4 Zhang, Y. and Gelb, B.D. (1996), 'Matching Advertising Appeals to Culture: The Influence of Products' Use Conditions', *Journal of Advertising*, 25(3), 29–46.

5 Lee, J.A. (1966), 'Cultural Analysis in Overseas Operations', *Harvard Business Review* (March–April), 106–14.

6 Zuurhout, M. and Heijblom, R. (1988), *Misrekeningen in Internationale Marketing. Twintig Praktijkgevallen (Misjudgements in International Marketing. Twenty Cases)*. Groningen: Wolters, Noordhoff.

7 Prystay, C. (2002), 'Selling to Singapore's Teens is Tricky– What Works in the US (Grunge, Anger, Rebellion) Doesn't Necessarily Click', *Wall Street Journal*, 4 October.

8 Kotler, P., Armstrong, G. and Wong, V. (2005) *Principles of Marketing, European Edition*. London: Pearson Education.

9 Mueller, B. (1996), *International Advertising, Communicating Across Cultures*. Belmont: Wadsworth Publishing Company.

10 Walliser, B. and Usunier, J.C. (1998), 'The Standardization of Advertising Execution: A Review of the Empirical Literature', in Andersson, P. (ed.), *Proceedings of the 27th Emac Conference, Marketing Research and Practice, Track 2: International Marketing*, Stockholm, 517–36.

11 Cutler, B.C., Javalgi, R.J. and White, D.S. (1995), 'The Westernization of Asian Print Advertising', *Journal of International Consumer Marketing*, 7(4), 24–37.

12 Anonymous (2002), 'Hitachi Expects . . . All Its Employees to be Able to Speak English', *Training Strategies for Tomorrow*, 16(1), 8–9.

13 Brassington, F. and Pettitt, S. (2003), *Principles of Marketing (3rd edition)*, Harlow, Essex: Pearson Education.

14 Hollensen, S. 2004, *Global Marketing, A Market-Responsive Approach*. London: Pearson Education; Keller, K.L. (2003), *Strategic Brand Management. Building, Measuring and Managing Brand Equity*. Upper Saddle River, NJ: Prentice Hall.

15 Usunier, J.C. and Lee, J.A. (2005), *Marketing Across Cultures*. Harlow, Essex: Pearson Education.

16 Mueller, B. (1996), *International Advertising, Communicating Across Cultures*. Belmont: Wadsworth Publishing Company.

17 Zuurhout, M. and Heijblom, R. (1988), *Misrekeningen in Internationale Marketing. Twintig Praktijkgevallen (Misjudgements in International Marketing. Twenty Cases)*. Groningen: Wolters, Noordhoff.

18 Brengman, M. (2002), *The Impact of Colour in the Store Environment. An Environmental Psychology Approach*. Doctoral dissertation, Ghent University, Belgium.

19 Pollay, R.W. and Gallagher, K. (1990), 'Advertising and Cultural Values: Reflections in the Distorted Mirror', *International Journal of Advertising*, 9, 359–72.

20 Caillat, Z. and Mueller, B. (1996), 'Observations: The Influence of Culture on American and British Advertising: An Exploratory Comparison of Beer Advertising', *Journal of Advertising Research*, 36(3), 79–88.

21 Zhang, Y. and Gelb, B.D. (1996), 'Matching Advertising Appeals to Culture: The Influence of Products' Use Conditions', *Journal of Advertising*, 25(3), 29–46.

22 Holzmüller, H.H. and Stöttinger, B. (1998), 'A Pragmatic Concept for Developing the Cultural Sensitivity of Marketing Managers', in P. Andersson (ed.), *Proceedings of the 27th Emac Conference, Marketing Research and Practice, Track 2: International Marketing*, Stockholm, 213–36.

23 Mueller, B. (1996), *International Advertising, Communicating Across Cultures*. Belmont: Wadsworth Publishing Company.

24 Walliser, B. and Usunier, J.C. (1998), 'The Standardization of Advertising Execution: A Review of the Empirical Literature', in Andersson, P. (ed.), *Proceedings of the 27th Emac Conference, Marketing Research and Practice, Track 2: International Marketing*, Stockholm, 517–36.

25 Walliser, B. and Usunier, J.C. (1998), 'The Standardization of Advertising Execution: A Review of the Empirical Literature', in Andersson, P. (ed.), *Proceedings of the 27th Emac Conference, Marketing Research and Practice, Track 2: International Marketing*, Stockholm, 517–36.

26 Hall, E.T. (1976), 'How Cultures Collide', *Psychology Today* (July), 66–97.

27 Usunier, J.C. and Lee, J.A. (2005), *Marketing Across Cultures*. Harlow, Essex: Pearson Education.

28 Hong, J.W., Muderrisoglu, A. and Zinkhan, G.M. (1987), 'Cultural Differences and Advertising Expression: A Comparative Content Analysis of Japanese and US Magazine Advertising', *Journal of Advertising*, 16(1), 55–62, 68; Ramaprasad, P. and Hazegawa, K. (1990), 'An Analysis of Japanese Television Commercials', *Journalism Quarterly*, 67 (Winter), 1025–33; Mueller, B. (1992), 'Standardization versus Specialization: An Examination of Westernization in Japanese Advertising', *Journal of Advertising Research*, 32(1), 15–24.

29 Hofstede, G. (2001), *Culture's Consequences* (2nd edition). Thousand Oaks, CA: Sage; Hofstede, G. (1991), *Cultures and Organizations, Software of the Mind*. London: McGraw-Hill.

30 Kim, U., Triandis, H.C., Kagitcibasi, C., Choi, S. and Yoon, G. (1994), *Individualism and Collectivism: Theory, Method, and Applications*. Thousand Oaks, CA: Sage Publications.

31 Zhang, Y. and Gelb, B.D. (1996), 'Matching Advertising Appeals to Culture: The Influence of Products' Use Conditions', *Journal of Advertising*, 25(3), 29–46.

32 Zandpour, F. and Harich, K. (1996), 'Think and Feel Country Clusters: A New Approach to International Advertising Standardization', *International Journal of Advertising*, 15, 325–44.

33 Hofstede, G.J., Pedersen, P.B. and Hofstede, G. (2002), *Exploring Culture. Exercises, Stories and Synthetic Cultures*. Yarmouth, Maine: Intercultural Press.

34 Hofstede, G.J., Pedersen, P.B. and Hofstede, G. (2002), *Exploring Culture. Exercises, Stories and Synthetic Cultures*. Yarmouth, Maine: Intercultural Press.

35 IP Peaktime (2005), *Television 2005. European Key Factors*. Neuilly-sur-Seine, Cedex, Brussels: IP.

36 European Advertising Standards Alliance (2003), 'Advertising self-regulation: the essentials', http://www.easa-alliance.org.

37 www.easa.iccwlo.org

38 *Advertising Self-Regulation in Europe, The Blue Book, 2005*. Brussels: European Advertising Standards Alliance.

39 'EU Enlargement Expands Opportunities for Advertising Self-Regulation', Press release of 20 May 2003 (www.easa.iccwlo.org).

40 'Latest News from Italy, Belgium, Ireland and the UK', Press release of 14 November 2002 (www.easa.iccwlo.org).

41 'Complaints Statistics 2004' (www.easa.iccwlo.org).

42 Eagle, L.C. and de Bruin, A.M. (2000), 'Advertising restrictions: Protection of the young and vulnerable?' Auckland, Massey University: Working paper 00.06; Gardner, C. (2004) 'Industry update', *International Journal of Advertising and Marketing to Children*, 5(3), 73; Clarke, B. (2003), 'The complex issue of food, advertising, and child health', *International Journal of Advertising and Marketing to Children*, 5(1), 11–16.

43 de Bruin, A.M. and Eagle, L. (2000), 'Children, the medium and the message: Parental perceptions of children directed advertising issues and regulation'. Auckland, Massey University: Working paper 00.14.

44 Eagle, L.C., Bulmer, S.L., de Bruin, A.M. and Kitchen, J. (2004a), 'Exploring the link between obesity and advertising in New Zealand,' *Journal of Marketing Communications*, 10(1), 49–67.

45 Berman, R. (2005), 'Sloth, not ads, is responsible for fat kids', *Advertising Age*, 76(16), 30.

46 Eagle, L.C., Bulmer, S.L. and Hawkins, J.C. (2003), 'The "obesity epidemic": Complex causes, controversial cures – Implications for marketing communication'. Auckland, Massey University: Technical report 03.03; Eagle, L.C., Bulmer, S.L., Kitchen, J. and Hawkins, J.C. (2004b), 'Complex and controversial causes for the "obesity epidemic": The role of marketing communications', *International Journal of Medical Marketing*, 4(3), 271–87.

47 Burr, L. and Burr, R.M. (1976), 'Television advertising to children: What parents are saying about government control', *Journal of Advertising*, 5(4), 37–41.

48 Chan, K. and McNeal, J.U. (2003), 'Parental concern about television viewing and children's advertising in China', *International Journal for Public Opinion Research*, 15(2), 151–66.

49 Spungin (2004), 'Parent power, not pester power', *International Journal of Advertising and Marketing to Children*, 5(3), 37–40.

50 Nathanson, A.I., Eveland Jr., W., Park, H.S. and Paul, B. (2002), 'Perceived media influence and efficacy as predictors of caregivers' protective behaviors', *Journal of Broadcasting and Electronic Media*, 46(3), 385–410.

51 Gray, O. (2005), 'Responsible advertising in Europe', *Young Consumers*, 6(4), 19–23.

52 Lascoutx, E. (2005), 'Food marketing to kids', Children's Advertising Review Unit (CARU) (2005). Retrieved 7 October 2005 from http://www.caru.org/news/2005/P034519.pdf

53 Burr, L. and Burr, R.M. (1976), 'Television advertising to children: What parents are saying about government control', *Journal of Advertising*, 5(4), 37–41.

54 de Bruin, A.M. and Eagle, L. (2000), Children, the medium and the message: Parental perceptions of children directed advertising issues and regulation. Auckland, Massey University: Working paper 00.14; Eagle, L.C. and de Bruin, A.M. (2000), Advertising restrictions: Protection of the young and vulnerable? Auckland, Massey University: Working paper 00.06; Eagle, L.C. and de Bruin, A.M. (2001) Marketing communication implications of children's new electronic media use. Auckland, Massey University: Working paper 01.24.

55 Walsh, A.D., Laczniak, R.N. and Carlson, L. (1998), 'Mothers' preferences for regulating children's television', *Journal of Advertising*, 27(3), 23–36.

56 Rijkens, R. (1999), *European Advertising Strategies. The Profiles and Policies of Multinational Companies Operating in Europe*. London: Cassell.

57 'Reclame voor Kinderen Moet' ('Advertising for Children is a Must'), *De Morgen*, 11 April 1998.

58 'Pools Parlement Verbiedt Reclame voor Kinderen' ('Polish Parliament Prohibits Advertising for Children'), *De Morgen*, 6 March 1999.

59 Helgesen, T. (2000), 'The Power of Advertising, Myths and Realities: Evidence From Norway', in Jones, J.P. (ed.), *International Advertising. Realities and Myths*. Thousand Oaks, California: Sage, 153–68.

60 Galloni, A. (2001), 'In New Global Campaign, Durex Maker Uses Humor to Sell Condoms', *Wall Street Journal*, 27 July.

61 Boddewyn, J.J. and Mohr, I. (1987), 'International Advertisers Face Government Hurdles', *Marketing News*, 8 May.

62 Phillips, C., Doole, I. and Lowe, R. (1996), *International Marketing Strategy. Analysis, Development and Implementation*. London: Routledge.

63 Agrawal, M. (1995), 'Review of a 40-Year Debate in International Advertising – Practitioner and Academician Perspectives to the Standardization/Adaptation Issue', *International Marketing Review*, 12(1), 26–48.

64 Levitt, T. (1983), 'Globalization of Markets', *Harvard Business Review*, 61(3), 92–102.

65 Zhang, Y. and Gelb, B.D. (1996), 'Matching Advertising Appeals to Culture: The Influence of Products' Use Conditions', *Journal of Advertising*, 25(3), 29–46.

66 Saatchi & Saatchi Business Communications, Belgium.

67 De Mooij, M. (2003), 'Convergence and Divergence in Consumer Behaviour: Implications for Global Advertising', *International Journal of Advertising*, 22, 183–202; De Mooij, M. (2000), 'Mapping Cultural Values for Global

Marketing and Advertising', in Jones, J.P. (ed.), *International Advertising. Realities and Myths*. Thousand Oaks, California: Sage Publications, 77–102.

68 Rijkens, R. (1992), *European Advertising Strategies. The Profiles and Policies of Multinational Companies Operating in Europe*. London: Cassell.

69 Rijkens, R. (1992), *European Advertising Strategies. The Profiles and Policies of Multinational Companies Operating in Europe*. London: Cassell.

70 Kotler, P. (2003), *Marketing Management (11th edition)*. Upper Saddle River, NJ: Prentice Hall.

71 Kotler, P., Armstrong, G., Saunders, J. and Wong, V. (2001), *Principes van Marketing*, Schoonhoven, Academic Service.

72 Keller, K.L. (2003), *Building, Measuring, and Managing Brand Equity (2nd edition)*. Upper Saddle River, NJ: Prentice Hall.

73 Fan, Y. (2002), 'The National Image of Global Brands', *Brand Management*, 9(3), 180–92.

74 Keegan, W.J. (2002), *Global Marketing Management (7th edition)*. Upper Saddle River, NJ: Prentice Hall.

75 White, R. (2000), 'International Advertising: How Far Can it Fly?', in Jones, J.P. (ed.), *International Advertising. Realities and Myths*. Thousand Oaks, CA: Sage, 29–40.

76 Keegan, W.J. (2002), *Global Marketing Management (7th edition)*, Upper Saddle River, NJ: Prentice Hall.

77 Kotler, P. (2003), *Marketing Management (11th edition)*. Upper Saddle River, NJ: Prentice Hall.

78 Rijkens, R. (1992), *European Advertising Strategies. The Profiles and Policies of Multinational Companies Operating in Europe*. London: Cassell.

79 Taylor, D. (2003), 'An Italian Teddy Weakens Global Brand Logic', *Marketing*, 27 February, 18; Neff, J. (2002), 'P&G Flexes Muscle for Global Branding', *Advertising Age*, 73(22), 53.

80 Fannin, R. (1984), 'What Agencies Really Think of Global Theory', *Marketing and Media Decisions* (December), 74–82.

Name Index

Subject Index